D1426869

THE STUART COURT MASQUE AND POLITICAL CULTURE

Court masques were multi-media entertainments, with song, dance, theatre, and changeable scenery, staged annually at the English court to celebrate the Stuart dynasty. They have typically been regarded as frivolous and expensive events. This book dispels this notion, emphasizing instead that they were embedded in the politics of the moment, and spoke in complex ways to the different audiences who viewed them. Covering the whole period from Queen Anne's first masque at Winchester in 1603 to *Salmacida Spolia* in 1640, Butler looks in depth at the political functions of state festivity. The book contextualizes masque performances in intricate detail, and analyzes how they shaped, managed, and influenced the public face of the Stuart kingship. Butler presents the masques as a vehicle through which we can read the early Stuart court's political aspirations and the changing functions of royal culture in a period of often radical instability.

MARTIN BUTLER is Professor of English Renaissance Drama at the University of Leeds. He is the author of *Theatre and Crisis 1632–1642* (Cambridge, 1984), and has edited *Cymbeline* (New Cambridge Shakespeare, 2005) and *The Tempest* (2007). He is a General Editor, with David Bevington and Ian Donaldson, of *The Cambridge Edition of the Works of Ben Jonson.*

THE STUART COURT MASQUE AND POLITICAL CULTURE

MARTIN BUTLER

CAMBRIDGE
UNIVERSITY PRESS

CAMBRIDGE UNIVERSITY PRESS
Cambridge, New York, Melbourne, Madrid, Cape Town, Singapore, São Paulo, Delhi

Cambridge University Press
The Edinburgh Building, Cambridge CB2 8RU, UK

Published in the United States of America by Cambridge University Press, New York

www.cambridge.org
Information on this title: www.cambridge.org/9780521883542

First published 2008

Printed in the United Kingdom at the University Press, Cambridge

A catalogue record for this publication is available from the British Library

Library of Congress Cataloguing in Publication data
Butler, Martin,
The Stuart court masque and political culture / Martin Butler.
p.   cm.
Includes bibliographical references and index.
ISBN 978-0-521-88354-2
1. English drama – 17th century – History and criticism.
2. Theater – Political aspects – Great Britain – History – 17th century.
3. Masques, English – History and criticism.
4. Politics and literature – Great Britain – History – 17th century.
5. Great Britain – Court and courtiers – History – 17th century.
6. Great Britain – Politics and government – 1603–1649.
I. Title.
PR678.M3B88   2008
792.60941′09032–dc22
2008026925

ISBN 978-0-521-88354-2 hardback

For James and Emily

Mendoza	And, Celso, prithee, let it be thy care tonight
	To have some pretty show to solemnize
	Our high instalment; some music, some masquery.
	We'll give fair entertain unto Maria,
	The duchess to the banished Altofront.
	Thou shalt conduct her from the citadel
	Unto the palace. Think on some masquery.
Celso	Of what shape, sweet lord?
Mendoza	What shape? Why, any quick-done fiction –
	As some brave spirits of the Genoan dukes
	To come out of Elysium, forsooth,
	Led in by Mercury, to gratulate
	Our happy fortune; some such anything,
	Some far-fet trick, good for ladies, some stale toy or other,
	No matter, so't be of our devising.
	Do thou prepare't. 'Tis but for fashion sake;
	Fear not, it shall be graced, man, it shall take.

John Marston, *The Malcontent*

Have I not seen the pomp of a whole kingdom, and what a foreign king could bring hither also to make himself gazed and wondered at, laid forth as it were to the show, and vanish all away in a day? And shall that which could not fill the expectation of a few hours entertain and take up our whole lives, when even it appeared as superfluous to the possessors as to me that was a spectator? The bravery was shown, it was not possessed; while it boasted itself, it perished. It is vile and a poor thing to place our happiness on these desires. Say we wanted them all: famine ends famine.

Ben Jonson, *Discoveries*

Earl of Essex Tedious orations, dotards on their knees;
I for one would yawn myself to death.

Benjamin Britten and William Plomer, *Gloriana*

Contents

Illustrations

Acknowledgements

This book has been a long time in the making. Much of the original research was done in 1990–1, when I was a Fellow of the Woodrow Wilson Center in Washington, D.C., at which time I believed myself to be working on a study of Ben Jonson. A Leverhulme research fellowship in 1994–5 enabled me to rethink the focus and to draft much of the present book, though it was set aside once I became swept up by *The Cambridge Edition of the Works of Ben Jonson*, which took over my energies for ten years. Having despaired of ever reviving this work, an Arts and Humanities Research Council research leave award has allowed me to return to it at last. I am grateful to these funding bodies for their generosity, and to those friends who encouraged me to believe that work which, to me, often felt like old hat was still worth pursuing.

Parts of this book draw on previously published essays. Chapter 4 uses material originally published in Malcolm Smuts, ed., *The Stuart Court and Europe* (Cambridge, 1996); chapters 1 and 6 draw on my contribution to D. Bevington and D. Holbrook, eds., *The Politics of the Stuart Court Masque* (Cambridge, 1998); chapter 7 uses material from P. Lake and K. Sharpe, eds., *Culture and Politics in Early Stuart England* (1994); chapter 8 draws on essays in *English Literary Renaissance*, 22 (1992) and 37 (2007), and *Medieval and Renaissance Drama in England*, 6 (1993); chapter 9 uses material from J. R. Mulryne and M. Shewring, eds., *Theatre and Government under the Early Stuarts* (Cambridge, 1993), and from *The Seventeenth Century*, 2 (1987); and chapter 10 draws on material published in *English Literary Renaissance*, 13 (1983), and in T. Healy and J. Sawday, eds., *Literature and The English Civil War* (Cambridge, 1990). I am grateful to the editors and publishers for allowing me to rework those essays here.

Versions of these arguments have been trialled in papers at seminars and conferences at the universities of Oxford, Reading, Warwick, Keele, Exeter, Chicago, and Massachusetts (Amherst); at the Institute of English Studies, University of London; the Shakespeare Institute, Stratford-upon-Avon; and the Folger Shakespeare Library. I am grateful to my audiences for their serious and provocative responses. Particular thanks go to colleagues at the University of Leeds, who have heard a lot of this in our research seminar over the years.

I have benefited considerably from the presence of a small masque industry at Leeds. David Lindley was working on this subject long before I arrived, and has been a marvellous inspiration and example. He read many early drafts, and his advice has been endlessly valuable, searching, and generous. In some ways this book is merely an extended conversation with him. I have also been fortunate to work with Karen Britland, first as Ph.D. supervisor, then as colleague on the Cambridge Ben Jonson, on which we laboured literally side by side. I have learned a huge amount from her, and am profoundly grateful for her thoughtfulness and loyalty. Amongst other colleagues, I greatly valued the help and advice of John Barnard, Michael Brennan, Jerry Brotton, the late Inga-Stina Ewbank, David Fairer, Paul Hammond, Markus Klinge, Tom Lockwood, James Loxley, Syrithe Pugh, and Jane Rickard. Amongst our students, I am particularly indebted to Susan Anderson and Lindsay Godson.

Beyond Leeds, I am conscious of three major debts: to Stephen Orgel, who read several chapters and encouraged me to continue; to James Knowles, for many interesting titbits and stimulating conversations; and to Kevin Sharpe, for his supportiveness even though we disagree over many things. It has been a privilege to read admirable work by Sophie Tomlinson, Sarah Poynting, Barbara Ravelhofer, Clare McManus, Gabriel Heaton, and Kevin Curran before it reached publication. Their ideas have helped greatly in giving focus to what I wanted to say. It is a privilege, too, to work again with Sarah Stanton, one of the heroines of British drama publishing.

Many other friends and colleagues have assisted with advice, references, off-prints, and ideas. I salute Bernadette Andrea, Jayne Archer, John Astington, Leeds Barroll, Anne Barton, David Bergeron, Jacques Berthoud, David Bevington, Keith Brown, Janet Clare, Liz Clarke, Tom Cogswell, Richard Cust, Anne Daye, Ian Donaldson, Mrs Janet Freeman, Caroline Hibbard, Lynn Hulse, Elliott Kendall, John Kerrigan, Peter Lake, Ted Leinwand, Leah Marcus, Ted McGee, Kate McLuskie, David Norbrook, the late John Orrell, Graham Parry, Ross Parry, John Peacock, Tim Raylor, Glyn Redworth, the late Conrad Russell, Jeanne Shami, Malcolm Smuts, Simon Thurley, Peter Walls, and Blair Worden. To all, my thanks. All the errors of fact and interpretation that remain are mine.

Finally, Jane, James, and Emily have kept this work in proportion and provided the continuity which so often it lacked. I cannot thank them enough for their love and patience.

A note on procedures

In the early seventeenth century, the English calendar was ten days behind the calendar on the continent, hence dispatches sent home by European diplomats carry dates ahead of those being used in England. English dating was further complicated by two modes of calculus, which marked the new year alternately on 1 January or on Lady Day, 25 March (with dates falling in January – early March expressed in the form 13 January 1603/4). These circumstances impact radically onto the material synthesized in the appendix, so, for the sake of clarity, I have standardized dates, anglicized continental dating, and taken the new year to begin on 1 January.

In this book I refer to Anne of Denmark as Queen Anne. In his biography of Anne, Leeds Barroll points out that she signed herself Anna, and in Scotland was known as Anna, Queen of Scots. However, Anne was the form by which her English subjects generally knew her – for example, she is named on the quarto title page of *The Masque of Queens* as 'the most absolute in all state and titles, Anne, Queen of Great Britain' – and so I have continued to use this name. In this I follow *The Oxford Dictionary of National Biography*, which also refers to her as Anne.

All quotations, from literary and non-literary texts, have been modernized and (where necessary) repunctuated. Since many texts are cited from modern-spelling editions, it seems inconsistent not to apply the principle of modernization to all quotations alike. If some are left unmodernized, a misleading impression is conveyed of their historical difference from quotations in modern spelling. The only exceptions are a few instances of citations from account books and the like, which are difficult to translate into modern forms, and where exactness of wording is crucial.

Line and page references for frequently cited texts use the following editions:

Ben Jonson, ed. C. H. Herford, P. Simpson and E. Simpson, 11 vols. (Oxford, 1925–52)

The Works of Thomas Campion, ed. W. R. Davis (1969)

The Poems of Thomas Carew, with his Masque 'Coelum Britannicum', ed. R. Dunlap (Oxford, 1949)

The Plays of George Chapman, gen. ed. A. Holaday, 2 vols. (Urbana and Cambridge, 1970–87)

The Poems and Masques of Aurelian Townshend, ed. C. C. Brown (Reading, 1983)

At the time of writing there are as yet no satisfactory modern editions of Daniel, Middleton, Shirley, or Davenant, but *The Vision of the Twelve Goddesses*, *The Inner Temple Masque*, *The Triumph of Peace*, and *Salmacida Spolia* are cited from *A Book of Masques in Honour of Allardyce Nicoll*, gen. eds. T. J. B. Spencer and S. W. Wells (Cambridge, 1967); the editors are, respectively, Joan Rees, R. C. Bald, Clifford Leech, and Terence Spencer. *Tethys' Festival* and *The Coleorton Masque* are cited from *Court Masques: Jacobean and Caroline Entertainments 1605–1640*, ed. D. Lindley (Oxford, 1995). Other masques I cite from the original printed texts, silently modernized. Place of publication is London, unless otherwise stated.

Where possible I have referred to aristocrats and monarchs by the titles that they bore during the periods under discussion, but I have occasionally telescoped chronology for the sake of clarity. I have preferred the spelling 'marquis' to 'marquess', on the authority of Fowler's *Modern English Usage* (and given the absence of 'marquess' as a headword in the *Oxford English Dictionary (OED)* – despite what *OED* says under 'Marquis', n.[1], 2).

The seventeenth-century Scottish court had had its own established festival

Introduction

This book studies English court festival under James I and Charles I in relation to the changing political and cultural climate of the time. It considers virtually the complete run of royal masques, from Queen Anne's first show at Winchester in 1603 to the last Whitehall festival, *Salmacida Spolia*, danced by Charles and Henrietta Maria in 1640 as the court geared up to confront rebellion in Scotland and the first parliament for eleven years.[1] It presents the story of the form while integrating it into an encompassing narrative of political and cultural transformation. The masques are a vehicle through which we can read the early Stuart court's political aspirations and the changing functions of royal culture in a period of often radical instability.

Masques were not confined to the early Stuart period. They were preceded by a rich tradition of Tudor festivity, which was at its most ostentatious under Henry VIII, and continued, in less ambitious ways, under his children. The image of Tudor monarchy was profoundly conditioned by Henry's Burgundian-style revelry, and by the entertainments associated with Elizabeth's Accession Day tilts and summer progresses into the country. But the Stuart accession in 1603 galvanized Whitehall's festivals, not least because, unlike Elizabeth, James often financed his own masques. This turned them into a cultural showcase for the new court, and introduced a note of competitiveness and conspicuous consumption which bespoke the ambitions of a dynasty keen to assert itself as a major player in Europe.

The sixteenth-century Scottish court had had its own established festival culture. James VI danced in masques and even wrote one himself, to celebrate the wedding of his cousin, Henrietta Stewart, in 1588.[2] Once in England, James never danced, but he was an occasional tilter and his queen took to the masque floor on numerous high-profile occasions. As the reign progressed, it quickly became apparent that Christmas festivals were to be the grandest annual fixtures in the court calendar, usually culminating with an expensive masque on Twelfth Night. Masques became the focus of extraordinary artistic effort and financial expenditure. They engrossed the energies of some of the period's most distinguished artists – poets like Ben Jonson, Thomas Campion, Samuel Daniel, and George Chapman, designers such as Inigo Jones and Constantino de' Servi, musicians like Alfonso Ferrabosco, Nicholas Lanier, and Henry Lawes, dancing-masters such as Jacques Bocan and Thomas Giles, and costume makers who are barely remembered today but whose names often survive in the financial records. The performers included representatives of the court's most entrenched aristocratic dynasties, many of them officials in the royal household, personal servants to the monarch, or aspirants to favour and preferment. Masques were not grossly expensive when considered in relation to the court's total outlay, but they were high-impact and attracted equivalent public attention.

Masques were performed before comparatively small audiences and were usually seen only once. They did not, then, function as political propaganda and information management in the way in which we understand those things today. Nonetheless, their spectators were drawn from the social elites from which the crown chose its officials and magistrates, who sat in parliament, and channelled royal authority into the realm at large. They were thus an important point of contact between the crown and its political class, cementing their bonds of loyalty and outlook. At the same time, masque nights were an opportunity for honouring the representatives of foreign powers, whether extraordinary ambassadors, who were temporarily present at Whitehall, or resident ambassadors who acted as their countries' representatives throughout the year. Although James and Charles tried to avoid using invitations to signal their favour to particular nations, the diplomats jostled ceaselessly for places of honour and their presence underlined that these were international occasions. Masques proclaimed the Stuarts' ability to command attention on the world stage and decked them in the symbolic forms of European kingship. Partly through their very considerable symbolic impact, Whitehall came to look like a centre of power equivalent in prestige to Paris, Vienna, and Madrid. Court protocol and its lavish festivals were signs that the Stuarts were a modern, forward-looking, cosmopolitan dynasty, capable of competing on equal terms with Bourbon and Habsburg.

It is true that spectators went to masques for the sake of other pleasures than the poetry, for the spoken sections took up a comparatively small part of the evening. Most of the time was given over to dancing, and the effect of the music, costumes, and spectacle must have been overwhelming. Ambassadors' reports and domestic feedback suggest that the poets' contributions were often misunderstood, inaudible, or ignored. The famous quarrel between Jonson and Jones, over the relative importance of the masques as drama or spectacle, was symptomatic of anxiety on this score. For many of those dancing or watching, the main attraction must simply have been to see and be seen: to enjoy the pleasures of court membership, show off wealth and status, and affirm one's sense of belonging to an elite community. Literary critics frequently write as if the words were central, but commonly spectators must have been less focused on the minutiae of the masque's verbal meanings than on the show of aristocratic display, which affirmed their stake in the Whitehall crowd. Masques celebrated the court as a place with which all of the king's leading subjects could feel a measure of identification. In this regard, the broad social ramifications of masquing were at least as important as its narrowly political meanings.[3]

That said, it is clear that masques always had some explicit political function. The king's presence inevitably politicized the occasion, and masque inventions usually took their point of departure from some aspect of royal policy or current events. Masque form – which was more variable than literary critics have tended to allow – was dictated by the political relationships between its participants: it changed according to whether the show was a presentation by the king or to him, or was some sort of conversation with him or amongst the family and friends surrounding him. There was often a mechanism to ensure that spectators understood the fable, by distributing printed or written sheets summarizing it,[4] or by printing the whole text, sometimes prior to the performance. There was also the beginning of an attempt to publicize court festivity beyond Whitehall's immediate territory, through printed texts, manuscript copies circulating from hand to hand, and letters of affairs sent into the country by the network of court correspondents, a process that became markedly more systematic under Charles I. If masques could never function as propaganda in the modern sense, they nonetheless worked to shape the image of the monarch and give prestigious expression to his values and priorities. They sought to underwrite his authority, foster confidence in his rule, affirm his ties with his nation, and invest him with political and personal legitimacy. The expense and time lavished by monarchs on masque preparations ensured that they were always culturally significant events. At the same time, even when the literary component was secondary to the dance and spectacle, it always framed the evening and gave meaning to its symbolism and aesthetic design.

My primary aim is to treat the masques' politics and aesthetics in an integrated way. The common but excessively atomistic conception of the form as a simple dyad in which antimasque was set against masque has given rise to a correspondingly simplified understanding of its political meanings. Sometimes masques are associated with a schematic and repetitious politics on the assumption that their form was itself stereotypical and inflexible. Alternatively, a simplified view of their meanings may arise if assumptions about the politics of the period are excessively rigid. This is a limitation of Jonathan Goldberg's remarkable study of Jacobean culture, which, despite its brilliant literary analyses, makes the masques seem stereotypical by adopting a one-dimensional view of Jacobean history, attributing an unrealistic political uniformity to the period, and failing to take account of historical change.[5] On the other hand, studies which focus on the minutiae of the masques' political functions have to ensure that they do not short-change their aesthetic dimensions. This is the Achilles' heel of Leeds Barroll's ground-breaking book on Queen Anne, which, while valuably contextualizing her masques by recreating their historical milieu in great density, pays little attention to their aesthetic qualities and gives scant impression of them as texts.[6] The present book attempts to do equal justice to the masques' historical and aesthetic aspects. It uses a methodology of detailed contextualization, locating each masque in relation to the moment of its performance, but tries to give adequate attention to both text and context, developing each in mutually supportive symbiosis, and ensuring that historical and cultural analysis are both pursued to sufficient depth. It aims to read the masques as texts in which the aesthetic and the historical are inextricably entangled with one another, and have equal claims on our attention.

The project of this book is to retrieve the complexity of the masques' politics, which were far more functional and substantive than they are often represented as having been. In part this is a matter of understanding masques as total events. The king was the centre of the occasion, but many people were involved in masque production, and there were many conflicting interest-groups in the Banqueting House. Royal consorts and children played a large part in masques' conception and performance, as did powerful courtiers and personalities such as Buckingham, all of whom brought their own priorities to the dance floor. No less significant were the spectators who, though silent in the texts, had their own distinctive investments in the occasion. Typically the king was the principal addressee, but the nature of the encounters that masques performed depended on who was dancing, who was paying, and whether the show was simple homage and celebration or an act of supplication, persuasion, or rapprochement. Sometimes masques were brought to Whitehall by outsiders, such as lawyers from the Inns of Court, and sometimes the monarch was entertained as a guest in spaces beyond his own palace; these occasions intruded new variables into the symbolic economy. Usually masques were constructed as projecting the king's world view, presenting the king for the sake of the king (as it were), but almost always some kind of conversation or dialogue was implicit. Masques stamped the king's authority onto his court, but the terms of that authority were constantly under negotiation.

It is also important to recognize that the stream of public action in which masques participated was open-ended, provisional, and inchoate, and that, by virtue of their location at the very centre of Stuart power, masques could not put complete aesthetic distance between themselves and the historical processes to which they alluded. They did not passively reflect a stable or pre-existing reality but were themselves part of an unfolding political narrative. They were rooted in the as yet unresolved tensions of their moment of performance, their fictions and songs being saturated with reference to matters that were topical or contingent. So although their primary purpose was to legitimate the king, they never inertly proclaimed kingly values, but performed real material functions in the life of the state. They helped to shape Stuart political culture, responding to current issues, inventing symbolic forms that articulated royal priorities, and devising fables which addressed the uncertainties of the moment. They were involved in and contributed to ongoing debates about policy and ideology, about the values and imperatives of kingship, and the court's ideals, aspirations, and objectives. With their conflict-based form, they sought to manage the outlook of their audience, arousing and discharging anxiety, encouraging identification between spectator and monarch, and endeavouring to create a climate of consensus and confidence. And by foregrounding the motifs of sudden transformation and social dancing – which suggested, respectively, decisive intervention or mutual rapprochement – they offered an arena in which symbolic solutions could be advanced for the problems, disagreements, and controversies of contemporary political life.

So my analyses treat the masques as acts of power as much as aesthetic performances, and endeavour to excavate the political work which each performed. They start from the assumption that the court's pleasures always had some political aspect, that their aesthetic design rested on and articulated Machiavellian imperatives. In the early seventeenth century, the idea was often voiced that panegyric ought to have some counselling function and convey advice as well as pleasure, that courtly entertainment should educate its spectators as well as entertain them. As Jonson put it in *Love's Triumph through Callipolis*, 'public spectacles either have been or ought to be the mirrors of man's life' and should always 'carry a mixture of profit with them no less than delight'.[7] This moralizing approach has been most fully developed by Kevin Sharpe,[8] but I shall be suggesting that the masques' justifications as channels of counsel were often at odds with their functions as purveyors of ideology. It is important not to take the masques' idealizing discourse at face value, but to understand how it arose from and intersected with the configurations of power, and to register the ritual and social dimensions of masque performance, the masques' ability to shape attitudes through collective action as well as explicit content. At the same time, the fact that festivity was a collaborative enterprise meant that what a masque did frequently ran athwart whatever limits any one of its producers – typically the poet – sought to put on it. A masque's *raison d'être* was ultimately configured around the monarch in whose service it was prepared, and in this respect Jonson, Jones, or any other participant was only an individual contributor to an enterprise of greater scope. Its meaning has to be triangulated in relation to the total event for which it was created.

On the other hand, what the masques failed to achieve was often as significant as what they accomplished. Much criticism has understandably focused on the masques' drive towards transcendence. The festive ideal was closure: masques emphasized harmony, unity, and consolidation. The aim of most masque fables was to sublimate conflict into aesthetic concord and make the king's will seem irresistible and divine. A magnificent court culture was thus a triumphant expression of royal prestige. But this book is just as interested in the points where that project broke down, the places where masques seem contradictory, unresolved, or embarrassed. At such moments, the tension between a masque's aesthetic objective and recalcitrant circumstance exposes the political gap which each was in the business of bridging. Such moments disclose how far kingly symbolism struggled to accommodate structural strains in the body politic. Seen in this light, the masques, and the political culture to which they belonged, present valuable opportunities for taking the court's temperature as it responded to changing historical conditions across four decades, and evaluating the success or otherwise of the image that the crown sought to sustain. As a series of snapshots taken at regular intervals through the period, each masque is uniquely revealing of the breadth of royal outlook and the degree of competence which, in successive years, the crown was able to project.

Of course, masques were always idealistic: they presented royal aspirations in the best light, and voiced what the monarchy thought it was doing or was capable of doing. This did not, though, make them mere fantasies. The old view no longer holds up that masques were froth on the tide of history, misrepresenting reality or distracting attention from it. Rather, the objective of each masque was to celebrate a functioning court, affirming the two-way tie between monarch and subjects, and creating an image of the king which seemed sufficiently in tune with the attitudes of his political elites and underlined the mutual investment that each had in the other. In the long term, that personal monarchy with which masques were identified would not endure; when the basis of Stuart authority collapsed, so did the masques. But in their complex responses to challenging circumstance, the masques uniquely demonstrated the strengths and sensitivities of Stuart government across a period when the crown was at the heart of English political life. And at the same time, their moments of discomfort, awkwardness, and excess point to the institutional weaknesses and political blind spots on which Stuart power would eventually founder.

CHAPTER I

Spectacles of state

These things are but toys, to come amongst such serious observations. But yet, since princes will have such things, it is better they should be graced with elegancy than daubed with cost.[1]

Francis Bacon's famous denial of the value of court masques, even as he begins an essay that lays down rules for setting out a masque as gloriously as can be, voices a contradiction endemic to the festival culture of the early Stuart court. By making space for masques in his 'counsels civil and moral', however briefly and with whatever show of reluctance, Bacon acknowledges the extent to which the serious work of statecraft, which in other essays he analyses with such subtlety and depth, could not be set apart from the apparently casual pleasures of princes. No less than travel, buildings, or gardens (the topics of three other essays), masques and triumphs were, for all their triviality, necessary themes in a complete portrayal of modern court life. Of course, Bacon's complaint, that masques were so far below serious consideration that space could barely be spared for them, is on one level a rhetorical pose. It allows him to approach the subject ironically, as if from the sidelines, and it is contradicted by the evidence of his personal involvement in the festivity that he affects to deplore. He himself wrote speeches to introduce the Earl of Essex on the Elizabethan tiltyard, and in 1614 he spent £2,000 on mounting *The Masque of Flowers* as a wedding gift for James's favourite, the Earl of Somerset.[2] Clearly, Bacon knew that masques had their uses, that they were intrinsic to the world of power and represented the pursuit of politics by other means. But Bacon's sense that, for all their costliness, masques were essentially toys – that there was a tension between their location at the heart of court life and their status as mere art or triviality – is a perception that recurs across the period, and resonates into the present. It points to a deep contradiction that all studies of masques confront, the difficulty of adequately evaluating a form in which the transcendent meets the contingent, extravagance tips into redundancy, and the purposeful and pleasurable are locked in indissoluble embrace. In no other literary medium are the confluences of art and power, imagination and event, quite so unsettling or emphatic.

These days there is little danger of masques being undervalued. Indeed, they have come to be regarded virtually as paradigmatic Renaissance texts, which give uniquely penetrating insights into the dominant cultural and political relationships of their time. Masques were central to the ritual world in which early modern court life took place. They were staged at the very heart of Whitehall, at key moments in the court calendar, and were intrinsic to royal protocol and self-display. With their deliberate and uneconomic wastefulness, they belonged to the systems of spectacle and patronage which Renaissance princes drew around themselves, and contributed to an aristo-cratic culture characterized by consumption and expense. Their visual and poetic forms introduced into England the symbolic language of modern European kingship, advertising the Stuarts' cultural capital, legitimating their government, and proclaiming the dignity of their new state. Twelfth Night festivals were thus not mere ephemera but showcased the new dynasty's power and prestige, and stood as leading examples of the pleas-urable 'work' associated with the early modern court. As today's studies of Renaissance culture have become preoccupied with the power of art and the arts of power, so masques have emerged as exemplary instances of Renaissance cultural production, in which the ineluctable entanglements of pleasure and politics, aesthetics and history are most fully revealed.

Not so long ago such a situation would have been almost unimaginable. For generations of critics, masques were an embarrassment, since their embedment in a particular and known history was so obvious and so compromising. Their frankly political character was fatal to their credibility as art, and prevented them from being read with any seriousness. At best they seemed a superior kind of propaganda, occasionally redeemed by flashes of lyricism and comedy. At worst, they were deplorably self-abasing, tasteless acts of sycophancy or misplaced ingenuity. Even sympathetic critics could not avoid projecting a whiff of disapproval about them. For example, C. H. Herford's thoughtful introduction to the masques in the monumental Oxford edition of Ben Jonson (1925–52) repeatedly pauses to regret that Jonson wasted his energies on 'soulless magnificence' and 'toys so perishable': 'The spectacle remains of the Titan playing with bubbles and butterflies and rainbows, and struggling, not with complete success, yet never with utter failure, to weave enduring art out of these unsubstantial materials.'[3] Herford's image of Jonson as a truant genius, squandering his time on unworthy objects, represents the attitudes of many for whom the artistic activity of masque-writing was fatally contaminated by its flattery of long-dead princes. His disparaging views were echoed in H. H. Child's review of the Oxford edition's masques, headed 'Embellishing a triviality': 'In his heart of hearts [Jonson] knew that he was attempting the impossible ... Jonson is seen in [this volume] to be constantly labouring to do what even he could never succeed in doing. Within the conventions of the masque he could not make a complete and thorough work of art.'[4] It would probably have been better, from this perspective, had Jonson written no masques at all. Behind such attitudes one readily detects the formalist assumptions of an older historicism in which the spheres of art and politics were taken to be distinct and antithetical, even incompatible. In such a system, art was not only separate from politics but defined in opposition to it. The artist worked in privacy and freedom, unshackled by political obligations, and the criteria for evaluating his work were purely aesthetic. The great vice was insincerity, and the task of art was to be organic, integrated, and aloof from everyday accidents. Unsurprisingly, this critical tradition could not deal with a form whose political involvements were perpetually on display, impairing what in literary terms could be rated as its achievements. It was impossible to evade the dilemma of having to deplore the poets' flattery of the great while praising the formal beauty and intellectual sophistication which, notwithstanding, masques also seemed to possess.

One necessary achievement of the remarkable critics who in the 1950s and 1960s first recovered the masques for modern scholarship was to make the case for their aesthetic coherence. This was variously seen in their diverse but complementary aspects as literature (expounded in Stephen Orgel's ground-breaking study, *The Jonsonian Masque*), as iconography (exemplified in the essays of D. J. Gordon), and as visual art (in the work of Roy Strong).[5] Initially this revaluation stayed within formalist coordinates, emphasizing the masques' structural integrity at the expense of, or in spite of, their overtly political dimensions. This was in line with the ahistorical assumptions of the then prevailing New Criticism,[6] though in fact Gordon and Strong were both products of the Warburg Institute, the scholarship of which did have a vigorous political side: the Warburg tradition sought to put art history onto a sociological basis and was formidably internationalist in outlook.[7] However, Strong and (particularly) Gordon tended to foreground the arcane aspects of masque symbolism, fostering a corresponding emphasis on their political mysticism and social elitism.[8] But since that time the firewall between literature and history has collapsed, and the historicisms which have subsequently emerged deny that art has any space which is not always already political. Far from wanting to deplore masque politics, more recent historicisms sidestep the old historicist dilemma at the outset by taking their entanglements with power as symptomatic and necessary – indeed, as a matter for celebration, even for a certain grim satisfaction. In this perspective, masques become almost totemic instances of the legitimating functions of early modern culture, and are frequently pressed into service as examples through which arguments about the politics of Renaissance literature are made. Particularly, in Stephen Orgel's more politicized later studies, notably his marvellous short book *The Illusion of Power* (1975), one sees masque criticism pioneering a 'New Historicism' that would soon turn into a critical tide. Masques became the key Renaissance texts in which the intersections of illusions and power were most compelling and conspicuous.[9]

In the 1970s and 1980s, the masques' characteristic motifs translated readily into New Historicism's familiar tropes, and were used to underpin the darkly Machiavellian emphases to which this work was often drawn. Performed by, with and to royalty, trading in stupendous images of sovereignty, staging ceremonial encounters in which monarch and courtier mimed the ties of obligation bonding England's political elites, and presenting acts of festive contest in which subversion was contained and disorder schooled into deference, masques were grist to the mill of a criticism that was preoccupied with the ways that culture instantiated power. If much New Historicism found its point of departure in the anecdotal and contingent, then the masques' ephemeral character – performed once and rarely repeated – made them a suitable case for treatment. If the expectation was that masque poets should (in Jonson's words) translate 'present occasions' into 'more removed mysteries',[10] then the form's frankly ideological nature was congenial. And with masques typically presenting disruptions and challenges to monarchy which, at the culminating moment, were reined in by the revelation of a hidden but potent authority, then they played out the mantra of a criticism which held that there was 'subversion, no end of subversion, only not for us'.[11] Masques thus became the leading edge of the Renaissance theatricalization of power, emerging as the classic instance of a process which co-opted literary, musical, and visual systems of representation into the service of early modern kingship. Disclosing sovereignty as a force that traversed the whole of society, absorbing contradictions and transcending contingencies, they not only participated in the royal theatre of power but actively performed and embodied it.

These days, then, masques arrive defined as the great examples of the tendency of Renaissance sovereignty to pull the age's aesthetic forms into its orbit. Chiming with that resonant Burckhardtian idea that the Renaissance state was a work of art, they are the works of art *par excellence* in which spectacle became a tool of state. Yet while this often inspiring criticism has reinvigorated court festival, it has continued to treat masque politics as essentially a subset of masque aesthetics, and shown little interest in relating them to the material culture of public institutions and ideological debate that mapped early Stuart political life – in short, to the detailed history. So a striking disparity arises between the New Historicist account of early Stuart kingship and the view which descends from political historiography. The literary critics' image of a triumphantly dominant royal power is a long way from the monarchy described by many historians, beset by insecurity and institutional weakness and troubled by financial shortfalls and political uncertainty. When the crown's structural problems do intrude into masque criticism – as, for example, they must when the Caroline years are being considered – a contradiction emerges between the claims that are made for the cultural influence of Stuart festivity and the fact of political collapse, which reinforces the old idea that masque politics were little more than royal fantasies writ large.[12] At the same time, New Historicists have tended to define masque politics in comparatively formulaic or schematic terms – for example, as the relentless and rather repetitive routing of 'disorder' by 'order' – without taking much notice of changing institutional conditions or the larger cultural climate. In work by David Lindley, David Norbrook, Leah Marcus, Leeds Barroll, and James Knowles, there is an important counter-current which addresses the masques' circumstances of perform-ance and wider historical context, though this research remains restricted to particular corners of the field or to individual case studies.[13] The aim of the present study is to create a consolidated narrative which traces the masques' development across the period and bridges the gap between them as literary texts and as events in a material history.

We can illustrate the strengths and limitations of the inherited tradition by looking at two of the most influential critical accounts, by Stephen Orgel and Jonathan Goldberg. Inevitably, all discussion starts with Orgel, whose work on court festival was path-breaking and exemplary, and uniquely prescient in discerning the future for Renaissance criticism more broadly: his early books were effectively New Historicism *avant la lettre*. Orgel's positions have shifted over time and make claims for masques on a number of fronts, but the move that I (admittedly unfairly) wish to isolate here is his emphasis on the poetics of space. In all Orgel's accounts, the physical relationships between masquers, king, and audience – the placement of the stage, dancing area, and auditorium – are crucial to his account of masque politics. His readings turn centrally on the assumption that dispositions of space define the relations of power enacted in the text. The king, seated directly opposite the vanishing point of the newly imported single-point perspective scenery, is always the dominant figure. He alone sees the action as it is meant to be seen, and the event is implicitly if not overtly centred on him. The masquers dance homage to him, and the audience watches the event and the king watching the event, their attentive spectatorship (and participation in the social dancing) being the means by which they are incorporated into the king's greater body, as proclaimed by the evening's harmonies.

In Orgel's model of court festivity, aesthetic and political economies mirror each other seamlessly.[14] The king's privileged visibility manifests his surveillance of his subjects: 'the centre of the spectacle was not the entertainment but the entertained, the monarch'.[15] Observing all and observed by all, he focuses the society created by the event, and the masque is a channel of social exchange in which masquers express their devotion and are confirmed in their own sense of prestige. At the same time, the fictions which the king contemplates shadow his power, showing disorder subdued by order, anarchy by authority, and sovereignty instantly and magically victorious. Yet, Orgel emphasizes, these fictions were no mere reflection of the king. Rather, the court was invited not so much to interpret the masques' images as to recognize them, and, in a sense, 'what the noble spectator watched he ultimately became'.[16] In depicting the political nation incorporated into the king's steady gaze, the masques revealed the court's true self, and fashioned courtly display into a statement of the impossibility of ever escaping from his all-embracing sovereignty. The crucial moment was always the 'revels', when members of the audience were taken out for social dancing, and the worlds of reality and representation became one.

Orgel's understanding of the masques as theatres of power was germane to his work from the 1960s, and was a crucial insight that opened the way for much subsequent criticism. It is unsurprising that it crystallized when it did, at a time when 'happenings' and environmental experiments were increasingly common in American theatre, though retrospectively it had much in common with the strategies of other critics who were coming to concern themselves with a poetics of space. Orgel's theatres of power are congruent with other visual paradigms that present the past as not so much a process as a geography. The carnival, the prison, the landscape tour, the great aristocratic household were all familiar New Historicist topoi.[17] Created by the methodology of thick description, such spatial metaphors recreate history as a web of cultural interconnectedness, and reorient the historical field from the diachronic to the synchronic, from a sequence of events and motives to a structure in which individual and collective identities are constituted.

Like these other spatial paradigms, Orgel's perspectival arenas make concretely apparent the masques' power relations. A limitation, though, is their tendency to efface their relationship to history as process. To these encompassing and densely articulated structures, narratives of micro- or macro-political change make little difference, so that one result of this paradigm is that every masque ends up doing more or less the same thing – i.e. legitimating the monarch. Incidental features differ, as each masque occupies a new occasion, but each testifies identically to the authority of the royal gaze, representing the court as reaffirming its unchanging sense of identity and purpose. In such a paradigm, the theatre of power is compellingly evoked but is strangely homogenized, immune to the processes of history, and endlessly replaying the same symbolic functions. At the same time, the reification of kingly power promotes a symmetry between what the court sees and what it is. Orgel argues that the poets had to devise fables in which the king's centrality in the performance was a metaphor for his centrality to the court, so that, when this was achieved, the masque became 'the expression of the monarch's will, the mirror of his mind'.[18] At such moments, it was 'a fiction within which the fable is true'.[19] Of course, Orgel stresses that such equivalences were not always achieved, and that when they failed masques lapsed into mere flattery. Even so, the notion that court theatre turned royal metaphors into 'reality' telescopes the political into the aesthetic and takes its idealizations at face value, potentially closing off other possibilities.

Another limiting aspect of this model is its insistence on the absolute primacy of the king's gaze. Although the correlation between the king's privilege and his position opposite the perspective vanishing point seems compelling in theory, it has become clear that these optical relationships were not stable in practice. John Orrell notes that although Inigo Jones's set designs look naturalistic within the conventions of single-point perspective, they did not transparently represent an imagined reality.[20] Rather, Jones handled perspective flexibly and creatively, and his scenes sometimes included double horizons or multiple vanishing points which stretched the visual space beyond what a single eye would 'naturally' see. The correspondence between the king's visual centrality and political privilege was thus in some respects pragmatic. Moreover, as Russell West argues, while single-point perspective asserted the king's dominance as viewer, its cost was to isolate him, underlining his solipsism and passivity. Although the spatial arrangements figured his dominance, he was 'the subject of monarchic perspectival vision' rather than governor of 'a wide range of points of view upon his own person'. His angle of vision was monocular rather than binocular – something that was further reinforced by James's reluctance to engage in masques as a performer. Unlike Elizabeth, who asserted her control by staging her royal presence and participating actively in her own festivals, James occupied a privileged view but was thereby 'less in command of the whole process of representation of his own royal self-hood'.[21] At the same time, the exclusive focus on the royal view marginalizes the other participants in the occasion, minimizing the perspectives of performers and spectators. Although the royal gaze was ubiquitous, it could never be the evening's sum total.

So while Orgel's model of court theatre has been very enabling, in some ways it restricts the masques' political range. Jonathan Goldberg's account of court festivity in *James I and the Politics of Literature* (1983) also represents the masques as performing a potent but limited range of ideological manoeuvres, but he focuses more directly than Orgel does on their textual-ity. Taking as his point of departure the assumption that cultural forms do not merely reproduce but actively instantiate their society's power struc-tures, he locates the masques within a discourse of sovereignty which shaped Jacobean representational codes, the ideologically saturated language which James's subjects spoke and in which, he argues, they were always already caught. This Jacobean discourse Goldberg characterizes as strategically fragmented. Stitching together a vast range of verbal, visual, and sculptural texts, he positions James as a kingly Machiavel whose power was embodied in a deliberate doubleness, a glorious emperor who was simultaneously a secretive inward politician. This generated a discourse remarkable for its divisions, a language in which James was, at one and the same time, hidden and disclosed, publicly on show yet ultimately invisible. This fragmentary, Machiavellian discourse Goldberg calls James's 'sustaining contradictions'.[22]

In Goldberg's analysis, the masques are the leading case of Jacobean doubleness. Goldberg seizes on their contrary perceptions, the vertiginous shifts between satire and ceremony, mystification and disenchantment, and reads them as both exposing James's authority and endorsing it. Yoking the scurrilous and the reverential, sacred and profane, masques mystified James's power even as they unveiled it. The same masques which hymned royal authority in their choruses returned in their antimasques images of court anarchy, yet both of these versions of rule James approved. To an older historicism, the conjunction of satirical antimasque and adulatory main masque was scandalous: the poets heaped praise upon the king while confusingly acknowledging the realities of politics and the mechanics of courtly myth-making. But for Goldberg the contradiction is enabling, since the antimasques' subversions were already in line with the 'duplicitous norm' of James's state. James allowed antimasque disorders just as he presided over the main masques' harmonies, since both were strategies within his authority's double vision. His poets demystified royal power, but in ways that were surprisingly cognate with mystified authority. They spoke for the king even (especially) as they seemed to speak against him.

Goldberg's account of the masques as conduits of the discourse that shaped Jacobean reality moves the framework of discussion away from politics and towards its representation. In doing so, it writes the masques into a particularly acute version of that vexing subversion/containment debate that followed New Historicism everywhere, and which was probably an unavoidable consequence of the slippage from politics to power, and the dissolving of power into the field of representation. Goldberg's stunning analysis of the masques as at one and the same time subversive and self-abasing interprets them as acts of rebelliousness which are countenanced in order that they might be contained, a position close to the celebrated argument of Stephen Greenblatt's 'Invisible bullets', in which the subversiveness of Renaissance texts is produced by the very order with which the texts were purportedly in conflict. And as so often in comparable analyses, in which power is not 'out there' to be contested but is dispersed around the whole discursive field and shapes social and cultural practices ubiquitously, the possibility disappears of anything that might once have been taken to signal change or conflict. With all transactions circulating in a liquid *laissez-faire* economy, and all encounters issuing in the same relentless closure, we do not see anything other than 'domination dominating'. The masques become testimonies to the prison-house of Jacobean culture, glittering occasions at which courtly elites danced in festive celebration of their own disempowerment.

Undeniably the masques were 'an inherently royal form' (as Goldberg puts it, referring to Jonson in particular).[23] They were tied to the legitimation of monarchy, whether overtly through their praise of kingly wisdom, or implicitly through their gestures of obedience. From any angle, their manoeuvres were circumscribed. But one may still feel that these two paradigms unhelpfully constrain the masques' politics. They involve what Alan Sinfield terms an 'entrapment model' of ideology, which foreshortens the belief-systems that it represents by assuming that those things which seem to challenge a structure of beliefs have been brought into being by the structure itself, and can only ever underpin the needs of the political dominant.[24] They tend to promote a formulaic idea of masque politics, which makes little space for acknowledging the day-to-day conduct of political life, or for exploring how masques responded to specific circumstance. Goldberg, in particular, presents James's 'sustaining contradictions' as fixed and supra-historical, as if they sprang up fully formed in 1603 and continued the same way until 1625, immune to chronology or change, and unaffected by sequence or context. Almost inevitably, such foreshortening implies that the aesthetic closures performed on the dancing-floor had little to do with the material business of state as it went on outside the Banqueting House. It barely disturbs the old view of the masques as courtly narcissism, hermetically sealed-off from reality, and breeding in Stuart kings a misleading sense of their endurance.

The dominant approaches, then, have continued to restrict the political work that can be associated with masques by maintaining a separation between them and the circumstances of their performance. Moreover, both views are vulnerable to Leeds Barroll's complaint that literary critics have tended to associate early Stuart kingship, unhistorically, with 'monolithic, hegemonic power':

One such assumption, often found in literary studies, has generally structured the English state as a binary, with the crown (synonymous with the 'state') in ideological opposition to those whom the crown rules. Such a polarizing of 'ruler' and 'ruled', supposing that the king and those around him contend with those whom they subjugate – the 'people' – has generated a concept of 'hegemonic force' in opposition to subversive counterforce.[25]

Barroll argues that tags like 'subversion and containment' or 'resistance and repression' imply that James and Charles ruled over an absolutist state in which power emanated from the monarch and political relationships took the form of oppositions, antitheses, and binaries. But this simplifies the mixed monarchy that early modern England was, for the Stuarts never possessed the personal absolutism that some literary critics have attributed to them. Although early modern Whitehall was more centralized than its European counterparts, the crown was financially weak and administratively it depended on aristocratic and provincial elites to channel its will into the localities. Unlike Louis XIV's Versailles, Whitehall was less the locus of absolute political hegemony than the main point of contact between Stuart England's competing but complementary social groups, whose cooperation the monarch needed in order to govern.[26] The king did not simply dominate, but ruled by an ongoing and reciprocal process of negotiation. Consensus was as central to the operations of power as conflict. As we shall see, this state of affairs gave masques a particularly sensitive public role. Being a channel of communication between the monarch and his elites, they performed enabling functions in articulating Stuart kingship, mediating between the crown and its partners, voicing royal priorities, registering disagreements, and forwarding the political conversation out of which the monarchy conjured its power. They did not reiterate a pre-determined kingly absolutism but participated creatively in the to and fro of practical political life, exploring the often vexed relationships between the crown, its servants, and political elites. This book, then, attempts to reconfigure the dancing-floor by putting the masques back into that material history. In the masques' manifold engagements with contemporary issues and events, we can read the shifting fortunes of early Stuart monarchy.

The Stuart court was a complex entity: it was a place, an institution, and a concept. In its simplest terms, it was embodied in the fabric of Whitehall and the other royal palaces, such as Greenwich and Hampton Court, which proclaimed kingly authority in their space and architecture. However, the court was not geographically stable, for the seat of government moved with the monarch, and where the king was, there the court had to be. At this level, the court was the king's establishment, his household in extended form. It comprised a huge aggregation of servants, ministers, and officials, from the service personnel at the bottom, paid by salaries, 'diet', or temporary hire, to gentlemen and great aristocrats at the top, who attended the crown out of social obligation and whose rewards came with the perks and advantages of office. This body of people included many overlapping groups, but there were two interlocking spheres in particular: the household attendants, grooms, gentlemen, and officers (known collectively as the Chamber) who waited on the king's person, and the secretaries, advisors, and politicians who, in their conciliar capacity, served the body politic. These two spheres were distinct in purpose but were often staffed from the same pool of personnel – for example, the Earl of Worcester was both James's Master of Horse and a privy councillor. However, in the early Stuart period this dual structure was further complicated by the emergence of a third, privileged space, the royal Bedchamber, which was dominated by a small group of the King's closest personal friends and formed territory to which even ministers and great aristocrats had limited access. Described by Neil Cuddy as the 'entourage',[27] the Gentlemen of the Bedchamber were, at first, almost all Scots, though they were less a political group than a tight-knit social circle, whose influence lay in the distribution of favour and reward. The entourage were the King's intimates rather than advisors: policy, more strictly defined, was made through a wider network of consultation (albeit the entourage became politicized during the years dominated by the Earl of Somerset and Duke of Buckingham, favourites who achieved public office as well as personal intimacy). And these distinctions were overlaid by the court's third aspect, its symbolic function as the fountainhead from which patronage, honour, status, justice, and reward were expected to flow. At this level, contemporaries were not mistaken in looking towards Whitehall as the kingdom's key locale. Its wealth and power made it the centre of national life.[28]

The court, then, was neither closed nor unified. It was a chaotic, frequently confusing structure, and was tied in intricate ways to the life of the realm. Literary critics have often postulated a cultural or political divide between 'court' and 'country', as if the court was somehow insulated or aloof from the rest of the nation. In fact, in an age before permanent parliaments, the court was the centre of government and locus of all decision-making, through which a tide of political transactions flowed, drawing colossal numbers of visitors to Whitehall. James may have preferred hunting to hard work, but the perpetual business of state was the daily fare of councils and committees, and when he was at Newmarket a stream of correspondence followed from his principal minister, the Earl of Salisbury.[29] In the next reign, the business of state expanded exponentially, largely because of Charles's hands-on approach. Unlike his father, Charles was a workaholic, who attended the Privy Council regularly and involved himself in the tiniest minutiae of affairs.[30] At the same time, the court was the nation's main social centre. Whitehall was the bastion of aristocratic influence, where conspicuous consumption and dignified leisure were pursued side by side with place-seeking and social climbing. The patronage system, which filtered into every corner of the national fabric, ensured the constant resort of gentlemen to court in search of favour and produced a corresponding outflow of offices and rewards, while as a marriage market Whitehall was the breeding-ground for alliances between noble dynasties and across social ranks. The court was not a closed cadre, but an agglomeration of elite and would-be elite groups, its spaces populated by established office-holders and outsiders gradually making their way – minor gentry, wealthy citizens, younger sons, educated professionals. Its rituals and etiquette marked the King's territory as separate, but were also channels of contact with the wider world, an intricate web of communication through which he maintained outreach with his subjects. His status as centre of the kingdom was actualized in his physical presence at court, which modelled his pervasive influence on the realm.

In addition to its permeability, the court was not a single entity, but plural. Unlike Elizabeth, James and Charles had families, and their consorts and children maintained separate households, with their own estates, officials, and companions. A large part of the two queens' time was spent in their own properties at Somerset House and Greenwich, and their establishments were institutionally distinct. Each had a hierarchy of officers that mirrored their husbands' households, and each fostered a separate cultural identity, through patronage, friendships, and personal style. Some European queens consort, such as Marie de' Médici, became powerful politicians in their own right, and, although Anne and Henrietta Maria never achieved quite such autonomy, the separations of personnel and personality associated with them put a significant tension at the heart of the court. If not exactly a rival centre of power, the consort's court prevented the royal voice from ever being unitary, and pulled politically and culturally in alternative directions. So too the arrival of a crown prince in 1603, and the household that was created for him, meant that the court had a reversionary interest for the first time in fifty years, with all its associated potential for oedipal conflict. The ideological divide between Prince Henry and his father was even more marked than that between James and Anne, and Henry's status as heir apparent made him the focus of a brief but vigorous princely cult. Consorts and children headed up little courts within the court, enriching and complicating the Whitehall mix, and making the articulation of authority far more involved than the simple validation of James's power. Of course there were many links between the royal households. Patronage and dynastic intermarriage ensured that the King's, Queen's, and Prince's entourages were never wholly distinct and that their memberships were frequently entangled. Still, although the King was the key figure, the court's internal structural divisions meant that it was not a single, monolithic hierarchy but a point of intersection between multiple and overlapping circles.

Beyond the royal family, favourites and powerful courtiers often acquired their own followings too. Under James, the groupings associated with the Howard dynasty and the friends and family of the Elizabethan Earl of Essex stood in tense relation to one another, divided by conflicts of personality, affiliation, and ideology. The two great favourites, Somerset and Buckingham, accrued huge personal influence over patronage and policy, each becoming a major power-broker in his own right. Other groups or affinities – such as the French and Spanish lobbies – were more inchoate, and shifted with the changing political configurations. Contemporaries were well aware of these distinctions, for their navigation was the essence of courtiership, and an attachment to the wrong patron could damage one's interests irretrievably. From a modern perspective, Whitehall's factionalism looks dysfunctional, and, at times, the co-existence of multiple centres of power could indeed be destabilizing. This structure threatened to become counter-productive under Buckingham, whose network of clients and dependants was so dominant that it provoked serious personal and political resentment. But factionalism was not intrinsically an evil, for as a way of accommodating differences and getting business done it was necessary to the structure of the early modern court. It created internal dynamism, by opening Whitehall up to connections that would otherwise have been marginalized or excluded, and encouraging a constant inflow of ideas and talent. At the same time, favourites were useful intermediary figures, who shielded the monarch and shared some of the burdens of office with him. There was, then, not one single 'courtly' politics at Stuart Whitehall, but a series of factions jostling for patronage and political influence. John Adamson characterizes European courts in this period as structured into 'foyers of power', which defined the successive levels of influence that individuals were able to achieve at the centre. Alternately complementing and competing with one another, these internal separations created a 'politics of access' which maintained energy and torsion within court life.[31] The court was never hermetically sealed, nor did it speak with a single voice.

It is difficult, when thinking of Whitehall as a topography, to draw the line that defines precisely where the court began and ended. In this period, other social sites were beginning to develop as gathering grounds for England's elites, which stood in ambivalent relation to the centre. The Inns of Court, the London playhouses, and the emergent West End were all frequented by the same people who attended the court, and were in some respects Whitehall's outlying territories, though in other regards their identity was constituted in antithesis to it. In a valuable study of court culture, Malcolm Smuts argues, perhaps over-generously, that London's whole cultural environment was essentially an extension of Whitehall.[32] Certainly London flourished economically and culturally because the court resided nearby, for the court's magnetic pull created a permanent community of social elites and service personnel in the capital. It is true, too, that court culture was not separate from the wider world, for Whitehall's patronage and spending helped to drive the cultural scene, and London's high society precipitated around the weekly calendar of balls and plays, feasts and gatherings at court and in private houses. But the idea that the court was a distinct territory with its own values and outlook was still taken for granted by contemporaries. Satirists depicted court and city as competing institutions, and the discourses of courtiership and urbanization pulled against one another, modelling civil values according to diverging principles and standards of behaviour. For example, Ben Jonson's *Cynthia's Revels* (1600) combines praise for Cynthia's ideal court with robust censure of individual courtiers for being effete, trivial, vain, time-wasting, and self-obsessed. Throughout Jonson's work and career, the oscillation between the opposed claims of courtliness and metropolitan urbanity is particularly emphatic.

Smuts's insistence on the court's open-endedness does, though, usefully underline that court culture was pluralistic and multi-faceted – that it was 'polycentric',[33] with several centres rather than one – and it draws attention to the courtly hinterlands, the satellite zones in London and beyond, such as the great aristocratic households which took their bearings from Whitehall and were in some respects miniaturized versions of it. Court culture percolated into the provinces because of noblemen like the Earl of Pembroke, who danced in masques then took Van Dyck portraits home to their country estates, while noblemen's mansions clustered along the Strand and courtiers bought houses in outlying suburbs, allowing courtly and urban culture to cross-pollinate. Courtly festivities followed monarch and consort as they visited their servants' homes in the city and country. In London, lords Hay and Buckingham feasted the court with masques, and Salisbury staged masques for James in Hertfordshire, as did the Crofts family when he arrived at Newmarket; Henrietta Maria mounted private shows with her ladies at Greenwich and Oatlands. The distinctively Stuart vogue for amateur theatricals in aristocratic houses in London and the countryside was another instance of the gradual dissemination of courtly forms. Moreover, since James and Charles recruited continental artists and surrounded themselves with the latest in European artistic fashion, the cultural climate over which they presided was assertively cosmopolitan. They may have travelled less widely than Elizabeth had done, but their courts' cultural impact was more wide-ranging and dramatic. There was no single court culture but a rich multi-cultural mosaic of competing modes.

So the image of the court which descends from the masques – integrated, harmonious, and unified – was some way from the actuality as lived at Stuart Whitehall. Undoubtedly a main function of festivity was to affirm the monarch's social and political power, by creating compelling images of his dominance at court and in the wider world. Masques performed gestures of homage to the king, proclaiming his authority, signalling correspondences between the body natural and body politic, and identifying his physical person with a principle of social and cosmic order. As his presence stilled storms, solved riddles, breathed life into statues, banished monsters, and exorcised interlopers, so the masques invested him with a quasi-magical legitimacy. Their characteristic device was to instil a sense of common purpose by manipulating anxiety, using fictions in which tension was aroused and suddenly and miraculously discharged. Typically, danger threatened and was averted, or strangers intruded and were expelled: the masques' dazzling epiphanies and instantaneous transitions from dark to light authorized royal government by testifying to the king's effortless command over those 'others' who contested or limited his power. Yet these images of perfect political competence cannot be taken as simple projections of a pre-existing reality, since a gap always intervened between their assertions of unity and the multi-layered textures of court life. Masques did not simply reflect royal glory but were symbolic transactions playing out the bonds between the monarch and his elites, while implicitly working to accommodate any differences that separated them. Each masque affirmed the king's sovereign power, but on the basis of a perpetually renewed dialogue with his subjects.

So, for example, at the simplest level, a masque might represent the court to itself, underlining its participants' sense of unity and celebrating their collective identification with the centre. But since Whitehall was not monolithic, much festivity was conducted across internal structural boundaries, and was energized by the court's areas of tension, with all their associated potential for debate, conflict, or resentment. The clearest examples of such disruption were Prince Henry's masques, the forms of which conflicted radically with his father's. For a brief but significant period, Henry functioned as a focus for alternative political aspirations to those encouraged by James. An able young man, fervent about the Protestant faith and keen to prove himself in the kingly arena of warfare, he acquired an enthusiastic personal following, and presided over a household at Richmond run on quite different lines from his father's. His festivals (discussed in chapter 6 below) showcased his military and religious ambitions, contradicting James's pacific and eirenical outlook. They were danced in homage to James but also in some sense challenged him, in that they asserted Henry's wish to be a power-broker in his own right, announcing a politics that was sharply at odds with Jacobean ideology. Henry's festivals thus unsettled his father's culture and iconography, creating a kind of legitimation crisis that was resolved only by his premature death.

No less striking were the festivals associated with the two queens, Anne and Henrietta Maria, both of whom were enthusiastic dancers, but whose masquing potentially disturbed their husbands' public profiles. Given the paternal emphases of Stuart culture, in which the king was symbolically identified as the father of the state, the wife's fate was always to be positioned as the subordinated partner, her gender difference testifying to her consort's superiority. Yet as Anne and Henrietta Maria developed their own festivals (discussed in chapter 5 below), so they acquired distinctive imageries that pulled against their husbands' cultures and staged active displays of female autonomy and Amazonian heroism that unsettled the gender hierarchies which normally underwrote kingly power. In the queens' masques, the two kings' authority was always triumphant, but it was none-theless problematized by their wives' forceful self-display. Female resistance was needed to affirm kingly control, the defeat of the feminine empowering the masculine monarch, but it backhandedly gave the consorts a crucial role in articulating royal identity. Its cost was the presentation of the royal marriage as under strain, with each king locked in conflict with his queen or in erotic dependence upon her.

Internal tensions are apparent even in masques staged by Gentlemen of the Bedchamber, the King's innermost circle of associates and a group amongst whom we might have expected the performers' relationships to be virtually equal. Despite the royal servants' similarity, their collective expressions of homage were never innocent of national or social differences. Rather, eyewitness reports of early Jacobean festivals always registered which dancers were English and which Scots, and, as courtiers gained or lost favour, so the performance of common devotion to a political father was compromised by the opportunities masques gave for self-promotion. In particular, in the years dominated by Somerset and Buckingham, masques became sites of struggle between aristocratic dancers intent on recommend-ing themselves, for whom theatrical performance was a means to enhance their status and demonstrate their prestige to the court as a whole. Although the mid-Jacobean masques (discussed in chapter 7 below) depicted the court as bound harmoniously into amity, they were riven by rivalries, as favourites and factions competed for reward. Moreover, these masques frequently debated the courtier's role, focusing on his duty of graceful self-fashioning, and on the place of the pleasure-principle in court life. They underlined the individual courtier's dependence on the King who could make or break him, but their energies came from the performer's disruptive desire and the unresolvable contradiction between his private aspiration and the solidarity of the group.

So the masques could never be passive reflectors of a complacent court, but always had some function of voicing or discharging tensions: royal authority constantly had to be staged or asserted. Indeed, it is a salutary reminder of the fluidity and breadth of Whitehall that a surprising number of courtiers who danced in the masques went on to fight Charles in the Civil War. A few examples will illustrate this. One remarkable case is the Earl of Holland, who danced in all the early Caroline masques, *Love's Triumph*, *Albion's Triumph*, *Tempe Restored*, and *Coelum Britannicum*. Brother to the puritanical Earl of Warwick (who later became parliament's admiral), Holland served Charles as Groom of the Stool and was close to Henrietta Maria, but he supported war with Spain and was an enemy of Charles's favourite advisors, Weston, Laud, and Strafford; at Strafford's trial he gave evidence for the prosecution. When war came, Holland oscillated between the two sides, acting first as a parliamentary envoy, then fighting for Charles at Newbury, then deserting again and joining the Presbyterian peers who wanted to broker a peace. He became distrusted by both sides and was executed for his part in the second civil war, but his hesitation between unpalatable alternatives bespeaks the difficulties faced by a courtier for whom participation in masques did not mean uncritical endorsement of the King.[34] Just as remarkable is the example of Lord Wharton – known as 'Sawpit' Wharton following a story that at Edgehill he fled from the battle and hid in a sawpit. Wharton was one of the lords who voted in the Short Parliament for grievances to be discussed before supply was voted, and he opposed billetting in the second Bishops' War, for which Charles rebuked him and Strafford said he should be shot for sedition. In the Long Parliament he joined the radicals, commanded a regiment at Edgehill, and supported the Independents down to Pride's Purge in 1648. He refused an invitation to join the Council of State, but remained in friendly communication with Cromwell; yet this young man danced in *Albion's Triumph*, *Coelum Britannicum*, and *Britannia Triumphans*, and was painted in shepherd guise by Van Dyck.[35] Or again, there was the Earl of Denbigh, who married Buckingham's sister and danced in *Coelum Britannicum* and *Salmacida Spolia*. He fought Charles at Edgehill, ended his career as speaker for the Lords (1648–9), and sat for a while on Cromwell's Council of State; Clarendon called him 'a person very ingrateful to the King'.[36] And one should not forget Philip Herbert, fourth Earl of Pembroke, who supported parliament throughout the 1640s and was elected to Cromwell's Council of State, but who was one of James's earliest favourites, danced in numerous Jacobean festivals, and, as Lord Chamberlain from 1626, supervised the arrangements for every Caroline masque.

The presence of such men amongst the masquers cannot be taken as a key to masque politics. Changed circumstances made for changed behaviour, and many courtiers found themselves in situations after 1642 which would have been almost unimaginable any earlier. Nonetheless, their appearance demonstrates the breadth of political opinion embraced by court festival – the way that Whitehall was a meeting ground for people of divergent attitudes and priorities, and who, once events polarized, moved in opposite directions on the political spectrum. It also suggests how crucial the masques were as points of internal contact, arenas in which symbolic displays of rapprochement, mediation, or accommodation could be performed. They depicted the court as happily united in homage to its head, marshalling their participants into attitudes of loyalty and support, and they created a climate of trust in the monarchy, underlining the personal identification between King and subject, master and servants. Nonetheless, this inner unity could not be taken for granted, and each masque's objective was to create the conditions for consensus, instilling confidence in the monarch, and finding the point of assimilation between King, courtier, and spectator. Each masque had to manage the potential tensions of its festive community, and – as we shall see – success was by no means guaranteed.

These considerations all relate to the masques' internal economy, their manipulation of social relationships within the court community. On another level, festivity also served extrinsic political functions, by giving prestigious expression to matters of policy, and to the values and ideals with which the monarchy sought to associate itself. Of course, they were not exactly public events in the modern sense of state propaganda, as there was only a limited attempt to publicize their content beyond the immediate spectatorship. Indeed, it was part of the ethos of court festival that access was limited to an elite group, membership of which confirmed one's closeness to the centre of power.[37] Nevertheless, it was important that the Christmas masques were state affairs: they were danced in the Banqueting House before a cross-section of the political nation – officials, counsellors, aristocrats, and magistrates – and with guests of honour drawn from the diplomatic community, whose presence made the performance an event on the international stage, news of which rapidly trickled back to Paris, Vienna, and Madrid. Not infrequently, court festival spilt out into public spaces. Magnificent celebrations were mounted for Princess Elizabeth's wedding in 1613, with masques, fireworks, and a river triumph; a grand tournament was held for her brother's coming of age in 1621; and in 1634 *The Triumph of Peace* began with a stunning procession through the streets from London to Whitehall. The newsworthiness of big occasions is evidenced by the publication in multiple printed editions of *The Triumph of Peace*, Elizabeth's marriage masques, and the first Jacobean masque (*The Vision of the Twelve*

Goddesses, 1604).[38] The ceremonials ordered for Prince Henry's investiture in 1610 were also carefully stage-managed, for his acclamation as heir designate was combined with a statement to parliament about the crown's financial needs, so that the festivity was coordinated with James's political ends. In the following reign, Charles used his masques even more systematically to underpin his political initiatives.

Within the Banqueting House walls, every masque involved some perspective on political issues, either through specific textual allusion or through imagery and dramatic fable, which ensured that performances resonated with current events. The aim was to invoke respect for the crown's political will, and instil confidence through the potency with which it was depicted. Masques were one of the most prestigious spaces for expounding Stuart kingly ideology. A distinctly superior image-making machine, they praised the values of Stuart rule, proclaiming its justice, wisdom, and authority, and promoting reverence towards it. Against this, Malcolm Smuts warns that masque fables should not be read as conduits of government, arguing that they were too optimistic and idealizing to be effective agents of policy. He says that, as 'symbolic allegories', masques 'offered little scope for political realism. Their function was to celebrate the monarchs' successes, not to remind them of unresolved difficulties or to enforce the mechanisms through which royal policies might be enforced.'[39] However, this perspective is excessively literalistic. Festivity did not present the Stuart 'reality', but put into circulation images of what James and Charles aspired to achieve, building ties of trust and common ground with their servants, and forging around the crown an ideology of peace, unity, and stability. Advertising the king's competence, instilling deference, and promulgating royal credibility, masques set out to foster confidence in Stuart government amongst precisely those spectators whose cooperation James and Charles needed for their rule to be a success.

But what constantly made things problematic was the divisiveness of the policies with which masques necessarily engaged and which created tensions within them. The earliest masques focused on the radical changes of 1603, the arrival of a Scottish king in England, and his wish to make the two realms a new constitutional entity, Britain. Unfortunately for James, British union was not a *fait accompli*, but aroused disagreements between and within the nations, and never became law in the form that he hoped. Unresolved differences over British identity bedevilled Stuart politics, and created the conditions for the collapse of Charles's government. As argued below (chapters 4 and 10), Britishness was the foundational trope for Stuart masquing and the single most important contribution that masques made to political discourse, for the Stuarts put their claim to British kingship at the core of their iconography. However, British identity could not be asserted without pain. In the early masques it is controversial and contested, while the later masques are troubled by gaps between these British tropes and the responses of Charles's constituent peoples. The issue here was the tension between the rhetoric of unity and Whitehall's internationalism, the fact that the Stuart court encompassed several nations, not just one. The masques' imagery has to be understood as a not always happy attempt to turn this conflicted identity into a singularity.

Just as vexed were the masques' international and religious dimensions. Unlike other Stuart cultural forms, masquing always had a European aspect, either explicit or implied. Masques were events on the world stage, intended for foreign consumption, their imagery putting the Stuarts in competition with Habsburg and Bourbon, and signalling their desire to be global players. Their emphasis on peace and stability was implicitly comparative, for it underlined the Stuarts' international standing and the values they espoused. James's self-image as the peaceful Solomon coordinated strong rule at home with constructive internationalism overseas, his pursuit of peace in both spheres being mutually reinforcing. His diplomacy bridged differences between Catholic and Protestant, while domestic confessional enthusiasms were damped down by an insistence on the disruptiveness of religious zeal. Under Charles, the emphasis on British peace was even more emphatically set against Europe's war-torn state. But the masques' pacifism was in tension with competing expectations about religious obligations, and with the hope, inside the court and without, that policy might be led by solidarity with co-religionists in Europe. Such disagreements erupted into the festivals for Prince Henry and for Princess Elizabeth's wedding: James's culture struggled to contain the disruptive enthusiasms of a son eager for war and a daughter whose marriage drew him uncomfortably close to Protestant Germany (see chapter 5 below). After 1619, the maelstrom of religious warfare into which the continent descended – initiated, in large measure, by James's new son-in-law – meant that Europe was the defining issue around which all other political matters turned. The later Jacobean masques (discussed in chapter 8) engaged repeatedly with the need to limit conflict, but could not escape the circumstance that the fortunes of James's German grandsons (who before 1630 were next heirs to the throne) were at stake. Later, Charles's wish to have a significant presence in Europe and his reluctance to engage in active warfare created an even more acute contradiction, between his images of heroically active kingship and the limits beyond which he would not go (see chapter 9). Stuart festivity was thus caught in an almost impossible double bind. The desire to promote Britain as a power to be reckoned with internationally was at odds with the ideology of peace and stability which for domestic reasons the Stuarts also needed to underwrite.

These contradictions lead to the question of precisely whom masques spoke for, and how their meanings were received. There always was an expectation that masques might have a counselling function, that festivity should educate as well as entertain. This idea is thematized in Jonson's masques, which frequently represent the poet as an intermediary between king and masquers, upholding royal fame while tutoring the king in the duties of office – though it is difficult to avoid the perception that humanistic pedagogy often took second place to the more urgent need to endorse royal policy.[40] On the other hand, masques which were presented to the court rather than by it had more freedom of manoeuvre, in that they were partly a conversation with royalty. So, for example, *The Triumph of Peace*, presented to Charles in 1634 by gentlemen from the Inns of Court, articulated an unusually challenging perspective on law and government, and the two shows the lawyers staged for the Palatine wedding are palpably different from *The Lords' Masque*, which was the court's 'internal' celebration. So too when the king moved around geographically, entertainments sometimes took the opportunity of talking back politely to him. This was the convention that obtained during progresses, when monarchs passing over the thresholds of towns or country houses could be welcomed and gently admonished. The hosts of a reception renewed their bonds with the dynasty, usually by handing over the keys, but sometimes reminded the monarch that kingship was a two-way street and subjects had priorities too. Of course, any royal encounter, inside or outside Whitehall, was limited by questions of tact, as the king could never be presented with meanings he was unwilling to endorse. The cancellation of *Neptune's Triumph* in 1624 is a striking example of what happened to a masque that, at a tense moment, overstepped the boundaries of the possible. The art of dialogue with the monarch was to find formulae through which all participants could communicate their point of view, defining areas of agreement and accepting mutual constraints, while for the king there might be some advantage in letting himself be manoeuvred into postures that expressed what people hoped for from him. Against this, though, is the possibility that the apparent consensus could conceal misunderstandings. Almost certainly at some masques the participants failed to intuit each other's points of view or to finesse their differences, so that problems in interpreting masques point to lurking tensions that could not readily be resolved. Still, the opportunities for masques to make meaning on several levels at once were substantial. There always had to be some kind of dialogue.

The bulk of this study follows this dialogue across the principal masques, chapters 4 through 10 presenting a narrative from 1603 to 1640 (except for chapter 5, which suspends chronology to explore festivals sponsored by the two queens). Each chapter covers around five years, so that the discussion highlights the changing contours of public life. Hence the masques' concerns shift as the political narrative shifts. The early Jacobean preoccupation with union soon gave way to the ideological uncertainties around Prince Henry and the Palatine marriage, and these were succeeded by the factional rivalries of mid-reign, and finally by the polarizations brought on by European war. In the next reign, Charles set the state on a new footing and the early masques supported his radical initiatives, but in the mid-1630s the failure of Scottish rule and its catastrophic consequences for England put festivity under strain again. The masques are thus an index of Stuart political consciousness. They demonstrate the court's developing response to public events, and its attempt to use culture to manage the royal image and promote or defend policy. Their various successes and failures – whether they transcend conflict effectively or not – help to disclose the strengths and weaknesses of Stuart government.

However, for a total picture we have to add in two complicating factors. One is that, by being occasions on which the whole court celebrated its sense of identity, masques had to encompass the needs of spectators as well as performers, a function which (I shall argue) gave them their emotional and psychological force. Masques have usually been seen from a top-down perspective, which treats the king's view as central, but while they staged his political power, they always had wider social resonance. They were no less meaningful occasions for the spectators, who are voiceless in the texts but whose presence at the performance was just as important, and they spoke beyond the throne to their experiences, dramatizing the issues of exclusion and belonging, identification and difference which were crucial for all Whitehall's habitués. Chapters 2 and 3 address this by sketching an anthropology of masquing, adopting a 'thick description' of festival practices in order to source the masques' core scenarios to Whitehall's inner symbolic economy, the structures and ceremonials which constituted the courtly *habitus* and around which the courtier's identity was constructed. The roots of masque form can be located in the court's ritual practices: a core function was to stage the anxieties about personal embodiment and social bonding experienced by the whole Whitehall community. Masques were powerful occasions not only because they promoted the king, but because they ritualistically played out the psychology of the courtier and his need to belong. They managed his involvement in this highly charged, high-risk environment, and their energies derive from the intense antagonisms and affinities of court life.

The other complicating factor is that, across the early Stuart period as a whole, masque form did not stand still, but altered with the shifting political climate. Masque aesthetics shaped royal responses to political change, but were themselves reshaped by transformations in the public sphere, and were accommodated to the changing relationship between crown and subjects. The common critical assumption that masques always took a strict cellular form, of masque and antimasque, and traded in rigid and absolute oppositions, ignores the fluidity of their structures over time. Jonson's masques come closest to the simple cell, with their sharp oppositions between witches and queens, satyrs and princes, but his schematic binaries did not fall fully into place before 1609 and lasted only briefly, after which he elaborated the form in new directions. Before 1609, the dominant masque scenario was the quest, not the combat. Festivals such as *The Vision of the Twelve Goddesses* and *The Masque of Blackness* were organized as processional structures, in which exotic outsiders arrived at Whitehall intending some gift or in search of a goal that gave their journey meaning. The action led towards incorporation of the unfamiliar rather than conflict with it: unlike the later, more confrontational masques, these devices showed strange visitors being absorbed, and there was an absence of physical transformation. Indeed, in *The Masque of Blackness*, this point – that the Ethiopian dames departed without losing their dark colouring – has been a critical stumbling-block, since many discussions assume that the masque lacks closure, as if the women's failure to transform signalled Jonson's underlying lack of faith in the court.[41] But such expectations derive from habits that developed later, when the antimasque/masque structure was more embedded and magical transformations had become germane. In 1605, there would have been no sense that the performance lacked anything. By 1610 Jonson had developed his more conflict-based form, but even here the binaries could be resolved in different ways: in *Oberon*, the grotesque satyrs who danced before Prince Henry's glorious arrival were not shut out but remained present throughout. And as, in later festivals, the number of antimasques increased, so their strict structural tie with the main masque loosened, producing that distinctive Caroline form, the masque as triumph, where a royal acclamation was preceded by any number of antimasque 'entries'. This reflected new technical possibilities and cultural influences, especially French practice where multiple *entrées* were the norm, but it also signalled changing relationships between monarch and masquers.

Moreover, while Jonson's model was influential, he was only one of many poets, and others developed more open-ended forms. From the start, Daniel's practice diverged sharply, his prefaces emphasizing far more than Jonson's that masques were collaborations and that, in performance, attention focused on masquers and audience as well as monarch. Jonson tended to disparage the performance, insisting that a masque's value lay in the ideological remainder that spectators took away, the 'more removed mysteries' instilled by the poet; in comparison, the bodily part was a 'carcass'.[42] But Daniel's prefaces insist that masques are just 'dreams' and their poets 'engineers for shadows'; their 'only life consists in show'.[43] Consequently, he refuses sharp oppositions between masque and antimasque. His masques underline their visionary aspect, emphasizing that meaning arises from the players' and audience's collective imaginings, and put much less emphasis on the monarch's controlling view. Intriguingly, in a correspondence now sadly lost, Daniel discussed with Fulke Greville – a writer with seriously conflicted attitudes about the court – how masques might benefit from 'improvements or reformations';[44] it is tempting to suppose that they had the 'Jonsonian' masque in mind. Similarly, Campion's masques often conflate antimasquers and masquers into the same persons, with the masquers having to reform themselves internally rather than defeat external antagonists, and they avoid instantaneous metamorphoses, using nuanced changes which move the performers only gradually towards perfection. In *Lord Hay's Masque*, the masquers slowly change from trees into men: the device emphasizes reconciliation rather than royal fiat, and presents resolution coming about through inner adjustments, not kingly command. The persistence of alternatives to the Jonsonian form meant that there was never one stereotypical resolution which all masques habitually reproduced.

One further development was also crucial: the courtiers' gradual invasion of the antimasque. In Jacobean festival the opposition between masque and antimasque was almost always social as well as moral. The masquers' prestige was built into their status as aristocrats, whereas the grotesque performers were marked as ideologically illegitimate because they were outsiders, i.e. professional actors. In the modern idealizing view, which takes the masques' hierarchies of status and ethics as mutually reinforcing, this separation is fundamental: the culminating moment is the disclosure of the masquers as the socially privileged representatives of the evening's moral values. Yet in practice this boundary was increasingly breached. In the late 1610s, a series of masques put aristocratic performers in grotesque roles and, in some cases, speaking parts. The best-known example is *The Gypsies Metamorphosed*, in which Buckingham and his friends played outrageously informal parts, but this was only one of several shows – some in the great festivals, other more casual or portable performances such as 'running' masques – that allowed courtiers to experiment with impromptu, informal, or inappropriately ribald roles. James Knowles, observing that many performers were connected to James's and Buckingham's intimate circles, calls them an extension of 'Bedchamber culture' into public space.[45] But even after Buckingham's death, the line between masque and antimasque continued to erode, and it became common in Caroline festivals, particularly in Henrietta Maria's masques, for antimasque entries to be led or performed by minor courtiers.[46] Such cross-casting completely undermined the idea that there was a sharp distinction between the world of ideals and the world of contingency, for in practice the simplistic binaries of praise and dispraise could not be kept apart. In this regard, performance and ideology were all too often at odds.

It goes without saying that masques were complex events. They functioned on many levels at once: their meanings were different for the king, masquers, and spectators, and their forms and resolutions were endlessly reworked. Critics have tended to decode them in relatively formulaic ways, and used this limited view of their meanings to write them off as irrelevant to the larger business of state. But we shall find that spectacle was a space apart, where performance responded to the pressure of events, and where political and social purposes intricately overlapped. In court festivity, symbolic solutions were applied to material problems, and this invested masques with a unique, if compromised, role in the transformation of Stuart monarchy. As spectacles in which the nature of Stuart kingship was renegotiated year after year, masques helped to invent the early modern state.

CHAPTER 2

Rites of exclusion

Sometime early in January 1604 – during the court's first Christmas season under England's first Stuart monarch – Ben Jonson and his friend Sir John Roe were shut out from the performance of a masque at Hampton Court. Roe wrote a bitter verse-letter about the experience, and fifteen years later Jonson retold the story during his sojourn with the Scottish poet William Drummond: 'Sir John Roe loved him and when they two were ushered by my Lord Suffolk from a masque, Roe wrote a moral epistle to him, which began that next to plays the court and the state were the best. God threateneth kings, kings lords, and lords do us.'[1] Unfortunately these details are tantalizingly vague, and we cannot be certain exactly why Jonson and Roe were excluded. It is tempting to suppose that the notoriously short-tempered poet provoked some incident that caused him to be ejected from the hall. It would be deliciously ironic if one of the first Jacobean masques was disrupted by the man who spent the next twenty years hymning Stuart order in his own Christmas festivals. The likelier scenario, though, is that Jonson and Roe never made it into the auditorium, but were refused admission at the door. This would explain the Earl of Suffolk's involvement, since, as Lord Chamberlain, he was head of James's household and had overall responsibility for controlling access to court festivals. Still, Jonson told Drummond that they were ushered 'from' the masque and Roe's poem speaks of being 'thrust out', which implies that they penetrated at least into the hall. Perhaps they got through the door but were ejected by senior staff inside, or maybe the crush inside was so great that several spectators were forced out to create space for the performance. Or maybe Jonson and Roe were involved in a scrimmage at the entry; given the demand for places, the Lord Chamberlain and his officials often had to assert their control with physical violence. Whatever the reason, the incident was sufficiently galling that Jonson not only narrated it to Drummond but ten years on recollected it again, in a speech by Lovel in *The New Inn*, distinguishing between true and false valour:

> I am kept out a masque, sometime thrust out,
> Made wait a day, two, three, for a great word,
> Which, when it comes forth, is all frown and forehead!
> What laughter should this breed, rather than anger,
> Out of the tumult of so many errors
> To feel with contemplation mine own quiet?[2]

In Lovel's analysis of the proper occasions for valour, anger at exclusion from a masque counts as heroic effort wasted on an unworthy object. But unlike Lovel, Jonson and Roe did not suffer patiently. Roe's poem and Jonson's inability to forget suggest how sharply their exclusion had rankled.

One uncertainty in this episode is the identity of the masque that Jonson and Roe failed to see. In the title of Roe's epistle,[3] the date is given as 6 January 1603 (i.e. 1604 by the modern calendar), but that evening the show seen by the court was merely a Scottish sword dance. The masque originally scheduled for Twelfth Night had been Samuel Daniel's *The Vision of the Twelve Goddesses*, but this was deferred to 8 January because of rivalries over precedence between the French and Spanish ambassadors.[4] Possibly the show was the sword dance,[5] but in the poem it is twice called 'the Queen's masque', which suggests that the date is wrong, and that Jonson and Roe were at Hampton Court for *The Vision of the Twelve Goddesses*. Daniel's *Twelve Goddesses* is the event that Jonson would have been interested in, since at the outset of James's reign Daniel was his rival for commissions and had landed this first major masque, which Jonson must have hoped to claim for himself. During the royal family's journeys south in 1603, both poets presented verses to members of the royal family, and Jonson's *Entertainment at Althorp* for Queen Anne and Prince Henry (June 1603) was calculated to display his talents as an inventor of festival devices. Nonetheless, Daniel's favour with the Countess of Bedford, the Queen's closest English friend and a patron whom Jonson had himself cultivated, carried the day and secured him the commission.[6] Yet despite Jonson's absence, Daniel must have got wind of his criticisms, since his printed text included defensive justifications of his iconography, and made a pre-emptive strike against 'captious censurers' who aspire to seem 'very deeply learned in all mysteries whatsoever' (194, 203). Such language suggests that Daniel was reacting against Jonson's elevated view of the philosophical functions of court festival, his belief in the ability of masque symbolism to endure, transforming 'present occasions' into 'more removed mysteries'.[7] Jonson's views were an implied attack on the relatively unambitious mode of Daniel's festival devices, but they did not appear in print until the publication of his part of the royal entry in March 1604 and the 1606 quarto of *Hymenaei*. Perhaps Jonson

had, after all, vented his criticisms at Daniel's performance, and so got
himself ejected.[8]

This specifically poetic rivalry colours Roe's poem 'To Ben. Jonson, 6 Jan.
1603', making it one of several early testimonies to the jostling for position
amongst those were keen to win court commissions. But the thrust of Roe's
epistle has less to do with poetic contests than with larger issues of access and
status. In Roe's memory, the envy of unsuccessful poets for the successful
is subsumed beneath a more wide-ranging social anxiety over 'who's in,
who's out':

> The state and men's affairs are the best plays
> Next yours. 'Tis nor more nor less than due praise.
> Write, but touch not the much descending race
> Of lords' houses, so settled in worth's place,
> As, but themselves, none think them usurpers.   5
> It is no fault in thee to suffer theirs.
> If the Queen masque, or the King a-hunting go,
> Though all the court follow, let them. We know
> Like them in goodness that court ne'er will be,
> For that were virtue, and not flattery.   10
> Forget we were thrust out. It is but thus:
> God threatens kings, kings lords, as lords do us.
> Judge of strangers, trust and believe your friend,
> And so me; and when I true friendship end,
> With guilty conscience let me be worse stung   15
> Than with Popham's sentence thieves, or Coke's tongue
> Traitors are. Friends are ourselves. This I thee tell
> As to my friend, and to myself as counsel.
> Let for a while the time's unthrifty rout
> Contemn learning, and all your studies flout.   20
> Let them scorn hell, they will a sergeant fear
> More than we that, ere long; God may forbear,
> But creditors will not. Let them increase
> In riot and excess as their means cease,
> Let them scorn him that made them, and still shun   25
> His grace, but love the whore who hath undone
> Them and their souls. But that they, that allow
> But one God, should have religions enow
> For the Queen's masque, and their husbands, for more
> Than all the gentiles knew, or Atlas bore!   30
> Well, let all pass, and trust him who nor cracks
> The bruisèd reed, nor quencheth smoking flax.[9]

This poem might well be read as continuing the literary arguments in the
hall. With its scorn for the audience's lack of learning (19–20) and its jibe

(28–9) about the number of religions in the masque (probably referring to the heterogeneous collection of goddesses that Daniel brought in),[10] it anticipates criticisms that Jonson was shortly to make in print. But the epistle moves beyond merely poetic rivalries to voice tropes of personal self-justification which are resonant of a larger and more widely shared social scenario – one in which anxiety about belonging to the court community is the inevitable counterpart of the ever-present possibility of being excluded from it.

Roe's distinction between good and bad poets is part of a broader opposition between the worth of those who are expelled and the worthlessness of those who remain, which represents the moral value of the court as a series of ethical polarities (ignorance/knowledge, flattery/friendship, guilt/innocence, riot/self-control, etc.). Although these distinctions are expressed ethically, their roots lie in social considerations, since the moral categories collapse so readily into social equivalents. Roe's polarities separate those who have achieved courtly access from those who are denied it, and in this manoeuvre social failure is taken for moral superiority. It is because Jonson and Roe are ejected from the celebrations in the hall that their claim to superior worth seems true: they are expelled because they are good, and good because they are expelled. Their assertion of difference from the people who have expelled them creates a compensatory sense of private authenticity, allowing Roe to scorn the worthlessness of the court that ejects him. But inevitably this defensive manoeuvre reinstalls the tenacious social anxieties which it purports to discharge. The vigour of Roe's protestation of indifference is suspect; indeed, the poem's distinctions *have* to seem absolute because his exclusion was not voluntary but thrust upon him. Consequently the intensity of his assertion of moral difference from the court signals covert identification with it and the continuing power over him of a desire to be admitted. His insistence on his own authenticity and the court's inauthenticity testifies to the persistence of a barely repressed wish to be taken in.

So Roe's critique of court celebration discloses backhandedly its own involvement in a world of social privilege which it purports to reject. Either you belong, it seems to say, in which case you celebrate your difference from those unfortunate enough to be excluded; or you aspire to belong, in which case your assertion of difference is a coded bid for acceptance. And this unacknowledged but scarcely hidden desire for inclusion is exemplified by the poem's contradictions. Roe's pose of superiority depends on his having been excluded, so he needs to be excluded in order to feel superior; yet his claim of superiority to the whole squalid affair is itself a strategy for admission on an alternative ticket. Roe's oscillation between the desire to belong and the parade of contempt for the worthlessness of the occasion composes in miniature the psychology of court festival as it affected all masque spectators, the embarrassment and damage to status which waited on the failure to secure entry. The care with which Roe maintains his pose of studied contempt towards the masque betrays his interest in admission to it.

Roe's social anxiety, his desire not to be excluded, is well seen in the poem's scatter-shot, the variety of targets against which it hits out. It is hard to work out where his anger begins and ends. Obviously Suffolk is one implied target, who is implicated in the reflections of lines 1–5 on the poverty of aristocratic honour. Such remarks were all the more undiplomatic given that Jonson may already have written a poem praising Suffolk and would benefit from his good offices in avoiding censure over *Eastward Ho!* (1605).[11] More generally, Roe's scepticism seems corrosive of the entire system by which aristocratic power is underpinned, and the poem quickly shifts into an attack on the court as a whole, before swerving into insulting remarks about the women masquers and, oddly, their husbands. It is as if the poet's outrage at being excluded is so extreme that it undermines the stance of detached righteousness, leaving him unable to fix his anger on a single object. At the same time, he exculpates the King and Queen from criticism, but of course the Queen was herself a masquer and so was implicated in the general attack. In any case, the royal couple's honour could not be unaffected by the claim that all their followers were flatterers. For all the reassurance that 'Like them in goodness that court ne'er will be' (9), royalty could not avoid being splashed by mud that was aimed at their servants. More worryingly, if everything is flattery except for the love of the worthy subjects who are excluded, then reserving King and Queen from personal blame offers them no protection. It only confirms the perception that the system over which they preside is no better than a debasing arena in which hungry placemen compete for opportunity.

It must have been this dark view of court ceremonial as an arena of power rather than a dance of gracious celebration which stuck in Jonson's mind in 1619 when he quoted Roe's most trenchant line: 'God threateneth kings, kings lords, as lords do us' (12). This perception called into question the governing ethos of court festival. By reading his expulsion as a link in a chain of violence reaching back up the hierarchy to the lords, king, and King of kings, Roe connected his exclusion with his society's encompassing forms of political enforcement. In doing so he demystified the event, presenting the masque in a way which, far from being enchanted by its harmonies, was radically disenchanted about them. Roe's verses view it not as an innocent source of aesthetic pleasure but a mechanism through which power was sustained and legitimated. His perspective represents the masque's gracefully hierarchical gestures as strategies of social control, and its courtly ceremonial as merely ornamental clothing decorating the exercise of force. Of course, his view reflected his treatment. Speaking as an ejected aspirant, it is not surprising he was reproachful. Still, his perspective is germane since the exclusion of some would-be participants was always the masques' defining condition: the legitimation of those taking part in the festival inevitably presumed the delegitimation of others who failed to meet the criteria for inclusion. However serenely masques lauded the legitimacy of the Stuarts, their margins and even their inner spaces were always sites of contention. The bright centre of the festival was shadowed by those who were denied a part in it.

It is a pity that the cluster of correspondents who were at Hampton Court, noting down the details of these first Stuart masques, were too preoccupied with the main spectacle to attend to this minor fracas. Still, even this limited information suggests that Jonson and Roe's bottom-up view of court festival would have been readily recognizable to the social elites who composed masque audiences. As we shall see, their experience was typical of the intersections of physical access, social ideology and aesthetic form that characterized all Stuart masques, and would have been shared by many other spectators attempting to pass through the same doors. It makes apparent the unspoken but understood social content of the gracious panegyric, the scenario of social competition and political enforcement, and the strategies of exclusion and inclusion on which the celebration of royal legitimacy rested. And it is a remarkable testimony to the coherence of festival structures across the period that, as early as the first Stuart Christmas, two would-be participants were already reading its rituals as forms of power. Theirs was a strikingly different perspective from much modern masque criticism, which has, until quite recently, tended to take the masques' mystifications at face value, and concurred with their celebration of kingly prestige. For those at the time on the margins of the hall, the celebrations may well have seemed significantly less pleasurable.

We do not know exactly how many people the masquing rooms could contain, but accommodation must often have been tight. The one visual record that survives showing a major court space prepared for an entertainment suggests how economical arrangements had to be. This is John Webb's plan of the Great Hall at Whitehall set up for a performance of *Florimène* in 1635 (figure 1). *Florimène* was not a masque but a pastoral with scenes and intermezzi, so the disposal of space cannot be taken as representative.

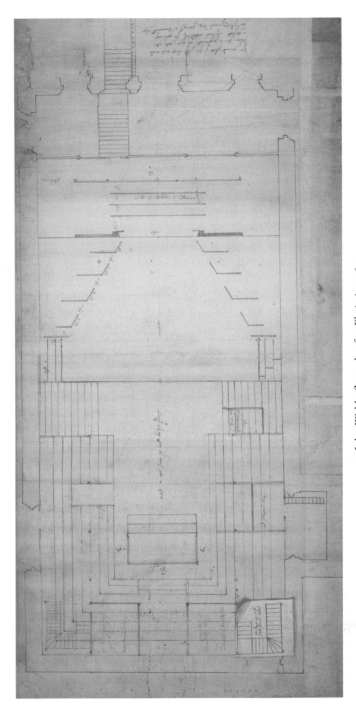

1 John Webb, floor plan for *Florimène*, 1635.

Florimène's stage was deeper than that used in masques, for it had both changeable flats and fixed V-shaped wings, and it was not necessary to reserve too much room on the floor of the hall, since the performers did not descend from the stage to dance with members of the audience. Nonetheless, at other times masques with scenery and social 'revels' were danced in this room, and the general set-up for the audience was similar.

Webb's plan nicely suggests the constraints put on space by the need to accommodate the stage and perspective scenery, and to ensure that the King had a clear view of the performance. The King sat on the dais or 'half-pace' in the centre of the auditorium, and spectators were arranged on the temporary seating or 'degrees' occupying that end of the hall. The *Florimène* plan has seven ranks of degrees rising from the floor, with a foot-platform at the front, and above them a separate gallery comprising four more ranks, supported by twelve posts marked as tiny squares in the middle of the degrees. The degrees are built across the main entrance to the room (at the top of the plan), with a vomitorium left clear to facilitate access at floor level. Access to the gallery is through two sets of stairs in the corners; the rather uncomfortable looking ladder in the bay window at the bottom of the plan probably led to the top level of the lower degrees.[12] This kind of fit-up, which was erected for each performance by the Office of Works and dismantled afterwards, was standard at the two Jacobean Banqueting Houses. The first Banqueting House (built in 1606 and burned down in 1619) had a permanent gallery supported by columns,[13] and the Works accounts for *The Masque of Beauty* (1608) mention 'making a great number of degrees on either side of the Banqueting House both below and in the galleries above'.[14] Inigo Jones's Banqueting House built in 1619–22 had a small permanent cantilevered balcony placed high enough around the walls for temporary degrees and galleries to be erected below it, as is indicated in the accounts for *The Masque of Augurs* (1622), which specify seven tiers of degrees below and four in 'the middle gallery' (i.e. the space between the degrees and the balcony).[15] In 1637 a new purpose-built Masquing Room was erected; Jones's notes on preparing the fit-up for the first show, *Britannia Triumphans*, mention 'degrees and galleries'.[16]

The two Banqueting Houses and the Masquing Room were handsome halls each measuring around 110 feet by 55 feet and with a floor area of some 6,000 square feet,[17] but the room needed for the stage and the social dancing left only half this free for seating. Although this was enough to accommodate a sizeable number, space was always at a premium. When Orazio Busino, chaplain to the Venetian embassy, saw *Pleasure Reconciled to Virtue* in the first Banqueting House in 1618, he estimated that the audience contained 600 ladies (and he complained of overcrowding, the embassy box being so 'uncomfortable that had it not been for our curiosity we would have given up or expired').[18] This implies a total attendance of around 1,200, and, although only an estimate, it is close to the capacity of 1,290 (of whom 470 are sitting in the galleries) that can be conjectured if we assume eleven tiers of seating and allow 18 inches space for each person.[19] It is also similar to the audience figures that modern scholars have deduced for comparable festival spaces in the Italian courts.[20] Other palace rooms used for masques were significantly smaller.[21] The Great Hall measured only 90 feet by 40 feet, and Webb's plan leaves barely 1,500 square feet for the audience.[22] The Paved Court Theatre which Jones built for *The Shepherd's Paradise* at Somerset House (1633) – not in itself a masque, but the space was reused for one – had an auditorium of 1,800 square feet, while the hall at Somerset House, used for masques by Anne and Henrietta Maria, was no more than 1,800 square feet in total.[23] In the event, there was plenty of room at *The Shepherd's Paradise* (Nathaniel Tomkyns told Sir Robert Phelips), but only because 'the difficulty of getting in ... being such or so apprehended, that there was a scarcity of spectators'.[24] In 1626, the Tuscan agent Amerigo Salvetti reported that when Henrietta Maria acted in Racan's *L'Artenice* at Somerset House it was all done 'as privately as possible', and access was restricted to 'a few of the nobility, expressly invited, no others being admitted'.[25] This was at one extreme of the spectrum, but more public occasions could also be tight. The temporary theatre built in 1605 for a royal visit to Christ Church, Oxford, had seating for just 550, plus standing room for 260 at the back.[26]

Inevitably, the premium on space made for difficulties of the Roe/Jonson kind. At *The Vision of the Twelve Goddesses*, the problems of access were compounded by the scenery which, unlike in the masques in subsequent years, was dispersed around the hall rather than concentrated at one end. As a consequence, reported Sir Dudley Carleton, seating was severely reduced: 'The hall was much lessened by the works that were in it, so as none could be admitted but men of appearance.'[27] Maybe this was why our two friends were ejected and, if so, others who fell equally short of being 'men of appearance' must also have been excluded. Matters were little better the following winter (1604–5). At the lost Whitehall masque *Hymen and the Four Seasons* the crowd was so large that some of the dancing was cancelled,[28] and at *The Masque of Blackness* the stage machinery was better arranged but admission, said Carleton, was chaotic:

The confusion in getting in was so great that some ladies lie by it and complain of the fury of the white staves. In the passages through the galleries they were shut up in several heaps betwixt doors and there stayed till all was ended; and in the coming out, a banquet which was prepared for the King in the great chamber was overturned, table and all, before it was scarce touched. It were infinite to tell you what losses there were of chains, jewels, purses, and suchlike loose ware, and one woman amongst the rest lost her honesty, for which she was carried to the porter's lodge, being surprised at her business on the top of the terrace.[29]

An enforced wait in the chambers outside the Banqueting House would have been a severe penalty, as masques typically went on until the small hours, while the woman who 'lost her honesty' was punished in a way that acknowledged the court's symbolic topography. Her removal to the porter's lodge, which in aristocratic houses marked the boundary between admission and exclusion, signalled her ejection to the event's margins.[30] Things were still badly run three years later, when during *The Masque of Beauty* (1608) 100 gentlemen found themselves imprisoned in the corridors, including Sir Horatio Vere, Sir John Holles, Sir William Slingsby, and 'a Danish lord who had stayed here long time purposely to see the Queen's masque and to carry the report of it unto his country [but] was there in safe custody and saw no more than if he had been in Denmark'.[31] Even worse was *The Masque of the Inner Temple and Gray's Inn* (1613), when the 'many hundreds of people'[32] who turned up to watch the masquers sail up the Thames from the city caused the palace galleries to become completely clogged. Spectators who left the Banqueting House to view the masquers arriving at the water gate were unable to get back in again, and inside the crush was so great that the floor could not be cleared for dancing. Eventually the performance was abandoned, and the masquers had to return five days later.[33]

In succeeding years, attempts were made to ease the pressure on space and reduce confusion. Attendance at the festivities for the Palatine marriage in 1613 was expected to be so great that women spectators were forbidden to arrive wearing bulky farthingales. The balcony that Jones built into his 1619 Banqueting House added some extra space above the temporary galleries. One rationale for the custom of repeat performances, which began with *The Irish Masque* (1613–14), was to increase access, and during James's reign most subsequent royal masques were repeated; the culminating instance was *The Temple of Love* (1635), danced on three occasions and possibly even a fourth. But there were limits to this strategy since masque splendour depended on resources being seen to be squandered in a single act of stupendous prodigality. That a masque be danced only once, then thrown away, was a testimony to princely magnificence, whereas to repeat it could suggest that its sponsors had an eye on economy. When in 1631 Charles returned to a single-performance model for his Christmas masques, one reason may have been that too many repeat performances were undermining the ethos of the form. His preferred, and entirely characteristic, solution to the access problem was to rationalize admission. He introduced a system of ticket entry, which was first used at *The Triumph of Peace* in 1634, and erected temporary turnstiles at the Banqueting House, a feature which probably became permanent at the Masquing Room built in 1637.[34] This allowed the numbers of people arriving and the routes by which they entered to be more strictly controlled, though at the cost of diluting the atmosphere of celebration. Not surprisingly, in the 1630s one encounters for the first time reports that some masques were under-attended.[35]

The people who bore the brunt of policing these boundaries, and maintaining order inside, were the Lord Chamberlain and his officials, who had overall responsibility for the court's public areas known collectively as the Chamber, and the Master of Ceremonies (plus a marshal of ceremonies, and two deputies) whose posts James created specifically to handle his court's burgeoning problem of diplomatic protocol.[36] Their authority on festival occasions was more than merely symbolic, and there are many allusions like Carleton's to 'the fury of the white staves' – the rods which they carried being insignia of office that could be used physically to create space where none existed. That violence was customary is seen in a scene from Beaumont and Fletcher's *The Maid's Tragedy* (1610), in which a court official, trying to keep interlopers out of a masque, wishes he had the same power as the lord who should have been on the door:

Diagoras. Stand back there, room for my Lord Melantius! Pray bear back, this is no place for such youths and their trulls, let the doors shut again! Ay, do your heads itch? I'll scratch them for you, so now thrust and hang. [*Knock within.*] Again, – who is't now? I cannot blame my Lord Calianax for going away. Would he were here: he would run raging amongst them, and break a dozen wiser heads than his own in the twinkling of an eye.
Within. I pray you, can you help me to the speech of the master cook?
Diagoras. If I open the door I'll cook some of your calves' heads. Peace, rogues.[37]

Jonson makes a joke of official violence in *The Irish Masque*, in which the visiting masquers, Irishmen who neither speak nor look like courtly guests, complain of being 'knocke[d] … o' te heads, phit te phoit stick' (10), but his comedy depends on the knowledge that the masque was itself being policed with comparable force. When in 1616 Sir Thomas Edmondes became Comptroller of the Household (another office with responsibility for policing court entertainments), he quickly acquired a reputation for severity. John Chamberlain reported that he 'doth execute the place with courage and authority enough but they say he doth somewhat too much flourish and fence with his staves, whereof he hath broken two already, not at tilt but stickling [i.e. acting as overseer] at the plays this Christmas'.[38] A similar reputation attached itself to the fourth Earl of Pembroke, who became Lord Chamberlain in 1626. Francis Osborne said he was 'intolerable choleric and offensive, and did not refrain ... to break many wiser heads than his own'.[39] This evaluation freely generalizes from an incident at *The Triumph of Peace*, when Pembroke broke his staff – which he holds in Van Dyck's family portrait at Wilton House – while trying to eject another literary intruder, the poet Thomas May.[40] But even Sir John Finet, Charles's Master of Ceremonies, described Pembroke 'storming' and swearing when the Spanish ambassador attempted to shoehorn twenty-one guests into *Luminalia* (1638) instead of the eight he was allowed.[41] After the fracas with May, the King intervened and made Pembroke recompense him with a £50 gift, but such episodes amply demonstrate the rigour with which the masques' boundaries were controlled. When the young lawyer Simonds D'Ewes tried to view *A Congratulation for the Prince's Return*, danced at York House in November 1623 to celebrate Charles's homecoming from Madrid, he and 'many others' were put out of the room by the Prince himself.[42]

This leads to the question of what qualifications were sufficient to guarantee access to a masque. Here we run into a problem of evidence, since it was in the nature of these events to attract comment primarily from the top downwards. Eyewitness reports are often full of detail about the royalty and great aristocrats involved in the masques but frustratingly unspecific about the lower end of the hall. The diary of Sir Humphrey Mildmay, a gentleman but not really a courtier, shows that he sometimes attended the Caroline masques,[43] and on special occasions young men residing at the Inns of Court seem to have had fairly free access.[44] Sir Thomas Knyvett expressed satisfaction at acquiring a ticket for *The Temple of Love* (1635), 'though [only] a country gentleman'.[45] It is, though, unclear whether status alone guaranteed admission and how low down the line was drawn: in 1610 Sir Richard Paulet, MP, entertained himself by mingling in the court garden with the crowd gathering for *Tethys' Festival*, but did not himself attempt to go in.[46] To a considerable extent, audiences must have been self-selecting, since spectators were expected to dress in finery of almost equivalent ostentation to the masquers. It would have been difficult to turn away ladies who arrived dripping with gems. Still, there must always have been the possibility that less space was available than could accommodate the numbers competing for it. The twenty-one Spaniards who attempted to gatecrash *Luminalia* evidently knew this, for they stayed in their coach during the negotiations with Sir John Finet, then drove off when he denied them admission.[47] On some occasions audiences were restricted to a very select few. For example, at the first performance of *Pan's Anniversary* (1621), in the Great Hall, no one was admitted 'under the degree of a baron'.[48] Others, though, were more permeable. Before *The Fortunate Isles* (1625), Finet instructed the French and Venetian ambassadors to enter Whitehall through the court gate rather than St James's Park, 'in regard of the inconveniency that would grow from the intrusion of multitudes of people by the way of the galleries if they were left open'.[49] He would not have issued this command had he not expected that some unwanted spectators would get in were an alternative route of access available.

It seems, then, that there was a three-fold hierarchy amongst visitors to a masque: those who were officially invited or had places guaranteed (ambassadors and their staff, the greater nobility and so forth), those without invitations who managed to achieve access (or under Charles, those who didn't have invitations but did have tickets), and a penumbra of people who arrived at the hall but failed to find places. This kind of calculus seems to be anticipated in John Chamberlain's letter to Sir Dudley Carleton discussing their strategy for ensuring admission to *The Masque of Beauty*. Shortly before the performance, Chamberlain wrote:

Sir, we had great hope of having you here this day, and then I would not have given my part of the masque for many of their places that shall be present, for I presume you and your Lady would find easy passage being so befriended, for the show is put off till Sunday by reason all things are not ready.[50]

This slightly confusing description defines two routes of admission. Chamberlain already had a place promised in the hall for himself ('my part of the masque'), but the Carletons seem to have intended arriving on spec and without any guarantee of getting placed. Since Carleton was well 'befriended' – presumably meaning he was known to the staff on the door – he was unlikely to be turned away. Nevertheless, access could not be assumed as a fait accompli, and even rising stars had to weigh up the risk of a refusal. For those lower down the ladder, attendance must have involved yet more improvisations. A highly complex scenario is sketched in Finet's account of the court party's arrival at *The Triumphs of the Prince d'Amour* (1636). This show was put on by the Middle Temple gentlemen in honour of the Palatine Prince, and was staged outside Whitehall in the Temple hall:[51]

Having passed the turn ['tourne'] door into the first court, they found there a guard made them on each side by above twenty gentlemen in the quality of Pensioners [to the lawyers' Christmas Prince], all richly apparelled, carrying in their hands their poleaxes. Passing forward, they entered another turn door into the hall and proceeding came to their repose in the Parliament Chamber, as they named it. The hall appointed to dance in, being in the meantime with much ado cleared of the pressing number of both sexes, then they were seated, in chairs all of one fashion to behold the representation.[51]

This narrative clearly delineates a separation between outer public space and inner spaces with different levels of privilege, the divisions between them being marked by doorways and turnstiles. On this occasion there were two turnstiles, which suggests that the interior areas had increasing gradations of privacy, and even those who made it into the central area could not count on getting sight of the performance. The need to clear the 'pressing number' of spectators to make room for the dancing indicates that some visitors who were initially present in the hall were subsequently turned out. It confirms Jonson's perception of the double risk spectators ran, that those who were not 'kept out' might still find themselves being 'thrust out'.

The uncertainties of access were compounded by the numbers of officials who were involved in policing the doors. At some occasions, success in admission might depend on connections with influential courtiers. King Charles himself took responsibility for placing the ladies at the Queen's masque of January 1627, and for Baron Oxenstierna and his party at the 1633 Somerset House masque.[52] James's favourite, Buckingham, seems to have wielded power at the doors, for when the Venetian ambassador, Girolamo Lando, was refused an official invitation to *The Masque of Augurs*, he was advised to solicit one from Buckingham instead.[53] Another influential official was the Earl Marshal, Arundel, who was consulted over seating at *Love's Triumph* (1631).[54] More commonly, though, access and seating were in the hands of the Lord Chamberlain's staff. In a typical example, at an event for the Palatine Prince in 1612 – a banquet, but similar in principle to a masque – admissions were controlled by the Master of Ceremonies, Sir Lewis Lewkenor, while the Lord Chamberlain was responsible for the ordering of places.[55] However, the division of labour did not always work so smoothly. As Comptroller of the Household, Sir Henry Vane caused embarrassment at *Britannia Triumphans* (1638) by letting the Spanish ambassador's gentlemen into seats reserved in the temporary Masquing Room for the French. Lewkenor's successor, Finet, had admitted the Spaniards to 'the first entry', but, left to their own devices, they took the opportunity to get past Vane at a door farther on.[56] Moreover, spectators were aware that securing a good seat might depend on the influence or goodwill of the official responsible for their admission. When Lando was told to refer himself to Buckingham, he crossly replied that he had always come 'by the right door of the Lord Chamberlain' and regarded any other means of entrance as an insult.[57] Sir Thomas Knyvett said that although he had a ticket for *The Temple of Love*, 'if I do not like my way of going in, I doubt I shall let it alone'.[58]

Once through the doors, visitors found themselves in an intensely hierarchical environment. The orderly arrangement of the space is well attested from the comments of Finet, the ambassadors, and other participants with a professional interest in protocol, who agree that seating for the most prominent spectators was always organized to respect nice gradations of precedence. The most desirable seats were at the head of the room, on either side of the king, and in general a strictly vertical arrangement prevailed, with the king sitting flanked by his great aristocracy in a visual projection of the hierarchies of the realm.[59] At *Hymen's Triumph* at Somerset House (1614), the royal family and French ambassador had the best seats, then the earls and barons sat 'on a great bench', and in front of them were the countesses, then the French ambassador's wife, then the baronesses.[60] At the banquet after *The Golden Age Restored* (1616), earls and barons sat in order of precedence, with the barons being subdivided into English, Scots, and Irish, an arrangement almost certainly mirroring the hierarchy earlier in the hall.[61] Frequent references to 'the lords' or 'the earls' in eyewitness narratives demonstrate that ranks of nobility were customarily bunched together,[62] and Finet made distinctions between 'public' seats amongst the lords and 'private' places elsewhere in the hall – with the clear implication that 'public' seats were more strictly controlled – and between 'right' and 'left', with the implication that places on the 'right' were more honourable.[63] Protocol further required that some groups be picked out. Busino noticed the privy councillors sitting together in a box for *Pleasure Reconciled to Virtue*; the Lord Chamberlain had a box over the entrance at *Time Vindicated* (1623); at *Albion's Triumph* (1632), seats were set aside for the Gentlemen of the Privy Chamber.[64] The next most desirable seats came below the barons: at *Mercury Vindicated* in 1615, the first person in this rank was the Lord Treasurer's son, Sir Thomas Howard.[65] It was also customary for the women to sit below the men, though this changed in Charles's reign, when men and women were separated horizontally rather than vertically. A new distinction appears in Caroline masques between the ladies' 'side' and the men's,[66] and some great ladies were granted boxes of their own. Henrietta Maria's French gentlewomen, led by her nurse, Madame Garnier, usually had places reserved above the Banqueting House entrance,[67] and Webb's floor plan for *Florimène* has boxes pencilled in for the Countess of Arundel, 'the Lady Marquise' (the Marchioness of

Hamilton), and Sir Thomas Edmondes.[68] Little wonder that spectators expected to arrive two hours before the performance in order to secure their seats.[69]

The clearest testimony to these distinctions comes from the ambassadors, whose willingness to squabble over fancied slights was so extreme that sometimes performances were postponed for days. The representatives of favoured powers were often given prominent positions close to the throne, and were intensely proud of such marks of prestige, which functioned as public expressions of respect to their nation from the British crown. For example, the Venetian ambassador wrote home that the attentions he received at *Hymen and the Four Seasons* 'discovered his majesty's real feelings' towards him (as he supposed) and 'demonstrated them to the whole court', and in 1610 Lewkenor had to produce the seating plan for *Tethys' Festival* to reassure him that his dignity was being fully acknowledged.[70] Unsurprisingly, the scope for dispute was endless, and was to some degree intrinsic to the occasion. The attendance of ambassadors from various nations testified to Whitehall's European standing, and was a direct consequence of the new internationalism of Jacobean policy. There had been nothing like it in Elizabeth's day, when there was no Spanish diplomatic presence at court after 1583 and rivalries were less acute. Protocol was particularly strained between the French and Spanish ambassadors since, as the representatives of Europe's two most powerful nations, neither was willing to give way to the other. A strategy developed whereby the two ambassadors received invitations every other year, and, when not invited, each would pretend to be sick so as to avoid acknowledging the favour done to the other. This charade worked so long as both agreed to participate, but it was easily sabotaged by non-cooperation, and by their subordinates, who were no less prone to squabbling. Finet admitted the gentlemen from the Venetian embassy to *Mercury Vindicated* on condition that they 'would not strive for places',[71] and frequently separate boxes were arranged, but these cordons were not always watertight. Busino complained that a Spaniard was put in the Venetian box at *Pleasure Reconciled*, and at *The Fortunate Isles* the King commanded that embassy staff be dispersed around the place, 'to avoid differences and wranglings'.[72] Matters were further complicated by antagonisms between the lesser powers, Venice against Flanders, Florence against Savoy, and by Spanish sensitivity to honours done to nations that they did not recognize, particularly the Dutch. In 1621, a busy season for international diplomacy, commissioners who arrived from Holland were not invited to *Pan's Anniversary*, which was the main festival that year, but fobbed off with a masque of gentlemen from the Middle Temple. In 1619 it had been decided that 'in regard of their troublesome punctilios' ambassadors should no longer sit next to the King but in their own boxes 'somewhat obliquely forward'. Nonetheless, at the Shrovetide performance of *Pan's Anniversary*, the Spanish ambassador Gondomar sat 'at the left hand of His Majesty under the state'.[73] Special arrangements also had to be made for non-resident ('extraordinary') ambassadors and their retinues, for royal relations from overseas, and for visiting foreign nobility. Being the daughter of a king, Pocahontas was 'well placed' at *The Vision of Delight* in 1617.[74]

Obviously the ambassadors' reactions cannot be taken as representative. Their obsession with protocol arose from professional considerations that made them hypersensitive about the hall's function as an arena for the display of status. But if it was only at the top of the room that etiquette counted this much, the ambassadors' anxiety about placing was symptomatic of the prevailing climate in the Banqueting House, attentive as people were to symbolic topographies that they all implicitly understood. Having successfully negotiated the demands of the door, spectators entered another environment that was scarcely less straitened, where they would find themselves once again competing for places. Although seats were prearranged for the important guests, the majority were placed at the time of arrival by what Finet calls the Lord Chamberlain's 'provident care'.[75] As everyone knew, the most prestigious seats were those closest to the King and lords; next came the degrees along the sides; finally, the galleries were universally regarded as least desirable. These distinctions are well seen in the placing, at the first performance of *Pan's Anniversary*, of the sixty French gentlemen who came with the Marquis de Cadenet's embassy. Cadenet himself was put with the King, his principal followers sat 'on a form behind the lords', more were in a box apart, and the rest had the better places on the degrees.[76] By contrast, the seats on the upper levels were much less sought after, being regarded as inconvenient and remote, and spectators who penetrated into the hall might yet find their evening spoiled if they were relegated to the margins. The Florentine ambassador was dreadfully disappointed when put into the gallery for *Mercury Vindicated*, and pleaded for a place among the lords.[77] At the Queen's 1627 masque, the Dutch ambassador's wife and daughters were unhappy about being placed on seats above and behind the King. They 'took exceptions against their being thrust up in a corner without respects', but since they had already declined to sit with the great ladies, pleading unfamiliarity with the English language, they were forced to make the best of it.[78] When the Moroccan ambassador was put in a box behind the King for *Britannia Triumphans*, Charles rebuked Finet for having placed him so 'obscurely'.[79] The one advantage of these locations was that the premium on space was less intense, and seating was relatively promiscuous. At *The Triumph of Peace* the gallery behind the dais was set aside for 100 gentlemen who had ridden through the city streets as part of the masquers' parade, and at *Coelum Britannicum* the ambassadors' gentlemen were allowed to choose their own seats in the gallery above the lords.[80] Nonetheless, no one had carte blanche to sit simply where they liked, and all were ultimately at the mercy of the gentlemen ushers. The ushers' task was to establish not only good order in the hall but the social protocols of the occasion as a whole.

The logic of the masques' exclusivity, then, placed the spectators in an inherently vulnerable situation. The flocking of visitors which signalled the magnitude of the event also meant that some would inevitably be turned away. But although contests over access were particularly fraught at the masques, they were intrinsic to the everyday fabric of court life, since as an institutional space Whitehall was, confusingly, both open and closed. Compared with the continental monarchies, the Stuarts lived in relative privacy. One of James's distinctive innovations was the establishment of the royal Bedchamber as the King's personal territory, where he was attended by his closest friends (mostly Scots), and where access was denied even to gentlemen who moved freely in the Privy Chamber. Even though Jacobean protocols were comparatively relaxed, James did not live his entire life in the public gaze, and the power of his favourites in the Bedchamber would be one of the reign's recurrent themes.[81] Charles intensified this process by tightening access, laying down stricter limits on the court's inner spaces, and commanding that the 'disorderly and unnecessary resort' of subjects to Whitehall be restrained and 'idle persons and other unnecessary attendants' should stay away.[82] These reforms were designed to create a climate of stateliness and decorum, and John Chamberlain noted that 'the court is kept more straight and private than in the former time'.[83] No one, said Edward Hyde, was seen 'in a place where he had no pretence to be'.[84]

Yet Whitehall was amphibious territory, and in the palace's outer, ceremonial rooms, the majesty of kingship continued to be staged in rituals of hospitality and power that conspicuously acted out the monarchy's public face. The business of state drew hundreds of people to Whitehall's public spaces on a daily basis, to petition, dance attendance, or simply to see and be seen, and both James and Charles kept medieval standards of hospitality, feasting each day hundreds of servants and hangers-on, who were entitled to diet or 'bouge of court', payment for their work through an allowance of victual. Early modern Whitehall was also more populous than Elizabeth's court, for James brought his Scots favourites south, and he and

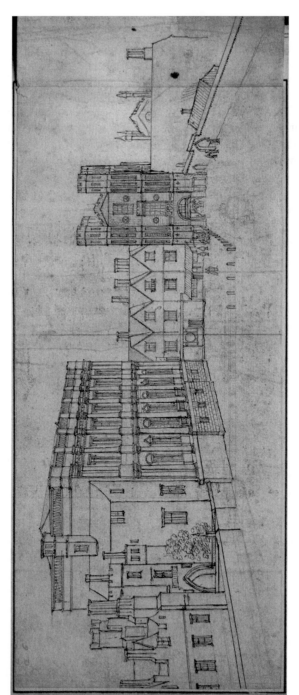

2 Wenceslaus Hollar, *The Banqueting House and Court Gate, c.* 1640.

Charles had consorts and children who needed their own establishments. Charles's household comprised over 1,800 people, of whom 900 might be on duty at any one time,[85] and numbers continued to expand, causing a knock-on development of lodgings and offices in Scotland Yard, at the palace's northern end.[86] Expenditure on the household departments and the vast quantities of diet that they needed exceeded two-fifths of Charles's peacetime budget.[87] 'The court is now filled with families of every mean courtier', complained George Garrard in 1637.[88]

This expansion in the court's public life was responsible for the Banqueting House's rapid and incremental development as a ceremonial space. By converting to stone the temporary wooden structure that he had inherited from Elizabeth, James signalled early on his intention of using masques as a recurring part of Whitehall's ceremonial. When that building was itself replaced, the new hall was even more ambitiously conceived as a ceremonial venue. More than just a masquing room, Jones's Banqueting House took on some of the functions of a Presence Chamber. Its scale was far grander than the existing Presence Chamber, and its main space was raised to the first floor, so as to communicate more conveniently with other court apartments on the *piano nobile*.[89] James and Charles used the room for Garter feasts, ambassadorial receptions, meetings with the two houses of parliament, ennoblements, touching for the King's Evil, distribution of the Maundy, and the ratification of treaties; the Petition of Right was presented to Charles here in 1628.[90] Inevitably, the overlap between these various functions created congestion – for example, in 1628 the Muscovy ambassador's reception was impeded by scenery that had been set up for a masque[91] – and this led Charles to erect yet another structure between the Banqueting House and the Great Hall, on the same scale but dedicated simply to the business of masquing. The trigger for this was the installation of the Rubens ceiling, which made the Banqueting House unusable for masques,[92] but it reflected an underlying trend towards greater complexity and differentiation in the ceremonial calendar. It was the closest Charles came to fulfilling his ambition of remodelling his court in imitation of the Louvre or the Escorial.

The topography of the Banqueting House announced its symbolic function, for it stood at the threshold of public and private, bridging the line between within the court and without. As Wenceslaus Hollar's drawing of the court's western aspect shows (figure 2), the Banqueting House formed Whitehall's frontage overlooking the main thoroughfare between London and Westminster. This public road bisected the palace buildings, separating the lodgings on the east from the cockpit, tennis court and tiltyard on the west. It ran in front of the Banqueting House, passed southwards under the Holbein gateway, and continued for 100 yards as an enclosed way between the palace walls themselves. Even more strikingly, the Banqueting House was the architectural hyphen between the royal apartments behind the Privy Gallery to the south (running east–west at first-floor level across the Holbein gateway) and the court gate, the unadorned fifteenth-century structure immediately to the north (visible on the left of Hollar's drawing). The court gate was the principal public access point to the whole palace, through which most of the visitors to the masques would have come. Here, said James Barlow, there was a 'continual throng' of gallants, ladies, and servants, and Finet arranged to meet the Dutch and Venetian ambassadors here, with 'a few followers … of the better sort', before the 1627 masque.[93] But access was also possible through the Privy Gallery, which linked the Banqueting House at its eastern end to the stairs down to St James's Park, and many visitors came to masques through the galleries, particularly those who were being specially honoured. At *The Golden Age Restored*, Pembroke and Lord Danvers escorted the ambassadors through the Privy Gallery, and for the second performance of *The Masque of Augurs* the Landgrave of Hesse was brought in by 'the back way through the garden'.[94] The gentlemen who were trapped in the corridors during *The Masque of Beauty* had attempted to make their passage through the King's bedchamber, and for *Time Vindicated* Finet mentions 'the entrance into the Banqueting House from the Prince's galleries'.[95] As we have already heard, at *The Fortunate Isles* the ambassadors were warned to use the court gate, since the back route through the Park would be closed to keep out unwanted guests. In 1631, Charles promulgated new orders limiting who could come into the privy lodgings on the very day that *Love's Triumph* was performed.[96] The Banqueting House thus marked several symbolic intersections between the King's private space and the public space of his subjects. It was a place where Stuart kingship and a more heterogeneous world came face to face.

At the court gate, the porters – two of whom, Walter Parsons and William Evans, were so large and intimidating that they occasionally starred as giants in the masques[97] – were supposed to filter out any undesirables who might otherwise infest the court. James's household ordinances required the porters to scrutinize all incomers, and ensure that servants seeking admission were 'comely and seemly' and that 'all other unfit persons, not allowed nor fit to come within our court' were excluded.[98] But these commands were under strain at the great ritual occasions, when the court attracted large gatherings of spectators as well as guests. Ambassadorial receptions were particularly prone to crowding. When the Muscovy ambassador arrived in 1617, the ceremonies in the Banqueting House were curtailed by 'the exceeding press of the people', and at Gondomar's welcome in 1620 an 'overthronging multitude' caused the terrace outside the Guard Chamber to collapse as Gondomar walked along it.[99] An 'overpressing multitude' hindered the Moroccan ambassador's welcome in 1637, and in 1641 Finet said the Dutch envoys could not even see the King in the Banqueting House, 'notwithstanding the Lord Chamberlain's ... best endeavours' (meaning that he used force).[100] For the reception of the Duke of Lorraine's agent in 1640 a rail was set up 'to keep off the intruding multitude', but 'the excessive numbers of intruders of all sorts' still caused chaos.[101] Rails were customary at Garter feasts, to protect the participants 'from the troublesome, yet usual, crowd and rapine of the people',[102] and similar arrangements were customary when the King dined in state in the Presence Chamber, for which a rail was also erected.[103] Public events outside Whitehall were no less disorderly. A banquet for Cadenet in the House of Lords in 1621 was spoiled by the 'unruly intruding multitude, as no officer was able freely to discharge his service'.[104]

On such occasions a contradiction was apparent between the public character of Whitehall's ceremonial and the expectation that nonetheless some kind of boundary had to be drawn. Unsurprisingly, resident ambassadors wishing to attend court festivities were often uncertain about whether access was open or closed. In 1637 the Spanish ambassador declined to attend the Garter feast without an invitation, even though Finet assured him that 'all that would might come to see it'.[105] Perhaps he was confused by Finet's gloss that, notwithstanding the free entry, the feast was technically private, since the King gave it as a gift to his Garter knights. Similarly, when invited to the wedding of Queen Anne's favourite, Lady Drummond, the Venetian ambassador hesitated over the informality of his invitation; Finet explained the event was private but would be celebrated with court revels as a mark of honour.[106] At such moments one senses an emerging contradiction between the desire to show munificence and the practical constraints created by the demands of economy and access. Ceremonial had to project the dignity of the King without publicity collapsing into promiscuity. At great festival times protocol might be relaxed, as it was for the two days of 'open court' kept for the Palatine marriage, with 'entertaining tables and free admittance to them of all worthy comers', 'for all people of fashion, as well citizens as others',[107] but presumably the porters and household officials must still have decided which visitors qualified as 'worthy' or not. The same ambiguity lurked in the apparently innocent dictum that access to the Presence Chamber was available to any 'gentleman of quality and of good fashion'.[108]

This issue pressed with particular keenness on the masques, since they were ambiguously positioned as public state festivals and household entertainments for the King's personal pleasure. From the beginning James enforced the principle that masques were private and invitations were at his discretion. When the French ambassador threatened to take his non-invitation to *The Masque of Blackness* as a political insult, he was told 'a masque is not a public function, and that His Majesty is quite entitled to invite any ambassador he may choose', for they come 'as private men to a private sport'.[109] Charles similarly refused to issue invitations to *Love's Triumph*, declaring it 'an entertainment intended only for the Queen's particular pleasure and satisfaction', and reiterated the principle several times that 'it had never been his custom to invite any ambassador to these entertainments'.[110] Probably this formula was adopted to forestall importunate ambassadors, but it encapsulated a central tension between the masque's status as a representation of the King's household at play and its function as an event for the political community at large. Such pronouncements preserved the fiction that masques were done simply for royal delight, but they flew in the face of the perception that in practice they were anything but private and that many spectators could scarcely be deemed guests. As Busino observed, the crowding at *Pleasure Reconciled to Virtue* undermined the pretence that the event was private, 'for though they claim to admit only those favoured with invitations, nevertheless every box was full'.[111] After 1634 the advent of ticket entry greatly simplified access; for example, Finet said the twenty-four tickets he secured for ambassadorial staff at *The Triumph of Peace* 'got them entrance and seats with conveniency'.[112] However, the problem with tickets was that they altered the character of the festival by exposing it to more mercenary transactions. Like invitations, tickets were notionally bestowed by the royal hosts,[113] yet at least one record survives of money changing hands.[114] Since the purchaser was the Earl of Northumberland it scarcely damaged the audience's dignity, but by creating a possible market for tickets, Charles unsettled the implied equation between the masque's image of royal honour and its function as an instrument of government. If tickets could be traded, it could no longer be claimed that admission was cognate with status.

What one would dearly like to know is whether anyone of acutely low rank ever made it into a masque. Almost certainly this never happened, but the notion that it might was one of the fantasies of social insubordination that was constantly evoked to police the boundary. A considerable number of plays in the period include episodes in which outsiders attempt to wheedle their way into court festivals; the topos is repeatedly used as shorthand to signify the social exclusiveness of court ritual. In Beaumont and Fletcher's *The Maid's Tragedy*, the door at a masque is held against 'youths and their trulls', and someone with a message for the cook; in Fletcher's *The Humorous Lieutenant*, ushers admit ladies and gentlemen to an ambassadorial reception but turn away citizens and their wives; in Field and Fletcher's *Four Plays in One*, citizens are ejected from a marriage feast, but their wives are let in 'at the back door';[115] in Jonson's *The Staple of News* a citizen slips into a masque by pretending to be one of the musicians;[116] and in *Cynthia's Revels*, a city wife is admitted at the court door but her husband is denied entrance. The common thread uniting these examples is that they all exaggerate and stereotype the social gulf separating those who get in from those who don't. As we have seen, in court festival it was typically ladies and gentlemen who battled with ushers at the doors, but in these fictional versions the gentry have easy admission and those refused entry are invariably citizens. It is difficult not to read this recurrent topos as staging the anxieties attendant on access, in which the dangers of exclusion are discharged by being projected onto competitors of manifestly lower status. The court door marks the line between those of securely privileged status and those who can only aspire to it. Even more strikingly, the plays rewrite social exclusion as sexual contest, for the courtier's privilege is often depicted as an erotic victory over city cuckolds whose wives are effectively stolen from them at the court entry: social insecurity is sublimated into sexual aggression. In a bilious history of the court printed in 1652, the republican controversialist Edward Peyton claimed that masques 'were used only for incentives of lust; therefore the courtiers invited the citizens' wives to those shows on purpose to defile them in such sort'.[117] Peyton's ludicrous testimony cannot be taken at face value, but it alludes to assumptions about the social functions of masquing that would have been readily understood. Jonson plays with the convention in *Chloridia*, when he has the dwarf postilion complain that he only managed to get into the playing space 'by the favour of one of the guard who was a woman's tailor, and held ope the passage' (155–6). The whole convention was playfully parodied by Henrietta Maria when she and her ladies visited the Middle Temple for the *Triumphs of the Prince d'Amour* dressed in costume as city wives.[118] The wit of her masquerade depended on the idea that the only citizen likely to get in was a beautiful woman who arrived unencumbered by her mate.

If in these theatrical examples the social anxieties and aspirations attendant on masquing seem almost embarrassingly obvious, they were foundational for the masques themselves, since the dialectic of inclusion and exclusion on which masquing turned was implicitly a structural counterpart to the social contests at the door. A series of masques build this perception into their form, using a scenario which shows outsiders being refused access. The antimasquers are low-born intruders who would enter the festival space if they could but are repulsed in order that the celebration can proceed. The most developed example is in Jonson's *Masque of Augurs*, where the antimasquers – a brewer's clerk, a bargee, an alewife, a showman, and some dancing bears – all hail from the disreputable London suburb of St Katharine's and attempt to blag their way past the Groom of the Revels, whose job it is to keep people like them out. They gain temporary admission by entertaining the court with their dances, but their vulgarity and poor hygiene are self-evident, and the bears, whose bodily habits are even worse, threaten literally to leave a mess in the hall. Eventually they are pushed out and the danger of contamination is expunged by the splendour of the evening's spectacle. Similar in effect is *The Triumph of Peace*, where the intruders burst in during the social dancing, interrupting not the start of the masque but the revels at their height. These visitors are a carpenter, painter, tailor, and four city wives, all of whom have helped to make the show behind the scenes, and now demand a proper sight of it. Finding themselves laughed at, they 'pretend' to be part of the masque and dance their way from the room, though their presence leaves a mental legacy. It is impossible to forget that they are necessary to the festival, that the celebration could not happen without their labour. This episode reasserts the social privilege of the participants, but at the cost of exposing the social mechanics that underpin the event.

Much the most interesting case is Jonson's *Love Restored* (1612). Here the figure trying to get in is the country spirit Robin Goodfellow, the very embodiment of festive mirth. In a long speech, Robin complains that he was turned away at the court gate, and had to climb over the wall by the wood-yard – that is, he breached the court by a back route, through its service area in Scotland Yard. Having reached the terrace outside the Banqueting House (where the woman was found 'at her business' in 1605) he was stopped by the guard, and he adopted a series of disguises linked to the masque's production in the hope of slipping in. He pretended to be a scene-shifter, a tire-woman, a musician, a feather-maker, and a 'wireman' (someone who hung the lighting), but in each of these disguises he was turned away. Those whom he saw getting in easily were different types – some foreigners (pre-sumably diplomatic staff) and 'a fine citizen's wife or two' (108) – but when he dressed himself as a city wife he ran into trouble, since it transpired that for women the price of admission was a groping by the guard. Eventually Robin accesses the room by pretending to be part of the show, and this is as it should be, for at a masque good-fellowship cannot be excluded. What really keeps him out, we discover, is Plutus, god of wealth, who has taken over the court in disguise as Cupid. The masque thus moves towards an affirmation of social amity, ejecting Plutus and his puritanical avarice and embracing love and good-fellowship: Robin's admission guarantees the masque's festive goodwill. But while the masque moves towards an affirmation of the court's political well-being, the social boundaries that Robin's narrative defines are less than comprehensive, and draw attention to the exclusions and provisos with which the masque is hedged. Robin may recover amity for the court but his presence is not a licence for all and sundry. On the contrary, good-fellowship only works if the community that celebrates it feels suitably homogeneous and bounded.

Such plots have to be used with extreme caution as data about who was admitted or excluded. Their depictions of vulgar intruders breaching the boundaries are unsupported by other kinds of evidence. We do not find court correspondents taking much notice of citizens, either within audiences or without.[119] But as indications of what people felt was going on, the social stakes that were implicit in masquing, they are invaluable, for they stage the underlying rationale of the occasion as a rite of social identity. They help to make apparent the general rule that the integrity of the masquing space was always defined by the imagining of dangers just over its border, that the event's sacredness was constituted by equivalent emphasis on the bad luck, profanity, or taboo that masque ritual warded away. So it is that masque after masque evokes a crowd of turbulent antimasquers pressing at the margins: not only citizens, but a vast array of witches, amazons, foreigners, exotics, alchemists, pigmies, satyrs, Ethiopians, puritans, Irishmen, drunkards, madmen, mountebanks, gypsies, monsters, and hybrids, figures that were brought into being in order for them to be beaten back beyond the boundary. Some of these characters are depicted as enemies like Plutus, who would destroy the festive community if they could. For example, the witches try to curse the court in *The Masque of Queens*, and the Evils of the Iron Age resist Astraea's return in *The Golden Age Restored*. Most, though, are simply eccentrics, disorderly outsiders who do not subvert the masquing space as such but whose presence within it is nonetheless seen as polluting or contaminating. Like Mary Douglas's definition of dirt, they are matter out of place.[120] They do not express 'real' threats to Whitehall's festivity, but function to draw the contested line between near and far, self and other, the marking of which was the perpetual business of the masques as rituals of social empowerment. Their supposed toxicity marks the limits of the festivity, and their disempowerment and dismissal is the structural precondition that allows the court to crystallize its sense of itself as a body. Their violation of masquing norms is the necessary transgression out of which the masquing community asserts its identity.

Inevitably, motifs such as these have sometimes been read as symptomatic of the court's vulnerability. Some critics imply that in beating away outsiders the masques were engaged in poignant political escapism, backhandedly acknowledging a tide in history that would shortly bear them down.[121] Yet while it is true that from the outside contemporaries often took masques as symbols of court luxury and excess, it is anachronistic and historically premature to project forwards to a political situation unimaginable until 1642. In the anthropological perspective being developed here, these fantasies of social transgression announced the court's power, not its fragility. Moreover, simplistic political allegorizing of the masques treats them misleadingly as sympathetic magic or acts of wish-fulfilling exorcism, and fails to acknowledge the real social functions that such rituals performed. Each masque was shadowed by a threshold of anxiety about belonging and exclusion that conscripted its spectators into the event, energizing and giving substance to the scenarios of empowerment and disempowerment in which the form traded. Indeed, whatever the political content of the masque fable, for the spectators the implied social agenda was likely to have been an equally compelling part of the evening. The perils of access marshalled the audience's anxieties and desires, provoking in them a psychological need for incorporation into the festive community, and creating a social dialectic that tied their sense of individual identity to the ideological legitimation of monarchy. From this point of view, the threat of exclusion was one of the mechanisms of coercion in which the masques so powerfully traded, albeit one that usually remained implicit, invisible except in the minds of the audience. Only with festivals like *The Masque of Augurs*, *Love Restored*, and *The Triumph of Peace*, which thematized the uncertainties of access and sublimated audience anxieties by projecting them onto characters who played out the fear of exclusion, was it openly apparent that the validation of the crown's political authority was inextricably entangled with the acts of social legitimation that were performed lower down the hall. The crown's power of validation was conjured out of the audience's need to belong.

Masques, then, depended on what could be called a 'social psychology' that underpinned their symbolic work. Their performances provoked a set of conflicts in the minds of their spectators that provided the raw material out of which the affirmations and rejections orchestrated in their fables were made, so that the thresholds they drew between the privileged and the excluded were informed as much by the social experience of the audience as they were by the need to legitimate the king. This psychology we have seen powerfully displayed in the behaviour of Jonson and Roe, and it is immanent in many of the stories touched on above. We also find it documented after the event in Francis Osborne's account of court festival written in the 1650s. Osborne was a hostile witness whose *Historical Memoirs* of James I depict masques as wasteful vanities, but, as the Earl of Pembroke's Master of Horse in the 1630s, he knew Whitehall's culture from within, and his reflections usefully pinpoint the conflicted mentality that they bred. Commenting on the indignity that Pembroke did to Tom May, Osborne focuses on the contradictory inner impulses that court festival provoked, the combination of eagerness for access and anxiety about exclusion:

So disobliging were the most grateful pleasures of the court, whose masques and other spectacles, though they wholly intended them for show, and would not have been pleased without great store of company, yet did not spare to affront such as came to see them: which accuseth the king no less of folly, in being at so vast an expense for that which signified nothing but in relation to pride and lust, than the spectators (I mean such as were not invited) of madness, who did not only give themselves the discomposure of body attending such irregular hours, but to others an opportunity to abuse them. Nor could I, that had none of their share who passed through the most incommodious access, count myself any great gainer (who did ever find some time before the grand night to view the scene) after I had reckoned my attendance and sleep: there appearing little observable, besides the company, and what imagination might conjecture from the placing of the ladies, and the immense charge and universal vanity in clothes, etc.[122]

What Osborne frankly calls 'madness' in the spectators is the seeming contradiction by which would-be participants found themselves in the position of being simultaneously welcome in the hall and unwelcome. As a member of Pembroke's staff, Osborne had easy admission: he viewed the scenery before the performances,[123] and distinguishes himself from those poor souls who, lacking formal invitations, had to attempt 'the most incommodious access'. Standing outside the struggles for place, he registers with relative detachment how much the exclusion of some spectators was not only likely but intrinsic, how much the privilege being celebrated positively required that some participants were seen to be excluded. In this respect, his analysis chimes with the disenchanted perspective of Sir John Roe. Both writers intuit that the masques' courtesies depended for their effect on the degree of discourtesy that happened at their margins, and that without the impertinences vented on those refused admission, the privilege they celebrated would have been less absolute. This is a perception that suggests how two-edged court festivity must have seemed to many of those attempting to secure places. However hostile Osborne's account, in perceiving that Whitehall's 'grateful pleasures' rested on 'affront[s]' and disobligations as well as civilities he identified what for the spectators within and observers without must always have been the unavoidable paradox. The court's inaccessibility and difference was the breeding-ground of their deference and desire.

CHAPTER 3

Rites of incorporation

On 1 January 1604, a week before Jonson and Roe were excluded from *The Vision of the Twelve Goddesses*, the court saw a masque at Hampton Court, the first such show in the forty-year sequence of Stuart Christmas revelry. According to Sir Dudley Carleton, who witnessed it, a 'heaven' was erected at the lower end of the hall, out of which came a Chinese magician who 'made a long sleepy speech to the King of the nature of the country from whence he came', then announced the arrival of 'certain Indian and China knights' whom he had brought in clouds 'to see the magnificency of this court. And thereupon a traverse was drawn and the masquers seen sitting in a vaulty place with their torchbearers and other lights, which was no unpleasing spectacle.' There followed some songs, and the eight masquers came up the hall to the King. The first, William Herbert, Earl of Pembroke, gave James a shield bearing an impresa with a poem explaining its meaning, and presented a jewel supposedly worth £40,000[1] – though Carleton believed that really the King intended to buy it after the performance from the financier Peter van Lore, 'but that is more than every man knew and it made a fair show to the French ambassador's eye, whose master would have been well pleased with such a masquer's present, but not at that price'. The other masquers presented shields and poems, and much attention was engrossed by Pembroke's brother, Philip Herbert, who was currently the Englishman uppermost in James's affections. Philip Herbert's impresa showed a horse in a green field, and the King asked him to interpret it. Herbert explained it was 'a colt of Bucephalus' race, and had this virtue of his sire, that none could mount him but one as great at least as Alexander. The King made himself merry with threatening to send this colt to the stable, and [Herbert] could not break loose till he promised to dance as well as Banks's horse' (Banks being a showman whose bay gelding was famous for its tricks). There followed the formal dancing, then the Queen and her ladies joined in the revels, after which the magician 'dissolved his enchantment' and revealed the masquers' identities for those who had not already guessed them.[2]

The text of *The Masque of Indian and China Knights* has not survived, but it remains important as the period's first major Christmas festival, which initiated motifs that would resonate through forty years' masquing, so embedded were they in the Stuart court's social protocols. Carleton's account of the festival tells us enough to show how explicitly it enacted Whitehall's structural relationships. The masquers were eight of the King's nearest personal friends, four of them English and four Scots.[3] The English were Sir Thomas Somerset (son to the Earl of Worcester, one of the messengers sent to Edinburgh to announce Queen Elizabeth's death, and now Queen Anne's Master of Horse), Sir Henry Goodere (who corresponded with James before the accession, and was amongst those first received 'into his service and care'),[4] and the two Herbert brothers, who were especially close favourites. Pembroke ended Elizabeth's reign in disgrace, but under James his upward career culminated in 1615 with his appointment as Lord Chamberlain. In 1603 he had already entertained James twice at Wilton; in July he was made a garter knight, and two weeks after the masque received his first significant office, the stewardship of the Duchy of Cornwall. Philip Herbert was an even dearer friend. Clarendon said he 'had the good fortune, by the comeliness of his person, his skill, and indefatigable industry in hunting, to be the first who drew the King's eyes towards him with affection', and 'pretended to no other qualifications than to understand horses and dogs very well, which his master loved him the better for'.[5] As for the Scots, they were James's two nearest blood relatives, the Duke of Lennox and his brother Lord Aubigny (sons of his boyhood friend, Esmé Stuart), with James Hay (future Earl of Carlisle and a courtier on whom astonishing gifts would be lavished) and Richard Preston (soon to be elevated as Lord Dingwall). Some of these eight would in time become significant office-holders, but at present they were strictly non-political: they were James's friends and companions, not office-holders or councillors. All the English were gentlemen of the Privy Chamber, while the Scots were gentlemen of the Bedchamber, and hence James's most intimate attendants (Philip Herbert was shortly after appointed to the Bedchamber, the first English courtier in that Scottish preserve).[6] The masque thus celebrated ties of love and affinity amongst James's inner circle, while bridging the gap between his English and Scottish establishments, a gap gestured at in the dancers' fictional roles as Indian and Chinese knights. Their disguises adverted to national distinctions that the audience would readily have recognized, and managed internal differences between the King's servants by displacing them onto more exotic identities, unified into a playful show of devotion to a now fully British court.

The eight masquers were virile young men, mostly in their twenties, and one cannot avoid speculating about the erotic content of their performances. It would have been impossible on the dance floor to separate their gestures of obeisance and homage to James from the staging of their bodily charisma as attractive royal servants. The Venetian ambassador called Pembroke 'a handsome youth, who is always with the king and always joking with him', and described how at the coronation he surprised onlookers by kissing James on the face, 'whereupon the king laughed and gave him a little cuff'.[7] Philip Herbert was an even closer friend, the first in a line of favourites that led to Somerset and Buckingham, and whose familiarity with James was provocatively intimate. At Herbert's wedding in 1605 the King gave the bride away, then visited the couple early the next morning 'in his shirt and his nightgown and spent a good hour with them in the bed or upon' (said Carleton, sardonically), 'choose which you will believe best'.[8] Herbert's impresa of Bucephalus traded on these associations, for it made a barely concealed allusion to his emotional bond with the monarch. Offering himself as James's mount, and protesting that he would throw off any rider less great than Alexander, it hinted in a deliciously insouciant manner at a homoerotic relationship. Exactly the same analogy was used by the Earl of Suffolk in 1611 when comparing Sir John Harington's failure at court with Somerset's success: 'Will you say … that the roan jennet surpasseth Bucephalus, and is worthy to be stridden by Alexander?'[9] Evidently Herbert's teasing impresa achieved its aim of drawing attention to his special devotion, for it led to the semi-private dialogue with James over its meaning, conscripting the event into a celebration of love between master and man. It must have seemed an intimate royal game, alluding to private confidences, and using codes that shadowed private relationships while hinting recklessly at unspoken content. Herbert momentarily made the event his own, rather as Buckingham did to the masques which he danced fifteen years later.

But this personal dialogue was only one element of the evening. For all performers, the festival must have affirmed their dependence on James, marshalling them into a ritual that was eroticized, playful, and ceremonious. With the whole court looking on, the masque staged the emotional bonds amongst the King's closest friends, playing out in intense form – at once symbolic and physical – the ties of obedience and affiliation that gave warmth to the larger social and political community. Further, by their choice of partners in the social dancing, the masquers affirmed the bonds between the King's household and the Queen's, since the ladies taken out to dance all belonged to the Queen's inner circle, her two ladies of the

Bedchamber (the Countesses of Bedford and Hertford) and five ladies of the Drawing Chamber.[10] The dances were thus not private acts of courtship but a public acknowledgement of Whitehall's new face and the appointments that had occurred since March. The gesture was reciprocated a week later when most of these same ladies, masquing in *The Vision of the Twelve Goddesses*, took out members of James's household. On that occasion, though, the men chosen were not youthful favourites but councillors and great office-holders, including the Earl of Worcester (who was Earl Marshal and Master of Horse), Lord Chamberlain Suffolk, Lord Admiral Nottingham, and Henry Howard (Privy Councillor and future Earl of Northampton). Most of these men shared close family connections and formed the court's most entrenched dynastic group.[11] Also taken out were several close friends of the Elizabethan Earl of Essex, men who fell under a cloud at the time of his revolt but moved back into positions of trust under the new monarch – Lord Treasurer Knollys, the Earls of Southampton and Devonshire, Sir Robert Sidney, and Lord Monteagle.[12] By highlighting these two affinities, and using the Queen's ladies as the channel between them, the event showcased the complex intersections over which James presided, the network of friends, kinsmen, allies, rivals, servants, and subjects who, during the festival, were bound in consociation. If the late Elizabethan court was notable for its strains and divisions, the parade of dance and counter-dance in James's first festivals presented a face of unity and common purpose.

Even in the absence of a text, *The Masque of Indian and China Knights* shows how powerfully Stuart festivals could articulate the court's collective identity, their ability to signal dependence and identification, association and belonging, and forge a unity knitted together from Whitehall's competing interest-groups. Strikingly, on this occasion the King was not the evening's sole focus. The masquers and their dancing partners were the stars, and the festival bracketed them within the overall courtly system, displaying in graceful aesthetic forms their relationships of subjection and obligation, service, competition, and friendship. Although (as the social and political apex of this community) James presided over the event, a range of formal and informal exchanges were presented that mapped onto the structural web of court life – between English and Scots, Privy Chamber and Bedchamber, King's and Queen's household, Howard and Essex. The masque's aesthetic and political task was to manage the personal and factional differences between the King's various 'families' and fuse them into an integrated whole. Nor was the audience's presence any less intrinsic. The spectators may have been silent in Carleton's narrative, but they were not merely passive. They were necessary to provide the context for Whitehall's self-display, and acted implicitly as the representative body of the social elite, standing as synecdoche for the greater nation. Since the masque was never printed, no attempt was made to disseminate it to a wider public other than by the circulation of eyewitness testimony through the channels of court correspondents. What counted was not what it said but what it did: it allowed the Whitehall community to celebrate its shared sense of belonging, drawing King, participants, and observers into an intimate experience of social affinity. Any political 'message' was subordinate to the articulation of this underlying ethos.[13]

Unlike the ceremonials described in the previous chapter, in which the masquing community asserted its identity by marking its separateness from those who were denied access to the event, the forms adopted by *The Masque of Indian and China Knights* were not confrontational. Although they foregrounded the masquers' exoticism and otherness, they validated them in terms of festive incorporation into the greater body of the court. This made the occasion as much a matter of social performance as it was of political purpose more narrowly construed. For the duration of the evening, the King, his friends, officers, servants, and courtiers joined in rituals of hospitality which affirmed Whitehall's collective identity, embodying it in symbolic gestures and transactions that played out the affective relationships uniting the participants. The show staged the court's internal bonds, its economy as a status-group, and underwrote both the courtiers' sense of belonging and the monarch's sense of ownership. As James M. Saslow comments on entertainments produced for the Medici family in sixteenth-century Florence, princely festivity 'served what Emile Durckheim, writing of religious rituals, termed a "latent function", that of bringing community members together in collective affirmation of their social bond independent of any manifest content'.[14] Of course, English masques were never quite as *laissez-faire* as this suggests. The reappearance in successive festivals of particular groups of masquers – such as the Earl of Suffolk's children or the Earl of Worcester's, or Henrietta Maria's Catholic ladies – suggests that performances were often driven by a strong 'family' content. Nevertheless, the forms used in *The Masque of Indian and China Knights* were endlessly recycled down to the Civil War: the entry of outsiders, their exotic and chivalric disguises, their approach, gift-giving, homage, and social dancing. The staying-power of these integrative motifs suggests that the assertion of group solidarity and collective self-identification was just as foundational to Stuart masques as was their commentary on national and international politics.

The Masque of Indian and China Knights was less antagonistic than many subsequent spectacles. It lacked grotesque or disruptive antimasquers who contested the performers' status, instead validating the masquers through their procession, presentation, and unmasking. In later years, the dyad of antimasque and masque would develop as the form of choice, and the dominance of this model in modern critical discussion has fostered a view of court festival as conflict-driven and propagandistic. The so-called 'Jonsonian' masque, with its topicality, promulgation of policy, and resolution of contradictions by a personal appeal to the monarch, was indeed politicized and focused expressly on the king. But too great an emphasis on dialectical structures and specific local meanings can efface the functions of social cohesion and self-definition that were so evident in *The Masque of Indian and China Knights* and crucial to court festival as a whole. For the participants – meaning monarch, masquers, and spectators alike – masques were one more component in Whitehall's daily etiquette, a periodic form of display germane to the courtly *habitus*. We only partially grasp their meanings if we ignore the way that their performances coalesced with the court's wider ritual practices. They were not isolated events but were intricately enmeshed in the recurrent ceremonial that bound together the life of king and courtier.

Court masques usually took place in a seasonal context, as part of the calendrical cycle shaping Whitehall's year. The customary masquing dates were 6 January – Twelfth Night or Epiphany – or Shrovetide, the day of carnival immediately before the austerities of Lent. New Year's night and Candlemas (the Feast of the Purification, 2 February) could also see masques, though Twelfth Night was always the major celebration, being the culmination of the Christmas festivities. As James himself told the ambassadors in 1613:

the last day should be taken for the greatest day, as it is understood in many other cases, and particularly upon the festivals of Christmas, wherein Twelfth Day or the festival of the three kings, which is the last, is taken for the greatest day; and in many places Tuesday is taken for the chiefest day of Shrovetide, wherefore the masque at court, composed for that day as being the greatest of all the festivals.[15]

In fact, this was a comparatively recent tradition: in 1604–5, the Privy Council, anxious that James was to repeat for *The Masque of Blackness* the levels of expenditure that had been incurred on *The Vision of the Twelve Goddesses* in 1603–4, advised him that 'many Christmases pass without any such note, dancing, comedies, plays, and other sports having been thought sufficient marks of mirth, except some great strange [= foreign] prince or extraordinary marriage fall in that time'.[16] But masques rapidly became a Christmas fixture, and by 1618 Orazio Busino was agreeing that Twelfth Night always saw the premier event, 'in accordance with an ancient custom of this royal palace'.[17] In the seventeenth century the gap between the court's seasonal celebrations and traditional observances that survived elsewhere in the country became increasingly marked. Nonetheless, court festivals were always coloured by a residue of calendrical custom, however attenuated, and this meant that the masques' formal and social characteristics were inevitably inflected by seasonal considerations. They belonged to a calendar of Whitehall ceremonial that was widely observed and ubiquitous.

The masques' embedment in the ritual year can be illustrated by listing the revelry for Christmas 1604–5, which is particularly well documented. This season saw three major events: the wedding of Philip Herbert and Lady Susan Vere, the creation of Prince Charles as Duke of York, and the Queen's show *The Masque of Blackness*. The wedding took place on 27 December, and Herbert was given 'all the honour could be done'. The bride was led to the chapel by Prince Henry and the Duke of Holstein (Queen Anne's brother), and gifts were given to the value of £2,500, including £500 in land from the King. The marriage was celebrated with 'bride cakes, sops in wine, giving of gloves, laces and points', and a banquet in the Great Chamber was followed by a masque in the Hall, *Hymen and the Four Seasons*, danced by eight gentlemen, including Pembroke, Hay, and Preston. This is now lost, though its title suggests that its themes combined the marital and calendrical. The couple were lodged in the Council Chamber, where the King woke them next morning. It was expected that on New Year's Day earldoms would be conferred, but these were put off. On 2 January James gambled in the Presence Chamber; Herbert threw the dice for him and 'had the good fortune to win £1,000, which he had for his pains'. Then three days were given over to the creation of the four-year-old Duke of York and eleven knights of the Bath, who were feasted in court, and a banquet and play were given by the Spanish ambassador for the Duke of Holstein, with gifts of fans and gloves for the ladies. The installation itself was on 6 January, performed in the Hall by nine earls and followed by a public dinner in the Chamber. Only then was the masque danced, in the Banqueting House, and there was talk of an 'after reckoning' to follow from the Duke of Holstein. Additionally, five plays were staged by visiting professional players during the holiday, and three more in the second week of January.[18]

Few Christmases were quite as busy as this, but the combination of state ceremonial, ritual observance, and social pleasure was characteristic. The habit of keeping a winter season continued to the Civil War, and under Charles it was formalized and extended, with Tuesdays and Thursdays being put aside for plays (in imitation of Spanish court practice),[19] and with the festivities being brought forward to the King's and Queen's birthdays in November, and drawn out after Epiphany (for Henrietta Maria's Shrovetide masque was usually framed as a gift reciprocating Charles's Twelfth Night show). Moreover, the fusion of different kinds of celebration staged in 1604–5 was customary, bringing together as it did masque, investiture, and wedding with feasting and game-playing. Under James, grand court weddings were commonly held at Christmas, for they added to the glory of the season – though doubtless they were encouraged because the costs would be borne by the couples' friends rather than the Exchequer. Whatever the reason, some of the highest-profile nuptials were seen at Christmas (the marriages of Lord Hay, 1607, the Earl of Essex, 1606, and Earl of Somerset, 1613), or at Shrovetide (Viscount Haddington, 1608, Princess Elizabeth, 1613), or at Candlemas (Viscount Roxborough, 1614).[20] Similarly, New Year often brought a round of promotions or investitures. The household of Prince Charles as Duke of York was inaugurated on 1 January 1611, the transfer of offices after Somerset's fall took place between 23 December 1615 and 4 January 1616, and George Villiers was created Marquis of Buckingham on 1 January 1618. For both kinds of event, Christmas or New Year were suitable dates of celebration because they marked times when the often peripatetic court was always gathered as a body, but they were also points of transition in the calendar, moments of induction or passage, shutting up the old year and inaugurating the new. Indeed, the title pages to Jonson's first printed masque and the masque section in his 1616 folio bore an epigraph from the discussion of New Year rituals in Ovid's *Fasti*.[21] Such associations were to the fore in *The Masque of Beauty* (1608), where the liminal god Januarius promised to 'renew' the 'happy rites' of James's reign (302–3). In *The Masque of Augurs* (1622), the festival that was staged to open the second Jacobean Banqueting House, seasonal omens were taken, the masquers dancing out their auguries for the coming year and the new ceremonial space. On this latter occasion, political and seasonal rituals knitted together seamlessly.[22]

The show which most explicitly capitalized on calendrical associations was Jonson's *Christmas his Masque*, staged at some point in the 1616–17 season. This was not strictly a masque but a pastiche of a Tudor mumming, performed by players rather than courtiers.[23] It had no social dancing, only a parade of characters with seasonal names such as Misrule, Carol, Gambol, New Year's Gift, Minced Pie, and Wassail, all bearing tokens of festival

customs such as playing cards, gingerbread, and the Christmas box, and led
in by their father Gregory Christmas, a hearty, Falstaffian figure of the kind
familiar in modern times. As Leah Marcus argues, Jonson's evocation of
timeless seasonal practices was politically useful at a moment when James
was using his proclamations and the *Book of Sports* to encourage the upkeep
of traditional holiday pastimes, as a way of discouraging divisive puritanical
sentiment and promoting deference and amity in the country at large.[24] In
fact, the show's attitude towards these customs was condescending – the
characters were all supposedly played by citizens, who feigned to have
brought Christmas to Whitehall in a gesture of loyalty – and it is difficult
to disentangle what is genuinely traditional in it from the traditions that
Jonson himself devised. Particularly, Father Christmas has no English
literary precedent before this show, so Jonson in a sense invented him,[25]
and the text has several of the earliest allusions to now-familiar Christmas
practices. *Christmas his Masque* was thus an example of the court using
seasonal motifs strategically, perhaps even creating them, rather than naively
participating in a nostalgic populism. Nonetheless, the trace of traditional
seasonal customs in Christmas masquing was strong. It recurred, for example, in Middleton's *Masque of Heroes* (danced at the Middle Temple in
1619), which presented the death of December and birth of the New Year,
and staged a controversy between corpulent Plum-Porridge and a thin
Fasting Day. Severity and Levity argued over the proper celebration of the
season in Middleton's *Honourable Entertainments* (a civic show, 1621), and,
in Thomas Pestell's *Coleorton Masque* (1618), Bob the Buttery Spirit complained about the decline of hospitality brought about by too much
puritanism.

All of these texts were agonistic. They presented symbolic contests
between carnival and Lent, and showed revelry triumphing over austerity
whenever it threatened seasonal good-fellowship. Even in *Christmas his
Masque* (the least confrontational of the four), interlopers from Friday
Street and Fish Street were denied access because their home addresses
linked them with self-denial. As such, these texts play out contrasts and
transitions that were implicit in many masques, which often turned on the
victory of the new over the old, the coming year over the past, and fertility
over restraint.[26] Typical is *The Masque of Flowers* (1614), which was organized as a struggle for precedence between winter and spring, and wine and
tobacco. The two sides entered in response to a challenge and sang songs
competitively at each other, after which the masquers were transformed
from flowers into men by the warmth of the kingly sun. Similarly, Jonson's
Vision of Delight (1617) presented a premature spring, with the winter

weather magically becoming unseasonably mild under James's influence, the change being announced by Peace, 'the opener of the new year' (129). Comparable transitions from winter to spring can be found, albeit in more coded form, in many other masques, notably *Mercury Vindicated, Pleasure Reconciled to Virtue*, and *Pan's Anniversary*. In each, James was interpellated into the festival by his association with the sun which, at the turning of the year, drives the court's seasons. As rites of winter renewal, masques celebrated the King's solar power, while reaffirming the cohesion, identity, and bondedness of the whole court community.

Agonistic motifs were even more germane to the marriage festivals, which were marked by tilts, debates, and combats, or were distinguished in formal terms by the presence of paired groups of participants, men against women, or bride's party against groom's. In *Hymenaei* (for the Essex wedding) and *The Lords' Masque* (for the Palatine wedding), two sets of masquers appeared, male and female; in *Hymenaei*, the symbolic movement from conflict into union was especially pronounced. In *Lord Hay's Masque* the masquers were all male, but the theme was a struggle for precedence between Apollo and Diana which reiterated the motif of gender rivalry. Whereas many non-nuptial festivals set masquers against antimasquers hierarchically, with the masquers inevitably emerging on top, these shows were more even-handed, their competing parties needing to work out a balance rather than subordination. The comparative provisionality of their resolutions acknowledged the social threat lurking in the transitions of marriage, the perils that were skirted while sexual taboos were temporarily suspended.[27] The same could be said of the combats on foot or horseback fought at weddings, as in the barriers at the Essex marriage, or the tilts held at the Palatine wedding, the Somerset marriage, and the royal nuptials of 1625.[28] In the Essex and Somerset combats, Jonson's text introducing the chivalric action stressed the two sides' symmetry, and the impossibility of knowing which was superior. Such devices bring to mind the marital rituals described by anthropologists in kinship communities, which celebrate weddings by symbolic struggles marking the transfer of the bride from one family to another, playfully discharging the feelings of insecurity and enmity that such exchanges entail. Wedding celebrations may see an attempt by the groom's kin to capture the bride, or a refusal by the bride's kin to relinquish her, often by concealing her – as in the superstitions still current today, which dictate that bride and groom should avoid seeing each other on the marriage morning, and that the bride should arrive last at the ceremony.[29] Jonson's *A Challenge at Tilt* (1613), with its two identical Cupids, each claiming that he was the 'real' god of love and setting bride's and groom's supporters at odds, was essentially a game of this kind. Its resolution sought to avert the occasion's potential for danger:

Let your knights – all honourable friends and servants of love – affect the like peace, and depart the lists equal in their friendships forever, as today they have been in their fortunes; and may this royal court never know more difference in humours, or these well-graced nuptials more discord in affections, than what they presently feel and may ever avoid. (221–7)

Jonson's admonitions were politically loaded – they alluded to factional rivalries that were provoked by the contentious Somerset marriage (discussed in chapter 7 below) – but to take this as the ritual's 'real' or only rationale misses the point. All court festivals were on some level apotropaic. They warded away the bad luck that threatened at moments of transition, the recurring liminal peril that provoked these symbolic contests.

While marital combats focused on the body of the courtier by providing an arena for the display of his prowess, the King had his own chivalric festival: the anniversary of James's accession (24 March) was usually marked with tournaments on the tiltyard, as Elizabeth's had been, as well as bell-ringing in local parishes. These tilts were public events, and attracted huge crowds of onlookers, most of whom would have been denied access to the masques. As well as celebrating the date, they helped to preserve the emotional tie between the crown and a nationalistic culture of Protestantism that was one of Elizabeth's legacies.[30] This role, though, James did not easily fulfil, and Stuart neo-medievalism gradually dwindled away and moved indoors, to be transmuted by the masques into a different model of courtiership, now exemplified as heroism on the dance floor. The Indian and China knights may have dressed as warriors, but their chivalry was expressed in terms which stressed the management of inner tensions rather than athleticism or military strength. The masquers' dignified comportment foregrounded their conquest of the passions and inward control of the self, and advertised their accomplishment as courtiers in their own right. Their refined bearing and decent social etiquette marked them out as legitimate participants in Whitehall society.[31] This first masque thus established the double social function of festivals, validating both the King's body and the social body at large. It marked the annual renewal of the King's power by manifesting his capacity to absorb difference, while promoting his individual servants, who danced out their contribution to his court's well-regulated ostent.

One recurrent motif which underlined the masques' function as a bonding mechanism was the gift or presentation, already encountered in the jewel

3 Engraved sword presented to Prince Henry, 1610.

and imprese that were offered at *The Masque of Indian and China Knights*, and the gloves and fans gifted by the Spanish ambassador at Christmas 1604–5. Early Jacobean masques constantly turn on gift-giving – what anthropologists call 'prestations', exchanges of offerings that point performatively towards an underlying legal or customary obligation. In *The Vision of the Twelve Goddesses* (1604), each of the female masquers presented a token which expressed her power: a sceptre for Juno, a scarf for Venus, a bow for Diana, a trident for Tethys, and so forth.[32] In *The Masque of Blackness* (1605), the Ethiopian women gave the King fans bearing mysterious imprese, and in *Solomon and the Queen of Sheba* (1606), James and King Christian of Denmark received caskets containing 'precious gifts', wine, cakes, and spices.[33] In *Tethys' Festival* (1610), Queen Anne gave Prince Henry a trident, a scarf, and a richly decorated sword that is now in the Wallace Collection and is, apart from Inigo Jones's designs, the sole surviving material remnant of any masque performance (see figure 3).[34] In *The Masque of Squires* (1613), the action turned on Anne's presentation of an olive branch, and in *Cupid's Banishment* (staged at Greenwich, 1617) she was given gifts of embroidery. Such symbolic exchanges largely disappeared from the post-Jacobean masques, except for the shields that were presented by Prince Charles to Henrietta Maria in the deliberately nostalgic *King and Queen's Entertainment at Richmond* (1636).[35] However, an attitude informed by gift-giving was always implicit in the displays of homage that, by dancing and making reverences, the masquers performed to the monarch. Even if no gifts were exchanged, the dancers' obeisance played out their dutiful relationship to the sovereign. Moreover, gifts were frequent currency lubricating the normal round of court entertainment – as at the play given by Henrietta Maria in November 1629 to celebrate the King's birthday, when boxes of sweetmeats were brought in between the acts to distribute amongst the guests.[36]

The exchange of gifts was one of Whitehall's most fundamental social rituals, for this practice expressed the wealth of the court community and the ties of obligation and clientage that bound it together. Luxury goods and material wealth were, for any early modern court, the most visible signs of its magnificence, and the Stuarts were no exception in assuming that prestige was best manifested in largesse. Prince Henry's sword, with its elaborately engraved HP motif (for *Henricus princeps*), exemplifies the combination of material worth and symbolic value that gift-giving fused together. Jewellery was indeed capital at this time, and the culture of display was intricately bound up with the assertion of aristocratic identity.[37] Stuart court portraits often depict members of the royal house wearing notable gems or standing with parts of the state regalia which embody both their sovereign authority and material inheritance, while jewels and plate were frequently exchanged at festival events such as weddings and diplomatic missions. Masques were prime occasions on which cripplingly extravagant sums could be seen to be carelessly squandered in the cause of dynastic aggrandisement. Not only were the performance costs prodigal, but the spectators themselves sported jewels and rich fabrics which enhanced the evening's ostentation. Sir Robert Sidney and Sir Ralph Winwood each spent £80 on suits to wear at masques, and jewellery was so far *de rigueur* that in 1640 Lady Nicholas declined to attend *Salmacida Spolia* because she lacked enough gems to appear well-dressed.[38] Carleton reported that many ladies lost 'jewels, chains, and purses' at *The Masque of Blackness*, while at *The Masque of Beauty* (said Chamberlain) one lady – 'and that under a baroness' – was wearing jewels rumoured to be worth £100,000, Arbella Stuart was even better dressed, 'and the Queen must not come behind'.[39] Although the scenery was expensive, the real material outlay was in the clothes of masquers and audiences. The spectators were producers as well as observers of the court's glory, for, while they consumed the theatrical display, their own show of wealth and status was genuinely part of the event: masque ceremonial centred as much on the encompassing social ritual as it did on the dramatic performance. Writing in 1656, the royalist historian Sir William Sanderson remembered this overwhelming opulence as the hallmark of pre-Civil War Whitehall:

> the splendour of the King, Queen, Prince, and Princess with the rest of the royal issue, the concourse of strangers hither from foreign nations, the multitude of our own people from all parts of our three kingdoms gave a wonderful glory to the court, at this time the only theatre of majesty, not any way inferior to the most magnificent in Christendom.[40]

Literally glittering in the candlelight, masque audiences embodied the economic power and sense of affinity of England's political elites.

The assumption behind such behaviour was that spending was necessary to manifest power, and that social capital could be accrued by deliberately wasting material wealth. Here we are on territory that has been charted in studies of ritual customs in archaic communities, particularly societies where an economy based on gifts and pre-capitalist practices still exists alongside or in place of a market-style economy. As in the 'Big Man' or 'charismatic' systems described by anthropologists, the uneconomic extravagance associated with masques had symbolic value. Its wastage was redeemed by the social prestige that it accumulated, or by the competition for attention that lavish spending advanced between rival patrons and clients.[41] The wastefulness of court ceremonial had prestige-value if not use-value: as Norbert Elias argues in relation to eighteenth-century France, it was subtended by codes of etiquette that marked out relationships of power, rank, and dignity which enmeshed the whole court society.[42] Such behaviour is also reminiscent of the 'potlatch' customs in archaic communities, which in the winter season indulge in a shocking expenditure of resources by way of wantonly extravagant consumption. The Chinook word 'potlatch' – which means both 'to nourish' and 'to consume' – is used of celebrations in which the feasting is not purely hospitable but carries an underlying spirit of competitiveness or antagonism, sometimes described as a 'war of property' or 'struggle of wealth'. The clan puts its prestige to the test by vaunting itself, laying waste to the very resources on which that prestige rests, and uses competitive feasting to articulate distinctions of status, defining the hierarchies of the group and marking out those beyond the tribe.[43]

Seen in these terms, the economic excess of masquing had as much to do with the self-definition of a community built around prestige and honour as it did with any more narrowly defined political objective. Certainly masques always involved the performers as well as the crown in expenditure on a grand scale, since dancers were expected to purchase their masquing costumes, and patrons underwrote their own shows on occasions outside the normal masquing season. It cost Buckingham £1,000 to welcome the King to his new house in Rutland (for which Jonson wrote *The Gypsies Metamorphosed*), and the Earl of Suffolk, claimed one of his daughters, 'spent in running at tilt, in masques and following the court about £20,000'.[44] James Hay, the great archetype of prodigality, was rumoured to have spent £22,000 on entertaining the French ambassador in 1617, hospitality which included *Lovers Made Men* and a feast so extravagant that John Chamberlain judged it 'rather a profusion and spoil than reasonable or honourable provision'.[45] Such wastage of material wealth would have been economically irrational but for the symbolic and social capital that it earned. Indeed, when Sir Francis Bacon paid £2,000 to mount *The Masque of Flowers*, he declined a £500 contribution from Sir Henry Yelverton, preferring to bear 'the whole charge with the honour'.[46] The demands of prestige over economics are seen even more starkly in the advice given to James by the Privy Council, when they discussed the cost of *The Masque of Blackness*. Although the councillors were anxious about the money, they advised James that if he wanted a masque he should 'resolve beforehand that the expense must be [his] own'. If he cancelled it simply for economy's sake, to the world at large it would seem 'neither safe nor honourable ... The saving of £4,000 would be more pernicious than the expense of ten times the value.'[47]

No less striking in this perspective are the affirmations of social reciprocation and mutual dependence that gift-giving involved. As Carleton noted, the jewel presented to James at *The Masque of Indian and China Knights* was intended to impress the French ambassador with the court's wealth, but this was a sham, for it was really being purchased by him, and the masquers only pretended it was a free gift.[48] What counted was not the monetary value of this fiscally redundant transaction but its show of political devotion and reciprocal regard, the affirmation of obligation and trust between monarch and courtiers. Studies of gift exchange have emphasized how widespread gift systems are, and how powerfully they function as mechanisms for establishing and maintaining bonds between members of the gift community. Gifts seem free and disinterested, but they operate in pre-capitalist societies in intensely self-interested ways. They perform functions of exchange and contract which constrain the partners no less than do legal undertakings in a market system, binding the donors to the donatees by virtue of the mentality of reciprocation that they create. Gift-giving puts the recipient in the giver's debt, and provokes an obligation to repay; the unrequited gift leaves the recipient wounded. More emphatically, a gift binds donor and donatee together by virtue of being a gift rather than a commodity. Not being an alienable object, a gift carries something of the donor into the recipient, creating a tie which is personal and ethical, even erotic, rather than aridly contractual. What matters, then, is not the value but the bond that the gift symbolizes. Gift exchanges mark out relationships between social partners rather than creating actual economic effects: Mary Douglas and Baron Isherwood call them 'shaking hands in a material way'.[49] They bring into being a community based on affective relationships in which a strong presumption exists that the partners in the gift transaction should each use their power to the benefit of the other.[50]

Early Stuart England was not a total gift economy, and had a well-developed commodity market.[51] Nonetheless, the gift model, and the mental assumptions that went with it, exerted great pressure in the social fabric, given the ubiquity of patronage practices and the huge repertoire of gift-giving customs associated with them. As the fountain of bounty, the King was the ultimate source of gifts, with his status expressed in his largesse, and at every level of society the conduct of day-to-day business was inflected by a language of gratitude, obligation, and love, and underpinned by the actual exchange of tokens between patron and client.[52] In the early seventeenth century, these assumptions were slowly eroding, the falls of Suffolk and Bacon on charges of peculation being evidence of a developing anxiety about where the boundary lay between lavish gift-giving and outright bribery. But down to the Civil War the custom continued to be observed that members of the royal household should mark their duty to the monarch by presenting gifts on New Year's Day, in return for which each officer received from the sovereign a corresponding gift of plate. This ritual dated back at least to Henry VIII's time, and reached its apogee under Elizabeth, from whose reign over twenty gift rolls survive recording the 200 or so presents that she received annually, and the precisely graded quantities of plate that she gave in return.[53] Many gifts took the form of clothes, or money in sums appropriate to rank (£20 from a duke, £10 from an earl), but others were frequently tokens symbolizing the relationship between monarch and servant: spices, fruit, and marzipans from kitchen staff, books from the royal printer, lute-strings from musicians. By James's reign, New Year rituals had become purely monetary and rigidly formulaic, and involved no face-to-face contact with the King. As the Earl of Huntingdon described the ceremonies for 1605, donors would offer purses with cash to the Lord

Chamberlain in the Presence Chamber, then visit the Jewel House and mark a piece of plate to a near-equivalent value, which was delivered to them in the afternoon by Jewel House staff, to whom a further gratuity was given.[54] Nonetheless, gift rolls survive down to 1640, and James's and Charles's annual expenditure on plate (combining gifts for diplomats with those for New Year) ranged from £2,500 to £7,000.[55] Henrietta Maria spent £2,500 annually on New Year gifts, and on 1 January 1613 the Palatine Prince dispensed ruinously expensive jewels around Queen Anne's and Princess Elizabeth's retinues.[56] It is difficult to see how such actions had any economic return for donor or recipient; rather, their value lay in the symbolic cementing of bonds and obligations. The association between New Year festivity and the annual ritual affirmation of social ties and its complex dance of gift and counter-gift must have been unavoidable. In his 'Epistle to the Countess of Rutland' (1600), Ben Jonson alludes to the familiar spectacle of New Year presents being exchanged at court, and avows that his verses are a gift worth more than mere gold.[57]

Under Elizabeth, court festivity was inextricably bound up with gift-giving, particularly because so much festival activity took place on progresses, during which the exchange of tokens was mandatory.[58] At her entry into London in 1559, Elizabeth received a purse of gold and a bible; at Norwich in 1578, a bevy of goddesses gave expensive presents; at Harefield in 1602, Sir Thomas Egerton presented jewels and a rich robe.[59] Often the theatrical shows mounted on progress were effectively gifts in themselves, or were little more than devices concocted to frame the presentation of a jewel worth considerably more than whatever the poet was paid. Under the Stuarts the crown travelled less but continued to receive offerings when entertained at London or further afield. When welcomed by Sir Robert Spencer at Althorp in Northamptonshire in June 1603 with an entertainment scripted by Jonson, Queen Anne was given a jewel by the Fairy Queen, in an action that carefully represented it as a mere trifle. This 'simple gift' (127)[60] the Fairy Queen offered to Anne out of gratitude to Spencer, who, since his wife's death, had allowed her the run of his estate:

> For which bounty to us lent,
> Of him unknowledged or unsent,
> We prepared this compliment,
> And as far from cheap intent
> In particular to feed
> Any hope that should succeed,
> Or our glory by the deed,
> As yourself are from the need. (138–45)

Jonson's convoluted syntax labours to discharge the contradictory meanings of the gift, for he could suggest neither that Queen Anne needed the jewel nor that Spencer expected some sort of return. Nonetheless, the implication was clear that obligations were being established on both sides – and less than a month later Spencer was raised to the baronage.

Similarly, at *The Entertainment at Britain's Burse*, commissioned from Jonson by the Earl of Salisbury in 1609 to mark the opening of his new luxury shops in the Strand, Queen Anne was given a silver plaque valued at 4,000 crowns, the King had a cabinet, Prince Henry a caparison for a horse, and the other members of the court party received rings.[61] Salisbury's munificence reflected his status as pre-eminent royal councillor and expressed his gratitude for extraordinary rewards: the motto over the shop read 'All other places give for money, here all is given for love.'[62] However, the pretence that the gifts were free was revealingly entangled in Jonson's text with the celebration of mercantile enterprise that the occasion also involved. The court was welcomed to this emporium by a shop-boy and his master, who praised their wares as if peddling them to potential purchasers and then presented gifts under colour of loaning them on approval, with an only half-facetious expectation that the recipients would eventually pay and be good customers in future. Jonson's speeches wittily exploited the gap between the event's commercial context and the gestures of personal obligation that gift-giving entailed. What might have been a demeaningly bourgeois economics was transformed by the exchange of gifts into an affair of honourable bounty cementing the King's relationship with his first minister and implying many more honours to come. Salisbury never danced in a masque himself – he was a bureaucrat rather than a favourite, and had physical disabilities – but he made up for it with a series of lavish entertainments welcoming James at his houses, each ostentatiously celebrating their mutual bond. The culmination came in 1607, when he gifted his entire estate at Theobalds in Hertfordshire to the King and received the old palace at Hatfield in return.[63] In Jonson's *Entertainment at Theobalds*, the Genius of the house lamented the loss of his old master, but was reassured that in the event's magical economy the exchange benefited all parties:

> O blessèd change,
> And no less glad than strange!
> Where we that lose have won,
> And, for a beam, enjoy a sun.   (130–3)

The material transactions encoded into the ceremonial forms could scarcely have been more emphatic. Master and servant were bound together by obligations so colossal that they could never be discharged.

Most festival gifts were given to the crown on progress, and functioned as threshold rituals that marked out the boundaries between monarch and subject, diplomatically negotiating their reciprocal bonds and obligations. The gestures of hospitality performed by James's hosts enacted symbolic versions of the contract by which he exerted power over his people, and variously sought to compliment and constrain him, and to forge mutually beneficial associations between host and sovereign. But the gift mentality was implicit in the masques too, not least because of their calendrical associations with New Year and Epiphany, the religious celebration of the Magi's presentation of gifts to the infant Christ, a story that combines symbolic prestation with explicitly political gestures of acclamation and homage.[64] Perhaps not surprisingly, the social obligations precipitated by gift-giving are central to the earliest surviving masque text, Daniel's *Vision of the Twelve Goddesses*. In this event, the Queen and eleven ladies, disguised as goddesses, were inducted by singers representing the Graces, who accompanied their presentation of gifts with a song expounding the action's wider significance:

> Desert, reward, and gratitude,
> The graces of society,
> Do here with hand in hand conclude
> The blessèd chain of amity:
> > For we deserve, we give, we thank,
> > Thanks, gifts, deserts, thus join in rank.
>
> We yield the splendent rays of light
> Unto these blessings that descend,
> The grace whereof with more delight
> The well-disposing doth commend,
> > Whilst gratitude, reward, deserts,
> > Please, win, draw on, and couple hearts.
>
> For worth and power and due respect
> Deserves, bestows, returns with grace
> The meed, reward, the kind effect
> That give the world a cheerful face,
> > And, turning in this course of right,
> > Make virtue move with true delight.   (353–70)[65]

The most striking aspect of this song is its elaborately formal number symbolism. It has three verses, each of three couplets, sung by three Graces as an accompaniment to masquers who enter in groups of threes, and its language foregrounds the relationship between the three ethical terms with which the Graces are associated – desert, reward, and gratitude – which are imagined as intricately linked together in an indissoluble chain.

Behind this conception lies a tradition descending from Seneca's essay *Of Benefits*, the foundational analysis of the social functions of obligation. Early in his treatise, Seneca invokes the iconography of the Graces to explain the three-way traffic of desert, reward, and gratitude. Why, Seneca asks, are there three Graces, who are always represented as young women, dancing hand in hand and laughing?

To this some answer that there ought to be three, because the one of them representeth him that bestoweth; the other, him that receiveth; the other, him that gratifieth and remunerateth the benefit. Others say that there are three kinds of benefits: the one of those who bestow the same, the other of those that restore the same, and the third of those that receive, and therewithal requite good turns.[66]

Seneca's analysis reiterates the essential point that gift-giving is reciprocal and provokes socially constitutive feelings of connectedness. The Graces' hand-in-hand dance corresponds to the inextricable linkage between giving, receiving, and requiting, and emblematizes the cycle of gratitude that gifts compel. The Graces are beautiful in order to express the delightful effects of gifts as they pass around the circle between giver and receiver: those who do good turns, receive them, and requite them will always be 'smiling and pleasant'. Daniel's Graces are moralized in precisely Senecan terms: singing with linked hands, they 'conclude / The blessèd chain of amity' ('conclude' here has the obsolete sense of 'comprise, sum up', *OED* I.2). They embody that tripartite connection which underpins the social fabric: worth deserves meed, power bestows reward, and respect returns 'the kind effect', to 'give the world a cheerful face'. As a gloss on the goddesses' presentation of gifts, the song represents the whole event as enacting the social impact of the new sovereign's bounty, the chain of connectedness which binds the court together. Daniel's preface says that his 'intent and scope' was 'only to present the figure of those blessings, with the wish of their increase and continuance, which this mighty kingdom now enjoys by the benefit of his most gracious Majesty, by whom we have this glory of peace, with the accession of so great state and power' (18–21). The endless, socially sustaining circulation of benefits and blessings, embodied in the show's gracious exchanges, thus became the evening's key motif. The masque acclaimed James, while re-affirming the stream of gift and counter-gift which underpinned his power. It played out the imagined community of his new Britain in mutually constitutive gestures of gratefulness and obligation.

The exchange of gifts gradually disappeared from the later masques, as Caroline court festivity became more systematically regulated. However, the roots of the show in the celebration of social bonds and affinities continued to be manifested in the custom that masque performances were always accompanied by feasting, which drew the audiences materially into the event. Masques typically ended with a collation, which consisted of comfits and other refreshments arranged in an adjacent room, and the convention was for the king to view the fare then leave it to the guests. Notoriously, though, it became common for the scramble for food to degenerate into an embarrassingly indecent free-for-all. The famous example is Orazio Busino's account of how *Pleasure Reconciled to Virtue* ended:

His majesty rose from his chair and, taking the ambassadors along with him, passed through a number of rooms and galleries and came to a hall where the usual supper was prepared for the performers, a light being carried before him. He glanced round the table and departed, and at once like so many harpies the company fell on their prey. The table was almost entirely covered with sweetmeats, with all kinds of sugar confections. There were some large figures, but they were of painted cardboard, for decoration. The meal was served in bowls or plates of glass; the first assault threw the table to the ground, and the crash of glass platters reminded me exactly of the windows breaking in a great midsummer storm.[67]

Busino's testimony may be exaggerated, but it is amply confirmed by other occasions. Carleton noted that at *The Vision of the Twelve Goddesses* the banquet was dispatched 'with the accustomed confusion', and that in the crush after *The Masque of Blackness* the whole table went flying; at *The Masque of the Inner Temple and Gray's Inn*, the Venetian ambassador was shocked to see how the banquet was 'rapaciously swept away'.[68] Comparable anecdotes tail off after the Jacobean period, perhaps because Charles's masques were better managed, or because the conventions for the general exeunt had changed. One rationale for the extra dramatic business or late entries that were increasingly contrived at the ends of masques may have been to allow the performers to rejoin their friends without being caught up in the near-riot that sometimes followed. Daniel said he devised the final sequence of *Tethys' Festival*, in which the lady masquers reappear having changed back into their normal clothes, in order to 'avoid the confusion which usually attendeth the dissolve of these shows'.[69]

It is tempting to see these fights over food simply as symptoms of the congestion discussed in chapter 2, which contradict the masques' celebratory ethos by replaying Whitehall's contests over access. Inevitably, there is an irony about the descent into chaos when it had been the aim of these festivals to show kingly power plucking order from disorder. Many masques depicted the court triumphantly banishing anarchy, only for much the same turmoil to re-erupt off-stage once the dancing was over. The irony is all the more acute in that collective feasting and the ritualized performance of the monarch's meals were core activities for early modern courts. Kings often ate in public, and the meticulous formalities that accompanied food consumption served to dignify the court's daily activity and give meaning to the courtiers' service: Buckingham, for example, was one of James's cup-bearers. Yet the contradiction between dignified masque and chaotic banquet was more apparent than real. Contemporaries accepted such behaviour because feeding frenzies were not unique to the masques but part and parcel of court hospitality, underpinning its lavishness and recklessness. So we find that at a banquet to celebrate the Treaty of Madrid in 1630 the 'disorderly multitude' fought over sweetmeats, which were thrown into the crowd by the courtiers, and that commonly, after guests departed from public dinners at Whitehall, the guard and inferior officers were allowed to 'scramble' or 'snatch' at the remains; this practice Sir John Finet calls 'the disordered custom of our court'.[70] Stuart monarchs were far from unique in tolerating scrambling for food. The practice expressed the deliberate wastefulness associated with festivity, the time of abundance that princely celebration strove to display (as when, during royal entries, fountains ran with wine or coins were thrown into the crowd). The masques' values of orderliness and control were thus only superficially at odds with the more energetic customs that manifested the sovereign's magnanimity, the 'licence' that accompanied royal 'liberty'. Indeed, the Savoyard ambassador was positively impressed by the demolition of the banquet after *The Masque of the Twelve Months*, which struck him as being 'according to the custom of great courts'.[71]

Such considerations are brought into focus by Jonson's intriguing but sometimes misrepresented remark in the preface to *The Masque of Blackness*, where he justifies his wish to see the text preserved in print by referring to the destruction that had already overtaken the performance's physical remains: 'Little had been done to the study of magnificence in these [spectacles], if presently with the rage of the people (who, as a part of greatness, are privileged by custom to deface their carcasses) the spirits had also perished' (5–9). Jonson's parenthesis has often been taken to mean that at the end of *The Masque of Blackness* the scenery had been violently torn down by 'the people'. Patricia Fumerton argues from it that despoliation of the fabric was a recurrent practice, and implies that masque performances were dogged by a popular violence which expressed the resentment of those who were excluded towards the monarchy that staged them.[72] But this seems unlikely to have been the case. No other evidence corroborates the destruction of *The Masque of Blackness* beyond Jonson's passing comment, and in many instances we know that the expensive scenery and costumes were carefully dismantled after the performance and stored away. Nor could such a 'custom' have prevailed after 1614, when the practice began of repeat performances. Rather than describing what specifically happened in 1605, it seems likely that Jonson was alluding to the general association between festival occasions and carnivalesque upheaval, a link that allowed spectators (rather than outsiders) to claim a space for themselves in the event by becoming its bodily consumers, taking material souvenirs or relics from it to be enjoyed now or treasured into the future. For example, it sometimes happened at European kingly enthronements that the *pallium* which protected the candidate, or the trappings of the horse which bore him, were looted after the ceremony – as at the end of the entry of Ferdinand II into Naples in 1506, when the baldacchino and the platform on which he sat were stolen, or at Charles V's 1536 entry into Siena, when his canopy was torn apart.[73] In England, a similar incident happened to Henry VIII, when, during a court entertainment of 1511, a pageant left outside the hall was ransacked by citizens, the looters going so far as to strip valuable fabrics from the bodies of the masquers themselves (some of which fabric, says Edmund Hall, Henry distributed freely, 'in token of liberality').[74] There was even a fight for possession of the baldacchino at Charles II's coronation in 1661, and a cloth of gold disappeared from James II's coronation in 1685.[75] Such carnivalesque violence did not express hostility or cupidity, but issued from the heightened emotional responses which court festival aroused. It marked the occasion as a significant transition in the royal calendar, and allowed the spectators to assert a direct stake in the celebration. By consuming the banquets violently, they shared in the occasion's fierce communion, and experienced their affiliations with the Whitehall community in intensely collective form.

How are we to interpret the symbolic functions of such practices? In an eloquent analysis of Tudor royal ceremonial, the anthropologist Clifford Geertz has compared the progresses and pageantry mounted by early modern monarchs to the forms of political legitimation that, he argues, obtain in all societies at all times:

At the political centre of any complexly organised society ... there is both a governing elite and a set of symbolic forms expressing the fact that it is in truth governing. No matter how democratically the members of the elite are chosen (usually not very) or how deeply divided among themselves they may be (usually much more than outsiders imagine), they justify their existence and order their actions in terms of a collection of stories, ceremonies, insignia, formalities, and appurtenances that they have either inherited or, in some revolutionary situations, invented. It is these – crowns and coronations, limousines and conferences – that mark the centre as centre and give what goes on there its aura of being not merely important but in some odd fashion connected with the way the world is built. The gravity of high politics and the solemnity of high worship spring from liker impulses than might at first appear.[76]

Applying to Elizabeth the idea of a 'theatre-state' developed from his fieldwork in Bali – where the artifice of court ritual was exceptionally intricate – Geertz models the legitimation of power in terms of the exercise of charisma. He presents political ceremonial as a liturgical theatre, in which power is asserted through what appear to be merely its trappings. Rituals seem inessential to the state, but are in fact its substance: they do not refer to anything beyond themselves, but personalize the state and invest it with authority. They mark out the prince (or prime minister, chief executive, or chairman of the board) as separate and sanctified, god-like and full of *mana*, embodying in his person the authority to which he lays claim. In this model, the prince is the 'exemplary' or 'glowing centre' from which all else is illuminated, bathing the state in a royal radiance that gives the subject's existence its meaning, and conferring an aura on those around him of 'being near the heart of things'. The state is a theatre, but at its most ritualized it becomes a kind of religion.[77]

In Stuart England, kingship could never be simply magical, for incipient absolutism was in conflict with strong constitutionalist traditions which understood the state as a mixed monarchy and kings as constrained by the inheritance of law. Geertz's charismatic kingship cannot, then, be mapped onto the masques. However, its combination of theological magic and political expediency does help to draw out the intersections between litur-gical and political reverence, and the larger social functions which these served. In a personal monarchy, kingship inevitably took on the trappings of a cult, instilling taboos and habits of respect that conditioned the subject's behaviour in the presence of the divine. Like all early modern monarchs, James and Charles were surrounded by protocol that proclaimed their sacredness and marked out their separation from their subjects. No matter how physically unimpressive the king was, etiquette made him an object of public gaze, investing his body with veneration and regard. Geertzian charisma helps to suggest why masques fell so readily into 'mysteries' and solemnities – 'the yearly rites / Are due to Pan on these bright nights'[78] – and foregrounds the ceremonial affect of the courtier's participation. Masques combined with and reinforced all the other religious and state observances that were intrinsic to early modern Whitehall – notably the king's public dining in the Presence Chamber, the procession preceding his attendance at the Chapel Royal on Sundays, the annual Garter feasts, the welcomes and dismissals of ambassadors, and the more irregular but no less august ceremonials set up for him to touch for scrofula, 'the King's Evil', which proclaimed a quasi-miraculous power. These rituals were the building blocks of a system of etiquette which ensured that the king's body was publicly visible at set times and was always approached with reverence. They imitated the protocols created around monarchs across Europe, and brought the king into direct contact with a sizeable public while underlining his sacramental aura as sovereign.[79]

Yet the prestations, feastings, and combats of the masques had a pay-off for the performers and spectators too, since they underwrote their membership within a community of peers and near-equals: they affirmed their sense of belonging, validating and even enabling their access to the courtly group. In this respect, they cut across the masque scenarios charted in the previous chapter, which tended to associate the king's power with the maintenance of anxiety, and stage royal authority as the cleansing of deviance. Those exclusionary motifs turned on a series of nested binaries – familiar and strange, domestic and exotic, civilized and savage, polished and coarse – that rehearsed wildness and excess, and showed otherness being expelled, in order to celebrate the monarch's protection of his state from the monstrous and alien: his role was thaumaturgic and apotropaic, healer and protector.[80] But against this exclusionary emphasis, the rituals of incorporation fulfilled competing social and symbolic needs. They allowed an emphasis on assimilation and bonding, trading on the participants' sense of their shared affinities, and working to accommodate the court's complex internal differences and rivalries; and they acknowledged that Whitehall was not a closed environment, and that masques could facilitate and manage change instead of simply celebrating a static social entity. In this respect, the customs accompanying masques were at one with the encompassing rituals of court life in being a repertoire of practices that the performers not merely observed but actively lived. They played out the courtiers' sense of their relationship to the monarch and to their fellow servants, and in doing so they helped to construct their identities, permitting them to advance claims for personal legitimation and public visibility that only intermittently intersected with the grander state themes of the masques. What from the King's perspective looked like effortless political magic was from the courtier's point of view urgent social traffic.

One text that recognized this double function and its potential for conflict, even before Stuart masquing got under way, was Ben Jonson's *Cynthia's Revels, or the Fountain of Self-Love* (1600). Staged three years before James's accession, this Elizabethan play directly anticipates key aspects of Stuart court festival. *Cynthia's Revels* depicts a fictional court that transparently mirrors Elizabeth's Whitehall, and culminates with a gift-giving and masque. Its main business is to satirize the frivolous pleasure-seeking and self-regard of Cynthia's courtiers. Their whole life is a play, for the demands of etiquette require them to theatricalize themselves, and they self-consciously stage their social competence, cultivating fashions and ladies' favours, and piecing out the time with games and wagers, self-promotion and back-biting – the degrading but necessary social traffic of Cynthia's court. The action concludes with a masque, and here the courtiers unwittingly demonstrate their unfitness to serve Cynthia. Two groups of dancers present her with imprese and a rich crystal globe, and masquerade under names which exemplify the qualities of the ideal courtier: Natural Affection, Pleasant Conversation, Wittiness, Simplicity, Good Manners, Good Enjoyment, Brave Spirit, and Good Nature. But when they unmask, it is evident that their persons do not bear out their masque roles, for their real names – Philautia (Self-Love), Gelaia (Laughter), Phantaste (Fantastic), Moria (Foolishness), Hedon (Voluptuousness), and so forth – proclaim their shallowness and triviality. They have veiled their bad qualities beneath the nearest positive courtly equivalent, resulting in a contradiction between social and theatrical identities. Cynthia shuts them from her presence, and imposes a penance: that in a counter-ritual they must sing a palinode which expresses their shame at having tainted her court.

Cynthia's Revels dramatizes the tension between court revel as a rite of social inclusion and as princely legitimation. It presents a masque gone wrong, in which the social function of festivity (to validate the courtier as an affiliate of the court) has come adrift from the political function (to under-write the prince). There is a disconnection between the praise of the court as an emanation of royal virtue and as a place to which any number of courtiers might aspire to attach themselves. Inevitably, the burning question is where the responsibility for this situation lies. The play unequivocally locates the fault in the shallow courtiers themselves: they have all drunk from the Fountain of Self-Love, a symbolic location associated with Narcissus, and so cannot see how much they lack the virtue to which they lay claim. Cynthia commissions the 'sports and triumphs' to purge the court: the masque will root out the 'follies [that] / Had crept into her palace' (sigs. I4v–K1r).[81] Still, the courtiers' assumption that service to the prince is best expressed in gracious revelry is not in itself a misapprehension – this is, after all, what courtiers are there to do – and at the moment when they unmask, it is implied that Cynthia, despite her apparent foreknowledge of the scheme, is genuinely disconcerted to discover that her court is not as she supposes. She is shocked at the disparity between roles and identities, and had taken the courtiers' compliments and gifts as a true image of reality. A conflict is adumbrated here between festivity's functions as an expression of royal power and as a mode of social being through which courtiers assert their membership of the court space. The courtiers' expectation that festivity can be used to perform their social affiliations – as Cynthia pejoratively puts it, to 'mix themselves with others of the court, / And without forehead, boldly press so far / As farther none' (sig. L3v) – is at odds with the monarch's need to affirm that inner space's sanctity. This is a conflict which would re-emerge in many later festivals.

Moreover, Cynthia herself is not free from danger, for she too is presented in terms that uncomfortably resemble her courtiers' self-love. The gift that she receives is a carved crystal, and, on looking into it, she discovers an image of herself as a shining deity, which she describes to her lady, Arete:

> O front! O face! O all celestial, sure,
> And more than mortal! Arete, behold
> Another Cynthia, and another queen,
> Whose glory, like a lasting plenilune [= full moon],
> Seems ignorant of what it is to wane.   (sig. K4)

Cynthia is momentarily overwhelmed by her own glory reflected back at herself, and this testifies to her superior insight, for she alone is capable of perceiving the goddess that she truly is. Yet like her courtiers' behaviour, the compliment admits considerable potential for narcissism. Jonson's syntax puts a gap between mortal ruler and immortal goddess, by underlining that the crystal's image is idealized and visionary. It reflects the secret, platonic truths hidden from the poor shadows of this world; nowhere is it suggested that Cynthia falls short of the goddess that she is acclaimed as being. Nonetheless, by receiving a mirror and contemplating a version of herself, her actions uncannily echo her courtiers' self-regard. Her visionary insight is the polar opposite to the Fountain of Self-Love, but it takes the form of an idealized narcissism that mirrors it, and resonates with the dangers of flattery and princely self-conceit. There is, in Jonson's humanistic terms, a lesson for the prince: that the idealizations of masques need not be taken at face value. The play punishes the courtiers, who must live better lives in future, but the shift in ritual style, from masque to palinode, points to conflicting obligations that festivity attempts to hold together. In court revelry, the tension between celebration and purgation could never be entirely discharged. It is not clear whether this is something that subsequent masques, as represented by this early capsule specimen, would adequately discharge.

Jonson was an outsider at the Elizabethan court, and his perspective on court festival was conditioned by humanistic expectations about moral counsel which, for him, changed significantly once he entered royal service. Certainly his subsequent masques give few hostages to fortune by radically compressing the space between ideal and actual. Nonetheless, *Cynthia's Revels* dramatizes tensions skirted by every masque, insofar as each encompassed multiple social and political functions: each had to celebrate the monarch, depict the court as an integrated unit, and give counsel and advice. Jonson was, then, prescient in acknowledging the possibility, indeed likelihood, of disjunctions between function and form. As we shall see, although James's and Charles's masques did not commonly break down as Cynthia's does, such a thing was not impossible. The intense aesthetic experience of masques validated the monarch's prestige, but the emotional energies on which their scenarios drew flowed from the social investments of the dancers, patrons, and observers, who also looked to festivity for their own species of legitimation. As a consequence, moments of fracture in court masques point to the conflicting purposes being pursued by their participants. While the following chapters concentrate more on the masques' political than social concerns, they will track the tensions that repeatedly played across them. In almost every festival, the recurrent issue would be how to correlate the aesthetic and the political. The constant and sometimes insurmountable task was to proclaim the king's centrality while accommodating it to the competing aspirations of the community of which he was head.

CHAPTER 4

The invention of Britain

On Shrove Tuesday 1618, the Jacobean court witnessed the oddest masque of the reign, Ben Jonson's *For the Honour of Wales*. This was a revised repeat of *Pleasure Reconciled to Virtue*, the masque which the court had seen on Twelfth Night but disliked.[1] *Pleasure Reconciled*, so spectators complained, had a dull fable, poor scenery, and – worst of all – lacklustre dancing. In preparing the masque for a revival, Jonson responded to criticism by deleting the opening antimasques, with their learned allegory of Hercules and Comus, and replacing them with a band of Welshmen who, vexed that the new Prince of Wales should be so shamed on his first appearance as principal masquer, came to Whitehall to speak up for their nation. Despite a tendency to lapse into Welsh and an inability to talk in turns without coming to blows, the Welshmen managed to sing a ballad listing Wales's delights, introduce two dances of Welsh folk and an antimasque of dancing goats, and tell the audience that the rocky scene, which in *Pleasure Reconciled to Virtue* had represented Mount Atlas, was now Mount Snowdon, and the performers all good Welshmen. Here, though, they ran into difficulty, since only the Prince and the Earl of Montgomery could plausibly be said to be Welsh. For the others, they fell back on more far-fetched claims to Welshness, based on supposed similarities with Welsh place-names. Buckingham and Hamilton

> is as good, noble, true Priton as any ever is come out of Wales …
> *Howell.* And the Howards, by got, is Welse as straight as any arrow.
> *Evan.* Houghton is a town bear his name there by Pipidiauke.
> *Howell.* And Irwin, his name is Wyn …
> *Rhyss.* Then Carr is plain Welse, Caerleon, Caermardin, Cardiff … And
>   Acmouty is Ap-mouthwye of Llanmouthwye.
> *Jenkin.* And Abercromy is all one as Abermarlys.
> *Evan.* Or Abertau.
> *Howell.* Or Aberdugledhaw.
> *Rhyss.* Or Aberhodney.

Jenkin. Or Abergavenny.
Howell. Or Aberconway.
Evan. Aberconway is very like Abercromy ...   (162–83)

Even though these linguistic links were quite fanciful, the presenters concluded optimistically that only 'a liddell hard s'ift has pit 'em aull into
Wales' (183–4).

Jonson's Welshmen were designed to pillory his critics, even as they
voiced their objections. Only minds as trivial as these, Jonson implied,
could prefer dancing goats to the original fare. But his Welshmen's idiocies
are striking because they hinged on an issue that was new and particular to
the political culture of the early Stuarts: how to find a coherent iconography
for the identity of the Jacobean court, given that James was a composite
monarch who ruled over several different peoples. Of course Wales was long
integrated politically and culturally with England, and Jonson clearly felt no
danger in joking at Welsh national difference. But his jokes remained
problematic because of the need to acknowledge not just two national
identities but three. Buckingham, Houghton, and the Howards could be
assimilated to Welshmen without too much strain, but matters were
complicated by the need to find spaces for the five Scottish masquers:
Hamilton, Carr, Irwin,[2] Achmouty, and Abercromby. By being playful
about differences between the English and the Welsh, Jonson inadvertently
drew attention to the more fraught dividing line separating both of these
nations from the Scots. It is hard not to feel that the linguistic contortions
consequent on the Scottish presence complicated the ritual event. Jonson
depicted James as presiding over a celebration which not only mocked
the people from whom his son's title derived, but which uneasily acknowledged the difficulty of finding a coherent language for describing brother-
hood between three nations. The letter-writer Nathaniel Brent commented
that Jonson's jokes were 'sufficient to make an Englishman laugh and a
Welshman choleric',[3] but by factoring in the wild card of Scottishness they
redirected attention towards that sensitivity about national difference
which, by situating Charles as political figurehead, the masque was ostensibly setting out to ameliorate.

I shall return to the question of Welsh difference later. For now, we can
simply note that the linguistic liberties which Jonson took in *For the Honour
of Wales* exemplify the tension between image and event that was so
besetting a problem in Stuart court entertainment. His jokes about
Scottish Welshmen testified to limits in the masques' symbolic programme
that commonly remained unacknowledged: they registered the persistent
gap between idealizing ceremony and the contingencies of multiple kingship

which it was one objective of this masque to efface. More importantly, that these tensions were so publicly displayed in a relatively peripheral masque suggests how fundamental the British issue was to Stuart masquing, across the period as a whole and in its earliest years in particular. As James never tired of being reminded, the arrival of the Stuarts at Whitehall created a monarchy which encompassed all of the island's peoples and made it possible for the first time to speak of Britain as a single state. In practice, the Stuarts' multiple kingship differed little from political circumstances which prevailed across early modern Europe, where composite monarchies created out of complex dynastic inheritances were the order of the day. Much the same balancing act was happening in other kingly confederations such as Spain, Poland, and, to a lesser extent, France.[4] But the claims to British particularism were enhanced by the situation of the British Isles, the geographical accident of separateness from the European mainland, which enabled the Stuarts to claim that their dynastic integration was validated by providence and nature.[5] When Charles commissioned the Banqueting House ceiling from Rubens, the scheme that he chose represented his father as the founding British monarch, pointing imperiously at the new political child, Great Britain, who in 1603 was miraculously born from two different mothers (see figure 4). This image built on James's celebrated speech to the 1607 parliament, which compared the Union to a baby that as yet was weak but over time would grow into a man, and played wittily on the fable of the Judgement of Solomon, by depicting the King commanding not that the child should be divided between the two mothers but that both women should recognize themselves as the true parent.[6] In determining that state ceremonial in the Banqueting House took place under images monumentalizing the miracle that was Stuart union, Charles showed how inextricably intertwined panegyric to his dynasty was with celebration of the bonds of international identity that Stuart kingship uniquely conferred.

These circumstances directly conditioned the ceremonial vocabulary of the masques, since they took up the British issue in terms that were equally foundational. Much that now seems inflated in Stuart panegyric cannot be understood unless it is remembered how revolutionary their arrival was. Repeatedly the masques returned to the trope – which can be traced back to Virgil's famous observation that Britain was a world by itself, 'et penitus toto divisos orbe Britannos'[7] – that Stuart Britain had a unique territorial integrity distinguishing it from other realms, both strategically and in terms of absolute superiority. By hymning James as Neptune, father to Albion, or by associating the realm with the Fortunate Isles, the classical paradise of western blessedness, the poets capitalized on the international status which

4 Peter Paul Rubens, *King James Perfecting the Union of England and Scotland*, from the
Whitehall Banqueting House ceiling, 1635, engraved by Simon Gribelin, 1720.

accrued to a multiple monarchy, and worked within the new frame of concepts that Stuart succession entailed. The Britishness of Stuart rule was the one factor which masques could not avoid addressing, and the early masques played a particularly sustained part in inventing a new discourse of British identity, preoccupied as they were with the consequences and symbolisms of being British. No other mode of political panegyric in James's early years was so obsessed with the topic of Union. As we shall see, the iconography and constitutional effects of Stuart succession were central concerns of the major masques in the first four Stuart Christmas seasons, *The Vision of the Twelve Goddesses* (1604), *The Masque of Blackness* (1605), *Hymenaei* (1606), and *Lord Hay's Masque* (1607). Additionally, the unique opportunity that the masques offered for staging gestures of international accord was seized upon from the start, as in that very first Christmas revel, *The Masque of Indian and China Knights*, which was danced by four English lords and four Scots; and on Twelfth Night 1604, when *The Vision of the Twelve Goddesses* was postponed, the substituted show was a Scottish sword dance arranged by the Duke of Lennox.[8] Subsequently Scots were only intermittently present in the lists of masquers, but three of the highest-profile masques in James's first decade (*Lord Hay's Masque*, *The Haddington Masque*, and *The Masque of Squires*) celebrated marriages between English and Scottish nobility, thus furthering James's policy of developing ties between the nations by promoting alliances amongst their aristocracies.

It exaggerates only slightly to say that Union was the ideological crucible out of which the masques were made. Certainly, the ability of the Stuart court to inspire confidence would be bound up with its capacity to project itself as a coherently British monarchy, and the arrival of a Scottish king at Whitehall necessitated the invention of an iconography to articulate the realm's changed identity, tying celebration of the Stuarts to myths of transformation and renewal, as if their arrival marked a turning point in history. From the outset James sponsored initiatives at many levels of political culture to express the ambitions of his kingship and put a new language of power into circulation. This iconographic project underlay the British imagery of the pageants at the first London entry in March 1604; the proclamation of the new name of Britain in October; the minting of a British coinage, including a twenty-shilling piece called a 'unite', in November; Francis Bacon's suggestion in 1605 that a British history should be commissioned; and the promulgation in April 1606 of a union flag for use by ships of the two nations.[9] But the early Jacobean masques were a crucial site of image-making. It must have seemed to contemporaries that a main reason for the lavish expenditure on them was their suitability for promoting the Union, and few could have missed how intensively they were used to project images proclaiming goodwill between the nations and the prestige of specifically British kingship. And as is shown by Jonson's Welshifying of the Scots, the issue of British identity pressed with special immediacy onto revels designed to be danced in a court which had suddenly become international. In order to celebrate early modern Whitehall, the masques had to devise a British symbolism which could mediate meaningfully between the often conflicting aspirations of the constituent nations that now met in the political arena.

However, between these prestigious images and the actualities of composite monarchy the fit was far from exact, and the strains of Union can be read in the difficulties the masques met as they sought to proclaim a coherently British identity in circumstances which often involved radically different ideas of British priorities. Though James's arrival resolved uncertainty over the succession, there were major differences of attitude towards the proposed Union within Whitehall and without, and its cost was a cultural dilemma over nationhood that was potentially almost as traumatic. This can be traced in the tracts written in 1603–5 for and against the Union, and in the bumpy ride Union had in the 1604 and 1606–7 parliaments (which debated, respectively, the realm's new name and Scottish naturalization). British unity may have been inscribed in the island's geographical separateness, but the fact that this was a personal union – one located in the king's body, and forged between dynasties rather than peoples and states[10] – meant that external separation did not automatically translate into an equivalent imagined national community. On the contrary, historians have come to see that Stuart affairs were conditioned by residual conflicts of interest and cultural self-consciousness among the British peoples, a situation that was the dynasty's major structural weakness. In one influential argument, Conrad Russell has suggested that the difficulty of coordinating the affairs of England, Scotland, and Ireland explains the intractability of Charles's troubles in the 1640s. Russell narrates the Caroline breakdown as a six-way split within and between the three kingdoms, whose multiple conflicts of interest presented the crown with problems of government which could not be managed in one realm without sparking off answering difficulties in the others.[11] Arguably, James's handling of multiple kingship was more sensitive than his son's. He nudged the two nations towards one another with cautious pragmatism, encouraging aristocratic intermarriages, introducing Scots into the English peerage, and dividing Household offices between the nations.[12] Still, the reports of Anglo-Scottish squabbles that form a rich seam in Jacobean correspondence suggest that even these devices had limited effect.

The problems with Union lay less in the national quarrels which it occasioned than in an ideological mare's nest of constitutional anxieties. Briefly, there were three areas of disagreement. First, Union aroused concern because it seemed to promote the crown's power at the expense of parliament, and because by altering the framework of the state it called inherited constitutional safeguards into question. In the 1604 debates, MPs were invited to ratify the change of name to 'Britain', but they worried that such an innovation would nullify the existing constitution and create a new kingdom, the rights and duties of which could not be known. Sir Edwin Sandys summed up these concerns with his pointed question, 'By what laws shall this Britain be governed?'[13] The same ground was rehearsed in the 1607 debates over Scottish naturalization, which similarly threatened a loss of legal separation. Such alterations, objected Sir Edward Coke, struck at the root of the constitution and could be made only by a conqueror: 'the king cannot change the natural law of a nation. This foundation is a firm foundation.'[14] As men anxious about the sanctity of English Common Law, Sandys and Coke were (so to speak) professionally uneasy at acts that seemed to put the King above it, but their resistance is comprehensible even if one looks no further than the unguarded rhetoric which some proponents of Union were already using. For example, in tracts fulsomely celebrating the accession, Sir John Skynner Douglas suggested that the English should submit to their Scottish King as to a ravishing lover – no one 'could refuse a nation so welcome, at an imbracement so necessary'[15] – while Sir William Cornwallis argued that England could not resist Union as it came fully formed, God making 'a new time settled in an instant'.[16] Not surprisingly, faced with a monarch whose Britishness seemed to put him outside inherited constitutional languages, common lawyers insisted that allegiance was due not to his person but to his greater body enshrined in the frameworks of English statute (and separations between English and Scottish law persist to this day).

Secondly, it quickly became apparent that the discourse of Union concealed differences between English and Scottish perspectives. Not only were some English xenophobic about the supposedly beggarly Scots,[17] but even sympathetic English statesmen thought of Britain as England writ large, an absorption of Scotland within an Anglocentric settlement. Conversely, Scottish voices on Union strove to envision it as a meeting of equals, in which the Scots' separateness was respected, not reducing them to the status of a dependent nation. When the Edinburgh lawyer John Russell complained that England craved 'nathing els bot the alteratioun of this estait, and sua to mak Scotland ane pendicle of thair realm',[18] he was anxious about

Union on the Welsh model, in which Scotland would become an English colony, as seemed to be immanent in English MPs' unwillingness to accept any arrangement other than annexation. Of course, unlike Wales, Scotland retained its parliament, and the Scots' trump card was that James was Scottish and could unravel the 'two kingdoms' argument by threatening to move back to Edinburgh.[19] Still, the legacies of these conflicts were that Union came out uneasily suspended between integration and incompleteness, and that the babel of different languages for talking about it in the tracts and debates was never satisfactorily clarified.

This, thirdly, made space for disagreement over how far Union should go. James's earliest statements spoke idealistically about perfect union, in which the merging of laws and parliaments would be cemented by a meeting of hearts and minds, but once he was faced with English foot-dragging he quickly fell back on more limited objectives, such as the change of name, repeal of hostile laws, and Scottish naturalization. But in the naturalization debates, even partial union ran into the sand when English lawyers appropriated James's language and argued that the best way to achieve naturalization was by a perfect union that would bring it about automatically – by which they meant English incorporation of Scotland. In 1607 this was a wrecking tactic and James, aware that perfect union could not be politically accomplished, rebuked parliament for suggesting it. Thereafter he built ties pragmatically between the nations, but that overarching unitary state which was his objective was effectively dead. United dynastically by the King's body, the two Stuart nations remained separate states with their own parliaments, legal codes, and churches, a regnocentric aggregation rather than the indissoluble entity that James wanted. After 1608, that ideal which in the symbolism of the masques was a marriage of hearts remained on the ground an uneasy cohabitation between uncomfortable and mutually suspicious bedfellows.[20]

In interpreting the early masques it is important to register the presence of these fractures within the notionally seamless discourse of Union, and how far the masques' praise of the King's body was complicated by the fact that as a multiple monarch James had more bodies than one. Critics have often played down this dimension, and taken the idealizing discourse of Union at face value. For example, Roy Strong writes about 'James's staggering achievement of uniting the British Isles under the sovereignty of one imperial diadem', and D. J. Gordon's classic essay on unionist imagery in *Hymenaei* reads it as celebrating a fully achieved or imminent historical outcome.[21] Gordon's essay was a landmark study, one of the first to demonstrate the philosophical seriousness of masque iconography – it compares *Hymenaei* with the unionist sermons and tracts and shows that Jonson synthesized a political rhetoric that was everywhere in 1603–5 – but it effaces the shortfall between what the masque represented and what was accomplished, and while it registers the metaphorical complexity of the languages of Union, it presents James's plan as an integrated, cogent project. But to understand *Hymenaei*'s politics properly, it is necessary to recover why Union was contentious, and how masques functioned as persuasion as well as celebration.

So we must read through the rhetoric to the ideological agenda which it served, and recognize that James's 'project' was not rigid but flexible, and shifted according to what he thought could be achieved. James told Cecil that Union was 'this great work' that he hoped would eventually be 'fully accomplished', and Cecil himself saw it in terms like those on Rubens's ceiling, as a 'beloved child' whose growth depended on careful nurture.[22] Only by acknowledging James's pragmatism and gradualism can we see how masques participated in the political process and helped to shape it. In this perspective, the Union debates were not a fixed background which the masques simply reflected but a series of shifting possibilities, deployed strategically. The masques are best considered neither as fantasy nor as propaganda slavishly reproducing a kingly line but as a series of attempts to respond creatively to some novel opportunities and problems. They set out to find a public symbolism which would be viable in unprecedented political circumstances, and to invent a common language that might bridge disagreements. Further (as we shall see), contemporaries were aware of the difficulties of translating the Union imagery into practice and, wary of iconographical persuasions, were anxious to scrutinize the meanings that might be read off the rhetoric. The problem with metaphors was that, however compelling symbolically, they had alarming political implications and invited demystification by those nervous about possible consequences. Too emphatic an acclamation of the revolution in the state ran the risk of activating all those anxieties that, in the long run, prevented the Union from going any further than it did. In this regard, the panegyrists of Union faced a double bind that was arguably insurmountable.

The masques that dealt directly with the Union fall into two groups: those (principally Jonson's) that embraced the accession as a radical overturning of inherited norms, and those that took a more cautious line and registered some of the reservations surveyed above. I shall consider the latter group first.

Daniel's *The Vision of the Twelve Goddesses* (8 January 1604) was constructed as a relatively simple act of visitation. Its central device was the descent of twelve ladies, dressed as deities and led by the Queen, from the summit of a mountain to the Temple of Peace, where they presented symbolic gifts expressing divine goodwill to the Stuarts. It began with speeches from Night, Somnus, Iris, and a Sybil, explaining that spectators would not see an action but a prophetical dream, and social dancing then followed until Iris recalled the masquers. Devised, financed, and performed by the Queen, this occasion (as Leeds Barroll emphasizes) focused as much on her power as on the King's.[23] James's role was comparatively minor, not least because, with scenery dispersed around the room, he did not sit in what would later become the usual commanding position opposite the vanishing point of the perspective. Nonetheless, as principal spectator at the most prestigious event of the first Stuart Christmas, the masque bore onto his image as well as Queen Anne's, and spectators might have read three levels of political statement from it.

To take the diplomatic meaning first, Daniel's masque was a gesture of friendship to Spain, and celebrated foreign policy changes since James's arrival. As several observers commented, it feted the Spanish ambassador, Don Juan de Taxis. He sat by the King, the Queen wore red favours in compliment to him, and he danced with her ally, the Countess of Bedford.[24] Extraordinary pains were taken to safeguard his status as principal guest. The French ambassador, Beaumont, had demanded an invitation to the masque, but to protect Spanish precedence it was put off for two days and replaced with a Scottish 'matachin' or sword-dance, a substitution which left Beaumont spluttering with rage.[25] In the masque itself, the Temple of Peace signalled favour to Spain, since it alluded to James's reversal of Elizabethan policy. Inheriting a wasteful and pointless war, his first act was to reopen channels to Madrid, and later in 1604 he entered into a peace which was the most visible sign of new counsels. In the context of the honours done to de Taxis, the Temple strongly evoked the coming treaty: Daniel's preface called the show one of the new 'ornaments and delights of peace' (12). The masque thus signalled the pragmatic and non-confessional posture towards Europe which would mark all future Jacobean policy.

At a domestic level, the action celebrated the new dynasty and the changed political prospects by recapitulating the accession in graceful symbolic forms. The goddesses' descent from the mountain translated the royal family's progress from Edinburgh into ceremonial gestures, ritualizing their transition from rocky northern kingdom to smoother southern plains. This was a reversal of the symbolic topography of Elizabethan revel: in *Proteus and the Adamantine Rock* (1595), a masque brought to Whitehall from Gray's Inn, Elizabeth was represented as the magnetic rock which kept her subjects' hearts from turning towards the potentially attractive monarch in the north.[26] Introducing the goddesses, Iris forecast the tropes of westering empire which were to become central to Stuart mythology, investing the dynasty as modern Virgilian monarchs presiding benevolently over political and cultural *renovatio*. She explained that the goddesses had left their Mediterranean homes, 'made now the seats of barbarism and spoil', for 'the western mount of mighty Brittany, the land of civil music and of rest' (257–60), setting up an opposition between James's secure rule and the inferior government of other times and places. Daniel's preface said that he wished 'to present the figure of those blessings ... which this mighty kingdom now enjoys by the benefit of his most gracious Majesty' (17–20). These were quite literally figured in the gifts which the goddesses brought, ranging from a sceptre (for rule) to a mine of gold (for riches) to a trident (for strength at sea), the divine blessings bestowed on Stuart power.

It was all the more striking, then, that the masquers adopted personae familiar from the repertoire of roles that Elizabeth herself had used and which would have unavoidably evoked her memory. Amongst the twelve goddesses were Diana, Vesta, Astraea, Pallas, Flora, Ceres, and Tethys, all names current in Elizabethan panegyric. Still more remarkably, the goddesses wore costumes which Ladies Suffolk and Walsingham had taken from Elizabeth's wardrobe, and cannibalized for this festival.[27] Clare McManus reads this as a visual usurpation by the new queen of her predecessor's memory, signalling Anne's appropriation of 'the now defunct Elizabethan courtly body'.[28] No less resonantly, given the ceremonious gift-giving which the goddesses performed, it would have been easy for the audience to read the masque as evoking the ghosts of a Tudor past in order to dramatize all the more forcefully their absorption into the Stuart renewal. As the goddesses delivered their blessings, so their action translated power from Elizabethan to Jacobean, conferring the symbols of wisdom, religion, justice, and so forth onto the new monarchy. It could not have escaped notice that the eleven masquers accompanying the Queen included the ladies who acquired the most intimate positions in her household during the scramble after offices,[29] nor that the men whom they took out to dance included James's principal privy councillors and several of the Earl of Essex's followers, who were eclipsed under Elizabeth but restored to favour by James (discussed in chapter 3 above).[30] With the move from a single Elizabethan goddess and her nymphs to a family of goddesses and their partners, there could scarcely have been a more visible statement of Whitehall's transformation since last Christmas. The masque mimed the demise of the old dynasty and its recreation in a new, legitimating change by casting it into ceremonial form. In dancing the measures, the masquers performed the harmonies of a new corporate dispensation.

Yet it is notable that Daniel did not disparage the Elizabethan past, nor figure James's arrival as cracking the moulds of the polity. On the contrary, the goddesses' rites of passage were explicitly transitional: they emphasized continuities as well as change, and their gestures of prestation situated James as a monarch who was not just acclaimed but carefully legitimated. With its parade of goddesses moving forwards in threes and accompanied by torch-bearers, this was a backward-looking event, which enfolded change in ceremonial forms belonging to the reign gone by. While power was ritually handed on, the goddesses' harmonious descent meliorated the trauma of the succession, mitigating the abrupt transition by a performance notable for its ceremoniousness. Gestures like these allayed English fears that dynastic change meant constitutional innovation, and they constrained James himself by representing his accession as an orderly inheritance. As if to pre-empt the anxieties of Sandys and Coke, the Stuarts were celebrated as legitimate successors but emphatically not as conquerors whose triumph had brought a new nation into being.

This ideological project impinged on the masque in several ways. For one thing, its allusions to the Union were restrained. Daniel was no opponent of Union,[31] and in the masque he gave space to links being forged between the nations. The gift left by Venus was 'th'all-combining scarf of amity' made up of diverse colours (301), and Concordia led the third group, danced by Elizabeth Stewart, the masque's sole Scottish performer, who had recently married an Englishman, the Earl of Nottingham. She was dressed in the colours of the two nations, red and white, embroidered with 'silver hands in hand', and presented a branch of 'parti-coloured roses' (86–9, 324). The description of Tethys as the ocean goddess who 'imbound[s] and circle[s] this greatness of dominion by land' (53–4) likewise signalled a British agenda, by invoking Britain's strategic strength when restored to island integrity. But Daniel used such concepts intermittently, and did not envision Britain as a new cultural departure or constitutionally integrated entity. Quite the reverse: Concordia's embracing hands implied that multiple kingship was amity, not unity, and Venus' scarf would not fuse but 'engird strange nations with affections true' (302) – language which reinforced cultural separateness even while signalling international friendship. Similarly, Juno offered a 'sceptre of command for kingdoms large' (290, 378), a gift which conceptualized James's realms in the plural, and Pallas' lance expressed kingly courage 'to get with glory, hold with providence' (297), advice which located multiple kingship not as nation-building but as dynastic ambition and territorial aggrandisement. Evidently, while the masque acknowledged that the realms were joined in the King's person, it presumed that a separation between nations would remain. Stressing concord rather than Union, and using the names 'Brittany' and 'Albion' indifferently (259, 344), it devised no new language for the British project.

In other respects this masque held back from naively endorsing Jacobean power. Although Night introduced the show as 'ancient rites', 'mysteries' which bespoke the divine sanctions of James's rule (224–5), Daniel's lengthy dramatization of its origins in a 'Vision' interpreted by the Sibyl counteracted simple mystification. By treating the masque as prophecy, he circumvented any easy identification between the images that were seen and the court that actually was, instead casting forward from the present to a glorious future that was still only conditional. When Iris closed the masque by explaining that the performers were not really goddesses, but that now the goddesses might 'grace this glorious monarchy with the real effects of these blessings represented' (417–18), she foregrounded the gap between representation and reality, insisting that the masque's praise of Stuart kingship should not be confused with its accomplishments to date. And by using a Sibyl to gloss the mysteries and mediate with the audience – however crude this seems in comparison with later shows which loftily refused to explain themselves[32] – Night ensured that the vision was seen as centred in the spectators' experience, and not solely in royalty. The Sybil, says Night, will

> describe the Powers that shall resort,
> With th'interpretation of the benefits
> They bring in clouds and what they do import.
> Yet make them to portend the true desire
> Of those that wish them[,] waking, real things ...   (231–5)

Night's language, and the insistence that the action was a dream, constructed the masque as a willed projection of communal desire. The spectators saw a vision brought into being by their community's corporate longings, one which emblematized the renewed state of which, collectively, they had been dreaming.[33]

Such reservations might have been picked up only selectively by the audience. In treating the accession as fulfilling English desires, eager for renewal after Elizabeth's declining years, Daniel underwrote recent changes, and devised rituals in which the anxieties they had raised could be managed, resolving the national trauma by refashioning it in celebratory forms.

Nonetheless, by emphasizing continuity and locating dynastic sanction in the community's collective will rather than in divine fiat, he articulated a kingly ideology different from that of masques soon to come. He represented sovereignty as legitimated by inherited tradition and operating according to political consensus, rather than as a non-negotiable and freely acting power. And with its culmination in the song of the three Graces (discussed in chapter 3 above), in which the gift-giving was related to a chain of benefits that tied giver and receiver in mutual interdependence, the masque enforced a view of Stuart society as an entity bound at all levels by reciprocal obligations. Three figures whose harmony rose from their dance's elegant but asymmetrical patterns, the Graces emblematized relations between King and people, and between the two conjoined states, in terms of concord, not unity. They allowed Daniel to insinuate a view of Stuart power that preferred balance to identity, in which distances between the nations did not simply collapse before an irresistible sovereign authority.

Three years later, Campion's masque for Lord Hay's wedding (6 January 1607) celebrated Union just as cautiously. This was one of James's symbolic matches between the nations, the bride being English (daughter to Lord Denny) and the groom one of James's closest Scottish favourites, 'the first meteor of that nature appearing in our climate' (as Anthony Weldon said).[34] Hay was Gentleman of the Bedchamber from 1603, and, once appointed Master of the Robes, he became a byword for Scottish prodigality. His marriage masque, presented to James as a gift from the performers who financed it,[35] was staged on the eve of the naturalization debates. Though measures had already been agreed which removed some practical obstacles, the critical constitutional matter, debated in parliament during February–April 1607, was whether Scots born before March 1603 were English subjects. This question uniquely focused the Union's constitutional logic, since it defined kingship in terms which profoundly affected the location of sovereignty: was allegiance due to the King's person or to his greater bodies that were the two separate systems of law? Observers felt that the legal principle was unlikely to be conceded given the mistrust between the nations. The French ambassador reported that 'This little sympathy, ... the differences of their laws, the jealousy of their privileges, [and] the regard of the succession, are the reasons they will never ... join with one another, as the king wishes'. John More similarly wrote that 'both Houses are occupied with the Union, wherein something may be done for the enlargement of commerce to content the king, but the point of naturalization sounds so harsh to the ears as the heart will hardly consent'.[36] In the event, the pessimists were correct, and when James's proposal for naturalization by statute failed to pass the Commons it lapsed altogether.

The hazards identified by Beaumont and More, jealousy and consent, were the central concerns of *Lord Hay's Masque*. More elaborate than Daniel's masque, this was structured as a contest for control of the dancing space between the masquers – nine Knights of Apollo – and the goddess Diana, whose grove dominated the set. The masque opened with flowers being strewn by Flora and Zephyrus, but their amiable songs were interrupted by 'stern Night' (217)[37] raging against the celebration. Night complained that Hay's marriage offended Diana: the bride was stolen from her nymphs, and she had angrily transformed Apollo's knights to trees. But Hesperus, patron of marriage, descended and reassured Night that Diana was being pacified by Apollo:

> Since the fair match was by that Phoebus graced
> Which in this happy Western isle is placed
> As he in heaven, one lamp enlightening all
> That under his benign aspect doth fall. (219)

Night made the trees dance, then released them with her wand. Dressed now in a 'false habit' of silver-green robes (222), they expiated their wrongs in solemn procession to Diana's tree of chastity:

> These green-leaved robes, wherein disguised you made
> Stealths to her nymphs through the thick forest's shade,
> There to the goddess offer thankfully,
> That she may not in vain appeased be. (224)

So this action involved another gift-giving, to the invisible goddess Diana. The masquers left their robes at her grove, and received glorious helmets in exchange.

As David Lindley has shown, this fable directly allegorized concerns about the Union.[38] Only one masquer was a Scot, but all the gentlemen were in intimate household positions around the King, and truly were Apollo's 'sons' celebrating a family event.[39] On the other side, Diana aroused associations with Elizabeth similar to those raised by the goddesses in Daniel's masque. She was a virgin; like Elizabeth she controlled her maids' marriages; and her tree of chastity recollected the political iconography of the last reign, recalling (for example) the design of the Armada medal. Though presiding over the masque, Diana did not actually appear, but she was all the more powerful for only being immanent. So while events centred on Apollo's marriage, its significant aspect was Diana's resistance. Her grove was set opposite James's seat, and the prestation was made not to him but to her. The marriage could only proceed when she was appeased, and she transformed the trees back to men, replacing their deceitful robes with martial helmets. Diana may have 'friendly smiled' (224), but her opposition was not incidental. The fable depended on her seeming a significant adversary, whose objections were not dissolved in kingly magic but had to be properly accommodated.

Another factor in this contest was Campion's powerful characterization of Night, with her gloomy house occupying half the stage,[40] and her threatening language:

> Vanish, dark veils; let Night in glory shine
> As she doth burn in rage; come, leave our shrine,
> You black-haired Hours, and guide us with your lights:
> Flora hath wakened wide our drowsy sprites …
> But they [the trees] shall tremble when sad Night doth speak,
> And at her stormy words their boughs shall break.   (217–18)

These 'stormy words' were corrected by Flora's genial songs, yet this was not simply the reining-in of a fierce female by another more amenable to reason. Flora and Night were complementary emanations of Diana, and Night's language evoked Diana's association with the chthonic deity Hecate, through which some Elizabethan poets had accessed a dark view of female power. The mythographer Conti (widely drawn on in the masques) analysed Diana as a three-form deity of contradictory aspect, for 'the moon, Hecate, and Diana are the same';[41] in his *Hymn to Cynthia* (1595), Chapman depicted Cynthia as a Titan, beautiful but terrifying, a pre-Olympian deity who disrupted patriarchal cosmography. Although Campion's Flora countered Night's objections, she did not overcome her, and before the Knights were retransformed Night showed her powers in a mysteriously Orphic way, by causing the trees to dance. Though Hesperus mediated between Diana and Apollo, Night was easily the most striking stage presence, and she and Flora departed together. This action permitted a complex, varied, and powerful image of active female agency.

It is not difficult to find political resonances here; if anything, the masque projected the moment's anxieties too nakedly. At this Anglo-Scottish event, the contest of female and male, Diana and Apollo, would have refracted tensions between Elizabethan and Jacobean, English and British. As Lindley points out, the description of the knights as thieves, and the gilding of the trees by Apollo's beams, alluded to the English belief that Scots like Hay had their hands in the exchequer. This prejudice was clearly visible in parliament's reluctance to grant the Scots full rights in England: in February 1607 James punished Sir Christopher Piggott for scandalously anti-Scottish words, and used his speech of 31 March to rebuke those who had described the Scots as trees transplanted out of barren ground into more fertile soil.[42] By even hinting at such matters Campion sailed close to the wind, and by making the knights leave their deceitful robes with Diana and affirm their temperance by processing around her tree, he was staging the sort of assurances that the English wanted:

> With spotless minds now mount we to the tree
> > Of single chastity.
> The root is temperance grounded deep,
> Which the cold-juiced earth doth steep:
> > Water it desires alone,
> > Other drink it thirsts for none:
> Therewith the sober branches it doth feed,
> > Which though they fruitless be,
> Yet comely leaves they breed
> > To beautify the tree. (225)

A promise to be temperate – that the knights desired water for the leaves and did not hanker after the fruit – would have been useful before the up-coming session. In the months before the 1610 parliament Cecil advised James to restrain his gifts because (he said) the absence of such restraint in 1607 had poisoned the debates over Union.[43]

So Diana's tree symbolically checked Apollo's heat: however vigorous his knights, their desires would be controlled. But this cut wider than the issue of Scottish profits. While the fable responded to fears about favours, the nuptial setting also made it an argument about blood – how freely the Knights would mingle with the nymphs, and how far English identity would be lost inside British. Hence Diana's purity rebuffed Zephyrus' amorousness: he told Night that 'If all her nymphs would ask advice of me, / There should be fewer virgins than there be' (218), a thoughtlessly negligent attitude towards Union which the action carefully put in its place. More centrally, the dramatization of the knights' transformation as a rebirth probably alluded to naturalization. This lengthy and ceremonious ritual reaffirmed their connections with Diana. First, with Night presiding, the trees sank into the stage and the knights emerged, while a song underlined a link with ancient mysteries:[44]

> Night and Diana charge,
> > And th'Earth obeys,
> Opening large
> > Her secret ways,
> While Apollo's charmed men
> > Their forms receive again. (222)

Then the masquers processed to Diana's tree and took their helmets, enrolling under her chaster banner. While the whole action effected reconciliation between Apollo and Diana, it reaffirmed ties with a prior dispensation. Night said they would resume their 'native forms' (221), and Hesperus proclaimed it as recovering lost identities: 'Knights of Apollo, proud of your new birth ... Your changed fortunes, and redeemed estate' (225). This laboured ceremony insisted on the distinctness of Diana and Apollo, by rehearsing the separateness of two identities. It implied that Anglo-Scottish mingling would not override Diana's legacy, and that, whatever the compromise, both partners' dignity must be respected.

Campion's fable, then, represented Union in terms which limited its alarming constitutional consequences. It foregrounded consensus and appeasement, working out a middle path between hostile positions. But was it therefore anti-Union, anticipating the debates shortly to come? Certainly it foreshadowed the case against naturalization, and defused royal arguments that would have collapsed English and Scottish identities together. But a lot depends on how one interprets the British framework within which the case for distinction was made.[45] Apollo needed Diana's consent before the marriage went forward, but once her anger was appeased his will prevailed, and, as Night admitted, she had to give way: 'Night must yield when Phoebus gets the day' (219). The masque's culmination was an acclamation of the integrated community over which, on these terms, Apollo would ultimately preside. Once the trees were transformed, the chorus sang a single couplet repeatedly from all corners of the room: 'Again this song revive and sound it high, / Long live Apollo, Britain's glorious eye' (223). With this echoing acclamation, the very earth resounded with praise of British monarchy, as if, in Joseph Loewenstein's words, it showed 'the natural reverence of a particular landscape for the monarch'.[46] Further, the epigrams prefaced to the printed text presented arguments for Union by gradualism rather than fiat. Comparing the marriage to the Scythian tribes who celebrated their alliances by drinking mixed blood, Campion remarked:

> O then, great monarch, with how wise a care
> Do you these bloods divided mix in one,
> And with like consanguinities prepare
> The high and ever-living union
> 'Tween Scots and English: who can wonder then
> If he that marries kingdoms, marries men?   (207)

Rather than treating Union as one body made miraculously from two, this epigram envisioned a developing consanguinity, two streams eventually flowing together as one. The same idea recurred in the Latin epigram to the bridal couple: 'The hope is that the new bride will bring forth an Anglo-Scottish heir; the one he begets later will be British: thus a new posterity, born from the two kingdoms, will make the noble ancestors on both sides famous' (210). In these terms British identity would prevail, though not in this generation. Their offspring would be Anglo-Scottish, but achieved Britishness would belong to grandchildren yet to come. These verses came down against retrospective naturalization, but the King could be consoled by the thought that a British state was the inevitable work of time.

So this masque performed multiple political functions. It served Union by dispelling anxieties about it, but it promoted partial union and the maintenance of separateness within the overall British project, and its attitude to royal power was less than reverential. James's project was not denied, but it needed consent and labour, not just command. And there are echoes of these sentiments in the more pragmatic royal posture which one finds in the parliamentary business of the ensuing weeks. In his speech of 31 March 1607, immediately after the failure of the naturalization proposals, James defended the gradualism of the Union that he had hoped for in terms recalling the masque:

Union is a marriage: would he not be thought absurd that for furthering of a marriage between two friends of his, would make his first motion to have the two parties be laid in bed together, and perform the other turns of marriage? Must there not precede the mutual sight and acquaintance of the parties one with another, the conditions of the contract, and jointure to be talked of and agreed upon by their friends, and such other things as in order ought to go before the ending of such a work?[47]

In stressing that, although marriage was a given, the contract remained negotiable, James retreated from and demystified the imagery of perfect Union which he had used in 1604. And he tactfully suggested that his drive for Union was characterized by pragmatic exchanges similar to those symbolically performed in Campion's Twelfth Night masque.

In contrast to these cautious masques, Ben Jonson's entertainments for 1605 and 1606, *The Masque of Blackness* and *Hymenaei*, developed a radical position that left less space for negotiation. These masques presented Britain as a revolutionary rather than evolutionary concept. Its legitimation was accomplished by James's magical power to transcend opposites and make impossibilities come true, a power rooted solely in the monarch himself and with which there could be little prospect of contest. The Union which Jonson envisaged was far more complete and irresistible than that imagined by Daniel and Campion, and the attitude towards Jacobean sovereignty was correspondingly more reverential. His masques assumed fewer opportunities were available for manoeuvre with the royal will, and presented themselves not as transactions with kingly power but as ritual enforcements of it.

Jonson's unionist iconography made few concessions to the past, or to English or Scottish anxieties. His imagery and fables shrewdly bypassed the local problems which Union aroused in parliament, and which preoccupied Daniel and Campion. He conspicuously ignored any reference to Queen Elizabeth, or to the English patriotic mythology which claimed Brute as the founding father of Britain and the Tudors in particular, and which, by implying that the English were the senior partners, was so offensive to the Scots.[48] In this his masques were out of step with other civic pageantry, such as Anthony Munday's 1605 Lord Mayor's show, *The Triumphs of Re-United Britannia*, which, drawing on mythical lineages, had subordinated Scottish pseudo-history to supposedly antecedent English traditions.[49] Jonson's masques thereby offered little support to specifically English nationalism. Equally, though, they refused the imperial vision favoured by the Scots, which identified the historic mission of Britain as promoting the international Protestant cause. Scots such as John Gordon and Robert Pont had argued that unity was required by the community of religious interest shared by two nations who had thrown off the Pope,[50] but this position Jonson ignored (and as a Catholic it would have been offensive to him, notwithstanding his Scottish ancestry). Instead, his mythologies appealed beyond national and confessional considerations to an idea of British kingship as a self-authorizing power before which local differences simply evaporated. They situated James himself as the mysterious locus of Union, the rationale for which could never be revealed, but which was one of the secrets hidden in his inscrutable royal will.

For Christmas 1604–5, Queen Anne commanded Jonson to prepare a masque in which she and her ladies could appear as blackamoors. Given the disparaging remarks which eyewitnesses left about their disguise,[51] many discussions represent her choice as an awkward obstacle that Jonson had tactfully to finesse. In the event, his fable utilized the masquers' pretended cultural difference as a motif which focused Union's dilemmas of identity, dilemmas which were resolved by the miraculous discovery of the British name. In *The Masque of Blackness*, twelve Ethiopian ladies arrived at the court in quest of a riddle. Their father, Niger, explained to the sea-god Oceanus that his daughters had become convinced that their skins were ugly and were searching for a transformation. A vision had instructed them

> That they a land must forthwith seek,
> Whose termination (of the Greek)

Sounds TANIA; where bright Sol, that heat
Their bloods, doth never rise, or set,
But in his journey passeth by,
And leaves that climate of the sky
To comfort of a greater light,
Who forms all beauty with his sight.   (188–95)

So far they had visited Mauritania, Lusitania (in Spain), and Aquitania (in France) without success. But on reaching Whitehall, their moon-goddess Ethiopia appeared and told them that the answer lay in this realm's new name – 'With that great name, Britannia, this blest isle / Hath won her ancient dignity and style' (246–7) – and that they would recover that paler beauty of which they were so envious in the beams of the British sun. Ethiopia's 'intemperate fires' (175) had scorched their skins, but, as the riddle promised, James's sun was identified by its temperateness. Since James's light 'refines / All things on which his radiance shines' (264–5), the masquers would be transformed to white by a year's washing and drying in the British climate.

While many discussions acknowledge this masque's British aspect, they often overlook how urgent the issue was. The question of what name the combined kingdoms would take was the talk of 1604. The Union tracts canvassed radically divergent positions, from Robert Cotton's view that 'Britain' was 'one such ancient name as most indifferently hath comprehended both the kingdoms', to Henry Spelman's that to change 'England' to 'Britain' would obscure a glorious title with a cloudy one.[52] Alternatives were debated by parliament in April, and the new style was assumed by proclamation in October, only eleven weeks before the masque (the word 'style', which Ethiopia used, was the legal term for a royal title, and was so used in the proclamation, as was the Virgilian tag about Britain being 'A world divided from the world' (247)). In inventing his fable, Jonson made the hinge the recovery of British 'style', and devised a riddle which expounded British identity by drawing directly on the most authoritative account of the name's meaning, William Camden's *Britannia* (1586). Camden's scholarly discussion compares 'Britannia' with the names Mauritania, Lusitania, and Aquitania, and argues that it was compounded from a Greek termination meaning 'region' (*-tania*) and a native word (*Brith*) connoting 'painted, blue(-coloured)'.[53] He particularly links it to the earliest historical accounts by Caesar, Tacitus, and others which called ancient Britain the temperate realm *par excellence*, citing the anonymous *Panegyric to Constantine* (fourth century AD) with its fulsome praise of Britain's mildness:

nature endowed thee with all the blessed gifts of air and soil; wherein there is neither excessive cold of winter, nor extreme heat of summer; wherein there is so great plenty of grain, that it serveth sufficiently both for bread and drink: wherein the forests are without savage beasts, and the ground void of noisome serpents ... and verily (that which for the use of our life we much esteemed), the days there are very long, and the nights never want some light, whiles those utmost plains by the seaside cast and raise no shadows on high, and the aspect both of sky and stars passeth beyond the bound of the night, yea the very sun itself, which unto us seemeth for to set, appeareth there, only to pass along and go aside.[54]

Jonson cites the *Panegyric* in a footnote to the riddle, and his rather opaque formula concerning Britain's sun, that 'doth never rise, or set, / But in his journey passeth by' (191–2), derives from it. Camden thus provided Jonson not only with the crucial detail of 'temperate air', but with a specific correlation between Britain's name and climate. Hence the temperance which the Ethopians found at Whitehall staged the recovery of a definingly British value, a climatological contrast that legitimated British kingship. In contrast to Ethiopia's 'heedless flames' (162), James was the temperate monarch, whose rule was authenticated by that quality associated with the other great prototype of imperial temperance, Augustus.[55] The promise that the scorched women could be redeemed in Britain was no trivial fantasy, but a version of the new national character as analysed by the leading authority on the subject.

But while the masque hailed 'Britain' as that 'new name [which] makes all tongues sing' (251), as everyone in the audience knew, parliament had refused to agree the change because the constitutional consequences were so formidable, and James had resorted to proclamation in lieu of a statutory enactment. The masque acclaimed James as a sun whose beams literally dispelled the clouds of opposition, but it rewrote recent events, flying in the face of his practical failure to achieve political consensus. Far from presenting a model of consensual change, the masque constructed James's sovereignty as irresistible and beyond contest. His magic name, Ethiopia promised, would perform miracles:

> For were the world, with all his wealth, a ring,
> Britannia (whose new name makes all tongues sing)
> Might be a diamond worthy to enchase it,
> Ruled by a sun, that to this height doth grace it;
> Whose beams shine day and night, and are of force
> To blanch an Ethiop, and revive a corse.[56]   (251–6)

Proverbially, to 'blanch an Ethiop' was to attempt the impossible, but in this fiction the miraculous British name changed black to white. At least one proponent of Union, Sir Thomas Craig, had used the Ethiopian analogy when arguing the need for uniformity of language between the nations, since without it their alienation would be unbridgeable. 'Sooner', he wrote, 'you may expect an Ethiopian to change his skin than a Frenchman to accept an English or an English-speaking king'.[57] Whether or not Jonson knew Craig's tract, he made a twist on the same linguistic conceit. By blanching the Ethiop, James's new style effaced even the most radical cultural difference.[58]

It is, of course, true that the masquers retained their blackness to the end, that their physical transformation was left for celebration next Christmas. To that extent the masque was gradualist and acknowledged that identities would not be instantly remade. Nonetheless, the absence of transformation did not indicate an uncertainty about the eventual change, since the action did end with the situation transformed. Only Niger returned to Ethiopia, and the ladies remained with Oceanus, to be washed ahead of incorporation into the line of 'Albion, Neptune's son' (361). Unlike the later contestatory masques, in which royal power was validated by scenic transformations happening in full view, this masque did not utilize changeable scenery and was not structured so as to require any physical alteration.[59] Jonson could have washed his Ethiops white had he wanted to; precisely this device was used in *The Gypsies Metamorphosed* (1621), in which the Marquis of Buckingham cleansed his sallow gypsy complexion to reappear as a glorious courtier. But physical transformation was not necessary here since the real political miracle, reinventing Albion as Britannia, had already occurred, and to solve the riddle it had not to be repeated, but recognized and admired. So although incorporation of the alien was not yet fully accomplished, it was already inevitable. Since James's light salved 'the rude defects of every creature', the masquers would, soon, 'for [their] pains, perfection have' (257, 346). It was a short step from such language to the constitutional claim that in James's person Union was already achieved and only needed perfecting.

So, unlike Daniel's and Campion's masques, this entertainment inculcated a radical ideology, in which Britain was transformed through the revolutionary power of kingship – what Loewenstein calls 'a plot of modernization'.[60] Far from invoking continuities with the past or constraining the future with advice, *The Masque of Blackness* abrogated history: the future was already immanent in a marvellous, transformational present. It might still appear that the figure of Ethiopia looked to the past, recollecting Elizabeth as a sort of 'Cynthia made alien'.[61] But although Ethiopia directed her ladies' wanderings, her role, unlike Campion's Diana, was permissive, not oppositional. She instructed Niger's daughters to join 'the Britain men'

(259), and in the final song she was eclipsed, acknowledging her shame before the Stuart sun: 'Dian, with her burning face, / Declines apace' (354–5). Ethiopia announced the new name, but the masque validated James's authority not by genealogies of power but by his magnificent singularity and radical break with the past. In this fable, the shock of the new was not so much ameliorated as embraced.

What the audience did find shocking was the disguise of the Queen and her ladies as Ethiopians. Recent discussions have focused on the challenge posed to inherited norms of feminine modesty by the Queen's reckless display of her body. Just as striking was the women's staging of racial alterity, a motif which resonated with the impact of James's arrival on the imagining of political identity. As Mary Floyd-Wilson suggests, Anne's role-play invoked anxieties about ethnic contamination provoked by the substitution of new Britain for old England. Her cosmetics perhaps recalled Camden's disconcertingly primitivist explanation that Britain was so named because the original inhabitants had painted their bodies, while the women's journey from Africa gestured at the perception of the Scots as ethnically other, specifically through their supposed descent from a common ancestor Scota, Queen of the Egyptians.[62] Black characters were by no means novel in court festivity. Henry VIII had first masqued as a moor in 1510, and dozens of pages dressed as moors would attend the masquers processing to Whitehall for *The Memorable Masque* (1613).[63] Scotland had a rich tradition of shows involving real or pretended Africans, from the black maidservant Ellen More, who presided over tournaments under James IV, to the sixty men dressed as moors who welcomed Queen Anne to Edinburgh in 1590.[64] But such confrontations between the exotic and the mundane were doubly frequent in early Jacobean Whitehall: the central device of *The Vision of the Twelve Goddesses*, *The Masque of Indian and China Knights*, and the lost show *Solomon and the Queen of Sheba* (1606) – in which Sheba and her ladies were probably in blackface[65] – was the presentation of James with tokens by figures who were alien, strange, and outlandish. Perhaps the earliest, paradigmatic instance of such encounters was James's surprising meeting on his progress southwards with men on stilts, who were taken for Patagonian giants.[66] On a literal level, such devices dramatized the circumstances of the new court, as from March 1603 Whitehall was besieged with strangers come to pay their respects. More crucially, encounters between the crown and figures from beyond the borders created a ceremonial space in which new relationships of difference and identity – between centre and periphery, normal and monstrous – could, at this founding moment, be symbolically enacted. With their obsessive polarizations between familiarity and strangeness, insider and outsider, the early festivals marked out lines of difference between the new monarchy and figures representing its others. The crossing of a dynastic threshold caused other thresholds to be tested and redefined.

Jonson's unique accomplishment in *The Masque of Blackness* was to conflate form and function by making the reinvention of national identity the goal of his fiction. By foregrounding the dynamic between alienation and incorporation, he crystallized the moment of crisis involved in the establishment of new nationhood. From the first, the masque focuses on questions of identity and difference. Its apparently casual opening, in which Niger tells Oceanus about his great labour in severing 'My fresh streams from thy brackish ... Though with thy powerful saltness thus far mixed' (127–8), obliquely announced the central theme: anxiety about miscegenation and the loss of separation which it threatened. The subsequent action dissolved the threat of the alien, instrumentalizing and domesticating it with the women's homage to the British crown, but not until the separation of self and other had been acutely compromised. As Ethiopians who longed to be British and British ladies wearing opulent dress but estranged in their looks, the masquers were suspended between categories, neither exactly black nor white but uncomfortably hybridized. Reports written by eye-witnesses amply demonstrate that the spectators were unable to decide whether to admire or be repelled by this 'ugly sight', 'a troop of lean-cheeked Moors'.[67] In mixing black with white and good water with bad, *The Masque of Blackness* staged a ritual which evoked anxieties about boundaries and the likelihood of contamination; fears about a regression to barbarism were projected onto outsiders, but aroused as well as assuaged. By bringing the normal and the estranged into alarming proximity, it risked the pollution of pure forms. The distaste is unmistakable in Carleton's report that when de Taxis danced with the Queen, he 'forgot not to kiss her hand, though there was danger it would have left a mark on his lips'.[68] And while Jonson's riddle disclosed the new identity through which anxieties would eventually be discharged, his strategy was to foreground rather than ameliorate the trauma of Union. James's arrival moved the nation to a revolutionary new order, and dissolved the security of inherited categories. In the masque's traumatic renaming, the lines separating black from white and alien from self were invoked that they might be seen to be in crisis.

A year later, Jonson's *Hymenaei* staged an action which depicted the power of sovereignty in no less revolutionary terms. Written for the adolescent marriage of the Earl of Essex and Frances Howard, *Hymenaei* celebrated an event that was avowedly a tool of state. As we shall see (chapter 6 below), James arranged this marriage for purely instrumental reasons. An intricate three-way alliance between the Howard, Devereux, and Cecil families, it was designed to build bridges across the court between rival factions, and create ties of friendship between competing aristocratic affinities. Further, it took place in the wake of the Gunpowder Plot which had increased the climate of international distrust: the Plot was perceived as an anti-Scottish conspiracy and sent prominent Scots hurrying back across the border.[69] *Hymenaei* responded to dynastic and national circumstance by showcasing a Union theme. Its frame was an archaeologically exact reproduction of a Roman marriage ceremony, recreated with obsessive authenticity and symbolism. But no sooner was the ritual under way than it was disrupted by the eight (male) Humours and Affections, who burst out of a globe representing the earth and the body of man. The subversives were disciplined by Reason, descending from the top of the globe 'as in the brain, or highest part of man' (129–30), and were reincorporated into the rituals by pairing with eight female Powers sent by Juno, goddess of marriage. With Order ranking the pairs, the ceremonies could conclude. Into this device, Jonson poured a wealth of emblematic analogies between union and marriage, from the mysterious anagrammatical correspondence between 'Juno' (goddess of marriage) and 'Unio', to the final ordering of the masquers into a perfect circle. Union was the grand principle holding the cosmos together, the sewer-up of discord in family, self, and state, that nuptial and philosophical circle being exemplified in the perfect binding of the British realms inside the Ocean's wedding ring (427–8). Written for a marriage which was overtly no love-match but a transaction of power – with a groom aged fifteen and a bride of thirteen, who were not expected to consummate their nuptials despite the epithalamion that closed the performance – *Hymenaei* was less embarrassed than any other masque in the period about proclaiming itself as ideological mystification. The specific identities of the married couple all but disappeared below a tide of symbolic detail designed to establish the political value of Union.[70]

In elaborating this symbolism, Jonson developed analogical tropes that (as Gordon has shown) were endlessly refracted in unionist literature, but he particularly harked back to James's first speech to the 1604 parliament, a thesaurus of symbolic topoi linking Stuart kingship to Union:

Hath not God first united these two kingdoms both in language, religion, and similitude of manners? Yea, hath he not made us all in one island, compassed with one sea, and of itself by nature so indivisible, as almost those that were borderers themselves on the late borders, cannot distinguish, nor know, or discern their own limits? ... whereby it is now become like a little world within itself, being entrenched and fortified round about with a natural, and yet admirable strong

pond or ditch, whereby all the former fears of this nation are now quite cut off ...
What God hath conjoined then, let no man separate. I am the husband, and all the
whole isle is my lawful wife; I am the head, and it is my body; I am the shepherd,
and it is my flock; I hope therefore no man will be so unreasonable as to think that I
that am a Christian king under the gospel, should be a polygamist and husband to
two wives; that I, being the head, should have a divided and monstrous body; or
that being the shepherd to so fair a flock (whose fold hath no wall to hedge it but
the four seas) should have my flock parted in two.[71]

Here were many of Jonson's analogies – the enclosed island, married couple,
head and body – already ransacked for ideological effect. But compelling
though the royal rhetoric seemed, MPs regarded it with suspicion. Although
such ideas appeared uncontentious philosophical commonplaces, they were
profoundly coercive, not least because they presumed that Union's objectives
could be taken as read. In the 1604 and 1607 debates, the implications of these
images were unpicked, as MPs denied that the King's singularity of person
required an equivalent incorporation between the realms. James's assertion
that he could not have 'a divided and monstrous body' was echoed by
proponents of Union, such as Sir John Hayward, who said the realm could
not have one body and two names, or the Earl of Northampton, who told
parliament there could not be two souls in one body.[72] But the objections
from Thomas Crew – that 'if [the kingdoms'] laws are several they are two
divided bodies' – and from Thomas Wentworth – that James was king of
England or Scotland but not both – refused the rhetorical manoeuvre that
telescoped the gap between dynastic and constitutional unity.[73] In the 1607
debates James tactically refined his analogy, insisting that although he wanted
'absolute and full union' and could not 'be the husband of two wives', he did
not desire 'confusion in all things' and the two realms would retain their local
privileges. But this cut little ice with English gentlemen who were inclined to
reject any model of the polity that was not unitary.[74]

In *Hymenaei* Union was represented as not susceptible to interrogation.
On the contrary, it was a 'mystery' celebrated by intensely hierarchical, even
hieratic, 'rites' from which the 'profane' were expelled so that Juno's liturgy
would be protected (67–73). When the Humours and Affections disrupted
the ceremonial, Reason told them to stay out of matters they did not
understand, and:

> inform yourselves, with safer reverence,
> To these mysterious rites;
> So want of knowledge still begetteth jars,
> And humorous earthlings will control the stars.   (151–4)

While meaningful within a scenario of microcosmic rebellion, Reason's words also rebuked those whose 'jars' in the state were hindering Union, and demanded their submission. Representing James's commands as beyond contest and accessible only through esoteric rituals, this masque unashamedly mystified royal power. And by making James the focal point for cosmic correspondences, it foregrounded his body as the mysterious source of Union. *Hymenaei* not only had the most highly wrought treatment of James's accession as a mystic marriage, it also hymned him in terms which put on show his bodily capacity as biological progenitor of a dynasty:

> 'Tis so: this same is he,
> The king and priest of peace!
> And that his empress, she,
> That sits so crownèd with her own increase!
> O you, whose better blisses
> Have proved the strict embrace
> Of union with chaste kisses,
> And seen it flow so in your happy race ...
> Sit now propitious aids,
> To rites so duly prized ...   (91–103)

Ostensibly a celebration of Essex's wedding, *Hymenaei* was more interested in James's progeny than the adolescent Earl's. Entirely reversing Elizabeth's iconography of English virgin impenetrability, *Hymenaei* rooted its symbolic and literal unions in James's happy sexual productivity. His fruitfully dynastic couplings with Anne would guarantee British 'increase'.

Similarly, by insisting its rites were perfect, *Hymenaei* presented images that, while seeming uncontentious, bore onto the Union controversy. Juno's combining force, dissolving diversity into identity and incorporating opposites into one, presented Union as a totalizing power: perfect union was divinely sanctioned and irresistible. Having disciplined the Humours, Reason expounded the symbolic meanings of the rituals, stressing Union's 'perfection' (197). Fire and water were carried to show that Hymen combined contrary elements; the bride's 'Herculean knot' (61) symbolized her marriage's indissolubility; and the five tapers which were lit referred to the number of complete unity, since five was composed of two unequal integers bound indivisibly together:

> Which, joinèd thus, you cannot sever
> In equal parts, but one will ever
> Remain as common, so we see
> The binding force of unity;
> For which alone, the peaceful gods

> In number always love the odds,
> And even parts as much despise,
> Since out of them all discords rise. (204–11)

Though esoteric, this numerically symbolic perfection had political resonance as an emblem for perfect Union, since by showing that exact equality between the partners would only produce endless mathematical contest, it made a virtue of asymmetry. The numerological argument effortlessly accommodated the otherwise problematic circumstance that James's Britain was a union of unequals.

Perhaps the feature which best demonstrated the masque's radicalism was its representation of Union as a process necessitating violence. As exemplified by the asymmetries between England and Scotland, Reason and Humours, husband and wife, Union was structured here not as balance but as mastery. The partners' relationship fixed them as dominant and subordinate rather than equals, and when Order ranked the masquers they were in a hierarchical chain all the more impressive for its intricate gradations (280–95). At the same time, Union had to resist attack from within and without. The opening song excluding the profane created a privileged space, marked off from a threatening external world, and the eruption of the Humours was an internal rebellion which showed the need for 'safer reverence' (151). Far from being a happy natural state, *Hymenaei*'s Union was strained and compelled, constantly exerting power against forces that would undermine it. As Hymen acknowledged, Union was 'that blest estate, / Which all good minds should celebrate' (107–8), implying that all good minds did not celebrate it; and since the achievement of unity presumed a prior state of division, it followed that Union had to be imposed. *Hymenaei*'s view of kingship was a long way from the consensual politics of Daniel and Campion. It represented sovereignty not as give and take between kings and their subjects, but as a constantly reiterated conquest.

The disregard for consensus continued in the masque's depiction of the nuptials not as happy feasting but as a sacrifice, performed by priests at an altar. This marriage was not a sentimental bond cemented by love but a rite of passage inflicted with pain, and, to symbolize this, the bride carried implements emblematizing domestic labour, and wore grey hair in token of ageing (55–8, 182–91). In Hymen's grimly threatening terms, the spectators would see 'two noble maids … to Union sacrificed' (105–6), and when the Humours interrupted they explained they wished to forestall violence, a 'disguised pretence' (said Reason) 'Of saving blood, and succouring innocence' (149–50). The masque's iconography thus instilled a view of Union as necessitating some losses, the surrender of a lesser good for the sake of a greater, and a psychology of sacrifice was projected in the fears of the bride, 'faint and trembling' for the blood she was about to shed (411–12).[75] Outside the masque Union's opponents were disinclined to be so passive, but *Hymenaei*'s iconography left little space for resistance. It implied that Union would be better for its inequalities, and stronger for being sealed with violence. Not just involving but requiring virgin singularity to be sacrificed, *Hymenaei* legislated for a Union based on power and kingly will. As it happened, on this occasion the bride and groom went separate ways, and James did not attend their bedchamber the next morning – as he had done at Philip Herbert's marriage in 1604[76] – to look for signs that virgin blood had been split. Still, one wonders whether *Hymenaei*'s position on Union did not arouse as many apprehensions as it allayed.[77]

After the 1607 parliament failed to accomplish closer statutory Union, the likely constitutional consequences of the accession were no longer so momentous and the British issue ceased to be so contentious. Scottish naturalization was achieved at law in Calvin's Case (1608), but further constitutional movement was negligible. Subsequent masques deployed British iconography more freely, and tropes such as Britain's association with the Fortunate Isles or James's identification as the British monarch Albion, or Neptune, became commonplace. Indeed, during Prince Henry's brief political summer, the idea of a resurgent British heroism was confidently invoked. Henry was represented as a specifically British prince in *Prince Henry's Barriers* (1610), a worthy descendant from the ancient Britons who 'made Caesar fly' (182) and who was supported in his chivalry by three Englishmen and three Scots,[78] while in *Tethys' Festival* (1610), written for his investiture as Prince of Wales, he was called 'Prince of the Isles' (an ancient Scottish title), presented with Astraea's sword, and greeted by the English and Welsh rivers. In *Oberon* (1611), he danced as the fairy prince, decked in symbolism which harked back to Elizabeth, but the curtain before the scene had images of England, Scotland, and Ireland, and the motto 'Separata locis Concordi pace figantur' (may what is separated in place be joined by harmonious peace).[79] But maybe the efflorescence of this iconography around Henry was a sign not of international acquiescence in British nationhood but of the presence in Whitehall of a Scottish prince whom even Englishmen could respect, and who seemed preferable to his father because of his enthusiasm for a nostalgically Elizabethan militarism. In fact, Henry's household was overwhelmingly staffed by Englishmen,[80] and, by hailing him as a new Arthur, *Prince Henry's Barriers* assimilated him to Anglocentric traditions. No other figure had such strong British attachments until the 1630s, when Charles's masques advanced him as a heroic Britannocles, but by then the coordinates of 'British' kingship were quite different (see chapter 9 below).

In masques staged after Henry's death, Anglocentricity continued to resurface in claims for integrated British nationhood. The jokes at the expense of Welsh pride in *For the Honour of Wales* attested to the attenuation of the old Tudor investment in a heroic Welsh past, and to complacent Jacobean perceptions of the Welsh as a culturally distinct but politically subordinated people, whose Union was effectively an annexation.[81] Unlike Scotland, Wales was entirely under the English system and administered by a few powerful families and the Council in the Marches – less a local institution than an outpost of English power. Under James there was a long-running attempt by the four English marcher counties to throw off the Council and have their affairs adjudicated at Westminster rather than Ludlow; the masque perhaps echoes this in its mockery of Evan, a long-winded Welsh attorney. As we have seen, Nathaniel Brent found Jonson's revisions 'sufficient to make an Englishman laugh and a Welshman choleric', but the lack of concern about Welsh sensitivities suggests this was one border which could be transgressed without hurting the British monarchy. By contrast, Milton's *A Masque at Ludlow* (1634) depicted the Marches as a place of real danger, while holding back from affirming that royal power alone could protect them (see chapter 10 below).

Rather more serious was the friction between the nations that was aroused four years earlier by Jonson's *The Irish Masque at Court* (29 December 1613). This was danced as part of the celebrations for the Anglo-Scottish marriage between Frances Howard and the Earl of Somerset (discussed in chapter 7 below), but it also alluded to the recent arrival at Whitehall of a delegation from the Irish parliament. This group came on a difficult mission. James had called a Dublin parliament to raise revenue and ratify the new Ulster plantation, but it broke down when Catholics withdrew in protest at a government attempt to pack it with Protestants, fearing, with some reason, that this heralded legislation extremely prejudicial to the Irish and Old English.[82] The masque pretended that the delegates had come not to negotiate but to pay their respects at the favourite's wedding. Four Irish footmen arrived, distinguished (like the Welshmen) by their broad dialect and ignorance of etiquette. They introduced their masters, who danced dressed in Irish mantles – the badge of colonial difference – but dropped their cloaks to reveal glorious masquing costumes underneath. Their transformation was preceded by a 'civil gentleman of the nation' (143), who praised James, and a bard, whose song prophesied the glories of Jacobean Ireland:

This is that James of which long since thou sung'st,
Should end our country's most unnatural broils;
And if her ear, then deafened with the drum,
Would stoop but to the music of his peace,
She need not with the spheres change harmony.
This is the man thou promised should redeem,
If she would love his counsels as his laws,
Her head from servitude, her feet from fall,
Her fame from barbarism, her state from want,
And in her all the fruits of blessing plant.   (156–65)

In the light of subsequent events, this prophecy seems patently designed to sanitize and reassure. James Smith notes that Irish bards were more commonly associated with Irish opposition to English culture, and with some reason David Lindley describes Jonson as reproducing 'the anaesthetic of official propaganda'.[83] Certainly Jonson shared the contemporary assumption that Irish 'barbarity' had to be regulated by English civility, though it is dangerous to measure him by standards out of his own time. The masque is best understood less as wanton falsification of colonial realities than as an image of what James's government thought it was achieving. In showing James as reforming the Irish mantle and bardic music, it reproduced the ideas of advisors such as Edmund Spenser and John Davies, both of whom believed that Irish pacification would be achieved only by eradicating such cultural differences.[84] Equally, the delegates' objective was to persuade James to take their grievances seriously by assuring him that in breaking his parliament they were not inciting rebellion, and, in this respect, symbolic gestures of loyalty met a pragmatic political need. Nevertheless – as the standard English speech of the 'civil gentleman' and bardic singer shows – in practice the incorporation of the Irish into a supra-national 'British' ideal meant subordinating their differences to English norms, and it is symptomatic of Whitehall's cultural blind spots that the ten masquers who represented the delegates were five Englishmen and five Scots. Chamberlain commented that, although the masque was repeated, the 'device, which was a mimical imitation of the Irish, was not so pleasing to many, which think it no time, as the case stands, to exasperate that nation by making it ridiculous'.[85] But it was not until the 1630s, when relations between English, Scottish, and Irish kingdoms began to break down, that the faultlines in the discourse of British nationhood became fully apparent.

Given the incompleteness of the Jacobean union and the uncertainty of convergence between the nations, it is unsurprising that the imagery of Britishness in these early masques sometimes seems tentative or compromised.

It was easier to praise the dynastic logic of the Union than to find an iconography that adequately accommodated the aspirations and fears of all those affected by it, and in representing the body of the King as the essential locus of Union the masques inevitably reproduced the problems as well as prestige of multiple kingship. Their moments of myopia or contradiction point towards underlying structural weaknesses in James's Britain that would eventually be catastrophic, not least the disconnections between the nations that troubled the supposedly unitary court announced in their imagery. Indeed, it may have been impossible to devise a British iconography that was entirely coherent or satisfied everyone without lapsing into blandness. But although politically the future was uncertain and it was generations before constitutional change came about on anything like the scale James wanted, culturally the idea of Union was gaining ground. As Tristan Marshall argues, while British nationhood proved elusive, the name of 'Britain' became increasingly commonplace,[86] and to this process the masques' ostentatious images of Britishness must have contributed. Moreover, by thematizing Union the masques not only flagged up the new identity but forced the pace of change, pre-empting developments elsewhere by putting the controversial topic at the centre of Stuart panegyric. Their legacy was to ensure that, however wide the gap between James's hopes and achievements, and however brief the period when a closer union was being pursued, early Stuart kingship would always be identified with the British project.

For the masques, Britain was the foundational issue around which crystallized many ideological and aesthetic factors that subsequently became customary. From the first, celebrations of Stuart monarchy took place in a different frame of reference from Tudor forms, and Britain was important to this shift for it gave Jacobean panegyric wider horizons than Elizabeth's, lifting court celebrations from the national and local to the international and cosmopolitan. As ruler of multiple kingdoms, James took his bearings from the grand continental monarchies, and his image of himself as the British monarch was calculated to avoid seeming narrowly nationalistic or confessional. The sudden efflorescence of court festival in 1603 reflected his enhanced sense of purpose, showcasing the dignity of his dynasty and the gloriously transformed state over which he reigned. At the same time, the focus on his body and progeny transformed the internal economy of court festival, situating monarch and performers in relationships of complex affinity rather than erotic servitude to a capricious queenly mistress. As father, husband, patron, and prince, James could be addressed in a wider repertoire of terms than was available for Elizabeth, while his command as a monarch was not problematized by gender or by any absence of biological productivity. The idea that he (and later Charles) was the powerful masculine principle that guaranteed the state's fruitfulness, unity, and continuance was a controlling motif of political culture down to the Civil War.

As we shall see in chapters 5 and 6, these internal relationships were complicated by the politics of Stuart family life. Unlike Elizabeth, James's fatherly authority could be brought into question by wifely disobedience or oedipal rivalry. Nonetheless, the impact of the British issue was irrevocable: it drew the masques into European festive modes that rapidly left behind Elizabeth's more localized panegyric. In making these changes, it seems clear that, of all those involved, Jonson responded most vigorously to the ideological consequences of Stuart succession. He seized on the emblematic potential of James's mysterious sovereign body, making it the centrepiece of *Blackness* and *Hymenaei*, and surrounding it with rituals that, by arousing and managing anxiety, confirmed the King as the symbolic, structural, and emotional centre of the new state. It is true that his masques presume a model of kingship that tended towards the autocratic, their artistic mode expressing political action as the exercise of transcendent sovereign will. Yet even Jonson was not single-minded about Union – witness his prosecution for jokes about the Scots in *Eastward Ho!* (1605) – and the differences of form and emphasis between *Blackness* and *Hymenaei* and the masques by Daniel and Campion show that Jacobean court culture encompassed a range of perspectives on power. Such differences were testimony to the persistence of unresolved competing attitudes at Whitehall, attesting that court culture did not simply ventriloquize the royal will but mediated between political elites, conscripting and orchestrating into a political body the members of this complex institution. The ability of court masques to conceptualize Union in multiple ways suggests that, in these early years at least, the conduct of Stuart monarchy was still comparatively pragmatic.

CHAPTER 5

The consort's body

On 27 July 1606, during a visit by James's brother-in-law, King Christian of Denmark, a disaster happened at a masque of Solomon and the Queen of Sheba staged for the two kings by the Earl of Salisbury. Salisbury was entertaining the court at Theobalds, his house in Hertfordshire, and his show complimented James by developing his favourite iconographical association with Solomon, a king renowned for wisdom and peace. James appears as Solomon the judge on the ceiling of the Banqueting House, but this entertainment alluded to the episode in 1 Kings 10, where Solomon is visited by the Queen of Sheba, who gives him gifts to honour his wisdom. Unfortunately, things did not go to plan. As the lady playing the Queen approached the throne, she tripped and deposited in Christian's lap a casket containing wine, cream, jelly, cakes, and spices. 'Much was the hurry and confusion' (wrote Sir John Harington, in a letter recounting the story); 'cloths and napkins were at hand, to make all clean'.[1] Then Christian tried to dance with the Queen but, being drunk, fell down and was carried to bed. Meanwhile more gifts were brought by three women playing Faith, Hope, and Charity, but they too were worse for wear. Hope could not speak, Faith 'left the court in a staggering condition', and Charity, having 'in some sort made obeisance', 'returned to Hope and Faith, who were both sick and spewing in the lower hall'. Next came Victory presenting a sword, but her weapon made James nervous, and, being intoxicated, 'she was led away like a silly captive, and laid to sleep in the outer steps of the ante-chamber'. Finally Peace entered but, 'contrary to her semblance', in the struggle to reach James she 'most rudely made war with her olive branch, and laid on the pates of those who did oppose her coming'. In scriptural exegesis, the Queen of Sheba's visit was usually seen as foreshadowing the three Magi, whose visit and gifts acclaimed the infant Christ. As Psalm 71 says, 'The kings of Tharsis and the islands shall offer presents; the kings of the Arabians and of Saba shall bring gifts; and all kings of the earth shall adore him; all nations shall serve him.' This is why the Queen of Sheba sometimes appeared in royal entries, including that given to Queen Anne at Edinburgh in 1590.[2] However, her arrival at Theobalds underlined how far James's court fell short of such exalted comparisons.

Harington's account of the masque cannot be taken at face value. Indeed, there is some question about whether he made it up, for his letter's addressee, 'Mr. Secretary Barlow', cannot be identified, and no other source records it, even though the festivities for Christian are thoroughly documented.[3] Harington, whose hopes for preferment under James were dashed, left a series of suspiciously polished epistles purporting to give an insider's view of Whitehall, all notable for their pose of sardonic disenchantment towards James and nostalgia for Elizabeth. His Aristophanic account of Christian's welcome is framed as a general case-study of the collapse of English manners under the new King, and is full of xenophobia and gender stereotyping:

The sports [for King Christian] began each day in such manner and such sort as well nigh persuaded me of Mahomet's paradise. We had women, and indeed wine too, of such plenty as would have astonished each sober beholder ... I think the Dane hath strangely wrought on our good English nobles, for those whom I never could get to taste good liquor now follow the fashion and wallow in beastly delights. The ladies abandon their sobriety, and are seen to roll about in intoxication.

Harington then describes the masque and its drunken actors, and draws a political moral:

I have much marvelled at these strange pageantries, and they do bring to my remembrance what passed of this sort in our Queen's days ... but I never did see such lack of good order, discretion and sobriety as I have now done; ... we are going on hereabouts as if the devil was contriving every man should blow up himself, by wild riot, excess, and devastation of time and temperance; ... I see no man, or woman either, that can now command himself or herself. I wish I was at home: *O rus, quando te adspiciam?*[4]

Like Hamlet on the ramparts, Harington sees kingly insobriety as an index of political decline, a process he associates with a loss of national identity and contamination by non-English habits: Christian's stained clothes, he says, 'defiled' the royal bed. The home space is invaded by the exotic, not only by Scottish and Danish intemperance, but by luxuries so Asiatic that they suggest 'Mahomet's paradise' (as Stephen Orgel notes, the Queen of Sheba would have been in blackface and oriental dress).[5] And while drunkenness – so frequently associated with the Danes in this period – signals foreign pollution, Harington no less forcefully links courtly decay with female exorbitance. In his account, royal luxury is signalled by too much wine and too many women, unruly ladies and effeminized men.

Christian is so unmanned by drink that he 'humbled himself', the cowardly James dare not look on a sword, and the hall is populated by ladies in various stages of vomiting, incontinence, and collapse. A superfluity of women, all lacking bodily discipline, is cause and effect of Jacobean dissipation. Court voluptuousness is inextricably entangled with female excess.

Assuming that this event was not entirely a fiction dreamed up by Harington, it is unclear who the women performers were, or even whether they were all women. Normally, female spoken roles would be taken by boy actors, though Christian would scarcely have danced with the Queen of Sheba had she been a boy, and the show's form – an entry and gift-giving – resembles previous female masques such as *The Vision of the Twelve Goddesses* and *The Masque of Blackness*.[6] Whether or not Harington reported what truly happened, his critique makes sense only if the players really were aristocratic women, for his claim is that the chaos in the hall was a capsule version of the court's effeminacy and excess. His misogyny is part of a general anti-courtly discourse which took the pleasures of masques as symptomatic of a morally and politically reprehensible lack of self-control. His perspective is close to that of the puritanical historian Arthur Wilson, who in 1653 said Jacobean Whitehall had been

a continued masquerado, where [Queen Anne] and her ladies, like so many sea-nymphs or Nereides, appeared often in various dresses to the ravishment of the beholders; the King himself being not a little delighted with such fluent elegancies, as made the nights more glorious than the days. But the latitude that these high-flying fancies and more speaking actions gave to the lower world to judge and censure even the greatest with reproaches shall not provoke me so much as to stain the innocent paper.[7]

Such extravaganzas were not in fact performed daily, but sea-nymphs did appear in *The Masque of Blackness* and *Tethys' Festival*, and Wilson references them in order to make a sexualized critique of James's relationship with his favourites. The connection is that masques demonstrate Jacobean Whitehall to have been rife with sexual misbehaviour. Queen Anne loved Pembroke, says Wilson, and James adored Philip Herbert and Somerset, the latter being 'an object more delightful' on whom 'his fancy ran with a violent stream'. It follows that self-indulgence was inevitable at a court given over to masquing's voluptuous pleasures, the mere report of which would have stained 'the innocent paper'. Wilson was less obsessed with foreign contamination than Harington was, but for him masques were no less spaces where proper gender relations broke down and men fell prey to effeminacy and lust. In the queen's 'masquerados', masculine self-control was overthrown by female ravishment.

Wilson and Harington were both hostile witnesses, but the trope was commonplace that masques attested to a creeping feminization of court culture, and to courtly women's unusual visibility and self-will. For Henry Hawkins, writing in the 1630s, masques were occasions when female beauty was triumphantly on display: 'Have you seen a stately masque in court, all set round and taken up with a world of beautiful ladies, to behold the sports and revels there? Imagine the stars, then, as sitting in the firmament to behold some spectacle on earth, with no other light than their own beauties.'[8] Other observers associated the same events with moral and social danger. In Webster's *The Duchess of Malfi* (1614), the Duchess's enemies repeatedly charge her with over-indulgence in masques, to insinuate that her household is unruly and her desires uncontrollable. Ferdinand warns her to 'give o'er these chargeable revels; / A visor and a mask are whispering-rooms / That were ne'er built for goodness' (1.1.333–5),[9] a threat Bosola echoes, predicting that lust will out though it 'do mask in ne'er so strange disguise' (2.3.76). Later, Ferdinand torments his sister with 'masques of common courtesans' (4.1.124), and one of the madmen cries 'Woe to the caroche that brought home my wife from the masque at three o'clock in the morning! It had a large featherbed in it' (4.2.104–6). None of these characters is exactly endorsed by Webster, but there is an undercurrent of misogyny in their assumptions about masques, which recurs even more forcefully in Middleton's *The Revenger's Tragedy* (*c.* 1606), a play obsessed by the connections between court festival and secret sexual incontinence. Both dramatists attest to a ready nexus of associations between revelry, lavish spending, and female provocation, and, given the prominence of women in James's festivals, such linkages were difficult to avoid. From the start, Queen Anne's masques aroused censure on just these grounds. Although her first show was merely a 'masquerade champetre' staged for Prince Henry in October 1603, it immediately met reproach, Anne Clifford recording in her diary that there was 'much talk of a masque which the Queen had at Winchester, and how all the ladies about the court had gotten such ill names that it was grown a scandalous place, and the Queen herself was much fallen from her former greatness and reputation she had in the world'.[10] This young diarist makes it sound as though the mere fact of female performance was scandalous, irrespective of the masque's content. From here it was only a short step to Dudley Carleton's notorious remark about *The Masque of Blackness*, that the women's 'apparel was rich, but too light and courtesan-like for such great ones'.[11]

If the association of masques with female transgression was a basic trope, much of this critical commentary was linked by an emphasis on masques as spectacle. It was visual display, particularly the disclosure of the female body, that shocked Wilson and Carleton. Wilson is especially bothered by what he calls masques' 'speaking actions', their status as pictures with light and motion which worked directly on the senses, by-passing censorship and appealing to the eye. He is exercised by their aesthetic of excess, their ability to stir up pleasure through extravagant effects, overwhelming the viewer by their sheer opulence. This all-too-forceful visual appeal permitted free rein for women actors to display their sexual desirability, giving their performances a resonance which is hard to recapture now but which for Wilson was the main issue: appreciation of masques could never be separated from their embodiment in the performers' persons. As Sophie Tomlinson notes,[12] Wilson's hostile appraisal of masques as dangerous speaking pictures was a reverse echo of Jonson's eulogy of the participants in *Hymenaei*, which put the same point more positively: 'such was the exquisite performance as – beside the pomp, splendour, or what we may call apparelling of such presentments – that alone, had all else been absent, was of power to surprise with delight, and steal away the spectators from themselves' (568–72). Stealing the spectators from themselves was what Anne and her ladies must often have seemed to do, as masque after masque praised their beauty and its power to make audiences admire them and draw partners onto the dance floor. Masques thus depended on the seductions of luxury, ostentation, and the exotic, making feminine bravery, beautiful costumes, beguiling movements, sensuous dancing, and sexual allure intrinsic to their aesthetics. The intensely realized female presence on which Anne's masques turned made them both glorious and disturbing.

The ethos of Anne's festivals was, then, bound up in unsettling ways with the display of female bravery. Nonetheless, the cultivation of sumptuousness as an end in itself was increasingly appreciated. The Winchester masque may have ruffled feathers but the French ambassador saw it as a foretaste of more beautiful festivals to come, and at *The Masque of Beauty* the Venetian ambassador praised 'the wealth of pearls and jewels that adorned the queen and her ladies, so abundant and splendid that in everyone's opinion no other court could have displayed such pomp and riches', adding that the splendour 'was worthy of her majesty's greatness'.[13] Such judgements came from foreign diplomats who knew all about continental festivals, but the vogue for female performance suggests that English audiences quickly caught up. Even Carleton was impressed by the richness of the women's gowns in *The Masque of Blackness*, which he thought becoming to 'such great ones'. The masques thus point towards shifting assumptions about gender and sexuality that were slowly taking hold across the whole

period, and things that seemed potentially shocking about female performance in 1603 were so far taken for granted a generation later as to be scarcely
worth mentioning. When Henrietta Maria took to the stage in 1625, she
performed more transgressively than Anne had ever done, but court correspondents reacted with conspicuously muted disapproval. Chamberlain,
noting that in *Artenice* she had a speaking part and some of her ladies wore
male costumes and beards, said 'I have known the time when this would
have been a strange sight, to see a queen act in a play, but *tempora mutantur
et nos*'.[14] His grudging tolerance suggests that, if not wholly accepted, female
performance was gradually becoming socially respectable.

William Prynne's *Histriomastix* (1633), with its provocative definition of
women actors as 'notorious whores', showed that this attitude was by no
means universal, but the enclosed nature of the court stage meant that
liberties were possible there which could not be taken in more public
environments. Masques were privileged spaces where new kinds of female
agency could develop, creating a repertoire of female performance that is part
of the back-story to the arrival of professional actresses in 1660.[15] Recent
scholarship emphasizes that, before the Civil War, masques were a principal
zone of female cultural production, that women had substantial artistic
leadership at court, and that performance allowed new modes of female
subjectivity and agency to emerge.[16] Much Stuart festival was actively
femino-centric. Whether or not Anne was the *fons et origo* of Jacobean
masquing (as has been argued),[17] she sponsored six masques in eight years,
and was responsible for innovations such as blackface disguising and the
invention of the antimasque. When in *The Masque of Queens* Jonson says that
'her majesty, best knowing that a principal part of life in these spectacles lay in
their variety, commanded me to think on some dance or show that might
precede hers, and have the place of a foil or false masque' (10–14), it is
unnecessary to assume that he ascribed to the Queen a formal innovation
that was really his own out of a misplaced sense of tact. Rather, knowing as we
now do that Anne's cultural patronage was discriminating and extensive
allows us to read this as a tribute to the creative partnership between poet
and a culturally influential patron – just as at *The Masque of Beauty* the
Venetian ambassador assumed she was 'authoress of the whole'.[18] Henrietta
Maria's creative control of her own festivals is amply attested, while other
aristocratic women, such as Lady Hay and the Countess of Bedford, sponsored court entertainments. Women's masquing no longer seems a frivolous
luxury but a bold and culturally necessary assertion of feminine capability.

This new historiography has shifted attention from the monarch to the
consort as patron and performer, who was as much the centre of the

occasion as the principal spectator to whom the dancing was addressed. The two queens' festivals not only celebrated their husbands but attested to their own status as powerful women, and this has led some scholars to read them as implicitly subversive, or as challenges to kingly authority.[19] Undoubtedly their masques always had potential for tension, given their cultural and political differences from their spouses. Each queen had her own household and moved in circles that overlapped with but pulled against her husband's, and each acquired a distinctive iconography, Anne's turning on the exotic, Henrietta Maria's on neoplatonic motifs of light and beauty.[20] More crucially, the relationship between the royal iconographies was dynamic, building instability into the processes of kingly legitimation. If James's kingship was cognate with his authority as husband and father, this depended in part on his wife's presence as the subordinated partner against whom his difference was established. Her love and loyalty testified to his vigorous male rule, though with the consequence that she was always cast as 'other' or potentially insubordinate. The queens' femininity was thus intrinsic to their consorts' legitimation, and worked in conflicting ways, either to fix them within their husbands' orbit, or to unsettle male authority by their association with the alien or by the attention which in performance they attracted. However, it remains a question whether each queen had a fully independent hand over her festivals. Henrietta Maria paid for her own masques, but Anne's were often jointly or wholly financed by James. In December 1604 the Privy Council advised James that for the sake of his honour he should fund *The Masque of Blackness*, despite other claims on his pocket,[21] and he seems to have paid for *The Masque of Queens*, *Love Freed*, and *Tethys' Festival*, the outlay for which was authorized by the Earls of Suffolk and Worcester.[22] The economics of masquing meant that, however much the queens' masques were in tension with the king, they always had to be at some level in negotiation with him.

The queens' masques do not exhibit outright subversion so much as an ongoing tension between female self-assertion and male control, a dialectic which is conditioned by anxiety about the power of the feminine at the same time as it creates space for feminine self-realization. They involve an alternative vision of Stuart power which promotes the claims of the female, necessitating a constant oscillation between promoting and managing women. This results in some uneasy manoeuvres by the poets, as they seek to contain the power of the feminine which, nevertheless, they are celebrating. For example, both Jonson and Daniel sought in their printed texts to ring-fence the splendour which the shows presented. The preface to Daniel's *The Vision of the Twelve Goddesses* carefully underlines that the blessings symbolized by the female masquers were traceable to the King, implying in retrospect, if not at the time, that Anne's empowerment ultimately came from James.[23] Jonson's text of *The Masque of Queens*, with its combative prose and weighty Latin marginalia, moves the focus even more emphatically from the masquers' bodies to the poet's role in creating their display. In his post-performance editorializing, Jonson supplants the memory of the shows with a pointedly literary recreation, drawing attention away from the dances to the labour of scholarship which breathed life into them.[24] Additionally, his frequent disparagement of masque performance, his insistence that visual display was the masque's carcass and quickly died, and that the words were its enduring soul, similarly diminish the impact of performance, and female performance in particular. In *Chloridia*, he scripted an apotheosis for women representing Fame, Poetry, History, Architecture, and Sculpture, but in his unprinted poem 'An expostulation with Inigo Jones', his perspective on such female glories was withering:

> I have met with those
> That do cry up the machine, and the shows,
> The majesty of Juno in the clouds,
> And peering-forth of Iris in the shrouds!
> The ascent of Lady Fame, which none could spy,
> Not those that sided her, Dame Poetry,
> Dame History, Dame Architecture too,
> And Goody Sculpture, brought with much ado
> To hold her up.[25]

Although this was an attack on Inigo Jones, the condescending middle-class epithets 'dame' and 'goody' were equally insulting to *Chloridia*'s female performers, and suggest how privately ambivalent Jonson was about the gender implications of an event which, nonetheless, he had scripted. Female performance involved a continual management of potential conflicts, a delicate negotiation over women's status in which neither monarch nor consort exactly had the upper hand. It inevitably drew attention to the limits and pressure points of Stuart paternalism.

Anne's masques were never explicitly political: they made no attempt to allegorize alternatives to James's policies. Her masquing was always framed within his British project, from the allusions to amity between the nations in *Twelve Goddesses*, to the Sphinx's riddle in *Love Freed*, about 'a world the world without', the answer to which, inevitably, was 'Britain' (285). Although her imagery was distinctive, it used the same eclectic classicism as James's, and made no ideological capital out of her Catholicism, even in masques by Jonson, who was a Catholic at this time. Yet Anne sat uneasily within the fatherly emphases of James's iconography, and her signature role was not Juno, wife of Jupiter, but Pallas, goddess of wisdom. When wedding rites were performed to Juno in *Hymenaei*, the goddess was not linked to the Queen, and in *Twelve Goddesses* Juno (played by the Countess of Bedford) stood only as companion to Pallas who, with her helmet, lance, and shield, presented a figure at odds with wifely obedience and Jacobean pacifism.[26] The masques staged by James's courtiers during the same period – *Hymen and the Four Seasons, Hymenaei, Lord Hay's Masque*, and *The Haddington Masque* – all adopt marital motifs and position James at the apex of sexual hierarchy in domestic and political spheres. In *The Haddington Masque* (214–35) James was a new Aeneas, a heroic prince exhibiting his ancestor's epic ardour and wielding the sexual power conferred by his mother, Venus. But Anne's reluctance to play Juno to James's Jove allowed her to avoid endorsing the postures of female submissiveness into which his marital imagery would have painted her. Instead, her role as Pallas underlined her agency and autonomy, and put her wisdom implicitly in competition with his status as Solomon.[27] Nor do her masques turn back to the Elizabethan chivalric motifs which could have offered an alternative model for voicing and discharging sexual tensions. Rather, James's passivity as non-performing principal spectator allowed the active function in Anne's festivals to be usurped by the women, and, for all their expression of female desirability, her masques were strikingly deficient in erotic charge. The women were represented as nymphs to be courted but also as a sisterhood conscious of their gender difference and confident in the authority that it conferred, remarkable for power as well as beauty. Anne did not resist James's bourgeois domesticity, but neither did she readily conform to it.

These emphases reflect Anne's ambiguous position at Whitehall. Her main concerns were to promote friendship with Spain and ensure marriages for her children that built ties between England, Spain, and Denmark (she was dismissive of the Palatine match before and after the event),[28] but her circumstances did not allow her to pursue political objectives in any sustained or systematic way. Her Catholicism remained largely private,[29] and although she was named to the council when James was absent from London in 1617,[30] foreign diplomats generally assumed that she was apolitical. The Venetian ambassador remarked that, although James apprised her of business, she did not 'mix herself up in affairs', and 'professes indifference' to them.[31] Nonetheless, she was a vigorous patron and fiercely protective of her personal space, and her circle's affinities were differently configured from her husband's. If James's inner circle was Scottish, with Cecil and the

Howards as his political agents, Anne's connections were to members of the old Essex faction, such as the Sidneys, Herberts, and Russells, relatives of the ladies and officials who staffed her household. Of course these networks were neither watertight nor mutually exclusive, and Anne acted as an important broker between dynasties and factions.[32] However, she actively obstructed James's minister Henry Howard, Earl of Northampton, and disliked his favourite Robert Carr and Carr's ally, Thomas Overbury. In the more polarized circumstances of the mid-reign, when Carr and the Howards achieved a near-monopoly of influence, she became identified with the anti-Carr grouping, and helped advance George Villiers as a rival favourite: Villiers's promotion to James's Bedchamber being done, symbolically, at her request. Her support was important to the anti-Carr faction, even if it occurred mainly in a private and domestic capacity.

Daniel's two masques expressed Anne's political and cultural prestige most forcefully. *The Vision of the Twelve Goddesses* was an almost entirely female affair. The only male speaker was Somnus (Sleep), who produced the vision, but it was interpreted by women: Night, Iris, a Sibyl, and the Graces – who, singing 'hand in hand' (355), were a pointedly self-sufficient image of women free from male interference. Iris explained that the deities had taken mortal forms for Anne's ladies were 'the best-built temples of beauty and honour' (412), and the Sibyl explicated their glories, marvelling that 'so great powers' should enter this 'humble roof' (284). This ensured that the Queen and her ladies were as much the focus of the masque as James, if not more so. The goddesses favoured him with blessings, but were independent entities who owed him no obligation, and their leader, Pallas, the 'glorious patroness of this mighty monarchy' (407), was the star. By contrast, James had nothing to do beyond receiving the Queen's radiance.

In *Tethys' Festival* (1610), the investiture masque presented to Prince Henry, James again shared the limelight with his wife. This was a family show, danced by Anne and Princess Elizabeth, and featuring the ten-year-old Charles, Duke of York, as Zephyrus, messenger of spring. Using aquatic motifs, it addressed James as Oceanus, King of the seas, but was led by Anne as Tethys, who brought in ladies named after rivers, her daughter being the nymph of Thames. The fiction praised James, but not extravagantly, and put Anne at its centre as 'that intelligence which moves the sphere / Of circling waters' (E4).[33] Surrounded by her children, she was mother of the dynasty, the watery imagery alluding to her fertility and harking back to Queen Elizabeth in her role as nature goddess, as in the Ditchley portrait.[34] Between dances Anne sat on her own dais, 'a little mount' crowned with a 'tree of victory' (F2v) – an emblem often used in her iconography and borrowed from Elizabeth's medals.[35] Daniel's verses emphasized the evening's fleeting pleasures, and that spectators should extract as much delight as they could from the shows as they were danced:

> Feed apace, then, greedy eyes,
> On the wonder you behold;
> Take it sudden as it flies,
> Though you take it not to hold;
> When your eyes have done their part,
> Thought must length it in the heart. (F3v)

These sentiments emphasized the transient joys associated with Anne's bodily performance, rather than James's lasting glory.

By contrast, Jonson's masques handled gender difference warily, representing the female anxiously, as if in need of containment. The masquers in *Blackness* and *Beauty* were richly costumed exotics; their presence was mysteriously ravishing, embodied in arcane hieroglyphics or in their dazzling throne of beauty. So seductive was their show that it 'move[d] each heart and eye / With the world's soul, true harmony' (*Beauty*, 373–4), but it was modulated by a sense of sexual danger. In *Blackness*, the singers admonished the 'daughters of the subtle flood' (306) not to engage too closely with their dancing partners:

> Come away, come away!
> We grow jealous of your stay.
> If you do not stop your ear,
> We shall have more cause to fear
> Sirens of the land than they
> To doubt the sirens of the sea. (295–300)

As Tomlinson notes, this song's warnings eroticized and unsettled the mixed dancing, emphasizing the women's 'dangerously open ears', and depicting the revels as an alluring encounter, 'a mutual enthralment arising from their entwining in dance'.[36] It reverses the sensual indulgence of its counterpart in *Tethys' Festival*, with its reckless invitation to pleasure. In *Beauty*, the women's seductiveness was distanced by Jonson's rigorously philosophical treatment of love as concept rather than emotion, but here again the songs reflected on the power of their eyes, seeking assurances that their Cupids would not run wild, be 'false', 'straying', deceitful, or impure (358–61). Such language was all the more remarkable given how emphatically the masque linked desire with physical motion around the hall. With the women's bodily power encapsulated in their throne's three-way movement and the 'curious squares and rounds' (302) of their teasingly sinuous dances, the songs' warnings pulled against the thrust of the fiction. They represented as morally problematic that sinuousness of motion which was central to the masque's aesthetic effect.

Far more than Daniel's masques, Jonson's festivals located Anne in a frame that foregrounded her status as consort. She may have danced seductively, but in these shows she did so under James's aegis, which remained the ideological reference point. Most of Jonson's festivals for Anne were shaped as quests, with James as the goal of her enterprise. He may have been the passive observer of her glorious display, but his presence resolved tensions and counterbalanced her self-presentation, her 'persuasive action' being comple-mented, if not entirely contained, by him as 'prime mover'.[37] In *Beauty*, the women were drawn to court by James's 'attractive beams, that lights these skies' (389); they commanded men's hearts, but his power was no less magnetic to them. In *Love Freed from Ignorance and Folly*, the fiction was even more confining. It replayed the gender structures of *The Masque of Blackness* by taking James as the answer to a riddle which released the women from imprisonment. The ladies were Daughters of the Morn who, led by Love, came from 'utmost east' (66) to seek Phoebus, whom the Orient Queen would wed. But they were caught by Ignorance, in the person of a monstrous Sphinx, and only the answers 'the king' and 'Britain' saved them. By making Love's enemy Ignorance, Jonson politicized what would otherwise have been simple romance motifs. The key to love was not desire but knowledge: it was necessary to love rightly by perceiving James's centrality to the world as Phoebus, the sun, and to admire his 'wisdom' (102) which was his kingdom's 'light and treasure' (288). This made the masque a fable of progress, as the characters moved from east to west and ignorance to civility, but also implicitly from female to male. The Sphinx who captured the (male) Cupid was female, and she was supported by twelve 'she-fools' (248). Cupid's first, incorrect answer to her riddling contraries was 'a lady' (185), and he only found the true answer with help from the muses' priests – poets and men of art like Jonson. This fable set up a complex oscillation between the masquers' oriental exoticism and the King's containing masculinity, James being no less powerful for his passivity. Indeed, he combined within himself the seemingly opposed principles of male and female:

> The contraries which Time till now
> Nor Fate knew where to join or how
> Are majesty and love; which there,
> And nowhere else, have their true sphere.   (292–5)

As the locus of majesty and love, James had absorbed the female and was mysteriously self-sufficient, the embodiment of both the maternal and the fatherly, a kind of super-parent to his admiring realm. Anne's ladies were released to dazzle the spectators with their beauty, but only after Ignorance had been chased away by Phoebus's fierce incandescence (204–5).

Love Freed was the most conservative fiction that Anne danced, but all Jonson's masques for her construed the relationship of King and Queen as inherently conflicted. Their ritual task was to manage the tension between his authority and her excess, juxtaposing male control with female self-assertion in an uneasy, unending dialectic. This tension was at its acutest in *The Masque of Queens*, where the stressful interaction of King and Queen was most fully worked out. This was the first masque to make its women Amazons, with the Countess of Bedford playing the Amazonian Queen Penthesilea, Anne as Bel-Anna, Queen of the Ocean – a role resonating with Queen Elizabeth's memory – and other ladies masquerading as martial heroines from history and legend. *Queens* further evoked the unruly feminine by introducing witches who disrupted the celebrations by casting spells to darken Whitehall. Their malice gave way before the queens' brightness, but their presence pointed to negative aspects of female performance that were at stake in the main masquers too. The witches were banished by Fame's trumpet, announcing Heroic Virtue in the character of Perseus, who would 'cut [them] off' (375) just as he had killed the gorgon Medusa. With the witches gone, the queens appeared in the Temple of Fame, then came down in chivalric style on chariots pulled by eagles, griffins, and lions (467–71). This was a clearer affirmation of female glory than Anne's earlier masques, with their mysterious hieroglyphics and revolving thrones. Not only had the women assumed heroic roles, they usurped festival forms normally reserved for men.

Critical debate focuses on whether the masque underwrote this display of female self-sufficiency or magnified the women in order to disempower them, by subordinating them to James's superior authority. Stephen Orgel develops the latter case, arguing that virtue had to be represented as masculine in *Queens* since the masque invoked the female as that which must be defeated so that James's king-centric order could be instated.[38] Perseus, the one male figure, stood at the structural hinge between antimasque and main masque, and held a shield that carried the head of a dead female monster. His association with Medusa qualified him to expel the witches, since his slaughter of the gorgon pre-echoed their defeat, but this meant that the masque's turn towards celebration depended on the repression of the feminine. The queens were not admitted until the monstrosity of disruptive female power had been exorcised: they could be accepted as martial heroines only after monstrous female display had been repudiated. From this point of view, the witches might be said to project the masque's political unconscious. Their disorderly behaviour expressed anxiety about female transgression which had to be discharged or held in check before the martial queens could be admitted. Anne's empowerment was thus qualified, for it was conditional on the dark side of femininity being subordinated by masculine control. Whatever praise she received, she was ultimately constrained by James's presence as onlooker. However, the irony of the masque (Orgel argues) was that James's authority as constructed by the fiction was more dependent on the female than it admitted. Perseus' virtue was betokened by the image of Medusa, and this put the dangerous woman at the heart of masculine self-realization. James may have wished his authority to be self-validating, but he could not avoid the open secret that the affirmation of masculinity called female transgression into being. Dangerous women were necessary, if only for the sake of male empowerment.

In Orgel's reading these tensions disclose the masque's misogyny, its project of disarming martial women. It is, he says, 'more a mirror of the king's mind than the queen's' and is 'a good example of absolutist mystification'.[39] Yet the same argument points to the disturbing impact of Anne's performance, on which James's validation rested. Since he could not affirm his power without at some level evoking the female, the theatrical consequence was to promote women's performance, setting masculine and feminine at odds. Moreover, Jonson ratcheted up the tension by depicting female virtue in terms far removed from the ideals of chastity, silence, and obedience that were normally invoked for women. The masquers' roles made for a display of transgressive female heroism. Led by the Amazon Penthesilea, the other women included Camilla (a Volscian queen who fought Aeneas), Thomyris (a Scythian queen who fought Cyrus), Artemisia (who supported Xerxes in battle), Hypsicratea (Queen of Pontus and enemy of Pompey), Zenobia (who led the Palmyrenes against Rome), Valasca (who usurped the Bohemian crown from her husband), the Ostrogoth Amalasunta, and the British warrior Boadicea. Had Jonson wanted to express female virtue conventionally, he could have chosen more passive forebears, but by opting for women remembered in history or pseudo-history – itself a departure in masques, which normally used allegorical or mythological figures – the imagery foregrounded military and political renown, and implied a continuum of male/female conflict. Of course, the witches' defeat betokened the masquers' ideological conformity, showing that punishments lay in wait for seriously unruly women, and the queens' histories were not spelt out in the hall (where allusion was made simply to their names) but were apparent only to readers of Jonson's narrative. Still, the costuming, with crowns, bared breasts, and military sashes, and the 'full triumphant music' (720), amply made the point that these were women to be reckoned with, not passive objects of the male gaze. The masque songs made no reference to James, and the presiding, female deity was the goddess Fame, whose 'brows the clouds invade' (727) though her feet were on the ground. It was 'her triumphs' (773) with which festivities ended.

The difficulties the masque had in reconciling the tensions in this project were apparent in Fame's genealogy as Perseus described it when scaring away the witches:

> So should, at Fame's loud sound and Virtue's sight,
> All poor and envious witchcraft fly the light.
> I did not borrow Hermes' wings, nor ask
> His crooked sword, nor put on Pluto's casque,
> Nor on mine arm advanced wise Pallas' shield –
> By which, my face aversed, in open field
> I slew the gorgon – for an empty name:
> When Virtue cut off Terror, he gat Fame.
> And if, when Fame was gotten, Terror died,
> What black Erinyes or more hellish pride
> Durst arm these hags, now she is grown and great,
> To think they could her glories once defeat?
> I was her parent, and I am her strength.
> Heroic Virtue sinks not under length
> Of years or ages, but is still the same
> While he preserves, as when he got, Good Fame.   (368–83)

In his character as Heroic Virtue, Perseus represents himself as Fame's father, a striking aspect of his claim being that Fame lacks a mother. Perseus is Fame's lone 'parent' (380), as if she was born through parthenogenesis, the mother being absorbed into the father, and the father projecting himself into an intense and quasi-incestuous relationship with his daughter.[40] Yet this victory is quixotic. The aphorism about Virtue begetting Fame in the act of killing Terror disturbingly conflates sexual congress with physical violence, as if Medusa's killing is the sexual act from which Fame is born; and Perseus' continuing power depends on recapitulating this act from moment to moment, for he cannot 'sink ... under length of years' – making him little more than a phallus, held perpetually erect as that primal scene is endlessly replayed. Additionally, Perseus' hyper-masculinity is troubled by the persistence of the feminine, particularly by the Erinyes, as he metaphorically calls the witches. In Greek myth, after Perseus killed Medusa he was pursued by her sisters, the other gorgons, but – perhaps through a Freudian slip that reveals the psychological work informing this little etiological fable – the masque substitutes the Erinyes or Furies for them.[41] The Erinyes were vengeful goddesses who pursued Orestes after he killed his mother, Clytemnestra, and whose anger was assuaged only by Pallas Athena – the goddess associated with Queen Anne, who gave Perseus his shield, and to whom he gave Medusa's head in token of thanks. It is difficult not to read this mythological slip, and the speech's knotty syntax and sliding pronouns, as symptomatic of Perseus' guilt towards the woman through whose death he asserts ownership of his daughter, Fame, and indicative of the masque's internal conflict as it praises the heroism of the martial queens while representing virtue as male violence towards the female. Perseus – who did not, in fact, kill Medusa 'in open field' but in her sleep, and with help from Pallas, the Graiae, and the nymphs – may look like a triumphant male, but he is besieged by assertive women: Medusa, the Erinyes, Pallas, Fame, the queens. Far from erasing the feminine, the masque positioned Perseus as endlessly at war with it. Jacobean kingship could not disentangle itself from the female as completely as the fiction seems to propose.

On the surface, *Queens* endorses the primacy of masculine power. Perseus boasts about his killing of Medusa and argues that, since James is more famous than Fame can proclaim (432–5), it is inevitable that heroines should gather in his honour. However, the manoeuvre which disrupts the masque's sexual politics is its failure wholly to repudiate the witches. In the sequence of Stuart festivals, *Queens* is especially significant as the first full exercise in binary form. This was the earliest occasion when antimasque and masque were set as polar opposites, structured into precise antitheses between witches and queens, spells and hymns, 'ugly hell' (24–5) and House of Fame. So exact was the symmetry that witches and queens mirrored each other perfectly: there were eleven witches led by a Dame, just as Queen Anne led eleven ladies, and the witches' grotesque dancing was a precise reversal of courtly dance codes, performed back to back and counterclockwise, as they 'do all things contrary to the custom of men' (447–8). Yet while Fame's trumpet blew the witches away, they were not destroyed but returned in the main masque, led in as the queens' captives and incorporated into Fame's (female) dispensation. As Jonson tells it

In the heat of their dance on the sudden was heard a sound of loud music, as if many instruments had given one blast. With which, not only the hags themselves but their hell into which they ran quite vanished, and the whole face of the scene altered, scarce suffering the memory of any such thing, but in the place of it appeared a glorious and magnificent building, figuring the House of Fame.   (354–60)

Here the operative word is 'scarce': the witches were not forgotten but continued to resonate in memory, and were brought in a second time, their power appropriated by the queens who triumphed over them.[42] By enslaving the witches, the queens validated James's order, but they also colonized space they had occupied, rendering the boundary between masque and antimasque permeable rather than absolute. So the masque's binaries were more exclusive in theory than in practice. While the witches' unruly female sisterhood stood as the opposing, mirror image to the queens, in some respects they were their subversive partners.

In the antimasque, the witches were depicted as the King's enemies. Their defeat attested to his sanctity, for as 'faithful opposites / To Fame and Glory' (132–3), they 'hate to see these fruits of a soft peace, / And curse the piety gives it such increase' (144–5). They disturbed his government by calling up storms, but despite their efforts he survived their malice. This paid tribute to James's well-known expertise in witchcraft, which Jonson further saluted by citing his *Demonology* (1597) in the marginalia, referring to it ahead of all the other scholarship on witch-lore that he quoted. James had personal reasons for this interest, for in the 1590–1 witch-panic it was claimed that witches raised the storms which prevented Anne from sailing from Denmark to Scotland, and that the Earl of Bothwell intrigued with them against him. James attended the interrogations, which seemed to substantiate the ideological point that the devil was the King's ultimate enemy, the sacrosanct status of the office meaning that the power of kingship and power of Satan inversely reinforced one another.[43] As James said, he attended the trials 'because I see the pride of these witches and their friends, which cannot be prevented but by mine own presence', and *Demonology* argued that only kings and magistrates could detect witches, since their authority was God-given: 'for where God begins justly to strike by his lawful lieutenants, it is not in the devil's power to defraud or bereave him of the office, or the effect of his powerful revenging sceptre'.[44] So when in *Queens* the witches attempted to repeat their crime, their failure to raise a storm demonstrated James's superior, divinely ordained magic. His presence prevented their spells from taking effect.

Yet as Diane Purkiss notes, the masque also supplied simpler motivations for the witches' failure.[45] They were defeated as much by their own incompetence as by James's magic: their irrational expectation that incantations would draw curses onto Whitehall. Jonson endowed them with folk-beliefs, superstitions, and popular follies (most backed up from classical sources but some taken from mere 'vulgar fable[s]'),[46] and each was named for an intellectual or moral flaw rather than supernatural evil: Ignorance,

Suspicion, Credulity, Falsehood, Murmur, Malice, Impudence, Slander, Execration, Bitterness, Rage, and Mischief (117–31). Their enmity was, then, partly a matter of intellectual delusion: they supposed themselves to have secret abilities, and failed to understand that no amount of charms would raise Hecate – hence their increasingly violent frustration when their magic failed. In the masque scheme, such stupidity was the obverse of James's royal wisdom, but it also echoed the more circumspect attitude towards witchcraft that he adopted after 1597, when he withdrew his general commission for prosecutions and focused on exposing cases of fraud or fantasy. One did not have to be a witch-expert to see that Jonson's witches were deluded, but the effect was to dilute the specifically sacramental aura of James's authority, redrawing the line between witches and queens in social rather than moral terms. If the witches were poor ignorant women and victims of their own stupidity, the aristocratic queens could not be faulted on the same grounds. They inhabited by right of status that terrain of power of which the witches could only dream.

Perseus' speech limits the queens' freedom by stressing their subordination to the monarch. Even as Bel-Anna took her seat in the House of Fame, she acted out her duty as consort:

> She this embracing with a virtuous joy,
> Far from self-love, as humbling all her worth
> To him that gave it, hath again brought forth
> Their names to memory, and means this night
> To make her once more visible to light;
> And to that light, from whence her truth of spirit
> Confesseth all the lustre of her merit.   (425–31)

The pronouns are ambiguous (there are no preceding referents), but 'him' probably means James, and 'that light' the intellectual and moral illumination emanating from him. Anne's fame is sourced to her husband's glory, and she disclaims improper agency by 'humbling ... her worth' to him. Even so, Perseus had only moments before affirmed that her promotion to the House of Fame was conferred by the other queens, not by her consort (414–24), and his terminology of 'worth' and 'merit' was uncomfortably at odds with the moral relativism that lurked in the concept of Fame, especially as exemplified by the heroines that Fame had promoted. In Virgil's *Aeneid*, to which Jonson specifically alludes,[47] 'Fama' is more properly 'rumour', the force that blows news around the world indiscriminately, promulgating truth and falsehood alike: fame can thus be good or bad, deserving or undeserved. The masque tidied up the concept by referring to

'Good Fame, that's out of Virtue born' (729), implying that only meritorious queens were remembered, but this begged the question of what virtues Anne's queens were celebrated for. Clearly, these 'brave', 'warlike', and 'bold' women (399–409) were not notable solely for moral integrity. Rather, to construct its line of famous queens, the masque advanced a form of female self-realization which it struggled to represent as humble obedience. In this respect the queens truly did carry on where the witches left off.

The Masque of Queens discloses strains in the management of James's authority which could not be readily ignored or discharged. The masquers did not displace James's ideological centrality, for the fable insisted on the priority of male power, both in myth and in practice. As Lawrence Normand points out, the name of the gorgon that Perseus killed means, etymologically, 'the queen'.[48] But neither were the women easily contained, and while the masque vindicated James's fatherly authority, it was everywhere disrupted by feminine assertion which, if not exactly subverting his power, did not straightforwardly endorse it either. This was a tension that arose ineluctably from the conflict-based model in which Jonson cast Jacobean paternalism. With James's fatherly rule expressed as the crushing of female disobedience, the power of the topmost partner was affirmed by the violence of the resistance which he overcame: the harder the struggle, the more emphatic his victory. But this was a recipe for instability, for it depended on the presumption of conflicts which could neither be resolved nor transcended. It locked James into an iconography that associated kingship with the assertion of force, and it fixed Anne into oppositional postures, her otherness being the necessary precondition out of which James's masculine authority was manufactured. *The Masque of Queens* thus signalled contradictions inherent in James's self-representation and marked a limit beyond which Anne's masquing could not go. In masques staged beyond the court, such as *The Coleorton Masque* in Leicestershire (1618), it was possible to have Amazons that upheld 'the precedency of female virtue' (220) and were unambiguously praised: 'Men match, though not exceed you' (290).[49] In this safely remote celebration, 'Juno [had] her will of Jove' (270). But it is symptomatic of the hotter temperatures generated by such things at Whitehall that when, in the same year, Lady Hay attempted to stage her own masque of ladies, with herself as queen of the Amazons, the occasion was cancelled at royal command.[50]

In one masque, at Shrovetide 1633, Henrietta Maria seems deliberately to have harked back to Anne's festive modes. In this show, for which financial records survive but no text, she and her ladies danced with swords and

5 Inigo Jones, costume design for *Love Freed*, 1611.

helmets, while the antimasquers were dressed as witches, furies, 'wanton women', 'roaring girls', and a queen of Vices who was perhaps their leader.[51] However, Amazons were not Henrietta Maria's usual style. She donned Amazon dress in *Salmacida Spolia* (see chapter 10 below), but in this show the Amazon helped the king, and the Shrovetide masque was virtually the only other instance.[52] As far as we can tell, it was relatively uncontentious. Payments for shepherd costumes, and the appearance of male courtiers as antimasquers (instead of professional actors), imply a light-hearted tone, while the polarity between queen of Vices and queen of Amazons suggests a moralistic affair. More importantly, evidence from the period as a whole indicates that Henrietta Maria's performances, for all their visibility, were more decorous than Anne's. When in *Chloridia* (1631) she received an

6 Inigo Jones, costume design for *Luminalia*, 1638.

apotheosis conferred by Fame, provocative implications like those in *Queens* were avoided. As the goddess Chloris, Henrietta Maria was beautiful but unthreatening, her power being used merely to discipline that rebel child, Cupid. Similarly, the contrast between Inigo Jones's designs for the two queens is very striking (see figures 5 and 6). Whereas Anne's ladies frequently and recklessly displayed their legs, shoulders, and décolletage, Henrietta Maria exposed her breasts only for *Chloridia*, and thereafter maintained unimpeachably decent coverage of her limbs. Indeed, so enveloping were the gowns for *Luminalia* (1638) that one wonders how her ladies' dancing skills could have been appreciated. Presumably their performance depended on collective patterns and elegant attitudes rather than the footwork, which must have been invisible.[53] Even when the ladies cross-dressed in *Artenice* and *The Shepherd's Paradise*, Jones designed generously cut skirts that were essentially variants of female costume.[54] They could hardly have been further from the 'whorish' displays of Prynne's imagination. Female excess was supplanted by new modes of modesty and restraint.

Henrietta Maria's more circumscribed approach to masque performance was necessitated by her comparatively dependent position. Only fifteen when she arrived in England in 1625, she was accompanied by a French household which buffered her with spiritual and social chaperones, and when a year later many of her French attendants were expelled, her establishment was integrated into the personnel of the English court (Charles surrounded her with established courtier families, especially the Villiers kinship network).[55] She was, then, less free to make her own identity than Anne had been. However, her household remained financially and structurally distinct from the King's, and she exhibited her own tastes from early on, reinforced by vigorous literary and artistic patronage that made her court a centre of richly cosmopolitan cultural activity.[56] Her self-presentation was shaped by the twin motifs of neoplatonic beauty and Catholic exemplarity, cultural strands that crossed the channel with her. This iconography was not incompatible with Charles's, and in most masques husband and wife were presented as partners, using imagery that underlined their reciprocal devotion. Nonetheless, her masques' repertoire of visual and intellectual motifs projected a political identity that diverged significantly from Charles's resolutely British and isolationist profile.

As Karen Britland emphasizes,[57] Henrietta Maria's culture was defined by her Bourbon heritage, and by her keen interest in continental affairs, driven by a relationship with her mother, Marie de' Médici, and her brother, Louis XIII, that was close, if fraught (because mother and brother were frequently at loggerheads, Marie eventually being forced into exile by Richelieu, her son's first minister). *Chloridia, Tempe Restored, Florimène, The Temple of Love,* and *Luminalia* all borrowed extensively from French and Médici festivals, and by appropriating these models they not only marked a new stage in the development of masque form but indicated an outlook characterized by strong awareness of European associations and priorities.[58] Unlike Anne's German relatives, who were comparatively minor players in Europe, the Bourbon kings were ranking powers, so that events in France impacted significantly onto English consciousness: Charles's foreign policy oscillated around the problem of how to avoid being outflanked by his great rivals, France and Spain. Henrietta Maria's Francophile masques foregrounded her status as a princess of France as well as England, and, unlike Charles's inward-looking festivals, referenced her identity to a wider European context. Her cultural difference was always presented as intrinsic, signalling international links that brought England friends and prestige, and spelling out her determination to keep Whitehall within the Bourbon–Médici dynastic orbit. It also gave her masques a more programmatic identity than had ever been the case with Anne's.

These preferences put Henrietta Maria near the centre of Whitehall's French lobby, which wanted close ties with France in order to counter-balance Spain and, perhaps, support for military intervention to recover the Palatinate, the hereditary lands in Germany belonging to Charles's brother-in-law, the Prince Elector, which he lost following his confrontation with the Habsburgs (see chapter 8 below). However, Charles's 'capacity to separate his decision-making from his personal affections'[59] meant that until 1639 Henrietta Maria's practical impact on politics remained limited, and her own politics were complicated by her Catholicism, by Whitehall's shifting and unfocused factionalism, by Charles's reluctance for war, and by the fact that after 1630, when Marie de' Médici was forced from Paris, her strongest overseas ties were with the opposition to Richelieu. While remaining 'energetically loyal to ... the French royal family and its associates',[60] Henrietta Maria was surrounded by Parisian exiles plotting to undermine the Cardinal, a situation which compromised her value as an advocate for a coherent overseas policy and helped to cloud Whitehall's already intrigue-ridden climate. Nonetheless, she was always unfriendly to pro-Spanish courtiers such as Portland and Windebank, and her circle attracted figures such as the Marquis of Hamilton and Earls of Holland, Northumberland, Leicester, and Carlisle, who were aggressively anti-Spanish and enthusiasts for the Protestant cause – and some of whom, in more divided times, were by no means loyal subjects.[61] Despite her religious differences, she shared the sympathy for the Palatine family, and was very attentive to her nephews, Charles Louis and Rupert, when they visited England in 1636 to solicit Charles's support. A little before, a draft for a masque in the French style had been sketched for her by the Lutheran poet Georg Rudolph Weckherlin, one of the secretaries for foreign tongues and a devoted supporter of the Palatines; it was probably not performed, but its themes of national moral reform anticipated the motifs of Carew's *Coelum Britannicum*.[62] So although the group around the Queen was very hetero-geneous and its politics were inconsistent, its effect was to entangle Charles in just those European affairs from which it was his instinct to distance himself.

The ideological impact of these political relationships was affected by the ethically and socially conservative aspects of Henrietta Maria's neoplatonism, and by her confessional situation as a Catholic princess living in a Protestant state. Undoubtedly the neoplatonic vogue with which she was identified had a feminist thrust, insofar as it licensed a secular woman-worship in which collective devotion was orchestrated into the service of a mistress admired for her virtue as well as beauty. Platonic love, which eventually percolated into every corner of the court's masques, plays, and romances, promoted what Tomlinson calls 'a cult of woman, or focus on the feminine'[63] of which Henrietta Maria was the centre and which gave her political activity social purchase. Often dismissed as mere preciosity or frivolousness – which it sometimes was – platonic love advanced the claims of women to be considered on an equal footing with men. It fostered a habit of idealized gallantry that emphasized female dignity, the woman's intellectual partnership with her admirers, and her moral leadership of her group. It thus enhanced confidence in the woman's ability to function freely in social life, though at the cost of sublimating her sexuality, and accepting strict ethical restraints. As Erica Veevers has shown, the cultural roots of platonic love were devotional, and lay in French Catholic spiritual practice, particularly the 'Devout Humanism' of St François de Sales, which sought to synthesize secular values of morality and civility with an aesthetic strain of piety associated with the Franciscan and Capuchin orders.[64] This brand of platonism combined elegant etiquette and social grace with high-minded ideals of discretion, chastity, and fidelity, allowing the practitioner to maintain inner devotion while participating outwardly in the pleasures of court life. In practice, these ideals were not always upheld (notably, by the Queen's gentleman usher Henry Jermyn, whose sexual continence fell well short), and platonic love was satirized by hostile observers as just another kind of coquetry. Nonetheless, it added to the options for women, and confirmed the reputation of Henrietta Maria's court as a space of intense female activity, while pinning that behaviour to moral and social codes that were supposed to be rigorously observed. Her portraits, with their characteristic combination of sartorial elegance and psychological inwardness, convey the image of a princess who legitimately occupies the role of leader of fashion because beneath this graceful exterior she is intelligent, poised, and serious.

Living in an establishment dominated by clerics and shaped by daily religious observances, Henrietta Maria was also acutely conscious of the obligations conferred by her faith. Indeed, at her departure from Paris, her mother gave her instructions urging her to follow the biblical example of Esther, and lead her husband and people back to the true church.[65] Unlike Queen Anne, she practised her religion openly, actively supporting Catholics, and fostering a Marian cult; her Catholicism was a visible aspect of her national difference. Inigo Jones built her a chapel at Somerset House where she was attended by twelve priests and public masses were held, her household becoming a place of resort for aristocratic Catholics. Sensing a shift in the religious climate, the Pope accredited two agents to her court, Gregorio Panzani and George Con, who built a *dévot* party at Whitehall, and some sensational conversions took place, such as Walter Montagu's and Lady Newport's. Charles tolerated all this activity since the Queen's religious freedom was protected by the marriage treaty. He was interested in the ceremoniousness of Catholic ritual and saw some value in fostering ecumenism, but he limited toleration to Whitehall's privileged spaces, and his personal commitment to Protestant doctrine was never in doubt.[66] However, Henrietta Maria's proselytizing aroused concern amongst a wider public which, unaware of the nuances, feared that Whitehall was becoming home to a Catholic fifth column. It conflicted with Charles's role as defender of the faith, and helped to undermine his credibility as a national religious figurehead.[67]

This impression was intensified by the Queen's masques, into which the language and imagery of Marian devotion frequently bled. The clearest example is Willliam Davenant's *Luminalia* (1638),[68] which presented her as the 'goddess of brightness' seated in 'a glory with rays' (18), chasing away darkness and making Britain a sanctuary for the muses and their 'prophetic priests' (2), the flamens and arch-flamens. The muses and flamens, said the argument, had been forced into hiding by 'barbarous Goths and vandals' (1), and while the idea of their return offered a generalized image of cultural renovation, Veevers points out how readily it resonated with the existence of an English Catholic underground now increasingly coming into public view.[69] Moreover, the masque's subtitle, 'The Festival of Light', alluded to the Purification (Candlemas), a feast associated with the Virgin and celebrated by the ritual lighting of candles, a practice which was defended in Anthony Stafford's recent treatise on the Virgin, *The Female Glory* (1635), and which some feared was creeping back into the English church.[70] Jones's design for the first scene was copied from a painting on an incident from the Virgin's life, Adam Elsheimer's *The Flight into Egypt*,[71] and the link was underlined by the poet Francis Lenton in *Great Britain's Beauties* (1638), which memorialized the performance with acrostics on the masquers, several of which play on 'Mary's blest name'.[72] *Luminalia* did not explicitly proselytize for Catholicism, but perhaps spectators understood it as endorsing similarities between the religions and possibilities for ecumenism. It unmistakably showcased the cultural values of Henrietta Maria's faith, and demonstrates how easily her masques' ornate rituals, privileging of visual display, and praise of female beauty could be taken as the secular counterpart to her religious beliefs.

The classic account of the conjunction of religion and aesthetics in Henrietta Maria's masques comes in the explanatory appendix added by Jones to the printed text of *Tempe Restored* (1632).[73] Here Jones explains that the Queen's performance as Divine Beauty was intended to lead the viewer towards spiritual elevation and moral refinement. Divine Beauty, he says, exemplified the power of a heavenly inclination, working through the physical body, to raise the soul into an enlightened idea of its material and spiritual well-being. A 'divine beam coming from above', her beauty chan-nelled spiritual influence to earth, and instructed viewers in 'all the happiness which can be enjoyed here below' (104) – a function dramatized in her relationship to Heroic Virtue, the role projected onto the King as principal spectator. The logic of Jones's analysis requires there to be a perfect equiv-alence between the masque's aesthetic and moral effect, since it was through the spectators' responses to the show's visual pleasures that their inner impulses were disposed into harmony: 'So that corporeal beauty, consisting in symmetry, colour, and certain unexpressable graces, shining in the Queen's majesty, may draw us to the contemplation of the beauty of the soul, unto which it hath analogy' (104). Jones's summary makes clear that he understood Henrietta Maria's masquing as legitimate in ways that Anne's was not, and that for him it was overtly ideological. He divides *Tempe Restored* into sharp hierarchies, between body and soul, above and below, inside and out, and this makes for a forcefully allegorical reading, the action's embodiment in imagery or performance being coordinated with a higher, ethical meaning which spectators were expected to decode. All Henrietta Maria's masques referred themselves to a divine master-narrative enshrined in the universe's aesthetic beauty, a beauty imitated in the harmonies of masque form. The disadvantage of such designs was their ineluctable drift towards the mystical: each masque tended to pull out of the here and now and into a spiritual frame of reference. However, this was mitigated by the neoplatonic insistence that the spiritual could be embodied in the corporal, and not merely symbolized by it, permitting the body to re-enter the masque as the incarnation of moral perfection. As *Luminalia* put it, Henrietta Maria was 'a terrestrial beauty in whom intellectual and corporeal brightness are joined' (13): her physical beauty not only pointed to moral beauty but manifested it, bringing heaven and earth into conjunction. This allowed the display of her person to be licensed as ethically desirable in itself.

From this perspective, Henrietta Maria's masques sought to hold up her beauty for love and admiration without drawing the observer into erotically turbulent waters. Here it is crucial that she was known to enjoy a happy domestic life, with her sexual desires amply fulfilled in marriage. Unlike

7 Peter Paul Rubens, *Landscape with St George and the Dragon, c.* 1630.

James and Anne, Charles and Henrietta Maria cohabited enthusiastically, and the masques brought this knowledge into play by staging each fiction as an erotic encounter between husband and wife. Since Charles liked to dance in his festivals, Henrietta Maria's masques took the shape of conversations with her husband more readily than Anne's had done, and each evoked the motif of the romantic quest. Charles led the way to this, since his panegyric had encouraged a turn towards romance. For example, Rubens painted an allegory of Charles as St George, exchanging tokens with Henrietta Maria over the dead body of the dragon, while grateful onlookers expressed their thanks and the sun broke through clouds over a distant landscape (see figure 7).[74] This impressive painting articulates Caroline values as Charles sought to project them *c.* 1629–30, depicting him as his realm's knightly protector and guarantor of its peace. The landscape incorporates recognizable buildings, including Lambeth Palace, home of the archbishop of Canterbury, and the dragon alludes in a general way to threats to Charles's people, whether warfare, corruption, or vice.[75] But, typically for Charles, this St George is detached from religious extremism (he is patron of England rather than Protestant champion, and the dragon is not obviously linked to the Pope), and the theme is subtly eroticized. St George is calm and relaxed after battle, and his relationship with the lady is central, emphasizing their mutual devotion and absorption in one another. Many other paintings would depict king and queen as a bourgeois partnership, surrounded by their children in harmonious domesticity, but here the sexual charge is palpable. Ringed by amazed spectators still recovering from their shock, the couple's private chemistry is the calm glowing centre, distilling the energies of freshly accomplished combat and drawing psychological depth into what is in other respects a public painting. The royal union was similarly enshrined as a romantic quest in poetic celebrations, such as Edmund Waller's verses on Charles's visit to Madrid, which have him falling in love en route with Henrietta Maria merely by glimpsing her dancing at the Louvre.[76] In the masques this motif became foundational for articulating Charles's sexual and political identity.

Caroline political culture used Charles's virtuous love for Henrietta Maria to express in domestic form the political values that ought to inform the public world. Husband and wife embodied authority and loving obedience (respectively), their mutual desire and esteem providing the private model for the subject's public relationship to the King.[77] In masque after masque, the King's power aspires to, and is tutored by, the Queen's love. However, this motif brought two problems: it ran the risk of effeminizing Charles, as a king in thrall to feminine allure, and for all the neoplatonic emphasis on the coordination of beauty with virtue, it endowed Henrietta Maria with a distinctly erotic power. Certainly those critics are wrong who see Caroline neoplatonism as a bloodless business; as Caroline Hibbard notes, the Queen spent half the 1630s in a state of pregnancy.[78] Even more literally than the celebration of James's paternal virility, Charles's political potency was encoded in his role as heroic physical lover. For example, Jonson's ode for Henrietta Maria's twenty-first birthday compares her to Venus wearing the ceston that made her sexually irresistible, then segues into Charles's performance on the tiltyard:

> See, see our active king
> Hath taken twice the ring
>   Upon his pointed lance;
> While all the ravished rout
> Do mingle in a shout,
>   Hey! for the flower of France![79]

These lines invoke the erotic implications of running at the ring with provocative literalness, wryly alluding to the private bodily satisfactions of

Charles's chivalry. As the final stanza suggests, the recent birth of a new prince showed that his 'pointed lance' had been successful in other tilts too. Similarly, in *Luminalia*, Davenant, comparing the King and Queen to angels, says their state is preferable because it is embodied: although angels are 'not perplexed with what we sexes call', the royal virtue is better 'because 'tis conjugal' (20). But this persistent sexualizing of the marriage put uncommon stress on Charles's ardour and private passions. By depicting him always as an amorous monarch, it risked exposing him to criticisms of uxoriousness.

These ambiguities beset the masques' presentation of Charles. In *Love's Triumph through Callipolis*, he danced in the person of Heroic Love, questing for union with Beauty. Here his heroism was expressed as desire, albeit desire legitimated by its intellectual control and virtuous objective. Whereas the antimasquers were foolish, frantic lovers, intemperate and sensual, Charles's love was 'chaste', 'the right affection of the mind, / The noble appetite of what is best, / Desire of union with the thing designed' (52, 54–6). The masque thus sanctioned his passion in its nuptial aspect, though at the cost of putting the masquers into avowedly sexual postures:

> Here stay a while. This, this
> The temple of all Beauty is!
> Here, perfect lovers, you must pay
> First fruits, and on these altars lay
> (The ladies' breasts) your ample vows,
> Such as Love brings, and Beauty best allows! (115–20)

Charles was admired for his vigour, but his masculinity was frankly sensual and had to be controlled by a worthy object. *Love's Triumph* sublimated the disruptive aggression of chivalry into the mutual orderliness of marriage, and by doing so it promoted Henrietta Maria into the icon of femininity that validated his exertions: 'Love must have answering love to look upon' (122).

A year later, in Townshend's *Albion's Triumph*,[80] sexual politics were more circumspectly handled. Charles was again a questing hero – Albanactus, dancing in honour of the goddess Alba – but this time he was subjugated by desire, 'subdued to love and chastity' (75), his relationship with the Queen pointedly subordinate. Cupid and Diana shot the masquers with arrows, and 'having conquered the conqueror' (75), the chorus urged the men to put off their fierceness:

> Ye worthies of this isle,
> That led by your brave chief

> In an heroic style,
> Have over-done belief,
>   Subdued by Alba's eyes,
>   Come down, Love's sacrifice!   (84)

The song urged the masquers to 'come down' literally from the stage to the dance floor, but implied that their masculine potency, displayed in their roles as Roman soldiers, would be moderated by the women, a dangerous tumescence contained by female virtue. Charles, the 'straight cedar, that hast stood / The shock of many a wind' (85), yielded phallic stiffness to his wife, and the chorus sang of a progeny that was born without any sexual act, apparently through a congress of the intellect that by-passed the body altogether:

> So hand in hand live many a day,
> And may your virtuous minds beget
> Issue that never shall decay,
> And so be fruitful every way.   (86)

In Carew's *Coelum Britannicum* (1634) these tensions were even more extreme. Here the entire premise was erotic: Charles's relationship with Henrietta Maria was so perfectly chaste that the gods themselves – normally busy with 'incests, rapes, [and] adulteries' (76)[81] – had decided to reform Olympus after the Caroline model. This wittily complimented Charles for his sexual control, but it meant that the masque was especially preoccupied with deviant or illicit sexuality, much of it voiced by the scoffing god Momus, who brought down the tone by cataloguing the Olympian pro- miscuity that needed to be reformed. Charles's sexual conduct was held up for imitation, but in bizarrely literalistic ways: to honour their 'great example of matrimonial union', said Momus, Jupiter had the name 'CARLOMARIA' set over his bedroom door (173–6). Such double-edged compliments spelled out the contradictions inherent in praising Charles's domestic chivalry while at the same time affirming his continence. The dangers of desire were further imaged in two seductive goddesses, Tiche (Fortune) and Hedone (Pleasure), and the heroic British knights led in by Charles were controlled as well as inspired by the Queen:

> For though you [the ladies] seem like captives led
>   In triumph by the foe away,
> Yet on the conqueror's neck you tread,
>   And the fierce victor proves your prey.
> What heart is then secure from you,
> That can, though vanquished, yet subdue?   (1042–7)

In the sensual eroticism of Carew's myth, Henrietta Maria's love was the hero's prize, her body a sexual Eden that, though infinitely pleasurable, was also free from guilt. Her love absolved Charles from the perils of lascivious sexuality while permitting him legitimately to indulge bodily pleasures. In this paradise's primal scene, she was both wife and mother, sensually overwhelming yet innocently enjoyable:

> These are th'Hesperian bowers, whose fair trees bear
> Rich golden fruit, and yet no dragon near ...
> Pace forth, thou mighty British Hercules,
> With thy choice band, for only thou and these
> May revel here, in Love's Hesperides.   (933–4, 944–6)

The British future lay in the King's blameless but productive sexuality, shedding 'On the ripe fruits of your chaste bed / Those sacred seeds of love' (1129–30).

Karen Britland observes how the mind/body dualism in Caroline masques worked to absorb Henrietta Maria's national and gender difference into celebration of Charles's heroic potency. Charles appropriated her 'generative capacities' for himself: his masculinity, 'predicated on the monarch's virile conquest of territories conceived as feminine', displaced biological productivity onto his wife while leaving him 'free to inhabit the realms of rational self-identity'.[82] However, as these examples show, the resulting iconography was neither stable nor lacking in tension. In praising Charles for perfect emotional control, the masques needed to place corresponding emphasis on the urgency and excess of his ardour; his outward calm was all the stronger for the violent feelings it kept in check. At the same time, by using this motif the masques advanced Henrietta Maria's status as Charles's intellectual equal, and as moral example for his immaculate yet sexually invigorating love. If Anne's signature role was the cross-dressed goddess Pallas, contesting her husband's political authority, Henrietta Maria was typically associated with the hermaphrodite, which expressed her unity with Charles but brought danger by its suggestions of emasculation. In *Coelum Britannicum* she combined with Charles to form 'Carlomaria'; in *Albion's Triumph* she was part of the 'Mary-Charles, whose minds within / And bodies make but Hymen's twin' (89); and *The Temple of Love* imaged her in Amianteros (chaste love), a figure composed of male and female halves – Sunesis (understanding) and Thelema (will) – in 'mixture ... made one' like the lovers on 'yonder throne'.[83] Hermaphroditism expressed her ambiguous relationship to Charles, inextricably bound to him as partner yet shadowing him with the threat of sexual enfeeblement. The masques had to negotiate this risky convergence between a monarch, whose authority was envisioned as a chivalry at once aggressive and restrained, and a consort whose femininity, though dutiful, was finding its own autonomous sphere of action.

The masques that most imaginatively explored this convergence were *Tempe Restored* (1632) by Jones and Townshend, and *The Temple of Love* (1635) by Jones and Davenant. Drawing on Balthasar de Beaujoyeulx's *Balet comique de la reine* (1581) but stiffened with a moral framework drawn from the Aristotelian philosopher Alessandro Piccolomini, *Tempe Restored* revolved around an opposition between Divine Beauty (Henrietta Maria) and Circe, the Homeric sorceress famous for transforming Ulysses' men into swine.[84] Circe was traditionally associated with the debasing power of sensuality, which makes men beasts, but here her function was more complex. The action opened with a young gentleman escaping from Circe's palace: the 'fugitive favourite' (95) – played by the page and future dramatist Thomas Killigrew – who had been transformed into a lion but managed to flee to the court for aid. He was pursued by Circe, who, accompanying herself on the lute, complained of being abandoned by him, and solaced herself with grotesque antimasques danced by her 'subjects' (96): Indians and barbarians, 'who naturally are bestial' (97), and half-transformed men with animals' heads. Then Harmony and fourteen Influences of the Stars announced the descent of Divine Beauty, who, in a particularly splendid sequence, came down with fourteen Stars, while eight Spheres sitting in clouds sang praises of her loveliness. Her arrival ensured that false love would be corrected, for 'fair and good, inseparably joined, / Create a Cupid that is never blind' (100). However, Circe's reign was not finished, for after the revels she returned to the stage and was attacked by Jupiter, Cupid, and Pallas, each threatening her with punishments. But she was unabashed by their rebukes and stood her ground, retorting that Jupiter and Cupid were no innocents, and that Pallas was a transvestite, a 'man-maid' (102). Although she resigned her power to the King and Queen, the dialogue and Jones's argument make it clear that she did so voluntarily.

Tempe Restored has attracted attention because it marks a theatrical milestone: it was the first English stage performance in which the performers' gender exactly matched their roles, and the first masque for which female performers other than the masquers are named, the text identifying Circe as 'Madam Coniacke' and Harmony as 'Mistress Shepherd'. Hitherto, all masques had involved some element of cross-dressing, for while court festival allowed aristocratic women to dance silently, female parts in the antimasques would be spoken by boys or professional male actors, as on the public stages down to the Civil War. *Tempe Restored* broke with tradition by creating a gender separation in the performance and casting women singers in the major female roles, while making a joke of the performance's one remaining instance of cross-dressing: Circe's sneer at Pallas as a 'man-maid' alluded to her traditionally transvestite appearance, and signalled that this female role was probably taken by a male singer, playing a goddess dressed as a man.[85] As if in a repudiation of Queen Anne's signature motif, the gender-bending Amazon was put down by the 'authentic' woman, but the effect remained radical since it was almost unprecedented for women to speak or sing on the English stage. Probably it reflects the practices Henrietta Maria knew from Parisian ballets, where women of lower social status were permitted to sing.[86] Clearly 'Madam Coniacke' was French, and Karen Britland plausibly associates her with Elizabeth Coignet, one of Henrietta Maria's ladies, who perhaps appeared in *Artenice* and some of the lost festivals of 1625–30. 'Mistress Shepherd' is harder to identify, but Britland suggests that she was Anne Sheppard, a dwarf employed in the Earl of Pembroke's household, who eventually married Richard Gibson the miniaturist (also a dwarf).[87] Male dwarfs frequently appeared in Caroline masques, and Anne Sheppard would have been an appropriate choice to accompany the fourteen Influences, for they were all young aristocratic children. So, like *Artenice* and *The Shepherd's Paradise*, *Tempe Restored* was a leading example of Henrietta Maria's sponsorship of festivals in which women began to find a theatrical voice.

Despite this theatrical radicalism, the masque occupied the usual domestic binaries. As Heroic Virtue, Charles was yoked with his consort, whose Divine Beauty inspired his love, and who eventually joined him on the dais to view the finale. The action set up a ladder of virtue that stretched from the ignorant barbarians, via the hybrid men-monsters, the fugitive favourite fleeing from beastliness and into rationality, and the divine but still incompletely grown Influences, to the royal couple who embodied the perfect moral qualities to which others could only aspire 'and therein [transcended] as far common men as they are above beasts' (104). But in other respects *Tempe Restored* disrupted some customary certainties. In particular, there was no clear separation between masque and antimasque. Not only did Circe return at the end, but her departure after the grotesque dances was merely a pause – she 'retire[d] towards the palace from whence she came' (97), as if resting but not conquered – and the fugitive favourite passed between the two worlds, showing they were contiguous, not mutually exclusive. Moreover, 'sullen Circe' (97) had unusual depth of character.

Although the masque's villain, a seductress and enchantress, she was a victim of love, her 'distempered heart ... stung with Cupid's dart' (97). Her song complaining about the fugitive favourite was a lament that set her in a long tradition of abandoned women and made complex emotional demands on the audience, and her abdication came about not because Jupiter and Cupid commanded it but because it completed her inner trajectory of betrayal, recrimination, and regret. Uniquely among antimasque figures, she learned something during the action and was allowed to develop like a dramatic character. Unusually humanized and capable of engaging interest, she was not entirely contained by the evening's closures: 'Thou hast thy will', she told Jupiter, 'and I have mine' (102). And if, as has been suggested, Elizabeth Coignet was the same person as the 'Frenchwoman, one of the Queen's chapel', 'that sings in masques at court', Circe must have been a complex figure indeed, for this lady was notable for being a 'very deformed gentlewoman, but of a voice incomparable sweet', and was celebrated to that effect in verses by Thomas Randolph.[88] Physically repellent but vocally entrancing, Circe was a living witness to the confusions of desire. Her contradictory singularity allowed her to evade the fixed categories into which masques normally corralled their participants.

In *Tempe Restored*, then, the normal moral separations did not obtain; nor, as a consequence, did the usual neoplatonic link between beauty and virtue.[89] Rather, Circe's world, though dangerous and inhabited by monsters, was still beautiful in itself. She lived in a palace, was addressed as a monarch, and sat, like Charles, in a 'chair of state' (95) to view the antimasques. Unlike masques in which the moral landscape of evil was reflected in dark or grotesque settings, her world appealed to the eye. Instead, as Jones's allegory and the fugitive favourite affirmed, the life of virtue was a matter of intellectual perception, of knowing how to distinguish between the 'appearance of beauty, either true or false' (103). Circe's world may have been inferior to Divine Beauty's, appealing only to the senses, but it was beautiful nevertheless and its powers of attraction, if less, were still real. As Jones's allegory said, Circe did not signify bad desire but 'desire in general, the which hath power on all living creatures, and being mixed of the divine and sensible [i.e. that which is perceptible by the senses], hath diverse effects, leading some to virtue and others to vice' (103). So the masque acknowledged that appetite was morally neutral, and that sensuality had a place even in the good life. The fugitive favourite may have fled from Circe, but desire was integral to the apprehension of virtue as well as of vice. The difference lay in the intellect, which adjudicated between good and bad impulses, symbolized by the figures of Invention and Knowledge on the proscenium (93), and dramatized in the favourite's dilemma, as he struggled to embrace 'reason' and shun 'sense' (95). And desire was equally appropriate for Divine Beauty, whose descent was as much sensually as spiritually overwhelming. The Spheres were moved to ecstasy by her, and hailed her as an 'image men adore' (101), whose visual presence compelled the eyes and made even heavenly music seem dull:

> I cannot blame ye if ye gaze
> And give small ear to what I say,
> For such a presence will amaze,
> And send the senses all one way. (100)

'How are we ravished with delight, / That see the best', they sang (101). The meaning may have been intellectual, but the language and performance were sensual. As Jones said, Divine Beauty appealed to the mind but the body and affections were essential 'instruments' (104). There was, then, no fundamental contradiction between Circe's physical appeals and the Queen's spiritual tutoring. They were differently placed rungs on the ladder to the divine, and in some respects mirrored one another.

So *Tempe Restored* effected a shift in masque ideology, away from customary ethical certainties and magical resolutions. The fugitive favourite feared Circe as an enchantress, but he knew that the real conflict lay elsewhere, for her power depended less on spells than on her victims' intellectual shortcomings:

> 'Tis not her rod, her philtres, nor her herbs
> (Though strong in magic) that can bind men's minds,
> And make them prisoners where there is no wall;
> It is consent that makes a perfect slave,
> And sloth that binds us to lust's easy trades. (95)

This was why he could escape from Circe's palace. He was not all bad, but had an apprehension of his slavery to vice that allowed him to choose reformation. Only men who lacked or misused this faculty of choice – the 'naturally' bestial barbarians, or the 'voluntaries' and 'willing servants' who were content to remain half-animal (97) – were incapable of breaking the spell. Little wonder that Milton seems to have remembered *Tempe Restored* in his *A Masque at Ludlow* (1634), and replayed Jones's fable in the capture of the Lady by Circe's son, Comus. But in Milton's fiction, human will-power alone cannot save the Lady, for it takes Sabrina's sacramental magic to release her captive soul. By contrast, in *Tempe Restored* the ethos was more unequivocally rationalist.[90] The fugitive favourite was responsible for his own moral status, and what counted was his 'consent', whether he made a good choice and was habituated to virtue or not. There is a striking difference here from the *Balet comique de la reine*, in which Circe's magical spells were real and irresistible. She charmed her victims motionless with her wand, and had to be countered with Mercury's moly; the French favourite blamed her, not himself, for his emasculation.[91] But in *Tempe Restored*, everyone had power to make themselves good or bad.

One consequence of this foregrounding of ethical rationalism was to reduce the masque's investment in Charles's kingly magic. In the *Balet comique*, Circe was the enemy of the monarch in particular. She aimed to prevent him from founding his golden age, and his force, rather than the gods', defeated her. At the same time, the French court women had little part in this conflict. The queen and her ladies were helpless victims of Circe's malice, frozen into immobility and needing rescue by the king. All this changed in *Tempe Restored*, which eschewed a gender politics of commanding males and subordinate females. Here the female actors had agency, and the fugitive favourite's sensual slavery was overcome by Henrietta Maria's miraculous beauty, which led men towards that happy conjunction of 'fair and good' (100). As for Charles, although the favourite fled to him for succour, he did not intervene in any practical way. Insofar as he embodied Heroic Virtue he was ideologically central, but his role was exemplary rather than active, the heroic 'prototype' (104), not the magic solution. So while the loving domesticity of King and Queen countered Circe and her favourite's sensual enslavement, the masque obliquely acknowledged continuity as well as difference. The royal couple had a purified, intellectually redeemed version of the relationship between witch and courtier, yet Circe's feelings were neither negligible nor disregarded, and the masque ended with a compromise: although Cupid and Jupiter thought they had won, the resolution depended on her consent, so both sides had their way. Moreover, Henrietta Maria had affinities with her, insofar as she wielded dazzling enchantments to which Charles was no more immune than the fugitive favourite was to Circe's. At the end Circe was not disabled, but handed on her power to 'this matchless pair' who became her 'heir' (102). *Tempe Restored* thus legitimated the Caroline marriage as the model of the state, but played out the sexual politics of that model with uncomfortable clarity. Heroism was a shared activity, and while this reassured the King he had conjugal support, it invested some of the responsibility in his wife. The monarch's virtuous self-restraint took strength from, but also depended on, his susceptibility to desire.

Three years after *Tempe Restored*'s momentous transformations, Henrietta Maria's erotic apotheosis came in *The Temple of Love*, a masque which cast

back to the orientalist excess of *Solomon and the Queen of Sheba*. Here she
played Indamora, Queen of the Indian realm Narsinga, leading out a double
masque of women and men, 'to guide those lovers that want sight / To see
and know what they should love' (A4).[92] Now specifically identified with
platonic love, and brought in by Orpheus, whose harp soothed rude winds
and troubled waves 'into a dance' (C3), she promised to cure the whole
kingdom by freeing it from false desire and teaching it to love properly. She
would disclose the true Temple of Love, which had been hidden by ancient
poets and modern magicians, who 'seduced the more voluptuous race / Of
men to give false worship in our own' (B1). Her arrival provoked regret in the
ancient poets, who realized how shameful their 'loose verse[s]' (A4v) had
been, and she saved the male masquers (noble Persian youths questing for
love), for they would have missed their way had she not cleared the fogs
concealing the temple. The point was not, as the magicians supposed, to deny
love's bodily part, but to harmonize body and soul in a code of conduct
reconciling sexual pleasure with moral restraint. This was an ideal that set the
woman as arbiter, and far from being esoteric or otherworldly, Henrietta
Maria's platonic leadership implied an ultimate power of surveillance over
men's minds. Since she was like 'the morning's light' or purified air, her
presence insinuated itself everywhere: 'her beams into each breast will steal, /
And search what every heart doth mean' (A4). Her objective was union with
the King, and the evening concluded with a hymn to the royal couple as the
perfect embodiment of chaste love, a fusion of understanding and will, male
and female, virtue and appetite. Through platonic love, opposed principles of
being would 'melt' themselves into a single hermaphrodite (C4v–D1).

This masque was much admired for its exoticism, its spectacular Indian and
Persian costumes which drew on imagery and rich material goods that were
part of a burgeoning trade to the far east.[93] Yet here the pejorative association
between female masquing, orientalism, and luxury, that created such tension
in Anne's masques, was recuperated and discharged. Henrietta Maria's oriental
display separated itself from the harem-like indulgences of the magicians, who
realized that if platonic love came in 'we may rid our temple / Of all our
Persian quilts, embroidered couches, / And our standing beds' (B2). Because
she guaranteed intellectual and ethical discipline, she could wield erotic power
without it seeming guilty of excess. As her ladies knew, their Persian lovers
would be both ardent and controlled: 'each shall wear, when they depart, / A
lawful though a loving heart, / And wish you still both strict and kind' (C4).
The masque thus offered a model for a court where orderliness and opulence
were mixed, allowing platonic love to function as moral code and as a socio-
political discipline ensuring the dominance of the royal will. By policing

8 Gerrit van Honthorst, *Mercury Presenting the Liberal Arts to Apollo and Diana*, 1628.

private behaviour, and licensing male self-assertion but bringing it under female restraint, court and state alike would be drawn into a decent conformity, united by the Queen's example. What, then, for Queen Anne was dangerous excess had been normalized for Henrietta Maria. Still, the gender implications of this model were voiced by the magicians, who could not believe that courtiers would be 'persuaded out of the use of their bodies' (B2v), and by the page who attended the Persian youths and feared his masters were now 'so modest too and pure, / So virginly, so coy, and so demure, / That they retreat at kissing, and but name / Hymen or love, they blush for very shame' (C1v). These characters were wrong, of course, and mistook restraint of the body for rejection: the desirability and compliance of the Queen's ladies was as important as their self-control. Nevertheless, their mistake pointed out how challenging to traditional ideas of male identity was the promotion of the Queen's values. The Caroline court may have started to transform the options for women; its cost was anxiety about effeminization amongst the men.

Gerrit van Honthorst's masque-like painting of Apollo, Diana, and Mercury (1628), now at Hampton Court, typifies the cultural politics of early Caroline visual art (see figure 8). It represents Charles and Henrietta

Maria as Apollo and Diana, and images Charles's wish to preside over a cosmopolitan court where peace, learning, and the arts could flourish. They sit at the top left; below, Buckingham pretends to be Mercury presenting them with a train of figures depicting the Liberal Arts, while at the bottom Ignorance and Envy – the two vices on the proscenium of *Tempe Restored* – are being pushed out of the frame. Here Charles and his consort are as a couple, but have little chemistry. Henrietta Maria is blandly characterized, a doll-like figure sitting back from the action, and while he holds her hand, it expresses ownership rather than love. The real emotional bond is between Charles and Buckingham: Buckingham, bathed in light, humbly solicits his master, and Charles leans forward and stretches out his other hand, to welcome the Liberal Arts but also in yearning for his favourite. Buckingham's wife appears too – she heads the procession, pregnant, bare-breasted, and playing that unromantic figure, Grammar – but marriage here is a tool of state, the women being mere adjuncts to the intense personal bond between the men, gazing into each other's eyes. Probably Buckingham commissioned the picture as a gift to celebrate the intimate partnership between generous King and loving servant.[94] But just a few months later he was dead, and the iconography was transformed. In all subsequent portraiture Henrietta Maria occupied the position originally reserved for him. She moved from the margin to the centre.

As Charles's consort, Henrietta Maria's status was always dependent on him, but her marginal place in Honthorst's allegory is revealing for what changed in her subsequent representation. The painting shows how completely the image of Charles in the 1630s shifted from homosocial to heterosexual gender relationships that eroticized the business of kingship and gave the Queen a crucial role in that iconography. In part this change reflects the prestige that came with the birth of Prince Charles, making her the mother of the dynasty and confirming her husband's status as progenitor of the Stuart line: before 1630, his sister's children were next in succession. But it also attests to a shift towards the domestic in Caroline iconography, which relocated the monarch on that boundary between public icon and private individual, depicting him as symbolic father of the nation and as family man, and drawing him into a world of privatized affections and intimacies. Its effect was to give Henrietta Maria a far greater presence than Anne ever had in creating the kingly image. She became not merely a dynastic child-producer but a role-model and domestic linchpin who was admired, loved, valued by her husband, and sexually active. Although portraits of the marriage present her as the subordinate partner, the relationship is deepened with tenderness on both sides, and her portrayal was reinforced by the psychological inwardness and private strength with which Van Dyck, in particular, invested her. Henrietta Maria benefited personally from the shift in cultural climate between Jacobean and Caroline, but also achieved a presence in the iconography of kingship greater than that of any previous English consort.

For Charles, the turn towards the domestic was more problematic. Unlike his father, he did not sit securely above the female, for his iconography was intricately enmeshed with it. His ability to command his private passions did have a political pay-off. It modelled in the domestic sphere that neostoicism which qualified him for rule in the public world, and was part of the encompassing exhibition of his personal discipline, his ability to maintain self-control whether in the bedroom, council chamber, or battlefield. The classic instances are Waller's poem on his calmness in the face of the sea-storm that nearly drowned him in Spain, and Clarendon's famous account of him receiving the news of Buckingham's death while at prayer, which stages the tension between studied public face and intense inner feeling (Charles remained unmoved in public but gave vent to passionate grief once in the privacy of his chamber).[95] The royal love affair allowed this dialectic to be played out daily, though its effect was to introduce into the iconography a tension between his identity as public figure and as private man. With Charles's personal strengths suggested by his ability to command the love of a good woman, and his susceptibility to emotion implying depths that the outward figure nonetheless kept largely concealed, his public persona was usefully humanized. Its cost, though, was to elevate the individual at the expense of the icon, shifting the imagery away from the sacramental and towards the rationalistic, and loosening the symbolic tie between his body and the body of the realm. Arguably, this was a step that helped to bring about the possibility of a more radical disconnection between these roles, not least by exposing Charles to criticisms of uxoriousness. The puritan historian Lucy Hutchinson later claimed that Henrietta Maria applied 'her great wit and parts, and the power her haughty spirit kept over her husband, who was enslaved in his affection only to her', and drew the moral that 'wherever male princes are so effeminate as to suffer women of foreign birth and different religions to intermeddle with the affairs of state, it is always found to produce sad desolations'.[96] Hutchinson was writing in the 1660s, by which time the Queen had long been demonized as an evil Catholic seductress. Still, the roots of that view lay in the royal love affair delineated in the masques.

There were no family pictures of James and Anne. Viscount Haddington owned a pair of individual portraits, but in her portraiture Anne is usually painted facing to the right, a device which ensures the pictures could not be hung as mirror images to her husband, and the only lifetime image in which she accompanies her husband is an engraving from early in the reign.[97] In no portrait does James ever seem to be holding his feelings in check – or, indeed, have many feelings to speak of. Rather, James's imagery represented him as displacing the feminine. His masques praised him for amazingly self-sufficient potency and overflowing bounty, a fantasy of plenitude and nurturing power which absorbed and replaced his wife's generative function. In *Hymenaei* the King was the mother whose 'sacred pain' (426) delivered the new British realm, and in *Mercury Vindicated* he was a glorious sun fathering his 'creatures' (206) on the goddess Nature. In *The Vision of Delight*, his presence caused a miraculously premature spring: his beams had 'got proud earth with child' (176). The most extreme version of this motif came in *Oberon*, danced to mark Prince Henry's coming to manhood, where James was hailed as a new creation:

> He makes it ever day and ever spring
> Where he doth shine, and quickens every thing
> Like a new nature, so that true to call
> Him by his title is to say, he's all. (354–7)

Not only was James nature itself, but *Oberon* tutored his son – whose marital future was rising on the political agenda – in the avoidance of love. The dialogue between the satyrs and the wanton nymph Echo, and the satyrs' taunting of the moon for her lovesickness, situated the feminine as that which needed to be repressed. A decade later, Charles's masques as Prince of Wales took a no less instrumental attitude to sexual passion. *Pleasure Reconciled to Virtue* urged him to leave 'the labyrinth of beauty' (295), and not 'grow soft or wax effeminate' (211); and *Neptune's Triumph*, performed after his return from Madrid without the bride he had gone to collect, celebrated his escape from sirens who had threatened the bond between father, son, and favourite. The iconography surrounding Charles as Prince demonstrates how radical was this shift in Caroline culture, and how novel was the space that opened up for feminized values. In their transformed gender relations, the Caroline masques shattered the iconography of masculine power and female resentment inherited from James and Henry. In doing so they imagined remarkable new roles for women, but started to unsettle some of that male authority which had been foundational for Stuart political culture. William Prynne's 'Women actors, notorious whores' testified to the power, and the unsettling impact, of that change.

CHAPTER 6

The revival of chivalry

On Twelfth Night 1606, the evening after *Hymenaei*'s mystical celebrations for the Essex–Howard wedding, a rather different performance took place at Whitehall. Two identically dressed women appeared in the Banqueting House, each claiming to represent Truth but acting as spokeswomen for propositions that were diametrically opposed. The first announced that marriage, 'the most honoured state of man and wife, / Doth far exceed th'insociate virgin life' (711–12), and argued that domestic union was a sanctuary outside which there could be no comfort or fruition. The second responded that, for a woman, marriage meant enslavement to another, and that loss of virginity brought the loss of her power of self-determination: 'Virgins, O virgins, fly from Hymen far' (823). Having reached this impasse, the two women called out champions to uphold their causes by combat. Thirty-two knights entered, and the evening passed in fighting at the barriers, first in pairs, then three against three. But as the combats reached their climax, they were interrupted by an angel, who announced the return of the first woman. Now magnificently dressed and borne in a chariot with Hypocrisy, Slander, and Vainglory at her wheels, she was revealed as the real figure of Truth, while her opponent, the defender of virginity, was 'mere Opinion, / That in Truth's forcèd robe for Truth hath gone' (922–3). Still, Truth consoled the knights that had striven so valiantly against marriage. They should not be discouraged at fighting for the losing side, since 'valour wins applause / That dares but to maintain the weaker cause' (920–1).

Jonson's *Barriers* occupied ideological terrain which had already been fully mapped in *Hymenaei*. It was inevitable that in a nuptial celebration virginity would defer to marriage, but this second subjugation of separateness to unity reiterated at a domestic level the political moral about Union which was promulgated on the previous evening. Nonetheless, this was more than a mere pendant to *Hymenaei*, since the terms of the combat alluded to the factional politics encircling the event – which the previous evening had largely passed over – thereby signalling tensions that would need more than angelic intervention to dispel them. The *Barriers* shifted the masque's transcendent concords into chivalric mode, and foregrounded their underlying conflicts by opposing virginity, with its Elizabethan resonances, to marriage. By doing so, they suggested concessions to the more 'forward' and confessionally motivated politics which were associated with one of the groups of combatants, the former Essexians, and which were at odds with the praise of peace that in other respects was the evening's main business. For all that Truth came down against militant virginity, the *Barriers* admitted that reconciliation through marriage was not endorsed by all participants.

James promoted the Essex–Howard marriage as a means of rapprochement at court, hoping to build bridges between rival factions. As the son of the Elizabethan earl whose 1601 rebellion ended at the block, the fourteen-year-old Earl of Essex occupied an ambiguous place. Before his fall his father had corresponded secretly with the Scottish King, promising to support his claim, and one of James's first acts in 1603 was to restore the attainted adolescent to grace, appointing him companion to Prince Henry and freeing from prison Southampton and others involved in the rebellion. Nevertheless, although the Essexians were back in favour, the positions of real power continued to be monopolized by the Howard family, the court's most entrenched dynasty, while the minister on whose advice James relied from early on was Robert Cecil, Earl of Salisbury – that politician against whose influence the 1601 rebellion was directed. The new marriage was contrived to stitch up these rifts of personality within the court fabric.[1] By marrying the Earl to Frances Howard, daughter to the Earl of Suffolk, an alliance was created between the Essexians and Howards, and a connection was opened to Cecil, whose son would soon marry Frances Howard's sister, and who was also close to the Prince. Additionally, the alliance had an ideological aspect, since Essex's followers were known for wanting an aggressive foreign policy, whereas the Howards favoured James's line of friendly co-existence with Spain. Fixing Essex within the orbit of the peace-loving Howards was a strategy that might contain his friends' more militaristic tendencies.

In the 1590s, the second Earl of Essex had cultivated the profile of a popular aristocrat eager for confrontation with Spain. His rebellion has been called 'the last honour revolt',[2] and in many respects it was impelled by the frustrations of men with strong military inclinations and a tendency to self-assertion, who were embittered by their exclusion from influence, and nostalgic for past glories. But Essex's circle also attracted 'an unusually high number of people with relatively radical political views',[3] and was distinguished by its enthusiasm for Europe. Many Essexians were convinced that

England was threatened by the ambitions of Catholic powers and that, for her freedom and for the faith, she needed to be vigorous overseas. Whereas Elizabeth held back from too deep an involvement in European warfare, the Essexians thought that England should maintain links with other Protestant states, and cultivate alliances to counterbalance the Habsburgs. After the death of Sir Philip Sidney, Essex assumed the mantle of anti-Spanish champion, and proved his military credentials at Rouen and Cadiz and in Ireland. And when he was not campaigning, Essex sustained this heroic image on the tiltyard, participating in the Accession Day tournaments which enabled courtiers to act out aristocratic fantasies of chivalric glory, scenarios which some, at least, hoped to translate into reality. Inevitably, Essex's association with the warmongers put him at odds with Cecil and reinforced the disruptive aspects of his tiltyard career.

The barriers of 1606 were less glamorous than an Elizabethan tilt, being merely a foot combat, but spectators cannot have missed how they evoked memories of the executed Earl. Eleven participants, most fighting in defence of virginity, had been knighted by Essex on overseas service in the 1590s,[4] and several were implicated in his revolt. Virginity's supporters wore Essex's colours and were led by the Earl of Sussex, who was arrested for complicity in the rebellion,[5] as was Sir William Constable, who had narrowly missed censure.[6] On the other side, the defenders of marriage wore the bride's colours, and included five Howards and several Howard clients.[7] Two, Lord Effingham and Sir Robert Maunsell, led the attack on Essex House in 1601, and the whole combat was overseen by the Earl of Worcester, who sat in judgment on Essex and now occupied the post he had coveted, Master of the Horse. The *Barriers'* division between Essex's friends and adversaries was not absolute (for in the intervening period some former allies had become friends with Cecil and the Howards),[8] but its relationship to the real aristocratic violence of 1601 could not have been missed. The encounter was a symbolic rehearsal of the fault-lines which the marriage was intended to heal, and a reminder of their origins in the personal and ideological conflicts of the 1590s.

The *Barriers* attempted to supply a safety valve for aggression, venting chivalric energies so that potentially explosive divisions might be stabilized. The combat staged the tensions between the two camps, translating factional oppositions into legitimate forms by permitting the Essexians a ceremonial articulation of their hostility, but the concluding entries abrogated court rivalries by remitting them to a third party, a frankly transcendental *deus ex machina*. At the same time, there was a subtle disparagement of the ethos of chivalric combat, and of the nostalgia for a patriotic Protestantism for which it was the vehicle. By framing the combat as a conflict between Truth and Opinion, Jonson camouflaged it as a debate about 'more removed mysteries'[9] but, to those involved, a struggle for precedence between virginity and marriage would have a frankly political resonance. In disclosing the champions of marriage as the party of Truth, the event came down against the disruptive individualism of Hymen's opponents, and signalled the shift there had been in political culture, the displacement of Elizabeth's cult of virginity by James's cult of marriage. Further, the whole combat was overshadowed by Jonson's humanistic devalorizing of knightly enterprise, which undermined the cleanly demarcated oppositions of the tiltyard. With Truth and Opinion identical to the eye, the distinction between them was established not by the knights' heroism but by the angel's superior insight. Effectively, the *Barriers* withdrew moral adjudication from the combatants on the Banqueting House floor and vested it in the King's transcendent vision. In the last, outrageous moments, Truth resigned her 'starry crown' to James, 'To show his rule and judgment is divine' (936).

Eyewitness accounts do not record what the Essexians thought about being once again on the losing side. Defeat in battle was not a problem in the chivalric code, since the idea was intrinsic that a knight's courage was no less admirable for having been overcome: hence Truth's observation that her opponents had shown valour in 'the weaker cause'.[10] Yet the thrust of Jonson's resolution was towards demilitarizing the public performances of both parties and the Essexians in particular. By instructing the losers that 'It is a conquest to submit to right' (931), Truth implied that the better heroism lay in submission and self-control. Treading a thin line between giving Essex's friends a dignified part to play and reaffirming the court's continuing disparagement of their politics and aspirations, the *Barriers* suggested the existence of tensions which could not be brought wholly into view but which were everywhere implicit. In this respect, Jonson's speeches disclosed structural difficulties that were to bedevil the political culture of the whole period, obliged as it was to reconcile the largely isolationist emphases of Stuart kingship with the subordinate yet persistent strain of sentiment at court that would have preferred to see greater interventionism. On this occasion, although the *Barriers* made space for chivalry, the mystique of a pacific and stable monarchy prevailed. However, in festivals over the next ten years the collision between these two tendencies would be more dramatic, and would need more complex resolutions.

The Stuarts' identification with peace, stability, and international conciliation has been frequently discussed and needs little reiteration here.[11] For Charles, the commitment to peace was imposed rather than assumed: he hankered after a strong role in Europe and his masques had a strain of chivalric self-dramatization that was at odds with his actual paralysis of will towards the continent (see chapter 9 below). But for *Jacobus pacificus* the pursuit of peace was of the essence, and he resisted alliances which might involve him in expensive overseas military commitments. The logic was partly financial, since (as Charles found in the 1620s) the crown's chronic indebtedness and administrative atrophy could ill bear the strains of war. But James was also wary of the explosiveness of Europe's religious differences, the Cold War situation in which Protestant and Catholic were ranged against one another, and he feared the consequences for kingly government should policy be driven by rival religious teleologies. He calculated that in these circumstances England's most prudential role was as a reconciler or mediator, and made his policy aim the maintenance of Europe's fragile peace. By holding the balance between Catholic and Protestant, and between the two great Catholic powers Spain and France, England would prevent divisions tipping into conflict, and check over-mighty principalities. To this end James strove for friendship, and eventually dynastic alliances, with Protestant and Catholic states alike, and returned lukewarm responses to invitations from abroad to take up the torch of European Protestantism.

These preferences were discouraging for those who felt that England ought to align herself with German Protestantism, help the Netherlands in their struggle with Spain, and exploit France's willingness to do anything to undermine her great neighbour. But James had no truck with the view that Europe's future was incipiently apocalyptic, a grand universal confrontation between godly and ungodly, nor did he believe that England had much to gain from warmongering. Although he continued Elizabeth's limited military support for the Dutch, he wished to preserve the status quo, not disrupt it. In any case, he rightly perceived that the conflict between Spain and the Netherlands was already moving into the extended truce that came in 1609. Closer alliance with the Dutch was problematic because they were trading and fishing rivals, and because they were a republican state in conflict with a monarchy, whose friendship led into ideologically turbulent waters. In early modern Europe, the threat to order seemed to come from religious zealotry, and James was anxious that too 'popular' a policy overseas would encourage those at home whose religious attitudes were tainted by populism. His instructions to Sir John Digby, ambassador to Madrid in 1617, required him to counteract 'a creeping disposition to make popular states and alliances to the disadvantage of monarchy'.[12] He wanted a Europe peacefully settled under stable and interlocking kingly dynasties, and good relations with Spain were preferable to Protestant activism both for the sake of peace and for more nakedly social considerations. By contrast with the Dutch, Spain was a congenial ally that (in Simon Adams's formulation) valued 'social order and monarchical legitimacy and stability' and whose friendship was cemented by respect for the survival of monarchy.[13]

The masques were ideal vehicles of this ideology, and the years of most prestigious festivity – 1603–10, 1614–23, and 1630–40 – coincided with periods in which English diplomacy was pursuing Spanish détente. When Daniel praised the Spanish peace in *The Twelve Goddesses* he was inaugurating a friendship which would be publicly signalled on successive Twelfth Nights; under James and Charles diplomatic correspondence overflows with complaints from French ambassadors that the honours in masque invitations were being stolen by their rivals. More importantly, the masques' allusions to secret kingly wisdom, their emphasis on transcending conflict, their ritualistic celebrations of harmony, and their linking of royal authority to dynastic strength, stability, and order all promoted submissiveness rather than enthusiasms of the sort likely to undermine Stuart peace.[14] Celebration of James as a glorious father who presided serenely over a settled kingdom was not calculated to encourage activism, but shaded into a preference for avoiding potentially destabilizing warfare. It also emphasized the singularity of the British state, and neglected links that might have been asserted between Britain and overseas Protestants. In this regard, the isolationist boast of *The Masque of Blackness*, that the new island state was 'A world divided from the world' (248), had more than poetic force. It expressed the practical implications of Stuart ideological preferences.

Against this, the pageantry of tournament and tiltyard which was so central to Elizabethan political culture had reinforced a different set of priorities. Historians have debated whether the tilts discharged or promoted the participants' aggressive tendencies. Chivalric service on the tiltyard bound an aristocratic caste into common devotion to their courtly mistress, while channelling potentially disruptive aspirations into forms remote from the realities of contemporary warfare.[15] But in articulating such fantasies, they also kept alive the expectation that aristocrats should give social and military leadership and, by fostering militaristic sentiments, they encouraged sympathy to a common cause with overseas states, such as the Dutch, who were menaced by Catholic neighbours. Additionally, the chivalric community itself stood in uneasy relation to the sovereign. During the Tudor period the crown asserted its role as the fountain of honour, yet the community of honour preserved some residual autonomy from the monarch's will, the prowess of knightly performances being in some measure self-validating. This left an unresolved tension in Elizabethan tournaments.

The passivity of the principal spectator could be turned to the Queen's disadvantage by the daring of those performing on the tiltyard floor.[16]

In Jacobean court culture, chivalric pageantry no longer had the same power.[17] The neo-medieval fictions that glamourized Elizabeth as a romance heroine presiding over the combats of knightly adorers had little to offer James, and, though a great hunter, he made no attempt to create a chivalric cult. He never tilted, though he ran at the ring at least seven times, the last in Christmas 1613 to honour the wedding of his favourite, Somerset.[18] These were not very successful occasions: in 1609 he had to buy Prince Henry a supper after losing to him at the ring, and in 1606, at a tilt staged for the King of Denmark, the two monarchs ran at the ring but Christian (said Carleton) 'had the good hap never almost to miss it, and ours had the ill luck scarce ever to come near it, which put him into no small impatiences'.[19] More significantly, Jacobean tilts had nothing like the ruinous Elizabethan outlay on furniture and dress, and only faintly echoed the old emblematic devices. As the reign aged, John Chamberlain complained the tilts were 'indifferently performed' or 'mean and poor whether you respect the number or cost'.[20] This suggests that glory on the tiltyard no longer seemed a route to favour, and that courtiers expected to get far less by staging elaborate chivalric transactions with the monarch. For all that Buckingham was painted by Rubens astride a rearing steed, he ventured on the tiltyard only once, to no great applause,[21] and after 1625 such festivals ceased altogether. In Caroline political culture, there was an absolute divide between Charles's support for the Garter cult and his image as an idealized English knight and his lack of interest in actually demonstrating practical skill in management of arms.

Yet despite these unpropitious conditions, chivalry was a long time dying. Almost forty tilts were held during James's reign, and Accession Day celebrations lasted to 1624.[22] A dozen or more courtiers performed regularly, and these included men known for their forwardness over Europe, such as Lennox, Arundel, Pembroke, Montgomery, Dorset, and Hay. The custom continued of presenting shields with esoteric impresas to the monarch, and considerable outlay went on retainers, devices, pavilions, and chivalric pageantry. Rich costumes were noted at Accession Day 1607, 'jousts of great pomp and beauty' in 1608, and 'indescribable magnificence' in 1613.[23] In 1609 Inigo Jones built an elephant pageant for Sir Richard Preston which crept with excruciating slowness around the tiltyard,[24] while at the June 1610 tilt one knight arrived in a thundercloud, and Lord Compton masqueraded in Sidneian manner as a shepherd knight sitting with his dog in a gold-encrusted bower, again designed by Jones.[25] The 1616 tilting cost the Earl of Rutland £150,[26] and a spectacular festival was mounted in 1620 for Prince Charles's first tilt (see chapter 8 below). But these tournaments lacked the developed poetic symbolism of Elizabethan shows, and the systematic political reflections for which it was the vehicle. With James setting little store by them, Jacobean tournaments did not mount any sustained symbolic conversation with the King, and without overtly programmatic features they lacked significance as public interventions, keeping chivalric forms out of the period's active political culture. However, all this changed during 1609–12, with the coming to maturity of Prince Henry. During Henry's brief political summer, England temporarily had an heir apparent who was as strongly wedded to pseudo-Elizabethan militaristic display as he was to forward and confessionally motivated politics.

When Henry died in November 1612 he was still only eighteen years old, yet he had already become the focus of a significant chivalric cult.[27] He was ambitious to make a political mark from an early age, asking for his estates to be made over in 1609, and commissioning a treatise from Richard Connock, one of his gentlemen, analysing the ages at which previous Princes of Wales had received their revenues, 'to prove that the same is as needful in these our days'.[28] This threatened James's finances and initially he stalled, but in June 1610 the investiture went ahead. Henry's revenues were settled in the autumn and gentlemen vied for household positions in November.[29] Thereafter he kept a sizeable court and clientage network that was potentially in competition with his father's. The Venetian Ambassador said he looks 'graciously on everyone and so everyone is his most devoted servant, and he can manage the king's most intimate and make them speak to the king just as he thinks best'.[30]

The most visible token of the political climate of Henry's court was his enthusiasm for military exercises. He first appeared on the tiltyard in 1606, aged twelve, the French ambassador noting that his pleasures were far from childish: 'He studies two hours a day, and employs the rest of the time in tossing the pike, or leaping, or shooting with the bow, or throwing the bar, or vaulting, or some other exercise of that kind; and he is never idle.'[31] At Christmas 1611–12 'he was every day five or six hours in armour'.[32] From the first, the iconography that developed around him centred on his athleticism and aptitude for arms. He was given armour by Sir Henry Lee, the Prince de Joinville, and Henri IV, and miniatures, portraits, and engravings depicted him en route to the tiltyard, at push of pike, or pausing on the edge of battle.[33] Such images traded on the expectation of a momentous future. At his death, Sir Thomas Edmondes's secretary wrote that his 'extraordinary great parts and virtues made many men hope and believe that God had

9 Robert Peake, *Equestrian Portrait of Prince Henry*, c. 1609.

reserved and destined him as a chosen instrument to be the standard-bearer
of his quarrel in these miserable times, to work the restoration of his Church
and the destruction of the Romish idolatry'.[34] In his remarkable equestrian
portrait by Robert Peake, he appears in armour decorated with rising suns
and has the figure of Occasion by his side, carrying his lance and helm
(see figure 9). Occasion's forelock is firmly tied to Henry's arm.

By 1610, Henry's court was becoming a gathering-ground for those
with attitudes that were out of step with Whitehall. A military lobby
collected around the Prince. The Venetian ambassador said 'he was obeyed
and loved by the military party' and his 'whole talk was of arms and war'.[35]

He corresponded with his German cousins on the Queen's side and gentle-men in the Dutch service,[36] and attracted former Essexians, notably the Earl of Southampton, who performed in *Prince Henry's Barriers* and *Oberon* (the only time that Southampton danced in a court masque).[37] James shrewdly appointed the young Earl of Essex as his companion. Henry was also interested in naval affairs, and when he joined the Privy Council he made naval reform his crusade. He visited the shipyards and had the *Prince Royal* built; in 1611 he wanted to be appointed Admiral.[38] This interest gave him a tie to Sir Walter Ralegh, at this time languishing in the Tower, and to Ralegh's associate Arthur Gorges. Henry consulted Ralegh on ship design, and Ralegh wrote for him on policy and war, stressing the interconnection between trade and strength at sea, arguing that Dutch seamanship was damaging English commerce, and that Spain might be challenged in the Americas.[39] This advice dovetailed with Henry's support for colonization. He supported the Virginia Company, and was 'Supreme Protector' of the North-West Passage enterprise; Robert Harcourt's Guiana expedition also received patronage.[40] He hoped that these enterprises would uncover sources of wealth and hurt Spain; the Venetian ambassador said the Spanish were anxious about their effect on trade.[41] The arguments from trade, religion, and policy all reinforced each other, and translated into the idea of a godly war against Spain's outlying possessions, which would be good for religion and commerce. Charles Cornwallis said Henry vowed that 'should the king his father be pleased upon any future occasion to break with Spain, himself … would in person become the executor of that noble attempt for the West Indies'.[42]

The protocols of Henry's court were also distinct from James's. On instituting his household he issued regulations reinforcing stateliness and order. Cornwallis said 'plenty and magnificence were the things that in his house he especially affected, but not without such a temper as might agree with the rules of frugality and moderation'.[43] Access was denied to unfit persons, and attendants were commanded to serve him reverently; everyone had to attend chapel daily and swear-boxes were set up. When Henry feasted his father at Woodstock in 1612, James was astonished at his house-hold's decorum, far exceeding anything he could command.[44] This rather prim splendour was reinforced by Henry's ostentatious piety, the 'rare tokens of a religious and virtuous disposition' that he famously displayed.[45] No small part of his attraction to contemporaries was the belief that he would prove a vigorously Protestant monarch. The tortuous negotiations for a marriage partner faced the obstacle of persuading him to love a Catholic, and just before the Palatine marriage it was rumoured that he intended to accompany his sister into Germany and seek a Protestant bride.[46] He was known to admire Henri IV, whose resistance to the Habsburgs was more determined than James's. The apocalyptic expectations that accrued to him can be gauged from John Holles's extraordinary letters lamenting his death. To Holles, the prince was 'our great Hercules', who would have cleansed the Augean stables at home and held up the faith abroad:

all brave undertakings by sea or land for the honour and benefit of this nation, the reformation and care of a sick, diseased, home state by upholding religion, bettering the policy, moderating the oligarchal greatness of court, of council, opening the passage to virtue with reward of merit to whosoever, in what sphere soever, is gone: our great Hercules hath taken up all these joys and many more up with him and as a worthless people hath left us to the jaws of the lion, the venom of the dragon, the insatiable rapine of the harpies, till the days of our misery be full answerable to our misgiving fears and the menacing prophecies of times past ... [He might have] laid such foundation of our safety with a true discovery of our stupid serenity, that we had been as *Diana inter nymphas*, once again the nation among all nations, a terror to God's enemies and ours, the triumph of the Church at home, and a sure haven to the distressed Church abroad.[47]

The event was traumatic for Holles since Henry's death dashed his worldly hopes. Still, the mythic status and fantasy of universal reform he associated with Henry vividly display the repressed political desires for which this untried youth had, for some, become the vehicle.

The problem in evaluating Henry's circle is that of knowing how to represent its dissident affiliations without exaggerating its status as a focus of 'opposition'. Roy Strong argues that James's and Henry's courts were in open tension with one other, that St James's Palace was a gathering-ground for courtiers who set themselves against royal Whitehall.[48] Certainly ambassadorial reports attest to friction. French and Venetian diplomats alike thought James was anxious about Henry's popularity and concerned to limit its effects. While Molin may have exaggerated that James was jealous 'that all his subjects place their hopes in him', La Boderie's judgment that Henry's reputation gave 'apprehensions to those who had the greatest ascendant at court' and that James controlled him by placing his own dependants around him is supported by the prospect of sweeping reform which Holles anticipated, and by James's reluctance to allow 'the rising sun' (in Molin's phrase) to have as large a household as he wanted.[49] Henry and Cecil did not get on, and Cecil had to cultivate the Prince: a story survives of him dissuading Henry from becoming President of the Privy Council, as it was 'dangerous to divide the government and to invest the son with the authority of the father'.[50] In Holles's memory, Henry's court already was a rival to James's: he lived 'with that order and majesty that [strangers] approached him rather as a king than a prince'.[51] Not surprisingly, after his death the same cult was not permitted to develop around Prince Charles. Charles's retinue was smaller than Henry's, and some of Henry's more outspoken advisors were refused further patronage.[52] Holles complained that although James promised to look after Henry's servants, many would be disappointed. 'The dispensers of these favours' would 'take the advantage of the king's wants and return us home also after the same unworthy fashion'.[53]

Yet it is too simple to posit, as Strong does, a direct antagonism between the Jacobean and Henrician courts. They are better seen as two followings or affinities in ongoing dialogue.[54] The Prince's autonomy was complicated by the fact that he was, quite literally, affiliated to the King. His challenge was possible only because James empowered him, and too naked a confrontation could not advantage him. There is also the difficulty of evaluating his public profile, which was generated by his position as the focus of other men's aspirations. The images that gathered around him were not so much expressions of his authentic personality as counters in the on-going struggle for influence over the heir, and for a stake in the reversionary interest. Different lobbies attempted to 'capture' the Prince and make claims on his friendship; he was courted just as assiduously by Cecil as by Ralegh.[55] And whatever the differences between son and father, Henry's apologists all dwelt on his respectfulness. Holles denied he wished to seize the sceptre, since despite his prowess he 'subjected himself as inferior in all things which fell either under his sense or understanding to his father's will and pleasure'.[56] Cornwallis said that 'so truly was he affected to the pleasing and satisfying of the King his father in all things' that he would ignore business that did not concern him, and if refused a request, 'with the least word, countenance, or sign given him of his majesty's disallowance, he would instantly desist from further pursuit of it'.[57] Such accounts suggest not confrontation but give and take between differently empowered partners in the political process.

Potential oppositions between Henry and James were further mediated by underlying communities of attitude. As we have seen (in chapter 5), Henry's cult rested on a misogyny that was cognate with James's own. Though coded as nostalgia for an Elizabethan past, his chivalric culture reproduced the same gender politics as his father's. Equally, although his militarism conflicted with Jacobean norms, its social coordinates were not troublesome, for the creation of a mystique of honour around the heir apparent was welcome. Henry cultivated royal dignity: his household's dress ran 'to an incredible excess', and he selected the Knights of the Bath that were to be made at his investiture, excluding those whose blood he thought inferior.[58] The consequences of his status for his politics can be seen during the 1610 parliament, in which he not only opposed the reform of wardship – the most notorious surviving feudal privilege, which would be abolished by the Long Parliament – but sought to become Master of the Court of Wards himself. This office, which controlled the education of young aristocrats, carried vast revenues and social power, and Henry disapproved of Cecil holding it, believing it should be in royal hands.[59] The revival of chivalry seemed to signal a resurgence of aristocratic militarism, but its cooptation by the prince diverted some of its subversive potential, reinvesting the sponsorship of honour within the royal house. Even Southampton experienced the limits of princely friendship, when during the creation of Henry's household he was ordered to leave court lodgings that Henry wanted for himself.[60] It is futile to speculate on how affairs would have been had he lived, but it seems unlikely that his leadership would have been congenial to those of radical social persuasions.

Nonetheless, these two royal circles pulled against each other, and for James there were inbuilt tensions in the ceremonial around his son. Elevation of the Prince was desirable, since his popularity bonded dynasty and nation, but as the reversionary interest he could have been the linchpin of an alternative state within the state, out of step with the dominant political culture. Disturbingly, Henry's culture sidestepped the filiations that should have fixed him as his father's son. He 'ever much reverenced' the 'memory and government' of Queen Elizabeth,[61] and this attachment reappeared in his festivals in Spenserean and other romance motifs that harked back to the previous reign's neo-Arthurianism. The result was not an overt challenge to James's culture, but neither was it exactly conformity. Rather, it presented a competition between two iconographies, each using different languages of legitimation, marshalling sovereignty after their own priorities, and pointing to aims that were in tension. It exaggerates Henry's autonomy to see his festivals as bids for power, but his legitimation inevitably had consequences for that of his father. The promulgation of James's iconography cannot have been unaffected by the emergence of a competing set of images which promoted a more forward kingship, and in this regard Henry's festivals were symptomatic of a developing legitimation crisis.[62]

Much Henrician festivity can be seen as an attempt to exploit but also to manage the phenomenon of the political heir, the problem of a figure whose empowerment depended upon yet contested the empowerment of his father. In 1610–12, James sought to limit Henry's ceremonial, denying him forms of legitimation which conflicted with his own. He was reluctant to allow the 1610 *Barriers* to be fought publicly, and he prevented Henry from processing to his investiture on horseback, because, said Giustinian, 'they did not desire to exalt him too high'. Henry also wanted to perform his 1611 masque on horseback, 'could he have obtained the king's consent'.[63] It is a revealing indication of his ambitions that, had he possessed more authority, *Oberon* might have been an equestrian ballet, perhaps on the model of Florentine carousels.[64] But he never achieved effective control of his own festivals, since the finances for all his masques were shared with either the King or the Queen.[65] As a consequence, all his performances were three-way conversations, in which his promotion went hand in hand with a dialogue between Prince and King, circumstances which make it hard to disentangle political statements being made by Henry from advice being given to him. Commentators have often ignored these conditions, and faulted his masques for lacking focus because they do not conform to unitary expectations imported from other texts.[66] But Henry's festivals all presumed a divided court, and in them conflict was not so much transcended as uncovered. Though anchored in myth, they exposed myth to history, the singularity of their legitimations being complicated by a fall back into the contingencies of narrative. The ideological work they performed was overtly on view, and the resolutions they worked towards were more than usually conditional.

The Twelfth Night *Barriers* of 1610 marked Henry's symbolic and literal entrance onto the court stage, and spectacularly showcased his talents. They cost almost £2,550, and over Christmas his six fellow challengers, and the fifty-six defendants who responded, were feasted at £100 a day.[67] Sir Thomas Edmondes commented that Henry 'beginneth to take great authority upon him', and predicted a great future for him 'out of the pregnancy of his spirit'.[68] The *Barriers'* fiction expressed these pretensions. It introduced Henry under the name Meliades, who in Arthurian romance was son to the Scottish queen by Meliadus of Lyonesse,[69] and surrounded him with prophecies about restoring British chivalry, from the Lady of the Lake, Merlin, and a stellified King Arthur. Such motifs fixed Henry in a lineage descending from militant Elizabethan Protestantism – the Lady of the Lake welcomed Elizabeth to Kenilworth on Leicester's behalf in 1576, and at The Hague in 1586 Leicester was greeted by Arthur as a star[70] – while their Spenserean associations made it seem as though the unfinished *Faerie Queene* (the first full text of which appeared in 1609) had been carried forward into the next generation. Further, as John Peacock has shown, Jones's visual designs put Henry into a setting which, through dense architectural allusion, associated him with religious and cultural reform.[71] Against this background, the Prince displayed his skill at sword and pike.

Jonson's speeches offered no simple adulation but a dialectic of praise and admonition. Henry was the exemplar of knightliness, for whom Chivalry awoke from sleep and called on the contestants to inundate the lethargic Jacobean court:

> Break, you rusty doors,
> That have so long been shut, and from the shores
> Of all the world, come knighthood like a flood
> Upon these lists, to make the field, here, good.   (396–9)

Henry's arrival miraculously restored Chivalry's ruinous house, and Arthur told the Lady of the Lake that this moment was James's crowning glory – a rite of passage which, by acting out the son's newly achieved manhood, perfected the father's state:

> Proceed in thy great work; bring forth thy knight
> Preserved for [James's] times, that by the might
> And magic of his arm, he may restore
> These ruined seats of virtue, and build more.
> Let him be famous, as was Tristram, Tor,
> Lanc'lot, and all our list of knighthood: or
> Who were before, or have been since. His name
> Strike upon heaven, and there stick his fame.   (81–8)

Henry's manliness effected a connection between the Stuarts and one version of the British past. With its Roman rather than romantic emphasis, Arthurian mythology sanctioned the new state in terms of the first authentically British kingship.

Against this, the speeches insisted on the need for aspiration to be controlled and safely directed. Arthur presented Henry with a shield rather than a sword, and his gloss was cautionary: the fates had wrought its decoration 'to show / Defensive arms th'offensive should forego' (98–9). Before Henry could fight, Merlin recounted a description of its decorations, dwelling on the primacy of defence over offence. The shield depicted Henry's heroic ancestors, and while it showed Cressy, Agincourt, and the Armada, prime space went to Edward I's and Edward III's support for industry and agriculture, Henry VII's care with cash, and Henry VIII's and Elizabeth's concern for the realm's defences. The lessons were that 'civil arts the martial must proceed, / That laws and trade bring honors in and gain, / And arms defensive a safe peace maintain' (212–14). Even warrior monarchs had to show self-control. Richard I, captured when he 'tempt[ed] [his] stars beyond their light' (236), had betrayed himself by recklessness; Edward I had a 'tempered zeal' (245); and the Black Prince's motto 'I Serve' (266) enshrined his caution and deference to his father. Whatever the combatants' knightly individualism, Merlin's review of history made restraint the true mark of legitimacy. It was a long way from the list of ambitious princes compiled by Connock.

Some commentators regard the *Barriers* as aesthetically incoherent, read-ing its divided praise of peace and war as a sign of Jonson's embarrassment with the commission, or as contradicting Henry's chivalry with political reality.[72] Such judgements presume too rigid a relationship between image and meaning, ignoring the contests over policy-making of which Henry was a focus. Merlin's advice resembles that given to Henry by Sir Robert Cotton in *An Answer … to Certain Propositions of War and Peace* (1609). Cotton's tract says that Henry was urged by 'some of his military servants' to pursue a war policy, so as to bring honour and spoil, and subdue domestic dissent. Cotton answers that the best princes 'preferred an unjust peace before the justest war' and went to war only as a last resort.[73] Citing many historical examples, he argues that Britain no longer had suitable allies, and that war disrupted trade and oppressed the people. Samuel Daniel presented similar views in his poetic 'Epistle to Prince Henry' (*c.* 1609–10),[74] which warned him that incursions into other kingdoms would cost 'more ado / Than all your conquests shall amount unto' (143–4). Though praising the need for arms 'both for your own defence / And terror to your potent neighbours' (170–1), Daniel argues that princely aggression did not 'square with the line of Christianity', and 'will your trouble, not your state increase' (153, 160). Cotton was a client of the Earl of Northampton and Daniel was servant to the Queen, both patrons with pro-Spanish tendencies. Their writings suggest how much Henry had become the focus of policy debate between rival camps. Strikingly, Jonson's speeches complimented two of the Howards, Nottingham and Suffolk, for valour against the Armada (311–14), underlining that love of peace was not a mark of cowardice.

At this precise moment Europe was uneasily poised between peace and war.[75] The truce of Antwerp had made England's military presence in the Netherlands superfluous and brought a scaling-down of military expendi-ture. But the fragile situation was exposed when the death of the Duke of Cleves (March 1609) sparked the Cleves–Julich crisis, a stand-off between the Habsburgs and their rivals over succession to the Duke's territories. Claims were laid by both Protestant and Catholic princes, and the situation escalated over the summer, with the Habsburgs invading Juliers, and Henri IV responding with a show of force. As Habsburg and anti-Habsburg inched into confrontation, even James reluctantly agreed in January 1610 to send 4,000 men. In the event, sabre-rattling paid off, but Europe was momentarily on the brink of a general crisis, and a conflagration might have followed had Henri not been assassinated in May 1610. Given the Cold War situation, this was a dress rehearsal for 1619, when another localized conflict over succession escalated into cataclysm. It amply demonstrated the momentous futures that were at stake in the debates around the Prince.

It was advantageous, then, to publicize English chivalry, and the Spanish ambassador must have been impressed by Henry's readiness,[76] but the moment's anxieties were equally apparent in speeches praising defensive arms. Though the shield depicted the trophies of British kings, Merlin said they showed the necessity of temporizing:

> [they] may make t'invite
> Your valour upon need, but not t'incite
> Your neighbour princes; give them all their due,
> And be prepared if they will trouble you.
> He doth but scourge himself, his sword that draws
> Without a purse, a counsel, and a cause.   (329–34)

This was not simply Jonsonian prudence, but a precise summary of the rationale for peace. It expressed the diplomatic line James held through the winter, as Henri tried to manoeuvre him into a war he did not want. Though speaking in 'mystic prophecies' (75), Merlin was far from apocalyptic, and lacked the taint of Protestant enthusiasm: previous kings had fought for religion, but against infidels, not fellow Christians (226, 240).[77] He located Henry's promise in some unspecified future, and the barriers tested whether he could control his prowess: true courage lay in knowing when to remain passive:

> Nay, stay your valour, 'tis a wisdom high
> In princes to use fortune reverently.
> He that in deeds of arms obeys his blood
> Doth often tempt his destiny beyond good.
>   (405–8)

Henry demonstrated his skill with arms, but the speeches subordinated military options to James's avoidance of potential catastrophe.

For the spectators, the barriers had a double aspect, as the display of Henry's valour pulled against his father's disinvestments in war. This tension was evident in the struggle over paternity between the King and the pageant's surrogate father and mother, Arthur and the Lady of the Lake – who in the sources is Meliades' lover but whom Jonson made his 'fostress' (155). The speeches framed the occasion with eulogy of James. The Lady hailed his new Britain, and Merlin praised him for being above the contingencies that shake other princes:

> Within his proper virtue hath he placed
> His guards 'gainst Fortune, and there fixed fast
> The wheel of chance, about which kings are hurled,
> And whose outrageous raptures fill the world.   (363–6)

After the barriers Merlin invoked an alternative, Jacobean model of valour:

> Look on this throne, and in his temper view
> The light of all that must have grace in you:
> His equal Justice, upright Fortitude
> And settled Prudence, with that Peace indued
> Of face, of mind, always himself and even.
> So Hercules, and good men bear up heaven.   (410–16)

This was a remarkable adjustment of Henrician values. True Herculean virtue, said Merlin, was not physical fighting but the secret heroics inside James's breast. Arthur's sanction was also hedged around with reservations about paternity. James – who in anagram 'Claims Arthur's Seat' (20) – was the true heir of 'my sceptre and my style'; since 'it is nobler to restore than make', Arthur's old Britain was 'outshone' by the new (77–81). Arthur stayed safely in the sky while Merlin took over, explaining that unlike old heroes, modern princes deal not with 'giants, dwarfs, or monsters … but men' (174). The speeches thus staged a contest over legitimation, in which power was authorized by James's political pragmatism rather than a heroic Arthurian mythos. Nonetheless, Henry's Arthurian lineage and assertion of an identity at arms created a tension that could not readily be resolved. His courage was enfolded within James's prudence, but at the cost of admitting the gap between the father's and son's rival criteria of legitimation.

It is uncertain whether Henry heard this message, since only a week later he was deep in plans for 'another triumph or show against the King's [Accession] Day in March'.[78] In the event, this tilt was staged with little pageantry, grand shows being held back for the investiture festivities in June.[79] By this time Europe had been transformed by Henri's death, an event overshadowing the prestige that the investiture was intended to display. Henri's death plunged the Prince into grief, but it defused the international crisis, and turned English attention back to home affairs.[80] The concerns of Daniel's *Tethys' Festival*, the masque presented by Queen

Anne to the new Prince of Wales, were emphatically domestic, as it was hoped that the ceremonials would help to obtain parliamentary supply, Henry's popularity persuading MPs to grant James a new fiscal settlement. In 1610 James's finances were approaching collapse, and Cecil had prepared a package, the Great Contract, that offered political concessions in return for a settled income. As things turned out, MPs were unconvinced that the concessions were worth the sums demanded, and remained fearful of what they saw as James's prodigality and unconstitutional attitudes. But when Cecil addressed them in February, he said parliament's business was two-fold, to settle James's revenues and witness the investiture. In March James presented his son to them, saying 'he desired to advance him for the service of the nation but could not do so without aids'.[81] So the investiture festivals were unique in being contrived to bear directly onto practical politics. They were explicitly part of the crown's parliamentary management.[82]

   These festivities did not lack chivalry. There was a water battle against a castle and Turkish ship, reportedly watched by 500,000 spectators, and a spectacular tournament featuring elaborate pageants, rumoured to have cost the tilters £1,000 apiece.[83] But Henry was refused an equestrian entry, and the installation staged a show of amity amongst the royal family, with James embracing him and Henry displaying 'submissive reverence'.[84] The peers presented Henry in the Court of Requests, and in a carefully managed ceremonial he was decked with the regalia. The rituals seemed timeless but had been manufactured for the occasion (no Prince of Wales had been invested for a hundred years),[85] and they were done in private, witnessed only by MPs and male noblemen.[86] The resemblance to a coronation underlined continuities to the past and the bonds linking crown, Prince, and nobility in the community of honour. James thus compensated for his own coronation's lack of impact – it had been muted by the 1603 plague – and emphasized that Henry was installed the constitutional way, in full view of parliament. The pomp, though, undermined the pleas of poverty, and suggested a contradiction between ostentation and frugality. Carleton said it was done after the fashion of Henry VII's investiture for Prince Arthur, 'who, you know, was a good husband', but at least one MP was shocked by the 'sumptuous and shining apparel' worn by these 'golden-feathered doves'.[87] Still, this was the most concerted attempt since the 1604 royal entry to make political capital out of a festival. Henry's coming of age was an opportunity to manufacture an image of Stuart kingship as a reservoir of British loyalty.

   The following evening's show was a social event, and offered a different kind of legitimation. *Tethys' Festival* congratulated Henry in ways that tellingly opposed the previous afternoon's political emphases. Devised as a marine masque, its first scene was a haven with ships at anchor, from which came Zephyrus (played by the Duke of York), eight naiads, and a triton, who presented Henry and James with gifts from Tethys, Queen of the Ocean. Then Anne was discovered in her ocean cavern with thirteen ladies, including Princess Elizabeth and Arbella Stuart, representing the British rivers. They processed in liquid meanders, and presented urns of flowers at a Tree of Victory. Finally, after the dances Tethys reappeared in a pleasant grove, from which Zephyrus conducted her to the King. Unlike the installation's monarchical symbolism and masculine codes of honour, this masque decentred the King's hierarchical and paternal gestures. It was a family celebration, affirming ties across the royal group, and replacing James's vertical gestures of possession with horizontal bonds amongst a female community. Zephyrus's gifts staged the kinship ties binding the royal family, and they were extended across the family of the nation in the gifts from the rivers. Such symbols contrasted with the installation by their disregard of the regalia of office or claims to divine sanction. They embedded King and Prince in a family network, celebrating their incorporation, not transcendence. Their political empowerment rose from the consensual gestures of love in which they participated.

Of course, *Tethys' Festival* situated James as supreme: his gift was a trident, identifying him as king of the Ocean. But the theme of maritime power complimented Henry by invoking his naval enthusiasm, and returned to the oceanic imagery used of Queen Elizabeth. In particular, the harbour scene showed 'the happy Port of Union' (192),[88] Milford Haven, where Henry Tudor had come ashore to challenge Richard III. The Prince was appropriately connected with another Welsh Henry, whose family union was the precursor to a union 'greater, and more glorious far than that' (195). This device gave the Prince his own historical geography, associating him with the far from peaceable Tudors, a patriotic history which could be seen as one lineage for his new title. The expectations which this created came into view when Zephyrus gave him Astraea's sword: even if 'not to be unsheath'd but on just ground' (205), Henry's acquisition of one of Elizabeth's symbolic attributes was at odds with his father's more cautious iconography. If for James monarchy of the waves signalled separateness from turbulence elsewhere, the celebration of the Tudor roots of Henry's title threatened to undermine isolationist emphases. James must have thought that by installing a Scottish heir as Prince of Wales in an English ceremony he could assert Stuart Britain's supra-national identity, but this Welsh imagery had resonances with a less quiescent politics.

The unusually concrete identity which *Tethys' Festival* created for the realm suggested a different perspective on sovereignty from the installation. Greeted as 'Lord ... of the Isles' (200–1) – one of the real titles with which he was invested[89] – Henry was directly attached to the land, an island prince welcomed by his rivers in gestures playing out this sovereign connection. Rather as Elizabeth stood on her realm in the Ditchley portrait, her body identified with the kingdom's topography, so homage to Henry literally flowed out of the land. His power came less from his lineage than from the realm's collective acclamations – and the representation of British rivers anticipated Michael Drayton's as yet unpublished *Poly-Olbion*, which delineates the nation through its waterways, local stories, and traditions rather than monarchical succession. By placing Henry in a historically and geographically specific landscape, *Tethys' Festival* ranged itself against Jonson's masques, which always delocalized their golden worlds, constituting them outside time and space. These images, derived from a specific moment of national identity-formation, represented Henry's sovereignty not as a given but as rooted in history. It put him back into the world of historical and political contingency from which his father's aim was to remove him.

Tethys' Festival, then, cut across Jacobean paternalism in important ways, problematizing the celebrations with rival languages of empowerment around the Prince. On the other hand, it was, if anything, even less hospitable than the *Barriers* to Henry's overseas ambitions. In the text's single sustained speech, Daniel counteracted Tudor expansionism by repeating the Epistle's warning against aggression. Zephyrus gave Henry a scarf embroidered with a map of the kingdom, 'wherein he may survey / Enfigur'd all the spacious empery / That he is born unto another day' (208–10), and a triton admonished him to be content with these boundaries:

> Which, tell him, will be world enough to yield
> All works of glory ever can be wrought.
> Let him not think to pass the circle of that field,
> But think Alcides' pillars are the knot:
> For there will be within the large extent
> Of these my waves and wat'ry government
> More treasure, and more certain riches got
> Than all the Indies to Iberus brought,
> For Nereus will by industry unfold
> A chemic secret, and change fish to gold.   (211–20)

This must have discomfited Henry. In urging him to stay behind the Pillars of Hercules, Daniel alluded to a symbol of imperial aspiration, the impresa of the Emperor Charles V. Hercules' Pillars, erected at the Straits of Gibraltar, marked the limits of the known world, but Charles's motto, 'Plus Ultra', voiced his wish to pursue imperial ambitions across the globe. The device was adopted by Henri IV, who presented himself as the Gallic Hercules, but Henry was being dissuaded from similar ambitions. Like Jonson's ascription of Herculean strength to James in the *Barriers*, Daniel channelled Henry's muscular iconography towards moderation. Using Hercules' Pillars as symbols of temperance, not aspiration, he restored the ethical meaning they bore before being appropriated by more ambitious monarchs.[90]

Moreover, the masque's praise for the British herring industry concurred with James's view of European rivalries as economic rather than confessional, an analysis that promoted friendship with Spain rather than Holland. In fact, in May 1609 – just as the Dutch were looking for British support in the Cleves–Julich crisis – James shattered goodwill by issuing a proclamation forbidding Dutch vessels from fishing in British waters except by licence. He was responding to Grotius's *Mare liberum* (March 1609), which raised constitutional temperatures by arguing that sovereignty of the sea was no one monarch's personal possession, and his proclamation drew protests from The Hague and played into the hands of Spain, who were pleased by such frictions.[91] Support for British fisheries was not unwelcome to Henry (Ralegh argued for it, and it was mentioned in Antony Munday's civic welcome, *London's Love to Prince Henry*),[92] but Daniel's formula severed the link between British sea power and hostility to Spain. By promising fish would bring 'more certain riches ... Than all the Indies to Iberus brought', he affirmed James's measures and argued against attempts to intercept Spanish fleets carrying treasure home from the Americas – always the pet project of Ralegh and others who held them as legitimate plunder for Protestants.

So *Tethys' Festival* underwrote Henrician imperialism no more than the *Barriers* did; nor would unqualified panegyric have been appropriate. In order to wrest money from parliament James needed to project an image of Stuart succession which would impress but not seem extravagant, and a balance was struck between exploiting Henry's hopefulness and giving hostages to fortune. To a limited extent this worked, since some of James's purposes were fulfilled. Although the Great Contract failed, Henry attended parliament with his father, and was judged to have been a 'mediator' with the Commons;[93] the masque text was printed as an appendix to the official narrative of the investiture.[94] Nonetheless, in *Tethys' Festival* Henry was not the subordinate political channel he had been at the installation, obediently transmitting his father's will. His iconography was in tension with James's and expressed the relationship between sovereignty and the nation in different terms. And inasmuch as the masque downplayed his aspirations, it perhaps projected an encompassing cautiousness about royal power, given the anxieties aroused that summer by the high-handedness of some of James's remarks to parliament.[95] On the proscenium was the figure of Neptune with his trident, and the words 'Regendo et retinendo' ('by ruling and restraining') (87–8). This Virgilian motto represented monarchs as legitimated by their inner discipline, but there was more than one direction in which it could be read. Whatever the masque's language, it represented the exercise of sovereign power as bound up with questions of proper control.

The masque which negotiated the fault-lines between father and son most creatively was Jonson's minor masterpiece and New Year offering, *Oberon, the Fairy Prince* (1611). The admiration that *Oberon*'s dazzling poetics have attracted has tended to lift it from its occasion, obscuring recognition of how densely it was embedded in its historical moment. Six months beyond the investiture, it celebrated Henry's achievement of his majority, the moment of financial independence. He was now acting on his own account, and had just finalized his household and published its regulations. As the Venetian ambassador sensed, a new force was about:

he is delighted to rule; and as he desires the world should think him prudent and spirited, he pays attention to the regulations of his house and is studying an order as to the cut and quality of the dresses of the gentlemen of his household … on the other hand he attends to the disposition of his houses, having already ordered many gardens and fountains and some new buildings.[96]

For Correr, the festival marked the inception of Henry's adulthood, which would prove whether he was as able as men hoped. Even more sanguine was the advice Henry received from Connock and other counsellors, who urged him to attend to the state's 'errors and confusions':

such is the case of this kingdom, as in standing still and continuing in this hectic whereof it labours, it must needs within few years fall into such an irrecoverable corruption, as in the eyes and understanding of man yieldeth no hope of help. And that, when as a state is brought to such terms, as in resting or adventuring the peril is the same, much better it must needs be to enter into action.[97]

From this point date expectations like those of John Holles, that Henry would be a Herculean reformer and cleanse the 'exuberated mortal impostume, which grows in the vitals of [James's] state'.[98] This was *Oberon*'s subject. It aimed not only to signal Henry as James's successor but to express the climate of reform with which he was increasingly identified.

Oberon had three scenes, arranged as progressively deeper revelations along the King's sight-line. It opened with forbidding rocks, before which satyrs led by Silenus waited impatiently for the fairy prince's arrival. The rocks parted to reveal a palace, guarded by sleeping sylvans, whom the satyrs taunted for unpreparedness. Then, as a cock crew twelve times, announcing a new year, the palace opened, disclosing Oberon and his knights amongst 'the nation of fays' (291). As masquers and fairies came forth, Silenus explained that fairyland was doing homage to the throne, and expounded James's kingly virtues. This deceptively simple structure has often been criticized as aesthetically and politically flawed. Stephen Orgel regards the shift of focus from Prince to King as a breach of decorum, which violates the unity of the event and exposes Jonson's failure to devise a fable complimentary to both. The fairy iconography invented for Henry, he feels, has little to do with the imperial panegyric of James, and causes a lurching gear-shift.[99] Jonathan Goldberg takes this further, seeing the felt loss of unity as a deliberate power-strategy, one of the 'sovereign contradictions' which, he argues, structured James's kingship. Goldberg reads the loss of decorum as necessary: such startling disruptions empowered the King, the masque's conflation of randy satyrs and surpassing monarch giving James a double persona, as king of wonder and sensual fulfillment alike.[100] But by searching for an illusory unity, these readings underestimate the exchanges which the masque hosted. They take insufficient account of its status as a transaction of power between royal competitors.

Exchequer accounts call *Oberon* 'the satyrs and fairies',[101] a phrase which usefully articulates the strategic divisions of a masque that brought together two sovereign iconographies. Henry's fairy role seems fanciful today, but was chosen less for its Shakespearean than Spenserean and Arthurian associations: in lieu of an equestrian ballet, it presented a chivalric ethos in sublimated form. In romance literature, Oberon – a version of the German 'Alberich' – is a prince of amazing powers but deceptively childlike appearance (he ceased to grow at the age of three). Appearing in the Charlemagne stories, his tale is entwined with Arthur's, as he is variously the son of Julius Caesar by Morgan le Fay or the donor to Arthur of rule in fairyland.[102] The masque foregrounded these associations. Henry emerged from fairyland in a chariot drawn by polar bears (linking him with Arthur's constellation, Arcturus) and the masquers were heroic knights, dressed in costumes which John Peacock has shown were modelled on Antonio Tempesta's equestrian portraits of the Caesars.[103] Silenus explained that they were preserved by Oberon's magic and returned once a year, being 'crowned with lasting youth' in 'seats of bliss' for the 'good they have deserved / Of yond high throne' (149–51, 325–7). This combined two romance topoi: the encounter between mortals and other-worldly beings, and the recovery of sleeping Arthurian heroes at moments of national need.[104] *Oberon* gave Henry an imperial role, figuring him as a returning champion of heroic renewal.

On the other side, the satyrs projected a version of the unregulated state which Oberon intended to reform. True to their nature, they were frisky, wanton, lustful, impatient, and aggressive, the embodiment of freely playing desire: 'fierce pleasure seekers', as Goldberg aptly calls them.[105] Though Silenus warned them to use 'Chaster language' (50), their talk fixated on drink, game-playing, and sex, and included an insultingly lewd song about Oberon's patroness, the moon; one wonders whether they really did have the erect phalluses which appear in Jones's costume design.[106] They expected their new leader to grant them unlimited licence:

Satyr 3.	Grandsire, shall we leave to play	
	With Lyaeus* now, and serve	*Bacchus
	Only Ob'ron?	
Silenus.	He'll deserve	
	All you can, and more, my boys.	
Satyr 4.	Will he give us pretty toys,	
	To beguile the girls withall?	
Satyr 3.	And to make 'em quickly fall?	
Silenus.	Peace, my wantons! He will do	
	More than you can aim unto.	
Satyr 4.	Will he build us larger caves?	
Silenus.	Yes, and give you ivory staves,	
	When you hunt, and better wine –	
Satyr 1.	Than the master of the vine?	
Satyr 2.	And rich prizes, to be won,	
	When we leap, or when we run?	
Satyr 1.	Ay, and gild our cloven feet?	
Satyr 3.	Strew our heads with powders sweet?	
Satyr 1.	Bind our crooked legs in hoops	
	Made of shells, with silver loops?	(76–107)

But as Silenus' remarks hinted, the satyrs found that Oberon's rule differed from their hopes. Contrary to expectation, his arrival refined grossness – 'Melt earth to sea, sea flow to air, / And air fly into fire' (300–1) – and transformed rudeness into dignified ceremonial:

> Give place and silence. You were rude too late;
> This is a night of greatness and of state,
> Not to be mixed with light and skipping sport.   (319–21)

This antithesis between amoral chaos and a chastely heroic discipline must have seemed a projection of Henry's aspirations. Indeed, the satyrs' discussion about enrolling themselves in his service referred directly to his newly created household. 'Ivory staves' were insignia borne by royal officials; leaping and running suggested his athletic amusements; and the 'larger caves' alluded to his new building at Richmond and St James's.[107] The one surviving eyewitness report, written probably by a member of the Spanish embassy, suggests that this is how it was understood: it mentions 'some dozen satyrs and fairies who had much to say about the coming of a great prince to be followed by a thousand benefits, in the hope of which the fairies danced about joyfully'.[108]

This action was potentially disruptive, but the masque handled it tactfully. Though anarchic, the satyrs did not critique Jacobean order damagingly. Called 'wantons', 'wags', and 'elves' (89, 198, 224), they were merely infants, children who were yet to come of age, and remained in that condition of indiscipline that Henry was praised for having left behind. Their education in civility allowed the masque to be a symbolic performance of the Prince's maturation. Similarly, the masquers' arrival was carefully depicted as homage to James, 'To whose sole power and magic they do give / The honour of their being' (331–2). As in the *Barriers*, James was the British King in 'Arthur's chair' (323), allowing the masque to accommodate father and son in a common mythology with space for acknowledging each other's status. Still, Henry was the heroic leader and active performer, while James's transcendence left him relatively passive. Such passivity was foregrounded in Silenus' praise, his warning to the satyrs to 'quake' before James:

> He is above your reach, and neither doth
> Nor can he think within a satyr's tooth;
> Before his presence you must fall or fly,
> He is the matter of virtue and placed high. (338–41)

Silenus punned on the supposed homology between *satyr* and *satire*, in order to claim that their rudeness testified all the more forcefully to James's supremacy. As King, James transcended whatever damage satyr/satire could do, his imperviousness to criticism attesting to his glory. In governing men 'by the sweetness of his sway, / And not by force' (346–7), this was an implied warning for Henry. But if James was above satire, Henry's engagement with it was all the more striking. Attended by heroes, and leading a chaster life than his followers expected, he was in a sense already spearheading satire's reformation.

There was, then, a question over whose agenda *Oberon* celebrated. The masque's fissures were less aesthetic lapses than signs of the fault-lines which it had to bridge, tensions that were overt in the conflicting signals about its affiliations. While James had an Arthurian persona, he was also figured as Pan, the Orphic nature-god who is mysteriously immanent in all things. As Silenus told the satyrs (with a pun on the mistaken etymology that believed 'Pan' meant 'the All'):

> He makes it ever day and ever spring
> Where he doth shine, and quickens everything
> Like a new nature; so that true to call
> Him by his title is to say, he's all.   (354–7)

This compliment was problematic, since although it made James a grand cosmic presence, it underlined his links to the satyrs, of whom Pan was patron deity (66). Identifying him with Pan gave him parental responsibility for the state of anarchy. On the other hand, Henry's imagery harked back to the previous reign's political culture. As fairy prince leading Arthurian knights, he was associated with Spenserean myths of legitimation, and although Elizabeth was never mentioned, her memory was recalled iconographically.[109] In two of Jones's designs, a stag held at bay by hounds appears at the entrance to the palace.[110] This, based on Philibert de l'Orme's celebrated frontispiece for Diane de Poitiers's Chateau d'Anet, alluded to the story of Actaeon, torn apart by his own dogs for having observed Diana naked, a myth usually interpreted as advising sexual self-control and warning against profaning sacred mysteries.[111] Actaeon's presence signalled the mysteries within the palace and the masque's opposition between disorderly lusts and militant chastity, but in terms recalling the Elizabethan cult of Diana. Further, the whole masque was lit by Diana's crescent moon, to which the satyrs appealed, hoping to replace Endymion in her affections (281). Rising at the opening and setting at the end, the moon framed the masque while tactfully acknowledging the greater Jacobean sun as its light-source. With its iconography exhibiting a double parentage, *Oberon* proclaimed more than one line of affiliation. It hinted at another lineage for Henry's empowerment than that of his father.

Of course, these transactions had limits. The masque never challenged James's power, but dwelt on Henry's homage. Henry could not subvert James without acknowledging the succession that empowered him, and although the satyrs constituted the antimasque they were not displaced by the masquers but remained for the revels. This failure to repudiate the satyrs has been taken as a flaw, a sign of contradictions that *Oberon* leaves unresolved.[112] But this is

10 Inigo Jones, costume design for Prince Henry as Oberon, 1610.

to impose onto the text misleadingly rigid expectations derived from a two-part antimasque/masque structure. *Oberon* did not make a simple opposition between legitimate and illegitimate rule, with sovereign power wiping out its enemies, but a gradual disclosure, with scenes opening successively and masquers coming forward from a position of depth. It worked by incorporation, not exclusion: the satyrs were less oppositional antimasquers to be repudiated than a problematic constituency who needed silencing so that Pan's praises could be heard. In effect, they were accommodated, reformed by Henry's arrival and kept within *Oberon*'s purified ethos. As Peacock points out, the satyric element persisted in subordinated form in Jones's designs for Henry, as a motif on his cuirass (see figure 10).[113] *Oberon* modelled political change as gradualism rather than cataclysm, and while legitimating James it took its bearings from the rising heir. This was not exactly to subvert Jacobean sovereignty, but it affirmed the place Henry would take within it, and suggested that his succession would have real political and ideological consequences. While not undermining James's authority, it signalled that the reversionary interest would have its own, competing priorities.

Henry never again danced in a masque, as the Christmas festivities for 1611–12 were frugal and before the next round he was dead. One can only speculate what his masques might have delivered had he spent the next fourteen years as monarch-in-waiting. As he eased into the responsibilities of power they might have become more pragmatic, but it seems unlikely that the differences between father and son would have lessened in the next, traumatic decade. As we shall see, as political polarizations became more acute at the end of the reign, fractures resurfaced even in masques danced by the altogether more conformable Prince Charles. But one reason why Whitehall's culture seems relatively homogeneous after 1612 was the absence of an assertive reversionary interest. Henry's death removed a focus for dissident elements at Whitehall that had kept the political culture dialectical. Had he lived, the existence of competing political communities with their own subcultures would have been more apparent than historically was the case.

One set of masques did carry forward Henrician emphases into these less propitious circumstances, the triumphs mounted in 1613 to celebrate Princess Elizabeth's marriage to the Elector Frederick V (the Palatine Prince). Frederick was in England for barely three weeks before Henry died, overshadowing the celebration of this momentous union. The wedding was deferred from Christmas to Shrovetide, but the festivals that were staged – a water tournament, and masques by Campion, Chapman, and Beaumont – were the most magnificent public shows that England had ever seen. The bill (from the Elector's arrival to Elizabeth's escort into Germany) reached the staggering sum of £93,000.[114] These festivities disclose the troubled afterlife of the cultural contests discussed so far. Henry was an enthusiast for the Palatine alliance, which was a political match of the kind he wanted for himself, and before his death he was involved in planning the celebrations. He was said to 'give order for everything ... concerning the following intended triumphs', and the Venetian ambassador reported that jousts and banquets were being prepared 'in obedience to the Prince's orders'.[115] Chapman's *The Memorable Masque*, when printed, was dedicated to Henry's Chancellor, Sir Edward Phelips. Strong argues that the plans changed direction after Henry's death and that, had they been staged according to his wishes, they would have been 'the climax of [his] festival policy'.[116] This ascribes a more coherent programme to Henry's festivals than they had when he was alive, and ignores the fact that festivity had to manage policy and not merely publicize it. Nonetheless, the wedding masques do reveal the strains of a neo-chivalric culture in the post-1612 climate. They celebrated a seemingly interventionist turn in English relations with the continent at the precise moment when the hopes pinned on the principal proponent of overseas activism had collapsed.

The Palatine match was welcomed by those who regarded England's interests as served by Protestant alliances. It caused a breach with Spain and strengthened the pretensions of a Calvinist prince whom some hoped might one day be Emperor.[117] John More said it happened '*malgre* the envy and malice of the devil and all his ministers', while Chamberlain noted how much it pleased 'all well-affected people, and what joy they take in it, as being a firm foundation for the stability of religion, which (upon what conceit I know not) was before suspected to be in *bransle*'.[118] But James was a reluctant Protestant champion, and his perspective was unenthusiastic. The death of Henri IV was a Spanish windfall that left England isolated, and France quickly concluded a double marriage with Spain, forcing England into the Protestant Union's arms and leaving Europe divided on confessional lines. From Madrid, John Digby commented 'we are now so straightened that I fear we shall rather follow necessity than election'.[119] But James's long-term aims remained conciliatory: to bridge religious polarities, keep Europe balanced, and avoid warfare that increased his dependence on parliament. These goals would be better achieved with Spain as a friend, and his priorities were shown in the alliances he was pursuing for his sons. The drawn-out search for a bride for Henry had, just before his death, seemed likely to settle on a Savoyard princess, and plans for Charles focused mainly on acquiring a Spanish *infanta* – choices that were financially desirable and bridged the confessional divide. So although James welcomed the Elector, the marriage did not signify a U-turn. Frederick was pushed home early to avoid expense, and he complained that James 'did not use him like a son, but rather like a youngling or childish youth not to be regarded'.[120] As for Anne, her demeanour to him was conspicuously remote.[121]

The consequence for the festivals was a conflict between the celebration and the limits within which excessive enthusiasm had to be restrained. The most notable instance of censorship – if such it was – was the so-called *Masque of Truth*, which is mentioned only in a foreign-language narrative of the nuptials.[122] It appears in a description of the celebrations written in French by D. Jocquet, a Huguenot living at Heidelberg.[123] Jocquet omits one of the three masques, Beaumont's *Masque of the Inner Temple and*

Gray's Inn, and replaces it with a description of a performance of apocalyptic dimensions. In this otherwise unknown show, a globe is discovered, upheld by the giantess Aletheia (Truth). The globe's usual supporter, Atlas, is suffering from exhaustion at the world's sinfulness, but the muses have led him to England where Aletheia was ready to take over. From the globe there issue three vast processions depicting Europe, Asia, and Africa, with queens figuring continents, princesses representing their regions, pages in national costumes, and the principal oceans and rivers. The cast has a hundred separately named participants, all of whom dance and offer gifts. Jocquet concludes with a stunning climax. As the muses urge the world to follow England's King in worshipping Truth, the globe splits apart and discloses a paradise. This is guarded by a threatening angel, but his flaming sword and death's head disappear when Atlas and the muses conduct the nations into Elysium.

As David Norbrook argues, although *The Masque of Truth* technically resembles other masques, its ambition and theme are unique. It configures the marriage not as a dynastic liaison but as an ideological alliance, its rationale being confessional accord between the nations and promotion of the faith. This was entirely at odds with other masques. Reversing Jonson's motto, *divisus ab orbe Britannos*, it presents the marriage as re-establishing England's global links on religious grounds.[124] Even more alarmingly, these associations sweep aside the usual social affirmations. Atlas resigns his power to Truth, and contrasts with his namesake elsewhere: in *Pleasure Reconciled to Virtue* Atlas looked on while Hercules modelled heroic enterprise for dancing courtiers, and in *Coelum Britannicum* Atlas' starry sphere was home to constellations of masquers led by the King. *The Masque of Truth* ends with panegyric to the King of kings rather than King James, its angel of death exposing the theological abyss below social forms, disenchanting the game of courtly manners. It is difficult to feel that James would have approved this, though it was more to the taste of that prince whom Joshua Sylvester lamented as 'The Church's tower, the terror of the Pope, / Heroic Henry, Atlas of our hope'.[125] Its radical appropriation of masque form discloses unexpected ideological possibilities in tropes which linked 'present occasions' with 'more removed mysteries'. These 'mysteries' would have led not to a secular monarch but to a Calvinist and politically militant God.

Could it have been performed? Arrangements for the wedding were fluid until quite late, and before his death Henry might have wanted to stage such a masque, of which Jocquet's text is the only trace.[126] Norbrook points to similarities with the civic pageantry, which was always more moralistic than court masques, and to Protestant poets associated with Henry, such as

Browne or Sylvester, who could have been its author. James was happy for the alliance to be seen as reinforcing solidarity with other Christian nations. The celebrations included a firework display themed around St George and the dragon, and a water-pageant in which Turkish ships were defeated and their 'bashaws' taken prisoner.[127] But these shows did not draw battle lines within Christendom, and it seems unlikely that even Henry could have mounted so contentious a masque without interference from his father. Writing for a European audience, Jocquet probably articulated what overseas opinion hoped James's rationale for the alliance was. As one of three continental accounts, his pamphlet expressed the view from Heidelberg, framing the events with a poem that depicted Frederick as Jason bringing the Golden Fleece home to a grateful people.[128] This expressed hopes in the Palatinate, where the triumphal arches were erected welcoming Elizabeth as a militant virgin in Gloriana's mould, and using Protestant imagery more emphatically than in England. German observers like André Paull thought that this marriage, 'contracted for the profit of all Christendom', had broken 'the damnable designs' of God's enemies,[129] but the Whitehall perspective was less eschatological. In the celebrations that definitely were staged, the space for representing the alliance as a blow for the faith was strictly limited.

One objective of the English celebrations was to contain the marriage's confessional associations: the emphases at home were social and dynastic. The limits of acceptability are well seen in the celebration for which James paid, Campion's *The Lords' Masque*. A double masque, of lords and ladies, this was especially spectacular, and its perspective seemed visionary. Its masquers descended from heaven to earth in the form of stars carrying lances,[130] and it culminated with a prophecy of Frederick's imperial future, spoken by a Sibyl drawing an obelisk 'dedicate to fame' on a golden thread (259).[131] Speaking in Latin, 'her native tongue' (261), she named his imperial destiny:

How the beautiful bride responds to the handsome husband! How full of power! She expresses her father in her face, the future mother of a male progeny, the mother of kings, of emperors. Let the British strength be added to the German: can anything equal it? One mind, one faith, will join two peoples, and one religion and simple love. Both will have the same enemy, the same ally, the same prayer for those in danger, and the same strength. Peace will favour them, and the fortune of war will favour them: always God the helper will be at their side. (260)

The use of Latin underlined the prophecy's religious aspect, since the enemy of Britannia and Germania could only be Roma. The Sibyl predicted a *translatio* of empire from south to north: envisioning the modern Caesar as conquering her Rome with a purified faith, she reversed the trajectories of religious history. This imagined a far from passive future for Frederick, though its implications were ambiguous. As he was only sixteen, his destiny was far off, and the songs emphasized offspring rather than heroism. Equally, since the enemy was not Spain but the Pope, this chimed with James's perspective, as he took his role as defender of the faith seriously. But, more importantly, the action had already framed the marriage in ways which ensured that potentially disruptive enthusiasms were firmly contained.

Containment came in two ways. The opening scene showed Entheus (poetic fury) being freed from Mania (insanity). Orpheus procured his freedom, and, although figuring the divinely inspired poet, Entheus stood here as art's harmonizing power, being introduced with wild beasts sitting tamely around him. The separation of Entheus from the 'frantics' signalled that the masque's acclamations were not tainted by unreasonable enthusiasm. Mania was anxious that, if her door were unlocked, 'All will fly out, and through the world disturb / The peace of Jove' (250), but Orpheus' harmonies ensured order would prevail. Whatever else was said, there would be no concessions to fanaticism. Secondly, the main action, in which the stars descended, was double-edged. This seemed 'a courtly miracle' (253), but its transgressiveness was emphasized. The stars were fires stolen from heaven by Prometheus, and although the 'flames in human shapes' (252) seemed divine, they were traitors to Jove, because of their 'theft' and 'stealth' (252–3). As a punishment, Jove had turned their dancing partners into stone – eight women whom Prometheus had made. These Jove released by degrees, in tranches of four, expressing the gradual cooling of his anger:

> Lo, how fixed they stand;
> So did Jove's wrath too long, but now at last
> It by degrees relents, and he hath placed
> These statues that we might his aid implore,
> First for the life of these, and then for more.   (256)

This twist on the myth was Campion's invention (in other versions Prometheus is punished by having an eagle peck his liver), and it made the transformation sequence an exercise in solicitation between Prometheus and Jove. As in *Lord Hay's Masque*, the central action staged a symbolic transaction of power, but whereas in the earlier show the kingly Apollo conciliated Diana, in *The Lords' Masque* the action testified unequivocally to Jove's authority. The dances could not proceed until Jove answered the chorus's prayers.

David Lindley interprets this sequence as a ritual enactment of dynastic politics. He notes that the dance at the midpoint, in which 'Each woman hath two lovers' (257), mimed Princess Elizabeth's situation in autumn

1612, poised between brother and husband. The ensuing action, in which Jove provided partners for the uncoupled men by changing the remaining statues, played out James's as yet incomplete schemes for his heir (the plans for Henry's marriage having been inherited by Charles). Prometheus and Entheus spelled matters out:

> Cease, cease your wooing strife; see Jove intends
> To fill your number up, and make all friends ...
> For all are sped, and now begins delight,
> To fill with glory this triumphant night.   (257)

As Lindley says, 'This is a precise summary of James's political intentions in his marriage plans for his children.'[132] Moreover, Campion's emphasis on the masquers' guilt gave the fable ideological purchase. With the masque staging Prometheus's contest with Jove, the praise of his sons was allowed only after Jove's anger was assuaged, so that the subversive heroics of Promethean aspiration were not so much licensed as forgiven. Whatever these virile heroes achieved, at the moment they asserted themselves they were subordinated to Jove's prior authority.

By this stage of his career Campion was moving into the Howard orbit, and his celebration of imperial potential within a carefully qualified frame expressed a view of the Palatine marriage that was acceptable to those concerned about peace. The masque represented the Elector as a suitable son-in-law, but by disparaging unruly enthusiasms and Promethean ambition it offered reassurance that England would not be drawn into dangerous religious commitments. And with its emphasis on James's all-competent sovereignty, it initiated a new iconographic turn. In this 'nuptial by his will / Begun and ended' (251), everything was subject to Jove's controlling power. It was Jove who sent Orpheus to release Entheus, transformed the statues, inspired the Sybil, and to whom the obelisk was dedicated. No previous masque had identified James with Jove or made so concerted an attempt to render his sovereignty godlike, yet in subsequent festivals such associations became clichés. Campion celebrated an alliance which threatened to unbalance Jacobean policy, but his fable suggested a hardening of attitude. He responded to troubling circumstances by creating tropes that were seminal for the more reverential treatment of monarchy in later masques.

It was left to the two Inns of Court masques to develop perspectives that addressed the religious dimension. Beaumont's *Masque of the Inner Temple and Gray's Inn* was much the simpler. It featured a group of Olympian knights, who appeared in their pavilions around an altar dedicated to Jove, preceded by nymphs, stars, Cupids, statues, and country folk introduced by Mercury and

Iris. Graham Parry calls this 'anodyne',[133] but its combination of militarism and piety projected a view of the marriage sympathetic to the Protestant agenda, and the country dance implied that it was welcomed beyond the court. The knights were dressed in 'veils', 'copes', and 'mitres' (289–90);[134] their pavilions looked like a military camp, and their dances were a temporary respite from their life of ascetic heroism. Jove's priests absolved them of any sins relaxation might breed, and they resumed their swords after the dances. This would have evoked Henry's memory, for he was sometimes hailed as an Olympian knight: in the funeral lament by Ralegh's friend Sir Arthur Gorges, *The Olympian Catastrophe*, he was seen as a chivalric hero plucked tragically from Olympus by the gods.[135] There was also a Spenserean aspect since, in a motif recollecting *The Faerie Queene* book 4, the nuptials were represented as uniting the Thames and Rhine, a theme pre-echoed in the masquers' decision to process to Whitehall by water. Of the performed masques, only this one envisaged the alliance as having military consequences, and the praise of royal power which was so emphatic in *The Lords' Masque* was absent. The fable was overseen by Jove, but a contest for precedence between Mercury and Iris (Jove's and Juno's messengers, respectively) ensured that Beaumont's Jove had less dignity than Campion's. His power did not abase those over whom it was wielded: the marriage delighted the whole state, not merely the monarch.

The performance which most clearly suggested Henry's hand was Chapman's *The Memorable Masque*, presented by gentlemen from the Middle Temple and Lincoln's Inn. It was disarmingly straightforward, presenting a scene of golden rocks that opened to disclose masquers dressed as Virginian princes. But structurally it was complex, since it addressed the marriage only indirectly, and had two distinct actions. One was the arrival of the Virginians to compliment the couple and associate their gold with the British Isles: this alluded to the likely profits of New World enterprise. The other was the reconciliation which the wedding made between Honour and Plutus, god of riches: this alluded to issues of equivalence between reward and merit. The two actions were held together by Plutus who, being involved in both, bridged antimasque and masque, but the structure was decentred, and its gestures of legitimation were oblique. For example, the masquers did not recognize James as the fount of power and had to be tutored in king-worship. The inconsistencies indicated an unusually complex relationship between masque and occasion.

D. J. Gordon sees the masque as elaborating Plutarch's discussion of the antithesis between Riches and Honour,[136] but it is important to emphasize how timely these concerns were. When in 1610 the Great Contract failed, Plutus became *the* Jacobean obsession, and as the crown sank into deficit

finance, James took desperate measures just to keep afloat. In 1611, he created
the new order of baronets in order to raise cash, provoking complaints that
honour was being put up to auction, particularly from lesser nobility who felt
it brought their precedence into question.[137] Meanwhile negotiations for
Henry's bride became money-driven: ostensibly the choice was a policy
matter, but it was evident that the suitor to offer the largest dowry would
do best. Henry's distaste for the whole business was well known. He said 'he
did not desire either to be bought or sold', and feared the money would 'not
come into his hands' but be 'scattered by the king's profusion'.[138] Complaints
about this figured in Jonson's *Love Restored* (1612) – discussed in chapter 7
below – in which Plutus disguises himself as Cupid, 'and in his belied figure
reigns [i'] the world, making friendships, contracts, marriages, and almost
religion, … usurping all those offices in this Age of Gold which Love himself
performed in the Golden Age' (172–8). But Chapman's Plutus differed from
the blind miser of classical precedent and from Jonson's crabbed puritan, for
he had wit and discrimination. Behind this shift lay the hopes for radical
initiatives which, in some quarters, the marriage aroused.

Plutus' good judgment appeared in the opening antimasque, a dialogue
with Capriccio, a fantastical traveller and 'man of wit' (20) who came to
court in the hope of benefiting from its riches. Capriccio was complex:
though no fool, he carried attributes (a bellows and spur) that linked him
to Ripa's emblem of Caprice, an image which reappeared as Levity in Henry
Peacham's *Minerva Britanna* (an emblem book written within Prince
Henry's circle). Peacham glossed Levity as

> Capriccio, or th'unstaid mind,
> Whom thousand fancies hourly do possess,
> For riding post, with every blast of wind;
> In naught he's steady, save unstableness.[139]

In the masque, Capriccio was a gold-digger, attended by baboons in Italian
dress, and with few deserving qualities: 'is it impossible that I, for breaking a
clean jest, should be advanced in court or council? Or at least, served out for
an ambassador to a dull climate?' (102–4). Though he was plausible, Plutus
saw through him, and dismissed him as unworthy of honour: 'I cannot
abide these bellows of thy head, they and thy men of wit have melted my
mines with them' (174–5). Since Capriccio was an outsider this was not a
critique of the court as such,[140] but it echoed Henry, who wanted his
household to be a college 'picked and chosen out of the best and rarest
spirits of Great Britain',[141] and those who felt that the scramble after cash
was undermining the link between honour, merit, and preferment. By

envisioning Plutus dispensing rewards honourably and denying them to undeservers, the antimasque's view of preferment was tactfully reformist.

The rest of the masque concerned Plutus' wealth, the 'womb of gold' (238) where the Indian princes appeared, and their conversion from sun-worship to king-worship. While reiterating masque tropes in which exotic aliens acclaimed James's sovereignty, the linking of political and ideological perspectives was more emphatic. The Virginians were noble but superstitious barbarians, whose conversion was political homage as much as Christian illumination. When they were disclosed, their priests turned their backs to James and invoked the setting sun, but were told to turn eastwards, where the true Phoebus sat, bringing 'heaven's true light / To your dark region' (333–4). This affirmed James's formal centrality, so much so that Gordon read it as a simple neoplatonic extension of Orphic ideas of kingship.[142] But this powerfully regno-centric action was problematic, since the missionary justifications for colonial enterprise appealed to those with a forward view of kingship, and had already been co-opted to promote Henry's cult. Tracts on exploration dedicated to the Prince emphasized that colonization brought the gospel to foreign peoples, and Henry planned to build a college for converting infidels at Henrico, Virginia.[143] Although complimentary to James, the masque gave kingship a theological rationale, suggesting that the marriage's religious dimension would make it famous even in Virginia. The 'golden world' (383) would subject 'black Error's night' to 'Christian piety' (331–2).

Although the masquers came from Virginia, they conflated two ventures. Their feathered dress was North American but their sun-worship and association with gold invoked another enterprise: Guiana. This was Ralegh's great project, his explorations having proved, he thought, that Guiana would rival Spanish Peru for wealth. The masque's scene, a rock that 'grew by degrees up into a gold colour, and was run quite through with veins of gold', opening to disclose 'a rich and refulgent mine' (119–20, 158–9), was based on Ralegh's narrative of his 1595 voyage, which described Guiana as literally gleaming: 'all the rocks, mountains, all stones in the plains, in woods, and by the rivers' sides are in effect through-shining, and appear marvellous rich, which being tried … are no other than *El madre del oro* (as the Spaniards term them), which is the mother of gold'.[144] In his panegyric *De Guiana* (1596), Chapman praised Guiana in terms like his masque ('Sit till you see a wonder, Virtue rich: / Till Honour having gold, rob gold of honour'), and the depiction of American riches chimed with the openings created in 1613 by James's temporary estrangement from Spain. Ralegh, hoping to be released from the Tower by playing on James's impecuniousness, had suggested that an expedition to Guiana might solve the money problem.[145] This was a project that Henry would have sympathized with, but James knew it would create conflict with Spain (as indeed happened on Ralegh's final voyage). Chapman's purely notional geography transposed the mines to Virginia, where they could be hymned without upsetting Spain, but the audience must have known which enterprise was more golden. This masque's solution for the cash-flow problem was indeed radical.

The Memorable Masque came closest of any of the 1613 festivals to the apocalyptic *Masque of Truth*, yet its radicalism had to be limited by tact. It could offer Guiana as a model for overseas enterprise only by conflating it with Virginia, and its promotion of religion was checked by its focus on the King's person. In comparison with *The Masque of Truth*, this would be a muted apocalypse, with the separations between Britain and the world overcome casually, not through deliberate policy. Britain, said Capriccio, was '*divisus ab orbe*', but since she stood 'fixed on her own feet and defies the world's mutability', as the globe turned, other nations would come round to her (296–7). This joke delicately reversed the trope of Jacobean separateness, but without relating it to any grand design. Britain's religious mission was voiced within limits, the global aspirations that would have been confidently presented in *The Masque of Truth* being elided. This indicated the ideological constraints affecting the Palatine marriage, though, by enfolding a radical agenda within a respectful performance, *The Memorable Masque* brought multiple perspectives to bear on it. The pull of Guiana against Virginia, and Plutus' concern for the proper distribution of rewards, indicated the divisions that Whitehall's culture had to bridge. Against this, *The Lords' Masque*, with its praise of Jove and containment of unruly enthusiasms, indicated that culture's likely future directions.

These tensions indicated the court's underlying transformation in the years after Henry's death. The Palatine marriage was an event on the continental stage; its triumphs were staged with one eye on Europe, and descriptions circulated in German and French.[146] But succeeding masques lost this dimension and increasingly turned to explore James's domestic rule and his relationship with his courtiers. In part this was because of changes in masquing personnel, but more broadly because politics had become dominated by the peace lobby. With Henry dead and Elizabeth absent, and with influence monopolized by the Howards, the warmongers were marginalized. As neither France nor Spain wanted conflict, an uneasy equilibrium prevailed, and James took advantage of this by embarking on a determined, if leisurely, pursuit of a Spanish bride for Prince Charles. These changed priorities were signalled in the masques after the Palatine wedding, all of which reinforced the attitude of *Love Freed*, that 'Britain's the world, the world without' (285). Masques re-engaged with European politics only at the end of the decade with the onset of the Bohemian crisis. However, this was a decisive shift, and it was rooted in a chain of consequences trailing back to 1613. Since the new war was triggered by Frederick's support for Bohemian Protestantism, the late Jacobean masques were embroiled in fall-out that followed, belatedly but inexorably, from Elizabeth's marriage. The crisis which they faced arose from just those ideological divisions which the 1613 festivities attempted to inhibit.

Although after Henry's death the chivalric ethos became gradually attenuated, his culture had involved a dialectic between two tendencies competing for space at Whitehall. The opposition between Henrician and Jacobean was not absolute, but Stuart festivity could not ignore the ideological differences which it entailed. James's culture strove to enclose Henry's forms, accommodating his militarism to its pacifism, but this was not easily accomplished. Particularly, Henry's codes of masculine self-assertion, which survived in sublimated form in subsequent festivals, were at odds with the ideology of self-control, poise, grace, and balance promoted by Jacobean ceremoniousness. If masques emphasized the triumph of reason over passion, and containment in outward and interior life, Henry's martial exercises unsettled that discipline, disrupting the otherwise seamless courtly display. This was something that James's culture could neither ignore nor entirely discharge but had to work around, even after Henry's death, when his ideas were kept alive by his political heirs. James's festivals had to find forms which promoted his kingship and accommodated those whose priorities diverged from his, and this made for a culture whose claims to transcendence could never be finally achieved, since its closures were always open to question. Only in the lull before 1619 was a temporary balance achieved between the images of consensus and the political performance.

CHAPTER 7

The dance of favour

On Twelfth Night 1612, a disaster happened at Jonson's *Love Restored*. Ironically, the masque's fiction was that something really was wrong with the performance, which the King's presence put right: the show was unable to get under way until obstacles presented in the antimasque were circumvented. The show opened with a masquer apologizing for delay caused by the boy playing Cupid catching a cold and being unable to speak, only to be interrupted by a figure who looked like Cupid but who, startlingly, railed against masquing and threatened to ban it. Then Robin Goodfellow appeared – supposedly the 'real' Robin Goodfellow – with a long tale about being kept out of court, and the stratagems he used to get in. Robin recognized the supposed Cupid for who he was, the money-god Plutus (often depicted like Cupid, as a curly-headed boy), who had stolen Cupid's ensigns and thrust him out, spoiling the celebrations. With Plutus discovered, the masquers brought Cupid on in triumph. He was dressed in a fur against the cold, but once warmed by the King's beams he discarded it, saying the revels would show the dancers' 'flamed intents' (255) from basking in the royal sun. But as Chamberlain reported, instead of the dances displaying James's nurturing fire, a shock followed: 'when they came to take out ladies, beginning [with my ladies] of Essex and Cranborne, they were refused, [and this gave] example to the rest, so that they were fain [to dance] alone and make court one to another'.[1] The dances should have displayed the concords of James's court and Love's victory over Money, but their non-performance embarrassingly subverted the masque's closures, revealing a gap between its aesthetics and other, more material agendas.

When Jonson printed the text, he suppressed any reference to this rebellion, and it is difficult to know what was at stake. The two named women were sisters, Frances Howard, Lady Essex, and Catherine Howard, Lady Cranborne, and it is tempting to suppose that their behaviour was a private plot, but since the other ladies followed suit this is unlikely (and Chamberlain's letter implies it embarrassed their father, the Earl of

Suffolk).[2] Possibly it was a sign of Prince Henry's hand, since they were married to associates of his, but this seems improbable since the masque was danced by a mixed company of gentlemen from his household and the King's: he would hardly have arranged for one of his own festivals to be spoiled.[3] A third possibility lurks in Chamberlain's observation that most of the masquers were Scots: maybe the refusal reflected tensions between the nations. Or perhaps the aristocratic women were offended by the low status of the gentlemen with whom they had to dance. Whatever the reason, their refusal is revealing for calling into question a series of principles that, though unspoken, were fundamental to masquing. It subverted the masque's aesthetic unity and proved its compliments were contrived, demonstrating that the dancers' apparent unanimity was riven with tensions, and exposing the fiction that their gracious movements embodied their regard for the King. It foregrounded the coerciveness of masquing protocols, uncovering the hidden rule that, when taken out, the women would always cooperate with their partners. And it exploded the form's collegiality, showing how easy it was for individual masquers to upstage their fellows, sidelining the main group with attention-seeking behaviour that captured the occasion for themselves. Small wonder that Jonson erased all memory of the performance from his printed text.

It is hard not to suppose that this female rebellion undermined the masque's politics, its aim of displaying the selfless service that characterized James's court.[4] *Love Restored* was responding to the parlous state of royal finance: reassuring James that with his courtiers' Love (Cupid) he could do without Money (Plutus), it took up the issue which more than any other dominated the mid-reign. After the failure of the Great Contract (1610), Whitehall descended into a scramble for cash that lasted the rest of the decade. In 1611 James created the order of baronets, simply so that the title could be sold; Prince Henry's marriage negotiations became an auction for the bride with the best dowry; and in December, a Forced Loan was instituted (a device by which money was 'lent' to the crown, but which was really a one-off unparliamentary tax).[5] *Love Restored* embraced the idea of economy, being ostentatiously inexpensive in comparison with previous Christmases, and endorsed the Forced Loan by advising the King not to 'crave / [Plutus's] aids, but *force* him as a slave' (249–50).[6] However, its main argument was that James did not need conventional finance, since his court was bound together by gratitude, the King's favours arousing the courtiers' selfless love. If the antimasque was ruled by Money and lacked Love, the main masque reintroduced Love under the sponsorship of good-fellowship. With Robin Goodfellow ejecting Plutus, the selfishness of money was replaced by the courtiers' serviceable gratitude, their dancing expressing the perfect equivalence of reward and merit.

But the women's attention-grabbing threatened to deconstruct the ideology of service. Cupid emphasized that the masquers would not 'rudely strive for place, / One to precede the other', but would display how the court was bound into 'one harmony'. Together, their individual honour, courtesy, valour, urbanity would figure the 'ornaments / That do each courtly presence grace' (254–68). But the women wrecked this. With the men dancing unhandsomely with each other, the images of concord must have seemed lop-sided, the symbolism of selfless cooperation contradicted by competition amongst the performers. The women do not seem to have wanted any rewards, or to have benefited from their behaviour. Nonetheless, they compromised the fiction that the dancers' devotion expressed Whitehall's love – that common loyalty which dissolved ambitions, antagonisms, and selfish ends. If the masque wanted to affirm the court's devotion in contrast to the mercenary gain that prevailed elsewhere, then the ladies' scene-stealing demonstrated that below this symbolic economy lurked a more material economy of self-promotion. Far from affirming that the courtiers' sole desire was to serve the King, the hijacking of *Love Restored* showed that, however elevated, the masque floor was just one more arena in which individuals competed for their own objectives.

Love Restored announced themes and forms that dominated the mid-Jacobean masques. After the celebrations for the Palatine marriage, court festival turned inwards, towards a culture of faction focused on the domestic sphere, in which rival favourites and affinities competed for access to royal bounty. This was partly due to a personnel shift, which was radically affected by Henry's death, Elizabeth's marriage and emigration, and Queen Anne's retirement from masquing, leaving the adolescent Prince Charles the only available royal dancer. Between the Palatine marriage and Charles's first masque, *Pleasure Reconciled to Virtue* (1618), no royal family member danced, and masques ceased to centre on the personalities and politics of the next generation. Instead, the prevailing mode followed lines set by *Love Restored*. The typical format was symbolic homage to the monarch danced by a group of prominent courtiers, such as Lennox, Pembroke, Dorset, and Buckingham, supplemented by a tail of lesser figures, such as Roger Palmer, James Bovey, Abraham Abercromby, and James Achmouty, minor courtiers who were valued for their athleticism ('the high dancers', as Chamberlain called them).[7] Even after Charles had emerged as principal masquer, court festival continued to showcase male courtiers, because of a taste in James's last decade for amateur performances outside the main Twelfth Night and Shrovetide occasions (of which Buckingham's *The Gypsies Metamorphosed* was the main example).[8] And until Henrietta Maria's arrival, there was no prominent woman sponsoring masques, so the female presence declined radically. The cancellation of *The Masque of Amazons*, intended for private performance in 1618 by ladies from Lord Hay's family, was symptomatic of how late-Jacobean masquing shifted into a pre-eminently masculine pursuit.[9]

The turn towards a culture of faction corresponded with the politics, dominated as the mid-Jacobean years were by the struggle for influence and reward. With the deaths of Salisbury and Henry, both in 1612, two strong figures disappeared from Whitehall, leaving a fluid state that was not resolved until the emergence of Buckingham as unchallenged favourite in 1616. After Salisbury's death, James kept power out of a single advisor's hands. He put the Treasury into commission and decided to be his own secretary, though in practice this role devolved onto the current favourite, Robert Carr, Viscount Rochester. For nearly three years, courtiers competed keenly for these posts, as rival affinities manoeuvred on behalf of their candidates. The situation stabilized in 1614, when Suffolk was appointed to the Treasurership, his office as Chamberlain going to Carr (now promoted to Earl of Somerset). This was a major structural change, for it politicized the role of favourite. Hitherto, Somerset and his predecessors had essentially been the King's intimate friends, but Somerset's receipt of a major household office (foreshadowed in his appointment to the Privy Council in 1612) marked the emergence of the favourite as a broker of policy and power as well as patronage, a transformation played out in the career of his successor, Buckingham.[10] Moreover, Somerset had kept in with the Howards' rivals, such as the Earl of Southampton (with whom he was in 'manifest faction'),[11] but he was now drawn into alliance with the Howards through a romantic attachment to Suffolk's daughter Frances, whom he married in December 1613 after the annulment of her union with Essex. This aggravated Essex's friends, since it was a victory for the conservative faction and insulted the Earl's masculine honour, and it affirmed the Howard stranglehold, giving them an alliance in the Bedchamber with the man with whom (said the Venetian ambassador) 'the King decides everything and in whom his majesty confides above all others'.[12]

Neither Somerset nor Suffolk held their places long, as each fell victim to the reign's two major scandals. In 1615 Somerset was brought down by revelations concerning the death of his friend Sir Thomas Overbury two years earlier. Overbury had been bitterly opposed to the Howards and to

Frances Howard's developing relationship with Somerset, and when evidence was found that his death in 1613 had been due to poison, the procurement of his murder was laid at Frances's door. Somerset seems to have been ignorant of the crime and protested his innocence at his arraignment in 1616, but he could not evade guilt by association and the affair destroyed him, and damaged the careers of his clients.[13] Then in 1619 his father-in-law was sunk by charges of corruption arising from an economy drive. In an investigation into the Treasury, Suffolk, his wife, and their officials were discovered to be enmeshed in peculation on an astronomical scale. Bribery and kickbacks were endemic to a bureaucracy in which remunerations were uneconomic and officials had to exploit the profits of their place, but Suffolk had used the Exchequer almost as a private resource and, at a time of mounting debt, had connived at extortion and misaccounting.[14] These events gave a point of purchase to rivals who wanted to unpick the Howard monopoly, and in 1616 Somerset's office of Chamberlain went to Pembroke, while George Villiers, the future Duke of Buckingham, quickly replaced him in the royal affections. In the following years Villiers shot higher than Somerset, and, ironically, acquired a monopoly of patronage even more complete than his had been.

With some justice, contemporaries perceived James's middle decade as a time of drift, its spectacular reversals demonstrating the high stakes to be played for and the absence of coordinated policy. Somerset's and Buckingham's careers exemplified the new political centrality of the favourite, and put the problematic practices of courtiership under intense scrutiny: the thin line between legitimate and illegitimate rewards, the lack of agreed standards of remuneration, the ambiguity about the King's emotional ties to his advisors.[15] With the damaging perspectives that it opened onto the King's friends, the Overbury scandal marked a low point, but the court was already perceived as a market of preferment. Although merit and reward were supposed to be equivalent (as brokers channelled royal bounty out towards deserving clients), few were unaware how much depended on a patron's whim. As one of Trumbull's correspondents noted, describing affairs at Salisbury's death: 'All our state is in several motions, some towards good, that's the King and some few, others only bending their affections and power to preserve a continual favour, which is the misery of our age. Everything uncertain, but the best hope declining'.[16] Equally revealing was George Calvert's view of Somerset as 'the *primum mobile* of our court, by whose motion all the other spheres must move, or else stand still; the bright sun of our firmament, at whose splendour or glooming all our marigolds of the court open or shut. In his conjunction all the other stars are prosperous,

and in his opposition mal-ominous.'[17] The increased numbers competing for
access and the high visibility of casualties also sapped confidence. Observing
in 1620 that, besides Suffolk and Somerset, Lord Admiral Nottingham,
Secretary Lake, Attorney General Bacon, and Lord Chief Justice Coke had
all been disgraced, Chamberlain glumly remarked 'it seems we live of late
under some rolling planet'.[18]

This extraordinary fluidity was symptomatic of the other structural
problem affecting the crown – the shortage of cash, which made it impossible to finance royal bureaucracy, and created the image of a spendthrift
monarch surrounded by courtiers gaping for hire. From the beginning
James languished under chronic money problems. Unlike the miserly
Elizabeth, he was a lavish spender and his rewards to favourites were a
recurrent complaint. His free gifts had risen to a value of £80,000 by 1611,
and he was generous even when money was short, paying off £44,000 in
debts for Haddington, Hay, and Montgomery in 1607, and lavishing
a third of a £50,000 loan in 1618 on gifts to four courtiers.[19] Some of his
largest departments were run by notoriously incompetent officials – like
Nottingham at the Navy and Suffolk at the Treasury – or men who prided
themselves on living in a high style (like Hay, who spent over £176,000 in
eight years at the Wardrobe).[20] But his problems were not solely his own
creation. He could not govern without rewarding his servants, and the
system was riddled with slack procedures, wastage, and graft, and inflation
was eating away at revenues while costs were increasing. Unlike his predecessor, he had a consort, children, and diplomacy to maintain, and the
household bills spiralled, topping £100,000 by 1614, nearly four times their
1603 level.[21] James plunged into deficit finance, and his debt reached
unprecedented heights. In 1610 he owed £500,000, with an annual deficit
of £46,000. Eight years on the debt had again almost doubled.

The 1610s saw several failed reforms: Salisbury's Great Contract, the
abortive attempt to manage the 1614 parliament, the sale of peerages, and
assaults on expenditure undertaken with varying degrees of conviction.
Much the most successful measures were spearheaded by Lionel Cranfield
in 1617–20, who sought to introduce good economic practice into the
household, rooting out fraud and trimming fat.[22] But even Cranfield
could not legislate against extraordinary expenditure nor counteract the
assumption that largesse was intrinsic to royalty, without which the King's
honour would be diminished. To those under threat of cutback, mercantile good management went against courtly magnificence, and Cranfield's
qualifications – his background in trade – made him appear 'insolent and
saucy' at court, 'out of [his] own element'.[23] As Sir Thomas Chaloner put

it, 'in the King's honour, some prodigality is not so dishonourable as a little spending'; even Godfrey Goodman felt that by niggling economies 'little was saved' but 'great dishonour [done] to his majesty'.[24] Such remarks echoed Salisbury's view that 'for a king not to be bountiful were a fault', or James's promise to parliament that, while he would restrain his gifts, 'a king's liberality must never be dried up altogether, for then he can never maintain nor oblige his servants and well-deserving subjects'.[25] In the discourse of reform, the conflict between good management and honour could never be entirely reconciled. The exemplar of these contradictions was Buckingham himself, who arrived as an agent for the forward party, a patron of Cranfield, and a proponent of economy, but who screwed more money out of his position than any previous favourite.[26]

Masques were crucial to Whitehall's culture of display, and were intimately involved in the competition for place conducted through extravagant spending. Testimonies to the careless ostentation of the King who could afford them, they were a stage for self-promotion and insinuation: successful performance would accumulate praise and social capital, enhancing a masquer's status in the eyes of peers and monarch. Of course, dancing in a masque never brought anyone a secretaryship, and a reminder of the difference in courtly styles is the fact that, while Frances Howard masqued several times, Somerset himself never took to the floor. Although Somerset first came to royal notice in an incident at a festival – as Hay's page, he broke his leg while presenting an impresa at a tilt, after which James began to enquire about him – his reluctance to stage himself publicly testifies to his more austere persona and, perhaps, to his relatively secure entrenchment in the King's affections.[27] By contrast, Buckingham's glamorously theatrical performances built on his personal charisma. As is suggested by the cut of his hose in William Larkin's portrait (see figure 11), he had no inhibitions about displaying his athleticism and physical grace, and his masques must always have been occasions for exchanges of intimacy with James. And for lesser aspirants to favour, these grand occasions held scarcely less promise. Few overextended themselves as sadly as Sir Henry Bowyer, who practised so hard for *The Masque of Squires* that he died from 'overheating'.[28] But it was a calculated gesture when Ralph Winwood wore an expensive new suit at the same masque, then gave Somerset a lavish gift, and horses to pull his coach to *The Masque of Cupids* at Merchant Taylors' Hall.[29] Winwood was hoping to achieve the secretaryship of state, an office that came his way three months later. Even more was at stake for those courtiers who aspired to places of personal intimacy with the monarch. A show such as *Lord Haddington's Masque* (1608), danced by noblemen of whom five were

11 William Larkin (attrib.), *George Villiers*, c. 1616.

Gentlemen of the Bedchamber, must have seemed like a private celebration amongst the King's nearest and dearest.

These circumstances make it difficult to draw a line on the masquing floor where pleasure ended and business began. Although masques showed the court at play, its everyday affairs apparently suspended, the business of solicitation and reward was going on nonetheless, the gestures of celebration and compliment being less disinterested than they appeared, not least because of the erotic undertow they facilitated amongst the King's closest circle. One commonplace in the courtesy books of sixteenth-century Italy was that pleasure was a courtier's business, in which he must take pains to succeed. Trivial though proficiency in revelling seemed, courtesy handbooks represented it as germane to self-promotion, the courtier's *otium* being the pursuit of *negotium* in aesthetically acceptable forms. As Francesco Guicciardini put it:

When I was young, I used to scoff at knowing how to play, dance, and sing, and at other such frivolities. I even made light of good penmanship, knowing how to ride, to dress well, and all those things that seem more decorative than substantial in a man. But, later, I wished I had not done so. For although it is not wise to spend too much time cultivating the young toward the perfection of these arts, I have nevertheless seen from experience that these ornaments and accomplishments lend dignity and reputation even to men of good rank ... Moreover, skill in this sort of entertainment opens the way to the favour of princes, and sometimes becomes the beginning or the reason for great profit and high honours.[30]

Similar perspectives were argued by Castiglione and Romei, for whom it was essential for the courtier to attract admiration through his audacious performances on grand occasions, the cultivation of an attractive grace being a way to achieve access. The implications of this for Jacobean masquing were profound. It meant that the apparently easy grace of the dances could always be exposed as an illusion, a patina of spontaneity designed to render as if natural what were in fact highly self-conscious performances. And from this perspective, the masques' vertical transactions between King and courtier were complicated by horizontal exchanges between the performers that were potentially more antagonistic than collegial. A masquer whose dancing was especially dazzling helped the evening to succeed, but his prominence came at the risk of sidelining the unity of the group. As *Love Restored* showed, masques demanded group solidarity and the illusion of improvisation, yet in significant respects their social agendas were in tension with their encompassing political ethos.

In contrast to the Palatine celebrations, with their eager crowds and imperial myth-making, the festivities for Somerset's wedding (Christmas 1613–14) were low-key and hedged with factional tensions. Perhaps the staggering expenditure incurred in February made economies necessary. The Inns of Court, said Samuel Calvert, declined to contribute anything, 'their expenses having been already extraordinary in shows, which they performed with greater affection than they can afford'.[31] In place of a collaborative masque, Francis Bacon gave Gray's Inn £2,000 to stage *The Masque of Flowers*, a gesture marking his personal obligations to the favourite. He had been promoted to Attorney-General, and although Sir Henry Yelverton offered to help pay, Bacon refused, lest it diluted the expression of his gratitude.[32] But elsewhere the royal wish for festivals met foot-dragging. The Lord Mayor had to be commanded to make a feast, and although this featured Middleton's *Masque of Cupids*, it was put together in four days and Middleton never printed it.[33] Presumably it could not be helped that the show for the marriage night, *The Masque of Squires*, was spoiled by the inexperience of its designer, Constantine de' Servi, who drew the invention 'into a far narrower compass than was from the beginning intended': the screeching wheels and visible ropes of his cloud machine provoked satirical comparisons with a portcullis.[34] But it is striking that the featured poet was Campion, now fully established as a Howard client, rather than Jonson, and that Jonson's contribution to the revelry, *The Irish Masque at Court*, made several ungracious jokes about the poverty of Campion's fable.[35] Problems were also encountered in mounting a tournament, since some of the invited tilters did not wish to participate in an event glorifying Somerset. Said the Savoy agent, 'many of them have refused because they are relatives of the Earl of Essex, and others have excused themselves, not being part of this faction'.[36] Frances Howard's cousin, Sir Edward Sackville, was allowed to tilt even though he had recently killed Lord Bruce of Kinloss in a duel. Suffolk pleaded with the King for his inclusion, since 'there is so few that will be willing to take his place if he go out'.[37] He also begged the Earl of Rutland and Lord Willoughby d'Eresby to dance in the masque; in the event Rutland joined the tilt, but Willoughby was not amongst the masquers.[38]

So for all the predictions, Somerset's marriage was celebrated with less bravery than was anticipated, and this relatively modest ostent led to fewer objections than might have arisen: Sir John Throckmorton was disappointed that the gifts came to only £10,000.[39] Nonetheless, it remained divisive because of the contests of personality and affinity which played across it, which conflicted with the rhetoric of amity expressed in the panegyrics. Since the Somersets married only weeks after Frances's first marriage was annulled, it was impossible for the celebrations not to become mired in political fall-out. Here it is important to distinguish what was public knowledge about the Somersets at the time of their marriage from the obloquy which overtook them two years later and which has led to modern judgments of the wedding as 'sordid' and 'scandalous'. As David Lindley points out, although the arguments at the annulment (summer 1613) focused on sensitive sexual matters, the accusations of murder, witchcraft, and adultery were still in the future, and it was only when the Overbury affair was uncovered in 1615 that the divorce came to seem the beginning of a history of moral decay.[40] The scandal attached to the Somersets in 1613 was the threat to Frances's reputation caused by the exposure of her intimate life, necessitated by the claim that her marriage to Essex was unconsummated, and this she confronted bravely, wearing her hair down at her second marriage in token of virginity. One of the aims of Campion's *Masque of Squires* was to vindicate the marriage from the forces of Rumour and Error.

If the event's ethical implications were less awkward than often supposed, it remained difficult to make the marriage a suitable general celebration, given the impact on the pursuit of favour of Somerset's hold on the royal affections. Somerset's intimacy with James was universally recognized. To the Venetian ambassador, he was 'further in the king's graces than any other subject', and at his promotion to Chamberlain James said 'he bestowed a place so near himself upon his friend, whom he loved above all men living'.[41] With Salisbury's death leaving a power vacuum, friendship translated into immense influence over everyday affairs. As de facto secretary, Somerset had 'the dispatch of all great businesses of state in his own hands' (said Throckmorton), and after the alliance with Suffolk 'all things are carried *in scrinio pectoris* between them two'. Edmondes thought he had 'so great a power of prevailing with the King as never any man had the like'.[42] Somerset repaid James's confidence by the skill with which he handled power. Observers noted his 'honourable virtues', 'discreet and noble' character, and 'modest nature'; the sobriety of his portraiture is quite unlike the gaudy iconography associated with Buckingham.[43] Nonetheless his influence provoked anxiety, and was an obstacle to other clients and aristocrats alike. As John Holles put it, since Somerset arrived 'we are all now become Pythagoras his scholars'.[44] Holles became a devoted client, but since Pythagoras' disciples observed a rule of five years' silence, he meant that under the new favourite circumspection was the order of the day.

Like the Essex–Howard union, the Somerset–Howard match was intended to be practical bridge-making, building connections across court divides. John More said there was 'a general reconcilement made between my lord of Howard and my lords of Pembroke, Southampton, etc. in this conjuncture',[45] a public rapprochement replayed in the social rituals for the wedding. For example, Pembroke and his brother Montgomery, former friends to Somerset but definitely not to the Howards, performed in both *The Masque of Squires* and the tilt. But the alliance drew Somerset away from former allies (Suffolk 'now guides the rudder of the state', wrote More), upset those who compared this marriage with Princess Elizabeth's (the shows, said Gabaleone, 'will surpass those put on for the Prince Palatine, a fact which is causing many people to talk'), and affronted Essex who, in the wake of the annulment, had 'become a great courtier'.[46] When Essex returned to court, he gravitated to the Queen's circle, where he could expect a friendly welcome: Anne's jealousy of Somerset was well known, and several of her servants had links to the Essexians.[47] These circumstances affected the marriage celebrations, for it became possible to hold the festivities at court only after Anne was persuaded not to snub them. Suffolk wished to celebrate the wedding privately at Audley End, but, Anne's consent being gained, it was changed to more public Christmas revelry at Whitehall. Still, those who expected the Queen to contribute to the celebrations were disappointed,[48] and, as if in rivalry to the favourite's marriage, she held her own high-profile festivities at Somerset House in February for the wedding of her lady, Jean Drummond, to Lord Roxborough. At her feast Essex stood conspicuously beside her,[49] and she invited the King to a performance of Daniel's pastoral tragicomedy *Hymen's Triumph*. With its depiction of innocent love amongst Arcadian shepherds and satire on the lack of 'virtue and desert' in today's 'fine herdsmen', this was a sensitively chosen text.[50] James may have hoped that Somerset's wedding would unify his court, but it was easy to read Anne's celebrations for *her* favourite's wedding as a riposte to James's. Not surprisingly, unlike the 1606–8 wedding masques, the 1613–14 festivities did not dignify the marriage with the rhetoric of unity. *The Masque of Flowers* was the only masque to invoke a specifically British theme.

All four surviving texts have intimations of strain. Although marriages were commonly celebrated with combats,[51] it is striking how obsessively the scenarios used for the Somersets turned on the reconciliation of conflict. *The Masque of Flowers* presented two challenges, between Winter and Spring, and tobacco and wine, which the main masque resolved with an apostrophe to James. The antimasque divisions were transcended by his nurturing light, which miraculously transformed the dancers from flowers to men. Similarly, although *The Irish Masque* was not originally meant for the wedding,[52] its depiction of servants squabbling for elbow room, each claiming to speak better than the others, reflected obliquely on the contests for access. The Irish servants' promise that the masquers would 'leap ash light … ash he tat vears te biggest feather in ty court' (93–4) linked the display of skills on the dance floor with sartorial self-promotion amongst the King's courtiers. And Jonson's *A Challenge at Tilt*, written for a tournament between the bride's supporters and the groom's, resembled the contests of the 1606 *Barriers* but invested the game with unusual levels of anxiety. In this fiction, two identical cupids each claimed to be the true Cupid: the issue was not the merits of marriage and virginity but whether the truth of love could ever be known. The cupids' contest unsettled the assumption that all was as it appeared, acknowledging that this was an unusually contentious marriage. Confusion was resolved into a higher unity by Hymen's revelation that the cupids were Eros and Anteros, the opposites whose amorous strife made love all the more binding. Their passionate reciprocation implicitly weighed Frances Howard's second marriage against her first, which had lacked just this sexual cement. Further, on the tiltyard the bride's relatives wore the groom's colours and the groom's friends wore the bride's, converting their rivalry into a more collegial emulation. Still, Hymen's hope that happy strife would be a model for future unity, and 'this royal court never know more difference in humours' (224–5), was more pious than real. Many spectators knew that some of those invited to tilt had stayed away.

These problems were addressed head-on in *The Masque of Squires*. The fable accommodated objections to the marriage, acknowledging at the outset the troubles which beset it and seeking as much to vindicate as celebrate it. In the antimasque, four squires recounted how their masters, twelve knights who were journeying from the four corners of the world to attend the ceremony, had been attacked by the enchanters Rumour and Error and the sorceresses Curiosity and Credulity. Six were turned into pillars and six scattered with storms, the disorder being depicted in confused dancing by figures representing winds, elements, and continents. Order was restored by Eternity, Harmony, and the Destinies, but it more specifically depended on Queen Anne's intervention: the Destinies presented her with a golden tree from which she plucked a branch, which magically dispelled enchantments and reunited the masquers. This fable transparently dramatized the Somersets' marriage as riding out storms of gossip and hostility. David Lindley describes it as 'typical ideological mystification', and speculates 'with what gritted teeth Anne performed the ceremony (or with what bated breaths the audience waited to see what she would do)'.[53] Yet Campion's fable was less collusive than this suggests, and less compromised by the requirement to mystify. The masque confronted the marriage's problems and attempted to manage them symbolically.

By demonizing opposition to the wedding, Campion did raise the ideological stakes, depicting Somerset's critics not as a political opposition but as part of the universal contest between error and truth. However, in other respects his strategy was not mystificatory, and in the printed text he disclaimed flattery, pointing out he had avoided using 'feigned persons … as satyrs, nymphs, and their like' to 'heighten invention' (268).[54] Rather, although the fable alluded to Catullus and Tasso, it presented not a veiled myth but an ornamented version of recent events, and while the masquers had romantic roles, the married couple lacked any special fictional aura. As honoured spectators the Somersets just played themselves (as it were), and although the masque began in the world of myth, at the masquers' arrival it moved back into the untransformed world of contingency. For the second half the scene changed to a view of the Thames, a device so mundane that the revels ended with an antic of watermen who arrived on barges to carry the performers home (275). If these vessels alluded to those that would shortly be ferrying some of the audience southwards, they were far removed from the floating shells in which masquers customarily made their departure, and suggest how little Campion's response to criticism was to gloss the marriage under glamorous fiction. Instead of alluding to more removed mysteries, he emphasized the separation of fiction and event, foregrounding the distance between the masquers and the enchantments from which they were rescued. Few masques were so little concerned to make their iconography self-sufficient, or to transform the world of everyday with a mythological covering.

   The masque also eschewed what would have been the easy scenario, of using the King to guarantee Somerset's safety. James was appealed to for 'relief' (269–70) yet the knights were not saved by his power. The fable left him passive, avoiding the irresistible royal magic familiar from earlier masques. Rather, the Queen rescued the knights, in token of her more than fictional influence over the nuptials: the crucial transactions were not between King and favourite but Somerset and his leading opponent. Inevitably the evening gave Anne little opportunity for refusal, since if she had not plucked the branch the fable would have ground to a halt (and at some point in advance she must have agreed to make this gesture). Still, by emphasizing her participation, the festival underlined how important her assent was, and rooted the celebrations in her action. Since the branch came from 'the Tree of Grace and Bounty' (273), her gesture implied an act of favour, putting Somerset in her debt; Gabaleone thought the tree was an olive, implying that it betokened a symbolic peace-making.[55] He also reported that she gave the branch to the Earl of Pembroke, who then began the dances by taking her out. This suggests that the performance enacted a chain of accommodation, with Pembroke mediating between the two rivals. A far from trivial gesture, the plucking of the bough must have seemed a public act of conciliation, which safeguarded Anne's position as well as Somerset's: the Spanish ambassador thought she 'danced in it to please the king and honour the bride and bridegroom'.[56] Further, since James's will was not directly invoked, her gesture turned it from a command performance to a communal event, and projected the audience's consent too. As someone from outside the fiction whose act allowed the masque to proceed, her participation made its resolution seem a matter of consensus. The solution was not imposed by royal force, but approved by the whole masque community.

So *The Masque of Squires* was not ideological whitewash, but staged a material transaction between competitors in the dance of favour. It formed a channel of symbolic exchange, and spectators probably read the fable of courtiers scattered by Rumour but reunited by the Queen's power as a statement of the reconciliation many hoped would prevail. But in the wake of the Essex divorce, one might still wonder what they made of a fiction which turned so centrally on anxieties about masculinity. Unlike the aggressively chivalric heroes of Henry's masques, these knights were curiously impotent. Helpless victims of enchantment, they could not effect their own rescue but were saved by female power (not only Anne, but the Destinies, and the female deity Eternity). The spectre of male impotence was re-invoked in the main masque, in a song which justified Frances's remarriage in terms of the future progeny which her first husband was unable to provide:

> [*Third singer*] What good can be in life
> 　　Whereof no fruits appear?
> [*First singer*] Set is that tree in ill hour,
> 　　That yields neither fruit nor flower.
> [*Second singer*] How can man perpetual be,
> 　　But in his own posterity?
> *Chorus* That pleasure is of all most bountiful and kind,
> 　　That fades not straight, but leaves a living joy behind.　(274–5)

This was pointed and legally correct, since it restated the grounds of the annulment, which were Essex's non-consummation and the union's incompleteness, the need for 'fruits' and 'posterity'. Yet it traded on sexual anxieties involved in the annulment, drawing attention to Essex's unhappy impotence and the favourite's frankly erotic success, his amorous hold on wife and monarch alike. Campion handled the issue tactfully, but one wonders whether Essex's friends thought it tactful enough. It hinted at one of the marriage's implications for courtly masculinity, that the celebration of Somerset's favour might spell the emasculation of just about everyone else.

With its uneasy gestures of reconciliation, *The Masque of Squires* staged a ritual for the temporary truce between the parties competing for favour in 1614. Unlike Jonson's apocalyptic reversals, Campion's more pragmatic affirmations fitted a court settling around a favourite who for the moment had James's affections and an alliance with the dominant faction. But the landscape was about to be transformed by the arrival of George Villiers. Villiers met James at Apethorpe in summer 1614 and was almost immediately appointed as a cup-bearer, then sworn Gentleman of the Bechamber, the first steps on a ladder that by 1625 led to a dukedom. His magnetism was a godsend to those courtiers who wanted to unpick Somerset's influence and promote more forward policies than the Howards', and a group of powerful sponsors collected around him, including the Queen, Pembroke, and Archbishop Abbot. This alarmed Somerset, who tried to hinder Villiers's promotion, and those whose futures depended on him. Shortly after Villiers's promotion to the Bedchamber, Holles retailed these developments to his brother with barely concealed anxiety:

Now, forsooth, there is a new favourite springing, who makes much noise and great expectation, that all the fortune-followers in that place seem to be distracted, and surely [although] the new man exceeds in number, the other [Somerset] fills less room but weighs more. And it may be the King's affection and others' malice to the other will bring forth something in his behalf, yet not in that proportion as he shall be able to raze out a Chamberlain and a Treasurer – both rooted by long service and many offices of great latitude in our state – out of the book of life, and turn the stream down another channel.[57]

Holles recognized that the new man had reforming credentials: his faction 'raised much smoke, and according to the manner of new brooms promise a cleanly house at first', but since it was composed of Essexians and malcontents, men from whom nothing new could be expected, they were unlikely to prevail.[58] This might have been the case if Somerset only had Villiers to deal with, but no one could have predicted the scandal that broke in October 1615, and on which his rivals immediately seized. As Holles reflected after the Overbury revelations: 'Pembroke expects to be Chamberlain, Villiers a baron and Master of the Horse; what other chips be gathered from the fall of this great oak I know not. Every bird of them will carry some straw or other to his nest, or else they have laboured in vain.'[59] Whatever one's judgment of the rights and wrongs of the Overbury affair – and it is unclear whether Somerset was aware of his wife's crimes, and unlikely that only Holles regarded him as someone of attested trust – the perception that justice would be entangled with private advantage was accurate.

This struggle for power created the climate for Jonson's masques of 1615 and 1616, *Mercury Vindicated from the Alchemists at Court* and *The Golden Age Restored*.[60] *Mercury Vindicated* was the first masque in which Villiers danced, and commentators recognized it was being used to enhance his profile. Chamberlain said that, despite his poverty, James found £1,500 for it, 'the principal motive whereof is thought to be the gracing of young Villiers and to bring him on the stage'.[61] In fact, just before the masque, in November 1614, Somerset blocked an attempt to place Villiers in the Bedchamber, arranging instead for Robert Ker, one of his own Scottish cousins, to be sworn and leaving Chamberlain unsure whether Villiers's career was already 'at a stand'.[62] Neil Cuddy suggests that James planned to open out the Bedchamber by taking two favourites, one English and one Scots,[63] and *Mercury Vindicated* certainly evened things out by giving starring roles to both gentlemen. Chamberlain said that the masque lacked invention but had 'excellent dancing, the choice being made of the best both English and Scots'.[64] Still, the uncertainty left courtiers guessing about the tide of favour, and John Donne was one of those trying to calibrate from the masque which patron had the best prospects. He wrote to Goodere in December that 'They are preparing for a masque of gentlemen, in which Mr. Villiers is and Mr. Ker, whom I told you before my Lord Chamberlain had brought into the bedchamber.' In a later letter, he mentioned his plans to dedicate a volume of poems to Somerset, and added: 'I have something else to say of Mr Villiers, but ... because new additions to the truth or rumours which concern him are likely to be made *by occasion of this masque*, I forbear to send you the edition of this mart, since I know it will be augmented by the next' (my emphasis).[65] Evidently Donne expected *Mercury Vindicated* would disclose the relative prestige of Villiers and Ker and the underlying state of Somerset's favour. Little wonder that Somerset tried to use his power as Chamberlain to sabotage the performance. He issued simultaneous invitations to the Spanish, Venetian, and Dutch ambassadors, even though he knew they would never tolerate being invited together, and also that it was not Spain's turn (Spain having been invited the previous season). The obvious imputation is that he hoped that such deliberately provocative invitations would lead to diplomatic meltdown and wreck the performance – and Sir John Finet's long and exasperated account of the ambassadors' reactions indicates that they nearly did.[66]

In *Mercury Vindicated* the pursuit of James's regard was theme and form. The masque depicted the attempts of Mercury (here both a god and a metal) to escape from the court alchemists, who were making their own artificial nature 'in a corner o' the court ... below stairs' (68–70). He saved himself by appealing to James, and was rescued by Nature, with Prometheus and the masquers. This fable staged a contrast between false productivity and true creation in senses at once material and social. The alchemists only created 'imperfect creatures' (183), but as the well-formed 'creatures of the sun' (206) the masquers attested to a filial relationship with a monarch who was more than figuratively 'their maker' (204). As the opposite of James's benevolent paternalism, the alchemists were linked to household misman-agement. Mercury described them as making absurd promises to the court's menials, in payment for which the officers skimmed off excess victuals from the larder, pantry, and scullery (65–90), a panorama of waste and favouri-tism amongst the court's under-officers which invoked the case for reform. But lest it reflect upon the King, Jonson emphasized that the alchemists operated below stairs and stood apart from the dominant ideology. Their imperfect creatures included a duellist, an astrologer, and a broker (148–72), and their poverty was sourced to the failure of their trade, armour-making, caused by the Jacobean peace (42). By contrast, Nature's creation in the main masque was validated by its perfection and by the masquers' exem-plary dancing. *Mercury Vindicated* accommodated a critique of shortcom-ings in the lower household to an affirmation of the legitimate pursuit of reward as it occurred, more obliquely but more glamorously, above stairs.

So this masque naturalized the competition for favour as normal to court life. The antimasque policed rewards, but the masquers themselves were overtly embarked in the contest. Nature's language rewrote Jacobean service as idealized filial devotion. The masquers were sons, peers between whom there was perfect horizontal equilibrium:

> Help, wise Prometheus, something must be done,
> To show they are the creatures of the sun,
>> That each to other
>> Is a brother,
> And Nature here no step-dame, but a mother.   (205–9)

This rhetoric of family identity rewrote horizontal rivalry as common dependency. Because they were all James's sons, they could not be com-peting with one another. Yet the songs readmitted courtly competition by the back door. In inviting the ladies to dance, Nature and Prometheus stressed how alluring the men's dancing was (240), and urged the masquers to 'show thy winding ways and arts, / Thy risings, and thy timely starts / Of stealing fire, from ladies' eyes and hearts' (213–15). Such language admitted courtship was an erotic strategy, the achievement of power through pleas-ure-giving, and represented as natural what covertly it acknowledged as contrivance, the skills that seemed intrinsic to a courtier's grace but which were carefully calculated and admired for their 'art'. Further, the occasion concluded with a song urging the masquers to pursue James's grace, since at court the only sin was to lack boldness in solicitation: 'No cause of tarrying shun, / They are not worth his light, go backward from the sun' (266–7). Given these sentiments, it is not surprising that Somerset was worried and Chamberlain felt the masque was memorable for its dancing. The fable unashamedly forwarded the competition between aspiring favourites, and showcased the bravest masquer's self-assertion.

A year later, *Mercury Vindicated*'s factional contests were replayed in *The Golden Age Restored*, but with brutal explicitness. By this date, the Overbury revelations were in full flood. The four poisoners, Richard Weston, Anne Turner, James Franklin, and Sir Gervase Elwes, had been executed; Sir Thomas Monson (Master of the Tower armoury) was under arraignment; and the Somersets had been in custody for three months. As the reign's most shocking scandal, its disclosures were still rocking Whitehall. Correspondence was full of speculation, and, as Foscarini wrote, 'the whole court is in a state of commotion'.[67] The burning issue was how far up the ladder the crimes might be taken. In the event the Somersets' trials were delayed until the summer, but at Christmas they were thought to be imminent and attention focused on whether the former favourite would be implicated. As Richard Lucy wrote to Trumbull, 'after Christmas we attend the revealing of great things and as great integrity of justice upon those which remain'.[68] Somerset's fall also caused the reign's biggest patronage shake-up. He lost his offices in November, and Pembroke and Villiers moved into the posts that Holles had predicted. Lower down the tree fevered jostling for plums was going on. Throckmorton advised Viscount Lisle that 'this great man's fall will raise your Lordship and some of your noble friends to your just and worthy demerits', and pleaded that since 'many good things [were] in his majesty's gift again … take this occasion of my service at this time to move for something for me unto his majesty'.[69] As Holles bitterly complained, 'some men's ruins are as necessary for prince's designs as other men's services'.[70]

Only Percy Simpson's mistaken belief that *The Golden Age Restored* was danced in January 1615 has prevented critics from perceiving how closely it shadowed the events of 1616.[71] At the opening, the goddess Pallas announced that Jove had decreed that the Golden Age and Astraea, goddess of justice, should return to earth. But before this could happen, the Iron Age and twelve Evils interrupted, declaring that they would subvert Jove's rule, and dancing to 'a confusion of martial music' (67). Pallas put them to flight by revealing her glorious shield, after which Golden Age, Astraea, and four English poets descended, followed by the masquers' discovery in a blaze of light, as 'semigods' preserved in Elysian bowers 'that justice dare defend, and will the age sustain' (128, 131). Such fictions were the common stock of European court ceremonial. Many princely courts were represented as oases of perfection to which Astraea had returned, and Jonson's iconography reached back through Prince Henry's heroic festivals to famous precedents in imperial panegyric by Virgil, Ovid, and Claudian. But on this occasion the myth of return was more precisely topical, as the ceremonial motifs tactfully yet transparently turned the winter's upheavals into symbolic action.

It would have been impossible for spectators not to read this as a reworking of current affairs. The family of Evils introduced by Iron Age – Fraud, Ambition, Pride, Scorn, Corruption 'with the golden hands' (39), and so forth, all following one another – alluded to the crimes of which Somerset was accused and to the dizzying network of conspiracy that shocked contemporaries (Foscarini reported a 'chain of accomplices' had come to light, and Throckmorton said no one could see 'the brim or bottom of this business').[72] There was besides an open reference to the murder in Iron Age's command for the 'babe last born, / Smooth Treachery', to appear (42–3) – an allusion so apparent that Percy Simpson decided it could *not* have been spoken in 1616.[73] The songs of the main masque stressed the Golden Age's innocent sexuality (177–97), a theme which, while common to Golden Age myths, was relevant to the lewdness with which the Somersets were tarred. And the celebration of the masquers as champions of justice belatedly but triumphantly installed around the throne could only have been understood as validating a new political order:

> Like lights about Astraea's throne,
> You here must shine, and all be one,
>   In fervour and in flame.
> That by your union she may grow,
> And you, sustaining her, may know
>   The age still by her name.   (206–11)

As the Tuscan diplomat Quaratesi reported, the Earl of Essex, 'who is continuously seen at court now', headed the dancers; this was his only recorded appearance in a Whitehall masque.[74] No less striking was the leading role given to Pallas – that goddess closely associated with Queen Anne's iconography – and the honours that were done to the invited ambassadors, from France, Venice, and Savoy. With Essex leading the masquers and representatives of the anti-Habsburg powers in the audience, the masque would have seemed a public celebration of some seismic political realignments.[75]

If history is written by the victors, then *The Golden Age Restored*, re-enacting political trauma as transformation into a new unity, is one of the clearest examples. Yet its very topicality – the way that the masque invested with the transcendence of myth a series of contingencies that were still in process – was problematic, and exposed the performance to tensions which, for all the triumphant closures, could not readily be erased. For example, the songs registered doubts about the reliability of the justice that was being celebrated. As everyone knew, there was no guarantee that James would proceed against his former favourite. His instructions to the judges emphasized the need to vindicate royal justice in language similar to the masque's, but the venom with which Chief Justice Coke conducted the trials, and the stress that he laid on the equity of royal justice, were designed to ensure that James would not back down if Somerset came in danger.[76] In the masque, this translated into praise that was coercive rather than complimentary:

> Look, look! Rejoice and wonder
> That you offending mortals are,
> For all your crimes, so much the care
> Of him that bears the thunder!
>
> Jove can endure no longer
> Your great ones should your less invade,
> Or that your weak, though bad, be made
> A prey unto the stronger;
>
> And therefore means to settle
> Astraea in her seat again,
> And let down in his golden chain
> The age of better metal.   (1–12)

Spectators would have connected this with the legal proceedings, yet its projection of justice as an act still to be accomplished, its emphasis on ensuring that 'great ones' were punished,[77] and its tactful invocation of Jove's justice made the panegyric strikingly conditional. Fictional distance allowed the masque to sidestep an absolute affirmation that Jove's and James's justice were identical. Rather, its praise was contingent on James achieving that ideal, and not until the end was he unequivocally acclaimed as divine (228–33). It is difficult not to feel that this 'delayed action' effect reflected less a concern about the propriety of directly aligning James with the godhead than an anxiety about his future intentions towards the favourite.

Similarly, one wonders what political implications spectators read into Astraea's arrival. Figuring chaste, imperial, and militant female power, Astraea had been central to Elizabethan iconography. Since she carried associations with a more ideologically forward position than James's preferences for peace, she was conspicuous by her absence from Jacobean panegyric; her return was sensitive at a moment when many predicted a fresh start. Somerset and Suffolk had been friendly to Spain and resisted talk of a parliament,[78] but Somerset's fall opened options harking back to earlier reigns. Trumbull anticipated a new parliament, household retrenchment 'and all abuses reformed which by corruption have crept into the government'; Foscarini thought the Spanish lobby would collapse; and Abbot expected Villiers's arrival to repair England's 'neglect'.[79] Unsurprisingly, the masque handled Astraea gingerly, subordinating her to Jove's control. In the final song she expressed loyalty to Whitehall's godhead (222–39), and at the outset Pallas – pointing out that the Golden Age was ruled by Jove's father Saturn – stressed 'Time not enjoyed his head of gold / *Alone* beneath his father' (15–16, my emphasis). This suggests an anxiety that the Golden Age be seen as Jacobean, rather than connoting Elizabethan nostalgia, though it paid implicit compliment to Queen Anne, in whose personal iconography the goddess Pallas and memories of Elizabeth both played a significant part (see chapter 5 above).[80] On balance the masque held in check the ghost of an Elizabethan past that Astraea threatened to invoke, but its caution shows how unsettling it was, how easily celebration of factional change slid into disparagement of the old world order.

Disparagement of the past was the greatest risk which this masque ran: how to represent Somerset's fall without denigrating the sovereign who promoted him and presided over the Age of Iron which was now redeemed. Although Somerset was far from universally lamented, the exposure of betrayal at the highest levels was not to James's credit, and he was concerned to limit the fall-out, not least by avoiding the humiliation of seeing a favourite go to the block.[81] In the masque this difficulty was neatly managed: the Evils were depicted not as criminals but subversives, implying that James himself was the target of their crimes. There was much speculation that the investigation would disclose some treason against the crown,[82] but in practice Somerset's guilt was never stretched this far. Nevertheless, this was how the Evils appeared, as guilty of 'insolent rebellion', 'profaner eyes' opposing the heavens (25–6). They were enemies of order, hierarchy, and Jove, and Iron Age was a demagogue, inciting his followers to usurp power:

We may triumph together
Upon this enemy so great,
Whom, if our forces once defeat
And but this once bring under,
We are the masters of the skies,
Where all the wealth, height, power lies,
The sceptre and the thunder.   (47–53)

The implied contradiction here suggested the risks of the masque, the imputations it had to avoid. Somerset's crimes were not treasonable, but by representing the Evils as rebels, the fable insulated James from blame by association. Far from having condoned crime at his elbow, James was the Evils' ultimate victim, his order threatened by them and his peace disrupted by their military dancing. This way his stature was safeguarded and the potentially damaging disclosure of courtly corruption displaced onto the less ideologically problematic issue of rebellion.

Even so, the problem of insulating the King pressed on the masque, since whatever Astraea and Golden Age meant for the future, their return was fraught with awkward questions about the past. In calling them down, Pallas tactlessly said they were 'long wished and wanted' (70), and Astraea and Golden Age seemed amazed at being restored, scarcely able to believe they might return (85–100). Welcoming the poets, Pallas said virtue was 'pressed' and arts 'buried' (120), while the invitation to the masquers to reveal themselves – 'O wake, wake, wake, as you had never slept' (134) – was even more troublesome, half-conceding as it did that good men were absent or asleep. As in some of Prince Henry's masques, the disadvantage of a fable of renewal was what it suggested about preceding times. Plainly, Jonson could not say that the reign was notable for corruption, and probably most spectators understood this as generalized advice against future factiousness. But the requirement to align praise of the present reformation with praise of the monarch created a tension which it was difficult to finesse without backhandedly acknowledging the factional contests on which this supposedly archetypal transformation rested. The trouble with celebrating 'the age's quickening power' (157) was that it invited awkward reflections about what the age was quickening from.

For all the seeming unity, then, fractures and tensions lay just below the surface. Jonson left the contradictions submerged, but their presence was a sign of the diverging perspectives between which he was negotiating. As panegyric to the King, *The Golden Age Restored* dignified James's rule by promulgating its ethical integrity, but its scheme was crossed by a politics of faction with which its declared purposes were at odds. The champions of

justice disciplined anarchic rebels, but this self-evidently recast courtly competition into moral terms. At the same time, in order to legitimate the
displacement of one faction by another, Jonson minimized the perception
that the gulf between iron and gold was less absolute on the ground than it
seemed in myth. Particularly, although the masque's praise for its heroes
emphasized their altruism, by the end of the evening the element of reward
within the renewal was acknowledged. In the antimasque, Corruption was
described as the Evil with 'golden hands' (39), but Pallas' final song –
reassuring the masquers that under Astraea 'want may touch you never' and
urging them to serve Jove 'as his bounty gives you cause' (214, 203) –
readmitted the material benefits of courtship and the masque's aim of underwriting the redistribution of largesse. These may have been rewards due to
faithful service, but they were rewards nonetheless, and they threatened to
contaminate the ethical plot by acknowledging that the heroes' honour rested
on kingly favour as much as on abstract ideals of goodness. For all its
celebration of moral reform, the masque was vexed by traces of a local politics
which its fable could neither mystify nor ignore. The all-too-concrete rewards
of virtue undermined the iconography of the Golden Age by disclosing that
even the reign of Astraea had links with material forms of gold.

The masques that chart Somerset's fall reveal the problems of court culture
in the mid-reign, the strains that affected an idealizing discourse when it
attempted to manage more mundane contingencies. They expose the contradictions between the symbolics of myth and the less than transcendent
circumstances which the masques had to accommodate: their formal and
linguistic fractures arose from structural uncertainties over cash, favour, and
service endemic to Jacobean courtship. But for the rest of the reign, the
now-ennobled Buckingham was near the centre of most festival activity,
and, unlike Somerset, with his relatively modest public profile, he readily
exploited its opportunities for exhibiting his histrionic skills. Even in
masques led by Prince Charles, the new favourite's dancing must have
compelled attention. For example, the day after Buckingham was elevated
to his earldom, Chamberlain noticed 'the new made Earl' was honoured in
The Vision of Delight, when he led off the revels with the Queen; and at *The
Masque of Augurs*, James publicly protested his love for him and took his
wife out to dance.[83] In such ways, the masques must repeatedly have marked
personal bonds between monarch and favourite. In the late-Jacobean period
there was an increasing number of informal shows put on at times other
than Twelfth Night and Shrovetide, and an upsurge in the variety and
playfulness of roles which courtiers took (including, for the first time, some

speaking parts).[84] Such changes are symptomatic of Buckingham's impact on court culture. His career demonstrated that successful amateur performance was one way to accumulate social capital. His activities on the dance floor were incidental to his political career, but did no damage to his status as favourite.

Modern critics have sometimes felt that in these shows the writers were playing games at the expense of their patrons' narcissism. Uncomfortable with what looks like collusion between poet and favourite, and reluctant to see the poets as directly involved in the struggle for influence, some have felt that Buckingham's masques must have been covertly satirizing their performer. Particularly, Jonson's *The Gypsies Metamorphosed* (1621), the show with which Buckingham welcomed James to his new house in Rutland by posing as the leader of a gypsy band who fleeces commoner and king alike, has been taken as evidence that some of the favourite's festivals were booby-trapped with irony.[85] Yet for all that *The Gypsies Metamorphosed* had the Villiers clan masquerading as disreputable charlatans, it traded on Buckingham's theatricality and erotic power. The irresistible glamour with which it invested him must have seemed empowering rather than undermining.[86] Buckingham played a thief, but his attractively self-confident gypsy, canting skills, pick-pocketing tricks, and carefree dancing allowed his crimes to be easily forgiven, for they were only amusing games. His gypsy band were vulgar but charismatic –

> They are of the sort
> That love the true sports
> Of King Ptolomaeus
> Our great Coryphaeus   (169–72)

– and his filching of keepsakes from yokels was trifling in comparison with his success in stealing ladies' hearts (425, 501). Accommodating Buckingham the opportunist to Buckingham the charmer, *The Gypsies Metamorphosed* staged a playful, self-consciously ironic version of the real relationship between King and favourite. While pretending to tell James's fortune, Buckingham wheedled silver out of him, and alluded openly to a royal bounty which he had already tasted:

> May still the matter weight your hand
> That it not feel or stay or stand,
>   But all desert still overcharge;
> And may your goodness ever find
> In me, whom you have made, a mind
>   As thankful as your own is large.   (346–51)

The Gypsies Metamorphosed did not so much satirize Buckingham's rapacity as underline his unprecedented intimacy with the monarch. Playing out his mastery of the theatrical arts of power, it typified the social functions of masquing in late-Jacobean Whitehall.

The occasion that proved Buckingham's courtly mastery was *Pleasure Reconciled to Virtue* (1618). The demonstration was all the more impressive for having been a high-profile royal occasion centred on Prince Charles: it was the Prince's first appearance as principal masquer, for which Jonson devised a weightily didactic invention. The masque turned on the educational idea that the masquers' revels tutored them in the right use of courtly pleasure. The antimasques featured Hercules, the prototype of the virtuously active hero, and invoked Xenophon's story of his arrival at a crossroads where he faced a choice between Virtue and Pleasure, towards which led divergent paths. Whereas Xenophon's Hercules chose Virtue rather than Pleasure, Jonson revised the fable, sketching out how the hero's integrity could be preserved while he temporarily gave way to delights. First Hercules disposed of a crew of riotous revellers devoted to Comus and led by his Bowl-bearer. As Hercules observed, their intemperate feasting brutalized them: 'these are sponges and not men' (94). Having resisted excessive indulgence, Hercules rested from his labour, but relaxation could not mean unreadiness, since once asleep he was vulnerable, menaced in a second dance by pigmies who, when he was awake, would have been no threat. By rousing himself and chasing the pigmies away, Hercules showed that off-duty did not mean off-guard. This two-pronged moral lesson framed the Prince's pleasures in the main masque. Though the masquers enjoyed their sports, they were led by 'Daedalus the wise' (243), and they descended from the 'hill of knowledge' (204), Mount Atlas, and returned to it at the end, promising 'to walk with Pleasure, [but] not to dwell' (327). Thus their evening of revelry did not undermine the life of virtue which they ought to live. Like Hercules, their sports were disciplined, free from the twin dangers of over-indulgence and over-confidence.

This educational fable was suited to the young Prince, and fashioned him after a less audacious image than his brother's. By denying that Pleasure and Virtue were inevitably opposed, Jonson repudiated the puritanical oppositions of Henry's more chivalric ideology. Even an 'active friend of Virtue' (168) could take time out. Evidently there was no intention of repeating with Charles's festivals the mistakes that were made with Henry's. Charles's investiture, in 1616, was much quieter than his brother's. He received a water pageant from the city (Middleton's *Civitatis Amor*) and processed to the Banqueting House with twenty-six young noblemen, but there was no masque nor, crucially, was parliament involved. Rather, said Chamberlain, the investiture was held 'within doors, for the sharpness of the weather and the prince's craziness [sickliness] did not permit any public show'.[87] Given Charles's delicate health, his disconnection from any 'forward' lobby, and the need to keep him subordinated, his first masque unsurprisingly identified his heroics as belonging to the mind. But by focusing on the dancers' indulgence in delight, *Pleasure Reconciled to Virtue* also thematized the festival occasion and addressed questions of moderation and restraint which cut against the conduct of court life more generally. In measuring Charles's legitimate revelry against the antimasquers' riot, the masque created a dialectic of freedom and restraint, indulgence and self-discipline which meshed with the crown's current preoccupation: its desperate need to find financial economies.

In 1617, the debt was at an all-time high, but James's spending was lavish. This year saw some extravagant feasting: Lord Hay spent £300 on his table every week and gave one banquet reputedly costing £22,000, while Chamberlain described the £600 dinner that celebrated Buckingham's marquisate as 'rather spoil than largesse'.[88] Cash was being drained by Charles's household and by James's progress to Edinburgh, for which he took a huge loan. 'The difficulty of raising money here augments daily', said the Venetian ambassador, 'but the natural prodigalities of his majesty have in no way diminished'.[89] In the autumn the merchant and financier Lionel Cranfield joined a Privy Council committee charged with making economies, and at Christmas reforms were announced for the household, the first department to be attacked. Cranfield's strategy was to manage the deficit not by limiting royal generosity but by scrutinizing the systems of reward. He argued that although 'the general received opinion is that the king's bounty hath caused ... [his] poverty', the true cause was wastefully uneconomic practices that frittered revenue away, and that economies could be made by reforming the custom of paying officials with meals at royal expense.[90] His investigations proved that the meals indented for were inflated out of all proportion, that more food supposedly entered Whitehall than was used, and that the officials' 'diet' – the meals which they purportedly consumed – had become gargantuan. Previous attempts at reform had foundered on internal resistance, and there were howls of anguish in December when Cranfield tore up the officials' own less ambitious proposals. He announced that diets would return to Elizabethan levels, and James signed his rules despite their resistance.[91] The new rules reduced diets by a third, though their impact on underlying attitudes about practices appropriate to princes was limited. As the officers complained, for all that economy was necessary, it was honourable for the court to be lavish with food and drink.[92]

Leah Marcus suggests that the antimasque of Comus has resonances with James's *Book of Sports*, the proclamation of May 1618 responding to attacks by godly magistrates on Sunday leisure pastimes. In the *Book of Sports* James defended the legality of his subjects' pleasures, and Marcus argues that Jonson was endorsing a *via media* between excessively licentious revelry and puritanical disapproval.[93] Undoubtedly Jonson's defence of innocent pleasures chimed with the *Book of Sports*'s image of a nation happily unified in festive amity. On the other hand, in January 1618 the critique of Comus would have cut particularly close to the Whitehall bone. Coinciding with the announcement of Cranfield's reforms, the masque urged the ethos of economy, creating a tie between reward and worth. Its riotous pleasure-seekers were disorderly consumers intruding into the court, their feasting uncontrolled by moral and social discipline. Jonson's Comus – unlike the elegant and youthful figure in Milton's *Masque at Ludlow* or Philostratus' *Imagines* (one source for the antimasque) – was a grotesque Bacchus, a walking belly dedicated to eating and drinking without measure. He was developed from Rabelais's account of Gaster, the 'gorbellied god', leader of an epicurean race of fat-bellied Gastrolators, who praises food and drink as the source of all arts and sciences.[94] Like the dancing bottles who followed him, Comus was the embodiment of consumerism:

> He, he first invented the hogshead and tun,
> The gimlet and vice too, and taught 'em to run,
> And since, with the funnel, an Hippocras bag
> He's made of himself, that now he cries swag …
> Hail, hail, plump paunch, O the founder of taste
> For fresh meats or powdered or pickle or paste;
> Devourer of broiled, baked, roasted or sod,
> And emptier of cups, be they even or odd.	(21–32)

In rebuking Comus's 'vicious hospitality' (92), Hercules distinguished proper from improper festivity in a manner pertinent to the sponsors of retrenchment. His intervention policed the Belly, critiquing the assumption that waste was a badge of privilege and drawing ideas of feasting into line with humanistic notions of virtuous living. Moreover, spectators would not have missed the allusion implied by making Comus's drunken Bowl-bearer the Belly's spokesman. If Hercules' great bowl had been misappropriated, it was answered by the presence among the masquers of James's cup-bearer, Buckingham, who waited on him at meals and whose support for Cranfield was well known. Hercules' cup would be retrieved from greedy consumers, and reinstated as 'the crowned reward / Of thirsty heroes after labour hard' (99–100).

In place of conspicuous consumption and aristocratic waste, the masque praised consumer control, a reformed state where rewards were proportionate to effort, a symbolic economy based on merit. It was stressed that Hercules' rest was an earned entitlement, 'labour's virtuous recompense' (180), and with James addressed as Hesperus, the western star, his court was the Hesperides, 'fair Beauty's garden' (210), accessible only by heroic toil. The masquers were introduced in terms that stressed the labour underlying their sports. Daedalus praised their dancing's prudence and control, describing how they 'interweave' their knots (254), 'figure out' gestures (257), and choose at each step between correct and incorrect paths. Thus the masquers' seemingly carefree grace did not signify moral negligence but the inner intellectual strenuousness on which that outward poise was founded:

> For dancing is an exercise
> Not only shows the mover's wit,
> But maketh the beholder wise
> As he hath power to rise to it.   (269–72)

Thus although the masquers enjoyed their liberty, it was achieved by successfully internalizing control rather than abandoning it. The spectators were asked to read through the dance steps to the hidden but essential discipline which underpinned them, constructing the masque's ideal society as a kind of meritocracy. The dancers' honour rested less on royal favour than on the correspondence between desert and reward. The King presided, but with the masquers praised for discipline, their validation depended on whether, through their dancing's labour, they deserved their places. As the final lines provocatively insisted, they needed inner virtue, not courtly status: ''tis only she can make you great, / Though place here make you known' (347–8).

This remarkable masque, then, insisted that the dancers needed to deserve their praise. The educational theme addressed to the Prince was underpinned by a larger argument, which asserted the claims of merit over place and measured courtly consumption against standards of discipline. Yet by conflating dancing and labour – by acknowledging that courtly 'play' performed social 'work' – the masque opened a channel through which virtue could be commmodified, and (perhaps unintentionally) underwrote the pursuit of favour through performance. On the one hand, the masque was demystifying, for it uncovered the dancers' grace as a contrivance, exposing the engineering beneath the seemingly effortless elegance. The chorus welcomed them as men 'born to know', mysteriously imbued with 'all lines / And signs / Of royal education and the right' (221–5), but the analysis of their dancing admitted that their poise was constructed, not inherent:

> Then, as all actions of mankind
>   Are but a labyrinth or maze,
> So let your dances be entwined,
>   Yet not perplex men unto gaze,
> But measured, and so numerous too,
>   As men may read each act you do,
> And when they see the graces meet,
>   Admire the wisdom of your feet.   (261–8)

On this reckoning, aesthetic admiration validated the masquers by approving their art, the intellectual control shown in their dancing. But on the other hand, by demystifying that grace as something that the dancers worked at, the masque opened the possibility that anyone might attain such validation, subordinating the criterion of inner virtue to the proof of external performance. In effect, *Pleasure Reconciled to Virtue* located the masquers' capital, both symbolic and real, in their own bodies. What they had to sell was themselves, and the endlessly graceful contrivance of their performance.

And this was how Buckingham famously turned the occasion to his advantage, when the dancing flagged and James nearly wrecked the evening by complaining it was insufficiently enjoyable. As the Venetian chaplain, Orazio Busino, reported:

The King, who is naturally choleric, got impatient and shouted out, 'Why don't they dance? What did they bring me here for? Devil take you all, dance!' Upon this the Marquis of Buckingham, his majesty's favourite, immediately sprang forward, cutting a score of lofty and very minute capers with so much grace and agility that he not only appeased the ire of his angry lord but rendered himself the admiration and delight of everybody. Inspired by this, the other masquers continued to display their powers one after another … though none matched the splendid technique of the Marquis.[95]

Generations of critics have seized on the gulf in Busino's account between what the masque promised and what it achieved, deducing that for all Jonson's strenuously articulated learning James was more interested in the height of the capers. Yet this is a dangerous incident from which to generalize: James's attentiveness was sapped by his poor health, and reports by other eyewitnesses agree that the masque was widely felt to be disappointing.[96] More to the point is what Busino suggests about the tension between the masque's discourse of reform and its effect of furthering that competition between reward-seeking courtiers which the fable was ostensibly in the business of policing. Jonson's critique of consumption tied reward to labour, but James's response demonstrated how much the evening's investments were still in a system of freely electing royal favour, and how much for Buckingham it was a forum in which to dance himself into his master's heart without forfeiting his rivals' admiration. Indeed, for Busino, this last point – that Buckingham promoted himself without damaging his relations with his peers, many of whom were competitors in the contest for reward – represented the occasion's real miracle. His dancing exhibited a mastery of the arts of self-promotion so absolute that it disarmed even those who might have been rivals. And in doing so, it signalled limits on the masque's educational project which made it difficult to promote an ideology of restraint from within a form that was a customary vehicle of aristocratic display. *Pleasure Reconciled* was a uniquely ambitious attempt to promote the criteria of courtly merit, but in positioning virtue as indistinguishable from the performance of virtue it left no standard by which it could be measured. For all its attempts to police favour, *Pleasure Reconciled* turned out at another level to have been peculiarly, if inadvertently, serviceable to it.

The structural fractures of these masques were symptomatic of the politicization of favour in the mid-Jacobean period, and the consequent instabilities in the patronage pyramid. With James's private friendships increasingly the focus of his public life, with his power to reward eroded by his poverty, and with claims on his bounty on the increase, the honour culture was becoming contaminated by fiscal and political considerations. In the masques this emerged as a contradiction between the idealizing discourses of courtiership (with their emphasis on innate grace, royal generosity, and control of courtly excess) and the acts of self-assertion which dancing allowed. The representation of courtship as a vertical exchange of gifts and services freely and reciprocally given was overlaid by horizontal transactions that were overtly market-driven. James's masques depicted Whitehall as the reservoir of honour, proclaiming its standing and rendering its largesse visible. But with their equation of social and economic capital, masques could not avoid the tensions to which the ethos of honour was subject, and as occasions for conspicuous consumption they unsettled royal authority even as they proclaimed it, their lavish expenditure squandering bounty in the act of performing it. The mid-Jacobean festivals thus had a double effect. While arraying the aristocratic community into postures of dependence on the crown, they provided a stage for the aspiration which their forms notionally harnessed. Their expression of James's fatherly rule was at odds with the filial ambition on which it depended, and which it checked with only varying success.

Our reading of these masques is inevitably affected by our historical vantage point, and it is unclear whether the strains that seem so prominent in retrospect appeared quite so acute to the participants. Arguably our difficulty here marks their fundamental distance from our own more professionalized culture, with its comforting (though in fact illusory) notion that individual labour translates directly into material reward.[97] Discussions of early modern patronage have emphasized how much the mental expectations of a community that lacked a paid bureaucracy were conditioned by now-lost assumptions about solicitation, dependency, and largesse.[98] In a world where access to power was limited, and the king, not the market, was the source of bounty, the conduct of business was bound up with ideas of honour and obligation, so that the disposal of rewards evaluated the individual's worth by measures different from today's meritocratic criteria. Public life was not an open arena of democratic competition but a network of moral and social obligations given meaning by the king's encompassing judgments. Liberality was a kingly virtue, for in bestowing favours the monarch drew the threads of the social fabric into their unity and rewarded those servants on whose emotional support he most relied. So those contests for position which loom so large to us may have seemed less troublesome to early modern audiences. They may have been more impressed by the spectacle of a fatherly king presiding benevolently over dances in which his courtiers' service was symbolically embodied and substantively expressed.

Yet there are some signs of double vision at the time. One symptomatic text is Middleton's *Inner Temple Masque, or Masque of Heroes* (1619). An entertainment for some 'worthy ladies' staged at the Inns of Court, this masque depicted its dancers as the Nine Worthies, 'deified for their virtues' (323–4).[99] Possibly Middleton had seen *Pleasure Reconciled to Virtue*, for he echoed Jonson's motifs, moralizing the masque choreography as an ideological performance exactly in Jonson's manner:

> Move on, move on, be still the same,
> You beauteous sons of brightness,
> You add to honour, spirit and flame,
> To virtue, grace and whiteness;
> You, whose every little motion
> May learn strictness more devotion;
> Every pace of that high worth
> It treads a fair example forth,
> Quickens a virtue, makes a story
> To your own heroic glory …   (342–51)

For Middleton's masquers as for Jonson's, dancing manifested control, a conscious dialectic between honour and virtue, pleasure and 'strictness'. Yet Middleton's language was less intellectual than moral: it stressed 'example' rather than grace, and its criteria for success were avowedly meritocratic. Harmony sang 'May your three times three blest number / Raise Merit from his ancient slumber' (352–3), and the heroes came from 'Virtue's court', where Time, rather than James, was 'king' (312, 332). As a private occasion involving no transaction with royalty, this masque had no need to observe rules of courtly decorum, and, crucially, its masquers were unconstrained by obligations of filial dependence. They answered to no one but themselves, and their dances were morally exemplary, not glamorously theatrical.

As for Jonson himself, in a poem of 1624 he too looked back at his long court career and reflected on the engineering that lay beneath its glittering surface. For twenty years, he said, he had

> eaten with the beauties and the wits
> And braveries of court, and felt their fits
> Of love and hate, and [come] so nigh to know
> Whether their faces were their own or no.[100]

Jonson created some of the court's most extended eulogies but, as this poem implies, he was sensitive to the gap between what its culture said and what contingently it did, the ambition and self-interest that its etiquette latently expressed. In the masques this contradiction figured as the unspoken but intrinsic tension between a courtier's outward poise and inner desire, which made the mid-Jacobean festivals at once unstable and dynamic. Typically, these masques both repudiated and advanced the pursuit of place, enabling a Machiavellian fascination with the arts of power, arts that were disavowed only on the surface. Hence *The Gypsies Metamorphosed* was pleasurable and compelling because of the risks it allowed for Buckingham, the bold combination of enchantment and scepticism with which it voiced his ambition. In representing him as James's creature, it characterized him as powerless and irresistibly empowered, with gestures of subordination that denied his appetite even while promoting it. So too the success of *Pleasure Reconciled to Virtue* depended on the masque giving that pleasure which its invention was in the business of restraining. Its virtue was accommodated to pleasure, but could not be achieved without it. In this respect, the masques were involved in an oscillation between restraint and desire, duty and intimacy, economy and spending which they were unable to resolve, and which issued in their peculiar strengths and ambivalences. In the event, the foreign policy crisis that was about to overtake court culture prevented these fault-lines from becoming even more acute than they already were. As it was, the mid-Jacobean masques were deeply involved in Whitehall's pleasurable contests, and testified to both the court's glory and its potential brittleness.

CHAPTER 8

The Jacobean crisis

If the spectators engrossed by Buckingham's dancing in *Pleasure Reconciled to Virtue* were witnessing a uniquely revealing display of the entanglements of social performance and Jacobean power, those looking for a more overt politics would have found a simpler message – signs of an increasingly close understanding between England and Spain. Negotiations for an Infanta for Prince Charles gathered pace in 1617. From Madrid Sir John Digby sent positive reports about the dowry likely to arrive with the Infanta Maria, and in London the Spanish ambassador, Count Gondomar, consolidated his friendship with James, and looked for ways to finesse the religious issue. So when in his account of *Pleasure Reconciled* Busino remarked how many Spaniards were in the audience, it clearly indicated the counsels ruling Whitehall. Gondomar sat by the king; Spaniards wearing gold chains – gifts from James to the embassy – sat with the privy councillors; more were in their own box; and Busino was offended when Sir John Finet asked the Venetians to make room for a stray Don ('by God, he placed himself more comfortably than all of us').[1] This was the last straw for the French ambassador, who was not invited. He protested about the preference shown to Spain and, receiving no redress, asked Paris for an early recall; Whitehall lacked French diplomatic representation for over a year. James, said Finet, was determined to honour Gondomar, 'the rather because a marriage between the prince and the Infanta was then in treaty'.[2] As Charles's first masque, *Pleasure Reconciled* announced his entry onto the international stage. It must have seemed a celebration of his coming to manhood and the future dynastic alliances awaiting him.

The status of the Spanish Match was, implicitly, the underlying concern of all the major court festivals for the rest of James's reign. Their overriding aim was to celebrate James's peace, and as this was premised on Anglo-Spanish friendship, their dances played out hopes of harmony with Madrid – as when Charles used the Shrovetide performance of *The Masque of Augurs* to show off a feather sent as a favour from the Infanta.[3]

But events were about to take a turn that would put Jacobean policy under acute strain and eventually destroy it. In May 1618, the Estates of Bohemia (the Protestant minority), reacting to the election of a hardline Catholic Habsburg, Ferdinand of Styria, as Bohemian King-Designate in succession to the moderate but ageing and childless King Matthias, threw two of Ferdinand's regents at Prague out of a window, and appealed for Protestant support.[4] This started a sequence of events that plunged the continent into thirty years of war, into which all major states, with the significant exception of England, were inexorably drawn. Spain was unable to stand by in a challenge to her Austrian cousins, and in any case the Twelve Years' Truce with Holland was shortly to expire. Meanwhile, in 1619, having repelled a Habsburg counter-attack, the Bohemians offered their crown to the Elector Palatine, James's son-in-law. Frederick rose to what seemed a defining moment for European Protestantism and was crowned in Prague in October, but barely a year later the Habsburgs drove him from Bohemia, then from his own lands in Germany. In summer 1620 troops from the Spanish Netherlands attacked the Palatinate, and in November Frederick was catastrophically routed at the White Mountain, outside Prague. He and Elizabeth went into exile at The Hague, Ferdinand (now elected Emperor) having promised their lands to his ally Maximilian of Bavaria. For the next twenty years the return of the Palatinate was the defining issue in English diplomacy.

The domino effect of these events drew a general war onto Europe which crystallized religious and ideological polarizations lurking just below the surface. In England, there was sympathy for co-religionists overseas, which developed a patriotic dimension after the disaster that overtook Princess Elizabeth. Archbishop Abbot hailed Frederick's election as a divine sign that 'that proud and bloody man' (Ferdinand) would be humbled and James honoured by his son-in-law's heroism: 'I am satisfied in my conscience that the cause is just [Abbot wrote] ... And when God hath set up the prince that is chosen to be a mark of honour through all Christendom to propagate his gospel, and to protect the oppressed, I dare not for my part give advice but to follow where God leads.'[5] From Paris the English ambassador Sir Edward Herbert wrote 'God forbid [Frederick] should refuse it, being the apparent way His providence hath opened to the ruin of the papacy', and at home Prince Charles had a 'wonderfully good affection to the cause', and avowed he had 'nothing to do at present but to think of the affairs of Bohemia and of my brother-in-law, nor does any thought find its way more readily into my mind'.[6] Others were more cautious, acknowledging the likely consequences. Chamberlain told Carleton 'it was a venturous part, and like to set all

Christendom by the ears', for 'one side [would] be utterly ruined'. Carleton responded gloomily that 'since the revolution of the world is like to carry us out of this peaceable time it is better to begin the change with advantage than with disadvantage'. Bohemia must be supported lest Ferdinand destroy the faith, and England could not sit still, since the Catholic powers would not remain mere onlookers.[7]

But James's view was different. The Palatine alliance belonged to a time when France and Spain were drawing together, and subsequent English diplomacy had concentrated on rebuilding friendships across lines of religion, and particularly on rapprochement with Spain. The prolonged and ultimately fruitless pursuit of an *infanta* has been seen as a sign of James's lack of grip, or vanity in wanting to be Europe's arbiter, but there was a lot to be said for forestalling a looming crisis. Though a committed Calvinist who fought theological battles on paper, James's political aims were to counteract the religious disagreements threatening to destroy the fragile peace and, wherever expedient, to promote *détente*. He did not share the eschatological notion that conflicts in Bohemia, Germany, and the Netherlands were part of a grand confessional design, which ranged Catholic and Protestant in apocalyptic confrontation, but treated them as independent issues that needed to be resolved separately. Since in 1619 there was hope that the other major powers would not seek a prolonged war, James's early efforts were devoted to finding an arbitrated settlement, but even after Spanish troops entered the Rhineland he continued to hold that resolution could be found through friendship with Madrid. With moves towards the marriage already under way, Spanish goodwill seemed guaranteed, and gave him diplomatic leverage, making the match conditional on restoring the Palatinate. At the least, in any conflict with Vienna, the Spanish Habsburgs represented the most influential friends he could have.

So James was unsympathetic to calls for intervention in Germany. Rather than creating a breach between London and Madrid, the loss of the Palatinate was for him, paradoxically, a reason for drawing closer to Spain. A special value of this policy was that it chimed with his more nakedly ideological preferences about legitimacy, hierarchy, and the respect due to princes. These were exacerbated by the Bohemian crisis, since Frederick had, arguably, colluded in the deposition of a hereditary prince and, as Carleton said, no one knew whether the Bohemians would return to a monarchy 'when they have once tasted of freedom'.[8] There was some doubt over whether the Bohemian crown was elective or hereditary, and, instead of supporting Frederick's actions, James at first demanded reassurance about their legality.[9] In January 1620, 'excessively displeased with these depositions of kings', he grilled Frederick's ambassador, Christoph von Dohna, showing 'by his looks and words that he did not hear without displeasure of the introduction by the people of the practice of dethroning kings and princes'.[10] Such considerations continued to weigh strongly. At Christmas 1620–1 he complained that 'his people [were] too republicaniz-ing', and was angry about 'this novelty of people conferring and taking away crowns at their pleasure'; the Marquis de Cadenet, on an embassy to London to justify French repression of the Huguenots, carried instructions 'to instill into his majesty's mind ideas calculated to increase his ill will towards republics and free states and towards those people who show themselves recalcitrant to monarchies'.[11] By contrast, any more activist response played into the hands of those who, from reasons of patriotic and religious zeal, desired a return to what were supposed to have been the godly policies of Queen Elizabeth. This would have involved England in closer relations with republican states such as Holland and Venice, and made James a financial hostage to parliaments unhappy about his closeness to Spain. Not surprisingly, he preferred the Spanish policy for reasons both international and domestic: that it damped down dangerously subversive enthusiasms at home and abroad.

Peace, Spain, and social order were the ideological nexus for court culture in the late Jacobean years. But the polarizations of opinion which these events created subjected the royal will to increasingly audible contest. Abroad, James's policy was undermined by Frederick's refusal to offer any apologies, Spain's reluctance to make concessions, and the escalation of the conflict into a multiple crisis. As the situation deteriorated without appease-ment delivering results, the marriage came to seem a cynical ploy to render England inactive, and James the dupe of Spanish double-dealing. At home, James's pro-Spanish position was maintained in the teeth of public unhap-piness, fuelled by an explosion of interest in events in Germany. In December 1620 there appeared the first in an avalanche of corantos on European affairs, which testified to the existence of a reading public hungry for news, and to the emergence of a new factor in the early modern polity, public opinion. At the same time, James's patience was tried by less polite commentary, libels, ballads, and pamphlets.[12] He responded to one libel, 'The Commons' Tears' (now lost), by writing his own verses, 'The Wiper of the Commons' Tears', warning people to mind their own business:

> Meddle not with your prince's cares,
> For whoso doth, too much he dares;
> I do desire no more of you,

But to know me as I know you.
So shall I love, and you obey,
And you love me in a right way;
O make me not unwilling still
Whom I would save unwilling kill.[13]

More practically, he introduced controls on the exchange of opinion, issuing proclamations in 1620 and 1621 against 'excess of lavish and licentious speech in matters of state'; in 1622 censorship of sermons was tightened.[14] The astonishing outburst of rejoicing at the collapse of the Spanish Match in October 1623, when Charles returned brideless from Madrid, indicates the levels of public dissent which at this stage of his reign James was trying to hold in check.

The masques of 1619–25 show the consequences for court culture of these ideological polarizations and narrowing political options. In response to the continental crisis, masques became preoccupied with European affairs and increasingly dedicated to promulgating non-intervention and peace, rehearsing James's perspective on events and investing it with dignity and persuasiveness. At the same time, the promotion of European peace was tied more tightly to the maintenance of kingly authority at home. Unlike the festivals of 1613–18, which focused on the courtier's life and its values, these masques set out more directly to instill obedience and respect. Typically, their actions were structured as the ejection of anarchic zealots by masquers representing order, deference, and control, and it was not fantastic grotesques but the monarch's own subjects who appeared as the enemy, an impudent rabble disrupting the otherwise serene Jacobean peace. If, in earlier masques, antimasquers embodied qualities in the court which in some way needed to be corrected before it could be celebrated, reformed to be reincorporated, in this more fraught climate the action was more emphatically exclusionary. The courtly heroes were presented not as overcoming inner temptations but as defeating with their innate, aristocratic virtue a threat to their own order, in the form of impertinence, ignorance, enthusiasm, and meddlesomeness coming from without. The implied ideological opposition – setting the transcendence and inscrutability of the royal will against the presumptuous vulgar who contested it – represented the outlook of a monarch who wished to limit the impact of the continental war and felt that the main threat to his power was unregulated zeal abroad and at home.

Much existing commentary on these masques has read their commitment to peace as morally reprehensible pusillanimity or, more charitably, as wishful thinking in an intractable situation.[15] Such judgments betray the staying-power of the Whiggish view of James as coward and procrastinator, and benefit from the wisdom of hindsight, which makes activism and intervention seem the only viable courses of action. But, however idealized these masques were, while the situation remained fluid they were not fantasies. Rather, they sought to present James's kingship as the fixed point in a turbulent world and, by promoting stable kingly government, to resist the drift towards confessional war. Nonetheless, as James was gradually overtaken by events, so these masques looked increasingly defensive, apologias for a monarchy whose intentions were too elevated to warrant full disclosure, and whose wisdom had to be stridently asserted rather than taken for granted. The images of consensus, prudent government, and royal peace in which they traded became hard-pressed, and, however impressively they were deployed, as the situation deteriorated they no longer seemed simply uncontentious. Far from representing the royal will as effortlessly transcending errors and follies, the masques themselves came to seem embroiled in political strain, vexed by struggles and ideological competition that contradicted the images of confident government they sought to project. It was almost inevitable that they came to read like acts of exclusion, in which an elite minority was embattled amidst the anarchy of an uncomprehending multitude. Less concerned to legislate about the court than for it, they were conditioned by, and contributed to, a significant hardening of attitude.

The earliest intimations of shifts in court culture, of splits and new tensions, came in a series of masques for 1619–20. The first to register the unsettled times was Chapman's *The Masque of the Twelve Months*, danced on Twelfth Night 1619.[16] On the surface, this was an affirmative ceremonial, which presented Prince Charles to his father as 'the darling of the year, delicious April' (184–5), a figure of generational renewal whose arrival rejuvenated a wintry court. The driving idea was that, by meeting together, James and Charles reconciled the contraries of 'majesty and love', 'youth and state' (33, 366). Charles was depicted as an emerging hero of gloriously masculine potential. 'The conqueror of charms' (19) into whose bosom Love had flown, he was introduced by Beauty, who issued from a fort shaped like a heart and decked with the Prince of Wales's ensigns, which swelled amorously at his arrival. His father was 'mild' but powerful, a monarch whose 'wisdom' guaranteed the realm's strength (307, 302); the harmony between the two expressed the concords of Stuart state. The fort, identified as 'the heart of the year' in which 'the whole world's chief virtues and beauties' were concentrated (149–51), was both bodily microcosm and epitome of the macrocosm, so that Charles's arrival refreshed public and personal worlds alike. His presence woke the sleepy fort, changed night into day, and winter to summer. Preceded by an antimasque of thirteen moons, his twelve suns, with their 'thousand coloured light', presented 'the full pomp of the year, / Contracted, yet much amplifièd here' (247–8).

In contrast to the contestatory politics of Chapman's *Memorable Masque* and other festivals for the previous Prince of Wales, *The Masque of the Twelve Months* was restrained, renewing rather than redefining the Jacobean generational structures. Its antimasques were not ideological contests but gracious inductions, from which figures who called the King's autonomy into question were absent. Charles was not a competitor for power, but a sharer and inheritor of his father's iconography. Figuring Charles and James as founts, respectively, of eroticism and of authority, the masque ritualized the rhythms of masculine renewal, affirming the succession, and celebrating the court's sense of future well-being. Since in this structure there were no internal strains to upset relations between the generations, Chapman created an external dynamic by setting up an opposition between the protected space of James's peace and the disorderly world beyond, in the unnamed but sinister influences pressing on the secure Jacobean state. His show initiated the ideological contrast between Whitehall and the world beyond that was to dominate all subsequent Jacobean masquing.

This basic trope, the warding-off of disaster, had fourfold reiteration. In the opening dialogue, Madge Howlet – an English version of Athena's owl – promised to police the realm against any dangers that might beset it. She would

> [keep] watch that no ill-looking planet
> Fasten his beams here; all ill-looking comets,
> In all their influences so much feared,
> Converting into good and golden dews
> That peace and plenty through the realm diffuse. (35–9)

Madge was alluding to a blazing star which had appeared in November and gave rise (said Simonds D'Ewes) to 'dismal conjectures'.[17] It was thought to presage some catastrophe or 'great war towards', especially as it came northwards out of Germany.[18] In the ensuing action this anxiety was sublimated into a musical contest between the harmonies of the Spheres and a military alarum given by the Pulses. The 'martial' Pulses (126) issued from the Heart beating their drums, but were tempered by Beauty. Taught to be passionate but not troublesome, their dangerous energies enlivened the sons of the Elements and Complexions. Then, in a supernatural charm spoken by Beauty, thirteen moons were drawn down from heaven, but Beauty warded off dangerous magic by emphasizing that her incantation was legitimate and the moons' approach was not fatal. This was not a deformed witch's sorcery but a 'royal charm' wielded by 'the goddess of proportion' (234, 220). Finally, after the masquers danced their entry, the presenters explained that they embodied the spirit of British heroism, and the sanctified separateness of the British Isles protected by James's person:

> These are no months, but that celestial seed
> Of men's good angels, that are said to breed
> In blessèd isles about this Britain shore,
> That heighten spirits bred here with much more
> Than human virtues …
>   For whose worth all
> These wonders in these isles angelical
> Are set in circle of his charmed command,
> Walled with the wallowing ocean, and whose hand,
> Charming all war from his mild monarchy,
> Tunes all his deeps in dreadful harmony.   (291–5, 303–8)

The masque's antithesis between happy security and threats to peace remained generalized, as the danger to James's power was nowhere made explicit. Nonetheless, the opposition between his 'mild monarchy' and intimations of 'war' was everywhere implied. Stuart peace was sustained amongst ubiquitous but unspecified dangers.

Clearly, *The Masque of the Twelve Months* reversed the politics of Chapman's *Memorable Masque*. That festival, for the Palatine marriage, had refused the tropes of British separateness which were so fundamental to the dynastic claims underpinning early Jacobean masquing. But by identifying Britain as the Fortunate Isles ('these isles angelical'), *The Masque of the Twelve Months* resurrected the tie between Jacobean sovereignty and an isolationist ethos at the precise moment when the long-term consequences of the Palatine alliance were becoming apparent. Late in 1618, events in Bohemia were being digested at Whitehall. Baron Dohna had arrived from Prague to solicit English support, and English Protestant enthusiasts were anxious about Spanish intentions and keen to show solidarity; there was talk of 4,000 men going to Bohemia under the Earl of Oxford and Lord Willougby.[19] But James did not intend to fan religious controversy while trouble was limited to Bohemia, and was anxious about its impact at home. He had already dismissed speculation about the urgency of the times. In conversation he called the comet 'Venus with a firebrand in her arse', and wrote a satire warning his subjects to keep their ideas under control:

> Wherefore I wish the curious man to keep
> His rash imaginations till he sleep,

Then let him dream of famine, plague and war,
And think the match with Spain hath caused this star ...
These jealousies I would not have a treason
In him whose fancy overrules his reason.[20]

His diplomacy was no less circumspect. Dohna received verbal promises of help but no action, as James talked only about a possible league and urged German princes to be cautious. With Ralegh recently executed, the Spanish party was dominant and James was in a 'lethargy', keener to return to his hunting than to embark on difficult business.[21] In this climate, by promoting an image of British vigour and heroic renewal *The Masque of the Twelve Months* countered the imputations of idleness, but kept in step with James's attitudes by representing Britain's strength as defensive, protected by its separation from danger. Talking to the ambassadors at the masque James refused to be drawn on 'the great disturbances in the world'. His view was that Bohemia's troubles might help the general peace by relieving pressure points elsewhere, and he steered conversation back onto the dancing.[22]

Such concerns were not yet the focus of *The Masque of the Twelve Months*, the business of which was to ritualize the succession, but they were implicit in it. By contrast, in Jonson's *News from the New World Discovered in the Moon*, danced a year later in the wake of Frederick's acceptance of the Bohemian crown, such political meanings were central. This masque was opened by two heralds, proclaiming tidings ostensibly brought to earth from the moon. Their items of news were fantasies that would convince only the gullible, but they were lapped up by a printer, chronicler, and factor, three sellers of novelty who expected a ready readership. Having ridiculed the newsmongers, the heralds introduced a dance of airy moon-creatures called Volatees, then announced the main masquers. They came from the unchanging but icy realms beyond the moon to serve James, and were restored to warmth by him. Although this did not directly refer to European affairs, its portrayal of men profiting from the hunger for information raised as transparently as could be done within masque protocols the excitements gripping the public early in 1620, and established an ideological opposition between the moonshine of news-mongering and the transcendent and enduring truth of the King.

Given the fledgeling nature of the newspaper industry, this masque's satirical thrust seems astonishingly prescient. Jonson was not attacking the yellow press as such, since the syndicates and newsbooks which he pilloried at greater length in *The Staple of News* (1626) were still several months into the future. The first coranto for the English market (in the strict sense of a digest of recent events) was published in Amsterdam in December 1620, and corantos did not begin to be printed in London until 1621; serial newsbooks date from 1622.[23] Jonson's three figures were all pre-journalistic types inhabiting a world about to be transformed by the onset of war. The printer was a producer of pamphlets whose news was small-scale and sensational; being neither specific nor verifiable, it could be endlessly recycled under different names (47–51, 63–7). The chronicler was an annalist whose undiscriminating records of affairs valued fullness of detail rather than analysis, the obvious models being the city chronographers John Stow and Edmund Howes (21–31).[24] And the factor was a professional writer of newsletters of the kind that had operated from London since the late 1590s and whose activities would greatly multiply in the 1620s.[25] In their dialogue they argued over whether news ceased to be news when it was printed (45–67). Don McKenzie explains this as a sign of the epistemological impact of print technology on the market-place,[26] but, more narrowly considered, the point of their disagreement concerned who was to consume news and hence what its social function would be. The factor – although he divided his news politically, into puritan, Protestant, and 'pontifical' (43–4) – was a gentlemen who spread news by letters, had a 'reputation' to maintain, and 'friends of correspondence in the country' (38–9). But when news was printed, it could be read by anyone, and the printer's readers were 'the common people; and why should they not ha' their pleasure in believing of lies are made for them, as you have in Paul's that make 'em for yourselves?' (52–5). The dialogue focused less on the production of news than its dissemination, the rapidly developing role of newsmongers as shapers of opinion. The danger against which the antimasque legislated was that anyone could thrust their noses into public affairs, exposing the conduct of power to discussion by those who ordinarily had no say in politics.

When newsbooks eventually began appearing, they responded to the public desire for information about Frederick and the Protestant commanders, and reflected English enthusiasms by concentrating primarily on the continental war. But even by late 1619, the sanctity of the *arcana imperii* was being undermined by the developing rift between the King's perspective and his people's, and the royal struggle to command respect. William Trumbull wrote that James's refusal to make any show of support for Frederick bred 'impudent calumnies' from 'every bad companion', and the Venetian ambassador said that, over Christmas, 'the profoundest silence has been enjoined upon all current affairs', so that 'anyone arriving in these islands would think that the people had lost their tongues'.[27] Faced with a son-in-law whose acts denied the principle of royal legitimacy, James commanded the clergy not to pray for him under the title of King of Bohemia, and forbade Dohna from attending 'The Running Masque' (January 1620) with him, lest another ambassador might refer to his master as 'King of Bohemia' in the royal hearing.[28] By being strictly legalistic over right and title, James hoped to preserve the status quo, but his response fell short of the support many would have preferred. Chamberlain said that a remark of Prince Maurice's was 'much talked of, that he is a strange father that will neither fight for his children or pray for them', and Sir Francis Nethersole (recently appointed envoy to the Protestant Union) was contemptuous, describing the directive to preachers as 'the inscrutable depths of his majesty's incomparable wisdom to amuse his son's enemies, and I trust will at last appear such to his friends as all good patriots wish and pray'.[29] Writing two days after the performance of *News from the New World*, Nethersole (if he had seen it) was evidently less than convinced by its defence of James's purposes.

The masque's project was to discredit the newsmongers: it disparaged their dissemination of news and ability to comprehend James's wisdom. Unlike *The Staple of News*, it emphasized stupidity more than cupidity, foregrounding the journalists' untrustworthiness. The printer reproduced any anecdote if it was 'good copy' (18), the chronicler detailed any ephemera that would fill paper, and the factor tailored news to his purchasers' politics. All three were taken in by ludicrous reports of a world in the moon, which ironically reproduced earthly lunacies. Jonson's moon had its own puritans – 'Doppers' (Anabaptists, from the Dutch *dooper* = dipper) and female Presbyterians, 'zealous women, that will out-groan the groaning wives of Edinburgh' (203, 216–17) – as well as a hermaphroditical *beau monde* making visits in coaches made of clouds. This airy and insubstantial world was summed up by the feathery Volatees and dispelled by the more grounded virtues of King James who, being sun to this moon, was its absolute antithesis:

> This is that orb so bright,
> Has kept your wonder so awake;
> Whence you as from a mirror take
> The sun's reflected light.
> Read him as you would do the book
> Of all perfection, and but look
> What his proportions be;
> No measure that is thence contrived,
> Or any motion thence derived,
> But is pure harmony. (336–45)

James's transcendence exposed the newsmongers' triviality and ignorance, setting them at the opposite pole to his glory. Their falsity was the reverse term which established his royal authority.

Not surprisingly, some commentators have regarded this masque as sycophantic, and deplored it for reinforcing James's supposedly reprehensible procrastination.[30] But such criticism mistakes the masque's priorities. In January 1620, with the other Protestant powers waiting on England's lead, James was trying to damp down enthusiasm for intervention and pursue remaining options for settlement within existing structures. The Privy Council felt that English involvement would escalate the conflict and provoke France to join the other side, whereas Louis might be pleased to see Ferdinand humbled if he was reassured that there would be no wider consequences.[31] The masque set out to make restraint seem a persuasive strategy, representing James as the guarantor of peace, the 'knowing king' (371) who sat untroubled amidst a turbulence that unbalanced mere ordinary men:

> But since the earth is of his name
> And fame
> So full, you cannot add,
> Be both the first, and glad
> To speak him to the region whence you came.   (358–62)

News from the New World served James's policy by representing him as uniquely prudent and far-seeing, his beams warming the masquers while he remained constant and unmoved. Still, his inaction was disliked by those who wanted greater decisiveness. Spain had asked England to mediate with Bohemia, but many who wanted to capitalize on this 'glorious and brave ... occasion' felt that, if war followed, English neutrality would only help the Habsburgs.[32] The impact of these emerging divisions is seen in the masque's structure, which was far more confrontational than earlier shows and stepped decisively away from consensus. Here the gulf between James's long-term perspective and the views of the newsmongers was represented as absolute, and such space as was once present for accommodation was absent. At stake was no longer James's legitimacy but, more problematically, his credibility.

Not the least sign of a loss of confidence was the stirring of divisions within the royal household. It became clear early on that Charles and Buckingham were more enthusiastic for war than James was. In February Nethersole called them 'good patriots, very zealous' on Frederick's behalf. Charles had 'great good will to his sister and the new king', and Buckingham promised to spend all his profits in Bohemia (he later gave £5,000 for the Palatinate). For the next four years they were both restive under Jacobean appeasement.[33] Inevitably this complicated the politics of

News from the New World: while affirming James's authority, it must have had an element of negotiation between father and son. And other evidence suggests that a kind of counter-culture was developing around the Prince. Over Christmas and Shrovetide, Charles and Buckingham were involved in a series of amateur theatricals at households in London and Newmarket, including repeat performances in various venues of the so-called 'Running Masque', possibly written by John Maynard, a client of Buckingham's.[34] As the hosts and performers of this show included prominent aristocrats sympathetic to the Protestant cause, such as the Earls of Oxford and Warwick and Viscount Doncaster (formerly Lord Hay), it seems likely that it functioned as an occasion for reinforcing the bonds amongst an aristocratic community under stress. The text of 'The Running Masque' is fragmentary and comparatively anodyne, but it signals its cultural allegiances by adopting the French style of multiple entries rather than the single Jonsonian antimasque, and it features Orpheus damping down the rebellious 'noise' (262) of a magician's infernal spirits and changing them into gloriously dressed courtiers. The potential for generational conflict was even more visible in a lost play performed by the Prince's Men 'in the presence of the king his father' shortly before the New Year. This, said the Venetian ambassador, presented a king who executed one of his two sons 'simply on suspicion that he wished to deprive him of his crown, and the other son actually did deprive him of it afterwards. This moved the king in an extraordinary manner, both inwardly and outwardly.'[35] The correspondence between this fiction of a king with two sons and the current relationships among the James–Charles–Frederick triangle was not exact, but its unpalatability to James suggests that it touched a nerve. Almost certainly he took it for some sort of reflection on his reluctance to intervene for his son-in-law.

Even more revealing was Middleton and Rowley's *A Courtly Masque Called the World Tossed at Tennis*, which had a command performance at Denmark House on 4 March 1620, shortly after the second performance of *News from the New World*, to mark the occasion when Charles came into possession of his late mother's property.[36] This was not really a masque but an unusually short play interleaved with dumb-shows and dancing. It lacked revels on the aristocratic model, and was current on the public stage in Prince's Men's professional repertoire, but its allegorical framework was carefully tailored to the Prince's outlook. Its action showed the world, originally owned by Simplicity, being passed successively to a king, soldier, sea-captain, churchman, and lawyer, with the devil at each juncture attempting unsuccessfully to take possession. All this was performed in riposte to a scholar and soldier, who opened the play by complaining the times were hostile to men of worth. By the end, the scholar had settled in the 'most glorious peace ... where the head / Of him that rules, to learning's fair renown, / Is doubly decked with laurel and a crown', but the soldier had recognized that virtue could be won overseas, in 'the most glorious wars / That e'er famed Christian kingdom' (F2v).[37] In this, he imitated Charles's example, 'the prince of nobleness himself', who 'Proves our Minerva's valiant'st hopefull'st son, / And early in his spring puts armour on' (F2). Soldiery and scholarship went hand in hand, but there would have been no doubt which appealed more strongly to the Prince.

No less remarkable was the choice of this Shrovetide for Charles's first tiltyard performance, an occasion which turned into a public display of staggeringly expensive ceremonial, witnessed by 'crowds of people' and a 'throng of coaches and troops'. Exceptionally for a period of austerity, a budget of £6,500 was found – vastly more than was spent on the masque – and ambassadors of six countries were invited. Charles was accompanied by Buckingham and thirteen other noblemen and (in what the Venetian ambassador called 'an unusual circumstance') was guarded by London's militia, '500 citizens, admirably armed, who appeared to accompany and serve his highness attracted by the special esteem which they have for his worth'.[38] In 1616 Charles's installation as Prince of Wales had passed with little public ceremonial because no one wanted to build up a new Prince Henry (see chapter 7 above), but the stage-management of the 1620 event, creating a heroic persona like his dead brother's, demonstrated how far the ground had shifted. Probably it was felt that a display of valour by the Crown Prince would restore confidence and send a signal to Spain about English preparedness, but it also suggested a difference of perspective between James and Charles that subsequent events would compound. Two days after the tilt James visited St Paul's, and spectators were disappointed when he appealed for money for the cathedral fabric rather than for Bohemia.[39] The perception that Charles wanted to embrace policies that James was reluctant about would eventually generate the most significant crisis in the reign's political culture.

For the next three years, James conducted an increasingly divisive holding action against the slide into war. After *News from the New World*, the crisis escalated alarmingly, first with Frederick's disastrous defeat at Prague (November 1620), then with the devastating advance of the imperial army, under General Tilly, through the Palatinate, a situation watched anxiously at home because the Rhineland fortresses besieged in 1621–2 were garrisoned by English troops. These events transformed the situation, as Frederick had lost his hereditary estates and attack on the Habsburgs had turned into conquest by the Habsburgs, but James was still reluctant to go to war. He wanted separate settlements at the war's individual flashpoints, and hoped that, if Frederick renounced his claim to Bohemia, Spain's desire for the marriage with Charles would induce her to restore the Palatinate. However, since he could not guarantee Spain would keep her word, he had to appear as though he were able to fight, and he put iron (and silver) into his diplomacy on receiving news of the defeat in Bohemia, by calling a parliament and Council of War for January 1621. This publicly signalled England's readiness to intervene, allowing James to fuel perceptions of himself overseas as a monarch whose people were pushing him towards military options. Yet his underlying hope was that the mere threat of intervention would be sufficient to halt territorial aggression and force Spain into delivering on her promises. Although parliament seemed a step into war, it was really designed to forestall it. If the sabre rattled loudly enough, the rapprochement with Spain and Europe's stability might be preserved.

This policy's disadvantage was that it fuelled domestic expectations that England would support the Protestant cause. Late in 1620 correspondence began to fill with rumour. In November the Venetian ambassador Lando wrote home that, although James was undecided about Bohemia, the 'generality' were hostile to Catholic states and suspicious of his ministers: 'They discuss the whole situation with more freedom than ever, expressing very lively opinions upon the welfare of the kingdom and the preservation of the religion which they profess. Perhaps this kingdom has never had its eyes so wide open ... [and] has never been so teeming with ideas and grievances as now'.[40] Buckingham's view was that 'whoever gives rein to the people will make the king of Bohemia laugh'. A week later Lando was reporting 'dangerous general excitement'. Gondomar could not walk the streets without 'insults of the populace', and panicked so completely that one night his household stayed awake and in arms and requested a guard from the Council, something the people regarded as a Spanish trick to make them 'barbarous' in James's eyes.[41] This was the point at which corantos started to appear, and letters were found in the streets threatening the people would display their wrath if James 'did not do what was expected of him'.[42] The most scurrilous surviving document is Thomas Scott's *Vox populi*, a tract masquerading as a report of Gondomar's secret consultations with Madrid, which seemed to expose the sensational reality beneath Spanish friendship. This circulated in November, and Gondomar, said Lando, 'foams with wrath in every direction'. A sequel was suppressed before it reached print and its author, Thomas Gainsford, was arrested.[43] James reacted with new controls on talk and preaching, and Drayton and Wither were among the poets complaining at this time that matters of state were now too sensitive to touch. When parliament met, in January, its first debate was on freedom of speech.

In this volatile situation, the masque for Twelfth Night 1621, Jonson's *Pan's Anniversary*, rehearsed the case for restraint.[44] It was a symptom of the escalating crisis that *Pan's Anniversary* was the first masque to be danced by shepherds and set entirely in Arcadia. It initiated the political use of pastoral masques, a mode that became more prominent in the next reign. It was also the first panegyric to develop the subsequently commonplace analogy between the ruling monarch and the great god Pan, who in the Orphic *Hymns* figures as the mysterious locus of cosmic harmony.[45] In early representations, such as Jonson's Highgate entertainment (1604), Pan appeared as a grotesque deity: amusing James with the praise of liquor, he was a local field god or puckish god of laughter in the tradition deriving from the Homeric *Hymn to Pan*. But in 1621, James was assimilated to the god in whose honour the rites were held, and associated with Orphic iconography that saw Pan as an immanent universal presence, a cosmic overlord haunting the recesses of nature and ruling all with a benevolent but invisible providence. With the songs shaped as hymns, Pan/James was worshipped as best of singers, hunters, leaders, and shepherds (172–89) – a formulation which foregrounded those parts of his iconography that accorded with James's hunting and poetry – and envisioned as presiding over a serenely untroubled Arcadia. The 'yearly rites' (5) of his worshippers celebrated 'the music of his peace' (68) and imitated social concords which Pan had himself instilled:

> come you prime Arcadians forth, that taught
> By Pan the rites of true society,
> From his loud music, all your manners wrought,
> And made your commonwealth a harmony.   (159–62)

The rituals thus embodied the perfect peace which it was their project to celebrate.

Into this pastoral serenity, the masque intruded a challenge from nine disruptive antimasquers. These men were not Arcadians but visitors from Boeotia, a country notorious in classical times for its inhabitants' stupidity (Pindar mentions 'the ancient taunt, Boeotian swine').[46] Significantly, the Boeotians did not precede the main masque but twice interrupted it. At their first appearance they were expelled 'with contempt' by the old shepherd who presented the rituals (158), then on return they were punished for impertinence by being transformed into sheep, so that worship of Pan could go ahead peacefully. Even more than in *News from the New World*, the structure was a contest between insiders and outsiders, which registered hardly at all as internal critique. And, for all the classical setting, the Boeotians were transparently contemporary citizens. Their leader, a fencer, was a gentleman,[47] but his unruly followers were artisans and mechanics with no place in a pastoral landscape: a tinker, tooth-drawer, juggler, corn-cutter, bellows-mender, tinderbox-man, clock-keeper, tailor, and clerk. Although it had no warrant in pastoral tradition, Jonson made the opposition between Arcadia and Boeotia a contrast between aristocrat and trades-man. Ostensibly the Boeotians had come from Thebes (85), but on the night they must have seemed to stumble in from Jacobean London, rather as if Overdo's lawless Smithfield were being disciplined by aristocrats from a Sidneian Penshurst.[48]

The action consisted of a literal and symbolic contest to the values of Arcadia. The Boeotians challenged the shepherds to a dancing competition, but they also threatened their social hegemony, since their undignified cavortings parodied the masquers' courtly ceremoniousness. Each Boeotian imitated one of the Arcadians' masquing skills. The tinker provided music and the juggler agility, the tooth-drawer kept their breath sweet and the corn-cutter directed their feet, the bellows-mender and tinderbox-man gave breath and fire, the clock-keeper kept them in time, and the mousetrap-man designed their 'cringes' (140), while the tailor was a 'prophet' (132) who pronounced the symbolic meaning of the event, and the clerk recorded it in shorthand. The Boeotians were guilty of absurd presumption: they emulated the Arcadians, but could only exhibit separately the graces which each Arcadian individually manifested. The old shepherd's warning tutored them in deference – 'beware of presuming, or how you offer comparison with persons so near deities' (154–5) – and their transformation into sheep reasserted the proper relations between stupid citizens and a 'hallowed troop of herdsmen' (257). It also vindicated Pan's power who, although a loving shepherd, was also a fearsome god. As the second hymn underlined, he was fearsome as well as kind, and could not be injured with impunity:

> But if he frown, the sheep, alas,
> The shepherds wither, and the grass.
> Strive, strive to please him, then, by still increasing thus
> The rites are due to him, who doth all right for us.   (200–3)

These lines, with their echoes of Old Testament warnings to recalcitrant shepherds,[49] were surprisingly stern, but they were borne out by the punishment which the Boeotians' indiscipline provoked. Pan's potentially shocking capacity for justice was subordinate to Golden Age tropes of peace, but the masque also emphasized that he must be reverenced and obeyed. Its concluding words urged shepherds to keep firm control of their flocks.

So although the action was genial, there was an underlying conflict between comedy and celebration. The antimasquers fulfilled the taste for amusement, but they ultimately had to be silenced for Pan's harmonies, most literally in the case of the tinker whose monotonous drumming announced their arrival (98–100). Doubtless the Whitehall audience would have associated his mindless pounding of a kettledrum with 'rough music', the unruly, plebeian noise of the charivari.[50] More crucially, the social contrast between courtier and citizen had a political edge, which emerged in the tailor who brought up the rear. He was another member of Jonson's gallery of puritans:

Nor can we doubt of success, for we have a prophet amongst us of that peremptory pate, a tailor, or master fashioner, that hath found it out in a painted cloth, or some old hanging (for these are his library) that we must conquer in such a time, and such a half time, therefore bids us go on cross-legged, or however thread the needles of our own happiness, go through-stitch with all, unwind the clew of our cares; he hath taken measure of our minds, and will fit our fortune to our footing. (131–40)

A 'prophet' like Busy in *Bartholomew Fair*, the tailor was an inspired enthusiast belonging to a trade noted for its puritanism. He shared his slogan about conquering 'in such a time, and such a half time' (from *Revelations* 12.14) with the deluded Anabaptist in *The Staple of News* (3.2.128). An ignorant fanatic, whose learning derived from a dilapidated moralistic tapestry, he was evidently the Boeotians' ideas man, and his 'philosopher' (141), the clerk, was an intellectual hanger-on, one of those Jonsonian ignorants in whom a little learning is a dangerous thing, who thought himself remarkable for being able to write *and* read (141–3). The tailor's presence implied the need to restrain both vulgar impertinence and religious fanaticism, and signalled the limits to James's pose of militancy. He indicated that James was unlikely to go to war out of emotional solidarity with German Protestantism, whatever expectations the new parliament raised, and that, however noisily sabres rattled, the overriding commitment was to peace. Confessional politics had no place in a strong, stable monarchy.

So *Pan's Anniversary* discredited popular religious enthusiasm, propounding an ideology that subordinated plebeian impudence to aristocratic control. But in 1621 this was contentious territory, and Chamberlain's eyewitness account indicates that some spectators were shocked by the masque's handling of religion: 'That night they had a ball at Whitehall, and on Twelfth Day were invited to the masque there, which was handsomely performed, but that there was a puritan brought in to be flouted and abused, which was somewhat unseemly and unseasonable, specially as matters now stand with those of the religion in France.'[51] The 'they' that Chamberlain referred to were an embassy led by the Marquis de Cadenet, who was guest of honour at the masque. Cadenet, a senior French nobleman, arrived unexpectedly in December, and he was sumptuously entertained, his visit sparking rumours of a change of alliances. Louis was capitalizing on James's need to put pressure on Spain, and Cadenet was welcomed by noblemen like Viscount Doncaster who hoped for an anti-Spanish front. But the real purpose was to ascertain English reactions prior to renewed moves against French Protestants at La Rochelle, and, if Paris was offering James much-needed support in Germany, the price was non-intervention in French affairs out of solidarity with co-religionists. Ditching the Huguenots was a gesture James could not afford to make, and the visit dissolved into acrimony. Cadenet was given 'a round answer' by James, who warned him that, though he could not support subjects in revolt against their monarchs, neither could he be unmoved by the persecution of fellow Protestants. The visit was marred by tiffs between the nobles, and Cadenet returned home with little accomplished.[52]

In relation to these issues the scenario of *Pan's Anniversary* became disconcertingly problematic. The masque was in hand before it was certain Cadenet would arrive, but once it became his welcome's centrepiece the tactlessness of its satire was apparent. Chamberlain may not have objected to a masque countering the growth of popular interest in politics, but he, and other spectators, were bothered by a caricature of Protestant extremism when the context foregrounded the state of religion in Europe at large. In effect, the masque was in danger of being shipwrecked on the diverging imperatives of Jacobean policy. James needed to damp down fervour for intervention at the same time as he wanted to license a posture of limited militancy, but Cadenet's arrival exposed the confusion over how seriously his policy was guided by considerations of the faith. Writing a masque that disparaged Protestant enthusiasm at a moment when James needed to reaffirm a circumscribed religious commitment, Jonson was in the unenviable position of having to accommodate incompatible options, and his use of the puritan to project an anxiety about the consequences of enthusiasm was wrong-footed by the residual need to uphold the faith when it was threatened in France. Chamberlain's discomfort demonstrated the ideological mare's nest towards which court festival was being propelled by the contradictory imperatives of the developing crisis. It was precisely the masque's success in articulating James's domestic agenda that caused it to be censured on grounds of confessional loyalty.

Such contradictions in James's political culture can only have undermined the effectiveness of his policy. He wished to project an image of war-readiness, but in Lando's view, despite the honours done to Cadenet, the crown's pro-Spanish preferences were self-evident: 'whereas the French ambassador has enjoyed these airy demonstrations, the Spaniard has that which is more solid and important, being more influential than ever over his Majesty or over those who guide him, making use for his own advantage of festivities, masques, and all distractions from business'.[53] When *Pan's Anniversary* was repeated at Shrovetide, it was frankly a Spanish triumph: Lando noted that Gondomar sat under the state beside the King 'with every imaginable honour' – in itself a violation of the policy by which no one ambassador was supposed to monopolize all favour at a masque. At the same time, the Dutch ambassadors, currently in London to promote English friendship now that the Twelve Years' Truce was expiring (but regaled by James with tactless complaints about fishing rivalries), were given an insultingly meagre welcome. They saw only a minor masque danced at Whitehall by some lawyers, and were honoured, said Lando, 'in very sparing fashion'.[54] The difference must have underlined the impression of royal detachment from the Protestant camp, and when a garbled report of the controversy over Jonson's puritan trickled down to the provinces via the letter-writer Joseph Mead, it too seemed to confirm everything that was feared:

I am told there was not long since (I suppose about New Year's tide) a play before his majesty wherein there was a puritan brought up, having long asses' ears, who should speak after this manner: 'Is it now a time to give lists, and make merry etc.? This should be a time of fasting and prayer, when the church of God is in so great affliction in Bohemia and Germany and other places, and not of masquing and music, etc.' I will not believe this was entertained with applause, and yet I am told so.[55]

It was only a short step from such an observation, which magnified the masque into an out-and-out attack on hot Protestants, to the feeling that the masques themselves were contributing to the absence of intervention in Germany.

Pan's Anniversary displays with uncommon clarity the problems masques faced in the new climate. At a time when a gulf was emerging between royal policy and popular temper it was difficult to present credible images of consensus, while the ideology of plebeian deference and royal control had the unfortunate consequence of representing the monarch as embattled against his own subjects. This placed a new and dangerous contradiction at the heart of court festival. The assertions of harmony were implicitly at odds with the exclusionary fables by which those assertions were made, and the images of autonomous sovereign authority were belied by the representation of that authority as significantly challenged. Beneath these difficulties lay an ideological conflict to which the masques were themselves contributing. It was not enough to invoke the monarch's political transcendence, since in the context of confessional war it was precisely that claim which was starting to look controversial. In this unstable climate, the strategies which the masques usually deployed to legitimate royal power ceased to seem irenic. Their rhetorical manoeuvres were no longer uncontentious but had themselves become part of the political debate.

The aftermath of *Pan's Anniversary* can be discerned in Jonson's masques for 1621–2 and 1622–3, *The Masque of Augurs* and *Time Vindicated*. In the months before Charles's journey into Spain, military options fell out of view, and measures were taken to silence dissent. The 1621 parliament ended in open breach, James responding to parliamentary calls for war against Spain by tearing the pages from the Commons journal. Observers expected to see him resorting to non-parliamentary finance, and Chamberlain drew the moral that resistance to royal power had backfired on its perpetrators: 'the wilfulness of the Lower House hath brought us to these terms, whereby we may see that *vanae sine viribus irae*, and that there is no disputing nor contesting with supreme authority'.[56] One sufferer was George Wither, who was imprisoned after the publication of *Wither's Motto*. This long and vitriolic indictment of late Jacobean England, which reputedly sold 30,000 copies, was a comprehensively disenchanted satire. It attacked no individuals by name but made it seem as if the whole state of things were awry and the times given over to flattery, pride, servility, and self-abasement, all affairs being governed by 'the minions of the time'.[57] For this Wither spent nine months in prison, James being determined 'to pare his whelp's claws'.[58] The ensuing year saw a battle between dissent and royal power: a deluge of outspoken sermons, 'libels and dangerous books' was met with proclamations commanding the nobility to return to their estates and with *Directions concerning Preaching* which forbade clergy from meddling with state affairs.[59] By December 1622, says Tom Cogswell, 'James had reasserted control and had ridden out a particularly alarming storm of popular criticism.'[60] Meanwhile expectations mounted that the Spanish

Match was about to be concluded. Lando reported that Dohna was 'beating the air', since ministers thought that 'once they have the daughter and her dowry nothing will be impossible with them for Spain'.[61] The degree to which confidence had ebbed is indicated by rumours that James was about to convert to Catholicism, but these were nothing in comparison with the shocking news of February 1623: that the Prince and Buckingham had donned false beards and false names and left for Madrid, to bring home the Infanta.

These circumstances help to explain the extreme polarizations apparent in the next masques, and the virtual abandonment of myth for almost unmediated images of dissent being confuted. *The Masque of Augurs*, danced on the very day that the 1621 parliament was dissolved,[62] focused on the inauguration of the new Banqueting House, the architectural symbol of Stuart permanence. In the glorious setting of a Roman college of augurs, Apollo, his poets and priests interpreted the omens as entirely auspicious. But this dignified ceremonial was preceded by the blundering arrival of seven citizens from St Katherine's (a poor docks area in London's East End) who thought James might prefer to be entertained by dancing bears. David Norbrook, arguing that Jonson felt privately distanced from the court he was celebrating, has suggested that their ursine cavorting and rollicking ballad about the pleasures of the East End were an implied satire on Whitehall's 'taste for riotous and farcical masques',[63] but it was more likely the citizens themselves who were put in their place. The citizens were jolly but, as the groom who admitted them observed, rather smelly (66–7), and their fun was low. Though amused by their account of how people came to St Katherine's to drink 'til they spew, and stink, / And often piss out our fire' (206–7), courtiers were unlikely to take up the invitation to visit.[64] Rather, the antimasque presented homely pleasures, disorderly and unrefined but essentially unthreatening, that would have pleased the monarch who promulgated the *Book of Sports* (that 1617 proclamation which, by licensing festive games on Sundays, sought to promote amicable relations in local communities). The groom threatened the citizens with the stocks (56–7), but wishing only to praise their neighbourhood and present love to the King (63), they avoided punishment through their entertainment's sheer humbleness. Though socially inferior, they offered no political challenge and, unlike the Boeotians, projected simple loyalty.

After this low induction, Apollo's remark that he had 'no vulgar ends' (283) moved the masque into a ritualized world where knowledge authorized power and peace was divinely sanctioned. The main masque was intensely learned, and larded with marginalia in the published text, and its structures were elaborately hierarchical, notably its main action, in which the augurs' dances were interpreted by the poets, validated by Apollo, and ratified by Jove. The political symbiosis between Apollo and his father –

> *Apollo.*   My arts are only to obey.
> *Jove.*   And mine to sway.   (441–3)

– shadowed the relationship outside the masque between James and Charles, and implied a model of authority in which the King's mighty commands were translated into action by a pyramid of subordinates. Even the birds whose behaviour the augurs interpreted were vertically ranked, the augurs judging 'how high / The vulture, or the hern did fly', and whether the swan, dove, or stork flew on top (352–5). Chiming with the classically arcaded buildings of the scene, these hierarchies suggested the sacredness, stability, and strength of Stuart power, Apollo's auguries directly reflecting James's transcendental foresight:

> Behold the love and care of all the gods,
> King of the Ocean, and the Happy Isles;
> That whilst the world about him is at odds,
> Sits crowned lord here of himself, and smiles …
> To see the erring mazes of mankind,
> Who seek for that, doth punish them to find.   (313–19)

Those 'erring mazes' were presented in the second antimasque, introduced by Vangoose, an Englishman who had turned Dutch through excessive admiration of the Low Countries, and which depicted 'straying and deformed pilgrims, taking several paths' (271–2). This subject reflected on the doctrinal unreliability of the world's faiths, the confusion above which James sat in wise detachment; it was diametrically opposed to the procession of the nations coming to enroll under the leadership of English Protestantism that was envisaged in *The Masque of Truth* (chapter 6 above). James's command of events had little to do with the religious obsessions of other men. Rather, Britain was so aloof from the 'tumult' of 'hatred, faction' and 'fear' (384–7) prevailing elsewhere that her peace was envied by the world:

> Thy neighbours at thy fortune long have gazed,
> But at thy wisdom, all do stand amazed,
>   And wish to be
> O'ercome, or governed by thee!

> Safety itself so sides thee, where thou go'st,
> And Fate still offers what thou covet'st most!   (404–9)

The immovability of James's peaceful and non-confessional policies could scarcely have been more emphatic.

Still more transparent was *Time Vindicated to Himself and to his Honours*, which, by abandoning the protective clothing of myth, forfeited even the pretence of aesthetic distance. The antimasquers were a group of grotesques, the Eyed, the Eared, and the Nosed, collectively the Curious – the very enemy named by James in his poem on the comet – who were led by Chronomastix (literally 'the Whipper of the Times'), a barely veiled lampoon of George Wither. With its devastating parody of Wither's interminably ambling couplets, the antimasque was a riposte to his indictment of 'the Times'. Chronomastix was self-loving and envious, his poetry mere scandal-mongering, and his followers a rabble who, reduced to eyes, ears, and noses, were the embodiment of mindless consumerism. Chronomastix listed 'prentices, clerks, seamstresses, fishwives, pudding-wives, chambermaids, and city ladies as his readership, and the dances presented his 'faction' (132): the 'Boss' of Billingsgate, a discarded magistrate, unlicensed printer, braggart soldier, and a pedantic schoolmaster who was a personal caricature of Alexander Gill, Milton's master at St Paul's School. They were all obsessed with malicious gossip, 'the impostures, / The prodigies, diseases, and distempers, / The knaveries of the Time' (50–2). Chronomastix was a rabble-rouser, a pathological malcontent who 'cares for nobody' (73) and encouraged the Curious to 'do what we list. Talk what we list. / And censure whom we list, and how we list' (81–2). His pleasurable antimasques were total anarchy, as the Curious prescribed the dances they wished to see:

Ears.	Let's have all the people in an uproar,
	None knowing why, or to what end: and in
	The midst of all, start up an old mad woman
	Preaching of patience …
Nose.	Something that is unlawful.
Ears.	Ay, or unreasonable.
Eyes.	Or impossible.
Nose.	Let't be uncivil enough, you hit us right.
Ears.	And a great noise.
Eyes.	To little or no purpose.
Nose.	And if there be some mischief, 'twill become it.

(225–8, 244–9)

A good antimasque would be to talk of the King or the state, and censure the Council 'ere they censure us' (210). Performed before a scene showing the

Banqueting House and the gateway fronting onto the public road through the palace, this masque depicted waves of sedition lapping at the very entrance to Whitehall.[65]

The apotheosis of Time's Whipper – the 'deifying of a pompion [pumpkin]' (200) – was answered in the main masque by James's apotheosis and by Saturn, Time himself, who discovered the masquers in the roles of Time's Glories released from obscurity by Venus (Love). Where Chronomastix served Infamy (99), the masque was presented by Fame, and the Glories brought 'harmony' and light (326), displaying value which Time's detractors could not see. Cupid defended the evening's innocent carelessness in contrast to the Curious's malicious pleasures, and Diana commanded the Glories to pass their time hunting, since that was a manly activity to 'keep soft peace in breath': 'Man should not hunt mankind to death, / But strike the enemies of man; / Kill vices if you can: / They are your wildest beasts' (531–5). The masque thus discharged anxieties by staging an action which anticipated history's judgments, sweeping away the merely contingent and proclaiming James's wisdom. But it is difficult not to register the tensions which the masque was attempting to discharge, not least because in vindicating James's times the masque had to allow that there was something they needed vindicating from. When Saturn's Votaries averred 'every public vow' was pleased by Venus once they had 'heard her why, and [waited] thy how' (302–3), and that the masquers proved 'what a glory 'tis to see / Men's wishes, Time, and Love agree' (313–14), their language elided the gap between the different versions of 'men' that were invoked in antimasque and masque. The fulfilment of 'Men's wishes' was premised on the disempowerment of whatever 'public' was spoken for by the antimasque.

It would be wrong to see these masques as attempting to escape from difficult 'realities' by justifying political structures that seem unpalatable today. Many spectators, for all that they disliked James's pro-Spanish position, must have been anxious about the war's social impact, and keen to see strong government. One instructive case is Sir Robert Naunton's reaction to his disgrace in 1621. Naunton was a proponent of a French alliance, but Gondomar contrived his removal from the secretaryship by exploiting indiscreet remarks he made to one of Cadenet's followers. This was a blow to the interventionist group on the Council, but, in appealing to the King, Naunton sought to distinguish his beliefs from those of more strictly ideological opponents to the marriage. He complained about being called 'a puritan, whose irregular scruples and fond opinions God and the world knows that from my first exercises in schools I have heartily opposed'.[66] For men like Naunton, the desire for overseas intervention did not mean any disbelief in domestic social control, and though preferring masques which promoted heroism, he may have been undisturbed by their emphasis on the need to maintain hierarchy. Nonetheless, the territory which the masques occupied was more fractured than before, their polarizations were more acute, and the appeal to common ground was harder to make. As Jonson may have found, even to address problems was dangerous. Chamberlain reported of *Time Vindicated* that 'Ben Jonson, they say, is like to hear it on both sides of the head for personating George Withers, a poet or poetaster as he terms him, as hunting after fame by being a chronomastix or whipper of the time, which is become so tender an argument that it must not be touched either in jest or earnest'.[67] One might suppose that James would have welcomed such satire, but Chamberlain implies that even to suggest that royal policies needed defending cut too near the bone. *Time Vindicated* made a powerful defence of censorship, but the point of restoring the times' quietness was that no discussions of troubles, not even sympathetic ones, could be heard. In these conditions the space for manoeuvre was severely diminished. The masques' alignment with the King was starting to look like a political and aesthetic liability.

All this was about to be transformed by the extraordinary events of 1623 – Charles's departure for Madrid in February, his discovery that the Infanta could not be had on terms to which he could agree, the agonizing wait at home, and the upsurge of national relief at his safe return in October. When Jonson wrote *Neptune's Triumph for the Return of Albion* (prepared for Twelfth Night 1624 but not performed), not only had the pro-Spanish posture collapsed, but, with the Prince and Buckingham demanding war and standing opposed to the King, the political landscape was redrawn. The momentousness of this transformation has not always been appreciated by literary historians, who have regarded Charles's Spanish pilgrimage as a quixotic act by a callow youth, and his return embarrassingly unencumbered by the Spanish bride that he had gone to collect as a disastrous step on that inexorable road to Civil War, an early premonition of the incompetence that would later cost him the crown. But Tom Cogswell's compelling revision of the historiography has resituated these events in relation to the struggle for political control at the end of James's reign and the belated emergence of a fully fledged reversionary interest.[68] If for the Prince the journey was a political coming of age, for James it was the severest challenge to his authority in the entire reign.

Cogswell argues that Charles went to Madrid, largely against James's will, out of eagerness to cut short the negotiations, and that he returned as the sponsor of a new policy and possessed of the undivided support of the man who only months before had been James's dearest dependant. Before Charles left it was already hoped that he might promote the intervention which the King had resisted. His wish to be a heroic leader – an enduring character trait – was well known, and Joseph Mead reported rumours that he pleaded with James 'to suffer himself no longer to be abused with treaties, desiring him, that since himself was old, and unfit now for actions of war, that he would give him leave to raise a royal army, and be the leader thereof himself, not doubting but to find the subjects ready'.[69] Whatever the truth, once on the spot in Madrid the marriage's diplomatic worthlessness became apparent. Charles left Madrid convinced that Spain had to be fought, and returned as leader of the war lobby, in uncomfortable alliance with former critics such as Pembroke. In the event, Charles and Buckingham were unable to muster sufficient support at Whitehall or to persuade James to break with Madrid. Instead, they determined to use the parliament called for February 1624 as their forum, with everything that implied about coordinating royal intentions with the pressure of national feeling. But it was also self-evident that Whitehall had undergone a sea-change, and James was in danger of being outflanked by his son. Bishop Goodman later wrote that Gondomar tried to frighten James by suggesting 'that the parliament would desire the king to retire to a private life, and follow his studies for his employment and his hunting for his recreation, and that he would repose the trust for managing the government unto his son, whom they found active and able to undertake it'.[70]

In *Neptune's Triumph for the Return of Albion*, Jonson directly allegorized Charles's homecoming, transparently reworking the whole episode as a myth of reunion. His masque opened with a dialogue between a Poet and a Cook, on the difficulty of pleasing one's customers. The Poet said his fable would depict Neptune's joy at his son's safe return from a hazardous journey, but he left it to the Cook to devise the vulgar antimasques. The main masque consisted of Albion's homecoming, and the greetings of the sea deities. Neptune was feigned to have sent Albion to Celtiberia to achieve a mysterious discovery, and Albion, accompanied by Hippius, his devoted 'manager of horse' (137), had escaped without falling prey to the sirens' temptations. Had the masque actually been performed, spectators would easily have decoded this as a version of the summer's events with Albion and Hippius as Charles and Buckingham, but, in the light of that winter's politics, the prevailing view that regards *Neptune's Triumph* as ideological misrepresentation cannot be sustained. In an influential reading Stephen Orgel has interpreted the masque as a text designed to save James's face. He argues it provided 'a context within which the fiasco may be seen as a victory' and replaced the realities outside the Banqueting House with an 'unrealistic' myth.[71] 'So is state discourse manufactured', comments Goldberg.[72] But in the context described above it was open to the masque neither to celebrate a unified court, nor to put a brave face on disaster. Whereas previous masques presented Charles as James's deferential son and successor, *Neptune's Triumph* had to negotiate the same relationship in the context of open collision between monarch and heir. Not surprisingly, Jonson's text was everywhere troubled by tensions which, while they could not be anywhere fully articulated, could neither be easily transcended.

The conflicts at stake can be suggested by looking at the development of the masque's fable. Its germ can perhaps be found in plans which Buckingham was nurturing in the summer for a canvas intended as a gift for Charles, memorializing the Spanish Match and his own role in it. His architect, Balthazar Gerbier, was developing this project before the critical policy shift came about:

I am advised, before my return from Italy, to make a pretty piece of the return from Spain with the Infanta; for instance, a triumph by sea representing a chariot with the Prince and Princess, Neptune driving his sea-horses, and your excellency as admiral of the sea in the front of the chariot, holding in your hands the reins; and to paint besides, on the margin of the water, the nymphs which shall represent England, which shall come in a dance to receive their Prince, with many angels flying in the air, some carrying the arms of Spain, and others things appropriate to their union. I think that this would be very beautiful, and tend to immortalize this action of yours, having brought the Princess by sea, and would be a beautiful present to be presented on the part of your excellency to the Prince.[73]

This confection was never painted, but it had many elements that resurfaced in *Neptune's Triumph*, though with their political valencies reversed (such as the genial English nymphs turning into dangerous Spanish sirens). It may have been the origin of what eventually became Jonson's sea-triumph, though its meaning in the summer was quite different. It would have celebrated Charles's achievement of a long-meditated alliance, and advanced Buckingham in the service of a prince who might shortly be king on his own account. As a gift from the favourite, it would have cemented his personal tie with the Prince, figuring Buckingham as Charles's servant but also holding the reins of power. In turning a version of this scheme into *Neptune's Triumph*, Jonson explored its implied networks of affinity, resituating Charles's triumph inside Neptune's commands, but the canvas suggests how much the masque's motifs centred on the younger men. The fable and its glorious performance were tied to the coming generation's political ambitions.

No less problematic was the applicability of this iconography to the event. Jonson organized his sea-triumph around a framework from Statius' *Achilleis*. From Statius came the inscription on the pillars fronting the scene, 'Sec[undo] Jov[i]' (that is, 'Second Jove', the title used for Neptune in *Achilleis* 1.48–9), and the banquet's location at Oceanus' palace (splendidly realized in Jones's design for the third scene). An unfinished epic on the life of Achilles, the *Achilleis* opens with Thetis, Achilles' mother, observing Paris' ships sailing towards Troy, and pleading with Neptune to raise a storm to overwhelm them, thereby averting the war and her child's death. But Neptune, who arrives from his banquet with Oceanus, admonishes her that this would disrupt Fate's decrees, particularly the war between Europe and Asia preordained by Jove. A positive reading might see this allusion as revising the classical source: as the modern, pacific Neptune, James's refusal to make waves guarantees his son's safe passage. But its implications carried over into Charles's part. Charles was no Paris, for he was immune to the sirens' charms; the implied parallel was with Achilles, the youthful hero shortly to prove himself in war. The mythical allusion seems poised between conflicting meanings for King and Prince. Returning to Neptune as to a nurturing parent, Albion was also marked out as a warrior hero, apted for a greater destiny by his avoidance of love.

Ostensibly this triumph was Neptune's. It was he who ruled the seas, whose 'great commands' and 'designs' (140, 369) Albion had performed, and who dispatched the floating island to waft him home. But this masque signalled a momentous departure, since here, for once, Neptune's foresight was not privileged: the monarch's secret purposes, which normally signified the impenetrability and irresistibility of his will, were for the first time in any Jacobean masque represented as shared. Albion not only did his task but actively participated in the hidden decision to undertake it. Although, as in previous masques, royal strategies were unexplained to the audience, their determination was ascribed not just to the King but to the whole royal party. As the Cook explained it, mighty Neptune

> late did please
> To send his Albion forth, the most his own,
> Upon discovery, to *themselves* best known,
> Through Celtiberia; and, to assist his course,
> Gave him his powerful Manager of Horse,

> With divine Proteus, Father of Disguise,
> To wait upon them with his counsels wise,
> In all extremes.   (133–40, my emphasis)

As Neptune's 'own', Albion was the subordinate partner, but no earlier masque ever suggested that a masquer might have a privileged insight into the royal will, let alone participate in policy-making as a joint enterprise. The Cook even implies that Hippius – that is, Buckingham – had an active role and shared, as advisor, in the decisions.[74] Further, it was hinted that Neptune might now delegate some of his cares to his son, Portunus noting that 'young Albion', on his return, will 'thy labours ease' (542). In fact, behind the scenes Charles had been involved in policy-making since 1621, when he began attending Privy Council meetings, and he and Buckingham had influence as senior figures in the Bedchamber,[75] but the fiction of all previous masques was that James's will was single and inviolable. So although the triumph notionally reaffirmed royal purposes, it did so in an entirely new way. Praise for James went hand in hand with a remarkable empowerment of Prince Charles.

Inevitably, the tension between father and son spelled trouble for the author, and the opening dispute between Poet and Cook over pleasing one's customers may be read as articulating Jonson's discomfort about dancing in this particular minefield. No less eloquent was the stress on Hippius' loyalty to Neptune (154–7, 410–12) – which, by its emphasis, crystallized precisely those intimations about Buckingham's disloyalty which they purported to dispel – and the masque's studied vagueness about the 'discovery' which it was celebrating, since what Albion had done could never quite come into view. As it would have been tactless to admit that all the merry-making was for the collapse of James's Spanish policy, Jonson had to make it sound as though the rejoicing was for Albion's return, leaving implicit the consequences that it had for future policy. Harmony was emphasized and the usual Jacobean tropes displayed: Neptune kept the earth 'in firm estate, / And, 'mongst the winds, [suffered] no debate', increasing 'our powers' and 'all the golden gifts of peace' (551–4). But the masque also dwelt on English naval strength, concluding with a prospect of the fleet 'ready to go, or come' and 'secure' Neptune 'both in peace, and wars' (510, 512), while a group of tars danced lustily, shouting 'hay for Neptune, and our young master' (522–3). Such features coincided with the policies of naval enhancement which Charles was shortly to be asking parliament to support with generous subsidies. His proposals were for a sea campaign, in which the principal enemy would be Spain, not Austria, whereas James would only countenance an expedition by land, with the limited objective of regaining the Palatinate, and with no naval dimension.[76] So the masque's marine aspect was deeply contentious. Although it carried forward the Jacobean emphasis on Britain as an island power, it avoided linking it with tropes of separateness. Instead, images of British isolation led into a timely emphasis on naval preparedness.[77]

Most crucially, Jonson's text exhibited an insoluble contradiction between the main masque's courtly joys and the popular acclamations incorporated in the antimasque in order that they might be disparaged. In the main masque, the Chorus, praising the 'incense' (390) flaming from the spectators on seeing the masquers, sang that Albion returned 'In answer to the public votes, / That, for it, up were sent' (353–4). However, the public votes shown in the antimasque represented popular rejoicing as the contemptible cavorting of plebeians – the dances being performed by, among others, a butcher, grocer, poulterer's wife, two dwarfs, a coranto-writer, a captain, and a 'fine laced mutton' (292), i.e. a prostitute. This was an extraordinary disavowal of the mood of national relief into which Charles sought to tap. The Poet explained that, although Albion came home in October, the courtly celebration was delayed to January to avoid bastardizing it with plebeian tumult. Contrasting his own songs with 'th'abortive and extemporal din / Of balladry', he said 'It was not time, / To mix this music with the vulgar's chime' (161–4). The muses waited for popular enthusiasm to subside before they opened their mouths, 'For they love, then, to sing, when they are heard' (174). There could have been no clearer statement of Jonson's problems in finding an accommodation acceptable to all participants, as this invention carried forward the anti-populist satire of preceding masques into a context where Charles was, nevertheless, exploiting the political advantage accruing to him from the national rejoicing. Charles's popularity was unprecedented, but it undermined his father and so had (in show at least) to be disparaged; and besides, popularity was a two-edged sword, since it bound him to anti-Catholic hopes that were disappointed a year later, when he married Henrietta Maria.[78] Seeking both to envision Charles's popularity and to constrain it, using tropes of peace but hinting at war, this masque was acutely over-determined. It was caught between the incompatible and diverging agendas of its participants.

In the event, this crisis of discourse was exposed in the most absolute way: James withdrew permission for the performance. At this distance it is hard to appreciate the seriousness of a masque's cancellation. Even monarchs fall sick and postpone their festivals, but *Neptune's Triumph* was the only Twelfth Night masque to be cancelled outright, and was abandoned at the latest moment, all the preparations being complete and 'many meetings' having passed for the dances.[79] The masque itself became an object of negotiation. James wished to uphold the convention by which ambassadors alternated as principal guests, so that honour could still be done to Spain, but the French ambassador seized the opportunity of playing a strong hand created by the policy hiatus. He humiliated James by refusing to participate in the usual charade in which ambassadors pretended to be sick, in order that one could be invited without it seeming an insult to the other. Furious negotiations took place but neither ambassador would budge, and a French threat that 'his country would not be friendly' if honour was done to Spain had the effect of forcing James into a declaration of preference, despite the protocols which were designed to avert the need for any such demonstration.[80] At the same time, James was anxious about how the masque might be interpreted, as rumours were circulating about its likely offensiveness: Salvetti, the Tuscan agent, wrote home that this Christmas 'intermedii [i.e. antimasques] … will be staged to poke fun at the Spaniards'. This had already happened in November, at a masque at York House (Buckingham's London home) written by Buckingham's client John Maynard. The Spanish delegation were invited but, said Chamberlain, they 'took offence at it, the main argument [being] a congratulation for the Prince's return'.[81] This could not be allowed in the Twelfth Night masque, and the Venetian ambassador reported that *Neptune's Triumph* originally carried 'some rather free remarks against the Spaniards', but these were removed at James's command.[82] Such royal interference was most unusual and showed how closely the masque was being scrutinized, but even with these changes it remained unproducible and was abandoned in the face of the embarrassment it would have involved. The whole episode was a unique demonstration of the relations between masquing and practical policy-making. It exposed the limits of acceptability outside which masques could not operate.

This was an unusually critical moment in James's reign. At no other time were his hold on power so uncertain, and the political options so perilous. Even so, it is remarkable that Jonson's masque should have been a casualty, as it shows how embedded it was in the struggle over policy, and how the tropes of loving inheritance defined in *The Masque of the Twelve Months* had become unworkable only five years later. In less polarized times, the masque might have been a symbolic act of appeasement, rapprochement, or conciliation, but the stakes were so high and the oppositions so acute that they prevented a performance that might bridge the positions of all those involved. The failure to stage *Neptune's Triumph* suggests how completely masques had been pulled into the policy vortex, and that it was impossible for them to escape unscathed as options collapsed. But even if the masque had been performed, the tensions in its fable would have been apparent, and it would inevitably have played out the competition for advantage in which the court was embroiled. One wonders whether for James cancellation was the course with fewest inconveniences. At the least, the failure to provide the customary Twelfth Night festivity was symptomatic of larger breakdowns within the political culture, and implied that this was indeed a moment of major historical crisis.

When *Neptune's Triumph* finally was performed, in 1625, it was in a revised version, shorn of its troublesome fable and antimasques and repackaged more comfortably as *The Fortunate Isles and their Union*. Although the text reproduced the main masque of *Neptune's Triumph* almost word for word, its new framework removed the tensions and silences that loomed so large in 1624. With Charles dancing as leader of the Macarii, inhabitants of the floating Fortunate Islands that were about to be joined to the British mainland, he was cast once more as homager to his father, dutiful and subordinate, and the iconography had returned to British insularity and utopian peace. There was no 'discovery' to be celebrated, nor any danger in 'public votes' (476); in 1625, such a phrase referred not to Charles's popularity but to the cash which had just been granted by parliament. The antimasque focused on the fanciful expectations of a Rosicrucian called Meerfool, mocking the hermetic utopianism of a transcendentalist movement which, as Frances Yates has shown, was associated with the prophetic Protestant enthusiasms that still clung to Frederick.[83] The fable now presented the masquers' voyage as alluding to dynastic union between the French lily and English rose (542–3). In the intervening year, Charles's naval strategy had been watered down into a limited land campaign, led by the mercenary General Ernst von Mansfeldt and forbidden by James from engaging any Spanish forces; the Bourbon marriage, intended as a grand Anglo-French alliance, delivered few military benefits and would be a source of future domestic strife. That Charles still expected great things is suggested by an unperformed entertainment, John Beaumont's *The Theatre of Apollo*, probably commissioned by Buckingham for private presentation, which showed James as Apollo, his son in a chariot drawn by Fame, and his daughter and her sons, Charles Louis and Rupert, in a chariot drawn by Peace. Beaumont's songs prophesied 'triumphant wars' for the Palatine family, based on hopes of military conquest: 'Earth, proclaiming you for kings, / New-found dominions to your sceptres brings'.[84] By comparison, the court's Christmas show was cautious, if not unadventurous. With relations between King and Prince stabilized and the scope of overseas action radically reduced, *The Fortunate Isles* was a throwback to the beginning of the reign.

Perhaps unsurprisingly, the 1620s brought the first sustained public complaints about the expense and politics of masquing. John Chamberlain's letters from this period repeatedly grumble about the waste of time and money (and no puritan he). In the 1619–20 season he complained that the court's revelry was too much after the French model but 'as in all other fantastical fashions so in this we strive to exceed and outstrip them', and in 1620–1 he noted that 'for all [James's] penury there is money given out and preparation made for a masque at court these holidays'.[85] Such observations suggest a perception, echoed elsewhere,[86] that too much festivity was going on, but his awareness that the problem had a political dimension is shown by his remark to Carleton that a transcript of Maynard's masque (the show that offended the Spaniards) 'were not worth the sending but that it is so free from flattery'.[87] Evidently he now felt that flattery was the norm and masques were guilty of excessive conformity to the royal line. Even more striking is the satirical poetry of these years, which strongly linked masques with unpopular policies. It is unsurprising that, after *Time Vindicated*, Wither complained about the court's masquing,[88] but much the same view was found in John Fletcher's epistle to the Countess of Huntingdon (*c.* 1624):

> Let me then
> Write something, madam, like those honest men
> That have no business; something that affords
> Some savour to the writer. Knights and lords,
> Pray, by your leaves, I will not treat of you,
> Ye are too tetchy; nor whether it be true
> We shall have wars with Spain (I would we might);
> Nor who shall dance i'th'masque, nor who shall write
> Those brave things done, nor sum up the expense,
> Nor whether it be paid for ten year hence.[89]

Fletcher was exercised about the extravagance and cost of revelry, but he was alert to the larger implications, the political imperatives that it served. He associated Christmas shows with Spanish appeasement, and would have preferred less dancing and more fighting. That such attitudes were becoming common is suggested by some anonymous verses that made the same complaint, more crudely, against James:

> At Royston and Newmarket
> He'll hunt till he be lean.
> But he hath merry boys
> That with masques and toys
> Can make him fat again.[90]

This writer was evidently as hostile to James's sexuality as to his politics, and represented his fault as over-indulgence in pleasure. Nonetheless, the masques were again a main focus of the satire, and even in this passing allusion were associated with withdrawal, passivity, and wasted resources.

These relationships were still clearer in an anonymous libel that circulated during the 1621 parliament, which attacked masques alongside Buckingham (under the name of Sejanus) and Sir John Digby (James's ambassador in Madrid):

> They say Sejanus doth bestow
> Whatever office doth befall,
> But 'tis well known it is not so,
> For he is soundly paid for all …
>
> When Charles hath got the Spanish girl
> The puritans will scowl and brawl,
> Then Digby shall be made an earl,
> And the Spanish gold shall pay for all …
>
> When the Banqueting House is finished quite
> Then James Sir Kingo we will call,
> And poet Ben brave masques shall write,
> And the subsidy shall pay for all …[91]

Though a popular satire, this poem was well informed about events, and had a sophisticated perspective on Jacobean ideology. Its author saw that peace, order, and Spanish gold went together, and felt that the masques had a principal role in disseminating this ideology. In his view, far from helping the crown communicate with its elites, masques had become part of the problem, by creating a political culture that was too closely tied to discredited policies. And even poet Ben, in verses written during these years though not printed until 1641, put a distance between his private opinions and his festive role. In 'An epistle to a friend, to persuade him to the wars' (1620),[92] he recommends avoiding the 'lethargy' and 'vicious ease' (1, 4) of London society by answering the drum beating in Europe; and in 'An epistle answering to one that asked to be sealed of the Tribe of Ben' (1623) he dismisses the 'Christmas clay / And animated porcelain of the court', contrasting true friends with those who are as superficial as 'the glorious scenes at the great sights' (52–3, 66). This implied attack on Inigo Jones was motivated by Jonson's disappointment at being excluded from plans for welcoming the Infanta at Southampton, but the poem still shows that there was an issue of credibility even for the man who supplied the scenarios of irresistible kingly power.

Of course, it was not inevitable that the masques should have provoked such criticism, and occasionally shows performed on Whitehall's margins and written by other poets than Jonson suggested alternative directions in which court culture could have developed. Even as *Pan's Anniversary* was being danced, a masque was in preparation by Viscount Doncaster to welcome Cadenet to Essex House two days later, which presented a less constrained, more open-ended aesthetic and political occasion than the Twelfth Night show.[93] This entertainment, tentatively ascribed to Chapman by Timothy Raylor, began with a borrowing from *The Golden Age Restored*: it showed nine giants, sons of Tellus (the earth), rebelling against Jove but stopped by Pallas, who turned them to stone. In contrast to the acute polarizations of Jonson's masques, these giants were eventually unfrozen again, and redeemed by Prometheus, who used his heavenly fire to re-transform them into heroes:

> by which we can
> Deal soul into cold stone, and raise up man
> Out of a punishment with moderate heat,
> Such as wise nature fancies. I'll beget
> Obedient life, and manners so refine
> As may discover that to be divine
> Which lent them shape and being, skillfully
> Recovering so my ruined ancestry
> From out this stony judgment, who shall wake
> Pleasures to those they frighted, and ne'er take
> A thought of roughness.   (174–84)

Inevitably, the giants' revivification was conditional on their obedience to the King. They were transformed by love, and Prometheus promised that their life would 'wear in serving you by whom I live, / Divinest powers' (185–6). Nonetheless, their rebellion was forgiven rather than dismissed, and the fire that re-animated them was not given freely, but stolen from Apollo, Venus, and Juno. The dances subordinated them to codes of courtly civility, but their double aspect, as both masquers and antimasquers, figures of service and of violence, invested them with divided allegiances. This masque broadly endorsed peace, but it held back from the confident assertions of kingly power that became so essential to James's festivals.

The Essex House masque attests to the persistence of dissident affiliations into late Jacobean court culture. Still, the festivals staged for James in this critical period for national and international politics display with singular clarity the difficulty for the masques of retaining aesthetic coherence and political credibility under the pressure of traumatic events. As the polarizations and divisions of the 1620s undermined the Jacobean consensus, so the masques were increasingly used to articulate the crown's political priorities, and became more and more identified with ideologically contentious positions. They must have seemed overwhelmingly to speak for the King, rather than to host dialogue with him. After James's death there was something of a hiatus in court festival, for masques were staged only sporadically in Charles's early years; the earliest Caroline masque text to survive is *Love's Triumph through Callipolis* (1631). The new King had bigger fish to fry, having gone to war with Spain and France simultaneously. But one wonders whether one reason for the masques' temporary absence was the overt partisanship into which they had fallen, undermining their effectiveness as tools of state, and bringing their aesthetic and political rationale into question. The masques were so closely associated with policies that seemed discredited that it was hard to reclaim them for common ground, while their association with the crown's political needs eroded their status as entertainments offering counsel as well as compliment. Although the late Jacobean masques presented the case for peace pragmatically and intelligently, it could not survive the deteriorating international situation, and in the long run they probably contributed to the conviction that James's policies were not negotiable and that criticism was increasingly taken for subversion. For all that they attempted to work out a coherent royal position, they ultimately helped to reinforce those polarizations which were gradually working to unsettle the early Stuart state.

CHAPTER 9

The Caroline reformation

In the season of 1626–7, Buckingham sponsored two masques which, however similar aesthetically, were politically at odds with each other. The first was staged on 5 November 1626 at York House, the Duke's London residence. Buckingham's visitors were led by Charles and Henrietta Maria, but the real guest of honour was the French ambassador, François de Bassompierre, who was in England to defuse the quarrels poisoning relations with France. Buckingham's feast, rumoured to have cost £6,000,[1] was calculated to compliment the Frenchman. Bassompierre was waited on by aristocrats, the music was French, the choreography was by 'Mr Montague the French dancer', and the Duke himself danced (said the Venetian ambassador) 'as he excels in posturing and agility'.[2] The centrepiece was an exhortation to Anglo-French accord. The masque culminated with figures of the kings and queens of France, Spain, and Savoy, placed beyond the English Channel but so true to life that Henrietta Maria could identify them, and her mother Marie de' Médici was set over them, who 'with her hand made a sign [to the English] ... to come and join themselves with her among the gods, and there to put an end to all the discords of Christianity'.[3] But by the time of Buckingham's second York House entertainment, barely six months later, all this goodwill had evaporated. The 15 May feast celebrated his departure to the navy at Plymouth, and focused on the political salvation he hoped for through military success overseas. In this masque Buckingham was assaulted by Envy, figured like Spenser's Blatant Beast 'with diverse open-mouthed dogs' heads, representing the people's barking'. Fame and Truth saved him from Envy, and it ended (said Contarini) with 'the putting to sea of the fleet, to inflame the King's ardour'.[4] Evidently Buckingham wanted to show that the hatred with which he was increasingly regarded would disappear once he returned victor, but spectators would not have missed the fact that France, currently blockading La Rochelle, was the enemy from whom this fame was to be plucked. With the earlier show's gestures of amity turned to declarations of war, there could be no clearer case of history eroding the certainties of myth. However transcendental the earlier affirmations, they had been completely overtaken by policy.

This *volte-face* is symptomatic of Charles I's problems, and helps to explain the paucity of masquing at the outset of his reign. Given the high profile of his later masques, it is striking that before 1631 he had so few. In significant respects the years 1625–31 were a trough between otherwise vigorous periods of masquing. There was indeed some expenditure during these years, particularly in the 1625–6 and 1626–7 seasons. The major events were the Queen's show of Gargantua and Gargamella presented to Bassompierre in November 1626, and her (unnamed) Whitehall masque of January 1627. However, little is known about these, and with the exception of Racan's *Artenice* (February 1626) – not really a masque but a play with scenes[5] – no texts survive, and no major writers were commissioned. After 1627 the record is even thinner. Charles made payments for a 'great masque' in February 1628, but it is uncertain whether it, or any of the other masques mentioned casually in 1627–8, was performed.[6] Buckingham's assassination in 1628 removed one of the principal patrons who, in Jacobean years, was behind much of the masquing not funded by the crown. The court continued to find money for drama, but it went on private entertainments and capital projects – on Charles's birthday in 1629, Henrietta Maria gave a play with scenery at Somerset House,[7] and the big event of 1630 was the opening of the refurbished Whitehall cockpit as a permanent royal theatre.[8] By contrast, for public aristocratic revelry, possibly 1628 and certainly 1629 and 1630 were blank.

Although less than a five-year gap, this was still a considerable change. In comparison with the elaborate Jacobean festivals, Caroline revelry was only intermittent. Almost certainly, the reason lay in the troubled politics of these years. Charles began his reign intent on war, as he wanted to revenge himself on Spain and force the Palatinate's return. But the naval campaign against Spain was a fiasco, the alliance with France foundered over religion, and the domestic whirlwind came in the 1625–9 parliaments, which protested against the costs of going to war with Europe's two great powers simultaneously. By 1630 Charles was desperately short of cash, and had enough on his hands without the distractions of dancing practice. At the accession, he was so deeply indebted that the coronation was staged (said Salvetti) 'without the magnificence characteristic of the ceremonial' so as 'to use the money for more needful purposes'.[9] Charles found £1,000 for Christmas and Shrovetide entertainments three years running,[10] but the expenses of double warfare left his finances exhausted.[11]

It is unsurprising that festivity disappeared and returned only after he made peace on all sides and rebuilt his revenue. A sustained festival culture centred on the King had to wait for more stable royal government in the 1630s.

Money aside, the swift back-pedalling at York House suggests a further explanation: the difficulties Caroline festival had in adapting a symbolic vocabulary inherited from the long Jacobean peace to the rapidly changing scenarios of war, and in sustaining that pose of royal competence in the face of Charles's spectacular reversals. The most damaging moments came in the tortuous relationship with France.[12] After the breach with Spain, Charles tried to make common cause with France, but Louis had his own ambitions, and the cost was high because he demanded religious concessions. In the marriage treaty, Charles promised a Catholic establishment for his wife, freedoms for Catholic subjects, and a loan of ships – only to find the Queen's servants colluding with parliament, his vessels being used to repress Protestants at La Rochelle, his diplomacy outflanked by Louis's secret accord with Madrid, and his people complaining that Catholicism was protected and nothing done against Spain. When Bassompierre arrived, relations were in crisis, as the Queen's servants had been dismissed, and troops were afoot for La Rochelle. Bassompierre set about ingratiating himself, paying 'great address' to everyone.[13] His 'prudent and amicable approaches' paid off: by October Salvetti detected a desire 'to complete the negotiations so as to establish good feeling between the two crowns'.[14] A compromise was reached over the Queen's household and the troops for La Rochelle were diverted to Germany, but no sooner had Bassompierre gone than, to Charles's outrage, Louis repudiated his agreements and impounded the English wine fleet. Six months later, with France once more the enemy, Buckingham's navy sailed south to a catastrophic engagement that left his reputation far from vindicated.

This story helps to unravel the implications of Buckingham's *Discords of Christianity*. It is difficult not to adopt an *ex post facto* view, as only weeks later it would have seemed an embarrassingly public miscalculation. Bassompierre wanted to prevent English interference in La Rochelle by displaying French goodwill, and to neutralize the Duke, whose hispanophile tendencies were thought to obstruct *détente*. Bassompierre effected Buckingham's reconciliation with Henrietta Maria, presented him with a personal plea from Marie de' Médici, and played on fears of English isolation.[15] He urged that if England broke with France only Spain would benefit, and Charles would regain the Palatinate if he relied on the family ties between brother monarchs brought by marriage to Louis' sister:

if the interests of this kingdom, his King's sister [Elizabeth], the King himself and the [Palatine] Princes his dependents and kinsfolk require peace with Spain, he offered the aid of his King and France to obtain it on honourable terms, thus seeking to remove the opinion that all the powers rejoice at seeing Great Britain involved in the war for their individual relief.[16]

As *The Discords of Christianity* showed, Buckingham absorbed these views. With its representation of family bonds radiating from France's Queen Mother and promise of miraculous transcendence of the differences symbolized by the Channel, it dramatized exactly the fears of isolation, and Bassompierre's solution, trust between royal affinities.[17] As Marie's daughter, the masque suggested, Henrietta Maria cemented Europe's dynasties, binding her husband to his brothers-in-law in France, Spain, and Savoy, and dissolving their antagonisms in happy loyalty to Henri IV's widow. This scenario Henrietta Maria reprised in her November masque, which foregrounded her role as European conduit by taking an invention from Rabelais.[18] However, as Charles discovered, marital affinities could not be relied on. The collapse of amity quickly exposed how much the imagery of dynastic unity elided differences of religion and nationhood. As Richelieu coolly wrote to Bassompierre, 'cette sorte … de ceremonie publique' was useful to string along rivals when one needed to gain time.[19] The shortcomings of Caroline policy and the iconography used to promote it could scarcely have been clearer.

Such failures were not within Buckingham's power to correct. Rather, the contradiction between his masques, and the instability of their imagery, signalled the exhaustion of inherited festive forms. With its depiction of Marie enthroned above international divisions, *The Discords of Christianity* harked back to James's iconography of peaceful royal transcendence and his faith in monarchy as the bulwark of order. Performed on 5 November, it set itself against the public bells and bonfires, proclaiming the need to put European unity above confessional nationalism. But with conflicts accelerating, Catholic military successes, and France and Spain jostling for advantage, such aspirations were unrealistic. France's transformation from treasured ally to perfidious enemy showed that the iconography of kingly prudence was hostage to the policy of others. It was also booby-trapped against warmongering monarchs because of its potential for disappointment. The masque on the navy left a credibility gap by creating expectations of military success that Buckingham failed to fulfil, while his prediction that he would defeat Envy by bringing back Fame proved overoptimistic. Earlier masques could present James as European arbiter because of his constructive disengagement: kingly transcendence could be plausibly depicted as a commitment to the long view. But the same omniscience was unavailable to a monarch whose decisions had immediate consequences, and whose foreign policy brought domestic instability. Evidently poets expected Charles's overseas credentials would legitimate him, as all three masques that we know about focused on Europe. Yet the wars caused chaos at home: the subsidies they needed, their dubiously legal funding, and the absence of any visible return translated into parliamentary deadlock, constitutional resistance, and debt. Even had there been victories to celebrate, the masques might not have reassured audiences anxious about forced loans. Charles put masques on hold because war showed how much festival needed to reinvent itself.

The 1630s brought a new turn towards festivals focused more overtly on the monarch's person and the domestic reformation that he sponsored. A crucial element in this was a retreat from the masques' international pretensions, a withering away of their status as commentary on Europe. Under Charles the expectation almost completely disappeared that masques should involve outreach or signal Britain's overseas priorities or friendships. This was, to say the least, a radical change. Every masque since 1619 had involved some kind of statement on Europe, but although the 1630s were a decade of busy diplomacy, Charles's festivals said almost nothing on foreign affairs. From time to time the ambassadors who traversed the continent were alluded to, but usually as a joke.[20] More frequently, Europe was seen with indifference or disinterest. The clearest sign of new directions was Charles's decision that, from 1630 onwards, the resident ambassadors should have no formal invitations to masques. The ruling was reviewed again in 1638, and Charles affirmed 'it had never been his custom to invite any ambassador to those entertainments'.[21] As a consequence, the official diplomatic presence at Charles's masques was astonishingly slight. Caroline festivals had ceased to address the international community.

Instead, Charles's masques represented Britain as admirable for its separateness: when Europe appeared, it was always in tropes elaborating on its otherness. Europe became that from which Britain was differentiated: a contrast was endlessly drawn between Charles's peace at home and shipwreck abroad, British serenity and European chaos. The *locus classicus* for this trope was Richard Fanshawe's 'Ode upon occasion of his majesty's proclamation', probably written to support Charles's 1632 edict commanding gentlemen living in London to return to their estates, and endlessly echoed in the 1630s masques.[22] After eight stanzas detailing Europe's sufferings, Fanshawe describes Britain as miraculously exempt:

> Only the island which we sow,
> A world without the world, so far

From present wounds, it cannot shew
           An ancient scar.
White Peace, the beautiful'st of things,
Seems here her everlasting rest
To fix, and spreads her downy wings
           Over the nest.
As when great Jove, usurping reign,
From the plagued world did her exile,
And tied her with a golden chain
           To one blest isle:
Which in a sea of plenty swam
And turtles sang on every bough,
A safe retreat to all that came
           As ours is now.[23]

Fanshawe's 'world without the world' shows continuity with Jacobean iconography, but while James linked his authority to the British state's marvellous self-identity, he had not suggested that this meant disengagement from Europe. By contrast, Charles's masques institutionalized the contrast between 'us' and 'them' that Fanshawe's poem implied. If the antimasque figures of James's masques were the witches, alchemists, and newsmongers who needed disciplining for national health, in Charles's masques the enemy was outside: Europe and the wider world were the antagonists against which British identity was defined. His festivals presented a parade of international stereotypes testifying to British superiority: French, Spaniards, Italians, Egyptians, Persians, Indians, pigmies, even (in the antimasques to *Florimène*) a native Canadian. James's masques had ethnocentric moments, but never made as emphatic a divide between home and abroad as did Charles's. If British Union was the foundational trope of the earlier reign, British exceptionalism was foundational for the next.

This remarkable change projects the paralysis of the will that overtook Caroline foreign policy.[24] After 1629, although Charles's survival was premised on minimal involvement in Europe's wars, he remained ambitious about playing a role in Europe, and was not averse to military options. This was, after all, a monarch who fought France and Spain, conducted two campaigns against the Scots, and in 1642 went to war with his own parliament. But the experience of the 1620s showed how little was to be gained in the present climate from active warmongering. War involved ideologically unpalatable alliances and financial dependence on parliament. At the same time, Charles's aims contracted. He had no wish to be the Protestant champion, a poisoned chalice that could be left to meteors like the Swedish King Gustavus, and focused more than ever on the single goal of restoring the Palatinate, an objective pursued not through campaigning but courtship of the powers that seemed strongest in Germany. This pushed him back towards Madrid, and while proposals for Swedish or Dutch leagues were rebuffed, the 1630 Anglo-Spanish treaty contained secret articles about future military cooperation.[25] Britain was turning into a non-combatant satellite of Spain: hamstrung by his inability to work with parliament, Charles attached himself to the ally that promised most, but kept out of conflicts that would destabilize him. Of course, Charles's options were limited, for France, Spain, and Holland were rivals as well as possible allies. Neutrality left the chance of future military action open, and by investing in the navy Charles built up British power in its one area of strength. But the moment to retrieve the Palatinate never came, and before 1635 Charles's competitors never altered their calculus for fear that Britain might intervene. The lack of long-term objectives meant that Caroline foreign policy was essentially reactive, and the initiative passed to France, who after Gustavus's death became the main anti-Habsburg focus.

The consequence for the masques was a deep tension between their pacifism and the residually heroic imagery in which Charles was still invested. They presented Britain both as a haven of peace and as a nation capable of war, with all the contradictions that this entailed. Discussion of the longer-term European prognosis was restricted to halcyon days at home and horrific war abroad, yet masques still depicted Charles as a warrior king, in fictions that implied military aspirations. As Roman emperor (*Albion's Triumph*), ancient worthy (*Coelum Britannicum*), or Britanocles, 'glory of the western world' (*Britannia Triumphans*), Charles adopted a symbolic language that harked back to his brother's festivals and broke from his father's imagery of humanistic scholar-king. It echoed the strain in Caroline portraiture that figured him in militarized guise as an armed leader, the outstanding instance of which is Van Dyck's equestrian portrait (figure 12). As John Adamson observes, this image is chivalric. Charles wears tilting armour with a lance-rest, and a squire holds his helm; the world of *The Faerie Queene* is not far away.[26] However, the associations are far from fanciful. His pose is imperial, modelled on Titian's portrait of Charles V, and presents him as an idealized, far-seeing general. Secure under Jove's oak, he holds the baton of command and gazes over an open landscape signifying the field of battle. The image seems composed, but its contradictory signals mark instabilities in Charles's culture which his festivity inevitably had to manage. Many accounts of the 1630s take the premium placed on quiet at face value and write off the militarism as fantasy. For example, Graham Parry describes the preference for armour as discordant against 'the

12 Anthony Van Dyck, *Charles I on Horseback, c.* 1635–6.

midsummer hum of dozens of court poets as they sang of the peace of England'.[27] But given Charles's conflicting objectives, this was a fundamental tension in his iconography, and his masques were torn between privileging the quiet state he could afford and the higher-profile kingship for which he remained ambitious. Praising his reign for peace, they, nevertheless, endorsed that common but non-Jacobean assumption that the decisive test of kingship was the ability to make war. The tension between Charles the connoisseur and Charles the monarch capable of maximum force was a legacy that each had to negotiate.

Much criticism of Charles's masques is overshadowed by foreknowledge of the disasters of the future. Despite their cultural prestige, the masques are often seen as fatally compromised by their monarch's political incompetence. In a famous essay, C. V. Wedgwood dubbed *Salmacida Spolia* 'the last masque', epitomizing the fortunes of a dynasty whose days were already numbered, its masquers dancing elegantly but ironically on the edge of apocalypse.[28] The same valedictory note recurs in Roy Strong's account of Caroline Whitehall as a 'confined arcadia', where the masques were fighting a futile rearguard action against disaster:

To understand the masques of Inigo Jones, which are so pure an expression of this decade, it is necessary to forget totally what happened after 1640 and to ignore, for the most part, Puritan opposition attitudes. It is essential to view these productions solely through the eyes of an optimistic king and his surveyor of works as they annually celebrated what they deluded themselves into believing to be the triumphant rule of a monarch by Divine Right.

In this view, the masques were on the wrong side of history, sliding inexorably into a revolution they could not escape. They gave Charles an 'illusion of control', but this was only 'a postponement of disastrous troubles to come', making their 'extravagant assertions of a mirage of power' seem 'faintly comic'.[29] And even in Orgel and Strong's *Inigo Jones: The Theatre of the Stuart Court*, with its groundbreaking defence of the masques' philosophical seriousness, masque politics are a 'profound irrelevance' which contradict the intellectual claims that are made for them. Charles's apotheosis was impressive but ineffective, for his Star Chamber decrees were 'as unreal as Inigo Jones's victory over gravity'. Outside the 'enclosed, idealistic realm of the Caroline autocracy', 'threatening clouds were already gathering', so the festivals worked as art but failed as politics. With the 'real' history going on elsewhere, the masques inevitably seem politically naive, if not a cause of the coming crisis.[30]

These judgments were generated by an older historiography that saw the 1630s as a 'highroad to Civil War', with the nation dividing inexorably between royalist and puritan and a beleaguered monarchy sinking under a tide of opposition.[31] Today's historians start from different coordinates. In 1629 Charles's subjects could not foresee the crises to come, and parliament's absence meant there was no 'opposition' in the old sense. Although Charles's rule foundered on frustrations and grievances, it was not destined to collapse. On the contrary, he seized the initiative and embarked on a modernization programme, living off his own resources and maximizing the crown's mechanisms of social control. Of course, antagonisms existed: the military disasters, emergency measures, and royal finance eroded confidence, and helped to confirm Charles's distrust of parliament as an institution whose criticism he increasingly took for subversion. But so long as his people cooperated, his power was not a mirage. The need was to instil confidence, and even if the masques idealized his new dispensation, they expressed a royal ideology that in the 1630s was being turned into political action daily. To situate them within a framework of accelerating resistance and read them as otherworldly overlooks their role in underwriting Charles's revolution in government.

Deadlocked with parliament, Charles turned in the 1630s to new strategies. A drive began to rescue royal finances: peace closed off one financial drain and rebuilt customs revenues by restoring trade, so that the crown was in surplus for the first time in generations. Household costs were pared back, while, in the absence of subsidies, other revenues were exploited that the monarch held through legal rights inherent in the crown – wardship and purveyance, monopolies, distraint of knighthood, and fines for forest encroachment. Such devices affirmed the crown's historic status at the same time as they raised cash. For example, royal forests were part of the King's ancient dignities, and Secretary Coke wrote of the crown's 'honour and power' in them.[32] Charles also began intense scrutiny of local and national affairs. Puritans were prosecuted and Privy Council business vastly increased.[33] Magistrates were commanded back to the provinces, and given a Book of Orders requiring them to crack down on the poor and idle, control alehouses and petty crime, oversee local employment, and attend to public works. A stream of proclamations on vagrancy, poor relief, overcrowding, exports, the plague, assay of gold, observance of Lent, and so forth announced Charles's intention of implementing the full force of statute. The Council enquired into local officers, monthly reports were demanded, and judges exhorted parish officials to be diligent.[34] If, as Dudley Carleton wrote, what the nation needed was 'the medicine of a wise and settled government',[35] Charles supplied this with a will. He began a vigorous reformation founded on strong central leadership and government efficiency. His influence was to reach every level of national life.

These new emphases were directly echoed in the masques. Caroline masquing occupied much the same ideological framework as Jacobean, but was harnessed more directly to the King's personality and the radical Caroline state. Unlike his father, Charles liked to participate in his own ceremonial, and this transformed the masques into dramatizations of his political enterprise. Magnificent representations of his power, they published his political and ideological priorities, proclaiming his justice, wisdom, and endurance, and making his kingship seem all-competent. This introduced a confrontational aspect absent from Jacobean masques – dissent was not just a transgression against generalized notions of order, but an affront to the will of the King himself. Advertising a style of government focused on the monarch's person, instilling reverence, and outlawing dissent as subversive, Charles's masques invested a regime intent on living off its own resources with the necessary moral force and political conviction. To the political elites on whose cooperation this enterprise depended, his masques must have seemed overwhelming.

Charles's masques made claims on two fronts. Firstly, they propounded his prestige by foregrounding his cultural achievements. Some historians have questioned the effectiveness of Charles's cultural patronage, pointing out that its impact was diluted by haphazard administrative structures and by the low public visibility of some of its products, such as statuary.[36] But the masques showcased his political culture, overcoming its physical dispersal by staging high-profile displays of its underlying coherence. Jones's designs ransacked the royal collections, copying ideas from Charles's astonishing treasury of pictures, statues, coins, and drawings, and displaying his status as a ranking European connoisseur.[37] Their monumental iconography foregrounded his public works, collating its architectural beauties and crystallizing their latent political symbolism. *Albion's Triumph* ended with a prospect of London dominated by Whitehall; *Coelum Britannicum* opened with ruined imperial buildings but ended with an image of Windsor Castle; *Britannia Triumphans* had a view of St Paul's Cathedral, the national shrine of Laudianism newly re-embellished by Jones; and *Salmacida Spolia* ended with a great imperial city, suggesting Charles's ambitions for redesigning London as a new seat of royal power. Jacobean masques occasionally invoked architecture in their myth-making, but never made so concerted an attempt to give cultural prestige to a political agenda. Charles's public works, the institutional environments of his power, were orchestrated into an order that was materially and aesthetically harmonious.

Secondly, the masques emphasized Charles's energy as a ruler by focusing on his programme of reform. The key instance was *Coelum Britannicum*, which alluded directly to his economies and improvements. This masque presented Jove's plan to purge the corrupt constellations from the heavens, and replace them with better. Jove was doing this, the fable explained, in emulation of Charles's domestic reforms, and new stars would be supplied by his courtiers. Charles's social measures were specifically alluded to: new court protocols, the proclamation for gentlemen to return to their estates, controls over monopolies, taverns, foodstuffs, and tobacco. No other masque referred quite so distinctly to policy detail, but in *Love's Triumph*, *Albion's Triumph*, and *Britannia Triumphans*, the governing trope was the same. Each celebrated a reformation, with Charles purging the world and transforming the state with irresistible dynamism. Of course, this reformation stopped short of a revolution. Britain was recovered from a decadent past rather than invented on new principles: idealized cities were refounded, but iconoclasm still figured as sedition or disruption. Nonetheless, the programme was not nostalgic. Both *Love's Triumph* and *Coelum Britannicum* drew on the anti-Aristotelian philosopher Giordano Bruno, who had imagined visionary renewal brought about by the guidance of potent and peaceable monarchs.[38] Charles was represented as a modernizer in heroic mode, a far-seeing leader who swept aside dross in a disciplined renovation. The wars and explosive politics of the 1620s would be replaced by domestic prosperity founded on forward-looking peace.

With this new ideological agenda, the Caroline masque reinvented itself as the triumph. Titles advertised the paradigm: *Love's Triumph through Callipolis*, *Albion's Triumph*, *The Triumph of Peace*, *The Triumphs of the Prince d'Amour*, *Britannia Triumphans*. No longer a drama but a parade in which Charles brought on conquered subordinates and loyal friends, the aim was to proclaim the monarch as leader. At his accession Charles missed an opportunity of investing his government with symbolic homage by cancelling the royal entry, but his masques repaired this deficit, presenting him as a ruler taking possession, a masculine emperor stamping his identity on a feminized state. The King was thematically and dramatically central, and his masques more overtly promulgated his power than negotiated with it. The clearest sign of a shift away from dialectic was the relaxation of the older cellular form, and a dilution of dramatic structure into multiple antimasques, culminating in the twenty grotesque 'entries' of *Salmacida Spolia*. This moved English festivity towards the Parisian *ballet du cour*, where multiple entries were the norm,[39] but also reflected the looser triumphal paradigm, which could be stretched to any number of episodes. Inevitably, the King's presence restricted the masques' variety. Most Caroline masques were devoid of event: nothing 'happened' other than that Charles arrived and was acclaimed. No longer a struggle in which the monarch looked from afar on symbolic contests that validated him, these masques represented kingship as immanent and embodied, and the antimasquers as dissenters whose resistance was futile. Not so much antagonists as unbelievers, the antimasquers' lack of vision was apparent at the moment of royal arrival. Effectively, the intimate structural link between masque and antimasque was removed, the grotesque entries endlessly reinforcing the

King's command rather than contesting with him dramatically. The limit on numbers lay in the poet's powers of invention rather than logic of argument.

Recently, Kevin Sharpe has argued that the proliferating antimasques allowed more space to address political issues, offering criticism as well as compliment. In this view, they were humanistic panegyric, which counselled the monarch under the sugar-coating of praise.[40] But it is difficult to see this as the prime rationale. The expository structure allowed for philosophic depth, but the triumphal form did not so much introduce a dramatic problem to which the crown accommodated itself, as elaborate in advance on the values with which Caroline kingship was associated. The King's visible sponsorship foreshortened the element of negotiation, making antimasques articulations of royal priorities rather than conversations. This shift was acknowledged in *Love's Triumph*, where Jonson calls masques 'the donatives of great princes to their people' (5–6), a definition that reoriented the form into a presentation by the prince, reversing the flow of traffic and implying that the dialogue was one-way. Carew's epigraph for *Coelum Britannicum* – 'Non habeo ingenium; Caesar sed iussit: habebo' (I have no skill to write, but Caesar has commanded me; well, I will have it)[41] – similarly identified the monarch as both sponsor and originator. There was also a new drive to disseminate the masques beyond the court. *Love's Triumph* was the first masque to be published in commercial format for twenty years, and all subsequent masques were promptly printed after their performances.[42] Under special circumstances some masques did talk back to the crown, but in Charles's ceremonial the imperative was mostly royal legitimation. His participation raised their status as political festivals but inhibited their freedom of manoeuvre. The need to legitimate the King was in tension with the agenda of advising him.

In other ways, the personal rule increased the masques' centralization. After Buckingham's death, masques ceased to be arenas where courtiers competed for attention. Only in *The Triumph of Peace*, when John Read was 'cried up for as handsome a man as the Duke of Buckingham',[43] and *The Triumphs of the Prince d'Amour*, when Richard Vivian was knighted, did individual masquers attract notice. Both of these were festivals presented to the court from outside, whereas in court a different climate prevailed. Charles's masques displayed Whitehall as orderly and peaceable, projecting the decent subordination of courtier to King who, as chief masquer, led off the event. They also became more disciplined occasions: the sole recorded casting dispute was Lady Carlisle's refusal to perform in *The Temple of Love*,[44] and it even became acceptable for courtiers to perform in antimasques. Crucially, masques became integrated into the Whitehall season, and were presented in pairs, one danced by Charles for Henrietta Maria, the other by her for him. Though more aggrandized than James's masques, Charles's were more rooted in his household's domestic life. Ceremonious compliments between King and Queen, they had effectively been privatized: subjects witnessed an intimate and often eroticized conversation in which the royal pair communicated lovingly with one another. So while masques proclaimed Charles's public agenda, they turned the form towards a cult of personality. In his intensely personalized culture, the state's good was collapsed into the King's desires, and each subject owed him an individualized loyalty. This equation, and its consequences, were the starting point for each of his masques.

Jonson's two Caroline masques have proved difficult to integrate with his Jacobean festivals and have often been neglected.[45] But *Love's Triumph through Callipolis* (1631) was a seminal event, which established the parameters for subsequent masquing. Fusing imperial power, erotic possession, and British exceptionalism, it departed emphatically from Jacobean norms, instituting motifs that were central to the fully developed Caroline form.

The ostensible occasion of *Love's Triumph* was the Treaty of Madrid, which ended five years' war with Spain. The articles were published in December, and Salvetti said it was danced 'in a manner of speaking, in celebration of the peace'.[46] His hesitation bespoke recognition of the ambivalence towards Europe around which Jonson manoeuvred. The royal position was embodied in Rubens's *Allegory of Peace and War* (figure 13), painted for Charles in 1629–30. Rubens was Philip IV's go-between in the negotiations, and his picture represents the treaty's benefits, affirming that peace would divert the horrors of war and restore the profits of trade. Shutting out an armed warrior and a deranged fury, Pallas Athene protects the happy family, whose prosperity figures as innocent if frankly sensual pleasures. Yet, said the Venetian Giovanni Soranzo, many regarded peace as dishonourable, were suspicious of Spain, and wanted alternative alliances. Soranzo thought Britain was financially incapable of new leagues: 'in this time of universal quiet and peace ... they do nothing here except to observe events in other places, and their preoccupation is to avoid calls upon them and expenditure'.[47] So the masque celebrated peace, but as a matter for solely British congratulation. All the ambassadors, including the Spanish ambassador, were refused invitations, and within the masque foreigners were ridiculed. The antimasquers were 'the four prime European nations' (33), and although Jones's designs adopted *commedia dell'arte* dress, the disregard of overseas sensibilities must have been palpable. *Love's Triumph*

13 Peter Paul Rubens, *Allegory of Peace and War*, 1629–30.

shifted to purely domestic delights, asserting that Charles and Henrietta Maria's love conferred universal happiness. As Amphitrite sang, 'Here, stay a while: this, this / The Temple of all Beauty is' (115–16). This trope was common – much European panegyric assured princes that they presided over a Golden Age – but public events were rarely telescoped into private desires so radically as here.

Love's Triumph made a neoplatonic contrast between Heroic Love – Charles himself, in quest of Divine Beauty (Henrietta Maria) – and its grotesque opposite, sensual love, whose 'sectaries, or depraved lovers' (23–4) obstructed his path. The 'confused affections' of this 'sensual school / Of lust' were expressed in their 'antic gesticulation' (30–2, 92–3), but harmony was established by fifteen virtuous lovers, hymned by Euphemus ('well-omened'), the goddess Amphitrite, and Euclia ('fair glory'). This fable was remarkable for its theatrical spareness. Although making an ideological contrast between unstable metropolitan obsessives and an elevated courtly pair, there was little action. The antimasque's drama was subordinated to celebration of the royal union, the main focus being the emotionally heightened meeting between chief performer and chief spectator. Their admiration of each other expressed their refinement, the songs elaborating their encounter into disquisition on love, unpacking its symbolism in terms of Charles's philosophical objectives. The thrust was thus visionary rather than dramatic. Somewhat like the Somersets in *The Masque of Squires*, Charles and Henrietta Maria did not have fictionalized alter egos but played versions of themselves. But unlike the Somersets, their roles were aggrandized and mystified, requiring spectators to read through the human figures to the ineffable union of Desire and Beauty which they embodied. This made for an unusually dematerialized form, with actions that were less events than testimonies to Charles's inherent superiority. The depraved lovers could not delay his triumph, for the masque lay in a transfigured present outside historical time and immune to contest, which removed the need for story by rendering the merely contingent redundant. It accessed eternal verities glimpsed behind the everyday, and with London re-imagined as Callipolis (the city of beauty), Charles's political aspirations were couched as a myth of private transcendence. Spectators would be marshalled into admiration, not so much participating in this vision as wondering at it.

So *Love's Triumph* developed an iconography that was both more personalized and more transcendental. Yet it would have been difficult for spectators to ignore the masque's function as government legitimation, since the purging of Callipolis alluded overtly to Charles's political programmes. In the early 1630s, control of London was a key issue. The disastrous 1629 parliament was followed by prosecutions of MPs, several of whom, including Jonson's friend John Selden, were still in prison. Another friend, Robert Cotton, was being investigated for allowing the King's critics to research precedents in his library.[48] No less newsworthy was Alexander Leighton, a fanatical puritan who, having asked parliament to pull down favourites and bishops, was publicly mutilated in November 1630. At the same time, Charles was developing his plans to make London a royal metropolis, with a proclamation that limited further building and set standards for future enlargement. James had attempted to restrict expansion by instituting a building commission, but Charles's initiative was more determined and politicized. He laid down specifications for new building, forbade the subdivision of mansions, and enforced all this with searches and Star Chamber prosecutions.[49] Stating that 'the uniformity of the buildings will bring much honour to the city' and prevent the 'unwholesome pestering of multitudes of poor people together', his proclamation linked aesthetic propriety to political control.[50] The urban programme was extended in the incorporation of the suburbs (1636), which brought labourers, aliens, and vagrants living in the margins and outside the customary jurisdictions within a new instrument of government.[51] Charles's personal authority would be manifested in a capital properly regulated, architecturally unified, and under common standards of orderliness.

The masque made no direct reference to London. In its philosophical programme, masquers embodying restraint, refinement, and self-control were set against distempered, turbulent, and chaotic grotesques. Yet the motif of a city purged of its humours enacted a symbolic contest between centre and margins, the King and those inimical to his will, which replicated the ideology of personal rule as seen in these early edicts. Heroic Love cast the plague of uncontrolled passions out of Callipolis's suburbs just as King Charles was ordering his metropolis:

> Vouchsafe to grace Love's triumph here tonight,
>   Through all the streets of your Callipolis,
> Which by the splendour of your rays made bright
>   The seat and region of all beauty is.
>
> Love, in perfection, longeth to appear,
>   But prays of favour he be not called on
> Till all the suburbs and the skirts be clear
>   Of perturbations, and th'infection gone.   (70–7)

The purging of 'infection' was highly topical, for 1630 was a plague year, which badly disrupted London life. As the chorus fumigated the Banqueting House, waving censers to 'vapour' away urban sickness (94), they linked Charles's harmonious love with a return to health in the streets. But with the antimasquers called 'sectaries', whose 'confused affections' lacked 'order and measure' (23–32), the fumigation also paralleled Charles's acts of political hygiene, his repression of London's trouble-makers. Metropolitan renewal thus played out the ideological assumptions underpinning Charles's aesthetic initiatives. Cleansing the body politic, it reasserted the dominance of centre over periphery, ruler over ruled, and projected a therapeutic model of kingship that expressed Charles's sense of good intentions towards his people. In doing so, it invented one of the characteristic tropes of Caroline iconography, for an opposition between royal purity and dissent as a sickness needing purgation was a recurrent topos down to *Salmacida Spolia*.

The rest of the evening focused on Charles's heroic body, with a fable of romantic chivalry that apotheosized his love for Henrietta Maria. Strikingly, in view of the platonic theme, Charles was not presented as a spiritualized being. On the contrary, the masque stressed his physical prowess, his qualifications for empire being inextricable from the couple's sexual satisfactions. Distinguishing Charles's 'chaste desires' (52) from the depraved lovers' brute passions, it praised his 'right affection of the mind, / The noble appetite of what is best', against those who, through lust, were 'slaves to sense, / Mere cattle, and not men' (54–5, 95–6). Yet while it emphasized that Charles wanted 'fruition' – 'no hopes / Are pure, but those he can perpetuate' (57, 64–5) – this claim rested on sensual foundations. The underlying motif was Theseus and the minotaur, a fable of heroic virility cognate with Charles's favourite myth of St George and the dragon. The bestial lovers, said the Chorus, were subhuman, but Charles was a new Theseus, with 'virtue to remove / Such monsters from the labyrinth of love' (98–9).[52] He would inhabit love's labyrinth, not as appetite's inhibitor but its perfect proponent, 'a rich perfume' or 'melting music, that shall not consume / Within the ear, but run the mazes round' (78–81). And while the royal union was glossed as a divine creation (155–65), the figure to whom events led was Venus, patroness of 'holy nuptial' (188). She conferred on King and Queen 'the arts / Of gaining and of holding hearts' (198–9), and presented a palm tree twined with lilies and roses. This alluded both to British peace and to the physical union from which it came. Caroline platonism has often been seen as intellectualized and pallid: Sharpe says platonic love was 'an ideal form of government' that signalled 'the ordering of nature' through 'the victory of reason over appetite'.[53] But this dilutes Charles's sensual empowerment: it would be truer to say that *Love's Triumph* incorporated platonic love in eroticized terms, not transcending appetite but embracing it. As Loewenstein points out, Callipolis was a resonantly Marlovian space for a triumph, with all its promise of aspiration and appetite.[54]

Perhaps these themes were provoked by the recent birth of a crown prince, an event which established his father's credentials as political parent. In affirming Charles's sexual vigour, *Love's Triumph* celebrated the succession. But more broadly, Charles's erotic imperialism pointed towards cultural fault-lines that would soon become ingrained. His sexualized heroism – the purified but still bodily pleasures of his power – was defined in opposition to 'sectaries' and ungrateful 'monsters' incapable of apprehending his perfection. This vision of Caroline kingship foregrounded recent traumas and polarizations; indeed, it positively demanded that polarizations exist for Charles to be validated. Of course, we cannot project back onto 1631 divisions which were still incomplete and hardened into political polarities only after the masques had gone. But even though *Love's Triumph* did not use the word 'puritan', its opposition between infectious eccentricity and decent centralized rule intuited latent cultural tensions, and

conscripted the masque for a characteristically Caroline agenda. Its ritualized character bespoke a regime with a preference for uniformity, which
regarded disorder as symptomatic of sickness needing strong political
medicine. Danced on a Sunday, it affronted Sabbatarian views: spectators
could not miss the connection between a chorus censing 'lustration' with
'solemn fires and waters' (84–5) and Laudian additions to church liturgy.
And its fable of a distracted metropolis cleansed by a powerful king
represented Charles as the audacious monarch who triumphantly brought
back settled government. In later masques the opposition between innovat-
ing royalty and uncomprehending people was a source of anxiety, but
in *Love's Triumph* it was the basis of legitimation. The opposition between
dignified rule and eccentric fanaticism displayed a newly invigorated
kingship.

A year later, Townshend's *Albion's Triumph* (January 1632) imitated
Jonson's frame in terms which more overtly connected with Charles's
reforms and allowed guarded reflections on the rhetorical strategies of
panegyric. A reconstruction of a Roman triumph, it depicted Charles as
an emperor attended by his consuls in front of archaeologically exact
imperial scenery: an atrium, forum, amphitheatre, and temple. Even more
than *Love's Triumph*, *Albion's Triumph* replaced dialectic with linear
structures. The antimasquers were dancers – gladiators, tumblers, and
'morescos' – who formed an 'interlude' (82–3),[55] a mere processional
episode. The structure turned again on the erotic bond between King and
Queen. As Albanactus, emperor of Albipolis, Charles sought the goddess
Alba, and their union, announced by Mercury and refined by Diana,
elevated him to godlike status. So delightful were his 'pleasures' (87) that
his land became an ideal haven: events concluded with the gods complaining that Britain was so secure they had nothing to do. Structurally, this
recapitulated *Love's Triumph* but with more focused imagery, and the
spectators were required simply to observe and wonder:

> Admire! but censure not their powers,
> That sink not with time's sandy hours,
> As mortal creatures do.
> And since the shaft that is addressed
> At heaven may hurt the shooter's breast,
> Be pleased and please us too.   (76)

The admonition was veiled, but its threat was evident.

John Peacock has explicated the masque's political and artistic contexts.[56]
Townshend named his main character after a pseudo-historical British king

and glossed the etymology of 'Albanactus', fancifully, as 'born in Scotland'
(75) – that is, Albania (in Brutan myth). This honoured Charles's northern
roots while echoing his plans for a progress to Edinburgh, a journey which,
though postponed to 1633, was a hot topic in 1631–2.[57] A Scottish parliament
and coronation would display Charles's British credentials, and here he was
imaged not just as a peaceful ruler but as Caesar, conqueror of nations,
returning with captive kings in his train.[58] Even more emphatic was the link
with the politicized aesthetics of Charles's growing art collection. He had
recently made his most important single purchase, the pictures and marbles
bought from Mantua for the staggering sum of £18,000, which came on the
market when the Gonzagas were ruined by warfare.[59] Charles beat off
competition from Marie de' Médici and Richelieu to secure a fabulous
haul, and its arrival at London, probably late in 1630, turned Whitehall
into one of Europe's greatest treasure houses at a stroke. Prominent in the
purchases were canvasses on imperial themes: the twelve Caesars by Titian,
now destroyed, and Mantegna's *Triumphs of Caesar*, now at Hampton
Court. *Albion's Triumph* was a poetic and architectural pastiche of these
monuments to empire, which decked Charles in the political symbolism of
antiquity. With its archeologically exact images of Caesar's return from
Gaul, Mantegna's *Triumphs* testified to the intersections of power, anti-
quarianism, and art, relationships that the masque affirmed. Jones's proscenium depicted figures of Theory and Practice, surmounted by royal arms
and the English imperial crown – the diadem worn by monarchs after the
coronation, which Mytens incorporated into portraiture of Charles.[60] The
statement of his political and cultural aspirations could not have been
clearer.

But matters were complicated by the dialogue between a common man,
Publius, and a philosopher, Platonicus, inserted between the first sight of
the triumph and the antimasquers' entry. Unusually in a court masque,
Publius and Platonicus ventriloquized audience voices, and their exchange
introduced a note of strain into the spectacle. Observers admiring the
triumph from afar but unable to catch all its details, they each showed
some resistance to the masque's idealizations, though from opposed points
of view. Publius, the common man, was an experiential materialist. His
attitude was that things merely say what they are, so when Platonicus said
there was a moral under every stone, he picked up a stone and was
disappointed to find nothing there. He was unresponsive to any allegory
that could be made from the pageantry; to him, it was just a glorious parade,
and its message about the conquest of vice, expounded by Platonicus, was
lost. Platonicus, though, was a philosophical idealist. He glossed the show's

inner meaning, but his sophisticated awareness of the need for interpretation introduced complications. He saw the triumph as an allegory honouring Charles (telling Publius that it showed Albanactus's victory over his
passions), but his acknowledgement of a space between material performance and ideological meaning intruded a hesitation about whether the
panegyric really did correspond to the values it displayed. Platonicus
asked Publius to describe the procession:

> *Publius.* Albanactus Caesar from his sumptuous palace through the high-streets of
>   Albipolis rid triumphing, on a chariot made –
> *Platonicus.* Of wood, perhaps gilt, perhaps gold. But I will save you all those
>   charges, if you will go on to the persons, and let the pageants alone.   (80)

For Platonicus, the real triumph was not outward trappings but the victory
of the mind: he told Publius he could understand the show without seeing
it. This was flattery indeed, for it allowed Platonicus to depict Albanactus as
an idealized conqueror, whose victories were more than merely physical.
But it also introduced a perception that the triumphs did not simply
embody Charles's inner qualities but were strategic representations of
what, for the sake of the fable, his inner qualities were supposed to be. In
reality, the masque's chariots might be nothing more than bits of wood,
'perhaps gilt, perhaps gold'.

The Platonicus–Publius dialogue is a remarkable moment, as the first
acknowledgement of possible consumer resistance to Charles's masquing
project. On the surface, the exchange underwrote the idealizations: probably spectators took it as dramatizing the gulf between those for whom
masques were incomprehensible shows and the sophisticated elites capable
of enjoying such mysteries. But Platonicus's answer was not especially
reassuring. His excessively intellectualized response to crude literalism did
not defend the truth of Charles's shows but argued that what mattered were
the ideological meanings that could be extracted. From this perspective,
their spectacle was redundant. If one read through the images to higher
'truths', their appearance was irrelevant; what counted was whether one was
convinced (or not) by their political claims. From here, it was a short step to
saying that Charles's mysteries had to be believed, even if one rejected their
expression. This is similar to the manoeuvre in Townshend's other masque,
Tempe Restored, which also problematized the gap between image and
meaning by contrasting Whitehall with Circe's sumptuous but dangerous
palace. Exploiting the perception that outward shows could not be trusted,
Tempe Restored introduced a tension by admitting the impossibility of ever

being sure that outward glamour corresponded with inner moral state. Of course, these masques sought to persuade their audiences that Charles really did embody the virtues that his festivals claimed: etiquette demanded that the fit between person and persona seem exact. Yet the visionary requirement that Charles's heroism was that which could never adequately be represented destabilized the equation, and opened the masques to the reservations voiced, from opposed directions, by these two spectators. It is symptomatic of the tensions latent in Caroline political culture that both the 1632 masques contained doubting Thomases. Neither entirely reconciled their praise of the King with their anxiety that the images used of him might not correspond with the public perception.

Of all Charles's masque poets, Townshend was the most ideologically distant from the monarch for whom he wrote, as is evident in his response to the death of Gustavus Adolphus in November 1632. For a brief but exciting period in 1630–2 the Swedish King became the long-desired Protestant champion, and news of his death in battle moved Townshend to write to Carew suggesting that Britain's poets should 'make a new flood' in lamentation.[61] His 'Elegy on the death of the King of Sweden' is not quite the radical document it is sometimes said to be. Though regretful for Gustavus's death, its enthusiasm for his generalship is tempered by an assumption that leadership is only the prerogative of kings. Still, its imagery of fiery pillars, rising suns, and fierce lions drew on Protestant apocalypticism, and its idea that princes would strive for Gustavus's spurs contrasts with Carew's circumspect reply. Carew's epistle 'In answer of an elegiacal letter upon the death of the King of Sweden' tactfully acknowledged Gustavus's deeds, but made a case for keeping England out of Europe. Shrewdly observing that Gustavus had made Germany one vast tomb, Carew praised the 'peace and plenty which the blessed hand / Of our good king gives this obdurate land'. His assertion that 'tourneys, masques, [and] theatres' were better themes than the German drum, bellowing 'for freedom and revenge', was a realistic assessment of war's effect. Were the Germans to recover their security, they too would 'hang their arms up on the olive bough, / And dance and revel then, as we do now'.[62] This was the attitude of Charles's early masques, and Gustavus's death reinforced it by showing with shocking clarity the risks of military action. Even Townshend's elegy did not question the wisdom of neutrality, and refrained from urging Charles to take up from Gustavus.[63] Nonetheless, his nostalgia for the royal warrior, and his enthusiasm elsewhere for 'the pure golden Princess Palatine',[64] aligns him with those who admired Gustavus's leadership and hoped for great things from it.

At the time of *Albion's Triumph*, Gustavus's campaign was at its height and Whitehall was agog with news of victories. He routed the imperial army at Breitenfeld in September and then swept down the Rhine. A Franco-Swedish league seemed likely, which, said John Pory, 'hath much troubled our grandees at court'.[65] Rumours of a new parliament were circulating, and the Earl of Craven, an enthusiast for the Palatines, began levying a private regiment.[66] But Charles was cautious and issued warnings against talk of parliament. Though willing to help Sweden financially, he was sceptical that Gustavus would help over the Palatinate, and was waiting for news from his envoys before reacting. Consulting Charles in December, Dudley Carleton found him in his gallery, arranging his Roman emperors in chronological order.[67] In these circumstances, the role of Albanactus promoted a different model of monarchy. With Charles seated in a grove, 'attended by fourteen consuls, who stood about him, not set in ranks, but in several gracious postures, attending his commands' (83), it cast him as a strong but peaceful autocrat, who made decisions with advice from a few peers, not a disorderly multitude. At the same time, the public climate explains why Platonicus's conversation with Publius was necessary, and Albanactus's heroism seemed in need of defence:

Platonicus. For a supplement to thy lame story, know, I have seen this brave Albanactus Caesar, seen him with the eyes of understanding, viewed all his actions, looked into his mind, which I find armed with so many moral virtues that he daily conquers a world of vices, which are wild beasts indeed.   (81)

Asserting that kingly victories happened in the mind rather than in battle, *Albion's Triumph* must have seemed conflicted and at odds with the prevailing mood. A magnificent statement of Charles's imperial aspirations, it made his conquests seem all the better for belonging to the domestic sphere. Little wonder that Platonicus was anxious to rebut Publius's disparagement, or that the masque seemed unable to shake off the problems broached in the antimasque. Unsurprisingly, the next time Charles wanted a masque, he turned not to Townshend but to a more like-minded poet, Carew.

No masques were staged during Christmas 1632–3, for Whitehall's theatrical energies went into Henrietta Maria's production of *The Shepherd's Paradise*, but the following year brought the two most magnificent Caroline festivals, Shirley's *The Triumph of Peace* and Carew's *Coelum Britannicum*. In these, Caroline revelry reached its greatest self-confidence. Each addressed Charles's now fully established political programme, and celebrated his stable royal government. *The Triumph of Peace* was mounted as homage from the Inns of Court, apologizing for the insult recently done to the crown by the puritanical lawyer William Prynne. Prynne's *Histriomastix* (1633) had given offence by its scandalous remarks about despotic rulers who patronized plays, and by its tactless reference to 'women actors, notorious whores', widely taken to mean the Queen. In February 1634 Prynne was prosecuted in Star Chamber and sentenced to life imprisonment and loss of his ears. *The Triumph of Peace* was danced four days before his trial, and its preface said the lawyers wished 'to present [their] duties' and celebrate 'the happiness of our kingdom, so blest in the present government' (1–4).[68] The apology could hardly have been richer. The evening began with a cavalcade through the city streets to Westminster, a modern Roman triumph which drew thousands of spectators. It was led by twenty footmen and a hundred mounted gentlemen each with two lackeys and a page, then came the anti-masquers with their music, then two chariots with the singers and more footmen, then four cars carrying the 'grand masquers', built (said Bulstrode Whitelocke) after 'the Roman triumphant chariots, as near as could be gathered by some old prints', with torches that 'made it seem lightsome as at noonday',[69] followed by 200 halberdiers. All the gentlemen wore £100 suits, so the cost of the procession alone was over £10,000. This was the most splendid public spectacle yet staged in London in a reign that, through royal insolvency, had not even seen a coronation entry. Charles was so gratified that he made the masquers walk twice around the tiltyard, and had everything repeated in Merchant Taylors' Hall at the city's expense ten days later. All 120 lawyers involved received invitations to see *Coelum Britannicum* later that month.[70]

Charles took *The Triumph of Peace* to signal the settled state of Caroline England and the happy unity between crown and political elites. Yet the masque was more complex, as its performers did not share his perspective on personal rule.[71] His government raised difficult legal questions, and in the 1640s lawyers anxious about the constitutionality of his fund-raising would be prominent amongst his opponents. In interpreting these doubts, it is important to underline that criticism of the legality of Charles's finance was not in itself opposition to the principle of prerogative rule. Although many believed parliaments were the best form of government, before 1641 there was no statute that required kings to call an assembly. Parliaments met only when the King needed to legislate or raise finance: if he had no legislative programme and could fund himself there was little incentive for consultation, so in ruling through his prerogative powers Charles was not stepping outside the law. Orgel and Strong therefore mistake the situation when they remark (apropos of Ship Money) that the basic question was 'whether the King could make the law without consent of parliament' and that

'[Attorney General] Noy had worked zealously to keep the issues out of the courts'.[72] On the contrary, Charles was obsessed with precedent and in some respects his rule was excessively legalistic. When developing his special measures, he repeatedly consulted with the judges and sought to test their legal validity; the 1630s have been well described as 'a decade of intense government by common lawyers'.[73] Almost certainly he took *The Triumph of Peace* to express the relationship between law and power that he thought he was upholding, but whether the lawyers saw it this way is another matter. The issue was not the illegality of his measures, but their political credibility: whether there was a point beyond which legal correctness no longer satisfied as political justification.

Charles's legalism emerged in three areas. He badgered the magistracy into enforcing the statutes controlling everyday life; he maximized his prerogative powers, such as wardship, forest laws, and distraint of knighthood; and he punished offenders against proclamations with exemplary fines. Technically legal though such measures were, they created anxiety because they seemed to undermine security of property, and because of the fiscal motives behind the parade of legalism. For example, the forest laws were virtually defunct, but their revival brought huge profits. One court sitting for the first time since Edward I's reign fined two landowners £80,000 for cutting timber and declared that seventeen towns had encroached on the royal forest; another extended the boundaries of Rockingham forest from six miles to sixty.[74] Similarly, the use of fines for breaches of proclamations, or for 'abuses' such as defective titles, made it seem that the law was being sold. John Pym said in 1640 that Star Chamber had become a court of revenue and 'many great nuisances have been complained of, but when there hath been money given, and compositions made, they are no more nuisances'.[75] Charles made huge profits from the Court of Wards, which administered his rights over the estates of minors, but they hurt the propertied classes: Edward Hyde wrote that many 'were exceedingly incensed … looking upon what the law had intended for their protection and preservation to be now applied to their destruction'.[76] The law was assumed to protect both royal authority and the subject's liberties, but as the crown's rights were all upheld against the subject's, so the issue of legality became mired in political anxieties. Looking back on distraint of knighthood, Hyde said that 'though it had a foundation in right, yet in the circumstances of proceeding it was very grievous', and displeased 'all persons of quality, or indeed of any reasonable condition throughout the kingdom'.[77] He also thought the judiciary was tainted by its support for 'acts of power, there being no possibility to preserve the dignity, reverence and estimation of the laws themselves but by the integrity and innocency of the judges'.[78] In 1634, such a loss of confidence was still some way into the future, but in raising the relationship between power and law, *The Triumph of Peace* occupied territory that would become bitterly contested.

The masque's planning brought together some extraordinary legal expertise. The 'Grand Committee' had some outstanding career lawyers, and a diverse range of opinion. Nearest the King was Sir John Finch, who as Speaker in 1629 was conspicuously loyal, and became Lord Keeper and a leading figure in Star Chamber; he was impeached in 1640 and fled the country. Close to him, though with credentials as royal critics, were William Noy and Sir Edward Herbert. Noy had led parliament's attack on monopolies, but as Attorney General he used his talents to create many of Charles's fund-raising devices, including Ship Money. Herbert, who managed Buckingham's impeachment, succeeded Noy in the same post. It was he who charged the Five Members (the King's most outspoken parliamentary opponents) with treason in 1641, for which he was impeached. Other committee members had contrasting careers. Edward Hyde would be a loyal friend to Charles, but in 1640–1 he led the attack on Ship Money and the prerogative courts. John Selden, a critic in the 1620s, made his peace in 1636 by providing Charles with the theoretical basis for sovereignty of the seas in *Mare clausum*, but he ended his career as a moderate parliamentarian sceptical of both sides in the struggle. As for Bulstrode Whitelocke, this Middle Templar was active in political life into the 1650s, and sat on Cromwell's Council of State. To these names, one could add the distinguished lawyers who viewed the masque at Whitehall. At least three of the future Ship Money judges were there: William Jones and Robert Berkeley, who gave judgment in favour, and George Croke, who became a minor hero by finding against. And even Simonds D'Ewes, the godly lawyer, friend of Prynne, and future Presbyterian MP, hired a coach to take him to Whitehall – though his autobiography suppresses any mention of attending so frivolous an event as a masque.[79]

This coalition shows how fluid politics still were, and how premature it is to suppose that in 1634 England was already polarized. Such an assumption has produced diametrically opposed readings of this masque. Orgel and Strong, taking the lawyers for opponents of the King, read it as an attack on the 'illegalities' of his rule, but are puzzled to find it was applauded at Whitehall, and conclude it must have been 'clumsy'.[80] Lawrence Venuti reads it regnocentrically, as a dramatization of Charles's proclamation to the gentry which impressed on his elites that his mandates had the force of law, but he cannot then account for its apparent criticisms other than as discontinuities within 'absolutist ideology'.[81] But by hardening Caroline culture into two 'sides', these readings simplify the situation. When opinion did polarize, the lawyers moved different ways, but in 1634 they still cooperated as royal servants contributing to the running of government; Charles could thus draw on a broad pool of talent, albeit one nursing anxieties about his rule. *The Triumph of Peace* allowed for debate over disputed issues within an encompassing politics of consensus: its commentary was not narrowly one-way.[82] A masque presented to Whitehall by visitors whose professional affiliations gave them some measure of ideological separation from the court, it enacted a highly charged symbolic conversation, staking out common ground on potentially divisive topics and building bridges between crown, advisors, and critics. Its theme was the interdependence of power and law, a binarism strongly asserted in its iconography. The proscenium depicted Minos and Numa, mythical kings renowned as lawgivers, and within the masque Charles and Henrietta Maria were addressed as Jove and Themis, that is, Divine Power and Divine Law, the origin and ordering principle of all things. And the principal characters were the Hours: Peace, Law, and Justice (Irene, Eunomia, and Dike). Children to Jove and Themis, and parents of the masquers, the Hours mediated between lawyers and King, expressing in their symbiosis the necessary conjunctions of authority and right. This iconography allowed performers and spectators to share disputed territory without discomfort. Complimentary to Charles, it nonetheless enabled the lawyers to insinuate their own views about good government.

Shirley's antimasques staged two problems: an audience in need of aesthetic unification, and a country in need of law. The framing device was presented by Confidence and his friends Fancy, Jollity, and Laughter, and Opinion with his family Novelty and Admiration. Though allegorically named, these figures were surrogates for the court spectators towards whom the lawyers were processing, and they were not a single constituency but two groups with diverging attitudes. Confidence – a 'gay man' (208) with slashed doublet, long hair and ribbons – and his friends were courtiers, but Opinion, with 'grave' face (171) and old-fashioned doublet and hose, was a country gentleman who had brought his family up to town. Assembling in the hall, they awaited the masquers' arrival with hostility. Opinion would 'like nothing' (280), and Fancy expected the lawyers' 'phlegmatic inventions' to be 'jeered to death' (226, 237). This disparagement projected a performance problem, of pleasing an audience at odds over taste, but also registered apprehensions about tensions between Whitehall and the lawyers. Such fears had been widely canvassed, by

Thomas Coke – 'the emulation that will be between the Inns of Court men and the courtiers you may easily imagine'[83] – and by George Garrard:

> They speak of £20,000 that it will cost the men of the law. Oh that they would once give over these things, or lay them aside for a time, and bend all their endeavours to make the King rich! For it gives me no satisfaction, who am but a looker-on, to see a rich commonwealth, a rich people, and the crown poor. God direct them to remedy this quickly.[84]

Garrard evidently thought the masque was the wrong gesture, an apology that only reproduced the underlying problem, and did nothing to address the crown's financial needs. Sir William Drake was even more lugubrious, expecting the lawyers would be scorned, for 'the courtier would be apt to scoff at the gentlemen, at which scoffs may be bred ill blood'.[85] In the event, the lawyers were applauded, but these fears suggest the performance was perceived as unusually sensitive, probably because it mined along one of the major fault-lines of the decade.

The antimasques depicted the pleasures and problems of the Caroline peace, focusing primarily on social disorders of the kind that Charles wanted his magistracy to address. Several episodes featured a tavern, with drunken gamblers, cheating beggars, and thieves. Although light-hearted, these images were not just celebratory, but alluded to the Book of Orders, and its criminalization of vagrancy, idleness, and insobriety. The antimasques concurred with Charles's programme by promoting discipline in the localities, and presenting social and moral regulation as going hand in hand. Moreover, at village level, alehouses were often seen as sources of disruption, and the Book of Orders coincided with an intensive drive against unlicensed taverns.[86] The problem with the tavern in the masque was that it was unlicensed:

> *Novelty.* A spick and span new tavern.
> *Admiration.* Wonderful, here was none within two minutes.
> *Laughter.* No such wonder, lady, taverns are quickly up. It is but hanging out a bush at a nobleman's door or an alderman's gate, and 'tis made instantly.
>
> (301–5)

Other antimasques focused attention on law enforcement in the provinces, and the lowly parish officers who fulfilled it, by showing thieves setting upon a merchant in a wood, and arrested by the constables. These episodes were nicely poised between approving Charles's peace and underlining that the rule of law was necessary to regulate it:

> *Opinion.* Are these the benefits of peace?
> Corruption rather.

Fancy. Oh, the beggars show
          The benefit of peace.   (328–30)

In the main masque, a disorderly peace was replaced by the controlling power of law. When Peace arrived, she banished the antimasquers and called on Law to support her: 'Appear, appear, Eunomia … / Irene calls. / Like dew that falls / Into a stream, / I'm lost with them / That know not how to order me' (505–11).

The fifth antimasque satirized six eccentric projectors bearing crazy inventions for which each wanted a monopoly: a jockey with a miraculous bridle, a farmer with a perpetual threshing machine, an adventurer with a submarine suit, a physician with a poultry scheme, and so on. This addressed one of the period's legal grievances, for patents and monopolies were deeply unpopular. They were attacked in the 1621 parliament, and in 1641 appeared in the Grand Remonstrance. It is important to note, though, that they were not simply illegal. They had arisen as devices to help innovation and protect new processes, but were open to abuse since they could be used to raise finance and reward favoured individuals, who received rights to exploit a product while paying a retainer to the crown. The Monopolies Act (1624) distinguished between different kinds of patent, and exempted new inventions from condemnation. The antimasque patents were of this kind: the antimasquers wanted to patent their unworkable inventions or impose them on the public. For example, Whitelocke glossed the jockey as 'a projector who begged a patent that none in the kingdom might ride their horses but with such bits as they should buy of him', and claimed that William Noy devised the dances to give Charles 'an information … of the unfitness and ridiculousness of these projects against the law'.[87] As Attorney General, Noy was responsible for licensing new monopolies, so his device expressed the discriminations his office was drawing, admonishing the King about the Statute of Monopolies and warning against countenancing any far-fetched scheme simply for hope of revenue. But Noy was not immune from his own satire: although he disapproved of racketeering, he had to get the best return for his royal master, and the general trend during the decade was towards domination by the economic motive. As Kevin Sharpe notes, 'many grants of monopoly were cynically exploited by courtiers for their own profit'.[88] Noy's antimasque was not so much an attack on the crown as an opportunity for it to disavow some of the scandalous practices with which it was associated, and it doubtless pleased participants such as Edward Hyde, who later expressed disgust with the 'projects of all kinds, many ridiculous, many scandalous, all very grievous … the envy and reproach of which came to the King, the profit to other men'.[89] But simply by alluding to patents, the masque drew attention to fiscal expedients which many of the audience disapproved of. Noy could not defend the crown's good practice without admitting there were abuses that it needed defending from.

The main masque that followed dwelt pointedly on the indispensability of law to peace. While deferential towards the King, the dialogue between Peace and Law moved the event into a conceptual frame that allowed the lawyers to insinuate their perspective on power. Irene (Peace) dismissed the antimasquers as disorderly, but emphasized that the remedy was control by Eunomia (Law). Without Eunomia she was 'lost' (510), and only she could bring Dike (Justice) to earth:

> *Irene.* Thou dost beautify increase,
>   And chain security with peace.
> *Eunomia.* Irene fair, and first divine,
>   All my blessings spring from thine.
> *Irene.* I am but wild without thee, thou abhorrest
>   What is rude, or apt to wound,
>   Canst throw proud trees to the ground,
>   And make a temple of a forest. (529–36)

Irene was the lead deity, but her words foregrounded the conditions of peace, that only through Eunomia could she be perfected. To an audience of lawyers, 'security' would have had constitutionalist implications: it referred not to foreign policy and outward threats but inner checks and balances, the safety of property and protection of ownership. Irene's sylvan justice, with some trees sanctified and others overthrown, presented legal priorities different from what was actually happening in Charles's woods. These associations accumulated as the dialogue proceeded:

> *Eunomia.* No more, no more, but join
>   Thy voice and lute with mine.
> *Both.* The world shall give prerogative to neither.
>   We cannot flourish but together.
> [*Chorus.*] Irene enters like a perfumed spring,
>   Eunomia ripens everything
>   And in the golden harvest leaves
>   To every sickle his own sheaves. (537–41)

Such sentiments were not 'an argument against prerogative rule',[90] for although the lawyers used the language of prerogative, it was not to urge the recall of parliament. Rather, they advanced the claims of law, that peace be regulated with strict legality, voicing the concern of the political elites that law should protect liberties of person and property. The harvest was golden because it respected the boundaries of mine and thine, while leaving 'to every sickle his own sheaves' expressed the political moral that lawyers anxious about forest law and distraint of knighthood were keen to emphasize. Of course, everything in this dialogue was governed by tact. Charles would not have disagreed with the view that peace had to be regulated by law: indeed, this was what he thought he was doing. Nevertheless, such language was rooted in a concern for the rights of the propertied subject, and set kingly power within a constrained framework. No disloyalty was implied, but a statement about the monarch's limits and duties certainly was.

The rest of the masque was more reverential. By calling Charles and Henrietta Maria 'Jove' and 'Themis', the lawyers coopted their profession into the structures of Caroline rule. As Divine Power and Divine Law, King and Queen were the lawyers' iconographical grandparents, fountains of those principles of justice which the masque was keen to advance. Their 'chaste embraces' (595) were again fulsomely hymned as a British blessing: Charles could not have been displeased with this. And yet in telling ways the masque held back from offering unconditional sanction. One was the royal identification with Jove and Themis, which carried a political point. Edward Hyde later criticized Charles for having eroded this distinction, between power and law:

In the wisdom of former times, when the prerogative went highest ... never any court of law, very seldom any judge, or lawyer of reputation, was called upon to assist in an act of power; the crown well knowing the moment of keeping those the objects of reverence and veneration with the people, and that though it might sometimes make sallies upon them by the prerogative, yet the law would keep the people from any invasion of it, and the King could never suffer while the law and the judges were looked upon by the subject as the asyla for their liberties and property.[91]

Although the separation of powers between administration and judiciary was less distinct than today, Hyde's views on the relations of power and law suggest that this iconography would have seemed an admonition as well as compliment, and suggest how one of the masque's organizers may have seen it. The royal love affair was conscripted into underlining the embrace yet separation that should obtain between justice and authority. No less striking was the anxious tone in which the Genius introduced the masquers:

> No foreign persons I make known
> But here present you with your own,
> The children of your reign, not blood;

> Of age, when they are understood,
> Not seen by faction or owl's sight,
> Whose trouble is the clearest light,
> But treasures to their eye and ear,
> That love good for itself, not fear.
> O smile on what yourselves have made ... (630–8)

This oddly circumlocutory address reflects the lawyers' need to divest themselves of associations with Prynne, but the hint that Charles might choose not to acknowledge his children cut two ways. The Genius claimed they would remain motionless until his looks inspired them to dance, forcing him to take responsibility for their animation. When they did move, it expressed a double tie, projecting their duty to Charles and his willingness to stand parent to law.

Even more remarkable was the masque's acknowledgement of its status as ceremonial, its self-consciousness about its ideological work. Shirley's most surprising innovation was an extra antimasque that erupted into the revels, disturbing the celebrations and calling their mechanics into question. At this unexpected moment, there was 'a great noise and confusion of voices within', and a crack, 'as if there were some danger by some piece of the machines falling' (672). Into the masque tumbled a carpenter, painter, guardsman, tailor, and the wives of an embroiderer, feather-maker, and property man, each protesting they had helped behind the scenes and demanding to see the dances. But having stopped the show, they resolved to escape embarrassment by pretending to be another antimasque and dancing their exit. This was an amusing episode, but symbolically it drew attention to the personnel who created the masque and now 'challenge[d] a privilege' (694), claiming recognition for their contribution to this collective exercise: 'What though we be no ladies, we are Christians in these clothes, and the King's subjects, God bless us' (700–1). If *The Triumph of Peace* emphasized consensus, building bridges between King and subject, its belated antimasque demonstrated how far everything rested on unseen but essential acts of collaboration. It demystified the machinery and exposed the ideological engineering, showing that Charles's myths depended on social cooperation. And in a most beautiful effect, it ended with the appearance of Amphiluche, the morning light, announcing the dawn. Most Stuart masques situated the monarch as transcendental, untouched by time: for example, *Coelum Britannicum* ends with the deity Eternity. But Shirley's uncharacteristic masque concluded by turning to the world outside, the quotidian pressures that bore onto masquing fictions. Charles's apotheosis was limited by the sun's tendency to keep on rising.

All contemporary observers agreed that Charles was delighted.[92] This masque must have seemed an impressive endorsement of his rule, and testament to the bonds uniting his monarchy with the lawyers. Expounding the symbiosis of kingship and law, it reflected Charles's own self-conception, his preoccupation with precedent and correctness. Indeed, the text was licensed for printing by his legal spokesman, the Lord Keeper, Sir John Finch.[93] Yet its differences from dominant festive forms testified to separations of attitude between which the text manoeuvred. Although the lawyers adopted Charles's triumphal devices, their iconography was emptied of imperial resonance. The procession – a parade to the King rather than by him – was an ambiguous homage, that promulgated a constrained image of kingship. A triumph without a hero, it did not express an emperor's glorious self-confidence but the checks and balances within which his power promised to contain itself. And, for once, Charles was not the only audience, since this masque went wider than Whitehall. Although danced at court, its parade was seen by hundreds of citizens, Whitelocke's 'multitude of spectators … loath to part with so glorious a spectacle'.[94] Not participants in the ordinary way, these onlookers turned *The Triumph of Peace* into that unique object, a masque that reached both courtly and plebeian audiences. Moreover, there was a special drive to promote it in print, for in circumvention of the customary printers' restrictions on the size of editions, three separate impressions, of several thousand copies, were published simultaneously.[95] Astonishing though it seems, *The Triumph of Peace* may well have been the period's most widely read literary text, perhaps reaching a larger initial readership than any other work of imaginative literature.

What these audiences made of it is a nice point. Sue Wiseman, noting the dozens of city marshals who policed the procession, questions whether the citizens really 'consumed' it. To them it was a display of conspicuous spending, 'a pageant signifying the richness and power of the court'.[96] Yet the visual symbolism that grouped the beggars next to the projectors in the parade was not accidental,[97] and those observers who remarked on it thought it displayed the lawyers' power as much as Whitehall's. William Drake's diary has the most explicit commentary:

A masque presented by the Inns of Court to the King, whereat the vulgar did much rejoice, saying that it showed the honour of the kingdom and it would much ingratiate the Inns of Court with the King and court; but men of judgment thought otherwise, for that the courtier would be apt to scoff at the gentlemen, at which scoffs may be bred ill blood. Besides, 'tis hazard as whether for their charges they will gain any other but envy, if they do it too well, or scorn, if not well enough; and

wise men wished a greater gravity and moderation in the Inns than to give way to
the spending of so great sums of money which might have been reserved for better
uses; neither did the condition of the present time befit such shows of magnificence, our neighbour countries being all in combustion about us, and his majesty's
only sister and her children wanting money to keep and preserve their country from
the spoil of their enemies.[98]

Drake shows that the masque was interpreted differently in different
quarters – gentlemen, courtiers, 'the vulgar' – and that all groups agreed
that more than a simple compliment was taking place. His own, rather
negative judgement chimes with that of George Garrard, who also thought
the occasion too much underlined the lawyers' power. Both detected here
an imbalance within the political nation: the masque witnessed the unity
between crown and elites, but also advertised the very tensions that it was in
the business of ameliorating. And this was exactly how one anonymous
eyewitness responded to the procession, writing verses that overflowed with
enthusiasm for the masquers and found a different moral from that which
Charles, presumably, read:

> Now did heaven's charioteer, the great day's star,
> In western ocean lave his weary car,
> And Cynthia, shining with her borrowed light,
> Sat queen of her great royalty – the night,
> When the four colleges of Law did bring
> Prepared triumphs to their sovereign King,
> So full of joy, that I was confident,
> When first I saw this goodly regiment,
> And all the glittering of this comely train,
> The silver age was now returned again ...
> These are the sons of Charles's peaceful reign,
> Whom yet if war's rude accent shall constrain
> To put on arms will quickly understand
> The laws of arms as well as of the land,
> And be as valiant in the midst of fight
> As they seemed glorious in the masque of night.[99]

Evidently this rhymer did not see the performance, for its praise of peace
would have dispelled his naive supposition that the cost indicated readiness
for more militarized engagements. But his verses demonstrate how, for one
spectator beyond Whitehall, the procession shifted the spotlight from the
King to the termers. For him, it testified to the lawyers' glory as much as to
Charles's.

The Triumph of Peace was the site of multi-faceted ideological and
aesthetic transactions. Addressing a contentious topic, defining common

ground and areas of disagreement, it managed friction points between
Caroline England's political constituencies. Promulgating a collective purpose while acknowledging inner disagreements, it made a symbolic accommodation, discharging anxieties, appeasing differences, and establishing
consensus. And inasmuch as its participants came away believing their
voices had been heard, it was a resounding success. It facilitated a conversation underlining mutual trust and reciprocation, and embraced diverse
audiences within a single event, modelling a community conscious of its
disagreements but holding them in check for the sake of the larger celebration. Whether its gestures made any difference to the conduct of policy is
harder to say. As the reactions cited above suggest, one consequence of the
symbolic consensus was to conceal potential disharmonies by eliding underlying conflicts. The resolution was achieved partly by representing as
negotiable differences which, in less celebratory contexts, would continue
to be sources of tension. But this is to anticipate polarizations that in 1634
were barely on the horizon. Rather, *The Triumph of Peace* displayed consensus in action, the give and take of politics, to which masques were
uniquely placed to contribute. While testifying to reservoirs of goodwill it
also voiced anxieties about Charles's government, allowing space for him to
acknowledge and thereby assuage them. The masque was thus a channel
through which his power was legitimated but also scrutinized by the larger
political community.

Two weeks later, the royal response to *The Triumph of Peace* was danced
at Whitehall: Carew's *Coelum Britannicum*. It is difficult to underestimate
this masque's importance, for it was perhaps the most accomplished festival
of the two reigns. Even more ambitious than Jonson's grandest inventions,
Coelum Britannicum benefited from some of Jones's most impressive
designs, and was justly described by Sir Henry Herbert as 'the noblest
masque of my time'.[100] Its unfamiliarity arises from its unusually demanding form – the main masquers were preceded by nearly a thousand lines of
dialogue – and from the modern eclipse of Carew, who has suffered with
Caroline court culture a kind of guilt by association. As John Kerrigan
argues, Carew is the principal casualty of retrospective approaches to the
pre-Civil War period.[101] Often written off as a typical courtier, effete,
hedonistic, and pusillanimous, he is overshadowed by a crisis that he
never lived to see, and his work has been evaluated as much by ideological
as by aesthetic criteria. This dramatically impacts onto *Coelum Britannicum*,
for even those who praise it tend to deflate it. For example, Graham Parry
says it 'attained a new peak of hyperbole' that marked 'the summer solstice
of royal confidence', as if it were danced in the teeth of imminent

collapse.[102] *Coelum Britannicum* was indeed outrageously hyperbolical. It elevated the masquers into stars to replace the existing constellations, which were found wanting in comparison with Charles's superior virtue. No fable more magnified Charles, or more invited irony. But the ironies that flow from a future as yet unmade should not diminish the masque's achievement. On the contrary, its power arises from its epochal claims: it presented Charles as inaugurating a new phase in history.

Coelum Britannicum was introduced by two gods, Mercury and Momus, whose sharply contrasting voices created an ambiguous frame. Events opened at maximum elevation with Mercury, bearing an embassy expressing Jove's admiration for Charles's earthly reforms, and announcing that Jove had decided to reform the heavens after his model, replacing the constellations with 'British stars' who would dispense 'a pure refined influence' (102–3). But he was quickly interrupted by Momus – god of ridicule and 'universal calumniator' (138), banished from the heavens for scurrility and fault-finding – who amplified this message in carnivalesque mode, ridiculing the gods' lubricity and elaborating the parallels between Jove's reformation and Charles's. Jove had banned monopolies and the sophistication of goods; new rates were imposed on Olympian commodities; the hours of heavenly taverns were changed and nectar confined to a standard strength (like Charles's proclamations on beer); Vulcan was barred from labouring on holidays, and Pan and Proteus from unlicensed piping (like Charles's proclamation on Sunday sports); the gods' families were forbidden from coming to the metropolis, and a new moral code was imposed on Jove's court, requiring decent heavenly behaviour – no adulteries, mutinous wives, or young pages in the bedchamber (228–76). Transmitted through Momus's disenchanted voice, Jove's reformation paralleled Charles's social initiatives, and the link was pressed home by Momus's announcement of an election of new stars in the language of royal proclamations: 'Oyez, oyez, oyez! By the father of the gods and the king of men: Whereas we have observed a very commendable practice taken into frequent use by the princes of these latter ages ... given at our palace in Olympus the first day of the first month, in the first year of the Reformation.' (421–5, 463–5). Almost identical public pronouncements must, under the personal rule, have been all too familiar.

Critics have speculated about Momus, and most take his voice as subversive. Annabel Patterson sees him as allegorizing Carew's own situation, insinuating a current of doubt about the Caroline project, and undermining it with sardonic commentary by letting in 'all the ironies and scepticism that formal compliment holds at bay'.[103] Joanne Altieri likewise argues that

Momus exposes the masque's idealizations as absurd, demonstrating its compliments were 'impossible to any literal world'.[104] Kevin Sharpe goes further, representing him as a satirist, truth-teller, and cynic who openly contests the masque's idealizations. His Momus is the voice of dissent uninhibited by deference, unimpressed by Charles's pretensions, and dousing Mercury's compliments with cold water that 'exposed the reality behind the masque'.[105] It certainly is true that Momus lacked any respect. His opinions could not be restrained by appeals to 'modesty' (124), and his scoffing language challenged customary decorum and scorned inherited obligations. Some of his remarks did seem to question Charles's reforms, such as his observations that Jove's orders were 'too strict to be observed long' (235), or that, though families were forbidden from frequenting the metropolis, women were still coming up on their own (241–6) – though this was a joke against women's resistance to male control rather than the proclamation to the gentry. However, the target of his insults was less the royal reformation than Jove's incompetent efforts to imitate it. They did not undermine Charles's dignity but demonstrated the need for a mythology more adequate to the modern British monarchy.

Momus's function was to repudiate the old iconography as incapable of voicing Charles's revolutionary aspirations. The figure most in awe of Momus was Mercury. As ambassador to the gods, Mercury needed to appear august, but Momus twitted him that, being god of thieves, he left behind a trail of 'pilfery' and 'petty larceny' (119–20) – from which insult Mercury never quite recovered. This was typical of Momus's impact, and he voiced similarly disenchanted accounts of Jove, Juno, Mars, Venus, and the other Olympians. Mercury rejected such gossip as 'scurrilous' (175), but Momus's brilliantly incisive satire offered a rich deflationary comedy. Throughout the masque he poured scorn on the divine, reducing the gods to fallible individuals:

Venus hath confessed her adulteries, and is received to grace by her husband … it is the prettiest spectacle to see her stroking with her ivory hand his collied cheeks, and with her snowy fingers combing his sooty beard. Jupiter too begins to learn to lead his own wife, I left him practising in the Milky Way; and there is no doubt of an universal obedience, where the Lawgiver himself in his own person observes his decrees so punctually; who besides to eternize the memory of that great example of matrimonial union which he derives from hence, hath on his bedchamber door and ceiling, fretted with stars, in capital letters engraven the inscription of CARLOMARIA.	(262–76)

The commentators who see Carew as debunking Charles assume that this satire on the gods was a coded attack on Charles, but the masque distinguished earthly from heavenly reformations, praising Charles's work and his superior precedent. It was the gods, always so unruly in their private lives, who needed to practise virtue, and the model for their reform – engraved over Jove's bedroom door – was Charles and Henrietta Maria's union, in imitation of whose 'exemplar life' 'immortal bosoms burn with emulous fires' (62, 68). Momus had fun at the gods' expense, but his disrespect legitimated the Caroline reforms by contrasting them with Jove's inadequate imitations. Thus it was not 'the mundane human world stripped of its abstract pretences' that Momus saw,[106] but the celestial world stripped bare. He was necessary as the figure who proved the old gods' shortcomings and validated Charles's modernizing ethos.

So Momus's attitudes were consonant with Mercury's. To Mercury, Charles and Henrietta Maria figured a new standard of virtue, a perfect love that put the gods to shame, their 'incest, rapes, adulteries' crying out for correction by a more rigorous ethics (76). Though more pungently expressed, Momus too believed that the constellations had to be removed because of their bad example:

> Because the libertines of antiquity, the ribald poets, to perpetuate the memory and example of their triumphs over chastity to all future imitation have in their immortal songs celebrated the martyrdom of those strumpets under the persecution of the wives, and devolved to posterity the pedigrees of their whores, bawds, and bastards; it is therefore by the authority aforesaid enacted that this whole army of constellations be immediately disbanded and cashiered. (207–15)

The only difference was that Momus spelled out the significance of this decision for the gods themselves. For Mercury, Jove's authority was still current, but for Momus Jove's reformation was equivalent to abdication. If the gods' problem was failure to achieve Charles's moral and social control, correcting their vices destroyed their authority. As Momus interpreted the decrees, Jove not only cleared out a few naughty constellations but repudiated the legacy of allegory and myth, the backward-looking inheritance of classical culture and its suspect values. The heavens had been peopled by 'immortal songs', but once these were recognized as the disgraceful inventions of 'ribald poets' (207–10), the basis of Jove's power collapsed. Jove's innovations were therefore symptomatic of an oedipal anxiety caused by the transfer of his authority to a new dispensation. His virtue was brought on by impotence, 'the decay of his natural abilities' (198), and he reformed because, being 'old and fearful', he 'apprehends a subversion of his empire, and doubts lest Fate should introduce a legal succession in the legitimate heir by repossessing the Titanian line' (230–3). Little wonder that Momus worried Mercury, for he was the voice of the new, a disrespectful radical expressing Charles's challenge to Jove. Mercury belonged to a disappearing order, for this was his 9,999th visit to earth (112). By contrast, Momus's proclamation dated from 'the first day of the first month, in the first year of the Reformation' (464–5), the epochal moment of Charles's revolutionary millennium.

Against this geriatric Jove, Carew set the new triumphant monarchy, led by its confident hero-king, whose values were elaborated in the long dialogues preceding his apotheosis. Before his entry, a series of pretenders to stellification arrived to present their rival claims to honour: Plutus (Riches), Poenia (Poverty), Fortune, and Hedone (Pleasure). Their self-justifying and deeply flawed rhetoric defined by opposites the purer ideology of Caroline kingship. In contrast to Riches, whose labours were sordid, miserly, competitive, and sacrilegious, Charles's virtue managed to be active without being self-seeking. In contrast to Poverty, who looked unworldly but was lazy, stupid, and servile, Charles could be contemplative without falling into abjection. Unlike Fortune, who was reverenced by the 'giddy superstitious crowd' (755), his eminence came from his inner wisdom, not the whims of popular caprice. As for Pleasure, she was universally admired but was the most dangerous candidate of all, the root of vice and origin of the decay into which the gods had fallen (830–1). Crucially, in a masque in which Charles played the glorious lover, Pleasure was the anti-type to his heroically empowering eroticism, projecting the negative capacity of the virtues for which he was praised. As the Queen's lover, Charles had a passionate forcefulness that was dangerously close to Hedone's 'effeminate' delights (827) and which, to be legitimate, was carefully distinguished from hers. Carew's critique of hedonism was thus not a disenchanted reflection on Whitehall's sensuality but the necessary proof that Charles could control his desires, ensuring his love was virile but chaste, ardent but not voluptuous. Pleasure had to be censured to avert the imputation that happy peacefulness signalled moral disarmament.[107]

Eventually these disputatious dialogues gave way to a fabulous patriotic romance, harking back to Arthurian motifs. Discovered like 'ancient heroes' inside a 'wild and craggy' mountain (886, 949), the masquers were lost leaders miraculously recovered from an antique past. Knights inspired by a burning love of the national mistress, they demanded from the ladies an answering tribute of desire:

> We bring Prince Arthur, or the brave
> St George himself, great Queen, to you,

You'll soon discern him; and we have
A Guy, a Beavis, or some true
Round Table knight, as ever fought
For lady, to each beauty brought.   (1030–5)

Their opponents were the constellations, cashiered for their wild lusts, whose dances expressed the now familiar Caroline opposition between monarchy and monstrosity. The Hydra, Dragon, Centaur, 'Goatfish', Gorgon, Crab, and 'Sagittar' were called down from the zodiac, and displayed as 'loathsome monsters and misshapen forms' (293, 297–8):

> They cannot breathe this pure and temperate air
> Where Virtue lives, but will with hasty flight
> 'Mongst fogs and vapours seek unsound abodes.
> Fly after them, from your usurped seats,
> You foul remainders of that viperous brood!
> Let not a star of the luxurious race
> With his loose blaze stain the sky's crystal face.   (392–8)

As in *Love's Triumph*, Charles was a royal knight chasing chimeras from his purified land, purging the air by his presence. A 'British Hercules', his paradise was free from serpents: 'These are th'Hesperian bowers, whose fair trees bear / Rich golden fruit, and yet no dragon near' (933–4, 944, 946).[108] These chivalric motifs culminated in the final scene, of Windsor Castle, symbolic home of the Order of the Garter. Charles had exploited the Garter's prestige as the prime order of knighthood. He had redesigned the badge, commissioned new plate for the chapel, revived the St George's Day ceremonials, and caused Van Dyck to design tapestries for the Banqueting House showing a Garter procession.[109] These were never woven, but by bringing Windsor to Whitehall *Coelum Britannicum* was the next best thing. Depicting the castle crowned by Religion, Truth, Wisdom, and Eternity, it identified Charles as the leader of British knighthood, whose piety validated national chivalry. As for the monsters, Momus consigned them to New England, 'which hath purged more virulent humours from the politic body than guacum and all the West Indian drugs have from the natural bodies of this kingdom' (387–90). With troublesome opponents expelled to the margins, whether monsters or men, the masque's purified Britain was guarded by a heroic king.

Probably spectators would have heard in these motifs a potent reworking of *The Faerie Queene*. With his combination of imperial ambition, pious aspiration, and erotic longing, Charles was a Red Cross Knight in modern guise. His arrival was announced by a Spenserean chorus of Kingdoms,

Druids, and Rivers, and the culminating action drew on reminiscences of the Garden of Adonis. Calling on time to cease, Eternity hymned the King and Queen's transcendence, as they looked down from Olympian height on the throng labouring beneath them:

> With wreaths of stars circled about,
> Gild all the spacious firmament,
> And smiling on the panting rout
> That labour in the steep ascent,
> With your resistless influence guide
> Of human change th'incertain tide.
>
> But, oh, you royal turtles, shed,
> When you from earth remove,
> On the ripe fruits of your chaste bed
> These sacred seeds of love;
> Which no power but yours dispense,
> Since you the pattern bear from hence.   (1121–32)

This apocalyptic compliment turned the couple into a Caroline Venus and Adonis. A 'royal pair' (1093) presiding over human aspiration and mutability, their union inspired their followers and mystically patterned their country's good. At the same time, reminiscences of Spenser allowed the eroticism underpinning their transcendence to be frankly acknowledged. The 'royal turtles' had a 'chaste bed' (1127–9), but the key to Charles's power was his biological productivity, a supremacy created by his knightly virility:

> … from your fruitful race shall flow
> Endless succession,
> Sceptres shall bud, and laurels blow
> 'Bout their immortal throne.   (1133–6)

Charles's budding sceptre punningly combined the symbolism of kingship with a phallic masculine fruition, providing the conclusive riposte to the old order's philandering and impotence. Jove's 'incests, rapes [and] adulteries' would be supplanted by Charles's decent but still potent apotheosis.

Coelum Britannicum moved Stuart masquing in an epic direction by co-opting radical reform and the national poem of chivalry into royal service. But this was no mere fantasy of lost Elizabethan glories: the masque recapitulated history in order to rewrite it, invoking immense archeological vistas to establish Charles's break with tradition. The whole evening opened with a scene of ruins like 'some great city of the ancient Romans, or civilised Britons' (38–9), which Jones compiled from prints of imperial buildings.[110]

The main entries were prefaced with a 'grave antimasque of Picts, the natural inhabitants of this isle' (879–82), performing an ancient war dance, after which a hill grew from the floor, like an accelerated version of geological time, bearing the British Genius and kings representing England, Scotland, and Ireland (883–9). The backward perspectives of history were compellingly evoked: telescoping the growth of seventeen centuries into a few moments, these images reconnected Stuart power to its remote origins and staged a teleology of dynasties. Yet the past was not seen nostalgically, but was invoked so that Charles could be liberated from it. The Roman past was glorious but ruined, linked to the superannuated mythology of the 'decrepit' heavens (1090); stupendously imagined, it could not be resurrected but was left behind by the Caroline power that supplanted it. So too the ancient kings attested to the historic British peoples' warlike character, but the central image was the emergence of a transcendental order without debts to the past. With Atlas' sphere erased and the old world returned to primeval blankness, a new self-legitimating dispensation appeared, a fresh start unencumbered by memories of the old. This revolutionary king's authority came not from the past or from Jove but from his own magnificent singularity.

James's early masques had stressed history's potential for anxiety (see chapter 5), but *Coelum Britannicum* took this motif to new heights, unleashing universal transformation and positively relishing the traumas of change. Charles's empire was without precedent, the apotheosis of the new. He disavowed pre-existing myths, eclipsed the heavens, and produced a sun 'in dead of night' (913). Although heralded by the 'ancient worthies of these famous isles', the masquers were 'modern heroes' unlimited by a historically specific identity, who represented a native culture suddenly at its moment of culmination and justifying itself by its deeds:

> Those ancient worthies of these famous isles,
> That long have slept, in fresh and lively shapes
> Shall straight appear, where you shall see yourself
> Circled with modern heroes, who shall be
> In act whatever elder times can boast
> Noble or great, as they in prophesy
> Were all but what you are. (856–62)

As in *Love's Triumph*, the masquers were their own example, unimpeded by the prior determinations of myth. The past from which they came was invoked in order to be exceeded, its prophecies fulfilled and heroes surpassed. Charles's rule was a moment of plenitude on which neither past nor future could improve, all times being collapsed into a marvellous here and now:

> Be fixed you rapid orbs, that bear
> The changing seasons of the year ...
> Make motion cease, and Time stand still,
> Since good is here so perfect, as no worth
> Is left for after-ages to bring forth.   (1087–8, 1094–6)

Although hubristic, this perfectly expressed Charles's disavowal of the chains and errors of the past. With the state re-founded and doubters consigned to outer darkness, the future belonged to his powerful, peaceful, and self-confident kingship.

When in *Love's Triumph through Callipolis* Jonson described the depraved lovers as antiquated 'pantomimi' (32), he was already intuiting what would become the dominant trope of these years: Charles as the arch-modernizer whose government was validated by an ideal of progress. *Coelum Britannicum* was the most audacious statement of this theme. It depicted Caroline Britain taking leave of a conflicted past and securing peace at home by convincing observers of Charles's vigour or, if necessary, by resorting to force. This would revive 'the politer arts and sciences' which – said Momus, in a characteristic repudiation of all preceding reigns – had 'not been observed for many ages to have made any sensible advance' (349–51). Such achievements depended on strong monarchy, focused in the person of Charles, whose credibility and kingly capital *Coelum Britannicum* displayed. And although hindsight has ironized these festivals, it is easy to see how their audiences, wearied by the conflicts of the 1620s and ignorant of the 1640s, would have been impressed by such triumphant images. Charles's early masques sought to propound his potency, presenting him as a vigorous and aspirational leader, and could hardly have been more impressive. As Salvetti said of *Coelum Britannicum*, it was 'truly royal', with 'the most lovely [scenes] that have ever been made in this realm'.[111] As a statement of royal power and visionary ambition, it could not have been improved upon.

Yet the ideological implications of this programme were worryingly divisive. *The Triumph of Peace*, addressing Charles from outside Whitehall, promoted a view of government as a reciprocal relationship between ruler and ruled, but the other Caroline masques left smaller space for negotiation. Charles's all-victorious kingship implied a top-down system with the monarch as perpetual conqueror, and required an enemy over whom his triumphs could be performed. The consequence was a reorientation of masque form along nakedly ideological lines, redrawing its customary structural hierarchies in terms of inner conviction rather than social order. James's masques, with their aristocratic masquers and plebeian antimasquers, were organized around social differentials, but Charles's drew sweeping divisions between the supporters and hinderers of kingship, with anyone who failed to acknowledge the power of his vision marked out as not quite 'one of us'. At the same time, the ritualism of Caroline ceremonial made the underlying direction of the regime's ideological sympathies clear. For all the masques' visionary dimensions, their theology was broadly rationalistic: Charles's success was measured in terms of secular achievements and celebrated with an orderly and harmonious liturgy. In this perspective, any obstacles to the reforming vision of the Caroline new way tended to get lumped together as varieties of fanaticism. It is hard to know whether this change was symptomatic of an underlying erosion of social consensus or whether the masques themselves, with their relish for a campaigning kingship, were helping to precipitate a new divisiveness. When *Love's Triumph* referred to its antimasquers as 'sectaries', it spoke volumes about the ideological differences on which the conduct of Caroline masquing had become premised.

One sign of the potential divisiveness of Charles's festival culture was the offence that was given by his willingness to dance masques on Sundays. *Love's Triumph* was danced on a Sunday, and the Earl of Carlisle received an anonymous letter pleading with him, 'being in so great grace and favour with his majesty', to intercede 'that no more masques should be upon the Lord's day, but on some other days'.[112] Whatever Carlisle's response, Charles continued to have Sunday shows. *Albion's Triumph* and *Britannia Triumphans* were danced on the Sabbath, and in 1640 Lady Carnarvon made it a condition of her participation in *Salmacida Spolia* that the masque should not take place on a Sunday.[113] Charles's lack of discretion was still being remembered in the Collier controversy of the 1690s, and was mentioned as a source of anxiety in Tom May's *History of the Long Parliament* (1647):

The example of the court, where plays were usually presented on Sundays, did not so much draw the country to imitation as reflect with disadvantage upon the court itself, and sour those other court pastimes and jollities which would have relished better without that, in the eyes of all the people, as things ever allowed to the delights of great princes.[114]

Yet there is little evidence of a sustained puritan campaign against masquing at this time. Indeed, May himself attended masques, and he implies that Charles's theatricals would have incurred no criticism had they been performed on any other day, while Carlisle's correspondent seems to accept that they were necessary to kingship. Prynne held that Henrietta Maria's acting made her a 'notorious whore', but public discomfort with Sabbath dancing did not produce substantial resistance to Caroline festivity. On the contrary, when *The Triumph of Peace* paraded through London's streets, the ordinary citizens thronged to see it.

It seems unlikely, then, that Charles's subjects shared the modern view that his masquing was a sign of political weakness. On the contrary, the masques were the showcase and platform for his ambitions. Nonetheless, this highly personalized form had vulnerable spots. It depended on Charles maintaining public confidence, and represented him in ways that implicitly pulled against each other. It situated him as both the nation's leader and its diagnostician, the embodied centre of the *polis* and the cure for its putative ills. At the same time, the masques' rationalist and visionary dimensions were in tension – their promotion of secular achievement and their sacramental view of monarchy – as were their images of triumphant nationhood and the exclusions and conquests out of which this triumph was created. Charles could not fulfil all these expectations at all times, and when his rule ran into difficulties their implicit contradictions became all too evident. As we shall see, this iconography worked so long as there was agreement about the objectives of government, and so long as Charles himself was not felt to be part of the nation's sickness. The rest of the personal rule would test the form to its limits when confronted by far more acute political difficulties.

CHAPTER 10

The Caroline crisis

On 24 February 1636, a royal party in fancy dress visited the Middle Temple to witness a masque given by the Prince d'Amour, the mock-ruler set up by the student lawyers to preside over their Christmas revels (actually a young Cornish gentleman, Richard Vivian). The group was led by Henrietta Maria and her principal ladies, the Marchioness of Hamilton and the Countesses of Denbigh and Holland, all dressed as citizens, attended by Mistress Bassett, 'the great lace woman of Cheapside'.[1] Also present were the Queen's young nephews, the Princes Charles Louis and Rupert, who were the guests of honour; her steward, the Earl of Holland; her master of horse, Lord Goring; and her servants Henry Percy and Henry Jermyn, 'somewhat disguised also'. Once in Middle Temple Hall, Charles Louis was welcomed by an ambassador sent from the Prince d'Amour, who promised him love and help from the lawyers:

> Thus whispered by my fears, I must impart
> For ceremony now what is his heart:
> Though with content of truth, I may report
> You have a numerous faction in his court.
> This palace, where, by sword then law maintained,
> His few but mighty ancestors have reigned,
> Is consecrated yours.[2] (2)

The show that followed backed up this protestation with a resolutely ardent military display. It opened with an antimasque of swaggering and debauched cavaliers 'of the cheaper quality, such as are said to roar, not fight' (4), all hanging uselessly around an alehouse, then replaced the alehouse with a temple of Mars and military camp, from which came eleven soldiers dressed in 'the old Roman shape', imitating those 'heroic Knights Templars, to which the palace of the Prince d'Amour was anciently dedicated' (8). These masquers were encountered by Cupid, who commanded them to prepare for love, and, after a second antimasque mocking five incompetent amorists – a Spaniard, Italian, Frenchman, Dutchman, and a 'foolish debauched English lover' (11) – they returned like 'a troop of noble lovers' (13). Finally, the scene changed to the Temple of Apollo, from which came twelve semi-naked savages bearing a banquet that declared them 'labourers on a fruitful soil, and what they carried did demonstrate a fruitful season' (15). As Charles Louis was offered the banquet, the priests of Mars, Venus, and Apollo invoked blessings, praying he would be 'rendered so divine / 'Twill be no sin t'implore your influence' (16).

The Triumphs of the Prince d'Amour (written by William Davenant, and probably without any input from Inigo Jones)[3] was remarkable as the most explicitly pro-war masque of the whole Caroline period. It was staged at a particularly sensitive moment in English affairs, and belonged to a group of festivals that strikingly disclosed the problems facing Charles's culture as the political climate began to heat up. Charles's nephews had recently arrived at Whitehall from The Hague, as part of a campaign to elicit more decisive support for their claim to the lands and electoral title forfeited by their father, the Elector Frederick V, in 1620 (he had died in 1632, and Charles Louis was now eighteen and Rupert sixteen). Charles Louis was received (wrote Lady Cornwallis) with 'a great deal of state in general, which hath given the world much satisfaction, and makes all men think that this journey will conduce much to the good of his affairs'.[4] He was popularly beloved for the sake of his mother, and was warmly embraced by courtiers who were enthusiasts for a more vigorous overseas policy oriented around ties of faith rather than strategic interest, and who felt there was a real chance of new counsels. The Venetian ambassador, Angelo Correr, reported that 'comedies, festivities, and balls are the order of the day here, and are indulged in every day at court for the Prince's sake, while all the greatest lords vie with each other in entertaining him'.[5] He saw the Queen's pastoral *Florimène*, and the Earls of Bedford, Essex, Warwick, Northumberland, and Craven – all advocates of war – were among those who gave gifts or banquets.[6] The court, said Correr, had 'not been in such a state for anyone for many years past'.[7] This would have been an opportune moment for decisive action, and for the first time since 1627 there were serious expectations of war. However, it was notable that Charles himself gave no masque for his nephew, who was present at Whitehall events only as an honoured guest. Instead, the entertainments that most enthusiastically canvassed the changing political options were staged in spaces away from the Banqueting House.

Charles Louis's arrival was timely because it followed hard on a revolution in international alignments.[8] The European situation was transformed in 1635 by two linked events, the Peace of Prague between Austria and

Saxony, and France's formal declaration of war against Spain. The Peace of Prague showed the futility of recent English diplomacy, for it undermined the German Protestant axis and confirmed Maximilian of Bavaria (who had seized the Upper Palatinate) as Elector Palatine. Since 1630 Charles had kept close to Spain in the hope that Madrid might pressurize Vienna into restoring the Palatinate, but the treaty showed this to be a pipedream. At the same time, by consolidating the imperial position, the treaty forced France into open alliance with the Habsburgs' enemies, redrawing the lines of conflict in simpler and more polarized form. Suddenly it looked as though England's best hopes for achieving its overseas aims lay with France, and the French lobby was galvanized. The Queen sent Walter Montagu to consult with Richelieu at Paris, and at Whitehall Charles met the French ambassador in the Queen's apartments. The diplomat Sir Thomas Roe argued Princess Elizabeth's case before him,[9] and in February 1636 the Privy Council debated proposals for a French league. Correr said that Charles Louis was welcomed 'by those who fervently desire a parliament' because his arrival would inevitably lead to war, as 'the King will not refuse to assume openly the protection of his nephew when he comes to ask it in person'; 'These ideas are occasionally maintained by the King and are constantly dinned into the Palatine's ears.'[10]

But Charles's view was rather different. He had no intention of becoming embroiled in a land war that would commit him to parliamentary subsidy. Rather, his great strategic asset was the Ship Money fleet. This set sail in May 1635, and, being financed by non-parliamentary levies, it gave him the ability for the first time to rattle the sword without becoming shackled to parliament. Although the fleet never saw any serious action, it was useful as a bargaining tool: it gave England control of the communications route along the Channel, which was crucial in any Franco-Spanish conflict, for Spain had no overland route of supply to its armies in Flanders. Sovereignty of the seas – that symbolic claim which Charles maintained by insisting that foreign ships vail their flags to English naval vessels – had practical force if it meant that England could hold the balance between the sides, purchasing alliances favourable to English interests while stopping short of commitment to land-based military action. At the same time, Charles doubted, perhaps rightly, that France really had much to gain from promises over the Palatinate. He feared a build-up of French power in Flanders and preferred to leave his options open, playing off potential allies against each other in the hope that he could persuade them to help return the Palatinate out of their desire to keep England friendly or neutral, and ultimately ensuring that English interests were represented in any general peace. In 1636, he sent out three separate embassies, to Paris, Madrid, and Vienna, partly as a delaying tactic and partly to see what could be wrested by diplomacy. It quickly became clear that nothing practical would come from Spain or Austria, and in early 1637 there was a strong expectation that England might at last join in a French alliance. But Charles dithered, and before events got that far, he was overtaken by the Scottish rebellion, and all prospects of overseas involvement collapsed. It is impossible to know whether Charles really intended the action that he talked about. Probably he simply hoped to take what diplomatic advantage he could from the change in international alignments, while holding back from any decisive breach with Madrid and avoiding any military commitments that were not capable of being disavowed. He was happy for the Palatine Prince to be offered command of a small fleet of ships, but the proposed objective was Spanish interests in the safely distant West Indies, and the fleet would sail under the Palatine flag so as to avoid an open conflict with Spain.[11]

It was all the more striking, then, that *The Triumphs of the Prince d'Amour* regaled Charles Louis with images of heroism by land. The conflict for which the masquers seemed so eager manifestly belonged to the European theatre. The priests of Mars sang of a pitched battle in which miraculously invincible knights chased the 'tame dejected foe' (7) from the field with irresistible slaughter, a scenario that took for granted the notorious horrors of the continental campaigns and was completely at odds with the nature and extent of naval action overseas that Charles was prepared to consider. The masque's strategic expectations were built into its title, which was written on the proscenium in French, and, as devotees of Venus, the knights implied their loyalty to the Queen, though it was a loyalty untrammelled by the dialectic of desire and self-restraint that was customary in Whitehall masques:

> Breathe then each other's breath, and kiss
> Your souls to union,
> And whilst they shall enjoy this bliss,
> Your bodies too are one.   (12)

Such amorous actions were far from the rarefied neoplatonism with which Henrietta Maria was usually associated, and projected a more recklessly engaged model of heroic action than Charles ever encouraged. This text entirely rejected the ideology of stoical restraint and calm self-control that figured in Charles's masques, putting in its place a zealous enthusiasm which threatened to put his lower-temperature kingship in the shade. Of course, such sentiments were licensed as expressions of love for one of the monarch's family. Devotion to Charles Louis helped to tie subjects to the crown, and the masque was distinctly lacking in confessional sentiment. The knights were motivated by the desire to win military and dynastic honour rather than by any fanaticism or religious principle. Still, it is tempting to conjecture that when the Prince d'Amour's ambassador expressed anxiety that his love for Charles Louis could be interpreted as treacherous by the Prince's 'jealous barons' (2), spectators might have caught a hint of a possible outcome for Charles himself. Certainly this show promoted expectations that, over the next eighteen months, he would struggle to fulfil.

There was always a risk in Christmas games like these that imitation of authority's forms would sometimes slip into parody and subversion. During the 1630s the Middle Temple authorities frowned on festive parliaments and mock kings for the impertinences that they always involved,[12] but the revival of Christmas revelry on an Elizabethan scale in 1635–6 must have been condoned from on high. The Prince d'Amour appointed household officials as well as a guard and two chaplains, dubbed knights, kept a favourite, and received petitions, in imitation of life at Whitehall. He was encouraged by aristocrats such as Holland and Pembroke (who lent him two cloths of state), and ran up expenses of over £2,000.[13] 'All this is done', said George Garrard, 'to make them fit to give to the Prince Elector'.[14] However, at times it must have been difficult to disentangle jest and earnest. The Prince's proclamations to his subjects included a command to imitate the pride of courtiers elsewhere, 'and especially in the court of Great Britain', a ruling he issued in parody of Charles's style, 'with the advice of our Privy Council only, not calling at the time (the haste of our occasions pressing us) our right trusty and well-beloved the states of our parliament'.[15] At some point he presided over a council that debated 'Queries of State' which skirted close to real-life issues, such as his right to levy money from his subjects, and whether it were better for subjects 'to replenish his coffers by a general contribution in parliament [rather] than by their denial to constrain him to raise money upon privy seals'. Amongst these 'Queries' were several that raised questions pertinent to the status of the Palatines as rulers deprived of their principality:

> Whether it derogate not from the power of an elected prince to hold his estate of sovereignty for any less time than term of life.
> Whether the peers that elect or a prince that accepts a limited dignity for lesser time commits the greatest error.
> Whether a man that hath ever commanded as an absolute prince can ever after his deposal or surrender conform himself to the obedience of a subject.[16]

These merely theoretical questions indicate how the lawyers' Christmas game was rooted in pedagogic exercises, but such matters of status were highly delicate, and had the potential to expose rifts between game and real life. Much of the protocol surrounding Charles Louis turned on the question of whether overseas ambassadors were prepared to call him 'Electoral highness' or not, since to do so would imply that they thought that Maximilian's claim to the same title was invalid.[17] Moreover, the Prince d'Amour had trodden embarrassingly on Charles Louis's toes over precedence. He wanted to maintain his pretence of kingship by sitting above him at the masque, but Finet would not hear of it, warning that 'when some speech fell to that purpose' the Elector had declared 'he would not be a prince in jest, as the other was'.[18] The Queen might casually put off majesty, but her nephew's sensitivity to insults showed just how uncertain his situation was. The Christmas prince intended to honour the Elector, but the blunder unwittingly exposed how much his fragile dignity depended on his uncle's willingness to act. Significantly, although Charles subsequently knighted the Prince d'Amour, he himself was not present at the Middle Temple show.

In the ensuing months Charles Louis' political prospects remained in suspense, though entertainments continued to come. Lady Hatton gave him two masques in March,[19] which have now disappeared, but may have been written by Henry Glapthorne, who had a family connection with her. Glapthorne did produce an enthusiastic speech of welcome for an entertainment 'at Mr Osbalston's' – perhaps Westminster School, where the headmaster was Lambert Osbaldeston (a man who would be vindictively persecuted by Archbishop Laud for supposedly slandering him). This speech greeted the Elector as 'a power inferior scarce to majesty' and prophesied that 'blest Delight / For this shall change her Tempe, and invite / The jocund Graces hither, to erect / Their palace here'.[20] Glapthorne's political outlook can be deduced from his lurid tragedy *Albertus Wallenstein* (c. 1635?), which dramatizes the recent death of the Bohemian general who had been the terror of Protestant nations, depicting him as a monster of cruelty and ambition. No less indicative was the command performance of the anonymous Elizabethan tragedy *Alphonsus, Emperor of Germany*, which Henrietta Maria arranged for the Elector at the Blackfriars in May.[21] This old-fashioned, sub-Marlovian play was evidently revived for the sake of its parallelism with his situation. Loosely founded on historical fact, it depicts a struggle for control of Germany between the Emperor Alphonsus, the imperial electors, and the heroic Englishmen Earl Richard and Prince Edward. Alphonsus is a Machiavellian Spanish tyrant and the electors are hopelessly divided over his claim to the crown. His fiercest enemy is the Palsgrave of the Rhine (Charles Louis's putative ancestor), and Alphonsus kills him, but the English nobles take revenge, Earl Richard eventually being elected the next emperor. The Queen also took Charles Louis to the Blackfriars to see Lodowick Carlell's preposterous tragicomedy *Arviragus and Philicia*, which, with its popular but dispossessed prince in conflict with a tyrannical usurper, similarly resonated with his troubles.[22] These plays, chosen for plots which echoed the Elector's situation, contrasted strikingly with his letters home to his mother complaining about the lack of effective progress.[23]

In the summer of 1636, as it gradually became clear that Charles's approaches to Vienna and Madrid were getting nowhere, the court visited Oxford, where they were welcomed with plays and disputations. But when they returned by way of the royal nursery at Richmond Palace, a special show was mounted for the six-year-old Prince Charles to show off his dancing. *The King and Queen's Entertainment at Richmond* is of unknown authorship but was probably arranged by the Queen's Chamberlain, the Earl of Dorset, whose wife was the Prince's governess and whose children also performed. The event focused almost exclusively on Henrietta Maria, addressing her as principal spectator, whereas Charles's presence was only passingly acknowledged. Doubtless this was because she was the Prince's mother, but it also reflected the show's desire to honour the outlook and personnel of the French lobby. A rambling, unfocused hodge-podge, it deliberately harked back to Elizabethan progress entertainments, opening with a country dance by rustics who wanted to show their devotion to the Queen but could not work out which person she was, then moving on to a pseudo-Elizabethan duet between a shepherd and shepherdess, who lamented that their love affair was crossed by family disapproval. The show's main subject was overtly Elizabethan: Prince Charles appeared in chivalric guise as the Spenserean knight Britomart, accompanied by a dwarf squire as in *The Faerie Queene*, and preceded by soldiers and a druid dressed 'after the old British fashion' (17).[24] He and his playmates wore Roman military costume, and were announced by a postilion who began speaking in Welsh, for that was 'the old British language' (23). Their squires presented shields bearing imprese to the Queen and, after the dancing, the closing song returned to the sentiments of the opening dialogue, by lamenting that once Henrietta Maria left Richmond the place would be plunged into darkness: 'Oh, then for pity haste you to come hither, / To keep those parts alive which else must wither' (30). Exactly the same tropes had been applied to Elizabeth forty years earlier.

The masque's politics were clear enough from its gratuitous mockery of 'one in the formal garb and habit of a Spaniard' who, reading 'some paper of instructions' and excessively absorbed by its 'punctilios and formalities', was ridiculed for his Pavlovian reactions to Spanish dance tunes, a pavane and a saraband (25). This was probably meant as satire on Spanish diplomacy and its endless delaying tactics. The masque's main antithesis, however, was between the Prince and an ancient British captain, whose warlike propensities had to be tutored by the Queen's civilizing grace. The captain was violent and profane, and enjoyed war's spoil and cruelty. He hoped Britomart would 'extend his arms as far as is / Or earth or sea, that he may think this kingdom, / As Alexander did the world's, / Too straight to breathe in' (21), and wanted him to rule by force rather than consent:

> Let him advise with us, and we will show him
> A nearer way how to be absolute:
> 'Tis but reserving a convenient guard,
> Some certain thousands of us 'bout his person,
> The thing is done; give us but pay enough,
> We'll warrant him he shall do what he list.

The Druid retorted that this counsel was fit for a soldier, but not a prince:

> If he [Britomart] hear us, we'll tell him
> A certain truth, that he which rules o'er slaves
> Is not so great as he that's king of free men.
> Oh, to command the wills of subjects rather
> Than bodies is an empire truly sacred,
> And the next way to rule in heaven itself!   (19)

The captain rebuffed this, and his 'tottered soldiers' came out in a wild dance, but seeing the Queen they quailed into 'a kind of timorousness' and offered her their weapons. In song, Apollo's priests 'attribute the taming of the soldiers' fierceness to the Queen's presence' (22–3).

The Richmond entertainment suggests how seriously conflicted were the court's war aims. Its Spenserean nostalgia, pastiche Elizabethanism, and praise of the Queen all served the outlook of the war lobby, and invoked a history reaching back through Tudor glories into a mythic British past. Henrietta Maria was invested with the mystique of her great predecessor, and by masquerading as a hopeful knight, Prince Charles projected an image of a warlike reversionary interest reminiscent of his dead uncle Henry. Yet the show's militarism was licensed by the Prince's youth, which conferred a pleasing air of fantasy, ensuring that its soldierly displays could not be taken for the real thing; and the move from British wildness to

Roman order imposed a narrative of civilization, with reckless militarism displaced by a more courtly chivalry that contained the soldiers' savagery. The Druid rebuked the captain for wishing to bring 'such harpies' as his soldiers into 'a peaceful kingdom':

> Sure you must have heard
> That this great king, to whom we now address us,
> Is such a one as, by his famed deeds,
> Poises the world about him, whilst he stands
> Unmoved in a firm peace of his own mind,
> As well as of his kingdom. (18)

Such language entirely reversed the aggressive emphases of the *Triumphs of the Prince d'Amour*, resurrecting the old Jacobean idea of Britain holding the balance between warring European nations. But how Charles could achieve 'famed deeds' while managing to keep everything in 'firm peace' was left unexplained, and the Druid's critique of the captain's plans for ruling by force was eerily reminiscent of the constitutionalist critique of the various legal expedients by which he was financing his kingship. Doubtless Charles believed he was truly a king who commanded the wills as well as bodies of his subjects, but the text had to finesse the tension between his confidence in the power of his mere presence to achieve his aims and the current pragmatic understanding of the need to strike up useful alliances. Probably the show was intended to reassure him that warmongering could be safely pursued, by containing the impact of military involvements within acceptable limits. Unfortunately, it also articulated the disabling contradiction in Charles's position, between his expectation that he could achieve his aims merely by threatening force and his reluctance to commit himself to action that would decisively back up those threats. It starkly demonstrates why, for all the expectations of these months, the promises made to his nephews remained unfulfilled.

The King and Queen's Entertainment at Richmond was shrewdly designed to appeal to Charles's sense of dynastic honour, since the Palatinate was important to him less for strategic advantage than for reasons of family reputation. However, in celebrating Prince Charles as the next heir, the performance implicitly acknowledged the downgrading of the Palatine cause as a policy imperative, for Charles Louis no longer had so significant a claim to the British throne, and the dishonour that his exile did to the crown had become less urgent. In the event, the Elector received none of the military or naval help that he sought. Early in 1637 a detailed *Manifest* was printed, setting out his wrongs, along with a short *Protestation* in Latin, English, and French, but negotiations with France were infinitely protracted as each side failed to manoeuvre the other into the war or peace that they wanted. Eventually Charles was diverted into the Scottish crisis, and plans for a fleet shrivelled into a proposal backed by the Earl of Arundel for Prince Rupert to lead an expedition to Madagascar, an idea his mother dismissed as 'one of Don Quixote's conquests'.[25] The only surviving traces of this are Van Dyck's portrait of the Earl and Countess of Arundel sitting by a globe turned towards Madagascar, and a poem by Davenant prophesying the island's conquest through the miracle of British kingship but giving little idea of what strategic advantage would be gained.[26] Charles's sense of dynastic loyalty was insufficient basis for an entire foreign policy, and the opportunity to demonstrate that he really meant what he said eventually slipped away. The princes left for home in June 1637, and the same year a satirical engraving, *The Kingly Cock*, was circulated, showing their uncle with his sword unbuckled and asleep in his chair, while the Spanish ambassador gave him toys and played tunes on his pipe, and the Palatine family and French king vainly attempted to rouse him.[27] It is one of several indicators that a significant gap had begun to develop between Charles's self-image as an honourable and decisive leader and the public perception of him, and it suggests how damaging to his credibility was his reluctance to translate his heroic aspirations into effective policy. A portrait of Prince Charles in armour was commissioned from Van Dyck in 1637 and widely copied,[28] but nothing came of the plans to celebrate his creation as a garter knight in 1638 with a public cavalcade through Westminster.[29] A birthday masque, written by Thomas Nabbes and depicting eight Princes of Wales as exemplary chivalric heroes, seems to have gone unperformed.[30]

Modern historiography no longer endorses the idea that in the 1630s Charles was fighting a rising tide of opposition and sinking progressively into disaster. The image the masques depicted, of a nation enjoying the benefits of peace and firm government, may have been idealized, but it did not radically misrepresent the reality, at least on the surface. Charles's foreign policy was hamstrung by his refusal to take any action that would shackle him to parliament, but down to 1637, when a revolt erupted in Scotland following the botched imposition of a new prayer book, he could indeed congratulate himself for presiding over a time of domestic stability and prosperity, in which his government had encountered few obstacles it could not overcome. This was largely because he had solved the cash problem, thereby removing his dependence on parliament. The peace policy produced an economic dividend, for it increased trade and brought massive customs revenues. With these behind him, Charles easily evaded the structural problem that had afflicted his father and beset his own government in the 1620s. By 1635 he was in surplus on his revenue, and the debt had started to fall; astonishingly, by the end of the decade, he had an income of nearly £900,000 a year, a large part of which came from Ship Money, which by 1640 had brought in £800,000.[31] He may have lacked the customary parliamentary grants, but Ship Money gave him an alternative means of taxation, and the absence of war meant that there was no pressing need for a new parliament. Had he not faced the ruinous expense of two military campaigns against the Scots, both of which failed, it is possible that he might have ruled independently well beyond 1640. As things were, the idea that his power was an illusion which the masques misleadingly encouraged him to entertain completely misreads the historical situation.

Of course, whether Charles's subjects had confidence in him to the degree projected in the masques is another question. Certainly there was more scope for political and ideological disagreement than the masques acknowledged, with their images of unity and uniformity, and to that extent they encouraged a misleading sense of achievement. The Palatine Prince's entertainments demonstrated how disruptive foreign policy was, and the occasions it presented for chipping away at confidence. Other problem areas were money and religion. The anxieties raised by the questionable legality of some of Charles's irregular financial measures have already been described (chapter 9 above); later in the decade, these focused increasingly on Ship Money. This was a defence levy normally paid by the maritime counties but which Charles extended to the whole country in 1634, asserting that it was necessary to his emergency powers and everyone benefited from its protection. Many felt that it was unconstitutional and undermined the security of property. Charles had in fact staged a consultation process with the judges, who declared Ship Money to be legal, and he successfully faced down resistance from the Earl of Warwick and Viscount Saye. Perhaps unwisely, he decided to make an example of a non-payer, John Hampden, and the trial which followed, running from November 1637 to June 1638, allowed the constitutional issues to be argued out in public, thereby politicizing the tax. The crown won, but only on a majority, with five of the twelve judges finding for Hampden (two on a technicality). This did not cause the levy to collapse, for Ship Money was collected energetically down to 1640; subjects recognized that, since its legal validity was proven, it could only be challenged in parliament. Nonetheless, as Richard Cust puts it, Hampden's case made it seem that a matter of legitimate leeway within the law had been stretched into 'a decisive extension of the royal prerogative'.[32] Ship Money became the poll tax of its day, the enormous short-term financial benefit being outweighed by the long-term political cost.

Equally fertile, in potential, were disagreements over religion, provoked by changes to English church practice promoted by Archbishop Laud. The Laudian church, with its preference for praying rather than preaching, for ceremonial order and doctrinal anti-Calvinism, represented an ecclesiastical settlement radically different from the reformed Protestantism to which James was wedded. Charles was a firm Protestant and set great store by his religious conscientiousness, but his doctrinal sympathies were with the anti-Calvinists, and he recognized the ideological advantages of Laud's liturgical changes, which he saw not as innovations but as the restoration of purer and more decent usages: increased reverence in ritual could instil reverence more widely. He endorsed the moves towards greater comeliness in doctrine, discipline, and architecture, and did not appreciate the depth of resistance to these changes and the anxiety that they bred. A fear that Catholicism was being reintroduced by the back door was intensified by the high-profile Catholic presence at Whitehall, especially around the Queen. So these years saw a series of disputes over altars, stained glass, kneeling for communion, and so forth, which, while individually minor, testified collectively to a growing climate of religious polarization. Laud's reforms cut away the theological middle ground, pushing religious moderates towards the radicals, and underlining the political link between bishops and crown. Since Charles believed himself to be defending the English church from popery, he was unsympathetic to complaints about creeping Catholicism, and took dissent as tantamount to disobedience. In the long term, the drive towards an unachievable religious uniformity was disastrous.

But these preconditions were transformed into real crisis only by a conjunction between Charles's religious preferences and the long-standing structural tension arising from the multiple monarchy. One problem for multiple kingship was that each of Charles's three kingdoms had a different religious settlement, and in the sixteenth century the Scottish Kirk had achieved a fuller reformation than the English Church. Charles wanted to engender unity between his churches, and having seen the Kirk in action in 1633, when he visited Edinburgh for his Scottish coronation, he determined to correct some of its (to him) unacceptable aspects. In July 1637, with characteristically little consultation, a prayer book reformed according to the English model was imposed on the Kirk, only to run into a storm of protest. This rapidly escalated into complaints about other aspects of church policy, including meddling English bishops, and Charles reacted with proclamations declaring his abhorrence of popery and his fidelity to the Scots religion, defending the prayer book, and threatening the protesters with 'high censure'.[33] But this threw petrol on the flames, for the Scots responded by drawing up a Covenant for the defence of religion, questioning the King's authority and implying the supremacy of statute, which within days was being subscribed to all over the north. In these events the gulf between Charles's vision of his church and his subjects' vision was dramatically exposed, but just as telling was the breakdown in political understanding between the constituent kingdoms. When Charles visited Edinburgh, he had been welcomed by pageants written by William Drummond depicting the 107 Scottish kings that ruled before him,[34] but for all his pretensions to Britishness, he was insensitive to Scottish sentiment. His perspective on northern affairs was shaped by a narrow circle of London-based Scots Catholics, and the ensuing negotiations failed to elicit Scottish trust.[35] Moreover, these faults had catastrophic consequences. Charles's inability to snuff out what turned into full-scale Scottish rebellion started a chain of events which eventually forced him to recall his English parliament, out of which came the collapse of English consensus, the spiralling crisis, and the drift into Civil War. None of these developments was inevitable in itself, but the conjunction of circumstances cruelly exposed his inflexibility and inability to engage in workable compromises.

These events form the context for the later Whitehall masques – *The Temple of Love* (1635), *Britannia Triumphans* (1638), and *Salmacida Spolia* (1640), each designed by Jones and scripted by Davenant – and explain why they exhibited the same contradictory combination of sentiments. The masques sounded an increasingly defensive note, insisting on the splendour of Charles's achievements while expressing surprise that these were not more generally appreciated. Although *The Temple of Love* preceded the onset of crisis, it was significant as the first masque to acknowledge that Caroline England might be something other than serenely untroubled. Sponsored by the Queen, it was a double masque with fifteen female dancers and nine of Charles's gentlemen headed by his cousin, the Duke of Lennox, and it was shown three nights running, and possibly a fourth. These multiple repetitions are usually put down to Henrietta Maria's desire to promote her platonic love cult, which was the main topic (see the discussion in chapter 5 above), but there may have been a wider agenda, for the masque was as crucial for the King as for her, its reflections on 'the queasy age' (B3)[36] being no less calculated to underwrite his virtues. With its admission that the times were 'queasy' and that some of the opposition Charles had to quell came from his own subjects, rather than being embodied in allegorical figures of disorder, *The Temple of Love* heralded a change that became more marked in *Britannia Triumphans* and *Salmacida Spolia*, shows that turned increasingly from the bare assertion of his prestige to justification of his values. In all these masques, the virtue of Charles's rule was no longer represented as self-evident or uncontentious. Rather, the tropes of reform and critical dialectic (so distinctive in earlier festivals) had disappeared, giving way to apology, vindication, and self-assertion. It was not enough for the King simply to be acclaimed: the basis of his rule had to be argued out. The state over which he presided was no longer represented as united, and Caroline government had to persuade, or overcome, an enemy within. The masques testified to changes that were eroding confidence in the royal image. If the state could no longer be represented as a happy consensus, it pointed to a public mood that was increasingly sceptical and confrontational.

The Temple of Love staged an act of royal vindication. It presented fogs of error, ignorance, and hostility, which cleared to reveal the pure truth embodied in the temple of the title and in the person of Henrietta Maria, playing the role of Indamora, Queen of Narsinga. This has been read by Erica Veevers as an allegory of the Queen's desire to promote Catholicism, supplanting a false temple with a true (perhaps alluding to her chapel at Somerset House, then under construction),[37] but the symbolism clearly had wide application. Divine Poesy, who announced Indamora, turned to Charles and linked the temple with Caroline rule more generally:

> Thou monarch of men's hearts, rejoice!
> So much art thou beloved in heaven
> That Fate hath made thy reign her choice,
> In which Love's blessings shall be given.
> *The Poets* Truth shall appear, and rule till she resists
> Those subtle charms, and melts those darker mists
> In which Love's temple's hid from exorcists.   (A4v)

While this permitted Platonic Love to be read as a vehicle for the Queen's civilizing power and code for religious illumination, from Charles's perspective it was a standard trope complimenting his secular government. Heaven's admiration for his virtue harked back to *Coelum Britannicum*, and Love's temple alluded to the bonds of unity which as King he expected to inspire, its 'blessings' being readily understood as the love that good kings could expect from their subjects. Such imagery was confessionally non-specific: as a religious motif, the preservation of temple and 'altar' (B3) pointed just as directly to Laud's beautification of the Church as to the recovery of a lost Catholicism. The triumphant emergence of the Temple of Love from the clouds of error must have appealed to King and Queen alike, and the masque's presentation of sovereignty stressed Charles's unchallengeable authority. His power, opposed by the mysterious magicians, was a

magical force, that blew back mists to reveal calm seas. With its strange
enemies, heavenly endorsement, and transcendental wisdom, the masque was
calculated to instil reverence for his kingship, as not subject to human
contest. The final song underwrote this by appealing to 'Charles the might-
iest and the best, / And to the darling of his breast, / Who rule by example
as by power' (Dɪv). This Janus-faced compliment – that the royal pair were
both good and powerful – left an ambiguity about the rationale for their
legitimacy. It implied that Charles was powerful because he was good,
instilling love by his life's example, but permitted the counter-perception
that his rule no less depended on force, or was no less forceful for being good.
Beneath the neoplatonic language was the merest hint of a threat. The
framework was ethical, but it instilled the idea that Charles was by his very
nature irresistible.

The figures attempting to impede his power were three magicians, of
'strange fashions' and 'deformed' in body (Bɪv), one fat, one thin, and one
with dog's ears.[38] Adepts who came from hell and were themselves 'sovereign princes' (Bɪv), they posed the usual generalized disruption to Caroline
peace, their mists hiding Indamora's temple and seducing 'the more voluptuous race / Of men to give false worship' (Bɪv) at their unchaste temple –
particularly the nine Persian youths whose affections they hoped to divert.
This fiction was distanced from reality by its fantasy orientalism and geographically non-specific setting, but was pinned to current concerns by one
pointedly topical allusion, included amongst the spirits raised by the magicians to 'infect the queasy age':

> To these I'll add a sect of modern devils,
> Fine precise fiends, that hear the devout close
> At every virtue but their own, that claim
> Chambers and tenements in heaven, as they
> Had purchased there, and all the angels were
> Their harbingers. With these I'll vex the world. (B₃v)

These men, when they arrived, were led by 'a modern devil, a sworn enemy
of poesy, music and all ingenious arts, but a great friend to murmuring,
libelling, and all seeds of discord, attended by his factious followers; all
which was expressed by their habits and dance' (Cɪ). Jones's otherwise very
full costume designs do not depict this character, but he was clearly meant
for William Prynne, whose *Histriomastix* (1633) had been taken as an attack
on the Queen's fondness for acting, and whose punishment was still comparatively recent news (he was pilloried, and lost his ears, in May 1634).
Moreover, Prynne was represented not as an isolated case of lunatic dissent

but, like Chronomastix in *Time Vindicated*, as leader of a 'sect' or faction. These were intended for radical Protestants, since the magician called them 'precise', and pointed up their fanaticism and self-righteousness. Not since *Pan's Anniversary* had a masque specifically attacked puritanism, and although the satire on Prynne was rooted in a particular case, it went further by treating him as symptomatic of a deeper malaise that needed ruthless suppression. So *The Temple of Love* implicitly acknowledged the existence of opinion hostile to Caroline government, which was not being easily dispelled. And by depicting puritans as 'devils' who 'vex[ed] the world', the masque helped to draw battle lines that would become increasingly significant, and to ingrain that habit of mind which historians have noticed in Charles, his tendency to take dissent for subversion and criticism for a challenge to his authority. Probably many in the audience would have regarded Prynne as a troublesome fanatic whose views were intolerable in an orderly state, but the underlying risk of such fictions was that they painted Charles into a corner where disobedient subjects came to be seen as potential enemies.

In this masque's analysis, the body of the state was ill – queasy – and in need of sovereign medicine. The illness was bred by the magicians, who regarded the sudden inexplicable onset of pure thoughts brought about by platonic love as itself a sickness. Platonic love they called the 'humorous virtue of the time', a 'humour [that] cannot last', and they resolved to 'infect' the age by calling up spirits of fire, air, water, and earth to unsettle its complexion (B2–3). The implied solution lay in Charles and Henrietta Maria, whose marriage was a perfect balanced unity, setting the 'pattern' for the whole nation (D1v). This image of Charles as the royal physician, patiently doctoring a sick state, would culminate in *Salmacida Spolia*, where it formed the governing idea. Here, though, it sat somewhat uneasily with those aspects of the text that spoke of Charles's irresistible force, and bespoke a tension – between Charles as benevolent monarch and as commanding autocrat – that in later masques became frankly disabling. The masque's discomfort with this conception was projected through the figure of an impudent Persian page who preceded the male masquers, proclaiming that because of platonic love his very flesh had turned to soul. He poked fun at his platonic masters for being 'so virginly, so coy, and so demure' that they dared not woo the ladies they came to dance with (C1v). The answer, of course, was not to get rid of the body but to regulate it rationally. In this perspective, platonics no less than puritans were 'a precise sect' (C1v) who needed to follow the King and Queen's superior example. Still, this model's shortcoming was its oscillation between exemplary admonition and outright suppression. The humours would be pressed down rather than discharged: the waves would be 'soothed' (C3), the lovers 'subdue[d]' (C3v), and their fires 'keep love warm, yet not inflame' (C4). While the image of the well-regulated body drew on time-honoured understandings of state-craft, it encouraged the notion that the only need was for peccant humours to be repressed. At the same time, it offered no hint of conciliation from the King's side, no notion that he had anything to do beyond displaying his perfect example. Since repressed impulses have a habit of returning, this position proved to be unhelpfully short-sighted.

Three years later, *Britannia Triumphans* was danced at the very moment that political cracks started to appear. In January 1638, Charles was attempting to contain the Scottish problem: his first proclamation on the prayer book was issued in December, and the Covenant was published in February. At the same time, Hampden's case was in full swing: the arguments were completed in December, and the judges' answers were awaited. The masque was designed to give Charles the strongest possible cultural support at this unprecedented political watershed. The proscenium before the stage featured figures symbolizing Naval Victory (a woman with a rudder and garland) and Right Government (a man with a sceptre and a book). Below were bound captives, and above were 'maritime fancies' (3),[39] such as tritons and children riding on seahorses and fishes. The subject, said the masque book, concerned Britanocles, whose 'wisdom, valour, and piety' had secured his own land and cleared the 'far distant seas, infested with pirates' (2). This alluded to the Ship Money fleet's multiple purposes: not only strategic control of the Channel but protection for merchant shipping against privateers in coastal waters, and the securing of Mediterranean trade routes against Moroccan piracy.[40] Fable and setting alike linked a show of strength on the high seas with a firm grip on recalcitrance at home, a theme which was implied in Jones's first scene (a view of London and the Thames dominated by St Paul's Cathedral, symbol of the unity of church and state) and powerfully reiterated at Britanocles' appearance, called forth by Fame:

> What to thy power is hard or strange?
> Since not alone confined unto the land,
>   Thy sceptre to a trident change,
> And straight unruly seas thou canst command!   (21)

As captain of the ship of state, Charles's accomplishments at sea exemplified his strengths as ruler. He was 'nature's admiral', whose arrival once again cleared 'misty clouds of error' (20), 'reducing what was wild' (25) into a decent order. The final scene was a calm seascape with a haven protected by a citadel, on which a 'great fleet', 'passing by with a side wind, tacked about and with a prosperous gale entered into the haven' (26). This was both a statement of real intent (Ship Money), a projection of political ideals (the fleet brought safely into harbour), and a metaphor for the arts of kingship. Judges who were not convinced by the arguments of Solicitor General Lyttleton might still be impressed by an insistence that Ship Money was bound up with national order.

Inigo Jones's iconographic version of the Ship Money arguments under-lined the increasingly dominant preoccupation with strength and legiti-macy, representing Charles as a vigorous and capable prince whose presence compelled his people's obedience. The ideological basis for this was argued out in the long antimasques that preceded Britanocles' arrival, which developed the justification for the ensuing apotheosis. These antimasques are highly revealing of the formal consequences of the narrowing political options with which Charles was faced, since they reacted directly to the need to manage the problem of dissent. They comprised an extended dialogue between Action and Imposture, discussing virtue, heroism, and right, and led into grotesque dances conjured up by Merlin, 'the prophetic magician' (8), followed by the arrival of the ancient hero Bellerophon mounted on Pegasus, and a burlesque chivalric interlude in which a knight and his dwarf rescued a damsel from a giant. Kevin Sharpe calls these speeches a 'debate' on the philosophy of rule,[41] but this rather overstates the discussion's openness. Rather, the dialogue set up an opposition between Charles's fame, exemplified by Action's reason, truthfulness, and magnanimity, and the besetting impudence of Imposture, whose presence interrupted Charles's celebration, tarnishing it with fantasy, scepticism, and contempt. The dialogue exposed Imposture's falsehood by assimilating him alternately to an anarchic libertarian populism and a gloomy and corrosive fanaticism.

Imposture spoke for two kinds of dissent. His first complaint against Action was the pyrrhonist one that everything was mere pretence. Whatever appearances were to the contrary, all men 'even from / The gilded ethnic mitre to the painted staff / O'th'Christian constable' (5) were only pursuing pleasure and self-satisfaction.[42] On this basis he credited no one's display of virtue, and held that any action which gave pleasure was good; his authority was Mahomet, who promised his followers women in paradise (6). These views, said Action, would appeal to gallants, usurers, and prostitutes. Imposture's other disciples were a 'rigid sect' of 'sullen clerks', 'disguised in a canonic weed' who 'by their reasons strict / And rigid discipline' impute a 'tyrannous intent to heavenly powers' (7–8). Their view was the opposite: that pleasure was worthless, good only came through denial, dancing and perfumes were sinful, and all the enjoyments that were free to beasts were denied to men. The anti-Calvinism of this satire was self-evident. Imposture offered two complementary moral attitudes – on one hand, pleasure-seeking anarchy, on the other, fanatical self-denial – and, in both, virtue was impossible, 'a mere name' (8). What this meant for the state, was illustrated by the masque with its grotesque entries raised up by Merlin and performed in 'a horrid hell' (10), showing the chaos that threatened when men were allowed to pursue their desires unchecked. Aside from four 'parasitical courtiers' (11), all the antimasquers were ordinary citizens enjoying pleasures such as ballads, performing apes, and vulgar music, and the culminating entries were a mountebank – parodying Charles's role as royal physician – and 'rebellious leaders in war': John Cade, Jack Kett, and Jack Straw, with soldiers whose apparel 'showed their base professions' (11). The citizens looked innocent enough, but the rebels raised the spectre of popular anarchy and rebellion, and Jones's costume designs also included sketches for Knipperdolling and John of Leyden, the 'kings' of the 1534 Anabaptist revolution in Germany.[43] These two are not named in the printed text, but the designs suggest the antimasques culminated with bogeymen figures, whose presence invoked fears of popular communism and apocalyptic millenarianism.

Against this nightmare scenario of populist revolt raised by a 'cozening prophet' (11), Action spoke for an ideology of virtuous heroism focused on an elite minority. He attacked Imposture for being 'most cheap, and common unto all' (4), and he was rescued by Bellerophon, a figure remembered for his valour in slaying monsters, who lamented the stupidity of men and accused Imposture of making music for 'the numerous world' to dance to 'when your false sullenness shall please' (12). Action put his faith in 'a few whose wisdoms merit greater sway' (8):

> There are some few 'mongst men
> That, as our making is erect, look up
> To face the stars, and fancy nobler hopes
> Than you allow, not downward hang their heads
> Like beasts to meditate on earth, on abject things
> Beneath their feet. (7)

All masques involved some social and intellectual hierarchy, with their opposition between privileged masquers and unprivileged antimasquers, but in *Britannia Triumphans* this social and numerical disparity became, for the first time, part of the political argument. It was the antimasquers' numerousness and stupidity that made them fearsome, whereas the masquers' superiority, and also their vulnerability, was proclaimed by their scarcity: a few good men outfaced by a mob, the 'prosperous, brave / Increasing multitude' (8). Here one senses the impact that events in Scotland were having on Caroline policy. The unsettling coalescence of dissent in two areas of government at once bred a crisis mentality that took criticism as subversion and calls for reform as a stalking-horse by which men might throw off royal government. In a proclamation issued early in 1639, before heading north with his army, Charles would claim he had treated the Scots with 'lenity and gentleness' but received only 'froward and perverse returns, notwithstanding all their specious pretences':

These disorders and tumults have been thus raised in Scotland and fomented by factious spirits and those traitorously affected, begun upon pretences of religion, the common cloak for all disobedience; but now it clearly appears the aim of these men is not religion, as they falsely pretend and publish, but it is to shake off all monarchical government, and to vilify our regal power, justly descended upon us over them.[44]

Although in January 1638 the military campaign was still some way off, the germ of this attitude was already present in the masque. The idea it instilled, that the age was not merely queasy but under attack from (in Merlin's words) 'the great seducers of this isle' (9), was helping to ingrain Charles's willingness to see a limited problem of government as an all-out challenge to royal authority. It made it seem as though not just national peace but his credibility as a monarch was under attack.

Britannia Triumphans did respond usefully to the crisis insofar as it made the case for the benefits of settled government on rational principles and showed Charles triumphantly riding out danger. He was a king with 'modern virtues' (19) – a point embedded in the 'mock romansa' (14) of knight, giant, and dwarf, a trivial parody of chivalry raised up by Merlin, which made his heroism seem altogether more stable and grounded. But the masque's conflicted attitude was implicit in the contradiction between its statements of confidence in him and the way that, nevertheless, it acknowledged those who continued to be unimpressed. As the fable's summary put it:

These eminent acts [of the King's] Bellerophon in a wise pity willingly would preserve from devouring time, and therefore to make them last to our posterity gives a command to Fame, who hath already spread them abroad, that she should now at home, if there can be any maliciously insensible, awake them from their pretended sleep, that even they with the large yet still increasing number of the good and loyal may mutually admire and rejoice in our happiness.	(2)

This double-edged paraphrase seems uncomfortably trapped between saying that Charles's virtue was visible to all and his critics were of no account, and that his virtue was apparent only to loyal worthies and his unpopularity was a real problem. The 'large yet still increasing number' of the loyal is at odds with the masque's conviction that most men are ignorant and the virtuous are a small minority, while the rhetorical aside expressing doubt that any could be 'maliciously insensible' to his fame denies that such people exist, while continuing to say that the masque is performed for their good; in any case, their indifference is only 'pretended', and hence not really significant. The problem is that the summary treats Charles as inherently glorious, but then cannot account for his critics' failure to admit it, other than by ascribing it to malice and disrespect. In this regard, it mirrors Charles's own bafflement with the Covenanters, insisting his authority over the Kirk was inherent, and making the crisis a test of 'whether we are their king or not'.[45] The non-negotiability of this position was signalled in the masque at the discovery of the Palace of Fame, on the balustrade of which were two figures, one symbolizing Science, the other Arms; and the repudiation of Spenserean chivalry in the mock romansa further underlined that the potential enemy was now not overseas but at home. Danced, provocatively, on a Sunday, the masque made a bullish response, facing down Charles's critics, and had the military campaign succeeded this might indeed have seemed justified. But its demonization of dissent as rebellion, the defensiveness with which it proclaimed Charles's competence, and its sensitivity to the vindication of royal honour were signs of entrenched attitudes that would be disastrous when, shortly afterwards, he found himself on the back foot.

Two years later, in January 1640, Charles and Henrietta Maria together danced the last masque of all, *Salmacida Spolia*. By this time Charles had experienced humiliating defeat in the north and was determined to regain lost ground, mount a second assault on the Scots, and reverse the unpalatable decisions taken at the Glasgow Assembly in the autumn; but he was painfully short of cash. He had, astonishingly, funded the 1639 campaign from his own resources – the first time an English king had ever gone to war without summoning parliament – but now he needed to raise a larger army and find funds to the tune of £1,000,000. In December, after much discussion, it was decided to call a parliament for April, the Privy Council reassuring him that these were circumstances in which his people could not fail to aid him. Secretary Windebank gave it as his opinion that, by doing so, Charles

might leave his people without excuse, and have wherewithal to justify himself to God and the world, that in his own inclination he desired the old way; but that if his people should not cheerfully, according to their duties, meet him in that, especially in this exigent, when his kingdoms and person are in apparent danger, the world might see he is forced, contrary to his own inclination, to use extraordinary means, rather than by the peevishness of some few factious spirits to suffer his state and government to be lost.[46]

Windebank's advice registers the discomfort involved in summoning the first parliament for eleven years, the last having dissolved in acrimony, betraying a tension between the insistence that this was an emergency moment and the uncertainty about whether MPs would indeed do 'their duties'. His words carry forward the anxiety of *Britannia Triumphans* about the state being riven with 'factious[ness]', expressing a scarcely veiled threat that if Charles did not get his way he would resort to 'extraordinary means' (perhaps help from Spain, which had been proposed by Strafford).[47] The sabre-rattling, then, was not only for the Scots. Nonetheless, many thought this was an opportune moment, a chance for Charles to rebuild his relationship with parliament. Clarendon later praised the Short Parliament's moderation, saying 'it could never be hoped that more sober or dispassioned men would ever meet together in that place, or fewer who brought ill purposes with them',[48] and in December Henry Vane expressed the general hopes:[49]

Although it may seem there are many reasons which might threaten some rubs and difficulties in the desired success of his majesty's gracious resolution ... yet there is great hope that *by his wisdom* all shall be overcome and carried so that so happy a meeting may be followed by a like conclusion, to the contentment and satisfaction both of the King and his subjects [my italics].[49]

Charles's wisdom was precisely that attribute which *Salmacida Spolia* represented as effortlessly overcoming his enemies.

Salmacida Spolia was unique in being a double masque, in which both King and Queen led the dancers. The principal spectator was Marie de' Médici, who since 1638 had been in England, somewhat reluctantly hosted by Charles; this arrangement suspended the usual convention whereby the masque staged a conversation between the royal lovers. With King and Queen dancing side by side, the element of compliment was removed, and the show was directed more emphatically at the political nation seated in the masquing house, the subjects whose support Charles needed to elicit at this juncture. The antimasque entries, too, were all played by minor courtiers. The masque was further unusual in its choice of dancers, for they had an uncommonly large proportion of men who in the months to come would emerge amongst the King's moderate critics or even opponents. Several, like the Duke of Lennox (a Scot), were loyal royalists who fought for Charles without hesitation, but the Earl of Newport had torn allegiances (he fought for Charles in 1642, but hated Strafford and joined the King's critics in the Short Parliament), Lord Paget was a waverer (he refused to fight the Scots in 1639, opposed Strafford and supported the religious reforms, but joined Charles at Edgehill, then made peace with parliament), and Lord Feilding was a firm opponent (he fought Charles at Edgehill, and ended up on Cromwell's Council of State). More strikingly still, the Earl of Lanark (another Scot) became secretary of state for Scotland shortly after the masque; he took the Covenant in 1644, and thereafter became a key mediating figure between Charles and his Scottish subjects.[50] Other masquers included the son of the Earl of Pembroke, who would side with parliament, and two sons of the Earl of Bedford, the leading moderate peer who was widely credited with persuading Charles to recall parliament, and who lived, says Conrad Russell, 'absolutely on the fault-line which was to divide the two sides'.[51] Intriguingly, Bedford's surviving papers contain extracts from *Salmacida Spolia*.[52] It is impossible to know whether the audience would have recognized these distinctions in 1640, for the underlying rifts in the court fabric only started to emerge as the crisis took hold, and all of these men had danced with Charles before. Still, their differences testify to the masque's complex political environment, and reinforce the impression Charles sought to convey of wanting to build bridges and appeal to men's loyalty across the developing divide. On the other hand, Karen Britland points out that the masquers who accompanied Henrietta Maria included several of her prominent Catholic ladies, whose presence reinforced the turn towards a pro-Spanish, hyper-Catholic position that she had taken since the failure of the French alliance.[53] Henrietta Maria responded vigorously to the prayer-book crisis, rallying support, appealing for a papal loan, and organizing Catholic contributions which, while financially useful, helped to create a political backlash. The masque dressed her and her ladies as Amazons, with plumed helmets and swords. It was a striking example of the masque's mixed signals.

Ostensibly, the theme was reconciliation. According to the ancient adages on the proscenium, 'Salmacida spolia', the spoils of Salmacis, were the fruits of victory won by persuasion, without bloodshed or sweat. This alluded to the fable of the Salmacian spring near the Greek colony at Halicarnassus in Asia Minor. So exquisite was its water that the indigenous tribes were drawn here to drink, and gradually fell into commerce with the settlers, by which their 'fierce and cruel natures were reduced of their own accord to the sweetness of Grecian customs' (76–7).[54] This myth of the harmonizing power of civilization (taken by Jones from Vitruvius)[55] was directly applicable to the crisis: it stated Charles's intention of subduing the rebels, but represented it as coming about by peaceful rather than warlike means. A second adage warned about the danger of Cadmian victories. This referred to Adrastus' siege of Thebes (founded by Cadmus), in which the city was saved but only at the cost of catastrophic losses on both sides: 'the allusion is that his majesty, out of his mercy and clemency approving the first proverb, seeks by all means to reduce tempestuous and sweet natures into a sweet calm of civil concord' (90–1). This conciliatory message was backed by figures on the proscenium depicting Commerce, Affection to the Country, and Forgetfulness of Injuries, though its implications were unsettling. The myth of Salmacis – a nymph who loved the boy Hermaphroditus and was fused with him while swimming in the stream – was more commonly understood as a fable of monstrous effeminization, and the tale of Greek settlers, when applied to Scotland, represented the Scots not as equals or fellow countrymen but as barbarians to be colonized. If this projected Charles's good intentions, it no less betrayed their underlying Anglocentricity.

Charles's role was pointedly conciliatory. He was not a triumphant Hercules, but Philogenes, lover of the people – perhaps harking back to his coronation medal, with its motto 'the people's love is the King's protection'.[56] The masque began with a tempest raised by a Fury, envious that 'the world should everywhere / Be vexed into a storm, save only here' (113–14), contrasted with a peaceful landscape presided over by the Good Genius of Great Britain. The Genius pleaded with Concord, who was threatening to depart, urging her to stay if only 'to please / The great and wise Philogenes' (160–1). Philogenes' virtues were forbearance in suffering his people's ingratitude, and his commitment to peace rather than force:

> Oh who but he could thus endure
> To live and govern in a sullen age,
> When it is harder far to cure
> The people's folly than resist their rage?   (176–9)

Curing the people's folly rather than resisting their rage suggested good intentions towards the new parliament, and cast Charles in the role of royal doctor, correcting 'the humours that increase / In [Britain's] full body' (119–20). The first of the twenty grotesque entries that followed was a Rosicrucian doctor, carrying ridiculous cures for pretended illnesses. The next scene showed a craggy route through inaccessible mountains, depicting 'the difficult pathway which heroes are to pass ere they come to the Throne of Honour' (284–5), and here Charles was revealed, surrounded by his lords, as the Chorus praised his forbearance:

If it be kingly patience to outlast
Those storms the people's giddy fury raise,
Till like fantastic winds themselves they waste,
The wisdom of that patience is thy praise. (345–8)

This underlined that Charles preferred to conciliate rather than avenge: 'Nor would your valour, when it might subdue, / Be hindered of the pleasure to forgive' (157–8). The final scene, of a great imperial city surmounted with crowds of deities and dominated by a huge bridge across a river, depicted the civilizing ideal as already achieved. It imaged Charles's aspirations as a version of the architecturally reformed metropolis that he was always ambitious to create, with the bridge anticipating that political connectedness for which the masque appealed. Still, there were limits to this accommodation, for the scene's design conveyed an inverted urban perspective, with imperial buildings in the foreground and vernacular architecture in the distance, as if London were being viewed from an idealized Westminster. It reversed the priority between centre and suburbs, and safely contained the city under the bridge's arches.[57]

The overt theme, then, was rapprochement, Charles's willingness to work positively with his people. Yet the masque as a whole showed few signs of compromise, for the pose of affection was everywhere in tension with distrust of the English and sabre-rattling for the Scots.[58] Charles's political determination was spelled out on the proscenium, with its figures of Resolution, Doctrine, and Discipline. These signalled at the outset that there was no room for manoeuvre over the Kirk, and Reason with a bridle embracing Appetite and children putting reins on a lion indicated that the desired political solution had to be firm government. For English subjects, peace was imagined as a return to traditional habits of amity. The prose narrative says that Concord and the Genius hoped to 'incite the beloved people to honest pleasures and recreations which have ever been peculiar to this nation' (173–5). This evidently referred to the *Book of Sports*: Concord and the Genius would instil social conformity by encouraging harmless pastimes of the kind protected by James in 1618, and again by Charles in 1633. For the Scots, the message was more dramatic. It is possible that Charles's appearance in the Throne of Honour was meant to allude to the up-coming parliament; from this perspective, the masque projected an image of unity and consensus with his political elites. Alternatively, the location of the Throne at the end of a 'difficult pathway' and amongst craggy mountains suggested his intention of returning northwards to subdue the rebels; and under the Throne lay tokens of inevitable conquest, military trophies and captives in chains. For all that the masque called Charles Philogenes, it made clear his willingness to achieve his objectives by force. Further, Jones said that his design for the difficult pathway was based on the grotto at Posillipo near Naples, a long tunnel famously cut through solid rock in Augustus' times (282–3). Like the prospect of a great city, it pointed up the link between technological achievement and political power. The Scots would be subdued by the twin imperatives of culture and empire.

So Charles's forgiveness was underpinned by the threat of what he could do were he so minded, his conciliation being limited by the conviction that his opponents' ultimate aim was to destroy kingly government. The masque displayed his qualifications for power, and expressed the real issue as being whether the King's or subject's will would ultimately prevail. As the Fury proposed, she would 'incense / The guilty, and disorder innocence' (121–2):

> The poor ambitious make, apt to obey
> The false, in hope to rule whom they betray,
> And make religion to become their vice,
> Named to disguise ambitious avarice.   (131–4)

In these terms, Charles's critics' complaints could only be understood as camouflage for rebellion, and the Covenant as merely a ploy. Moreover, Britland points out that Marie de' Médici's presence generalized the Scottish problem, for her troubles – an exiled queen whose blessings had proved 'too great to last' (294) – linked Charles's little local difficulty to a larger European crisis in which every royal regime was currently under stress.[59] The Fury would have brought such disruption into Britain, were it not for Charles's resolute kingship, and for his wife, daughter of Henri IV, 'the chief and best / Of modern victors' (304–5). Henrietta Maria's love for Charles reiterated Marie's effect on Henri, for her beauty had inflamed his valour and her 'Tuscan wisdom' taught him 'how to thrive' (308). This was a tribute to Marie's Florentine dynastic roots, but it also highlighted her daughter's increasing ascendancy as a policy-maker, and Marie's 'Tuscan wisdom' alluded unmistakably to the great master of statecraft, Machiavelli. In *Salmacida Spolia*, the partnership between husband and wife now functioned overtly as a metaphor for strong government. The dangerous female demon of the antimasque was answered by Charles's Amazonian queen, whose military dress and Machiavellian insight gave him the power necessary to assert his will. The closing chorus hymned their anticipated success in terms that were magnificently ambiguous:

> All that are harsh, all that are rude,
> Are by your harmony subdued,
> Yet so into obedience wrought
> As if not forced to it, but taught.   (455–8)

The crucial concession in Davenant's syntax – 'as if' – made this praise devastatingly open-ended. The language stressed harmony and education, but the grammar left it impossible to know whether Charles's unruly subjects were subjected willingly or unwillingly. Evidently those who would not be 'taught' would still find themselves being 'forced'. The crucial thing was for obedience to be restored, and Charles's will to be effected in both men's minds and their bodies.

What would have been the audience's response? The one suggestion of an alternative perspective to the King's lies in some verses 'to be printed not sung', included in the text before the third scene, 'inviting the King's appearance in the Throne of Honour' (309–10). We cannot now tell whether these lines were unperformed for reasons of space or tact, but if we wanted to identify an element of 'talking back' to Charles, they might seem likely candidates. Their meaning, though, essentially reiterated the rest of the text. They endorsed Charles rather than offering an alternative perspective, and urged him to go boldly through the difficult pathway, attacking 'o'erweening priests' for supposing that they knew 'distant heaven' better than he did (321–3) – presumably this meant the Scottish ministers whose preaching supported the Covenanters.[60] This suggests that at this moment of crisis many spectators saw the situation in similar terms to Charles, bearing out his expectation that an English audience would respond positively to calls for help and see the need for unity against the Scots. The masque projected values which many would have wanted to preserve: peace, royal honour, the economic, cultural, and political achievements of Stuart monarchy. But at the same time it struggled to contain the contradictions that lurked barely disguised beneath its surface. While striving to invoke trust in Charles as a benevolent monarch, it also represented him as a commanding ruler whose will must not be disobeyed. It acknowledged problems in his state, but put all the blame on the subjects' 'giddiness'. It stressed that his virtue qualified him to 'rule alone' (363), yet left him looking perplexed that his subjects were so ungrateful. These tensions were deeply disabling, for they undermined the masque's aesthetic unity and political coherence. If Charles's rule was so perfect, why were his subjects disaffected? And if he was confident about the 'beloved people' (173), why should the masque need to make intimidating gestures? By exposing the gap between Charles's pose of conciliation and his intention of ruthless action, the masque made the contradictions in his position starkly apparent: it was unable to reconcile the declarations of trust in him with the admission that confidence needed to be compelled. Affirming peace in military gestures, showing Britain as both serene and troubled and Charles as both loved and feared, it was profoundly implicated in the contradictory initiatives of this moment of crisis. Its affirmations of godlike control were disrupted on every level by strains that could not be effectively discharged.

Just two months after the second performance, the first parliament for eleven years convened, to be opened with a speech from Lord Keeper Finch that reads like a paraphrase of *Salmacida Spolia*. Finch appealed to the members for speedy cooperation and warned that Charles was determined to wrest back control of Scotland, while striving at the same time to insist on his fatherly love and preference for constitutional rather than warlike ways:

> Out of his piety and clemency [his majesty] chose rather to pass by [the Scots'] former miscarriages, upon their humble protestations of future loyalty and obedience, than by just vengeance to punish their rebellions … It is a course his majesty takes no delight in, but is forced unto it; for such is his majesty's grace and goodness to all his subjects, and such it is and will be to them – how undutiful and rebellious soever they are – that if they put themselves into a way of humility becoming to them, his majesty's piety and clemency will soon appear to all the world.[61]

Finch's hesitations between expressions of love for the people and a bullish insistence on the need to suppress rebellion exposed the confusions of royal policy. Charles could not pose simultaneously as forgiving father and as bringer of retribution, appealing for unconditional loyalty while determining on war and blaming his subjects for its consequences. For their part, Lords and Commons professed their willingness to serve but declined to advance money before they had discussed grievances. They refused Charles's suggestion to vote money first in order to see how accommodating he could be, even though Finch promised 'you cannot express so much dutiful affection … as he will requite and reward with graciousness'.[62] Instead, the debates came to focus on the matter at issue in the masque, the question of trust. Messages from the King pleaded 'If they will not trust me at first, all my business this summer will be lost, and before the year goeth about I must be trusted at last', but as Sir Francis Seymour for one put it, 'if he had satisfaction for Ship Money he should trust the King with the rest'.[63] The King expected the urgency of his needs to be self-evident, but parliament chose to insist that domestic grievances had to be attended to. Not surprisingly, Charles came to feel that he was again being obstructed by a few ill-affected individuals, and, signally lacking that patience which the masque boasted, he dissolved parliament after just three weeks. In a declaration published shortly after, he complained that he had acted 'with all the expressions of grace and goodness which could possibly come from him', and needed no mediator for the Scots other than 'the tender affection he hath ever born to that his native kingdom'.[64] But parliament was unimpressed by royal ultimatums and unwilling to be bounced into offering supply, while Charles's reluctance to negotiate and his expectation that parliament should promptly accede to his will undermined the pose of conciliation. The Short Parliament demonstrated, amongst other things, how little *Salmacida Spolia* had managed to instil that confidence which was its main objective.

Salmacida Spolia has often been treated as the ultimate example of courtly escapism, the futile magic of a dynasty trying to exorcise unpalatable political realities. In fact, it was far from being a fantasy, and the situation was far from desperate. Consciously designed for a moment of crisis, the masque sought to occupy the ideological high ground, voicing the King's desire for resolute action and dictating terms to parliament about the campaign that he wished to fight. Had Charles managed parliament more flexibly and convinced his subjects that the situation demanded unity, the outcome could well have been different, as it would also have been later that spring had his generalship been more effective; even two years further on, civil war was not necessarily the only possible outcome. The masque expressed Charles's conviction of the need to seize the initiative, his determination to impose his will, and his insistence that if the Scots continued to disregard his mercy any consequences would be their fault. It was a characteristic response by a king with an acute sense of honour, whose instinct in a tight corner was to demand obedience or fight. The trouble was that, given the erosion of trust, these were the wrong priorities. Charles needed to find middle ground and convince his subjects of his trustworthiness, but *Salmacida Spolia* testified more to his sense of injury and disappointment. It failed to register either the strength of feeling against the prayer book, or his subjects' reluctance to support a war in its defence, or parliament's determination not to let slip an opportunity of voicing its accumulated grievances. It attempted to rally support behind the King as the focus of unity, but on the basis that his case was unanswerable and that a failure to help was tantamount to rebellion. The point was not that Charles was in denial about the crisis, but that his attitude was insufficiently pragmatic. The masque's conflicted language showed how far short it came of accommodating the differences that it hoped to bridge.

Salmacida Spolia returns us full circle to the Christmas season of 1603–4. If *The Vision of the Twelve Goddesses* had brought Queen Anne down from rocky mountains to the pleasant English plain, *Salmacida Spolia* returned to the mountain, but now in a mood of uncertainty and discord. It marked the collapse of the British vision which for nearly forty years the masques had taken for granted. Charles's inability to see his Scottish subjects as anything more than barbarians to be colonized or crushed signalled a remarkable shortfall in the rhetoric of union: it evinced the dynasty's failure to make the British ideal a reality by ruling in such a way as to make all subjects feel they had a common stake in the state. Similarly, the gulf between *Salmacida Spolia*'s imagery of imperial civility and the tempests and rebellions threatened by the Fury no longer expressed Charles's kingship in terms of his inherent legitimacy. Rather, it drew attention to the act of will by which his rule had to be sustained: the monarch who easily dispelled all obstacles in his path was displaced by a more querulous and insistent figure, less confident about his accomplishments or about receiving the respect that ought to be his due. The political and cultural achievements of the Caroline state were undeniable. The ideals of stability, continuity, and transformation which Charles's festivals proclaimed were desirable, and by underlining their potential fragility the later masques showed how sensitized were their political antennae. But *Salmacida Spolia* failed to register the cost of these achievements, or to recognize that they had not taken root in all men's minds alike. It did not adequately acknowledge that Charles's values were ideologically contentious, and that the nation encompassed political and cultural differences that could not easily be pressed into uniformity. By presenting Charles's government as single-minded and not for turning, and by reinforcing his negative attitude towards dissent, it helped to precipitate that crisis of confidence which it had every intention of resisting. In the festive conversation, the two sides were increasingly talking past one another.

It is perhaps surprising that the later Caroline masques did not function in a more politically productive or enabling way. The spectacle of king and subjects dancing together in gracious accord and acknowledging their mutual dependence should have been a forum which fostered trust, particularly between the crown and those social elites who, for all their reservations about Charles's political objectives, had no wish to plunge the nation into crisis. Festivals such as *The Triumph of Peace* and *The Triumphs of the Prince d'Amour* demonstrated that masques could reach out to groups with different priorities, enabling genuine debate and rapprochement. *Salmacida Spolia*, with its array of moderate aristocrats and future opponents dancing beside the King, ought to have functioned as a statement of Charles's wish to build goodwill on all sides. But on the whole Charles failed to capitalize effectively on such opportunities. He was out of sympathy with the aims of those who wanted a more determined overseas policy: the conflicted representations of chivalry in the Palatine entertainments are very revealing on this score. At the same time, in representing domestic events, the Whitehall masques came to articulate more insistently a non-negotiable opposition between enthusiasm and order, turbulence and discipline, which reinforced rather than ameliorated society's tendencies towards polarization. In the event, the later masques may unwittingly have helped to precipitate that crisis of confidence which they had every intention of resisting. In this respect, the structural and ideological tensions of *Salmacida Spolia* are symptomatic of a wider political failure. Charles's inability to find effective common ground with his traditional masque audience is one of the pointers suggesting that 1640 was indeed a moment of political and cultural implosion.

Of course, no one had any answers to the problems of 1640; that is, in part, why the Civil War happened. The masque poets cannot be berated for failing to anticipate a conflict that no one could foresee, nor for pulling punches in front of a monarch prone to defensiveness and sensitive about his honour. In this regard, the masques were casualties of political rifts which had already started to open up, and which no form of discourse was able to bridge. The contradictions of the later masques, which seem so glaring in retrospect, are symptomatic of the common ideological blind spots of the moment. Yet one may still feel that there were missed opportunities here which, if seized with more determination, could have helped to enlarge the outlook from the throne. Charles clearly understood and sought to exploit the masques' political potential, but used them to reiterate policy aims that seemed increasingly divisive and partisan. So while the later masques did not retreat from politics, they could not supply a fund of constructive criticism which might have helped him reclaim his public image. Rather, they ingrained tendencies that were already inherent, and encouraged Charles to write himself into a corner where he lacked the space necessary to renegotiate his options. When the crisis came in 1640 and Charles found himself without those resources of goodwill and personal prestige which a different monarch might have inspired, it partly reflected a failure to make his festival culture work on a truly national and inclusive scale. And it was Charles's inability to use his culture to more constructive political ends that prevented the masques from liberating themselves from the aesthetic contradictions in which they had finally become embroiled.

When, in May 1640, the court felt so insecure that arms were brought over from the Tower, they were stored, with unconscious irony, in the basement of the masquing house.[65] With the onset of war, the court decamped to Oxford, and although the festival tradition trickled on there in an attenuated way, no more masques were staged at Whitehall.[66] In *A Deep Sigh Breathed through the Lodgings at Whitehall*, James Barlow described the state of the palace as it stood in 1642. He focused on the strange sensations aroused by the silence of the buildings and the freedom he now had to walk into the masquing house without being challenged, and explore spaces to which no spectators had previously had access:

Now you may go in without a ticket or the danger of a broken pate; you may enter at the King's side, walk round about the theatres, view the pulleys, the engines, conveyances, or contrivances of every several scene, and not an usher o'th'Revels or engineer to envy and find fault with your discovery, although they receive no gratuity for the sight of them.[67]

Barlow was astonished by the literally disenchanting effect induced by uncovering of the stage mechanics, the pulleys and contrivances that created effects which had once seemed so magical, and by the emptiness of the rooms, the loss of aura caused by the absence of social and topographical taboos that had previously been so absolute. If the court's power and the masques' iconicity came from the protocols that protected Whitehall's spaces – the boundaries, zones of privilege, and restrictions of access that Barlow's free-ranging exploration violated – the elaborate social codes that protected royal privacy had collapsed, leaving the court empty and the intruder free to move around territory where the old intricate hierarchies no longer applied. All that survived were the literal mechanics of kingship, the thrones, scenery, and engines that anyone could play with, and which now stood revealed as mere theatre. Parliamentarian pamphleteers such as George Wither were quick to point the moral:

The Queen will not have so many masques at Christmas and Shrovetide this year as she was wont to have other years heretofore, because Inigo Jones cannot conveniently make such heavens and paradises at Oxford as he did at Whitehall, and because the poets are dead, beggared, or run away, who were wont in their masques to make gods and goddesses of them, and shamefully to flatter them with attributes neither fitting to be ascribed or accepted of; and some are of opinion that this is one of the innumerable vanities which hath made them and us become so miserable at this day.[68]

Wither's remarks take revenge for the drubbing he had received in *Time Vindicated*, and tell us what masques looked like in retrospect, when they had come to seem so much hot air. But, however flimsy the masques appeared from the vantage of 1642, the political conversations which they had enabled down to this point had been complex and substantial. It was with the collapse of royal authority that they ceased to be any more than flattery and vain shows.

Were there other forms that court festival might have taken in this period, other ways that the court could have been celebrated which would have ameliorated rather than reinforced the difficulties that overtook it after 1637? The one festival text which no one would willingly let die is, of course, Milton's *Masque Presented at Ludlow Castle* (1634), known since the eighteenth century, rather misleadingly, as *Comus*. *Comus* belongs to a large body of provincial festivity which this book has not had space to consider, but which can be invoked briefly for the sake of the light that it casts over the tradition of masques at the centre. Although staged on the Anglo-Welsh border and focused on the tribulations of three adolescents, this was, as John Creaser has argued, a state occasion.[69] It was designed to inaugurate the service of the children's father, John Egerton, Earl of Bridgewater, as President of the Council in the Marches and Lord Lieutenant of the marcher counties, and was, therefore, part of Charles's campaign to tighten channels of government across the nation at large – hence, on one level, its allusions to rural riot and 'the shaggiest ruffian / That lurks by hedge or lane' (392–3),[70] the kind of masterless figure that Charles was determined to bring under control. Although Bridgewater was appointed in 1631, he did not arrive in Ludlow until 1634 and stayed only briefly, conducting most of the business through deputies.[71] Nonetheless, as a local magnate and privy councillor he was expected to tighten up the administration of the border, and the Council was reconstituted and expanded, bringing the energies of the personal rule into this outlying territory. The masque was danced at Michaelmas, the beginning of the law term and the day on which all members of the marcher administration would be assembled in honour of Bridgewater's 'new-entrusted sceptre' (56). However, the one circumstance which differentiates *Comus* from other state events is that it remained unprinted until 1637, whereas, had it been a Whitehall masque, it would, in this period, have moved into print as soon as it was performed. Instead, Henry Lawes's preface to the quarto privatizes what in 1634 had been political, by emphasizing that the (as yet anonymous) author had deliberately withheld it from view. Moreover, the 1637 text expands on the Ludlow version, presenting Milton's developing personal response to the polarizations of the 1630s. If in performance *Comus* was part of Caroline state culture, in print it became detached from it.

As one might expect, *Comus* was constituted in telling ways against the Whitehall masques, both participating in the masque tradition and distancing itself from it. In naming the character Comus, and locating the Attendant Spirit in the garden of the Hesperides (7), Milton probably had *Pleasure Reconciled to Virtue* in mind. Comus's identity as son of Circe and Bacchus, and his animal-headed followers, alluded to *Tempe Restored* (a masque in which Alice Egerton had danced). The final lines echoed, and revised, a passage in Townshend's masque,[72] and there were echoes of *Coelum Britannicum* too.[73] The song in which the Attendant Spirit announced his descent from the heavens resembled the opening of *The Fortunate Isles*, and the mythological carapace – Oceanus, Neptune, Tethys, Leucothe, Parthenope, and so forth – overlapped with the watery iconography of Jacobean masquing, with Sabrina's 'silver lake' (785) harking back to *The Masque of Blackness*. Comus's journey into Wales through the 'Celtic and Iberian fields' (80) reversed the trajectory across Celtiberia of Prince Charles in *Neptune's Triumph*, and recollected the Ethiopian dames' travels through Lusitania and Aquitania in *Blackness*. The encounter between Comus and the 'foreign wonder' (252), as he called the Lady, replayed the courtly dialectic of domestic and exotic, though with the twist that here the aristocrat was the estranged visitor, whereas Comus considered himself to be at home. Milton's pastoral mode picked up from the pastoralism of *Artenice* and *The Shepherd's Paradise*, albeit in a less bland manner, while the final scene, a view of 'Ludlow town and the President's castle' (878 SD), echoed the view of Windsor in *Coelum Britannicum* and anticipated that of St Paul's Cathedral in *Britannia Triumphans*. The Lady's song and speeches breached masque decorum, but followed precedents set in *Tempe Restored* and other non-court theatricals such as *Cupid's Banishment* (performed for Queen Anne at Greenwich in 1617 by members of a ladies' academy). On the other hand, the length of these speeches, which made the show more a cross between a masque and a play, and the downgrading of the dances to a position after the conflicts had been resolved, were significant adjustments to the usual masque economy. Comus was baffled by strenuous rhetoric and elevated song, rather than by the spectacular entries and symbolic choreography of court masquing.

Milton's fable presented an occasion for dancing, but critiqued revelry in terms similar to, though more searching than, *Pleasure Reconciled to Virtue*. Comus and his 'glistering' crew (112 SD) embodied uncivil, intemperate, and barbarous pastime in need of proper discipline. The Lady took their 'riotous and unruly noise' (112 SD) for the sound of 'ill-managed merriment':

> Such as the jocund flute or gamesome pipe
> Stirs up among the loose unlettered hinds,
> When, for their teeming flocks and granges full,
> In wanton dance they praise the bounteous Pan,
> And thank the gods amiss.   (191–6)

This has been read as a riposte to the *Book of Sports*, and Charles's encouragement of dancing rather than praying on Sundays,[74] though it is important to note that Milton was not against revelry per se, but mounted a defence of well-managed merriment. This was, after all, a masque which concluded with country dancing, though dancing of a decent and appropriately moderate kind: 'Back, shepherds, back, enough your play, / Till next sunshine holiday' (879–80). More striking is the Lady's riposte to Comus's arguments in favour of shameless pleasure-seeking, which moved beyond the local case into a general censure of an aristocratic culture characterized by prodigality and conspicuous consumption:

> If every just man that now pines with want
> Had but a moderate and beseeming share
> Of that which lewdly-pampered luxury
> Now heaps upon some few with vast excess,
> Nature's full blessing would be well dispensed
> In unsuperfluous even proportion,
> And she no whit encumbered with her store;
> And then the Giver would be better thanked,
> His praise due paid, for swinish gluttony
> Ne'er looks to heaven amidst his gorgeous feasts,
> But, with besotted base ingratitude,
> Crams, and blasphemes his Feeder. (716–27)

These utopian words reactivated the humanistic perspective on festival, in which a function of revelry was to allow ethical counsel to be voiced amidst the celebration. Couched as a critique of improper self-indulgence and social injustice, the speech cut far more forcefully than Jonson's masques ever had done against the association of aristocratic revelry with deliberate wastage. Arguably, the Lady's perspective was itself extreme. The masque lined up with virtuous temperance rather than abstinence, and was framed by the occasion itself, of harmonious feasting in honour of an orderly aristocratic family. In any case, since the Lady's arguments appeal for social equity to be extended to 'every just man', her words are less radical than they sound: the 'loose unlettered hinds' would not have qualified for such charity.[75] Nonetheless, these words spoken by a woman riveted to her chair, refusing out of principle to participate in a feast proffered in a princely hall, reversed many of the customary assumptions about the social value of revelry and the compliance of courtly ladies. It politicized the critique of conspicuous consumption, weighing prodigality against criteria of equity, and it allowed the celebration to be seen, for a moment, as if from the perspective of those normally excluded from the festivity.

Comus's immobilizing of the Lady was reminiscent of that frequent device from events such as *Lord Hay's Masque* and *The Lord's Masque*, where a masquer frozen into a statue was released by the warmth of princely favour. Here, though, the prince's power was conspicuous by its absence. Although Ludlow was the children's ultimate destination, their father had nothing to do with their release. This was achieved by the flower haemony – plausibly glossed by Cedric Brown as an allegory of the word of God[76] – and by the river goddess Sabrina, a deity belonging to the locality. Sabrina's chaste ceremoniousness mirrored the Lady's essentially private, inner heroism, manifested in outward immobility rather than triumphant self-display, and she had no connection with Bridgewater's authority or with the monarch's power extending from the centre. The magic that saved the Lady came from other sources than the King. Probably Lawes felt that Milton's text failed to honour the performers enough, since he adjusted it to give the brothers something to say in the final rituals, whereas Milton had left them silent and passive. But throughout the masque, the usual social and political courtesies were gently deflated. The boys were ambitious to prove themselves as heroes, but were rather helpless and had much to learn about the workings of evil, while their appeal to the stars to 'unmuffle' (318), which in another masque might have produced a scene change, went unanswered – rather like the Lady's song to Echo which, untypically, had no echoes in it. If other masques presented a formal contrast between vice and virtue, where an absence of dramatic interaction allowed the masquers' heroism to be assumed rather than demonstrated, Milton created a world of conflict in which virtue was not invulnerable and its foe was formidable. Comus was seductive as well as dangerous, and although the children made it to Ludlow, his palace remained standing and he lived to fight another day. With earth an untransfigured 'dim spot' (25) and the children playing themselves rather than idealized heroes, this show discouraged the two-way traffic that regularly elevated courtly masquers into gods; the Attendant Spirit's epilogue affirmed that 'feeble' virtue would need heaven to 'stoop' to her (907–8). The work of moral strenuousness could not be conveniently transcended. Rather, the 'crown that virtue gives' would come only to her 'true servants' (29–30).

Could the recruitment of Milton to the reservoir of masque poets have helped to counteract some of the shortcomings of Charles's festival culture as it fell into crisis? Although Milton's brilliant adaptation shows him to have been a keen student of festival forms, and his other work in the 1630s (such as the provincial masque *Arcades*) was by no means out of step with Caroline culture, it seems unlikely that he would have achieved or wanted a career as a masque poet at court. The adjustments he made at Ludlow were probably too radical to please at Whitehall, and the changes he incorporated in the masque's printed text only sharpened its already manifest conflicts. *Comus* showed no discourtesy to kings but put no faith in them either, and its scriptural frame of reference (such as 'the sun-clad power of chastity', added in the 1637 revision) was at odds with the classicizing language of most other masques. Where Jonson's masques were held together by the figure of the laureate poet – an avatar of the author himself, mediating usefully between king and Fame, upholding monarchy and upheld by it – Milton's equivalent was the good shepherd Thyrsis, a figure whose trajectory ran along a different path. And what Milton made of masque form pointed towards a different conception of festivity's social function, in which transfiguration and apocalypse were not rituals binding together courtly communities in this life but states reserved for the individual soul in the next. In his epilogue, the Attendant Spirit addressed the spectators not as members of a group but as if 'in private conscience',[77] using divisive language that undermined the expectation that masques should celebrate the individual's absorption into the social collective:

> Mortals that would follow me,
> Love virtue, she alone is free. (903–4)

Or, in words added to the 1637 text, 'List, mortals, if your ears be true'. Milton's 'if', with its separation between those who have ears to hear and those who merely belong to the world, marked a gulf between ritual affirmation and the private obligations of the individual that called into question all the usual assumptions underpinning festive forms. It was a gulf down which, as events accelerated, the whole festival tradition would eventually disappear.

A calendar of masques and entertainments, 1603–1641

This calendar lists all the principal masques and entertainments produced for royal or aristocratic audiences during the Jacobean and Caroline periods. It is intended to supply a chronological framework for this study, and is as comprehensive as possible within those limits. It includes all masques and entertainments for which texts survive, and lists the most significant of those for which we have documentation but no text.

To be included, a text must normally have involved a dramatic presentation and a dance, and must have been intended for a particular occasion. However, for the sake of completeness I have listed the most important of Henrietta Maria's amateur theatricals even when these were more properly plays rather than masques or entertainments. I have also included some aristocratic theatricals performed privately at great houses in London and the provinces. Welcomes which took the form of little more than an address to the monarch do not appear, nor do tilts, running at the ring, or barriers (except those which had specifically dramatic presentations), nor plays, dinner entertainments, or balls given as gifts from courtiers to king, queen or prince (unless they had specific masque elements). I have not attempted to accommodate the period's vast civic pageantry, except for occasions on which major theatrical presentations were made to royalty.

The list is based on the calendars of E. K. Chambers, *The Elizabethan Stage*, 4 vols. (1923), IV.75–130; G. E. Bentley, *The Jacobean and Caroline Stage*, 7 vols. (1953–68), VII.16–128; and C. E. McGee and J. C. Meagher's four indispensable compilations: 'Preliminary checklist of Tudor and Stuart entertainments', *Research Opportunities in Renaissance Drama*, 27 (1984), 47–126; 30 (1988), 17–128; 36 (1997), 23–95; and 38 (1999), 23–85. A few corrections have been made to these extremely full and very reliable sources, which are discussed in the notes. I also include some corrections to Orgel and Strong's *Inigo Jones: The Theatre of the Stuart Court* (1981), given this publication's importance as a reference tool. For ease of reference I list items year by year, though if this were a true court calendar it should more properly be divided according to season.

In listing performance venues I have not distinguished between the successive Banqueting Houses at Whitehall; but, briefly, the second Elizabethan Banqueting House survived until 1606; the first Jacobean Banqueting House functioned from 1608 and burned down on 12 January 1619; and Inigo Jones's Banqueting House was inaugurated with *The Masque of Augurs* in 1622 but was not used for masques after 1635, when the Masquing Room came into use. 'The Hall' is used to denote the great hall at Whitehall. The name of the queen's residence was officially changed from Somerset House to Denmark House on 4 March 1617, but as the older name continued to be used in the subsequent documentation I have referred to it as Somerset House throughout.

In the fifth column I have attempted to give some account of the sponsorship of each masque, although the nature of the documentation and the complex scenarios in which masques were performed mean that these designations are inevitably imprecise. The name in this column is usually the paymaster, or whoever otherwise footed the bill, but in the case of the royal Christmas and Shrovetide masques, which were usually referred to as sponsored by the dancer who led out the masquers, I have given the name of the principal performer where that information seems to be more relevant. It should be noted that masques described in correspondence as the 'queen's masque' or 'prince's masque' were often funded wholly or jointly by the king. For the Inns of Court I use the abbreviations IT (Inner Temple), MT (Middle Temple), GI (Gray's Inn), and LI (Lincoln's Inn).

In the final column I list ambassadors who were present in an official capacity. It should be remembered that often when ambassadors were not publicly honoured they were still present as private individuals. I list only the ambassadors of the major European powers, and take no account of diplomatic agents for such states as Florence and Savoy who, though present and sometimes actually invited, were not generally accorded the same privileged spectatorship.

Date	Title	Poet	Venue	Sponsor	Ambassadors
1603					
25, 27 June	A Particular Entertainment of the Queen and Prince	Jonson	Althorp	Sir Robert Spencer	
9<>16 October	Masque for Prince Henry[1] (lost)		Winchester	Queen	
1604					
1 January	The Masque of Indian and China Knights (lost)[2]		Hampton Court	Duke of Lennox	France
6 January	Masque of Scottish Lords (lost)		Hampton Court		France
8 January	The Vision of the Twelve Goddesses	Daniel	Hampton Court	Queen	Spain, Poland
15 March	The Magnificent Entertainment given to King James[3]	Dekker, Jonson, Middleton	London	The city; the Italian and Dutch merchants	
1 May	A Private Entertainment of the King and Queen	Jonson	Highgate	Sir William Cornwallis	
27 December	Hymen and the Four Seasons[4] (lost)		The Hall	Earl of Pembroke	Venice

[1] Omitted by McGee and Meagher; details in Chambers, *Elizabethan Stage*, I.171, Nichols, *Progresses of James I*, I.291, and *The Diaries of Lady Anne Clifford*, ed. D. J. H. Clifford (Stroud, 1990), 27 (this last is incorrectly linked by Meagher and McGee to *The Vision of the Twelve Goddesses*). The masque is unlikely to have been performed before 9 October as it is described in Sir Thomas Edmondes's letter of 17 October but passes unmentioned in his preceding letter (Nichols, *Progresses of James I*, I.290).

[2] Lennox's sponsorship is established by two letters of Dudley Carleton, 22 December 1603 and 15 January 1604, indicating that 'the Duke' organized the first masque and was responsible for inviting the French ambassador (see Chambers, *Elizabethan Stage*, III.279, and Lee, ed, *Dudley Carleton to John Chamberlain*, 55). Possibly Lennox also arranged the Scottish 'matachin' on Twelfth Night, to which the French ambassador was invited. Mary Sullivan (*Court Masques of James I*, 6n, 11) incorrectly interprets 'the Duke' as the Duke of Holst.

[3] There is some confusion about this in the literature: it is often called the 'Coronation Entertainment', but the coronation was held on 25 July 1603 and the formal entry was postponed until March 1604 because of plague. In reprinting his contribution in his 1616 *Works*, Jonson called it 'Part of the King's Entertainment in passing to his Coronation' but this is not how it is named in the 1604 texts.

[4] More usually referred to as *Juno and Hymenaeus*, but Carleton's description suggests that, although the setting was the Temple of Juno, Juno herself did not appear. The masquers were discovered seated in the temple and were brought in by performers representing Hymenaeus and the Four Seasons. See Chambers, *Elizabethan Stage*, III.377.

1605					
6 January	*The Masque of Blackness*	Jonson	Banqueting House	Queen	Spain, Venice
1606					
5 January	*Hymenaei*	Jonson	Banqueting House	The masquers	Spain, Flanders
6 January	*Barriers*	Jonson	The Hall		
24 July	*The Entertainment of the Two Kings*	Jonson	Theobalds	Earl of Salisbury	
27 July	*Solomon and the Queen of Sheba*⁵ (lost)		Theobalds	Earl of Salisbury	
31 July	*Royal Entry*	Marston and others	London	The city	
1607					
6 January	*Lord Hay's Masque*	Campion	The Hall	The masquers?	
22 May	*An Entertainment of King James and Queen Anne*	Jonson	Theobalds	Earl of Salisbury	
16 July	*Merchant Taylors' Entertainment*	Jonson	Merchant Taylors' Hall		
August	*The Entertainment at Ashby*	Marston and Skipwith	Ashby	Earl of Huntingdon	
1608					
10 January	*The Masque of Beauty*	Jonson	Banqueting House	Queen	Spain, Venice
9 February	*The Haddington Masque*	Jonson	Banqueting House	The masquers	France, Flanders
5<>11 May	*Entertainment at Salisbury House* (lost)	Jonson	Westminster	Earl of Salisbury	
1609					
2 February	*The Masque of Queens*⁶	Jonson	Banqueting House	Queen	France
11 April	*The Entertainment at Britain's Burse*	Jonson	Westminster	Earl of Salisbury	

⁵ The date of *Solomon and the Queen of Sheba* is suggested in a report that a masque was staged on the Sunday night (the two kings, James and his brother-in-law Christian of Denmark, were at Theobalds from 24 to 28 July). See H. N. Davies, 'The limitations of festival: Christian IV's state visit to England in 1606', in *Italian Renaissance Festivals and Their European Influence*, ed. J. R. Mulryne and M. Shewring (Lampeter, 1992), 325. For the possibility that it may all have been an invention by Sir John Harington, see chapter 5, note 3.

⁶ The extracts from Audit Office accounts referring to work on stage and scenery printed by Herford and Simpson (*Ben Jonson*, x.494) and repeated by Orgel and Strong (*Inigo Jones*, 1.131) do not belong to *Queens* but to *The Masque of Beauty*. See *Malone Society Collections*, 10.22.

Date	Title	Poet	Venue	Sponsor	Ambassadors
1610					
6 January	*Prince Henry's Barriers*[7]	Jonson	Banqueting House	Prince	Spain, Venice
31 May	*London's Love to Prince Henry*	Munday	London	The city	
5 June	*Tethys' Festival*	Daniel	Banqueting House	Queen	Spain, Venice, Holland
1611					
1 January	*Oberon, the Fairy Prince*	Jonson	Banqueting House	Prince	Spain, Venice
3 February	*Love Freed from Ignorance and Folly*[8]	Jonson	Banqueting House	Queen	France, Venice
1612					
6 January	*Love Restored*[9]	Jonson	Banqueting House	Prince	
30 August	*Entertainment for the King*[10] (lost)		Woodstock	Prince	

[7] For the ambassadors, see J. Orrell, 'The London stage in the Florentine correspondence, 1604–1618', *Theatre Research International*, 3 (1977–8), 165, 165. Chamberlain (*Letters*, I.293) mentions that the Queen was planning a masque at Candlemas or Shrovetide, and this is confirmed in HMC 75 (*Downshire MSS*), II.216, but it never came to anything (unless these are the first stirrings of *Tethys' Festival*). For the confusion over Inigo Jones's design for an elephant pageant, which Orgel and Strong date incorrectly to 24 March 1610 but which actually belongs to 1609 (*Inigo Jones*, I.176–7), see chapter 6, note 24 above.

[8] Orgel and Strong erroneously describe *Love Freed* as the Queen's Twelfth Night masque for 1610, put off for one year (*Inigo Jones*, I.229). This misinterpretation was probably created by an ambiguous remark of Percy Simpson's that the Queen's masque was 'originally planned for Christmas 1610' (*Ben Jonson*, X.527), by which he meant Christmas 1610–11, not 6 January 1610. Simpson's misleading comment summarizes information reported by the Venetian ambassador: *Love Freed* was intended to be danced early in the 1610–11 season (i.e. before the performance of *Oberon*) but was put off, first to Twelfth Night and then subsequently to Candlemas. The details are correctly given in Chambers, *Elizabethan Stage*, III.386 (though at IV.386 Chambers himself slips by calendaring the masque under 2 February). Notwithstanding these confusions, the Queen did in fact consider staging her own Shrovetide masque in 1610, though nothing came of it: see Chamberlain, *Letters*, I.293.

[9] Queen Anne was also preparing a masque for this season, but it was cancelled owing to the death of the Queen of Spain: see Chamberlain, *Letters*, I.316, 321. John Thorys (HMC 75, *Downshire MSS*, III.181) described this as a joint masque between Queen and Prince, with six men and six women.

[10] The devices are mentioned, without a specific date, by Chamberlain (*Letters*, I.379). The court was at Woodstock from 26 to 31 August, but this was probably the same event as the great feast on 30 August described by Sir William Cornwallis (Nichols, *Progresses of James I*, II.*462).

1613

Date	Masque	Author	Venue	Patron	Ambassadors
14 February	*The Lords' Masque*	Campion	Banqueting House	King	France, Venice, Holland
15 February	*The Memorable Masque*	Chapman	The Hall	MT & LI	
20 February	*The Masque of the Inner Temple and Gray's Inn*	Beaumont	Banqueting House	IT & GI	
27–28 April	*The Caversham Entertainment*	Campion	Reading	Lord Knollys	
4–8 June	*Entertainment at Bristol*		Bristol		
26 December	*The Masque of Squires*	Campion	Banqueting House	King	Spain, Flanders
27 December, 1 January 1614	*A Challenge at Tilt*	Jonson	Whitehall		
29 December, 3 January 1614	*The Irish Masque at Court*	Jonson	Banqueting House	King?	

1614

Date	Masque	Author	Venue	Patron	Ambassadors
4 January	*The Masque of Cupids*[11] (lost)	Middleton	Merchant Taylors' Hall	The city	
6 January	*The Masque of Flowers*[12]	Daniel	Banqueting House	Francis Bacon	France, Venice
3 February	*Hymen's Triumph*[13]		Somerset House	Queen	
10<>15 August	*Antimasque at Rufford*[14] (lost)		Rufford Abbey	Sir George Saville	

[11] Possibly two masques were involved: Stow's *Annals* refers to 'two several pleasant masques', and Middleton was paid for 'the late masque of Cupid and other shows lately made', although this last phrase could refer to his other civic entertainments from September and October 1613 (Chambers, *Elizabethan Stage*, III.443).

[12] It is usually stated that the ambassadors of France and Venice were present at *The Masque of Flowers*, on the basis of Sir John Finet's narrative. However, Finet's confusing and inconclusive account of the protracted negotiations surrounding this occasion leaves room for doubt, and Gabaleone's report implies that neither ambassador saw anything of the Somerset wedding celebrations (J. Orrell, 'The London court stage in the Savoy correspondence, 1613–1675', *Theatre Research International*, 4, 1978, 79, 82). Chamberlain's letter of 5 January, before the performance of *Flowers*, is uncertain about who will attend (*Letters*, 1.499).

[13] Sir John Finet gives a date of 2 February for *Hymen's Triumph*, but as John Chamberlain, writing in the very midst of the events, twice gives a date of 3 February he is more likely to have been correct (*Letters*, 1.504, 507).

[14] Erroneously dated by McGee and Meagher to August 1615. See *Malone Society Collections*, 6.III.

Date	Title	Poet	Venue	Sponsor	Ambassadors
1615					
6 and 8 January	Mercury Vindicated from the Alchemists at Court[15]	Jonson	Banqueting House	King	Venice
13 January	Ulysses and Circe	Browne	Inner Temple	IT	
19<>21 February	Spanish Ambassador's Masque[16] (lost)		Spanish embassy	Spanish ambassador	
1616					
1 and 6 January	The Golden Age Restored[17]	Jonson	Banqueting House	King	France, Venice
8 June	The Merchant Adventurers' Entertainment (fragmentary)	Jonson	London	Merchant Adventurers	
4–6 November	Civitatis Amor	Middleton	Chelsea and Whitehall	The city and Inns of Court	
1 November <> 31 December	Masque at Greenwich[18] (lost)		Greenwich		
25 December <> 6 January 1617	Christmas his Masque	Jonson	Whitehall	King	
1617					
6 and 19 January	The Vision of Delight[19]	Jonson	Banqueting House	King	France, Holland
17 January	Masque for the Earl of Buckingham (lost)		Middle Temple	MT	

[15] The ambassadors of Spain and Holland were also invited to *Mercury Vindicated* but questions of precedence at the masque forced them both to withdraw (Chamberlain, *Letters*, 1.569–70).

[16] *Letters of John Chamberlain*, 1.582.

[17] For the long-standing confusion over the dating of *Mercury Vindicated* and *The Golden Age Restored*, see the introductions to the texts in *The Cambridge Edition of the Works of Ben Jonson*. The ambassadors were invited to the first performance of this masque, but thinking Twelfth Night to be the more prestigious date they preferred to attend the second (Sullivan, *Court Masques of James I*, 237).

[18] *Malone Society Collections*, 10.27, 28. S. P. Cerasano and M. Wynne-Davies identify these payments with the performance of *Cupid's Banishment* at Greenwich in May 1617. See their *Renaissance Drama by Women: Texts and Documents* (1996), 76.

[19] For the ambassadorial presence, see Orrell, 'Florentine correspondence', 175.

Date	Title	Composer	Venue	Sponsor	
19 February,	*Balet de la revanche du mépris d'Amour*[20]	Mailliet	Somerset House		France
4 March?	*Lovers Made Men*	Jonson	The Wardrobe	Lord Hay	
22 February	*Cupid's Banishment*	White	Greenwich		
4 May	*Entertainment at Brougham Castle*	Campion	Brougham Castle	Earl of Cumberland	
6 August	*Entertainment at Houghton*[21] (lost)		Houghton Tower	Sir Gilbert Houghton	
17 August	*Masque at Woodstock*[22] (lost)		Woodstock	Prince?	
August or September					
1618					
1 January	*Masque of Amazons* (lost) (unperformed)		The Wardrobe	Lord Hay	
2 and 9 January	*The Wedding of the Farmer's Son*[23] (lost)	Jonson	Enfield and Theobalds	Earl of Montgomery	
6 January	*Pleasure Reconciled to Virtue*[24]		Banqueting House	Prince	Spain, Venice

[20] The title-page of this ballet claims it was danced 'devant la royne de la grande Bretagne. Imprimé à Londres ce 28. Janvier 1617', and Chamberlain records Queen Anne seeing 'a kind of masque or antique' presented by her French musicians at Somerset House on 19 February (*Letters*, 2.56). Assuming that the date on the title page is indeed that of performance (in itself an unusual thing), perhaps the text was published in advance of the staging, as was the case with some of the quartos of Jonson's masques in the 1620s (though the case is complicated by the possibility that the date might be given continental-style, and hence mean 18 January in England). The Works Accounts record a payment of £42 to Inigo Jones for erecting scenery for a masque for the Queen, and for renewing it before the masque was repeated for the King; and also that Anne gave James a feast on 4 March, at which a play was acted by 'Anthony Cossarre and his fellows the French comedians' (*Malone Society Collections*, 6.63-4, 10.27), which was probably, though not certainly, a repeat of the same performance (this was the occasion on which Somerset House was renamed Denmark House). See also M.-C. Canova-Green, *La politique-spectacle au grand siècle* (Paris, 1993), 222.

[21] See *The Journal of Nicholas Assheton*, ed. E. R. Raines, Publications of the Chetham Society, 14 (1848), 41-5.

[22] Unrecorded by Bentley, *The Jacobean and Caroline Stage*, and McGee and Meagher, 'Preliminary checklist of Tudor and Stuart entertainments', but see *Malone Society Collections*, 10.28.

[23] In Bentley this appears as two different entertainments, *The Marriage of the Farmer's Son* and *Tom of Bedlam* (*The Jacobean and Caroline Stage*, v.1372, 1422). But it is evident from the reports of newsletter-writers (PRO SP 14/95/11, 12 and 14) that only one entertainment was involved, which was danced at Enfield on 2 January then repeated for the King at Theobalds on 9 January.

[24] A problem is created by a payment in the Chamber Accounts for making the Banqueting House ready for 'three several masques' in December 1618 – January 1619, which suggests that more masques were staged in these months than are recorded here. F. P. Wilson and R. F. Hill (*Malone Society Collections*, 10.29) assumed that the cancelled *Masque of Amazons* was one of these, but this is impossible as it was intended not for the Banqueting House but the Wardrobe. Its sponsor was Lord Hay, who as Master of the Robes had control of the Wardrobe; it was prepared but cancelled as a result

Date	Title	Poet	Venue	Sponsor	Ambassadors
2 February	The Coleorton Masque[25]	Pestell	Coleorton	Sir Thomas Beaumont	
2 and 19 February	The Masque of Mountebanks[26]		Gray's Inn, and Banqueting House	Gray's Inn	
17 February	For the Honour of Wales[27]	Jonson	Banqueting House	Prince	
1619					
6 January, 8 February	The Masque of the Twelve Months[28]	Chapman	Banqueting House; The Hall	Prince	Venice, Holland, Bohemia
6 January <> 2 February	The Inner Temple Masque, or Masque of Heroes	Middleton	Inner Temple	IT	
22 April	Masque of Warriors (lost)		Dutch embassy	The 'Artillery men'	
30 December	The French Ambassador's Masque[29] (lost)		French embassy	French ambassador	Holland

of royal disapproval. However, three masques were staged in the Banqueting House across this season as a whole: *Pleasure Reconciled to Virtue*, *The Masque of Mountebanks*, and *For the Honour of Wales*. The last two were danced in February, but the simplest solution is to assume that, despite its date, the December/January payment refers to these three. See also note 26 below.

[25] For the attribution and auspices, see P. J. Finkelpearl, 'The authorship of the anonymous "Coleorton Masque" of 1618', *Notes and Queries*, 238 (1993), 224–6.

[26] McGee and Meagher say the King attended the first performance of *The Masque of Mountebanks* at Gray's Inn, but this is a misreading of John Chamberlain's letter of 7 February 1618 which says that the guest of honour was the Lord Chancellor, Francis Bacon (*Letters*, II.136). It should be noticed, from Chamberlain's letter of 21 February, that the Grayans had intended to bring their masque to court on 16 February (Shrove Monday) but were prevented from doing so since there was no time to rearrange the Banqueting House for the repeat of Prince Charles's masque the following evening (*Letters*, II.142). This shows that both *For the Honour of Wales* and *The Masque of Mountebanks* were danced in the Banqueting House, and bears onto the interpretation of the documentation discussed at note 24 above.

[27] Erroneously listed as 18 February by McGee and Meagher, 'Preliminary checklist of Tudor and Stuart entertainments'.

[28] For the identification and dating of *The Masque of the Twelve Months*, see M. Butler, 'George Chapman's *Masque of the Twelve Months* (1619)', *English Literary Renaissance*, 37 (2007), 360–400.

[29] See J. Orrell, 'Amerigo Salvetti and the London court theatre, 1616–1640', *Theatre Survey*, 20 (1979), 1–26 (5); and M. Butler, 'Jonson's *News from the New World*, the "running masque," and the season of 1619–20', *Medieval and Renaissance Drama in England*, 6 (1993), 153–78 (171, 173). Orrell is mistaken in describing this event as the first performance of 'The Running Masque'; 'The Running Masque' was first given by Buckingham a few days later in requital of the French ambassador's feast.

3, 4, 5, 7, 8, and 10(?) January; various dates in February	'The Running Masque'[30]	Maynard?	London and Suffolk	Marquis of Buckingham	France
6 January, 29 February	News from the New World Discovered in the Moon[31]	Jonson	The Hall	Prince	France, Venice, [Holland, Bohemia]
17 February	Masque at Saxham (lost)[32]	Crofts family	Saxham	Sir John Crofts	
February	The Prince's Masque (lost)[32]		Saxham	Prince	

[30] The repeat performances of the 'Running Masque' have produced confusion and are considered in full in my essay 'Jonson's *News from the New World*, the "running masque," and the season of 1619–20'. The first five London performances in January are all well documented, and the final performance at Somerset House on January 10 was projected but may have been put off due to the imminence of the progress into Suffolk (Chamberlain, *Letters*, ii.282; misreported as 9 January on p. 159 of my essay). However the Works Accounts record that a dancing-floor was laid at Somerset House 'for the Prince and noblemen to dance upon' during the period October 1619 – September 1620, which could have been for this occasion (*Malone Society Collections*, 10.31). Concerning the performances for the court at Newmarket we have only John Chamberlain's report (from London on 12 February) that 'the running masque ranges over all the country, where there be fit subjects to entertain it' (*Letters*, ii.288); but see additionally note 32 below. For text and authorship, see J. Knowles, 'The "running masque" recovered: a masque for the marquess of Buckingham', *English Manuscript Studies 1100–1700*, 8 (2000), 79–135.

[31] Incorrectly listed as 7 January by Bentley, 'Preliminary checklist of Tudor and Stuart entertainments', and Orgel and Strong, *Inigo Jones*. For the correct date, see Butler, 'Jonson's *News from the New World*, 155. For the venue, see *Malone Society Collections*, 6.119. The ambassadors of Holland and Bohemia were invited to the Shrovetide performance.

[32] The Crofts family entertained the court at Saxham (near Bury) on 17 February, but payments from the Prince's Wardrobe for this season also refer to 'his highness' masque at Berry' (see J. D. Knowles, 'Masques in the 1619–20 season', *Notes and Queries*, 237, 1992, 369–70), as well as a passing mention of 'his highness' masque at Newmarket'. Possibly, (1) these masquing costumes relate to the single occasion at Saxham (as Chamberlain's report that 'the King, Prince, and all the court go thither ashroving' could imply that there were performances or at least disguises both by hosts and by visitors (*Letters*, ii.288)); or (2) the court was entertained at Bury *and* Newmarket (NB: at some point the Prince sent a message back to London that 'the maskers' were to attend him at Newmarket (*Malone Society Collections*, 6.147–8)). I am inclined to suppose that the Newmarket and Bury payments refer to a single masque and that alternative (2) is the likeliest. Some of these could, of course, refer to performances of the 'Running Masque', although the Prince is not elsewhere listed as a performer in this and the Wardrobe accounts seem to imply a new set of costumes.

Date	Title	Poet	Venue	Sponsor	Ambassadors
4 March	A Courtly Masque Called the World Tossed at Tennis[33]	Middleton and Rowley	Denmark House	Prince	France; Spain, Flanders
5 August	Entertainment at Salisbury[34]		Salisbury		
1621					
6 January, 11 February	Pan's Anniversary[35]	Jonson	The Hall	Prince	France
8 January	The Essex House Masque	Chapman?	Essex House	Viscount Doncaster	France
13 February	Middle Temple Masque (lost)		The Hall	MT	Holland
3, 5, and 31 August <> 9 September	The Gypsies Metamorphosed[36]	Jonson	Burley, Belvoir, Windsor	Marquis of Buckingham	
>14 December	The Visit of the Nine Goddesses[37]	Carew?	Saxham	Sir John Crofts	
1622					
6 January and 5 May	The Masque of Augurs[38]	Jonson	Banqueting House	Prince	Spain, Venice

[33] For the date, see chapter 8, note 36 above.

[34] Apparently this was performed twice: see *Malone Society Collections*, 6.118. Masques were planned by Sir Edward Zouch for the King's visit to Woking, later in the progress (*CSPD 1619–1623*, 175), though there is no subsequent record of these.

[35] For the dating of *Pan's Anniversary*, see M. Butler, 'The politics of early Stuart pastoral: Ben Jonson's *Pan's Anniversary*', *ELR*, 22 (1992), 369–404. The French ambassador extraordinary attended the Twelfth Night performance, and the ambassadors of Spain and the Spanish Netherlands attended at Shrovetide.

[36] The date of the Windsor performance is uncertain, but is limited by the King's movements within this period. The likeliest dates within this ten-day period were the two Sunday evenings, 2 and 9 September.

[37] For the identification of this masque, see C. E. McGee, '"The Visit of the Nine Goddesses": a masque at Sir John Crofts's house', *ELR*, 21 (1991), 371–84. The date cannot be later than 14 December since James saw it before he returned from Newmarket to Whitehall, and he was already at Royston on 15 December (Chamberlain *Letters*, II.415, 417).

[38] There has been a doubt over the date of the repeat performance, created by a discrepancy between the reports of John Chamberlain (who says it was repeated on 5 May) and Sir John Finet (who dates it to 6 May). Bentley accepted Finet's date, but Chamberlain's is confirmed by Simonds D'Ewes (*The Diary of Simonds D'Ewes 1622–1624*, ed. E. Bourcier, Paris, 1984, 76). McGee and Meagher, 'Preliminary checklist of Tudor and Stuart entertainments', record a performance on 20 May, but this seems to be a ghost created by John Chamberlain's initial report that the repeat was to be delayed nearly a whole month (*Letters*, II.433).

19 January	*Time Vindicated to Himself and to his Honours*	Jonson	Banqueting House	Prince	France, Venice
18 November	*A Congratulation for the Prince's Return* (lost)	Maynard	York House	Duke of Buckingham	Spain
1624					
6 January	*Neptune's Triumph for the Return of Albion* (unperformed)	Jonson	Banqueting House	Prince	[Spain]
5 August	*A Sylvan Masque* (lost)	Maynard	Burley	Duke of Buckingham	
19 August	*The Masque of Owls*	Jonson	Kenilworth	Prince	
December<> March 1625	*The Theatre of Apollo* (unperformed)	Beaumont	Whitehall	Duke of Buckingham?	
1625					
9 January	*The Fortunate Isles and their Union*	Jonson	Banqueting House	Prince	France, Venice
Summer	*Royal Entry* (cancelled; lost)	Jonson and others	London	City of London	
20 November	*French masque*[39] (lost)		Whitehall	Queen's ladies	
1626					
21 February	*Artenice*[40]	Racan	Somerset House	Queen	

[39] Mentioned in a letter from Katharine Gorges to Sir Hugh Smyth, 7 December 1625, in Bristol Record Office; cited by Karen Britland, *Drama at the Courts of Queen Henrietta Maria* (2006), 32.

[40] Shrove Tuesday. Some ambiguities in the records raise the possibility that another masque was performed at Candlemas (2 February): Salvetti's 21 December dispatch mentions a 'masque of ladies' in preparation for Candlemas (Orrell, 'Amerigo Salvetti', 10), and on 1 February Sir Nathaniel Bacon was expecting 'the Queen's masque … in the manner of a play, she being a special actor in it' for 2 or 3 February (Bentley, *The Jacobean and Caroline Stage*, IV.548). But in most records *Artenice* is considered the main event of the season and Bacon's description certainly fits it exactly; Salvetti may be referring to a provisional date which was subsequently put back. Orrell, noting that the Venetian ambassador described *Artenice* as 'a pastoral followed by a masque' (*CSPV 1625–1626*, 345), suggests there may have been two planned events which were conflated on the day ('Amerigo Salvetti', 11), but this is a very cautious solution and the overwhelming weight of the documentation seems to treat the pastoral as the only event.

Date	Title	Poet	Venue	Sponsor	Ambassadors
5 November	The Discords of Christianity[41] (lost)		York House	Duke of Buckingham	France
16 November	Gargantua and Gargamella[42] (lost)		Somerset House	Queen	France
1627					
14 January	The Queen's Masque[43] (lost)		Banqueting House	Queen	Venice, Holland
1 May	May Day masque	Rachel Fane	Apethorpe		
15 May	The Departure of the Navy[44] (lost)		York House	Duke of Buckingham	
1628					
6 January	'The Running Masque' (unperformed?)[45] (lost)		Whitehall		

[41] For the subject, see Orrell, 'Amerigo Salvetti', 12. Finet, *Finetti Philoxenis*, erroneously dates this event to 15 November.

[42] The details of the subject are in a letter of 3 December 1626 printed by T. Birch, *Court and Times of Charles I*, 2 vols. (1848), 1.180, concerning 'the great masque on Thursday was sennight' i.e. 16 November. The date is correctly given with supporting citations by Bentley, *The Jacobean and Caroline Stage*, VII.62; the Chamber Accounts say that the occasion was the Queen's birthday (16 November: *Malone Society Collections*, 6.123). See also Orrell, 'Amerigo Salvetti', 12; Finet, *Finetti Philoxenis*, [192]. Orgel and Strong cite the letter from Birch but miscalculate the reported day of performance, attributing it to 24 November and thereby creating a fictitious occasion (*Inigo Jones*, 1.389). W. R. Streitberger's statement in *Malone Society Collections*, 13.96, that there was another masque on 26 November appears to be an error.

[43] Wrongly listed by Bentley as performed at Somerset House; he is misled by a costume list in *Malone Society Collections*, 2.332–4, which actually refers to the masque of 16 November 1626 (see Orrell, 'Amerigo Salvetti', 13). The Works Accounts record work done 'in the Banqueting House at Whitehall for a masque for the Queen's Majesty' (*Malone Society Collections*, 10.37; also 6.123; Finet, *Finetti Philoxenis*, 198–9; and Birch, *Court and Times of Charles I*, 1.185). Karen Britland tells me that NA LC 5/38 has a payment of £1,026 12s 3d made to the Earl of Denbigh in 1636 for 'divers necessaries by him furnished for the Queenes Masque performed at Xmas 1626'. Possibly the recently discovered masque fragments by Aurelian Townshend belonged to this occasion: see Britland, *Drama at the Courts of Henrietta Maria*, 225–8.

[44] For the subject, see Orrell, 'Amerigo Salvetti', 14, and Birch, *Court and Times of Charles I*, 1.226.

[45] Known only from a letter of 2 January 1628 (Bentley, *The Jacobean and Caroline Stage*, V.1404), projecting that a running masque was expected to take place shortly. See the following note.

24<>26? February	Inner Temple Masque[46] (lost)	Inner Temple and Whitehall?	IT
26 February	The King's Great Masque[47] (unperformed?) (lost)	Banqueting House	King
12 August	Queen's masque[48] (lost)	Wellingborough	
December	Unknown masque[49] (lost)	Banqueting House	

[46] The court was at Newmarket, and this masque, mentioned on 12 January as likely to happen at Shrovetide, may not have taken place (Birch, *Court and Times of Charles I*, 1.312). During December 1627 – January 1628, the Templars set up a Christmas Prince in festivities which culminated in a minor riot in the city on Twelfth Night (see Birch, *Court and Times of Charles I*, 1.311-13, and H. L'Estrange, *The Reign of King Charles*, 2nd edn, 1656, 70). These revels may have created the expectation that a masque would be taken to court, either on 6 January or at Shrovetide, and proceedings taken in the Court of Requests by John Stone, of the Inner Temple, against Francis Tippesley, masquing suit maker, describe an Inner Temple festivity of December 1627, for which 44 'whiffling suits' and 104 vizards were rented, and which the lawyers intended taking to Whitehall (quoted in Sullivan, *Court Masques of James I*, 172-3). However, no definite evidence survives to show that this was done.

[47] A 'great masque' is mentioned by Joseph Mead in a letter written from Cambridge on 12 January 1628. He describes a forthcoming Shrovetide masque by the Templars, 'over and besides the King's own great masque, to be performed in the Banqueting House by an hundred actors' (Birch, *Court and Times of Charles I*, 1.312). Preparations were made, since the Works Accounts refer to 'a new masque intended to have been performed' (*Malone Society Collections*, 10.38-9), and £1,200 was disbursed, including £500 for six masquing suits: McGee and Meagher, 'Preliminary checklist of Tudor and Stuart entertainments: 1625-1634', *Research Opportunities in Renaissance Drama*, 36 (1997), 44. But there is a surprising absence of eyewitness testimony, which makes it impossible to say with certainty that this festival was staged.

[48] See B. Ravelhofer, 'Bureaucrats and courtly cross-dressers in the *Shrovetide Masque* and *The Shepherd's Paradise*', *English Literary Renaissance*, 29 (1999), 75-96. Ravelhofer transcribes extracts from the accounts in NA LR 5/64-65 in her Ph.D. dissertation, 'The Stuart masque: dance, costume, and remembering' (University of Cambridge, 1999).

[49] Sir John Finet mentions that on 7 December he found the Banqueting House blocked with scenery 'formerly built for a masque', and further that this was 'a work of late and future use', implying that the show was to be repeated. This occasion is otherwise unknown, but the report is very circumstantial, and the Banqueting House was not likely to have been scaffolded for anything less than a masque. See A. J. Loomie, ed., *Ceremonies of Charles I: The Notebooks of Sir John Finet 1628-1641* (New York, 1987), 49.

Date	Title	Poet	Venue	Sponsor	Ambassadors
1629					
1630					
c. 1630	*Masque at Wiston* (lost)[50]	Suckling	Wiston	Earl of Cranfield	
1630<>1634	*Arcades*	Milton	Harefield		
1631					
9 January	*Love's Triumph through Callipolis*[51]	Jonson	Banqueting House	King	
22 February	*Chloridia*[51]	Jonson	Banqueting House	Queen	
1626<>1633?	*The Ballet of Vices and Virtues*[52] (draft; unperformed?)	Weckherlin			
1632					
8 January	*Albion's Triumph*	Townshend	Banqueting House	King	
12 January	*The Queen's Entertainment*[53] (lost)	Davenant?	Lord Goring's	Lord Goring	
14 February	*Tempe Restored*[54]	Townshend	Banqueting House	Queen	
October	*Masque 'in a country village'*[55] (lost)			Queen	

[50] See *The Works of Sir John Suckling: The Non-Dramatic Works*, ed. T. Clayton (Oxford, 1971), 28.

[51] It appears that *Chloridia* was kept in rehearsal with a view to a possible repeat performance in May, although the repeat probably never happened: see *Malone Society Collections*, 13.110, and Orrell, 'Amerigo Salvetti', 16.

[52] See L. Forster, 'Two drafts by Weckherlin of a masque for the queen of England', *German Life and Letters*, 18 (1964–5), 258–63.

[53] Reported by J. P. Feil, 'Dramatic references from the Scudamore papers', *Shakespeare Survey*, 11 (1958), 108. Possibly a masque was presented on 3 September 1634, when Goring again entertained the Queen with 'comedies, dancing, music, and other agreeable pastimes' (Bentley, *The Jacobean and Caroline Stage*, VII.94).

[54] Ravelhofer transcribes a tirewoman's bill covering the period April–June 1632, which mentions work done for the Queen and Lady Stamford's daughter (Elizabeth Grey) 'For a Masque' ('The Stuart masque: dance, costume, and remembering', appendix, 8). It seems likely, though, that this relates to *Tempe Restored*, in which Elizabeth Grey appeared, rather than some extra, unspecified, and otherwise unrecorded show.

[55] Not in Bentley; see *CSPV 1632–1636*, 15–16, and McGee and Meagher, 'Preliminary checklist of Tudor and Stuart entertainments, 1625–1634', 68. It is not clear that either of the other two documents reported by McGee and Meagher relate to this entertainment. The payment from the Works Accounts belongs to the period October 1631 – September 1632 (in which case there could have been another, otherwise unreported entertainment

1633				
9 January	*The Shepherd's Paradise*	Montagu	Somerset House	Queen
5 March	*Masque of Vices, Furies and Witches* (lost)[56]		Somerset House	Queen
21 May	*The King's Entertainment at Welbeck*	Jonson	Welbeck	Earl of Newcastle
15 June	*The Entertainment of the High and Mighty Monarch, Charles, King of Great Britain*	Drummond	Edinburgh	City of Edinburgh
1634				
3 and 13 February	*The Triumph of Peace*	Shirley	Banqueting House and Merchant Taylors' Hall	Inns of Court
18 February	*Coelum Britannicum*	Carew	Banqueting House	King
30 July	*Love's Welcome at Bolsover*	Jonson	Bolsover	Earl of Newcastle
17 August	*The Queen's Galanteria*[57] (lost)		Holdenby	Queen
August	*The Chirk Castle Entertainment*	Salusbury	Chirk	Sir Thomas Middleton

staged by the Queen at Nonsuch), while the payment to Lady Carnarvon's coachman probably relates either to *Albion's Triumph* or *Tempe Restored*. Further, although McGee and Meagher call this 'The Queen's Country Village Masque', the Venetian ambassador says only that the rehearsals were taking place in the country near to London (at Greenwich? Nonsuch?) – in which case the performance may have been at Whitehall.

56 Bentley assumes that this was a repeat performance of Montagu's *The Shepherd's Paradise*, first seen on 9 January and intended to be repeated on 2 February (*The Jacobean and Caroline Stage*, vii.86), but several different sources establish that it was a distinct masque, now lost. See J. Orrell, 'Productions at the paved court theatre, Somerset House, 1632/3', *Notes and Queries*, 223 (1976), 223–5, and 'Amerigo Salvetti', 18–19; *Malone Society Collections*, 10.44–5, 13,122; Loomie, ed., *Ceremonies of Charles I*, 138; Ravelhofer, 'Bureaucrats and courtly cross-dressers', and 'The Stuart masque: dance, costume, and remembering' (transcribing accounts in PRO LR 5/63–66).

57 Not in Bentley. See H. Berry, 'The Globe bewitched and *El Hombre Fiel*', *Medieval and Renaissance Drama in England*, 1 (1984), 225; Ravelhofer, 'Bureaucrats and courtly cross-dressers', and 'The Stuart Masque: Dance, Costume, and Remembering' (transcribing accounts in NA LR 5/63–66). The date of performance is established by Sir John Finet's report (Loomie, ed., *Ceremonies of Charles I*, 165–6).

Date	Title	Poet	Venue	Sponsor	Ambassadors
29 September	A Masque presented at Ludlow Castle (Comus)	Milton	Ludlow	Earl of Bridgewater	
December<> December 1643	The Christmas Antimasque[58]	Cavendish		Earl of Newcastle	
1635					
10, 11, 12, and 14 February[59]	The Temple of Love	Davenant	Banqueting House	Queen	
August	Pastoral (lost)[60]		Oatlands	Queen	
21 December	Florimène (antimasques only survive)	Townshend (antimasques)	The Hall	Queen	
1636					
January<> December	Mr Moore's Revels		Oxford		
24 February	The Triumphs of the Prince D'Amour[61]	Davenant	Middle Temple	MT	

[58] Not in Bentley. See W. Cavendish, Dramatic Works, ed. Lynn Hulse (Oxford, 1996), xi.

[59] James Knowles queries whether the fourth performance took place, since the only record is Sir Humphrey Mildmay's diary, which refers to seeing 'a pretty masque of ladies' on Valentine's day (Bentley, The Jacobean and Caroline Stage, III.217). However, there are no records of any other masque during this season. See Knowles, 'The faction of the flesh: orientalism and the Caroline masque', in The 1630s: Interdisciplinary Essays on Culture and Politics in the Caroline Era, ed. I. Atherton and J. Sanders (Manchester, 2006), 136 note 70.

[60] See Ravelhofer, 'Bureaucrats and courtly cross-dressers'; 'The Stuart masque: dance, costume, and remembering'.

[61] There is a confusion in the records, as James Howell predicted the performance would be on Tuesday 23 February, Herbert gives the date as 'Wensday the 23', and the published title page and George Garrard's letter both supply 24 February. The simplest explanation is that the performance was postponed one day (Davenant's preface says it was postponed at least once), and that Herbert got the day right but the date wrong. See Bentley, The Jacobean and Caroline Stage, III.219, VII.102.

Date		Author	Place	Host	
27 February	*Corona Minervae*	Kynaston	Covent Garden	Sir Francis Kynaston	
1 March	*The Palatine Prince's Masques* (lost)	Glapthorne?	Lady Hatton's	Lady Hatton	
12 September	*The King and Queen's Entertainment at Richmond*		Richmond	Prince	
December<> January 1637	*Masque at Ampthill*[62] (lost)		Ampthill	Countess of Devonshire	
1637					
1 January	*Masque of Ladies*[63] (lost)	Heywood	Hunsdon	Earl of Dover	
April	*Masque of Comus* (lost)[64]		Skipton	Earl of Cumberland	
1638					
7 January	*Britannia Triumphans*[65]	Davenant	Masquing Room	King	Morocco
6 February	*Luminalia*	Davenant	Masquing Room	Queen	
29 May	*A Presentation Intended for the Prince* (unperformed)	Nabbes			
1639					
1640					
6 January	*Masque at Bretby*	Cokayne	Bretby	Earl of Chesterfield	

[62] See Knowles, 'The "running masque" recovered', 91 and note 45. The dowager Countess of Devonshire was de facto head of the Devonshire branch of the Cavendish family.

[63] See Heywood's *Pleasant Dialogues and Dramas* (1637), 245–6. This was performed on 'last New Year's night', though it is not clear whether this definitely means New Year 1636–7. Hunsdon is in Hertfordshire.

[64] Not in Bentley. See M. Butler, 'A provincial masque of *Comus*, 1636', *Renaissance Drama*, n.s. 17 (1986), 149–73. I am grateful to Lynn Hulse for correcting my error over the date of the account-book entries (1637, not 1636).

[65] Erroneously dated as 17 January by Orgel and Strong (*Inigo Jones*, II.661).

Date	Title	Poet	Venue	Sponsor	Ambassadors
21 January, 18 February	*Salmacida Spolia*[66]	Davenant	Masquing Room	King	
January<> December	*Raguaillo d'Oceano*	Fane	Apethorpe		
1641					
6 January	*Masque at Knowsley*	Salusbury	Knowsley	Lord Strange	
31 December	*Antimasque of Gypsies*	Salusbury	Chirk Castle		

[66] The correct date of the second performance (Shrove Tuesday) was established by Wayne H. Phelps, 'The second night of Davenant's *Salmacida Spolia*', *Notes and Queries*, 224 (1979), 512–13.

Notes

INTRODUCTION

1. This study confines itself to Whitehall and other satellite spaces associated with the court. Although I occasionally refer to masques performed elsewhere, there is not room to do more than gesture towards the full range of festival activity in aristocratic households in London and across the provinces. This topic will be greatly illuminated with the appearance of James Knowles's forthcoming book on aristocratic culture.

2. *The Poems of James VI of Scotland*, ed. J. Craigie, 2 vols. (Edinburgh, 1955–8), II.134–45. See also Michael Lynch, 'Court ceremony and ritual during the personal reign of James VI', in *The Reign of James VI*, ed. J. Goodare and M. Lynch (East Linton, 2000), 71–92.

3. The imbalance towards the literary in discussions of masques has been considerably redressed by five recent studies: John Peacock's *The Stage Designs of Inigo Jones: The European Context* (Cambridge, 1995); Peter Walls's *Music in the English Courtly Masque, 1604–1640* (Oxford, 1996); Skiles Howard's *The Politics of Courtly Dancing in Early Modern England* (Amherst, Mass., 1998); John Astington's *English Court Theatre, 1558–1642* (Cambridge, 1999); and Barbara Ravelhofer's *The Early Stuart Masque: Dance, Costume and Music* (Oxford, 2006). The literary-critical bias of the present book is not intended to imply any disregard for the valuable perspectives developed by these scholars.

4. This practice cannot be definitely proven, but it seems likely that the verses 'to be printed, not sung' included with *Salmacida Spolia* (1640), and the list of medical cures promised by Wolfgangus Vandergoose, were intended for distribution at the performance. *Neptune's Triumph* (1624) opens with a figure representing the poet distributing 'the argument'. In the masque staged at the end of Middleton's *Women Beware Women* (1621?) the duke has a summary of the argument which he compares with the performed action. Ravelhofer (*The Early Stuart Masque*, 3–4) gives other examples of plays containing masques in which abstracts or summaries are distributed, including Middleton's *No Wit, No Help Like a Woman* (1611?) and Shirley's *The Constant Maid* (1638).

5. Jonathan Goldberg, *James I and the Politics of Literature* (Baltimore, 1983).

6. J. Leeds Barroll, *Anna of Denmark, Queen of England: A Cultural Biography* (Philadelphia, 2001).

7. *Ben Jonson*, VII.735.
8. K. Sharpe, *Criticism and Compliment: The Politics of Literature in the England of Charles I* (Cambridge, 1987). For the humanistic tradition of *laudando praecipere*, see O. B. Hardison, Jr, *The Enduring Monument: A Study of the Idea of Praise in Renaissance Literary Theory and Practice* (Chapel Hill, 1964), and E. W. Talbert, 'The interpretation of Jonson's courtly spectacles', *PMLA*, 61 (1946), 454–73.

1 SPECTACLES OF STATE

1. F. Bacon, *The Essays or Counsels Civil and Moral*, ed. B. Vickers (Oxford, 1999), 88.
2. See P. E. J. Hammer, 'Upstaging the queen: the Earl of Essex, Francis Bacon, and the Accession Day celebrations of 1595', in *The Politics of the Stuart Court Masque*, ed. D. Bevington and P. Holbrook (Cambridge, 1998), 41–66.
3. *Ben Jonson*, ed. C. H. Herford, P. Simpson and E. Simpson, II.250, 261, 334.
4. *The Times Literary Supplement*, 15 November 1941, 566, 569.
5. The obviously missing terms here are music and dance, but for an early treatment see D. Cunningham, 'The Jonsonian masque as a literary form', *ELH*, 2 (1955), 108–24. This shortfall has now been made up by the work of Peter Walls and Barbara Ravelhofer.
6. I refer here to Stephen Orgel's early work, exemplified by *The Jonsonian Masque*. Orgel's later studies are more emphatically politicized.
7. See E. H. Gombrich, *Aby Warburg: An Intellectual Biography* (1970); and R. Woodfield, ed., *Art History as Cultural History: Warburg's Projects* (Amsterdam, 2001).
8. See Strong, *Art and Power: Renaissance Festivals 1450–1650* (Woodbridge, 1984), 62, on festivity 'attuning' the court to 'a magical universe full of occult influences'. For Gordon, see the essays collected as *The Renaissance Imagination* (ed. S. Orgel, 1975), and the warts-and-all portrait in Frank Kermode's memoir, *Not Entitled* (1996), 173–94. The important work of Frances Yates on sixteenth-century festival had a similarly ambivalent impact: see David Norbrook's comments in *Poetry and Politics in the English Renaissance* (2nd edn, Oxford, 2002), 2.
9. An extract from *The Illusion of Power* is the lead item in the anthology *The New Historicism Reader*, ed. H. Aram Veeser (New York, 1994). For a rigorous, if unattractively hostile, critique of Orgel's work from a post-Marxist theoretical perspective, see Lawrence Venuti, *Our Halcyon Dayes: English Prerevolutionary Texts and Postmodern Culture* (Madison, Wis., 1989), 165–72. The other pioneering critic who should be acknowledged here is Louis Montrose, particularly for his essay 'Gifts and reasons: the contexts of Peele's *Araygnement of Paris*', *ELH*, 47 (1980), 433–61.
10. *Ben Jonson*, VII.209.
11. S. Greenblatt, *Shakespearean Negotiations* (Oxford, 1988), 65.
12. This problem is marked in the last chapter of Orgel's *The Illusion of Power*, and in Orgel and Strong's *Inigo Jones; The Theatre of the Stuart Court*, 2 vols. (1973).

See the discussion in chapter 9 below. Kevin Sharpe's *Criticism and Compliment* addresses the topic from a historian's perspective, though he goes too far the other way by taking the masques' idealizations at face value.

13. Lindley, *Thomas Campion* (Leiden, 1986) and *The Trials of Frances Howard* (1993); Norbrook, 'The reformation of the masque', in *The Court Masque*, ed. David Lindley (Manchester, 1984), 94–110, and '"The Masque of Truth": court entertainments and international Protestant politics in the early Stuart period', *The Seventeenth Century*, 1 (1986), 81–110; Marcus, *The Politics of Mirth: Jonson, Herrick, Milton, Marvell and the Defence of Old Holiday Pastimes* (Chicago, 1986); Barroll, *Anna of Denmark*, and the various essays by James Knowles cited in the subsequent chapters of this study.

14. It must be emphasized that this equivalence disappears in Orgel's later work. See 'Jonson and the Amazons', in *Soliciting Interpretation: Literary Theory and Seventeenth-Century English Poetry*, ed. E. D. Harvey and K. E. Maus (Chicago, 1990), 119–39; and 'Marginal Jonson', in D. Bevington and P. Holbrook, eds., *The Politics of the Stuart Court Masque* (Cambridge, 1998), 144–75.

15. Orgel, 'The spectacles of state', in *Persons in Groups: Social Behaviour and Identity Formation in Medieval and Renaissance Europe*, ed. R. C. Trexler (Binghampton, N.Y., 1985), 114.

16. *The Illusion of Power* (Berkeley, 1975), 39; slightly adapted from *The Jonsonian Masque* (Cambridge, Mass., 1965), 7.

17. See Alan Liu, 'The power of formalism: the New Historicism', *ELH*, 56 (1989), 721–73; and compare Rudolph Starn and Loren Partridge, *Arts of Power: Three Halls of State in Italy 1300–1600* (Berkeley, 1992), and Reinhard Bentmann and Michael Muller, *The Villa as Hegemonic Architecture*, trans. T. Spence and D. Craven (1993).

18. *The Illusion of Power*, 45. Thomas M. Greene argues a similar position in 'Magic and festivity at the Renaissance court', *Renaissance Quarterly*, 40 (1987), 636–59.

19. *The Jonsonian Masque*, 66.

20. J. Orrell, *The Human Stage: English Theatre Design, 1567–1640* (Cambridge, 1988), 228–44.

21. R. West, 'Perplexive perspectives: the court and contestation in the Jacobean masque', *The Seventeenth Century*, 18 (2003), 33.

22. Goldberg, *James I and the Politics of Literature* (Baltimore, 1983), 116.

23. Goldberg, *James I*, 65.

24. A. Sinfield, *Faultlines: Cultural Materialism and the Politics of Dissident Reading* (Oxford, 1992), 39.

25. Barroll, *Anna of Denmark*, 2.

26. For the French court, see Norbert Elias, *The Civilizing Process*, trans. E. Jephcott, 2 vols. (Oxford, 1978–82), and Peter Burke, *The Fabrication of Louis XIV* (New Haven, 1992).

27. Neil Cuddy, 'The revival of the entourage: the Bedchamber of James I, 1603–1625', in *The English Court: From the Wars of the Roses to the Civil War*, ed. D. Starkey (1977), 173–225. See also Cuddy's 'Anglo-Scottish union and the

court of James I', *Transactions of the Royal Historical Society*, 39 (1989), 107–24, and 'Reinventing a monarchy: the changing structures and political function of the Stuart court, 1603–88', in *The Stuart Courts*, ed. E. Cruickshanks (Stroud, 2000), 59–85.

28. R. G. Asch, 'Court and household from the fifteenth to the seventeenth centuries', in *Princes, Patronage and the Nobility*, ed. R. G. Asch and A. M. Birke (Oxford, 1991), 1–38; J. Adamson, 'The making of the ancient regime court', in *The Princely Courts of Europe 1500–1750*, ed. Adamson (1999), 7–41.

29. See Alan Stewart, 'Government by beagle: the impersonal rule of James VI and I', in *Renaissance Beasts*, ed. E. Fudge (Urbana, Ill., 2004), 101–15.

30. K. Sharpe, *The Personal Rule of Charles I* (New Haven, 1992), 262–73.

31. Adamson, 'The making of the ancient regime court', 17. See also *The World of the Favourite*, ed. J. H. Elliott and L. W. B. Brockliss (1999), especially the essays by Linda Levy Peck and Pauline Croft.

32. R. M. Smuts, *Court Culture and the Origins of a Royalist Tradition in Early Stuart England* (Philadelphia, 1987), 53–72.

33. The term is James Knowles's, from 'The "Running masque" recovered: a masque for the marquess of Buckingham (c. 1619–20)', *English Manuscript Studies*, 8 (2000), 81.

34. B. Donagan, 'A courtier's progress: greed and consistency in the life of the Earl of Holland', *Historical Journal*, 19 (1976), 317–53; B. Manning, 'The aristocracy and the downfall of Charles I', in *Politics, Religion and the English Civil War*, ed. Manning (1973), 35–80. As Groom of the Stool, Holland waited on Charles's bodily needs; this was one of the highest Bedchamber offices, though it carried no political influence.

35. B. Dale, *The Good Lord Wharton* (1901); G. F. Trevallyn Jones, *Saw-Pit Wharton* (Sydney, 1967).

36. E. Hyde, Earl of Clarendon, *History of the Rebellion and Civil Wars in England*, 6 vols. (1888), IV.278; C. Feilding, *Royalist Father and Roundhead Son* (1915).

37. See Adamson, 'The making of the ancient regime court', 33–9.

38. See Lauren Shohet, 'The masque as book', in *Reading and Literacy in the Middle Ages and Renaissance*, ed. I. F. Moulton (Turnhout, 2004), 143–68.

39. *Court Culture and the Origins of a Royalist Tradition*, 255. Smuts's view is critiqued in David Harris Sacks's insightful essay, 'Searching for "culture" in the English Renaissance', *Shakespeare Quarterly*, 39 (1988), 465–88.

40. Here this study differs radically from Kevin Sharpe's *Criticism and Compliment* (1987), which argues that moral and political counsel took priority.

41. For example, Stephen Orgel argues that 'nothing really happens' at the climax of *Blackness*, the true dramatic conclusion being reserved for *The Masque of Beauty* three years later (*The Jonsonian Masque*, 127–8). Clare McManus calls the masquers' transformation 'an unfulfilled promise' (*Women on the Renaissance Stage: Anna of Denmark and Female Masquing in the Stuart Court (1590–1619)* (Manchester, 2002), 11).

42. Terms from the preface to *Hymenaei*, 18–19; *Masque of Blackness*, 8.

43. *The Vision of the Twelve Goddesses*, 201; *Tethys' Festival* (in *Court Masques*, ed. Lindley, 1995), 32, 54.
44. Noticed by Norbrook, 'The reformation of the masque', 96.
45. Knowles, 'Jonson in Scotland: Jonson's mid-Jacobean crisis', in *Shakespeare, Marlowe, Jonson: New Directions in Biography*, ed. T. Kozuka and J. R. Mulryne (Aldershot, 2006), 264. Other examples include *The Wedding of the Farmer's Son* (1618), 'The Running Masque' (1620), *The Entertainment at Salisbury* (1620), and *The Essex House Masque* (1621).
46. The earliest example is *Gargantua and Gargamella* (1626), performed by Buckingham, Holland, and Sir George Goring; the best-known is *Tempe Restored* (1632), which had a major speaking part for Thomas Killigrew. A host of courtiers appeared in the antimasques for *The Masque of Vices* (1633), *Luminalia* (1638) and *Salmacida Spolia* (1640). Caroline masques also have prominent parts for the court dwarves.

2 RITES OF EXCLUSION

1. *Ben Jonson*, 1.136. Roe was a second-generation gentleman, whose family were wealthy citizens moving into court service. He was grandson to a lord mayor, and had a military career in Ireland and the Low Countries; the diplomat Sir Thomas Roe was a cousin. See *Ben Jonson*, 1.223–5, and John Donne, *Poems*, ed. H. J. C. Grierson, 2 vols. (Oxford, 1912), II.cxxxiii–cxxxv.
2. *The New Inn*, 4.4.177–88.
3. See the collation in Grierson's *Poems of John Donne*, 1.414–15.
4. See M. Sullivan, *Court Masques of James I* (1913), 9–17, and E. K. Chambers, *The Elizabethan Stage*, 4 vols. (Oxford, 1923), III.280–1. Briefly, the French ambassador, the Comte de Beaumont, had been guest of honour at *The Masque of Indian and China Knights* on 1 January, but he also wanted an invitation to the more prestigious Twelfth Night festival, an honour James was reserving for the Spanish ambassador, Don Juan de Taxis. In the event Beaumont was circumvented by a ploy: he was invited for Twelfth Night, but the masque was put off and staged for de Taxis two nights later. Beaumont subsequently claimed to have told James that if de Taxis had turned up on Twelfth Night he would have killed him (Sullivan, *Court Masques of James I*, 14).
5. As argued by Chambers, *Elizabethan Stage*, III.279. If the sword dance was organized by the Duke of Lennox, as seems likely from Sir Dudley Carleton's account (see note 2 to the appendix, 360 above), Jonson might have got in, since he may already by this date have established his friendship with Lennox's brother Aubigny. The dance of cherubs in *The Haddington Masque* (also an Anglo-Scottish celebration) was called a 'matachina' by John Chamberlain, just the word that Carleton used for the 1604 sword dance. See *Dudley Carleton to John Chamberlain 1604–1624: Jacobean Letters*, ed. M. Lee, Jr (New Brunswick, 1972), 54; *The Letters of John Chamberlain*, ed. N. E. McLure, 2 vols. (Philadelphia, 1939), 1.255.
6. See Barroll, *Anna of Denmark*, 66–8. Daniel dedicated the printed text to Lady Bedford, with an acknowledgement that she obtained the commission for him.

See *The Vision of the Twelve Goddesses*, ed. J. Rees, in *A Book of Masques*, ed. Spencer and Wells, 209–12.

7. *Ben Jonson*, VII.209.

8. On the context of this exchange between Jonson and Daniel, see the rather different accounts by Joseph Loewenstein, 'Printing and "the multitudinous presse": the contentious texts of Jonson's masques', in *Ben Jonson's 1616 Folio*, ed. J. Brady and W. H. Herendeen (Newark, Del.: 1991), 168–91, and John Peacock, 'Ben Jonson's masques and Italian culture', in *Theatre of the English and Italian Renaissance*, ed. J. R. Mulryne and M. Shewring (Houndmills, 1991), 73–94.

9. My text is based on *Ben Jonson*, XI.371, modernized and collated with Grierson's *Poems of John Donne*, 1.414–15. I have occasionally improved the punctuation for clarity. There are disputed readings at lines 12, 22, and 29 (where Grierson reads 'far more' rather than 'for more'). 'Popham' (16) is Sir John Popham, Chief Justice of the King's Bench from 1592 to 1607, who was notorious for his severity; 'Coke' is Sir Edward Coke, at this time Attorney General, who had recently prosecuted Essex and Raleigh for treason. The final line echoes Isaiah 42.3: 'A bruised reed shall he not break, and the smoking flax shall he not quench: he shall bring forth judgment unto truth' (repeated in Matthew 12.20).

10. Loewenstein, 'Printing and "the multitudinous presse"', 171.

11. Epigram 67. The poem is hard to date. Loewenstein thinks it celebrates Suffolk's appointment as Lord Chamberlain in May 1603 ('Printing and "the multitudinous presse"', 171–2). Since Jonson refers to him as 'Howard' rather than 'Suffolk' it could predate the grant of his earldom in July 1603. The Simpsons date it *c.* 1605–6, after the *Eastward Ho!* affair (*Ben Jonson*, XI.12). Ian Donaldson (Ben Jonson, *Poems*, ed. Donaldson, 1975, 37n.) and Colin Burrow (editor of Jonson's poems for the *Cambridge Edition of the Works of Ben Jonson*, gen. eds. D. Bevington, M. Butler and I. Donaldson) think it celebrated Suffolk's appointment as Treasurer in 1614.

12. J. Orrell, *The Theatres of Inigo Jones and John Webb* (Cambridge, 1985), 134–43. I am indebted to the late John Orrell for detailed advice about the interiors of Stuart masquing spaces. Many references in these two paragraphs come from my correspondence with him.

13. It is mentioned by the chaplain to the Venetian embassy, Orazio Busino, in his eyewitness account of *Pleasure Reconciled to Virtue* (1618).

14. NA E351/3243. See also HMC 75 (Downshire MSS), III.I.

15. NA E351/3255.

16. Orgel and Strong, *Inigo Jones*, II.695.

17. S. Thurley, *Whitehall Palace* (New Haven, 1999), 82; Orrell, *Theatres of Inigo Jones*, 151.

18. Orgel and Strong, *Inigo Jones*, I.282.

19. This is John Orrell's figure (private correspondence). John Astington estimates the capacity at 1,300 spectators: *English Court Theatre 1558–1642* (Cambridge, 1999), 163.

20. See J. M. Saslow, *The Medici Wedding of 1589* (New Haven, 1996), 150. At 180 feet by 65 feet, the Uffizi theatre was more spacious than the Banqueting House; the auditorium alone was 130 feet long (Saslow, 79). Many contemporary estimates of audience numbers are wildly exaggerated. In 1608 the French ambassador Antoine de la Boderie ludicrously complained that honours done to the Spanish ambassador at the *Masque of Beauty* were witnessed by 10,000 people (Sullivan, *Court Masques of James I*, 38). The Teatro Medici at Florence and the Mantuan court theatre were said to hold up to 5,000 or 6,000 spectators, though capacity was more like 1,300: see A. M. Nagler, *Theatre Festivals of the Medici* (New Haven, 1964), 104, 120, 178. Henry VIII's May Day ceremonies in 1515 were witnessed by 25,000 people, but this was an outdoor event: S. Anglo, 'The evolution of the early Tudor disguising, pageant and masque', *Renaissance Drama*, n.s. 1 (1968), 25.

21. Orrell, *Theatres of Inigo Jones*, 151.

22. Orrell, *Theatres of Inigo Jones*, 141–2. Astington estimates the capacity of the degrees drawn by Webb at around 400 people, and 450 in the Paved Court Theatre (*English Court Theatre*, 163).

23. Orrell, *Theatres of Inigo Jones*, 80, 115. The plans for *The Shepherd's Paradise* included an open floor between the degrees and the front of the stage, and were modified for the performance of a lost masque on 5 March 1633 (see the appendix, p. 373 above, and the sources cited there).

24. G. E. Bentley, *The Jacobean and Caroline Stage*, 7 vols. (Oxford, 1941–8), IV.918; Herbert Berry, 'The Globe bewitched and *El Hombre Fiel*', *MaRDiE*, 1 (1984), 223–4.

25. Bentley, *The Jacobean and Caroline Stage*, IV.549. In the 1620s scenic performances at York House (Buckingham's London residence) were staged in a room 35 feet by 35 feet: see B. Gerbier, *A Brief Discourse Concerning Three Chief Principles of Magnificent Building* (1662), 42. Gerbier actually writes 'a room not above 35 foot square', but presumably means a square with sides of 35 feet.

26. Orrell, *Theatres of Inigo Jones*, 25. This is the figure for spectators, and one also has to add in the court party.

27. Lee, ed., *Dudley Carleton to John Chamberlain*, 55.

28. *Calendar of State Papers, Venetian* [hereafter *CSPV*] *1603–1608*, 207.

29. Lee, ed., *Dudley Carleton to John Chamberlain*, 68.

30. On the social symbolism of gateways, see Felicity Heal, *Hospitality in Early Modern England* (Oxford, 1990), 28–36. In great houses, the porter's lodge was the place where punishments were administered: see Massinger's *The Duke of Milan*, 3.2.62–3, and *A New Way to Pay Old Debts*, 1.1.136 (*Plays and Poems*, ed. P. Edwards and C. Gibson, 5 vols., Oxford, 1976).

31. BL Stowe MS 169, fols. 247–8; letter of Dudley Carleton, 18 January 1608. I am grateful to James Knowles for this reference.

32. *The Marriage of Prince Frederick and the King's Daughter the Lady Elizabeth* (1613), B4.

33. Chamberlain, *Letters*, 1.426. There was a similar problem with an entertainment for the King at Merchant Taylors' Hall in 1607, at which 'the multitude

and noise was so great that the lutes nor songs could hardly be heard or understood'. See J. Nichols, *The Progresses, Processions, and Magnificent Festivities of James I*, 4 vols. (1828), II.137–8.

34. Turnstiles first appeared at Buckingham's York House masque in November 1626, at which (said the French ambassador) 'on y entroit par un tour, comme aux monastères sans aucune confusion' (F. de Bassompierre, *Journal de ma vie* (Paris, 1870–7), III.274), but when they reappeared for *Coelum Britannicum* George Garrard called them 'a new way of letting [spectators] in by a turning chair' (Bentley, *The Jacobean and Caroline Stage*, III.107–8). They are also documented for *The Triumphs of the Prince d'Amour* in the Temple, and for *Britannia Triumphans* (A. J. Loomie, ed., *Ceremonies of Charles I: The Notebooks of John Finet 1628–1641* (New York, 1987), 196, 241). For tickets, see *The Knyvett Letters 1620–1644*, ed. B. Schofield, Norfolk Record Society 20 (1944), 88; Loomie, ed., *Ceremonies of Charles I*, 148–50 (*Coelum Britannicum* and the repeat performance of *Triumph of Peace*); Bentley, *The Jacobean and Caroline Stage*, III.108 (Garrard to Thomas Wentworth, on *Coelum Britannicum*: 'they let in none but such as have tickets sent them beforehand'); and James Barlow's *A Deep Sigh Breathed through the Lodgings at Whitehall* (1642), A3v.

35. *The Earl of Strafford's Letters and Dispatches*, ed. W. Knowler, 2 vols. (1739), II.148 (*Britannia Triumphans*: only partially quoted in Bentley, *The Jacobean and Caroline Stage*, III.200); Historical Manuscripts Commission, Report (hereafter *HMC*) 77 (*De Lisle and Dudley MSS*) VI.233 (*Salmacida Spolia*, Shrovetide performance, explaining that the reason people failed to attend was 'hard usage . . . at the former dancing').

36. Loomie, ed., *Ceremonies of Charles I*, 20–5. Tilts were controlled by servants of the Knight Marshal (who, for much of our period, was the Earl of Arundel) and the yeomen of the guard. At the tilt for the Palatine marriage they used their staves to 'abate the too forward unruliness of many disordered people, which otherwise would have much troubled the tournaments' (*The Marriage of Prince Frederick and the King's Daughter*, B2v).

37. F. Beaumont and J. Fletcher, *Dramatic Works*, gen. ed. F. Bowers, 10 vols. (Cambridge, 1966–96), II.36.

38. Chamberlain, *Letters*, II.47.

39. F. Osborne, *Historical Memoirs on the Reign of Queen Elizabeth and King James* (1658), sig. **r.

40. Bentley, *The Jacobean and Caroline Stage*, V.1158.

41. Loomie, ed., *Ceremonies of Charles I*, 242.

42. *The Diary of Sir Simonds D'Ewes*, 170.

43. Bentley, *The Jacobean and Caroline Stage*, II.672–81. Mildmay saw *The Temple of Love* and mentions *The Triumph of Peace* and *Coelum Britannicum*. It is unclear whether he saw the last two: he says he 'saw the stately masque' on 3 February 1634 (i.e. *The Triumph of Peace*) but this might have been only the procession of masquers moving through the streets. Mildmay also saw several plays at court, and on at least one occasion was unable to get in, 'the play being full' (3 February 1638).

44. For example, *The Triumph of Peace* was attended by the King's Bench justices Jones, Berkeley, and Croke and by Sir Simonds D'Ewes, the future Presbyterian MP (Tucker Orbison, 'The Middle Temple documents relating to James Shirley's *Triumph of Peace*', *Malone Society Collections*, 12, 1983, 60, 70), and in diary entries covering his years at the Middle Temple, D'Ewes mentions hearing descriptions of *The Masque of Augurs* from friends (*Diary*, ed. E. Bourcier (Paris, 1977), 56). In 1634, all the lawyers who performed in *The Triumph of Peace* were invited by the King to see *Coelum Britannicum* (Bentley, *The Jacobean and Caroline Stage*, III.107). Before the performance, George Garrard was worried that some of the younger lawyers would let the side down as they were new to London and had not yet seen 'any dance or masque at the court, neither know what belong to it': HMC 12 (*Cowper MSS*), II.34.
45. *The Knyvett Letters*, 88.
46. L. Shohet, 'The masque as book', in *Reading and Literacy in the Middle Ages and Renaissance*, ed. I. Moulton (Brussels, 2004), 163, quoting Paulet's diary in the Hampshire Record Office. Paulet did purchase a printed copy of the masque.
47. Loomie, ed., *Ceremonies of Charles I*, 242.
48. Quoted by Sullivan, *Court Masques of James I*, 126 (incorrectly attributed to *News from the New World*).
49. J. Finet, *Finetti Philoxenis* (1656), 144.
50. Chamberlain, *Letters*, I.252.
51. Loomie, ed., *Ceremonies of Charles I*, 196.
52. T. Birch, *The Court and Times of Charles I*, 2 vols. (1848), I.185; Loomie, ed., *Ceremonies of Charles I*, 138.
53. *CSPV 1621–1623*, 216; Finet, *Finetti Philoxenis*, 91.
54. Loomie, ed., *Ceremonies of Charles I*, 138.
55. Finet, *Finetti Philoxenis*, 9.
56. Loomie, ed., *Ceremonies of Charles I*, 241. For the Masquing Room, see Orrell, *Theatres of Inigo Jones*, 155.
57. Finet, *Finetti Philoxenis*, 91.
58. *The Knyvett Letters*, 88.
59. The earliest evidence I have found for such hierarchies is the organization of the theatre built at Christ Church, Oxford, for James's 1605 visit: see Orrell, *The Human Stage*, 127.
60. J. Orrell, 'The London court stage in the Savoy correspondence, 1613–1675', *Theatre Research International*, 4 (1978–9), 83.
61. Finet, *Finetti Philoxenis*, 31–2.
62. For example, Finet, *Finetti Philoxenis*, 24, 71; Loomie, ed., *Ceremonies of Charles I*, 99, 121, 148.
63. Loomie, ed., *Ceremonies of Charles I*, 122, 240.
64. Orgel and Strong, *Inigo Jones*, I.282; Finet, *Finetti Philoxenis*, 115; Loomie, ed., *Ceremonies of Charles I*, 119.
65. Finet, *Finetti Philoxenis*, 24.

66. Loomie, ed., *Ceremonies of Charles I*, 119, 135. In 1629, the Queen's ladies all sat together at a court play (76).

67. Loomie, ed., *Ceremonies of Charles I*, 121. For the identification of Garnier as Henrietta Maria's principal French gentlewoman, see Karen Britland, *Drama at the Courts of Queen Henrietta Maria* (Cambridge, 2006), 55–6.

68. Lady Arundel was England's first countess, and also had boxes at *Britannia Triumphans* and *Salmacida Spolia* (see Loomie, ed., *Ceremonies of Charles I*, 240, 272). Lady Hamilton was a niece of Buckingham's, the wife of Charles's Master of Horse, and Lady of the Bedchamber to Henrietta Maria.

69. Busino mentions a two hours' wait (Orgel and Strong, *Inigo Jones*, I.282); the ambassadors attending the Queen's masque in 1627 were told to turn up at six o'clock (Finet, *Finetti Philoxenis*, 199); and at *Albion's Triumph* in 1632 they were placed two hours in advance (Loomie, ed., *Ceremonies of Charles I*, 119).

70. *CSPV 1603–1607*, 206; *CSPV 1607–1610*, 508.

71. Finet, *Finetti Philoxenis*, 19.

72. Orgel and Strong, *Inigo Jones*, I.282; Finet, *Finetti Philoxenis*, 144.

73. Finet, *Finetti Philoxenis*, 59; Sullivan, *Court Masques of James I*, 243. The Venetian and Dutch ambassadors sat together in a box for *The Masque of the Twelve Months*: J. Orrell, 'Amerigo Salvetti and the London court theatre, 1616–1640', *Theatre Survey*, 20 (1979), 14.

74. Chamberlain, *Letters*, II.50.

75. Finet, *Finetti Philoxenis*, 16. Finet's narrative of *Britannia Triumphans* also makes it clear that some seating arrangements were fluid until the last moment (Loomie, ed., *Ceremonies of Charles I*, 240–3).

76. Finet, *Finetti Philoxenis*, 71.

77. Finet, *Finetti Philoxenis*, 19.

78. Finet, *Finetti Philoxenis*, 199.

79. Loomie, ed., *Ceremonies of Charles I*, 242.

80. Loomie, ed., *Ceremonies of Charles I*, 149, 150.

81. Cuddy, 'The revival of the entourage', 173–225; 'Reinventing a monarchy: the changing structures and political function of the Stuart court, 1603–88', in E. Cruickshanks, ed., *The Stuart Courts* (Stroud, 2000), 59–85.

82. Quoted in J. Richards, '"His nowe majesty" and the English monarchy: the kingship of Charles I before 1640', *Past and Present*, 113 (1986), 70–96; and Sharpe, *Personal Rule*, 217. See also Sharpe, 'The image of virtue', in Starkey, ed., *The English Court*, 226–60.

83. Chamberlain, *Letters*, II.609.

84. E. Hyde, *The History of the Rebellion*, ed. W. D. Macray, 6 vols. (Oxford, 1888), IV.490.

85. G. E. Aylmer, *The King's Servants* (1974), 27.

86. S. Thurley, 'The Whitehall plan of 1670', *London Topographical Society* (1998).

87. Aylmer, *The King's Servants*, 27; cf. J. Adamson, 'The Tudor and Stuart courts 1509–1714', in Adamson, ed., *The Princely Courts of Europe* (1999), 95–117.

88. W. Knowler, ed., *The Earl of Strafford's Letters and Dispatches*, 2 vols. (1739), II.129; quoted in Thurley, *Whitehall Palace*, 93.

89. See A. Daye, 'The Banqueting House, Whitehall: a site specific to dance', *Historical Dance*, 4 (2004), 5. Anne Daye's interpretation of the space differs from that argued for here.

90. Thurley, *Whitehall Palace*, 84; Per Palme, *Triumph of Peace: A Study of the Whitehall Banqueting House* (Uppsala, 1957), 15; Birch, *Court and Times of Charles I*, 1.366.

91. Loomie, ed., *Ceremonies of Charles I*, 49.

92. Gerbier (*A Brief Discourse*, 40) says that the room lacked 'conveyances for smoke, and capacities for echoes'.

93. Barlow, *A Deep Sigh*, A2; Finet, *Finetti Philoxenis*, 144, 199.

94. Finet, *Finetti Philoxenis*, 31–2, 106.

95. BL Stowe MS 169, fol. 248; Finet, *Finetti Philoxenis*, 115–16. Possibly 'prince's galleries' could be a misprint for 'privy galleries'. For one sightseer coming in through the Park in 1585, see V. von Klarwill, *Queen Elizabeth and Some Foreigners* (1928), 319–22.

96. Birch, *Court and Times of Charles I*, 11.91.

97. J. Knowles, 'The "running masque" recovered: a masque for the marquis of Buckingham (c. 1619–20)', *English Manuscript Studies*, 9 (2000), 79–135. As Knowles points out, the two are described in Thomas Fuller's *History of the Worthies* (1662), 'Monmouthshire', 54; and T. S., *Fragmenta Aulica* (1662), 45–6.

98. Society of Antiquaries of London, *A Collection of Ordinances and Regulations for the Government of the Royal Household* (1790), 304.

99. Finet, *Finetti Philoxenis*, 39, 63.

100. Loomie, ed., *Ceremonies of Charles I*, 234, 297.

101. Loomie, ed., *Ceremonies of Charles I*, 277. For a picture showing the reception of the Prince de Ligne in 1660, see Thurley, *Whitehall Palace*, 87. The Prince's train is being brought through the centre of the Banqueting House, the great English officers and ladies line the sides, and the balcony is full of public onlookers.

102. Elias Ashmole, quoted in Palme, *Triumph of Peace*, 132.

103. Adamson, 'The Tudor and Stuart courts', 104.

104. Finet, *Finetti Philoxenis*, 69.

105. Loomie, ed., *Ceremonies of Charles I*, 217.

106. Finet, *Finetti Philoxenis*, 13.

107. Finet, *Finetti Philoxenis*, 11; *The Marriage of Prince Frederick and the King's Daughter*, B3v.

108. BL Stowe MS 562, quoted in Palme, *Triumph of Peace*, 112.

109. *CSPV 1603–1607*, 214; R. Winwood, *Memorials of Affairs of State*, ed. E. Sawyer, 3 vols. (1725) 11.44.

110. Loomie, ed., *Ceremonies of Charles I*, 98, 240; and cf. 150.

111. Orgel and Strong, *Inigo Jones*, 1.282.

112. Loomie, ed., *Ceremonies of Charles I*, 148.

113. Henrietta Maria issued her own invitations for her masques, and usually asked the French ambassador and the agent of Savoy to come in their capacity of

'domestics' within her household (Christine of Savoy was her sister); see Loomie, ed., *Ceremonies of Charles I*, 32–3. The protocol of her masques therefore sometimes cut across that of Charles's. Sir Thomas Knyvett had his ticket for *The Temple of Love* directly from her: see *The Knyvett Letters*, 88.

114. R. J. Alexander, 'Some dramatic records from Percy household accounts on microfilm', *REED Newsletter*, 12.2 (1987), 14 (a payment of 40 shillings for 'tickets to see the masque' by Algernon Percy, tenth Earl of Northumberland, 1634).

115. Beaumont and Fletcher, *Dramatic Works*, VIII.243.

116. *The Staple of News*, 1.5.127–30.

117. Peyton, *The Divine Catastrophe of the House of Stuart* (1652), 47. For a 'real-life' example, compare the feast and play presented by the Lord Mayor to new Knights of the Bath at Drapers' Hall in 1616, at which the courtiers put the citizens wives' 'to the squeak', Sir Edward Sackville attempting to rape one behind locked doors (Chamberlain, *Letters*, II.35). At the second performance of *The Triumph of Peace*, staged at Merchant Taylors' Hall in the city, Finet said the citizens were admitted by ticket, together with 'the better and handsomer sort' of their wives and daughters (Loomie, ed., *Ceremonies of Charles I*, 149).

118. Bentley, *The Jacobean and Caroline Stage*, II.219.

119. The exceptions are occasions on which masquers visiting the court from outside paraded through the city streets and were viewed by city crowds, the notable example being *The Triumph of Peace*, which created huge interest in 1634. But the spectatorship of these crowds established all the more forcefully the privilege of the audiences who actually got to see the show.

120. I refer to *Purity and Danger: An Analysis of the Concepts of Pollution and Taboo* (1966).

121. The classic statement is Veronica Wedgwood's ironizing account of *Salmacida Spolia* as 'The last masque' in her *Truth and Opinion* (1970), 139–56. This attitude is widespread in older criticism, but remains implicit in some recent accounts.

122. Osborne, *Historical Memoirs*, sigs.**r-*r.

123. It was common for distinguished guests who were unable to attend the masque to view its rehearsals or scenery in advance of the performance. See HMC 78 (*Hastings MSS*) II.73–4; Loomie, ed., *Ceremonies of Charles I*, 272; and Campion, *Works*, 222n. (describing faults in the performance of *Lord Hay's Masque* caused by a failure to reset technical devices which had been shown to visitors before the performance).

3 RITES OF INCORPORATION

1. This figure was a gross exaggeration. In 1603, £40,000 would have covered the running costs of the late Queen's household, while the entire crown income that Salisbury attempted to secure in the Great Contract of 1610 was only £200,000. See J. Cramsie, *Kingship and Crown Finance under James VI and I* (Woodbridge, 2002), 69, 95.

2. Chambers, *Elizabethan Stage*, III.279–80; Lee, ed., *Dudley Carleton to John Chamberlain*, 53–4.
3. The Herberts were technically a Welsh dynasty (as their titles of Pembroke and Montgomery announce), but their family had long been anglicized, and their main residence was at Wilton in Wiltshire.
4. B. H. Newdigate, *Michael Drayton and his Circle* (1941), 81.
5. E. Hyde, *The History of the Rebellion*, ed. W. D. Macray, 6 vols. (Oxford, 1888), I.74.
6. On the distinction between the Privy Chamber (staffed by four dozen attendants) and the Bedchamber (staffed by only ten gentlemen), see Cuddy, 'Reinventing a monarchy', 67–75.
7. *CSPV 1603–1607*, 105.
8. Lee, ed., *Dudley Carleton to John Chamberlain*, 66.
9. Nichols, *Progresses of James I*, II.414.
10. For full details, see Barroll, *Anna of Denmark*, 81–7.
11. Henry Howard was uncle to Suffolk, and Nottingham was their cousin through the line descending from the second Duke of Norfolk (d. 1524). The obvious absentee from this group is Robert Cecil, James's most important advisor: see p. 80 below.
12. Southampton and Monteagle took part in the rebellion and were both imprisoned. Sidney was Essex's brother-in-law, Knollys was his uncle, and Devonshire was a close friend, but all had kept aloof from the rebellion. Sidney had been made Lord Chamberlain to Queen Anne, and so was head of her household.
13. See Adamson, ed., *The Princely Courts of Europe*, 33–8.
14. Saslow, *The Medici Wedding of 1589*, 14.
15. Finet, *Finetti Philoxenis*, 8.
16. HMC 9 (*Salisbury MSS*), XVI.388.
17. Orgel and Strong, *Inigo Jones*, I.282.
18. Sullivan, *Court Masques of James I*, 22–5; Lee, ed., *Dudley Carleton to John Chamberlain*, 66–8; Winwood, *Memorials*, II.44; Chambers, *Elizabethan Stage*, IV.119. Carleton's narrative is slightly confusing. It looks as though the banquet for the Duke of Holstein was presented on 3 January ('Thursday last'), not at the end of December (as Carleton's sequencing of events seems to imply).
19. I am grateful to Ralph Giesey for this information.
20. This custom was not kept up in the next reign, though there was a grand court wedding at Christmas 1634–5, between Lord Charles Herbert and Lady Mary Villiers, for which a play with scenes was staged (Henry Killigrew's *The Conspiracy*).
21. 'Salve festa dies, meliorque revertere semper': Ovid, *Fasti*, 1.87 (Hail, happy day, and ever more return still happier).
22. For a similar argument about Lord Mayor's shows, see Lawrence Manley, *Literature and Culture in Early Modern London* (Cambridge, 1995), 277–8.
23. For a full account, see the introduction to my edition of *Christmas his Masque* in *The Cambridge Edition of the Works of Ben Jonson*, gen. eds. D. Bevington, M. Butler, and I. Donaldson (forthcoming), where I argue that the show was

staged by the Prince's Men, and that, except for Christmas himself, the performers were children.

24. Marcus, *The Politics of Mirth*, 76–85. The historical roots of masques in folk drama and ritual are treated in Enid Welsford's *The Court Masque* (1927), though in an uncritical Frazerian spirit as if the masque was a survival of ancient fertility cults.

25. There was, of course, a tradition of Christmas princes and lords of misrule; the masque alludes to this, though without a precise literary precedent.

26. See Douglas Lanier, 'Fertile visions: Jacobean revels and the erotics of occasion', *Studies in English Literature*, 39 (1999), 327–56.

27. See Douglas, *Purity and Danger*, ch. 9.

28. For the 1625 combats, see Alan Young, *Tudor and Jacobean Tournaments* (1987), 208. The source, a French pamphlet of 1648, is not corroborated by any other record.

29. See Arnold Van Gennep, *The Rites of Passage*, trans. M. N. Vizedom and G. L. Caffee (1960).

30. D. Cressy, *Bonfires and Bells: National Memory and the Protestant Calendar in Elizabethan and Stuart England* (1989), 57–9. See also R. Strong, *The Cult of Elizabeth: Elizabethan Portraiture and Pageantry* (1977), 129–63; Young, *Tudor and Jacobean Tournaments*, 205–8. The custom was quietly dropped after 1625.

31. Cf. M. James, *Society, Politics and Culture: Studies in Early Modern England* (Cambridge, 1986), 392–3.

32. On this occasion, the gifts were deposited in the performance space, not given directly to the King.

33. Chambers, *Elizabethan Stage*, 1.172.

34. See J. Mann, *European Arms and Armour* (1962), 263–4; and B. Thomas, O. Gamber, and H. Schedelmann, *Arms and Armour: Masterpieces by European Craftsmen from the 13th to the 19th Century* (1964), 70. Queen Anne still owed £9,000 for this sword and other jewels in November 1611 (*Calendar of State Papers, Domestic Series* [hereafter *CSPD*] *1611–1618*, 91).

35. Shields and other gifts were presented to the Countess of Derby during *The Entertainment at Ashby* (1607); gifts were also central to the 1627 Apethorpe masque: see Marion O'Connor, 'Rachel Fane's May masque at Apethorpe, 1627', *English Literary Renaissance*, 36 (2006), 90–113.

36. Loomie, ed., *Ceremonies of Charles I*, 75.

37. On the social function of jewellery, see Peter Burke, 'Renaissance jewels in their social setting', in A. G. Somers Cocks *et al.*, *Princely Magnificence: Court Jewels of the Renaissance, 1500–1630* (1980), 8–11; and the essays by Somers Cocks and Janet Arnold in the same volume. On the use of clothes to signal economic wealth, see A. R. Jones and P. Stallybrass, *Renaissance Clothing and the Materials of Memory* (Cambridge, 2000).

38. Ravelhofer, *The Early Stuart Masque*, 130 (citing *Sidneiana*, ed. S. Butler, 1837, 89–90); Chamberlain, *Letters*, 1.496; *CSPD 1639–1640*, 352.

39. Lee, ed., *Dudley Carleton to John Chamberlain*, 68; Chamberlain, *Letters*, 1.252–3. There was much anxiety about the loss of jewellery in the crowd or

while dancing. Frances Howard lodged a ring with her friend Mary Woods because she was afraid of losing it at a masque (Lindley, *The Trials of Frances Howard*, 51, citing NA SP 14/51/133); Robert Sidney lost two diamonds worth £40 at *Blackness* (Ravelhofer, *The Early Stuart Masque*, 130). See also the impecunious Gertrude in Jonson, Chapman, and Marston's *Eastward Ho!*, who fantasizes about finding a jewel worth £100 in the streets early in the morning: 'May not some great court lady, as she comes from revels at midnight, look out of her coach, as 'tis running, and lose such a jewel, and we find it?' (5.1.88–90).

40. W. Sanderson, *A Complete History . . . of James I* (1656), 366–7.
41. For this comparison, see Werner Gundersheimer, 'Patronage in the Renaissance: an explanatory approach', in *Patronage in the Renaissance*, ed. S. Orgel and G. F. Lytle (Princeton, 1981), 3–23; and Mary Douglas, *Natural Symbols: Explorations in Cosmology* (1970), 156. Pierre Bourdieu, in *Outline of a Theory of Practice*, trans. R. Nice (Cambridge, 1977), chapter 4, discusses the way that, in pre-capitalist societies, the accumulation of material wealth brings a corresponding obligation to show 'generosity': symbolic capital can only be earned by expending economic capital. See also P. Fumerton, *Cultural Aesthetics: Renaissance Literature and the Practice of Social Ornament* (Chicago, 1991).
42. N. Elias, *The Court Society*, trans. E. Jephcott (Oxford, 1983), 78–145.
43. The classic discussions of potlatch are by Marcel Mauss, *The Gift: Forms and Functions of Exchange in Archaic Societies*, trans. I. Cunnison (1954), and Franz Boas, *Kwakiutl Ethnography*, ed. H. Codere (Chicago, 1966), 77–104. See also Lewis Hyde, *The Gift: Imagination and the Erotic Life of Property* (1979), and Elias, *The Court Society*, 67–8.
44. J. Orrell, 'Buckingham's patronage of the dramatic arts: the Crowe accounts', *REED Newsletter*, 5.2 (1980), 9; L. Stone, *Family and Fortune* (Oxford, 1973), 285. The £1,000 budget for *The Gypsies Metamorphosed* paid for the whole royal visit, of which £100 went to Jonson and £200 to the composer and performer, Nicholas Lanier.
45. Chamberlain, *Letters*, 2.57. Almost certainly Suffolk's and Hay's expenses are exaggerated, but they show what people thought was the case.
46. Chamberlain, *Letters*, 1.493.
47. HMC 9 (*Salisbury MSS*), XVI.388. See the analysis in Barroll, *Anna of Denmark*, 100.
48. A comparable device was used in 1618 when the King gave the Russian ambassadors a gift of £600. In fact, this was paid for by the Muscovy Company (Finet, *Finetti Philoxenis*, 55–6).
49. Mary Douglas and Baron Isherwood, *The World of Goods* (1979), 68.
50. For these ideas, see Mauss, *The Gift*; Hyde, *The Gift*; Raymond Firth, *Symbols: Public and Private* (1973), 368–402; Marshall Sahlins, *Stone Age Economics* (1974), 149–83; Natalie Zemon Davis, *The Gift in Sixteenth-Century France* (Oxford, 2000); Alan D. Schrift, ed., *The Logic of the Gift: Towards an Ethic of Generosity* (1997); and Bourdieu, *Outline of a Theory of Practice*.

51. However, the commodity market was not yet autonomous and value-free, and was itself coloured by ethical considerations. At a time when long-distance trade was difficult, cash in short supply, and the global economic system still very fragmented, financial transactions depended on notions of credit, reputation, and trust that carried a strong personal and moral charge. See Craig Muldrew, *The Economy of Obligation* (Basingstoke, 1998).

52. The fullest discussion is by Linda Levy Peck, *Court Patronage and Corruption in Early Stuart England* (Boston, 1990), 12–46.

53. See A. J. Collins, *Jewels and Plate of Queen Elizabeth I: The Inventory of 1574* (1955), 100–12, 249–52; J. Arnold, *Queen Elizabeth's Wardrobe Unlock'd* (Leeds, 1988), 93–110; J. L. Nevinson, 'New Year's gifts to Queen Elizabeth, 1584', *Costume*, 9 (1975), 27–31; Gabriel Heaton, 'Performing Gifts: The Manuscript Circulation of Elizabethan and Early Stuart Court Entertainments' (unpublished Ph.D. dissertation, Cambridge, 2003).

54. See Nichols, *Progresses of James I*, 1.471. Nichols prints several gift rolls in his *Progresses and Public Processions of Queen Elizabeth*, 3 vols. (1823).

55. I am grateful to Malcolm Smuts for these figures, which are based on the Exchequer Order Books, NA E403/2744–2759.

56. Caroline Hibbard, 'Henrietta Maria in the 1630s: perspectives on the role of consort queens in *Ancien Régime* courts', in *The 1630s: Interdisciplinary Essays on Culture and Politics in the Caroline Era*, ed. I. Atherton and J. Saunders (Manchester, 2006), 105; HMC 75 (*Downshire MSS*), IV.2.

57. *The Forest*, 12.

58. The classic discussion is by Louis Montrose, 'Gifts and reasons: the contexts of Peele's *Araygnement of Paris*', *ELH*, 47 (1980), 433–61. See also Mary Hill Cole, *The Portable Queen: Elizabeth I and the Politics of Ceremony* (Amherst, 1999); and F. Heal, 'Giving and receiving on royal progress', in *The Progresses, Pageants, and Entertainments of Queen Elizabeth I*, ed. J. Archer, E. Goldring, and S. Knight (Oxford, 2007), 46–61.

59. Arnold, *Queen Elizabeth's Wardrobe Unlock'd*, 83–4.

60. Jonson, *A Particular Entertainment of the Queen and Prince their Highness at Althorp*, in *Ben Jonson*, VII.125.

61. J. Knowles, 'Jonson's *Entertainment at Britain's Burse*', in *Re-Presenting Ben Jonson: Text, History, Performance*, ed. M. Butler (Basingstoke, 1999), 114–51. Not all of these details are evident from the text, but they are spelled out in the Venetian ambassador's eyewitness report (*CSPV 1607–1610*, 269).

62. *CSPV 1607–1610*, 269.

63. See James Knowles, '"To raise a house of better frame": Jonson's Cecilian entertainments', in *Patronage, Culture and Power: The Early Cecils, 1558–1612*, ed. P. Croft (New Haven, 2002), 181–98.

64. See Gordon Kipling, *Enter the King: Theatre, Liturgy, and Ritual in the Medieval Civic Triumph* (Oxford, 1998), ch. 3.

65. I cite the edition by J. Rees, in *A Book of Masques*, ed. Spencer and Wells (accidentals emended).

66. Seneca, *De beneficiis*, trans. Thomas Lodge (1614), 1.3. For the iconography, see Edgar Wind, *Pagan Mysteries in the Renaissance* (rev. edn, 1967), 26–52.
67. Orgel and Strong, *Inigo Jones*, 1.284.
68. Lee, ed., *Dudley Carleton to John Chamberlain*, 56, 68; Chambers, *Elizabethan Stage*, III.235.
69. *Court Masques*, ed. Lindley, 63.
70. Loomie, ed., *Ceremonies of Charles I*, 97, 165, 167.
71. Orrell, 'The London court stage in the Savoy correspondence', 83.
72. Fumerton, *Cultural Aesthetics*, 159–62.
73. S. Bertelli, *The King's Body: Sacred Rituals of Power in Medieval and Early Modern Europe*, trans. R. Burr Litchfield (University Park, Pa., 2001), 99–100.
74. J. Dillon, *Performance and Spectacle in Hall's Chronicle* (2002), 41.
75. Bertelli, *The King's Body*, 100.
76. C. Geertz, 'Centers, kings, and charisma: reflections on the symbolics of power', in *Rites of Power: Symbolism, Ritual, and Politics since the Middle Ages*, ed. S. Wilentz (Philadelphia, 1985), 15; for the anthropological context, see his *Negara: The Theatre-State in Nineteenth-Century Bali* (Princeton, 1980).
77. Geertz, 'Centers, kings, and charisma', 14.
78. Ben Jonson, *Pan's Anniversary*, 3–4. For an extreme version of these ideas, see Vaughan Hart, *Art and Magic in the Court of the Stuarts* (1994).
79. See Adamson, 'The Tudor and Stuart courts', 101–5; Richards, 'His nowe majesty', 70–96; Marc Bloch, *The Royal Touch*, trans. J. E. Anderson (1973); and, for a wide survey, Bertelli, *The King's Body*.
80. See Skiles Howard, *The Politics of Courtly Dancing in Early Modern England* (1998), 110–16; and Tom Hayes, *The Birth of Popular Culture: Ben Jonson, Maid Marian, and Robin Hood* (Pittsburgh, 1992), 39–49.
81. I quote from and reference the 1601 quarto of the play. Herford and Simpson's edition rather unhelpfully reproduces the revised text printed in 1616.

4 THE INVENTION OF BRITAIN

1. Contemporary reactions to the masque are summarized in *Ben Jonson*, x.575–7.
2. John Chamberlain identifies Sir William Irwin as a Scot: 'The Lord Sheffield in a doting humour hath married a young Scottish wench, daughter of one Sir William Urwin that was a kind of dancing schoolmaster to Prince Henry' (*Letters*, II.220–1). Irwin was sworn as a gentleman-usher of Prince Charles's Privy Chamber in 1613 (Birch, *Court and Times of James I*, I.257).
3. *Ben Jonson*, x.577.
4. See especially J. H. Elliott, 'A Europe of composite monarchies', *Past and Present*, 137 (1992), 48–71.
5. On the emergence of a unified cartographic image of Britain, see Richard Helgerson's *The Forms of Nationhood* (Chicago, 1992), 105–47 – though Helgerson's narrative of a progressive shift from a king-centred to a land-centred view of the state neglects the distinction between England and Britain, and the dependence of British identity on dynastic factors. One of the prime pro-Union

arguments, made in James's speech of 31 March 1607, was that Union closed the 'back door' with Scotland which was England's strategic weakness before 1603, undermining Elizabethan ideas of England as virginal, enclosed, and inviolate. For the name 'Britain' before 1603, see S. T. Bindoff, 'The Stuarts and their style', *English Historical Review*, 60 (1945), 192–216; D. Hay, 'The use of the term "Great Britain" in the middle ages', *Proceedings of the Society of Antiquaries of Scotland*, 89 (1955–6), 55–66; and M. J. Enright, 'King James and his island: an archaic kingship belief?' *Scottish Historical Review*, 55 (1976), 29–40.

6. John Morrill, 'The fashioning of Britain', in *Conquest and Union: Fashioning a British State 1485–1725*, ed. S. G. Ellis and S. Barber (1995), 18; Palme, *Triumph of Peace*, 233–7; R. Strong, *Britannia Triumphans: Inigo Jones, Rubens, and Whitehall Palace* (1980). A more paradoxical interpretation is argued by Gordon in *The Renaissance Imagination*, 38–41.

7. *Eclogues*, 1.66. See J. W. Bennett, 'Britain among the Fortunate Isles', *Studies in Philology*, 53 (1956), 114–40; and Wind, *Pagan Mysteries in the Renaissance*, 222–30.

8. Chambers, *Elizabethan Stage*, III.279–80.

9. See *Stuart Royal Proclamations*, vol. I *(1603–1625)*, ed. J. F. Larkin and P. L. Hughes, vol. II, ed. J. F. Larkin (Oxford, 1973–83), 94–7, 101, 135; B. Galloway, *The Union of England and Scotland 1603–1608* (Edinburgh, 1986), 58–89; and R. Woolf, *The Idea of History in Early Stuart England* (Toronto, 1990), 55–64. See also K. Brown, 'The vanishing emperor: British kingship in the seventeenth century', in *Scots and Britons: Scottish Political Thought and the Union of 1603*, ed. R. A. Mason (Cambridge, 1994), 58–87; and H. Trevor-Roper, 'The invention of tradition: the highland tradition of Scotland', in *The Invention of Tradition*, ed. E. Hobsbawm and T. Ranger (Cambridge, 1983), 15–41.

10. For this crucial distinction, see Benedict Anderson, *Imagined Communities: Reflections on the Origin and Spread of Nationalism* (1983).

11. See especially two essays and two books by Russell: 'Why did Charles fight the Civil War?' *History Today*, 346 (June 1984), 31–4; 'The British problem and the English Civil War' *History*, 72 (1987), 394–415; *The Causes of the English Civil War* (Oxford, 1990); and *The Fall of the British Monarchies 1637–1642* (Oxford, 1991). Russell has been criticized for Anglocentricity, in that he invokes these issues mainly to explain difficulties in London: see Peter Lake's review in the *Huntington Library Quarterly*, 57 (1994), 167–97. For other perspectives, see *The Scottish National Covenant in its British Context*, ed. J. S. Morrill (Edinburgh, 1990); Linda Colley, *Britons: Forging the Nation 1707–1837* (New Haven, 1992); K. M. Brown, *Kingdom or Province? Scotland and the Regal Union, 1603–1712* (Houndmills, 1992); R. G. Asche, ed., *Three Nations – A Common History?* (1993); A. Fletcher and P. Roberts, eds., *Religion, Culture and Society in Early Modern Britain* (Cambridge, 1994); Ellis and Barber, eds., *Conquest and Union*; B. Bradshaw and P. Roberts, eds., *British Consciousness and Identity: The Making of Britain 1533–1707* (1998); G. Burgess, ed., *The New British History* (1999); and A. I. MacInnes and J. Ohlmeyer (eds.), *The Stuart*

Kingdoms in the Seventeenth Century (2002). Scholarship on the Union debates is well represented by B. P. Levack, *The Formation of the British State* (Oxford, 1987), and Galloway, *The Union of England and Scotland*.

12. On the Household, see Neil Cuddy's 'Anglo-Scottish union and the court of James I', and 'The revival of the entourage'.

13. *Commons Journals*, 1.187. For detailed analyses of these debates, see Galloway, *The Union of England and Scotland*, and Levack, *The Formation of the British State*.

14. Quoted by Conrad Russell, 'The Anglo-Scottish Union 1603–1643: a success?' in *Religion, Culture and Society in Early Modern Britain*, ed. Fletcher and Roberts, 246.

15. J. S. Douglas, *Rapta Tatio* (1604), sig. D2v.

16. W. Cornwallis, *The Miraculous and Happy Union of England and Scotland* (1604), sig. E3.

17. For a sustained attack on the Union on account of Scottish poverty, see Sir Henry Spelman's 'Of the Union', in *The Jacobean Union: Six Tracts of 1604*, ed. B. R. Galloway and B. P. Levack (Edinburgh, 1985).

18. *The Jacobean Union*, ed. Galloway and Levack, 97. This issue is discussed by Jenny Wormald, 'The creation of Britain: multiple kingdoms, or core and colonies?' *Transactions of the Royal Historical Society*, 6th series, 2 (1992), 175–94; Brown, *Kingdom or Province*; and R. A. Mason, 'Scotching the Brut: history and national myth in sixteenth-century Britain', in *Scotland and England 1286–1815*, ed. Mason (Edinburgh, 1987), 60–84.

19. As he did on 2 May 1607 (*Commons Journals*, 1.366–8). See also *A Collection of Several Speeches and Treatises of the Late Lord Treasurer Cecil*, ed. P. Croft, *Camden Miscellany* 29 (1987), 309.

20. Jenny Wormald has argued that hostility between the nations presented enduring obstacles to Union; see 'The creation of Britain', and 'The union of 1603', in *Scots and Britons*, ed. Mason, 3–16. Russell is more optimistic in 'The Anglo-Scottish Union 1603–1643', 238–56.

21. Strong, *Britannia Triumphans*, 19; Gordon, '*Hymenaei*: Ben Jonson's masque of union', *Journal of the Warburg and Courtauld Institutes*, 8 (1945), 107–45; reprinted in *The Renaissance Imagination*, 157–84.

22. HMC (*Salisbury*) xvi.362–4; quoted by John Morrill in *The Nature of the English Revolution* (Harlow, 1993), 95; *A Collection of Several Speeches and Treatises*, ed. Croft, 310.

23. *Anna of Denmark*, 89–90.

24. Sullivan, *Court Masques of James I*, 194 (citing the report of the French ambassador Beaumont).

25. Sullivan, *Court Masques of James I*, 12–17.

26. See *Gesta Grayorum*, ed. D. S. Bland (Liverpool, 1968), and M. Axton, *The Queen's Two Bodies: Drama and the Elizabethan Succession* (1977), 85–7.

27. See Carleton's account, and Lord Shrewsbury's letter cited in Chambers, *Elizabethan Stage*, iii.280, 278.

28. McManus, *Women on the Renaissance Stage*, 108.

29. Barroll, *Anna of Denmark*, 91–3.
30. For this list, see Chambers, *Elizabethan Stage*, III.280. Southampton and Monteagle had been imprisoned and fined for their parts in Essex's revolt, and Devonshire (= Mountjoy) and Sidney had been close associates. For the Essexians, see chapter 6 below.
31. In his historical writings, Daniel describes the medieval conflicts between English and Scots as futile in the light of events to come. See J. Rees, *Samuel Daniel* (Liverpool, 1964), 153–4.
32. The classic statement of intellectual elitism comes in Jonson's contribution to the 1604 royal entry, which was overtly a riposte to Daniel's more self-explanatory device. See *Ben Jonson*, VII.91.
33. In 'Ben Jonson's masques and Italian culture', John Peacock relates Daniel's dream format to the masque's background in Italian aesthetics. I do not dispute his learned analysis, but draw out here its ideological consequences.
34. Anthony Weldon, *The Court and Character of King James*, in *Secret History of the Court of James the First*, ed. W. Scott, 2 vols. (Edinburgh, 1811), I.330. Weldon (on the whole a hostile witness) presented Hay relatively positively: 'he was a most complete and well-accomplished gentleman, modest and court-like, and of so fair a demeanour, as made him be generally beloved' (332). For Hay's subsequent political career, see R. Schreiber, *The First Carlisle* (1984).
35. Lindley argues that it was financed by Cecil, Suffolk, and Exeter (see D. Lindley, *Thomas Campion* (Leiden, 1986), 176–7, and 'Who paid for Campion's *Lord Hay's Masque*?', *Notes and Queries*, 224, 1979, 144–5). But it seems likelier that the finance was a collective affair involving all those who participated, as was usually the case with marriage masques. For example, the cost of *The Haddington Masque* (£3,600) was split twelve ways between the dancers (see Chambers, *Elizabethan Stage*, I.211–12). Suffolk, who had two sons dancing, would certainly have contributed, but there is no hard evidence for Cecil's or Exeter's involvement.
36. W. Notestein, *The House of Commons 1604–1610* (New Haven, 1971), 211–12; HMC 75 (*Downshire MSS*), II.23.
37. Page references are to T. Campion, *The Works*, ed. W. R. Davis (New York, 1967).
38. See Lindley, *Thomas Campion*, 176–90, and 'Lord Hay's masque and Anglo-Scottish Union', *Huntington Library Quarterly*, 43 (1979), 1–11.
39. Two were gentlemen of the Privy Chamber, one was a carver to the King, and a fourth was a gentleman pensioner. The Scot was Sir Richard Preston.
40. The stage plan included in Campion (*Works*, ed. Davis, 206), cannot be trusted. Davis's interpretations of the terms 'screen' and 'dancing place' are particularly misleading.
41. N. Conti, *Mythologiae* (1567), 82; quoted by Philippa Berry, *Of Chastity and Power: Elizabethan Literature and the Unmarried Queen* (1989), 129. This paragraph draws heavily on Berry, especially 41–2.
42. James VI and I, *Political Writings*, ed. J. P. Somerville (Cambridge, 1994), 165.
43. *A Collection of Several Speeches and Treatises*, ed. Croft, 310.

44. I describe the transformation as Campion narrates it in the text, but in performance it worked out less well, since a technical fault caused the trees to become stuck.

45. Lindley argues that the masque reflects the views of Cecil, Suffolk, and Exeter. But there is no proof of Cecil's or Exeter's involvement (see note 35 above), and in any case earlier historiography has exaggerated Cecil's anti-Union stance. He was alarmed by the establishment of a wholly Scottish Bedchamber, but as a principal councillor he had no difficulties of access, and he worked diligently for Union. See Pauline Croft, 'Robert Cecil and the early Jacobean court', in *The Mental World of the Jacobean Court*, ed. L. L. Peck (Cambridge, 1991), 145–60. In 1610, he told James that in the long term the Union was inevitable: 'law and nature [are] fully resolved to bring forth and nourish that child, which must be the life and strength of this island' (*A Collection of Several Speeches and Treatises*, ed. Croft, 310).

46. J. Loewenstein, *Responsive Readings: Versions of Echo in Pastoral, Epic, and the Jonsonian Masque* (New Haven, 1984), 97.

47. James VI and I, *Political Writings*, 163.

48. See Mason, 'Scotching the Brut'.

49. Munday wrote that 'Scotland yielded out of Tudor's race, / A true-born bud, to sit in Tudor's place': *Pageants and Entertainments*, ed. D. M. Bergeron (New York, 1985), 15.

50. See, for example, John Gordon, *A Panegyre of Congratulation for the Concord of the Realms of Great Britain*, trans. E. Grimstone (1603); Gordon, *ENOTIKON or a Sermon of the Union of Great Britain* (1604); and Robert Pont, *Of the Union of Britain*, in *The Jacobean Union*, ed. Galloway and Levack.

51. See *Ben Jonson*, x.448–9.

52. R. Cotton, *Discourse of the Name of Britain*, NA SP 14/1/3; Spelman, 'Of the Union', in *The Jacobean Union*, ed. Galloway and Levack.

53. For full discussion, see T. Worden, 'The rhetoric of place in Ben Jonson's "chorographical" entertainments and masques', *Renaissance Forum*, 3.2 (1998), 1–25.

54. W. Camden, *Britain*, trans. P. Holland (1610), 3. This discussion of the name is the opening section of Camden's history.

55. For Augustus as the temperate emperor, see especially H. Erskine-Hill, *The Augustan Ideal* (1983).

56. Richmond Barbour points out that the image of Britain as a diamond in the ring of the world is another Camden echo. See 'Britain and the great beyond', in *Playing the Globe*, ed. J. Gillies and V. M. Vaughan (Delaware, 1998), 129–53.

57. T. Craig, *De unione regnorum Britanniae tractatus*, ed. C. S. Terry, *Scottish History Society* 60 (Edinburgh, 1909), 288. Craig anticipated the masque's concern with temperance in his argument that it would be cheaper for the Scots to have James at a distance: 'The nearer the sun is to the earth and the more direct its rays, the more oppressive to mankind and harmful to vegetation are its rays. When its rays fall obliquely, temperature is more equable and the earth brings forth a more fertile harvest' (451–2).

58. In *English Ethnicity and Race in Early Modern Drama* (Cambridge, 2003), 116–17, Mary Floyd-Wilson cites James's *True Law of Free Monarchies* to suggest that 'blanch' is a Scots legal term meaning the king's power to convert a debt into allegiance. This meaning is not glossed in the *OED*.

59. See the discussion of this point in chapter 1 above.

60. Loewenstein, *Responsive Readings*, 96.

61. Loewenstein, *Responsive Readings*, 101.

62. Floyd-Wilson, *English Ethnicity and Race in Early Modern Drama*, 118–25. The masque's use of hieroglyphics adds an Egyptian element to the dancers' Ethiopian identity.

63. *The Marriage of Prince Frederick and the King's Daughter the Lady Elizabeth* (1613), B3v.

64. See the excellent account of these entertainments by Bernadette Andrea, 'Black skin, the Queen's masques: Africanist ambivalence and feminine author(ity) in the masques of *Blackness* and *Beauty*', *English Literary Renaissance*, 29 (1999), 246–81; and also McManus's *Women on the Renaissance Stage*, 75–6, 83–4. Other valuable analyses include Hardin Aasand, '"To blanch an Ethiop, or revive a corse": Queen Anne and *The Masque of Blackness*', *Studies in English Literature 1500–1900*, 32 (1992), 271–85; Yumna Siddiqi, 'Dark incontinents: the discourses of race and gender in three Renaissance masques', *Renaissance Drama*, n.s. 23 (1992), 139–64; Lynda E. Boose, '"The getting of a lawful race": racial discourse in early modern England and the unrepresentable black woman', in *Women, 'Race', and Writing in the Early Modern Period*, ed. Margo Hendricks and P. Parker (1994), 35–54; Kim F. Hall, *Things of Darkness: Economies of Race and Gender in Early Modern England* (Ithaca, N.Y., 1995); Barbour, 'Britain and the great beyond'; and Kathryn Schwartz, *Tough Love: Amazon Encounters in the English Renaissance* (Durham, N.C., 2000). It may be worth adding that although C. H. Herford disparaged the Queen's command for 'blackamoors', he was well aware that black characters were already common in court entertainment (*Ben Jonson*, ii.265).

65. See chapter 5 below. There is a good discussion by Kim F. Hall, 'Sexual politics and cultural identity in *The Masque of Blackness*', in *The Performance of Power: Theatrical Discourse and Politics*, ed. S. E. Case and J. Reinelt (Iowa City, 1991), 3–18.

66. Nichols, *Progresses of James I*, 1.94. Palladia, or giants protecting the safety of the house or city, often appeared as liminal figures in inaugural rituals, for example at the Kenilworth entertainment (1575) and at royal entries by Henry V, Henry VIII, Philip II, and Queen Elizabeth: see Manley, *Literature and Culture in Early Modern London*, 224, 251.

67. *Ben Jonson*, x.448.

68. *Ben Jonson*, x.448.

69. See J. Wormald, 'Gunpowder, treason and Scots', *Journal of British Studies*, 24 (1995), 157–64. The Venetian ambassador said that in November the Scots were fleeing London in droves (*CSPV 1603–1607*, 304).

70. See Lindley, *The Trials of Frances Howard*, 21; and Marie Loughlin, '"Love's friend and stranger to virginitie": the politics of the virginal body in Ben

Jonson's *Hymenaei* and Thomas Campion's *The Lord Hay's Masque*', *ELH*, 63 (1996), 833–42.

71. James VI and I, *Political Writings*, 135–6.

72. J. Hayward, *A Treatise of Union* (1604), 35; Galloway, *The Union of England and Scotland*, 109. Many other examples could easily be cited: much the most elaborate is John Gordon's sermon *ENOTIKON* (1604).

73. Russell, 'The Anglo-Scottish Union 1603–1643', 246; *Commons Journals*, 1.336 (17 Feb. 1607).

74. I am summarizing Russell's acute analysis of the debates of April–May 1607: 'The Anglo-Scottish Union 1603–1643', 246–8. Campion's Latin epigram prefacing *Lord Hay's Masque* invokes the polygamy topos, and adds a hint of incest, that James cannot marry his kingdoms when they are both his daughters. But then he concludes that the miracle of Union is that James, uniquely, can do such things.

75. Although in fact, as everyone knew, the adolescent bride and groom were not going to be put to bed together that night. This later became crucial to the Essex annulment.

76. Lee, ed., *Dudley Carleton to John Chamberlain*, 66.

77. The representation of virginity surrendering to marriage, and the absorption of singularity into unity, was underlined in the *Barriers* performed on the following evening (discussed in chapter 6 below).

78. The Englishmen were Arundel, Southampton, and Sir Thomas Somerset; the Scots were Lennox, Hay, and Preston. See *Ben Jonson*, x.513.

79. *Ben Jonson*, x.522.

80. See the complete list in *A Collection of Ordinances and Regulations* (1790).

81. On Stuart Wales, see C. A. J. Skeel, *The Council in the Marches of Wales* (1904); A. L. Dodd, *Studies in Stuart Wales* (Cardiff, 1952); P. Williams, 'The activity of the Council in the Marches under the early Stuarts', *Welsh History Review*, 1 (1961), 133–60; and G. Dyfnallt Owen, *Wales in the Reign of James I* (Woodbridge, 1988).

82. H. Kearney, 'The Irish parliament in the early seventeenth century', in *The Irish Parliamentary Tradition*, ed. B. Farrell (Dublin, 1973), 88–101; J. C. Beckett, *A Short History of Ireland* (6th edn, 1979), 61–70; and A. Clarke, 'Pacification, plantation, and the Catholic question, 1603–23', in *A New History of Ireland*, ed. T. W. Moody, F. X. Martin, and F. J. Byrne, vol. III (Oxford, 1976), 187–232. On James's policy towards the British periphery, see M. Lee, Jr, *Great Britain's Solomon: James VI and I in his Three Kingdoms* (Urbana, Ill., 1990), ch. 7.

83. J. M. Smith, 'Effaced history: facing the colonialist contexts of Ben Jonson's *Irish Masque at Court*', *ELH*, 65 (1998), 299; D. Lindley, 'Embarrassing Ben: the masques for Frances Howard', in *Renaissance Historicism*, ed. A. F. Kinney and D. S. Collins (Amherst, Mass., 1987), 260.

84. See A. R. Jones and P. Stallybrass, 'Dismantling Irena: the sexualizing of Ireland in early modern England', in *Nationalisms and Sexualities*, ed. A. Parker, M. Russo, D. Sommer, and P. Yaeger (New York, 1992), 157–71.

85. Chamberlain, *Letters*, 1.498.
86. T. Marshall, *Theatre and Empire: Great Britain on the London Stages under James VI and I* (Manchester, 2000), 185.

5 THE CONSORT'S BODY

1. J. Harington, *Nugae antiquae*, ed. H. Harington and T. Park (1804), 1.348–54 (350).
2. See Kipling, *Enter the King*, 159–61, and McManus, *Women on the Renaissance Stage*, 73. The Queen of Sheba also figured in royal entries at Ghent in 1458 and Bruges in 1515.
3. See Lee, *Great Britain's Solomon*, 130; J. Scott-Warren, *Sir John Harington and the Book as Gift* (Oxford, 2001), 185–8. However, Neville Davies points out that there are considerable discrepancies between the official narratives of the visit and comments in contemporary letters and diaries: see 'The limitations of festival: Christian IV's state visit to England in 1606', in *Italian Renaissance Festivals and their European Influence*, ed. J. R. Mulryne and M. Shewring (Lampeter, 1992), 319–20. Clare McManus, noting that female speaking parts would ordinarily have been played by boys, argues that the whole occasion was a satirical fiction invented by Harington: 'When is a woman not a woman?' *Modern Philology*, 105 (2008), 437–74.
4. The Latin tag is from Horace, *Satires*, 2.6.60: 'O my country home, when shall I behold you?'
5. S. Orgel, 'Marginal Jonson', in *The Politics of the Stuart Court Masque*, ed. Bevington and Holbrook, 153. See also Hall, *Things of Darkness*, 138–40.
6. McManus points out that Queen Anne was absent from the Theobalds celebrations, as she had recently given birth and had not yet been churched ('When is a woman not a woman', n. 17).
7. A. Wilson, *The History of Great Britain* (1653), 53–4.
8. H. Hawkins, *Parthenia Sacra* (1633), 114–15. See D. Clarke, 'The iconography of the blush: Marian literature of the 1630s', in *Voicing Women: Gender and Sexuality in Early Modern Writing*, ed. K. Chedzgoy, M. Hansen, and S. Trill (Keele, 1996), 121–2.
9. Line references are to J. R. Brown's Revels edition (1964).
10. *The Diaries of Lady Anne Clifford*, ed. D. J. H. Clifford (Stroud, 1990), 27; Chambers, *Elizabethan Stage*, 1.171n.
11. Chambers, *Elizabethan Stage*, iii.376.
12. S. Tomlinson, *Women on Stage in Stuart Drama* (Cambridge, 2006), 19. My argument here does little more than summarize Tomlinson's excellent discussion.
13. Chambers, *Elizabethan Stage*, 1.171n; *CSPV 1607–1610*, 86.
14. Chamberlain, *Letters*, ii.630.
15. This topic is exhaustively treated by Sophie Tomlinson in *Women on Stage in Stuart Drama*.
16. The pioneering studies are by Barroll, *Anna of Denmark*; McManus, *Women on the Renaissance Stage*; Karen Britland, *Drama at the Courts of Queen Henrietta*

Maria (Cambridge, 2006); and Tomlinson, *Women on Stage in Stuart Drama*. See also the essays collected in Clare McManus, ed., *Women and Culture at the Courts of the Stuart Queens* (Basingstoke, 2003). Earlier work significantly anticipating these more substantial studies includes Suzanne Gossett's '"Man-maid, begone!": women in masques', *ELR*, 18 (1988), 96–113; Marion Wynne-Davies's 'The queen's masque: Renaissance women and the seventeenth-century court masque', in *Gloriana's Face: Women, Public and Private, in the English Renaissance*, ed. S. P. Cerasano and M. Wynne-Davies (1992), 72–104; Barbara Lewalski's *Writing Women in Jacobean England* (1993); and Kathryn Schwartz's *Tough Love: Amazon Encounters in the English Renaissance* (Durham, N.C., 2000).

17. This case is eloquently made by Barroll and McManus, though both downplay the importance of masques during the period 1603–13 that were not sponsored by Queen Anne – *The Masque of Scottish Lords, The Masque of Indian and China Knights, Hymenaei, Lord Hay's Masque* and *The Haddington Masque*, as well as the household entertainments given by Sir William Cornwallis and the Earl of Salisbury.

18. *CSPV 1607–1610*, 86.

19. See especially Wynne-Davies, 'The queen's masque', and Lewalski, *Writing Women in Jacobean England*.

20. See Britland, *Drama at the Courts of Queen Henrietta Maria*; and Erica Veevers, *Images of Love and Religion: Queen Henrietta Maria and Court Entertainments* (Cambridge, 1989).

21. See the letter drafted by Cecil in HMC 9 (*Salisbury MSS*), xvi.388–9; analysed in detail by Barroll, *Anna of Denmark*, 99–100.

22. *Ben Jonson*, x.492, 528; Orgel and Strong, *Inigo Jones*, 1.191–2.

23. See the passage quoted at chapter 3, p. 82, above.

24. See L. S. Meskill, 'Exorcising the gorgon of terror: Jonson's *Masque of Queenes*', *ELH*, 92 (2005), 181–208.

25. B. Jonson, *Poems*, ed. I. Donaldson (Oxford, 1975), 'Ungathered Verse', 34.31–9.

26. There is a contemporary engraving of Anne as Pallas in the British Museum collection: see F. O'Donoghue, *Catalogue of Engraved British Portraits*, 6 vols. (1908), 1.55.

27. Pallas is further associated with Anne in *The Masque of Queens* and *The Golden Age Restored*.

28. See the (possibly unreliable) testimony of James Howell: 'nor do I hear of any legacy that she left at all to her daughter in Germany, for that match some say lessened her affection to her ever since, so that she would often call her Goody Palsgrave' (*Epistolae Ho-Elianae*, 1645, 1.2.7).

29. See A. J. Loomie, 'King James's Catholic consort', *Huntington Library Quarterly*, 34 (1970–1), 303–16; McManus, *Women on the Renaissance Stage*, 92–6.

30. McManus, *Women and Culture at the Courts of the Stuart Queens*, 85.

31. *CSPV 1603–1607*, 513; *1610–1613*, 313.

32. L. L. Peck, *Court Patronage and Corruption in Early Stuart England* (1990), 68–72.

33. S. Daniel, *Tethys' Festival, or the Queen's Wake* (1610); printed as an appendix to *The Order and Solemnity of the Creation of the High and Mighty Prince Henry . . . Prince of Wales* (1610).

34. James Knowles, '"To enlight the darksome night, pale Cinthia doth arise": Anna of Denmark, Elizabeth I and the images of royalty', in *Women and Culture at the Courts of the Stuart Queens*, ed. McManus, 42. See also Tomlinson, *Women on Stage in Stuart Drama*, 37; and Philippa Berry and Jayne Archer, 'Reinventing the matter of Britain: undermining the state in Jacobean masques', in *British Identities and English Renaissance Literature*, ed. D. J. Baker and W. Maley (Cambridge, 2002), 119–34.

35. Knowles, 'To enlight the darksome night', 21–2; McManus, *Women on the Renaissance Stage*, 15, 206.

36. *Women on Stage in Stuart Drama*, 23.

37. Tomlinson, *Women on Stage in Stuart Drama*, 35.

38. S. Orgel, 'Jonson and the Amazons', in *Soliciting Interpretation: Literary Theory and Seventeenth-Century Poetry*, ed. E. D. Harvey and K. E. Maus (Chicago, 1990), 119–39; Orgel develops this reading further in 'Marginal Jonson', 171–2. Some of the intellectual ground that Orgel's reading assumes is laid out in Stuart Clark's *Thinking with Demons: The Idea of Witchcraft in Early Modern Europe* (Oxford, 1997), 91–3, 644–6; and see Clark's earlier essay, 'Inversion, misrule, and the meaning of witchcraft', *Past and Present*, 87 (1980), 98–127.

39. Orgel, 'Jonson and the Amazons', 133.

40. See Goldberg, *James I and the Politics of Literature*, 87–8.

41. See Apollodorus, *The Library*, 2.4.2–3.

42. Tomlinson, *Women on Stage in Stuart Drama*, 32; Diane Purkiss, *The Witch in History* (1996), 205.

43. See the pamphlet *News from Scotland* (1591); Stuart Clark, 'King James's *Daemonologie*: witchcraft and kingship', in *The Damned Art*, ed. S. Anglo (1977), 156–81; and Christine Larner, *Enemies of God: The Witch-Hunt in Scotland* (1981).

44. *Calendar of State Papers Scottish, 1589–1593*, 524; *Demonology*, 2.6.

45. Purkiss, *The Witch in History*, 202–3. See also L. Normand, 'Witches, King James, and *The Masque of Queens*', in *Representing Women in Renaissance England*, ed. C. J. Summers and T.-L. Pebworth (Columbia, Miss., 1997), 115.

46. *Masque of Queens*, marginalium 10; see also marginalium 12.

47. At 453–4, Jonson cross-references *Aeneid* 4.173–7, where Fama is said to have 'her feet on the ground, and her head in the clouds' – a wording that Jonson incorporates into the first song (727–8), probably by way of her treatment in Cesare Ripa's *Iconologia*, one of his habitual sources for masque iconography. Doubtless Jonson remembered that Virgil's passage relates to another famous but problematic queen, Dido.

48. Normand, 'Witches, King James, and *The Masque of Queens*', 117. *OED* traces the name to the present participle feminine of the verb μέδειν (to protect, to rule).

49. References are to the text edited by Lindley in *Court Masques*.
50. Bentley, *The Jacobean and Caroline Stage*, v.1288–9. Chamberlain commented that neither the King nor the Queen approved of this masque (*Letters*, ii.126).
51. The documents in NA LR 5/63, 5/65, and 5/66 were identified and transcribed by Barbara Ravelhofer, 'The Stuart Masque: Dance, Costume and Remembering' (unpublished Ph.D. dissertation, Cambridge, 1999), appendix, 25–40. See also Ravelhofer, 'Bureaucrats and courtly cross-dressers in the *Shrovetide Masque* and *The Shepherd's Paradise*', *English Literary Renaissance*, 29 (1999), 75–96; and *The Early Stuart Masque*, 178.
52. The exception was the 1628 Wellingborough masque (apparently unperformed), for which helmets and wooden swords were manufactured. See Britland, *Drama at the Courts of Queen Henrietta Maria*, 64–5.
53. See Ravelhofer, *The Early Stuart Masque*, 178–9.
54. Orgel and Strong, *Inigo Jones*, ii.527, 532. Sarah Poynting observes that the women who cross-dressed or took speaking parts were not the great titled ladies who danced in masques, but a younger and lower-status group. See '"In the name of all the sisters": Henrietta Maria's notorious whores', in *Women and Culture at the Courts of the Stuart Queens*, ed. McManus, 170–1.
55. See Caroline Hibbard, 'The role of a queen consort: the household and court of Henrietta Maria, 1625–1642', in *Princes, Patronage and the Nobility: The Court at the Beginning of the Modern Age, c. 1450–1650*, ed. R. G. Asch and A. M. Birke (Oxford, 1991), 393–414.
56. See Caroline Hibbard, 'Henrietta Maria in the 1630s: perspectives on the role of consort queens in *Ancien Régime* courts', in *The 1630s: Interdisciplinary Essays on Culture and Politics in the Caroline Era*, ed. I. Atherton and J. Sanders (Manchester, 2006), 97–100.
57. Britland, *Drama at the Courts of Queen Henrietta Maria*, 74–5.
58. Britland's *Drama at the Courts of Queen Henrietta Maria* is the definitive treatment of this topic. See also John Peacock, 'The French element in Inigo Jones's masque designs', in *The Court Masque*, ed. Lindley, 149–68; M.-C. Canova-Green, *La politique-spectacle au Grand Siècle: les rapports franco-anglais* (Paris, 1993); Axel Stähler, 'Between tiger and unicorn: *The Temple of Love*', *Journal of the Warburg and Courtauld Institutes*, 61 (1998), 176–97; and Melinda Gough, 'A newly discovered performance by Henrietta Maria', *Huntington Library Quarterly*, 65 (2002), 435–47.
59. Richard Cust, *Charles I: A Political Life* (2005), 285.
60. Hibbard, 'Henrietta Maria in the 1630s', 101.
61. Malcolm Smuts, 'The puritan followers of Henrietta Maria in the 1630s', *English Historical Review*, 93 (1978), 26–45. See also Hibbard, 'The role of a queen consort'; and Kevin Sharpe, *The Personal Rule of Charles I* (1992), 173–9, 537–41. In the 1640s Hamilton was a royalist, but Northumberland supported parliament, Holland changed sides more than once, and Leicester became a neutral (Carlisle died in 1636).
62. L. Forster, 'Two drafts by Weckherlin of a masque for the queen of England', *German Life and Letters*, 18 (1964–5), 258–63. The ballet dates c. 1627–33. See

also David Norbrook, '"The Masque of Truth": court entertainments and Protestant politics in the early Stuart period', *The Seventeenth Century*, 1 (1986), 97–100; and Anthony B. Thompson, 'Licensing the press: the career of G. R. Weckherlin during the personal rule of Charles I', *Historical Journal*, 41 (1998), 653–78.

63. Sophie Tomlinson, 'She that plays the king: Henrietta Maria and the threat of the actress in Caroline culture', in *The Politics of Tragicomedy: Shakespeare and After*, ed. G. McMullan and J. Hope (1992), 190.

64. Veevers, *Images of Love and Religion*, 14–23; cf. Britland, *Drama at the Courts of Queen Henrietta Maria*, 6–13.

65. Britland, *Drama at the Courts of Queen Henrietta Maria*, 6–8; Alison Shell, *Catholicism, Controversy, and the English Literary Imagination 1558–1660* (Cambridge, 1999), 155–6.

66. Sharpe, *The Personal Rule of Charles I*, 306–7; Cust, *Charles I*, 145–7.

67. See Caroline Hibbard, *Charles I and the Popish Plot* (1983).

68. Page references are to W. Davenant, *Luminalia* (1637).

69. Veevers, *Images of Love and Religion*, 146. Cf. Britland, *Drama at the Courts of Queen Henrietta Maria*, 168–76.

70. Veevers, *Images of Love and Religion*, 143–4.

71. Peacock, *The Stage Designs of Inigo Jones*, 204–5.

72. Lenton, *Great Britain's Beauties, or the Female Glory Epitomized* (1638), 5. Lenton's subtitle makes the connection with Stafford's *The Female Glory* explicit. He also wrote a religious poem, 'Queen Esther's Hallelujahs', a subject perhaps alluding to Henrietta Maria's status as the English Esther: see Jerome De Groot's life of Lenton in the *ODNB*.

73. Page references are to *The Poems and Masques of Aurelian Townshend*, ed. Brown. Although the speeches and songs were written by Townshend, the printed text states that the subject, allegory, descriptions, and 'apparatus of the scenes' were 'invented' by Inigo Jones; to all intents this was a masque by Jones rather than Townshend (104–5). The situation is different with *Albion's Triumph*, where Townshend was responsible for the 'invention and writing' (90).

74. This painting dates from 1629–30, but did not enter the Royal Collection until 1635, when Endymion Porter purchased it on Charles's behalf. See C. Lloyd, *The Queen's Pictures* (1991), 104.

75. See Veevers, *Images of Love and Religion*, 187–90; Roy Strong, *Van Dyck: Charles I on Horseback* (1972), 59–63; Malcolm Smuts, *Court Culture and the Origins of a Royalist Tradition in Early Stuart England* (Philadelphia, 1987), 247–9.

76. E. Waller, 'On the danger his majesty (being Prince) escaped in the road at Santander'. The romance elements are discussed by Britland in *Drama at the Courts of Queen Henrietta Maria*.

77. This is thoroughly discussed by Sharpe, *Criticism and Compliment*.

78. Hibbard, 'Henrietta Maria in the 1630s', 96. During the period 1629–40 she gave birth eight times.

79. Jonson, *The Underwood*, 67.37–42.

80. Page references are to *The Poems and Masques of Aurelian Townshend*, ed. Brown.
81. Quotations are from *The Poems of Thomas Carew, with his Masque, 'Coelum Britannicum'*, ed. Dunlap.
82. Britland, *Drama at the Courts of Queen Henrietta Maria*, 72–3.
83. W. Davenant, *The Temple of Love* (1635), D1r–v.
84. For discussion, see Britland, *Drama at the Courts of Queen Henrietta Maria*, 90–110; Tomlinson, 'She that plays the king', 50–8; Axel Stahler, 'Inigo Jones's *Tempe Restored* and Alessandro Piccolomini's *Della Institutione Morale*', *The Seventeenth Century*, 18 (2003), 180–210; Melinda Gough, '"Not as myself": the Queen's voice in *Tempe Restored*', *Modern Philology*, 101 (2003), 48–67; and James Knowles, '"Can ye not tell a man from a marmoset?": apes and others on the early modern stage', in *Renaissance Beasts: Of Animals, Humans, and Other Wonderful Creatures*, ed. Erica Fudge (Urbana, Ill., 2004), 138–63.
85. See Gossett, 'Man-maid, begone!', 108–10.
86. Gough, 'Not as myself', 51.
87. Britland, *Drama at the Courts of Queen Henrietta Maria*, 92–7.
88. Roy Booth, 'The first female professional singers: Madam Coniack', *Notes and Queries*, 242 (1997), 533. The verses 'Upon a very deformed gentlewoman', printed in *Poems, With 'The Muses' Looking Glass' and 'Amyntas'* (1638), survive in manuscript copies with the alternative titles quoted above referring to the Frenchwoman. This identification is accepted by Britland, Tomlinson, and Knowles, though it cannot be absolutely proven, for there could have been more than one female singer in the masques. It is not exactly confirmed by Jones's allegory, which mentions 'The description of [Circe's] person, of extraordinary beauty, and sweetness of her voice' (103). The fugitive favourite implies that Circe comes into court 'in a mask' (95), though no mask is visible in Jones's costume design for her (Orgel and Strong, *Inigo Jones*, II.501–2).
89. See Stahler, 'Inigo Jones's *Tempe Restored*', which analyses the Aristotelian roots of Jones's allegory. Nonetheless, the presentation of Henrietta Maria as beautiful because good preserves some neoplatonic aspect.
90. This point is strongly emphasized by Knowles in 'Can ye not tell a man from a marmoset?'
91. *Le balet comique de la royne*, 1581, trans. Carol MacClintock and Lander MacClintock, *American Institute of Musicology, Musicological Studies and Documents*, 25 (1971), 41–2.
92. References are to I. Jones and W. Davenant, *The Temple of Love* (1634 [1635]).
93. See James Knowles, '"The faction of the flesh": orientalism in the Caroline masque', in *The 1630s*, ed. Atherton and Sanders, 111–37.
94. C. White, *The Dutch Pictures in the Collection of Her Majesty the Queen* (Cambridge, 1982), 55.
95. *Selections from Clarendon*, ed. G. Huehns (Oxford, 1955), 93. Waller also wrote a poem on this famous incident.
96. L. Hutchinson, *Memoirs of the Life of Colonel Hutchinson*, ed. J. Hutchinson (1908), 71. Hutchinson was only born in 1620, but she might have seen some

masques; her father, Sir Allen Apsley (d. 1630), was Lieutenant of the Tower, and she lived near London until 1641. See also Frances E. Dolan, *Whores of Babylon: Catholicism, Gender, and Seventeenth-Century Print Culture* (Ithaca, N.Y., 1999), 125, which considers the development of these tropes around Henrietta Maria in detail.

97. R. Strong, *The English Icon: Elizabethan and Jacobean Portraiture* (1969), 264; A. M. Hind, *Engraving in England in the Sixteenth and Seventeenth Centuries*, vol. II: *The Reign of James I* (Cambridge, 1955), 181. The only exception is a single image of James and Anne by Jan Wierix, probably produced abroad (Hind, *The Reign of James I*, 57). All the other engravings either pre-date the Stuart accession, or post-date Anne's death.

6 THE REVIVAL OF CHIVALRY

1. As noted by the Venetian ambassador: *CSPV 1603–1607*, 308. See also Cuddy, 'Anglo-Scottish union and the court of James I', 109–15; Lindley, *The Trials of Frances Howard*, 13–17; Roy Strong, *Henry Prince of Wales and England's Lost Renaissance* (1986), 42, 44–5; and L. L. Peck, *Northampton: Patronage and Policy at the Court of James I* (1982), 15–21.
2. M. James, *Society, Politics and Culture* (Cambridge, 1986), 416. On the Essex circle, see also J. H. M. Salmon, 'Seneca and Tacitus in Jacobean England', in *The Mental World of the Jacobean Court*, ed. Peck, 169–88.
3. David Norbrook, *Poetry and Politics in the English Renaissance* (1984), 129.
4. Lord Monteagle, Sir John Gray, Sir John Leigh, Sir Robert Maunsell, Sir Henry Goodere, Lord Gerrard, Sir Robert Carey, Sir Robert Drury, Sir Carey Reynolds, Sir Richard Houghton, and Sir William Constable. Additionally, Sir William Woodhouse commanded a regiment at Cadiz; and Lord Willoughby, though only twenty-three, had already fought in Holland, and was son to an Essex client. The identification of Willoughby in *Ben Jonson* (x.439) is erroneous, being caused by gross confusions in the old *DNB* article. For correct details, see the new *DNB*, and HMC 66 (*Ancaster MSS*), xxix.
5. Sussex commanded a regiment at Cadiz and was drawn to Essex through his inability to obtain court office. He frequented Essex House, but was out of town when the rebellion took place (James, *Society, Politics and Culture*, 434; *CSPD 1598–1601*, 546).
6. Constable was arrested after the rebellion but bailed and not tried. Herford and Simpson (*Ben Jonson*, x.430) incorrectly identify him with the William Constable who was made Baronet in 1611 and subsequently became a Forced Loan refuser and Regicide; this was a younger namesake from the same family. Amongst the other knights, Sir Robert Killigrew's father was connected with the Essexian Sir Henry Neville and used his influence to protect him in 1601 (*The House of Commons 1558–1603*, ed. P. W. Hasler, 3 vols. (1981), II.395). It should also be noted that Sir Oliver Cromwell, who fought for virginity and was uncle to the future Protector, was not, as sometimes stated, the same man as the Lord Cromwell who was involved in the Essex revolt.

7. Sir Thomas Monson, Master Falconer and Chancellor to Queen Anne, was a client to the Earl of Northampton (*ODNB*; *The House of Commons 1558–1603*, ed. Hasler, III.67); Sir Roger Dallison was a Howard client; his corrupt practices as Master of the Ordnance were concealed by them (L. Stone, *Family and Fortune*, Oxford, 1973, 280).

8. Several Essex knights fought on the side of marriage, but only Lord Monteagle had a connection with the revolt (he was imprisoned and fined £6,000). In 1606 Monteagle was in high favour, as he had uncovered the Gunpowder Plot, which Jonson celebrated in an epigram to him. Sir John Gray likewise moved into court service. He took no part in the rising but was entrusted with custody of the prisoners; under James he became a gentleman of the Privy Chamber (*The House of Commons 1558–1603*, ed. Hasler, II.224). Sir Henry Goodere became a gentleman of the Privy Chamber in 1603. Sir Robert Maunsell joined Essex on the Cadiz and Islands voyages, but he was related to the Earl of Nottingham and aligned with the court party in local politics. In 1601 he helped arrest the Essexians (*The House of Commons 1558–1603*, ed. Hasler, III.12; A. H. Smith, *County and Court: Government and Politics in Norfolk 1558–1603*, Oxford, 1974, 304). On the other side, the one anomaly was Lord Gerrard, who was friendly with Cecil and in 1601 proclaimed Essex a traitor. But in the 1590s his career as a soldier and knight marshal had kept him close to Essex, and the Earl visited his home. He was an Essexian who in the crisis opted for loyalty (*The House of Commons 1558–1603*, ed. Hasler, II.184–5).

9. *Ben Jonson*, VII.209 (from Jonson's preface to *Hymenaei*). This is how it was read by D. J. Gordon, who said the *Barriers* affirmed 'the eternal Unity which is the ground of the universe' (*The Renaissance Imagination*, 183). This takes Jonson's Truth at face value, and colludes in the masque's ideological mystification.

10. See James, *Society, Politics and Culture*, 315–16.

11. For some full treatments, see M. Lee, Jr, *James I and Henri IV* (Urbana, 1970) and *Great Britain's Solomon*, ch. 9; T. Cogswell, *The Blessed Revolution: English Politics and the Coming of War 1621–1624* (Cambridge, 1989); and the important work of Simon Adams: 'The protestant cause: religious alliance with the West European Calvinist communities as a political issue in England, 1585–1630' (unpublished D.Phil. thesis, Oxford, 1973); 'Foreign policy and the parliaments of 1621 and 1624', in *Faction and Parliament*, ed. K. Sharpe (Oxford, 1978), 139–71; and 'Spain or the Netherlands? The dilemmas of early Stuart foreign policy', in *Before the English Civil War*, ed. H. Tomlinson (London, 1983), 79–101.

12. *The Letters and Life of Francis Bacon*, ed. J. Spedding, 7 vols. (1861–74), VI.157–9; quoted by Adams, 'Foreign policy', 141.

13. Adams, 'Foreign policy', 141.

14. Compare Norbrook, 'The reformation of the masque', 97–8.

15. See Smuts, *Court Culture and the Origins of a Royalist Tradition*, 20–1, and A. Young, *Tudor and Jacobean Tournaments* (1987).

16. James, *Society, Politics and Culture*, 332–3. See also Richard McCoy, *The Rites of Knighthood* (Berkeley, 1989); and Berry, *Of Chastity and Power*, ch. 4.

17. I draw here on the best recent treatment, Young's *Tudor and Jacobean Tournaments*, 37–42. See also J. S. A. Adamson, 'Chivalry and political culture in Caroline England', in *Culture and Politics in Early Stuart England*, ed. P. Lake and K. Sharpe (Houndmills, 1994), 161–97.

18. See Chamberlain, *Letters*, 1.496; and Young, *Tudor and Jacobean Tournaments*, 38. The other six occasions were: the two cited in note 19 below; the tilt after *The Vision of the Twelve Goddesses* in 1604 (see *The Journal of Sir John Wilbraham*, ed. H. S. Scott, *Camden Society Miscellany*, 10, 1902, 66); a match with the Prince and Duke of Brunswick in April 1610 (HMC 75, *Downshire MSS*, 11.276); the celebrations for 5 November 1611 (*CSPV 1610–1613*, 238); and the wedding celebrations for Princess Elizabeth, February 1613 (Nichols, *Progresses of James I*, 11.549). Possibly James participated in other tilts; for example, the payment for a standing for Queen Anne at the 1604 Accession Day tilt implies that James was performing (C. E. McGee and J. C. Meagher, 'Preliminary checklist of Tudor and Stuart entertainments 1603–1613', *Research Opportunities in Renaissance Drama*, 27 (1984), 61).

19. *CSPV 1607–1610*, 246; Lee, ed., *Dudley Carleton to John Chamberlain*, 87. See also *CSPV 1607–1610*, 243.

20. Chamberlain, *Letters*, 1.590, 617; 11.152.

21. At Prince Charles's first tilt, in 1620, the general challengers were the Prince, Buckingham, and Hamilton, but the honours went to Charles and the Earl of Dorset (Chamberlain, *Letters*, 11.298).

22. For full listings, see Young, *Tudor and Jacobean Tournaments*, 205–8, and McGee and Meagher, 'Preliminary checklist of Tudor and Stuart entertainments 1603–1613' and 'Preliminary checklist of Tudor and Stuart entertainments 1614–1625', *Research Opportunities in Renaissance Drama*, 30 (1988). These lists supplement that in Orgel and Strong, *Inigo Jones*, 1.179–80. A tilt was planned for 1624, but was cancelled because two riders were injured in rehearsal.

23. McGee and Meagher, 'Preliminary checklist of Tudor and Stuart entertainments 1603–1613', 77, 85; HMC 75 (*Downshire MSS*), IV.74 (absent from McGee and Meagher).

24. See Orgel and Strong, *Inigo Jones*, 1.176. Orgel and Strong attribute this design to the 1610 tilt on the basis of a letter dated incorrectly in Nichols's *Progresses of James I*: the correct date (given in Birch, *Court and Times of James I*, 1.91) is 1609. Birch's dating can be confirmed internally, since the letter mentions three events from March to April 1609: the censure of Lord Balmerino, and the publications of James's *Apology* and Lancelot Andrewes's *Tortura Torti*. Additionally, by the following year Sir Richard Preston had become Lord Dingwall. Preston was Prince Henry's tutor in arms (T. Birch, *The Life of Henry Prince of Wales*, 1760, 21).

25. Orgel and Strong, *Inigo Jones*, 1.178. The report of the 1610 pageants is in HMC 55 (*Various Collections*), III.261.

26. Orgel and Strong, *Inigo Jones*, 1.180.

27. See Birch, *The Life of Henry Prince of Wales*; E. C. Wilson, *Prince Henry and English Literature* (Cornell, 1946); J. W. Williamson, *The Myth of the*

Conqueror: Prince Henry Stuart, A Study of Seventeenth Century Personation (New York, 1978); Strong, *Henry Prince of Wales*; and Timothy V. Wilks, 'The court culture of Prince Henry and his circle 1603–1613' (unpublished D.Phil. dissertation, Oxford, 1987).

28. P. Croft, 'The parliamentary installation of Henry, Prince of Wales', *Historical Research*, 65 (1992), 180; R. Connock [Connak], *A Collection of the Names of all the Princes of the Kingdom of England* (1747), sig. B1v. Connock's preface asks the Prince to protect him from any royal displeasure that may follow from making these arguments. He was auditor of the Duchy of Cornwall, and became Henry's Solicitor General.

29. *CSPV 1610–1613*, 78. Connock calculated Henry's revenues at over £51,000 (*A Collection of the Names*, 50–60). His household list, running to some 250 names, is printed in *A Collection of Ordinances and Regulations*, 313–39.

30. *CSPV 1610–1613*, 265.

31. Quoted in Birch, *The Life of Henry Prince of Wales*, 76.

32. Chamberlain, *Letters*, 1.330.

33. These images are reproduced by Strong, *Henry Prince of Wales*: see plates 22, 23, 33, 42, 45, and 48.

34. Winwood, *Memorials*, III.410.

35. *CSPV 1610–1613*, 450.

36. For correspondence with Clement Edmondes, Sir Edward Cecil, and Sir Edward Conway, see Birch, *The Life of Henry Prince of Wales*, 43, 153–5, 181. Henry entertained the Duke of Brunswick and Prince of Anhalt in 1610, and the Prince of Hesse in 1611 (*CSPV 1607–1610*, 465, *1610–1613*, 78; HMC 29, *Portland MSS*, IX.26–7).

37. HMC 75 (*Downshire MSS*), III.1–2. Southampton sometimes joined in the revels (as at *The Vision of The Twelve Goddesses*), but *Oberon* is his only recorded appearance as a masquer.

38. *CSPV 1610–1613*, 52, 227, 240, 264–5, 283.

39. P. Lefranc, *Sir Walter Raleigh écrivain* (Paris, 1968), 256–9, 596–601; Ralegh, *Works*, ed. T. Birch, 2 vols. (1751), II.71–107, 359–61; Ralegh, *Excellent Observations and Notes Concerning the Royal Navy and Sea Service* (1650). For Gorges's dedications to Prince Henry, see H. E. Sandison, 'Manuscripts of the "Islands Voyage" and "Notes on the Royal Navy"', in *Essays and Studies in Honour of Carleton Brown* (New York, 1940), 242–52; and J. Gibson, 'Civil war in 1614: Lucan, Gorges, and Prince Henry', in *The Crisis of 1614 and the Addled Parliament*, ed. S. Clucas and R. Davies (Aldershot, 2003), 161–76.

40. Williamson, *The Myth of the Conqueror*, 51–2; R. Harcourt, *A Relation of a Voyage to Guiana*, ed. C. A. Harris, Hakluyt Society, 2nd series, 60 (1928), 51.

41. *CSPV 1610–1613*, 405; and compare 265, 402.

42. Cornwallis, *A Discourse of the Most Illustrious Prince, Henry, late Prince of Wales* (1641) in *The Harleian Miscellany*, ed. W. Oldys, 10 vols. (1808–13), IV. 336. Cornwallis was Prince Henry's Treasurer.

43. Cornwallis, *A Discourse of the Most Illustrious Prince*, 335.

44. *A Collection of Ordinances and Regulations*, 338; W. H. [William Heydon?], *The True Picture and Relation of Prince Henry* (Leyden, 1634), 9. The Venetian ambassador stressed that Henry formulated his household regulations himself (*CSPV 1610–1613*, 106).

45. W. H., *The True Picture*, 2.

46. *CSPV 1610–1613*, 450. Ralegh also gave him marital advice, suggesting the best match would be a French princess: *Works*, I.249–80.

47. HMC 29 (*Portland MSS*), IX.35–6. See also 8–11, 26–7, 31–9.

48. See *Henry Prince of Wales*, of which this is the overarching argument.

49. *CSPV 1603–1607*, 513–14, *1607–1610*, 516; Birch, *The Life of Henry Prince of Wales*, 90, 109–10.

50. Birch, *The Life of Henry Prince of Wales*, 194. This story is retailed in Robert Johnston's Latin history of Great Britain (1642), and certainly Henry's appointment to the Privy Council in 1611 was a significant event, though Johnston might be confusing the story with Salisbury's attempt to dissuade him from demanding his revenues too early. See HMC 75 (*Downshire MSS*), III.155; Croft, 'The parliamentary installation of Henry, Prince of Wales', 180, and, generally, 'Robert Cecil and the early Jacobean court', 140–2.

51. HMC 29 (*Portland MSS*), IX.9.

52. Wilks, 'The court culture of Prince Henry', 220–1.

53. HMC 29 (*Portland MSS*), IX.34.

54. Strong exaggerates the polarization between Jacobean and 'Henrician' culture, playing up Henry's credentials as a far-seeing and ideologically motivated connoisseur, and playing down James's abilities. His image of James, as a 'bloated pedantic middle-aged father, careless of affairs of state, prepared to accept appeasement at any price, bent on the pleasures of the chase, totally unaesthetic, whose penchant for handsome courtiers was hardly becoming', is a caricature (*Henry Prince of Wales*, 15). Additionally, he does not distinguish between what Henry was personally concerned to achieve and expectations that were projected onto him, and he credits gossip, hearsay, and retrospective mythologizing. There are important corrections in Wilks's excellent dissertation, 'The court culture of Prince Henry'.

55. See Croft, 'Robert Cecil and the early Jacobean court', 140–2.

56. HMC 29 (*Portland MSS*), IX.11.

57. Cornwallis, *A Discourse of the Most Illustrious Prince*, 334; cf. W. H., *The True Picture*, 3.

58. *CSPV 1610–1613*, 106, *1607–1610*, 516.

59. *CSPV 1607–1610*, 227; and see 451.

60. *CSPV 1607–1610*, 206.

61. HMC 29 (*Portland MSS*), IX.10.

62. Cf. William Hunt, 'Spectral origins of the English revolution: legitimation crisis in early Stuart England', in *Reviving the English Revolution*, ed. G. Eley and W. Hunt (1988), 305–22.

63. *CSPV 1607–1610*, 401, 496; *1610–1613*, 79. Another reason for abandoning the procession was the security scare caused by Henri IV's assassination (Croft, 'The installation of Henry, Prince of Wales', 186–7).

64. See R. Strong, *Art and Power: Renaissance Festivals 1450–1650* (Woodbridge, 1984), 56.

65. For *Prince Henry's Barriers* and *Oberon*, the documents in *Ben Jonson*, x.509–11 and 519–22 show Henry's officers Sir Thomas Chaloner and Sir David Murray negotiating with the Exchequer over payments. The Revels accounts call *Love Restored* 'The Prince's masque', but the bills were paid by the King (*Ben Jonson*, x.531–3). *Tethys' Festival* was paid for jointly by King and Queen, and the unperformed masque of Christmas 1611–12 was planned jointly by Prince and Queen (HMC 75, *Downshire MSS*, III.181).

66. The classic instance, discussed below, is the often reiterated dissatisfaction with *Oberon*, but *Prince Henry's Barriers* has been similarly criticized. Strong gives a one-sided account of the *Barriers* and *Tethys' Festival*, complaining they were not militaristic enough. He assumes that they should have been straightforwardly interventionist, and since they weren't he dismisses them as 'floundering' or 'blunted' (*Henry Prince of Wales*, 144, 156).

67. Chamberlain, *Letters*, 1.293. The Simpsons calculate the cost at £2,466, but overlook the armoury bill of £81 (*Ben Jonson*, x.511). Their account (II.203, x.512) also muddles the January *Barriers* with the June investiture. The sources give the number of defendants as, variously, fifty-six or fifty-eight.

68. HMC 75 (*Downshire MSS*), II.199.

69. See M. C. Williams, 'Merlin and the prince: *The Speeches at Prince Henry's Barriers*', *Renaissance Drama*, n.s. 8 (1977), 221–30.

70. See J. Peacock, 'Jonson and Jones collaborate on *Prince Henry's Barriers*', *Word and Image*, 3 (1987), 173.

71. Peacock, 'Jonson and Jones collaborate', 172–94.

72. See, for example, Norman Council's influential essay 'Ben Jonson, Inigo Jones and the transformation of Tudor chivalry', *ELH*, 47 (1980), 259–75; and Strong, *Henry Prince of Wales*, 142–4. My own reading is close to Williamson's in *The Myth of the Conqueror*; and cf. W. T. Furniss, 'Ben Jonson's masques', in R. B. Young, W. T. Furniss, and W. G. Madsen, *Three Studies in the Renaissance* (New Haven, 1958), 124–7.

73. R. Cotton, *An Answer made by Command of Prince Henry to Certain Propositions of War and Peace* (1655), 6. This tract circulated extensively in manuscript: see S. Daniel, *The Brotherton Manuscript*, ed. J. Pitcher (Leeds, 1981), 21, and n.28.

74. Daniel, *The Brotherton Manuscript*, 131–7.

75. The best account is Lee, *James I and Henri IV*, 142–67.

76. *CSPV 1607–1610*, 410.

77. John Peacock points out that Jonson's Latinized form of Henry's *nom-de-guerre* suppressed its religious significance. Its original form, 'Moeliades', could be anagrammatized as 'Miles a Deo' ('Jonson and Jones collaborate', 173–4).

78. Chamberlain, *Letters*, 1.293.

79. Orgel and Strong, misled by Nichols's misdating of the elephant pageant (see note 24 above), confusingly treat this tilt as if it was an exceptional occasion (*Inigo Jones*, 1.177). In fact there were no pageants in March 1610: the two most elaborate tournaments in these years were the 1609 Accession Day tilt and the

investiture tilt (6 June 1610). Strong has a more correct account in *Henry Prince of Wales*, 158–9, but he misdates the investiture tilt, and mixes up the 1609 and 1610 Accession Days (151–2).

80. *CSPV 1610–1613*, 153; and Strong, *Henry Prince of Wales*, 76.
81. *CSPV 1607–1610*, 451.
82. Croft, 'The parliamentary installation of Henry, Prince of Wales', 177.
83. HMC 75 (*Downshire MSS*), 11.317; 55 (*Various MSS*), 11.361. The figures are exaggerated: the entire population of London at this time was less than 500,000.
84. HMC 75 (*Downshire MSS*), 11.316.
85. Croft, 'The parliamentary installation of Henry, Prince of Wales', 183–4, 190–1.
86. Some ladies were present, but confined to the gallery; see HMC 55 (*Various MSS*), 111.260. For the limited entry, see Birch, *Court and Times of James I*, 1.112.
87. Birch, *Court and Times of James I*, 1.112; HMC 55 (*Various MSS*), 111.260.
88. I quote *Tethys' Festival* from *Court Masques*, ed. Lindley. Aside from Strong, the only serious discussions are by John Pitcher, '"In those figures which they seeme": Samuel Daniel's *Tethys' Festival*', in *The Court Masque*, ed. Lindley, 33–46; and Berry and Archer, 'Reinventing the matter of Britain', 119–34.
89. E. C. Williams, *Anne of Denmark* (Harlow, 1970), 44.
90. See E. Rosenthal, 'Plus ultra, non plus ultra, and the columnar device of emperor Charles V', and 'The invention of the columnar device of emperor Charles V', *JWCI*, 34 (1971), 204–28, and 36 (1973), 198–230, respectively; and C. Vivanti, 'Henri IV, the Gallic Hercules', *JWCI*, 30 (1967), 176–97. This image is central to Daniel's 'Epistle to Prince Henry': see *The Brotherton Manuscript*, 132.
91. Lee, *James I and Henri IV*, 143–4; G. Edmundson, *Anglo-Dutch Rivalry during the First Half of the Seventeenth Century* (Oxford, 1911), 19–27; R. Tuck, *Philosophy and Government 1572–1651* (Cambridge, 1993), 169–79.
92. Ralegh, *Works*, 11.71–90; Munday, *Pageants and Entertainments*, 35–44.
93. HMC 75 (*Downshire MSS*), 11.330; *CSPV 1610–1613*, 24. The Speaker of the House of Commons, Sir Edward Phelips, was later given a top appointment in Henry's household (*CSPV 1610–1613*, 93).
94. See *The Order and Solemnities of the Creation of Prince Henry, Prince of Wales, Whereunto is Annexed the Royal Masque* (1610).
95. For representative reactions, see Chamberlain, *Letters*, 1.300; *CSPV 1607–1610*, 439, 496, 499–500; and W. Notestein, *The House of Commons 1604–1610* (New Haven, 1971), 255–434.
96. *CSPV 1610–1613*, 106.
97. Connock, 'Advice to Prince Henry', in *A Collection of the Names*, 69, 71. Internal indications date this tract to the time immediately after the investiture.
98. HMC 29 (*Portland MSS*), 37.
99. Orgel, *The Jonsonian Masque*, 88–91.
100. Goldberg, *James I and the Politics of Literature*, 123–6.

101. *Ben Jonson*, x.521.
102. *The Boke of Duke Huon of Burdeux*, trans. Lord Berners, ed. S. L. Lee, Early English Text Society, extra series, 40–1 (1883), xxxi–xxxii, 603. This translation, made in 1534, was available in a 1601 reprint.
103. Peacock, 'Jonson and Jones collaborate', 187–8. One observer said their costumes were 'as the Roman emperors are represented': HMC 75 (*Downshire MSS*), iii.1.
104. The myth of sleeping heroes also recurred in compressed form in the sequence in which the satyrs rouse the guards.
105. *James I and the Politics of Literature*, 123.
106. See Orgel and Strong, *Inigo Jones*, i.221. This detail Jones carried over from the source for his design, an antique scene by Marcantonio Raimondi: see Peacock, *The Stage Designs of Inigo Jones*, 142–3. The satyrs had conspicuously erect phalluses in the staged revival at Case Western Reserve University, 1992, though this was probably a touch by the director, Barry Rutter, who used similar costumes in his 1988 production of Tony Harrison's *The Trackers of Oxyrhynchus*.
107. A library was arising at St James's, and expensive works were in hand at Richmond (Strong, *Henry Prince of Wales*, 107). Jones had already been appointed Surveyor to the Prince.
108. HMC 75 (*Downshire MSS*), iii.1.
109. In Spenser's *Faerie Queene*, Oberon is the father of Gloriana (2.10.75–6; and see 2.1.6).
110. See Orgel and Strong, *Inigo Jones*, i.212–15. These were part of Jones's first design for the palace, and were rejected in favour of a second, more syncretic version: for the best analysis of this, see J. Peacock, 'The Stuart court masque and the theatre of the Greeks', *JWCI*, 56 (1993), 207–8. Though the designs were not used, they show how Jones's and Jonson's imaginations were working.
111. Peacock, 'The French element in Inigo Jones's masque designs', 151–2; A. Blunt, *Philibert de L'Orme* (1958). For the Diana cult around Henri II's mistress, see F. J. Baumgartner, *Henry II King of France 1547–1559* (Durham, N.C., 1988); Françoise Bourdon, *Diane de Poitiers et le mythe de Diane* (Paris, 1963); and Berry, *Of Chastity and Power*, 47–53.
112. See Goldberg, *James I and the Politics of Literature*, 124.
113. Peacock, 'The Stuart court masque and the theatre of the Greeks', 207.
114. BL Add. MS. 58833, cited in R. M. Smuts, 'Public ceremony and royal charisma: the English royal entry in London', in *The First Modern Society: Essays in English History in Honour of Lawrence Stone*, ed. A. L. Beier, D. Cannadine, and J. Rosenhein (Cambridge, 1989), 69–93, 89. Chamberlain claimed that the fireworks and water tournament alone cost £9,000 (*Letters*, 1.428).
115. Strong, *Henry Prince of Wales*, 176; *CSPV 1610–1613*, 447.
116. Strong, *Henry Prince of Wales*, 175.
117. See the contemporary analysis in HMC 75 (*Downshire MSS*), iii.251–2, and the reports of the 1612 election (291, 293). The best modern accounts are

C. P. Clasen, *The Palatinate in European History* (Oxford, 1966); Adams, 'The protestant cause'; Lee, *James I and Henri IV*, 168–85; and Cogswell, *The Blessed Revolution*, 12–20.

118. HMC 75 (*Downshire MSS*), IV.41; Chamberlain, *Letters*, 1.427.

119. HMC 75 (*Downshire MSS*), III.278.

120. Chamberlain, *Letters*, 1.449. For the accelerated departure, see HMC 75 (*Downshire MSS*), III.444.

121. Chamberlain, *Letters*, 1.404; Williams, *Anne of Denmark*, 156.

122. D. Norbrook, '"The Masque of Truth": court entertainments and international Protestant politics in the early Stuart period', *The Seventeenth Century*, 1 (1986), 81–110. My discussion does little more than replay Norbrook's brilliant analysis.

123. D. Jocquet, *Les Triomphes, Entrees, Cartels, Turnois, Ceremonies, et aultres Magnificences faites en Angleterre et au Palatinat pour le Marriage et Reception de Monseigneur le Prince Frederick V* (Heidelberg, 1613).

124. Norbrook, 'The masque of Truth', 101.

125. J. Sylvester, *Lachrimae lachrimarum* (1612), sig. A2.

126. The choice of Campion's, Chapman's, and Beaumont's masques was not fixed until January 1613: see HMC 75 (*Downshire MSS*), IV.2.

127. Nichols, *Progresses of James I*, II.537–41.

128. Jocquet, *Les triomphes*, sig. A4. The other two narratives were a German pamphlet, *Beschreibung der Reiss* (Heidelberg, 1613), and a French newsbook, *Troisième Tome du Mercure François* (Paris, 1616). On the basis of differences in the transcription of the songs, Norbrook suggests ('The masque of truth', 84) that the French version derived from an independent source, indicating that the *Masque of Truth* existed outside Jocquet's account. But I cannot find any differences between the two, and it is more likely that the Paris account was worked up from Jocquet's.

129. J. R. Mulryne, 'Marriage entertainments in the Palatinate for Prince Elizabeth Stuart and the Elector Palatine', in *Italian Renaissance Festivals and their European Influence*, ed. Mulryne and Shewring, 173–96; HMC 75 (*Downshire MSS*), IV.108.

130. The lances are mentioned in diplomatic reports: see *A Score for 'The Lords' Masque' by Thomas Campion*, ed. A. J. Sabol (Hanover, N.H., 1993), 27. English, French, and German observers all dwelt on the masquers' identity as chivalric knights.

131. References are to the text in Campion, *Works*, ed. Davis.

132. Lindley, *Thomas Campion*, 209.

133. G. Parry, 'The politics of the Jacobean masque', in *Theatre and Government under the Early Stuarts*, ed. J. R. Mulryne and M. Shewring (Cambridge, 1993), 106.

134. References are to the text edited by Philip Edwards in *A Book of Masques*, gen. eds. Spencer and Wells.

135. A. Gorges, *Poems*, ed. H. E. Sandison (Oxford, 1953).

136. D. J. Gordon, 'Chapman's *Memorable Masque*', in *The Renaissance Imagination*, 194–202. See also David Lindley, 'Courtly play: the politics of

Chapman's *Memorable Masque*', in *The Stuart Courts*, ed. E. Cruickshanks (Stroud, 2000), 43–58.

137. Chamberlain, *Letters*, 1.325.
138. *CSPV 1610–1613*, 328, 300–1; and see R. Strong, 'England and Italy: the marriage of Henry Prince of Wales', in *For Veronica Wedgwood These*, ed. R. Ollard and P. Tudor-Craig (1986), 59–87.
139. H. Peacham, *Minerva Britanna* (1612), 149.
140. Though the name was sometimes used to mean frivolous courtiers: see John Castle's letter of 19 November 1616: 'some of the capriccios of the court, that would gain the name of wits by traducing the best things of others' (Birch, *Court and Times of James I*, 1.441).
141. W. H., *The True Picture*, 30–1.
142. Gordon, *The Renaissance Imagination*, 201.
143. Strong, *Henry Prince of Wales*, 60; D. Kay, *Melodious Tears: The English Funeral Elegy from Spenser to Milton* (Oxford, 1990), 12.
144. W. Ralegh, *The Discovery of the Large, Rich and Beautiful Empire of Guiana* (1596), sig. 2r; and compare 67–8, 83.
145. S. R. Gardiner, *History of England ... 1603–1642*, 10 vols. (1883–4), II.380.
146. See Norbrook, 'The Masque of Truth', and *A Score for 'The Lords' Masque*', ed. Sabol.

7 THE DANCE OF FAVOUR

1. Chamberlain, *Letters*, 1.328. This letter is damaged, and this section has extensive lacunae. The words in square brackets are my conjectural amplifications of missing passages.
2. This point is speculative, and involves filling in Chamberlain's gaps. I assume Suffolk was the father who 'said he repented that he had not entreated ... and his daughter to dance'.
3. Chamberlain calls the performers 'gallants chosen out of the King's and Prince's men' (*Letters*, 1.328). In Jonson's folio, they are 'gentlemen the King's servants', but the Revels accounts call it 'the Prince's masque' (*Ben Jonson*, VII.377, X.531). It is sometimes assumed that Henry himself danced, and this seems likely, though nothing in the documents indicates it.
4. See M. Butler, 'Ben Jonson and the limits of courtly panegyric', in *Culture and Politics in Early Stuart England*, ed. Lake and Sharpe, 100–4. For some different readings, compare J. Fischer, '*Love Restored*: a defence of masquing', *Renaissance Drama*, n.s. 8 (1977), 231–44; and Marcus, *The Politics of Mirth*, 29–38.
5. S. R. Gardiner, *History of England 1603–42*, 10 vols. (1883–4), II.134–65; R. Strong, 'England and Italy', 59–87; Chamberlain, *Letters*, 1.323; J. Cramsie, *Kingship and Crown Finance under James VI and I* (Woodbridge, 2002), 117–50.
6. Jonson closely echoed Salisbury's sentiments about forcibly raising cash. Salisbury told the 1610 parliament 'there is no greater a slave than money and not worthy to be accounted among wise men, it being good for nothing but use' (*Proceedings in Parliament 1610*, ed. E. R. Foster, 2 vols. New Haven, 1966, 1.6).

7. For Palmer and Bovey, see *Ben Jonson*, X.599, 607, 637, 650–1. Palmer was Prince Charles's cup-bearer. James Bovey (*pace* the Simpsons, in *Ben Jonson*, X.429) was a son of the Serjeant of the King's wine cellar, 'a boy of spirit, a good rider, lutenist, dancer, etc'; in 1617 Charles paid for him to be brought back from the Hague after he ran away (*CSPD 1611–1618*, 437). Chamberlain listed Achmouty and Abercromby among 'the high dancers' and 'such like dancing companions' (*Letters*, 1.496; 11.128). Abercromby would receive considerable financial rewards from the crown, such as an unusually large New Year's gift in 1627 (BL Egerton MS 2816).

8. For fuller discussion, see M. Butler, 'Jonson's *News from the New World*, the "running masque", and the season of 1619–20', *MaRDiE*, 6 (1993), 153–78.

9. NA SP 14/94/83 (Sir Gerard Herbert to Sir Dudley Carleton, 31 December 1617), 14/95/3 (Nathaniel Brent to Carleton, 2 January 1618).

10. Alastair Bellany, *The Politics of Court Scandal in Early Modern England* (Cambridge, 2002); and James Knowles, 'Crack kisses, not staves: sexual politics and court masques in 1613–1614', in *The Crisis of 1614 and the Addled Parliament*, ed. S. Clucas and R. Davies (Aldershot, 2003), 143–60. See also Cuddy, 'The revival of the entourage', and Pauline Croft's reservations in 'Robert Cecil and the early Jacobean court', 145–6.

11. Birch, *Court and Times of James I*, 1.248. See also Peck, *Northampton:*, 30–3; and P. R. Seddon, 'Robert Carr, Earl of Somerset', *Renaissance and Modern Studies*, 14 (1970), 48–68.

12. *CSPV 1613–1615*, 219 (dispatch of 7/17 October 1614).

13. The indispensable treatments are Lindley's *The Trials of Frances Howard*, and Bellany's *The Politics of Court Scandal*. For one client of Somerset whose career was damaged by his fall but who remained loyal, see *Letters of John Holles*, ed. P. R. Seddon, 3 vols. (Nottingham, 1975–86), and HMC 29 (Portland MSS), IX. The equivalent poetic example is George Chapman, whose court hopes ended with Somerset's disgrace.

14. The fullest treatments of the 1617–20 financial reforms are F. C. Dietz, *English Public Finance 1558–1641* (2nd edn, 1964); M. Prestwich, *Cranfield: Politics and Profits under the Early Stuarts* (Oxford, 1966); P. R. Seddon, 'Household reforms in the reign of James I', *Bulletin of the Institute of Historical Research*, 53 (1980), 44–5; R. Lockyer, *The Early Stuarts* (Harlow, 1989), 71–94; Peck, *Court Patronage and Corruption*; and Cramsie, *Kingship and Crown Finance under James VI and I*. On Suffolk, see A. P. P. Keep, 'Star Chamber proceedings against the Earl of Suffolk and others', *English Historical Review*, 13 (1898), 716–29.

15. The fullest treatment of this topic is Peck, *Court Patronage and Corruption*.

16. HMC 75 (*Downshire MSS*) 11.344.

17. Birch, *Court and Times of James I*, 1.191.

18. Chamberlain, *Letters*, 11.325.

19. Peck, *Court Patronage and Corruption*, 34; Lockyer, *The Early Stuarts*, 72; NA SP 14/95/3. See also *CSPV 1610–1613*, 12.

20. Dietz, *English Public Finance 1558–1641*, 405.

21. Peck, *Court Patronage and Corruption*, 34.
22. Prestwich, *Cranfield*, 199–252; R. H. Tawney, *Business and Politics under James I* (Cambridge, 1958), 152–83. And compare G. E. Aylmer, 'Attempts at administrative reform 1625–40', *English Historical Review*, 72 (1957), 246–59.
23. Chamberlain, *Letters*, II.150.
24. Seddon, 'Household reforms in the reign of James I', 54; Goodman, *The Court of King James the First*, I.320.
25. James I, *Works*, 320. Cf. L. L. Peck, '"For a king not to be bountiful were a fault": perspectives on patronage in early Stuart England', *Journal of British Studies*, 25 (1986), 31–61.
26. See Roger Lockyer, *Buckingham* (Harlow, 1981), 48–50, 71–5.
27. For Somerset's sober self-image, see A. R. Braunmuller, 'Robert Carr, Earl of Somerset as collector and patron', in *The Mental World of the Jacobean Court*, ed. Peck, 230–50.
28. Chamberlain, *Letters*, I.497.
29. Chamberlain, *Letters*, I.496, 499.
30. *Maxims and Reflections*, trans. Mario Donandi (Philadelphia, 1965), 86; quoted by Frank Whigham, *Ambition and Privilege: The Social Tropes of Elizabethan Courtesy Theory* (Berkeley, 1984), 22–3. For similar sentiments from Castiglione and Romei, see Whigham, 47 and 89.
31. HMC 75 (*Downshire MSS*), IV.267. The lawyers went on collecting money for the Palatine celebrations for a long time: see T. Orbison, 'The Middle Temple documents relating to George Chapman's *The Memorable Masque*', *Malone Society Collections*, 12 (1983), 1–30; and J. R. Elliott, 'Musical and dramatic documents from the Middle Temple', *Malone Society Collections*, 15 (1993), 171–94.
32. Chamberlain, *Letters*, I.493; and see the discussion by E. A. J. Honigmann in *A Book of Masques*, ed. Spencer and Wells, 151–4.
33. Chamberlain, *Letters*, I.499; HMC 75 (*Downshire MSS*), IV.286; Orrell, 'The London court stage in the Savoy correspondence', 82.
34. Campion, *Works*, ed. Davis, 268; J. Orrell, 'The agent of Savoy at the *Somerset masque*', *Review of English Studies*, n.s. 28 (1977), 301–4.
35. For Campion's patronage, see Lindley, *Thomas Campion*, 64–6, 210–11.
36. Orrell, 'The London court stage in the Savoy correspondence', 80. One possible refuser was George Clifford, son to the fourth Earl of Cumberland. See the letter to him from Carr printed by T. D. Whitaker, *The History and Antiquities of the Deanery of Craven* (1812), 365, warning that his father's affairs would suffer if he excused himself (the date is wrong, since Carr signs himself 'Rochester', which puts the letter in the period 1611–13, and hence probably for this tilt). I am very grateful to James Knowles for this reference.
37. NA SP 14/75/37, fol. 64.
38. NA SP 14/75/15, fol. 59. See Chambers, *Elizabethan Stage*, III.246.
39. HMC 75 (*Downshire MSS*), IV.286. Compare Chamberlain's moderate remarks in *Letters*, I.495, 498. Philip Gawdy's account mentions 'great gifts of plate' (BL Egerton MS 2804, fol. 208).

40. Lindley, *The Trials of Frances Howard*. See also Lindley's 'Embarrassing Ben: the masques for Frances Howard', *English Literary Renaissance*, 16 (1986), 343–59.
41. *CSPV 1610–1613*, 142; Chamberlain, *Letters*, 1.548. Thomas Lorkin reported some even more effusive remarks: Birch, *Court and Times of James I*, 1.336.
42. HMC 75 (*Downshire MSS*), IV.221; Chamberlain, *Letters*, 1.515; HMC 75 (*Downshire MSS*), IV.385. Somerset is often referred to simply as 'the great lord': see Chamberlain, 1.606, and HMC 75 (*Downshire MSS*), IV.470.
43. HMC 75 (*Downshire MSS*), III.285–6, 412; *CSPV 1610–1613*, 135. See also Goodman, *The Court of King James the First*, 1.215 ('truly he was a wise, discreet gentleman'); and the evidence collected in Braunmuller, 'Robert Carr, Earl of Somerset as collector and patron'.
44. HMC 29 (*Portland MSS*), IX.32. Holles became a firm follower of Somerset, remaining loyal even after his fall.
45. HMC 75 (*Downshire MSS*), IV.252.
46. HMC 75 (*Downshire MSS*), IV.285, 385; Orrell, 'The London court stage in the Savoy correspondence', 81.
47. For Anne and Carr, see the great quarrel narrated at HMC 75 (*Downshire MSS*), III.83; and Lindley, *The Trials of Frances Howard*, 84. Her Vice-Chamberlain was a Sidney, Lord Lisle; and see Barroll, 'The court of the first Stuart queen', in *The Mental World of the Jacobean Court*, ed. Peck, 200–5.
48. Chamberlain expected that the Twelfth Night masque, *The Masque of Flowers*, would be financed by the Queen (*Letters*, 1.487), though it was paid for by Bacon.
49. HMC 29 (*Portland MSS*), IX.31. For the changes of plan around October–November, see HMC 75 (*Downshire MSS*), IV.242, and Chamberlain, *Letters*, 1.481, 485: correspondents repeatedly treat the two weddings as parallel events. For the pastoral, see Daniel, *Hymen's Triumph*, ed. Pitcher (1994), v–xvii; Orrell, 'The London court stage in the Savoy correspondence', 82–3, and *The Theatres of Inigo Jones and John Webb*, 14.
50. Daniel, *Hymen's Triumph*, 517, 492. This whole passage contrasts a disappearing Golden Age simplicity with the 'corrupted humours' of today's favoured shepherds in terms which, though conventional, were applicable to the Jacobean patronage system.
51. See 72–3 above.
52. *The Irish Masque* was the celebration in hand before it was decided to make Somerset's wedding the centrepiece to Whitehall's Christmas. See Lindley, *The Trials of Frances Howard*, 128.
53. Lindley, *The Trials of Frances Howard*, 138–9.
54. References are to Campion, *Works*, ed. Davis.
55. Orrell, 'The agent of Savoy at the *Somerset Masque*', 304n. It is worth noting that it was customary for gentlemen newly admitted to James's Bedchamber to be presented to him by the Queen, the fiction being that they were appointed at her recommendation. This was done with Villiers (R. Lockyer, *Buckingham*. 1981, 19–20).

56. Sullivan, *Court Masques of James I*, 89 (quoting a dispatch from Sarmiento to Inoiosa, 1/10 January 1614, NA Spanish Transcripts, 2/35).
57. HMC 29 (*Portland MSS*), ix.65.
58. HMC 29 (*Portland MSS*), ix.72–3.
59. HMC 29 (*Portland MSS*), ix.94.
60. For the dating of these masques, which is crucial to their interpretation, see the introductions in *The Cambridge Edition of the Works of Ben Jonson*. Much critical discussion of them has been nullified by Percy Simpson's mistaken conviction that they were performed in reverse order to that in which they were printed.
61. Chamberlain, *Letters*, 1.561.
62. Chamberlain, *Letters*, 1.559; and compare HMC 75 (*Downshire MSS*), v.58.
63. Cuddy, 'The revival of the entourage', 215.
64. Chamberlain, *Letters*, 1.570.
65. J. Donne, *Letters to Several Persons of Honour* (1651), 149, 198 (letters of 13 and 20 December 1614).
66. The chaos surrounding the diplomatic invitations is wearisomely described by Finet (*Ben Jonson*, x.554–7) and Foscarini (*CSPV 1613–1615*, 317–18, 328), and confirmed by Chamberlain (*Letters*, 1.570). Finet was adamant that Somerset should have known better, and implies very strongly that his action was malicious.
67. *CSPV 1615–1617*, 62 (3/13 November 1615).
68. HMC 75 (*Downshire MSS*), v.390.
69. HMC 77 (*De Lisle and Dudley MSS*), v.340, 344.
70. HMC 29 (*Portland MSS*), ix.171.
71. This section compresses material from 'Ben Jonson and the limits of courtly panegryic', and from M. Butler and D. Lindley, 'Restoring Astraea: Jonson's masque for the fall of Somerset', *ELH*, 61 (1994), 807–27.
72. *CSPV 1615–1617*, 79; HMC 75 (*Downshire MSS*), v.373.
73. *Ben Jonson*, x.546
74. A. M. Crino, 'Il processo a Lord e Lady Somerset per l'assassinio di Sir Thomas Overbury nelle relazioni di Francesco Quaratesi ed di Pompilio Gaetani', *English Miscellany*, 8 (1957), 261.
75. *Ben Jonson*, x.547.
76. For full illustration of these strategies, see Butler and Lindley, 'Restoring Astraea', 810–14; and Lindley, *The Trials of Frances Howard*, 159, 186.
77. David Lindley points out that anxiety was expressed at Weston's trial that the law be not made 'a net to catch the little fishes or flies and let the great go', and repeated in sermons and reports ('Restoring Astraea', 813 and note 16).
78. *CSPV 1613–1615*, 512; *1615–1617*, 37.
79. HMC 75 (*Downshire MSS*), v.224, 386; *CSPV 1615–1617*, 79.
80. This connection is made by Barroll, *Anna of Denmark*, 150–1.
81. In June 1616 the Somersets were sentenced to death, but James commuted this to imprisonment.
82. HMC 75 (*Downshire MSS*), v.386, 392, 409, 415, 419.

83. Chamberlain, *Letters*, ii.49 (and compare Lockyer, *Buckingham*, 28); *The Diary of Sir Simonds D'Ewes*, ed. Bourcier, 56–7. There are difficulties with D'Ewes's report. D'Ewes did not personally see the masque (he was upset that it was danced on a Sunday), and nowhere else in his English reign is James mentioned as dancing. Possibly Buckingham's wife was taken out by the Prince (cf. D'Ewes's remarks on p. 78 about favours shown to him at the masque by Charles), but even if not, the comments testify to what observers supposed was going on.

84. See chapter 1, 32–3 above.

85. See D. B. J. Randall, *Jonson's Gypsies Unnmasked* (Durham, N.C., 1975), and, more broadly, D. Norbrook, *Poetry and Politics in the English Renaissance* (1984), 224.

86. See M. Butler, '"We are one mans all": Jonson's *The Gipsies Metamorphosed*', *Yearbook of English Studies*, 21 (1991), 253–73; and 'Jonson's *News from the New World*, the "running masque", and the season of 1619–20'.

87. Chamberlain, *Letters*, ii.31–2; also *Letters from George Lord Carew to Sir Thomas Roe*, ed. J. Maclean, *Camden Society Publications* 76 (1860), 54–5; and full references in McGee and Meagher, 'Preliminary checklist of Tudor and Stuart entertainments 1614–1625', 40–2. The further entertainments included plays, and barriers performed by gentlemen from the Inns of Court. An entertainment by the Lord Mayor for the newly ennobled KBs ended scandalously when the courtiers took liberties with the citizens' wives (Chamberlain, *Letters*, ii.35).

88. Prestwich, *Cranfield*, 160; Chamberlain, *Letters*, ii.127.

89. *CSPV 1617–1619*, 87.

90. Tawney, *Business and Politics under James I*, 145–7; and see Prestwich, *Cranfield*, 199–252.

91. For the officers' resistance, see *The Letters and the Life of Francis Bacon*, ed. Spedding, v.275, 280–1, 283–5; and NA SP 14/94/52 (Gerard Herbert to Carleton, 6 December 1617) and 14/95/12 (Nathaniel Brent to Carleton, 10 January 1618).

92. NA SP 14/94/52.

93. Marcus, *The Politics of Mirth*, 108–20; and see 'The occasion of Jonson's *Pleasure Reconciled to Virtue*', *Studies in English Literature 1500–1900*, 19 (1979), 271–93. Referring to the attempt to suppress Sabbath game-playing in Lancashire that provoked James to issue the *Book of Sports*, Marcus interprets Comus as representing 'rioting Lancashire Catholics', the pigmies as 'the proud, inhospitable spirit of puritanism', and Hercules as King James mediating between them (*Politics of Mirth*, 115–16). However, the masque revolves around hospitality, not Sabbatarianism, and James figures as Hesperus, not Hercules. Marcus also posits an ecclesiastical allegory defending the Jacobean church; this turns on Busino's reference to musicians dressed like priests with mitres, alluding to Anglican bishops. But it was conventional for masque musicians to dress as priests: cf. Walls, *Music in the English Courtly Masque*, 7–12.

94. Jonson's dependence on Philostratus and Rabelais is detailed in *Ben Jonson*, x.587–9.
95. *CSPV 1617–1619*, 113–14.
96. On James's melancholy, see Chamberlain, *Letters*, II.121, Brent's letter to Carleton, 2 January 1618 (NA SP 14/95/3), and Williams, *Anne of Denmark*, 194. Others complained that the masque's fable and scenery were dull (*Ben Jonson*, x.576–7).
97. Stanley Fish explores Jonson's poetry from this perspective in 'Author–readers: Jonson's community of the same', *Representations*, 7 (1984), 106–24.
98. See especially Peck, 'For a king not to be bountiful were a fault', and *Court Patronage and Corruption*; Cuddy, 'The revival of the entourage'; and Lockyer, *Buckingham*.
99. References are to the text edited by R. C. Bald in *A Book of Masques*, ed. Spencer and Wells.
100. *Ben Jonson*, VIII.200.

8 THE JACOBEAN CRISIS

1. Orgel and Strong, *Inigo Jones*, 1.282; see also Sullivan, *Court Masques of James I*, 112. For the progress of the Spanish Match in 1617–18, see Gardiner, *History of England 1603–1642*, III.37–8, 58–64, 102–7. The discussions were suspended shortly after, because of the non-negotiability of the religious differences, but events in central Europe soon put the Infanta back on the agenda.
2. *Ben Jonson*, x.585. There is a great deal of confusion in this part of the Simpsons' commentary. Their note on this passage from Finet, relating it to Finet's comments on the 1616 masque (*Ben Jonson*, x.547) – itself wrongly identified as *Mercury Vindicated* – is incorrect, as they have confused the French ambassador's objection to Gondomar's 1618 masque invitation with his objection to an audience given to Gondomar in 1616. Similarly, their quotation from Finet at x.569, incorrectly linked to *The Vision of Delight*, really relates to *Pleasure Reconciled*.
3. Chamberlain, *Letters*, II.433.
4. On the European crisis, the classic narrative from England's point of view is Gardiner's *History of England 1603–1642*, III.261–398, IV.172–230, 272–411. See also J. V. Polisensky, *The Thirty Years War*, trans. R. Evans (1971); G. Parker, *The Thirty Years' War* (1984); C. H. Carter, *The Secret Diplomacy of the Habsburgs 1598–1625* (New York, 1964); R. E. Schreiber, *The First Carlisle: Sir James Hay, First Earl of Carlisle* (Philadelphia, 1984) and *The Political Career of Sir Robert Naunton 1589–1635* (1981); Cosgwell, *The Blessed Revolution*; and the seminal work of Simon Adams: 'The Protestant Cause,' 'Foreign policy', and 'Spain or the Netherlands? The dilemmas of early Stuart foreign policy'.
5. *Cabala, sive scrinia sacra* (1654), 169.
6. S. R. Gardiner, *Letters and Other Documents Illustrating the Relations between England and Germany at the Commencement of the Thirty Years' War*, Camden Society, second series (1868), 12–13, 142, 148.

7. Chamberlain, *Letters*, II.263–4; Lee, ed., *Dudley Carleton to John Chamberlain*, 271, 272.
8. Gardiner, *Letters and Documents*, 7; and compare Sir Edward Herbert's mention of 'the untamed Germans' (65).
9. Gardiner, *Letters and Documents*, 26, 57–8; Chamberlain, *Letters*, II.265–6; *CSPV 1617–1619*, 358–9.
10. Gardiner, *Letters and Documents*, 90, 148.
11. *CSPV 1619–1621*, 490, 520, 510.
12. Cogswell, *The Blessed Revolution*, 20–35.
13. *The Poems of James VI of Scotland*, ed. J. Craigie, 2 vols. (Edinburgh, 1958), II.186.
14. *Stuart Royal Proclamations*, I.495–6, 519–21; Fuller, *The Church History of Britain*, 1655, 9.100, 108–9. There were also instructions to the clergy in 1620 not to mention matters of state in their sermons.
15. For some representative assessments, see P. R. Sellin, 'The politics of Ben Jonson's "*Newes from the New World Discover'd in the Moon*"', *Viator*, 17 (1986), 321–7, which calls that masque 'an utterly reprehensible performance from any enlightened political or humanitarian point of view'; and Parry's 'The politics of the Jacobean masque', which describes 'the preposterous glory' of these masques as 'a good way of escaping from the unpleasantness of the season outside' (111, 113). Sara Pearl's excellent essay 'Sounding to present occasions: Jonson's masques of 1620–5', in *The Court Masque*, ed. Lindley, 60–77, is less moralistic.
16. For the identification, authorship, and dating of this masque, see M. Butler, 'George Chapman's *Masque of the Twelve Months* (1619)', *English Literary Renaissance*, 37 (2007), 360–400. Line references are to the text edited in that essay.
17. S. D'Ewes, *Autobiography and Correspondence* ed. J. O. Halliwell, 2 vols. (1845), I.122.
18. Chamberlain, *Letters*, II.185. For full references, see Butler, 'George Chapman's *Masque of the Twelve Months*'.
19. Birch, *Court and Times of James I*, II.137; *CSPV 1617–1619*, 427, 428–30, 440–5, 463. Matters were exacerbated by reports that Spain was fitting out a fleet (actually for use against Algiers pirates).
20. Birch, *Court and Times of James I*, II.110; *The Poems of James VI*, II.172.
21. *CSPV 1617–1619*, 463; see also Gardiner, *Letters and Documents*, 166.
22. *CSPV 1617–1619*, 432–3.
23. The best treatments are by F. Dahl, *A Bibliography of English Corantos and Periodical Newsbooks 1620–1642* (1952), and M. A. Shaaber, 'The history of the first English newspaper', *Studies in Philology*, 29 (1932), 551–87. See also Shaaber, *Some Forerunners of the Newspaper in England 1476–1622* (2nd edn, 1966); L. Hanson, 'English newsbooks, 1620–1641', *Library*, 4th series, 18 (1938), 355–84; J. Frank, *The Beginnings of the English Newspaper 1622–1660* (Cambridge, Mass., 1966); F. S. Siebert, *Freedom of the Press in England 1476–1776* (Urbana, ed., 1965); L. Rostenberg, 'Nathaniel Butter and Nicholas

Bourne, first "Masters of the Staple"', *Library*, 5th series, 12 (1957), 22–33; and J. Raymond, *The Invention of the Newspaper: English Newsbooks 1641–1649* (1996), 7–8.

24. Sellin ('The politics of Jonson's *Newes from the New World*', 325–6) suggests that Jonson was thinking of such works as the massive state annals of William Camden and the Dutchman Emmanuel van Meteren, but these were works of critical historiography, not popular chronicles.

25. See especially R. Cust, 'News and politics in early seventeenth-century England', *Past and Present*, 112 (1986), 60–90; and F. J. Levy, 'How information spread among the gentry, 1550–1640', *Journal of British Studies*, 21.2 (1982), 11–34. A good Jacobean example would be John Pory; John Chamberlain was not a professional newsmonger but a correspondent with friends at court.

26. See D. F. McKenzie, '*The Staple of News* and the late plays', in *A Celebration of Ben Jonson*, ed. W. Blissett, J. Patrick, and R. W. Van Fossen (Toronto, 1973), 83–128.

27. Gardiner, *Letters and Documents*, 67; *CSPV 1619–1621*, 90.

28. Schreiber, *The First Carlisle*, 34; *CSPV 1619–1621*, 112; Gardiner, *Letters and Documents*, 133.

29. Chamberlain, *Letters*, II.284; Gardiner, *Letters and Documents*, 133–4.

30. Particularly, Sellin's 'The politics of Jonson's *Newes from the New World*'. The value of this essay is undermined by its confusion of *News from the New World* with 'The Running Masque', leading Sellin to suppose that James saw nearly a dozen repeat performances.

31. Birch, *Court and Times of James I*, II.189.

32. Birch, *Court and Times of James I*, II.189 (letter probably addressed to Viscount Doncaster and attributed by Birch to Thomas Murray).

33. Gardiner, *Letters and Documents*, 178, 148; Birch, *Court and Times of James I*, II.191; R. Lockyer, *Buckingham*, 85. See also Cogswell, *The Blessed Revolution*, 58–69.

34. For the text, see James Knowles's 'The "running masque" recovered: a masque for the marquess of Buckingham', *English Manuscript Studies 1100–1700*, 8 (2000), 79–135. See also M. Butler, 'Jonson's *News from the New World*, the "running masque", and the season of 1619–20', 153–78.

35. *CSPV 1619–1621*, 111. Previous discussions of this incident (such as my own in *Theatre and Crisis 1632–1642*, 1984, 6) have missed the point by presuming that James saw it as a reflection on his relations with the long-dead Prince Henry.

36. The occasion is implied by the induction, in which Richmond and St James's palaces lament that the Prince is moving to Denmark House. James awarded Denmark House to Charles in September 1619 (*CSPD 1619–1623*, 129); it seems likely that the housewarming was the ball and banquet that Charles hosted the following March (Chamberlain, *Letters*, II.292–3). On 8 March, the Prince's Men received payment for four court performances (Bentley, *The Jacobean and Caroline Stage*, VII.35).

37. Middleton and Rowley, *A Courtly Masque* (1620).

38. *CSPV 1619–1621*, 190, 225, 227; Chamberlain, *Letters*, II.294, 298–9; *Malone Society Collections*, 6.118; Young, *Tudor and Jacobean Tournaments*, 74.
39. Chamberlain, *Letters*, II.299–300.
40. *CSPV 1619–1621*, 489–90.
41. *CSPV 1619–1621*, 497, 501–2.
42. *CSPV 1619–1621*, 496.
43. *CSPV 1619–1621*, 491; S. Adams, 'Captain Thomas Gainsford, the "Vox Spiritus", and the *Vox Populi*', *Bulletin of the Institute of Historical Research*, 49 (1976), 141–4.
44. For my re-dating of *Pan's Anniversary* (usually given as 19 June 1620), see M. Butler, 'Ben Jonson's *Pan's Anniversary* and the politics of early Stuart pastoral', *English Literary Renaissance*, 22 (1992), 369–404, and the introduction to this masque in *The Cambridge Edition of the Works of Ben Jonson*.
45. For a full discussion of the iconography, see Butler, 'Ben Jonson's *Pan's Anniversary*', which sets out this argument at greater length. Jonson also suppresses the tradition which linked Pan with King Midas, who was given ass's ears after he preferred Pan's music to that of Apollo – a fable with implications that flattered neither Pan nor princes.
46. *Olympian* 6.151. See also Horace, *Epistles*, 2.1.244, and Juvenal, 10.50.
47. As is shown by the bill for his costume: *Ben Jonson*, X.605–6.
48. A corn-cutter, a tinderbox-man, and a puritan appear in *Bartholomew Fair*; a mousetrap-man is a ghost character in the list of characters; and a fencer and a tooth-drawer are mentioned in the Induction.
49. For example, Zechariah 10.3 and 13.7; Jeremiah 51.23; and Ezekiel 34.
50. See D. Underdown, 'The taming of the scold', in *Order and Disorder in Early Modern England*, ed. A. Fletcher and J. Stevenson (Cambridge, 1985), 116–36.
51. Chamberlain, *Letters*, II.333.
52. *CSPV 1619–1621*, 498, 526–7, 533–4; *CSPD 1619–1623*, 212–13; Nichols, *Progresses of James I*, IV.630–5; Gardiner, *History of England*, III.388–91; Adams, 'Foreign policy', 152–3; Carter, *Secret Diplomacy of the Habsburgs*.
53. *CSPV 1619–1621*, 533–4.
54. *CSPV 1619–1621*, 579; Sullivan, *Court Masques of James I*, 242–3.
55. Birch, *Court and Times of James I*, II.228 (Mead was writing from Cambridge in February).
56. Chamberlain, *Letters*, II.421. See also *CSPV 1621–1623*, 198.
57. G. Wither, *Wither's Motto* (1621), sig. A8v. Four editions of this poem were printed simultaneously, and so great was the demand that the Warden of the Stationers' Company, Matthew Lowndes, was found to be selling it surreptitiously even after he had himself fined Humphrey Marriott for printing it without licence. See *The Carl H. Pforzheimer Library*, 3 vols. (New York, 1940), III.1124–6.
58. Birch, *Court and Times of James I*, II.266.
59. Birch, *Court and Times of James I*, II.355; *Stuart Royal Proclamations*, I.561–5, 572–4; Fuller, *The Church History of Britain*, IX.110.
60. Cogswell, *The Blessed Revolution*, 34; and see 20–35 more generally for a brilliant evocation of these months.

61. *CSPV 1621–1623*, 516.
62. Parliament had been prorogued in December, but the dissolution itself was ordered on 6 January.
63. Norbrook, *Poetry and Politics*, 224.
64. The ballad itself did not appear in the quarto edition, and was perhaps added for the masque's second performance. See *Ben Jonson*, VII.626, and the *Cambridge Edition of the Works of Ben Jonson*, 'Textual Analysis'.
65. See the scene design reproduced in Orgel and Strong, *Inigo Jones*, 1.356–7.
66. G. Goodman, *The Court of King James the First*, ed. J. S. Brewer, 2 vols. (1839), II.228.
67. Chamberlain, *Letters*, II.473.
68. Cogswell, *The Blessed Revolution*. For rather different readings of the story, drawing more extensively on Spanish sources, see Glyn Redworth's *The Prince and the Infanta: The Cultural Politics of the Spanish Match* (New Haven, 2003); and A. Samson, ed., *The Spanish Match: Prince Charles's Journey to Madrid, 1623* (2006).
69. Goodman, *The Court of King James the First*, II.250.
70. Goodman, *The Court of King James the First*, I.386–7.
71. Orgel, *The Illusion of Power*, 71, 77. See also *The Jonsonian Masque*, 91–9.
72. Goldberg, *James I and the Politics of Literature*, 71.
73. Goodman, *The Court of King James the First*, II.265 (original in French; J. S. Brewer's translation). On Gerbier's other work for Buckingham, see Lockyer, *Buckingham*, 213–15.
74. In their commentary, the Simpsons took the inclusion of Proteus in these counsels to refer to Sir Francis Cottington, a courtier with strong Spanish credentials, whose reputation as a political dissembler is mentioned by Clarendon (*Ben Jonson*, X.665). They are followed by Orgel and Goldberg, who develop this by describing Cottington as 'an accomplished secret agent' (*The Illusion of Power*, 72; *James I and the Politics of Literature*, 71). But although Cottington travelled to Madrid with the Prince, Proteus cannot have represented him directly or been played by him (as Buckingham played Hippius), since in the masque he was one of the principal soloists, and would have been played by a professional musician. In fact the reason for Jonson foregrounding Proteus – a god particularly associated with shape-shifting – was not any allusion to Cottington, but the circumstance, widely remarked in contemporary reports, that Charles and Buckingham had gone to Madrid in disguise. See my commentary to the forthcoming Cambridge edition. It may be added that Cottington's own role in the affair was ambivalent: see M. J. Havran, *Caroline Courtier: The Life of Lord Cottington* (1973), 70–6.
75. R. Cust, *Charles I: A Political Life* (Harlow, 2005), 9–10; Redworth, *The Prince and the Infanta*, 43.
76. The strategic implications are analysed in Cogswell, *The Blessed Revolution*, 57–76.
77. Patricia Fumerton argues that the masque's real subject is the legitimation of England's overseas trade (*Cultural Aesthetics*, 195–201). But this is not the aspect of English sea-power that was on most people's minds early in 1624.

78. For contemporary comment, see J. Birch, *The Court and Times of Charles I*, 2 vols. (1848), I.119–43.
79. Chamberlain, *Letters*, II.538.
80. *Ben Jonson*, X.659 ('the ambassador ... entreated the Earl of March to present [an answer] to his majesty in these words: that about two years since upon the like occasion, he had received the like message, but knowing how strongly his majesty stood then affected to the alliance with Spain, he would give him no distaste but with excuse of his indisposition kept himself absent, that if he should now again do the like, he should in the sight of the world put a scorn upon himself and do an unanswerable wrong to the king his master ... He humbly beseeched his majesty to proceed plainly and fairly without using any more colourable or alternative invitations').
81. J. Orrell, 'Amerigo Salvetti and the London court theatre, 1616–1640', *Theatre Survey*, 20 (1979), 8; Chamberlain, *Letters*, II.527.
82. *CSPV 1623–1625*, 196.
83. F. Yates, *The Rosicrucian Enlightenment* (1972).
84. *The Theatre of Apollo*, ed. W. W. Greg (1926), 9. For discussion, see Britland, *Drama at the Courts of Queen Henrietta Maria*, 19–20, 27–30.
85. Chamberlain, *Letters*, II.282, 332.
86. Particularly in the work of first-generation historians hostile to the Stuarts, such as Arthur Wilson's *History of Great Britain* (1653) and Anthony Weldon's narrative of how James was content to be diverted from serious business by courtly fooling (*The Court of James I*, 1650). Obviously too biased to be taken at face value, Weldon is contradicted by the evidence that James – whose preferred leisure was always hunting – sometimes disliked these theatricals: for example *Pleasure Reconciled to Virtue*, and *The Marriage of the Farmer's Son*. Weldon was answered in detail by Godfrey Goodman in *The Court of King James the First*, though the fact that Goodman took this seriously enough to respond to it suggests that he felt there was a kernel of truth.
87. Chamberlain, *Letters*, II.532.
88. G. Wither, *Britain's Remembrancer* (1628), sig. H5v.
89. HMC 78 (*Hastings MSS*), II.58–9. See G. McMullan, *The Politics of Unease* (Amherst, Mass., 1994), 17–29.
90. Bodleian MS Malone 23, fol. 20v. Quoted in P. Thomson, *Shakespeare's Professional Career* (Cambridge, 1992), 172.
91. Quoted by Richard Cust in 'News and politics in early seventeenth-century England', 66–7, from a transcription in the diary of William Davenport of Chester.
92. For the dating of this poem (which affects its interpretation), see M. Butler, 'The dates of three poems by Ben Jonson', *Huntington Library Quarterly*, 55 (1992), 279–84.
93. Timothy Raylor, *The Essex House Masque of 1621: Viscount Doncaster and the Jacobean Masque* (Pittsburgh, 2000).

9 THE CAROLINE REFORMATION

1. Birch, *Court and Times of Charles I*, 1.166. This was a gross exaggeration; the real figure was nearer £200. See J. Orrell, 'Buckingham's patronage of the dramatic arts: the Crowe accounts', *REED Newsletter*, 5.2 (1980), 15.
2. Orrell, 'Buckingham's patronage', 15; *CSPV 1626–1627*, 21.
3. Orrell, 'Amerigo Salvetti', 12; Birch, *Court and Times of Charles I*, 1.166. I refer to 'Savoy' for the sake of clarity, though the figures in question, Victor Amadeus and Christine of Piedmont, were still only heirs to the duchy (they succeeded in 1630).
4. Birch, *Court and Times of Charles I*, 1.226; *CSPV 1626–1627*, 239.
5. *Artenice* ended with a masque-like discovery and dance: see Orrell, *The Theatres of Inigo Jones and John Webb*, 81–4.
6. For details, see notes to the appendix, 373–4 above.
7. See Loomie, ed., *Ceremonies of Charles I*, 75–7; J. Meautys, *The Private Correspondence of Jane Lady Cornwallis 1613–1644* (1842), 217–18; *Malone Society Collections*, 2.351; Orgel and Strong, *Inigo Jones*, 1.396–403. It has long been known that there was a play with scenes at Somerset House sometime in 1629–30, but not the proper date. This can now be established from Finet and Cornwallis.
8. Bentley, *The Jacobean and Caroline Stage*, VI.282; Orrell, *The Theatres of Inigo Jones and John Webb*, 90–112.
9. HMC 11 (*Skrine MSS*), 44.
10. The minimum costs can be calculated from the documents summarized in Orgel and Strong, *Inigo Jones*, 1.383–4, and McGee and Meagher, 'Preliminary checklist … 1625–1634', 30, 41, 44.
11. See Sharpe, *Personal Rule*, 105–6.
12. T. Cogswell, 'Prelude to Ré: the Anglo-French struggle over La Rochelle, 1624–1627', *History*, 71 (1986), 1–21. See also Cogswell, 'Foreign policy and parliament: the case of La Rochelle', *English Historical Review*, 99 (1984), 241–67; and S. Adams, 'The road to La Rochelle', *Proceedings of the Huguenot Society*, 22 (1975), 42–30.
13. *CSPV 1625–1626*, 575.
14. HMC 11 (*Skrine MSS*), 86, 89. See also the Salvetti transcripts, the detailed reports in *CSPV 1625–1626* and *1626–1628*; Bassompierre's own narrative in *Journal de ma vie*, 4 vols. (Paris, 1870–7); and H. Noel Williams, *A Gallant of Lorraine*, 2 vols. (1921), II.467–501.
15. *CSPV 1625–1626*, 574.
16. *CSPV 1625–1626*, 577. See also 566: 'My king … has two brothers-in-law; he wishes rather to be a suppliant to the one who shuns his friendship [i.e. Charles], than to embrace the other who desires it and constantly urges him to form some union [i.e. Philip]'.
17. See the account of the masque in S. R. Gardiner, *History of England 1603–1642*, V.145. Some of Gardiner's details are wrong: he assumes Frederick and Elizabeth were represented, but the masque depicted only Marie de Médici's

immediate family. For similar themes elsewhere in Marie de Médici's iconography, see R. F. Millen and R. E. Wolf, *Heroic Deeds and Mystic Figures: A New Reading of Rubens' 'Life of Maria de' Medici'* (Princeton, 1989), 160–3, and Britland, *Drama at the Courts of Henrietta Maria*, 25–7. It's worth noting that France/Savoy was also a fault-line. Savoy was a small but significant principality abutting France to the east, and Louis was concerned to keep control of it, by force if necessary.

18. Birch, *Court and Times of Charles I*, 1.180.

19. Quoted in Cogswell, 'Prelude to Ré', 16.

20. For example, in *Chloridia* and *Coelum Britannicum*.

21. Loomie, ed., *Ceremonies of Charles I*, 98, 240. For independent confirmation, see *CSPV 1629–1631*, 464, and Orrell, 'Amerigo Salvetti', 14.

22. The title dates the poem to 1630, but the proclamation to which it refers was issued two years later. See J. Loxley, *Royalism and Poetry in the English Civil Wars* (Basingstoke, 1997), 46–7.

23. Fanshawe, *Poems and Translations*, ed. P. Davidson, vol. 1 (Oxford, 1997), 56.

24. For two detailed and contradictory discussions of Charles's foreign policy, see L. J. Reeve, *Charles I and the Road to Personal Rule* (Cambridge, 1989), 226–74, and Sharpe in *Personal Rule*, 65–104. See also M. Alexander, *Charles I's Lord Treasurer* (1975), 148–57.

25. Sharpe, *Personal Rule*, 76.

26. J. S. A. Adamson, 'Chivalry and political culture in Caroline England', in *Culture and Politics in Early Stuart England*, ed. Lake and Sharpe, 161–97. See also R. Strong, *Van Dyck: Charles I on Horseback* (1972).

27. Parry, 'Van Dyck and the Caroline court poets', in *Van Dyck 350*, ed. S. J. Barnes and A. Wheelock (Washington, D.C., 1994), 251.

28. Wedgwood, 'The last masque', in *Truth and Opinion*, 139–56.

29. Strong, *Splendour at Court* 219, 233, 247–8.

30. Orgel and Strong, *Inigo Jones*, 1.49–50, 72, 75; see also Orgel's 'Plato, the Magi, and Caroline politics: a reading of *The Temple of Love*', *Word and Image*, 4 (1988), 663, which calls the masques 'self-congratulatory'. This perspective has a strong hold in art history. For example, Francis Haskell calls Van Dyck's portraits 'quintessential representations of a refined and doomed culture at its peak': 'Charles I's collection of pictures', in *The Late King's Goods*, ed. A. MacGregor (1989), 224.

31. G. R. Elton, 'A highroad to civil war?', in *Studies in Tudor and Stuart Politics and Government*, 3 vols. (Cambridge, 1974), II.164–82. For some revisionary accounts, see Reeve, *Charles I and the Road to Personal Rule*; Sharpe, *Personal Rule*; and Richard Cust's two studies, *The Forced Loan and English Politics 1626–1628* (Oxford, 1987) and *Charles I: A Political Life*.

32. Quoted in Sharpe, *Personal Rule*, 117.

33. L. M. Hill, 'County government in Caroline England', in *The Origins of the English Civil War*, ed. C. Russell (1973), 66–90; T. G. Barnes, *Somerset 1625–40* (1961); A. Fletcher, *Reform in the Provinces: The Government of Stuart England* (1986); Sharpe, *Personal Rule*, 262–73.

34. See A. Fletcher, *Reform in the Provinces: The Government of Stuart England* (New Haven, 1986).

35. Quoted in Sharpe, *Personal Rule*, 52.

36. R. M. Smuts, 'The political failure of Stuart cultural patronage', in *Patronage in the Renaissance*, ed. G. Fitch Lytle and S. Orgel (Princeton, 1981), 165–87; J. Richards, '"His nowe majestie" and the English monarchy: the kingship of Charles I before 1640', *Past and Present*, 113 (1986), 70–96.

37. See Peacock, *The Stage Designs of Inigo Jones*; and D. Howarth, 'Charles I, sculpture and sculptors', in *The Late King's Goods*, ed. MacGregor, 73–113. *The Late King's Goods* gives an unrivalled sense of the richness of Charles I's collections.

38. A wider case for Bruno's influence is made by Hilary Gatti, 'Giordano Bruno and the Stuart court masques', *Renaissance Quarterly*, 48 (1995), 809–42, though many of her suggestions are unpersuasive.

39. See, particularly, John Peacock, 'The French element in Inigo Jones's masque designs', 149–68.

40. Sharpe, *Criticism and Compliment*, 192 (and compare 26–7).

41. Ausonius, 1.4.11 (trans. H. G. Evelyn White). Compare Townshend's remark at the end of *Albion's Triumph*: 'for the invention and writing of the masque … my excuse and glory is, the King commanded and I obeyed': *The Poems and Masques of Aurelian Townshend*, ed. Brown, 90.

42. The exceptions which prove the rule are *Time Vindicated*, *The Masque of Augurs*, *Neptune's Triumph*, and *The Fortunate Isles*, which appeared in fugitive quarto formats not designed for commercial sale. The dating of the printed Caroline masques, which is always old-style, indicates that they were published at the time of performance, or shortly afterwards.

43. Bentley, *The Jacobean and Caroline Stage*, v.1158.

44. Bentley, *The Jacobean and Caroline Stage*, III.217.

45. The two best accounts of *Love's Triumph* are by Orgel and Strong, *Inigo Jones*, 1.63–6, and Karen Britland, *Drama at the Courts of Henrietta Maria*, 66–73.

46. Orrell, 'Amerigo Salvetti', 15. For the treaty's publication, see *Stuart Royal Proclamations*, ed. Larkin and Hughes, II.306–7; and *Articles of Peace … in a Treaty at Madrid* (1630).

47. *CSPV 1629–1632*, 448, 463.

48. The most helpful account of these months is by Reeve, *Charles I and the Road to Personal Rule*, 118–71.

49. See N. G. Brett-James, *The Growth of Stuart London* (1935), 195–6, 223–47; H. M. Colvin, ed., *The History of the King's Works*, vol. III, part I (1975), 129–60; and Sharpe, *Personal Rule*, 407–12.

50. *Stuart Royal Proclamations*, II.287.

51. V. Pearl, *London and the Outbreak of the Puritan Revolution* (Oxford, 1961), 9–42; R. Ashton, *The City and the Court 1603–1643* (Cambridge, 1979), 163–71.

52. The Theseus connection surfaces in the inclusion of Amphitrite, wife of Poseidon, for Poseidon was sometimes associated with Aegeus, Theseus' father. However, Jonson's text calls Amphitrite the wife of Oceanus (101).

53. Sharpe, *Criticism and Compliment*, 203.
54. See Loewenstein, 'Personal material: Jonson and book-burning', in M. Butler, ed., *Re-Presenting Ben Jonson: Text, History, Performance* (Basingstoke, 1998), p. 106.
55. References are to *The Poems and Masques of Aurelian Townshend*, ed. Brown. Jones's designs show that the procession was originally intended to include barbarian captives (absent from the printed text).
56. See *The Stage Designs of Inigo Jones*, 302–14; and 'Inigo Jones and the Arundel marbles', *Journal of Medieval and Renaissance Studies*, 16 (1986), 75–90.
57. See *CSPD 1631–1633*, 192, 207, 250, 270, 271; *CSPV 1629–1632*, 619; and Birch, *Court and Times of Charles I*, II.144.
58. The captive kings are mentioned by Publius (66) and included in Jones's designs, so were probably part of the procession.
59. See David Howarth's account in *Splendours of the Gonzaga*, ed. D. Chambers and J. Martineau (1981), 95–101. Howarth gives a figure of £30,000, though this does not agree with the calculations in W. N. Sainsbury, *Original Unpublished Papers Illustrative of the Life of Sir Peter Paul Rubens* (1859), 321. See also *The Late King's Goods*, ed. MacGregor, 205–6, 212.
60. Compare Orgel and Strong, *Inigo Jones*, II.458–9, with *The Late King's Goods*, ed. MacGregor, 259–60. This crown was probably made for Henry VIII: see A. J. Collins, *Jewels and Plate of Queen Elizabeth I* (1955), 10–12, 264. Even if the crown on the proscenium was not this specific diadem, in the taxonomy of regalia it clearly is an imperial crown, as Townshend's text requires (75).
61. *The Poems and Masques of Aurelian Townshend*, ed. Brown, 48–9.
62. *The Poems of Thomas Carew with his Masque 'Coelum Britannicum'*, ed. Dunlap, 77. For discussion, see M. P. Parker, 'Carew's politic pastoral: Virgilian pretexts in the "Answer to Aurelian Townshend"', *John Donne Journal*, 1 (1982), 101–16; and R. A. Anselment, 'Thomas Carew and the "harmless pastimes" of Caroline peace', *Philological Quarterly*, 62 (1983), 201–19.
63. Sharpe argues Townshend wanted war and reads the 'Elegiacal letter' as 'an implicit critique … of royal policy' (*Criticism and Compliment*, 176). But this is not evident in the poem, and Loxley's view is nearer the mark: that its most striking feature is its failure to allude to Britain (*Royalism and Poetry*, 23–4).
64. *The Poems and Masques of Aurelian Townshend*, ed. Brown, 50.
65. Pory to Scudamore, 24 December 1631 (NA C115/M35/8387).
66. See Birch, *Court and Times of Charles I*, II.153, and the citations in Sharpe, *Personal Rule*, 703.
67. Reeve, *Charles I and the Road to Personal Rule*, 178. For a sceptical reading of Sweden's usefulness to England, see Sharpe, *Personal Rule*, 78–82.
68. References are to the text edited by Clifford Leech in *A Book of Masques*, ed. Spencer and Wells.
69. B. Whitelocke, *Memorials of English Affairs* (1682), 20. For a full contemporary description, see J. Limon, 'Neglected evidence for James Shirley's *The Triumph of Peace* (1634)', *REED Newsletter*, 13.2 (1988), 2–9.
70. T. Orbison, 'The Middle Temple documents relating to James Shirley's *The Triumph of Peace*', *Malone Society Collections*, 12 (1983), 34.

71. See W. J. Jones, *Politics and the Bench: The Judges and the Origins of the English Civil War* (1971); J. P. Kenyon, *The Stuart Constitution* (1966); and G. Burgess, *The Politics of the Ancient Constitution* (Basingstoke, 1992).
72. *Inigo Jones*, 1.63, 65.
73. Jones, *Politics and the Bench*, 94.
74. Jones, *Politics and the Bench*, 97.
75. Kenyon, *The Stuart Constitution*, 201–2.
76. E. Hyde, *History of the Rebellion*, ed. W. D. Macray, 6 vols. (Oxford, 1888), 1.199.
77. Hyde, *History of the Rebellion*, 1.85.
78. Hyde, *History of the Rebellion*, 1.88.
79. Orbison, 'Middle Temple documents', 60, 70; D'Ewes, *Autobiography and Correspondence*, 11.105.
80. Orgel and Strong, *Inigo Jones*, 1.64.
81. L. Venuti, *Our Halcyon Days: English Prerevolutionary Texts and Postmodern Culture* (Madison, Wis., 1989), 180–211.
82. Indeed, planning had to be cooperative, for Inigo Jones re-used the same stage for *Coelum Britannicum* two weeks later. See *Malone Society Collections*, 10, 46.
83. HMC 12 (*Cowper MSS*) 11.34.
84. W. Knowler, ed., *The Earl of Strafford's Letters and Dispatches*, 2 vols. (1739), 1.177.
85. Huntington Library MS HM 55603, fol. 22v. I am grateful to Tom Cogswell for this citation.
86. P. Clark, *The English Alehouse: A Social History 1200–1830* (1983); P. Wrightson, *English Society 1580–1680* (1982), 167.
87. Orgel and Strong, *Inigo Jones*, 11.541–2.
88. Sharpe, *Personal Rule*, 258. See also W. J. Jones, '"The great Gamaliel of the law": Mr Attorney Noy', *Huntington Library Quarterly*, 40 (1977), 197–226, and *Politics and the Bench*, 92–5.
89. Hyde, *History of the Rebellion*, 1.85.
90. *Inigo Jones*, 1.66.
91. Hyde, *History of the Rebellion*, 1.85.
92. Bentley, *The Jacobean and Caroline Stage*, v.1157–9; Orgel and Strong, *Inigo Jones*, 11.538.
93. Bentley, *The Jacobean and Caroline Stage*, v.1156.
94. Orgel and Strong, *Inigo Jones*, 11.543.
95. See W. W. Greg, '*The Triumph of Peace*: a bibliographer's nightmare', *Library*, 5th series, 1 (1946), 113–26.
96. S. Wiseman, *Drama and Politics in the English Civil War* (Cambridge, 1998), 118.
97. The documents disagree over the order of the procession. Whitelocke and Folger MS Z.e.1(25) follow the order laid down by the sequence of the antimasques, but the printed text has the beggars following the projectors (J. Limon, 'Neglected evidence' for James Shirley's *The Triumph of Peace* (1634)', *REED Newsletter*, 13, 1988, 2–9).

98. Huntington MS 55603, fol. 22v (spelling and punctuation modernized). It is unclear whether Drake wrote before or after the event.

99. Quoted in M. B. Pickel, *Charles I as Patron of Poetry and Drama* (1936), 147.

100. Bentley, *The Jacobean and Caroline Stage*, III.107.

101. J. Kerrigan, 'Thomas Carew', *Proceedings of the British Academy*, 74 (1988), 348.

102. Parry, *The Golden Age Restor'd*, 194, 196.

103. A. Patterson, *Censorship and Interpretation* (Madison, Wis., 1984), 109.

104. J. Altieri, *The Theatre of Praise: The Panegyric Tradition in 17th-Century English Drama* (Newark, Del., 1986), 84, 87. See also her 'Responses to a waning mythology in Carew's political poetry', *Studies in English Literature 1500–1900*, 26 (1986), 107–24.

105. Sharpe, *Criticism and Compliment*, 238.

106. Altieri, *The Theatre of Praise*, 81.

107. On this point see Loxley, *Royalism and Poetry*, 204–7.

108. The Herculean connection is developed by having Atlas and the sphere as the main scene of the antimasques: Charles's new Hesperides are safer than the old. Carew may have been harking back to *Pleasure Reconciled to Virtue*, which used the same group of myths.

109. Strong, *Van Dyck: Charles I on Horseback*, 59–63; *The Late King's Goods*, ed. MacGregor, 272–3.

110. Peacock, *The Stage Designs of Inigo Jones*, 314–21.

111. Orrell, 'Amerigo Salvetti', 21.

112. Birch, *Court and Times of Charles I*, II.89.

113. Bentley, *The Jacobean and Caroline Stage*, III.213.

114. T. May, *History of the Long Parliament of England* (1647), part 2, 7. See also [G. Ridpath,] *The Stage Condemned* (1698). For plays on Sundays, see M. Butler, 'Another Sunday play at Charles I's court', *Notes and Queries*, 228 (1983), 430–1.

10 THE CAROLINE CRISIS

1. Knowler, ed., *Strafford's Letters*, I.525. See also Loomie, ed., *Ceremonies of Charles I*, 196, and G. Holles, *Memorials of the Holles Family 1493–1656*, ed. A. C. Wood (1937), 236. This was the second of three occasions on which the masque was performed. I have discussed the entertainments in this section in much greater detail in M. Butler, 'Entertaining the Palatine Prince: plays on foreign affairs 1635–1637', *English Literary Renaissance*, 13 (1983), 319–44.

2. Citations are to W. Davenant, *The Triumphs of the Prince d'Amour* (1635 [1636]).

3. See Peacock, *The Stage Designs of Inigo Jones*, 236. The other Twelfth Night masques in this period were all Jones–Davenant collaborations, with Davenant supplying the words but Jones having overall responsibility for the invention as well as design.

4. J. Cornwallis, *The Private Correspondence* (1842), 241.

5. *CSPV 1632–1636*, 491.

6. Knowler, ed., *Strafford's Letters*, 1.504; D'Ewes, *The Autobiography and Correspondence*, II.138; A. Collins, *Letters and Memorials of State*, 2 vols. (1746), II.472; *CSPD 1637*, 251; Bodleian MS North c.4, fol. 7.

7. *CSPV 1632–1636*, 486.

8. The most recent discussions are by Sharpe, *Personal Rule*, 509–36; Cust, *Charles I*, 124–33; and Ian Atherton, *Ambition and Failure in Stuart England: The Career of John, First Viscount Scudamore* (Manchester, 1999), 171–219. For the wider background, C. V. Wedgwood's *The Thirty Years' War* (1938) is still useful.

9. *CSPD 1635–1636*, 243.

10. *CSPV 1632–1636*, 469, 511.

11. Atherton, *Ambition and Failure*, 17; Cust, *Charles I*, 129–30.

12. See the examples cited in Butler, 'Entertaining the Palatine Prince', 326–7.

13. Knowler, ed., *Strafford's Letters*, 1.506–7, 525; HMC 55 (*Various MSS*), VII.411; Holles, *Memorials of the Holles Family*, 236. Holles, who was the Prince D'Amour's Comptroller, improbably claimed that the total cost was £20,000.

14. Knowler, ed., *Strafford's Letters*, 1.507.

15. L. Hotson, *Shakespeare's Sonnets Dated and Other Essays* (1949), 239–44.

16. F. S. Boas, ed., *The Diary of Thomas Crosfield* (1935), 83–4.

17. *CSPV 1632–1636*, 489; Atherton, *Ambition and Failure*, 180.

18. Loomie, ed., *Ceremonies of Charles I*, 196.

19. Knowler, ed., *Strafford's Letters*, 1.506.

20. H. Glapthorne, *Poems* (1639), 2.

21. Bentley, *The Jacobean and Caroline Stage*, V.1285–8.

22. Bentley, *The Jacobean and Caroline Stage*, III.113–14.

23. *CSPD 1636–1637*, 172.

24. Citations are to *The King and Queen's Entertainment at Richmond* (Oxford, 1636).

25. *CSPD 1636–1637*, 559.

26. W. Davenant, *The Shorter Poems and Songs*, ed. A. M. Gibbs (Oxford, 1972), 10–21; S. J. Barnes, N. de Poorta, O. Millar, and H. Vey, eds., *Van Dyck: A Complete Catalogue of the Paintings* (New Haven, 2004), 437.

27. Reproduced in Butler, 'Entertaining the Palatine Prince'. This high-quality engraving, by Crispin de Passe, was apparently printed in Holland, but the English verses accompanying it indicate it was intended for circulation at home. It must post-date January 1637, as it shows the Earl of Arundel returning empty-handed from Vienna.

28. O. Millar, *Tudor, Stuart, and Early Georgian Pictures in the Collection of Her Majesty the Queen* (1963), 105–6; Barnes *et al.*, eds., *Van Dyck: A Complete Catalogue*, 481–3 . This may be a studio portrait, with the head only by Van Dyck. Both of these catalogues list the many copies and engravings.

29. Sharpe, *Personal Rule*, 220–2. In the event, the Prince was installed privately at Windsor.

30. Nabbes, *A Presentation Intended for the Prince*, in *The Spring's Glory* (1638), F–G2.

31. Sharpe, *Personal Rule*, 105–30; Cust, *Charles I*, 125, 191.

32. Cust, *Charles I*, 194.
33. Sharpe, *Personal Rule*, 790. For detailed analyses of the intersection between the British and theological problems, see Conrad Russell, *The Causes of the English Civil War* (Oxford, 1990) and *The Fall of the British Monarchies 1637–1642* (Oxford, 1991).
34. W. Drummond, *The Entertainment of the High and Mighty Monarch, Charles, King of Great Britain* (Edinburgh, 1633), 13.
35. Cust, *Charles I*, 227.
36. References are to I. Jones and W. Davenant, *The Temple of Love* (1634 [1635]).
37. Veevers, *Images of Love and Religion*, 133–42.
38. Orgel and Strong, *Inigo Jones*, II.605, 616.
39. References are to I. Jones and W. Davenant, *Britannia Triumphans* (1637 [1638]).
40. K. R. Andrews, *Ships, Money, and Politics: Seafaring and Naval Enterprise in the Reign of Charles I* (Cambridge, 1991), 128–59; N. A. M. Rodger, *A Naval History of Britain* (1997), I.379–94.
41. Sharpe, *Criticism and Compliment*, 248.
42. 'Ethnic' here means 'heathen': see *OED*, 'Ethnic', A1.
43. Orgel and Strong, II.696–7. Orgel and Strong call these 'rejected designs', but that for John of Leyden is a fully worked-up fair copy, not merely a sketch.
44. *Stuart Royal Proclamations*, II.662–3.
45. *Stuart Royal Proclamations*, II.665.
46. R. Scrope, ed., *State Papers Collected by Edward, Earl of Clarendon*, 2 vols. (Oxford, 1773), II.81.
47. Cust, *Charles I*, 250.
48. Hyde, *History of the Rebellion*, I.183.
49. *CSPD 1639–1640, 459.*
50. The text calls him 'Earle of Leimricke', and Orgel and Strong wrongly identify him as William Villiers, second Viscount Grandison of Limerick. Grandison was Buckingham's half-brother and danced in *Coelum Britannicum*, but there was no Earldom of Limerick. William Hamilton had been created Earl of Lanark in 1639; the title was variously spelled 'Lanrick' and 'Lanerick': see G. E. Cockayne and V. Gibbs, *Complete Peerage*, 14 vols. in 13 (1910–98), VI.263; and *A Book of Masques*, ed. Spencer and Wells, 369. Lanark also masqued in *Britannia Triumphans* and *Luminalia*; he was younger brother to Charles's Scottish favourite, the Marquis of Hamilton. For Grandison's career, see the *ODNB* article on his daughter, Barbara Palmer, née Villiers.
51. *ODNB*. Of the two sons, William Russell led the parliamentary campaign in the south-west and fought at Edgehill, but subsequently oscillated between the two sides.
52. Personal communication from Conrad Russell.
53. Britland, *Drama at the Courts of Henrietta Maria*, 187–8.
54. References are to the text edited by T. J. B. Spencer, in *A Book of Masques*, ed. Spencer and Wells (1967).
55. Vitruvius, *The Ten Books on Architecture*, trans. M. H. Morgan (New York, 1960), 54–5.

56. Cust, *Charles I*, 190.
57. John Peacock makes this point in *Stage Designs of Inigo Jones*, 108–9.
58. In *Criticism and Compliment*, 251–6, Kevin Sharpe argues that *Salmacida Spolia* presents Charles with the case for moderation at this moment of crisis. As will be seen, my reading suggests that this masque's politics were far from moderate.
59. Britland, *Drama at the Courts of Henrietta Maria*, 180–1.
60. Some have taken this to mean Laudian priests: see T. J. B. Spencer, *A Book of Masques*, 340–1; and M. Butler, 'Politics and the masque: *Salmacida Spolia*', in *Literature and the English Civil War*, ed. T. Healy and J. Sawday (Cambridge, 1990), 69 – a paragraph I here withdraw. In context, the allusion can only be to the Scottish ministers encouraging the Covenanters.
61. J. Rushworth, *Historical Collections* (1680), 2.1116–17.
62. *Journal of the House of Lords*, 4.63.
63. E. S. Cope and W. H. Coates, eds., *Proceedings of the Short Parliament, 1640*, Camden Society Publications, 4th series, 19 (1977), 189.
64. *His Majesty's Declaration to all his Loving Subjects* (1640), 7–8.
65. Sharpe, *Personal Rule*, 907.
66. See M. Lloyd, *The King Found at Southwell, and the Oxford Jig Played and Sung at Witney Wakes* (1646). Some on-going continuities are traced by Dale B. J. Randall in *Winter Fruit: English Drama 1642–1660* (Lexington, Ky., 1995), 157–83, and Sue Wiseman in *Drama and Politics in the English Civil War* (Cambridge, 1998), 114–36.
67. *A Deep Sigh*, A3v.
68. *Mercurius Rusticus, or a Country Messenger* (1643), 10. See David Norbrook, *Writing the English Republic: Poetry, Rhetoric and Politics 1627–1660* (Cambridge, 1999), 87.
69. John Creaser, '"The present aid of this occasion": the setting of *Comus*', in *The Court Masque*, ed. Lindley, 111–34. For other criticism along these lines, see especially Maryann McGuire, *Milton's Puritan Masque* (Athens, Ga., 1983); David Norbrook, *Poetry and Politics in the English Renaissance* (rev. edn, Oxford, 2002; first published 1984), 224–69; Cedric C. Brown, *John Milton's Aristocratic Entertainments* (Cambridge, 1985); Leah Marcus, *The Politics of Mirth*, 169–212; Michael Wilding, *Dragon's Teeth: Literature in the English Revolution* (Oxford, 1985); Barbara Lewalski, 'Milton's *Comus* and the politics of masquing', in *The Politics of the Stuart Court Masque*, ed. Bevington and Holbrook, 296–320; and Sophie Tomlinson, *Women on Stage in Stuart Drama*, 71–7. Stephen Orgel argues against the masque's status as state occasion in 'The case for Comus', *Representations*, 81 (2003), 31–45.
70. These words are not in the printed version. I cite *Comus* from the Bridgewater manuscript, which supplies the text as performed in 1634, compared where necessary with the early quarto, *A Masque Presented at Ludlow Castle* (1637). References are to the transcription in J. S. Diekhoff, ed., *'A Maske at Ludlow': Essays on Milton's 'Comus'* (Cleveland, OH, 1968). The history of Milton's revisions is extraordinarily complex, and is complicated by the fact that the performance text was probably adapted by Henry Lawes. The definitive

account is by S. E. Sprott, *John Milton, 'A Maske': The Earlier Versions* (Toronto, 1973).

71. Brown, *Milton's Aristocratic Entertainments*, 27–8.
72. Milton: 'Or, if virtue feeble were, / Heaven itself would stoop to her'; Townshend: 'Where Divine Beauty will vouchsafe to stoop / And move the earth, 'tis fit the heavenly spheres / Should be her music, and the starry troop / Shine round about them like the crown she wears'. Noted by Brown, *Milton's Aristocratic Entertainments*, 3.
73. Milton: 'We that are of purer fire / Imitate the starry choir'; Carew: 'Jove is tempering purer fire, / And will with bright flames attire / These glorious lights'. Noted by McGuire, *Milton's Puritan Masque*, 41.
74. See Marcus, *The Politics of Mirth*. For a valuable account emphasizing Milton's recuperation of lawful games, see Blair Hoxby, 'The wisdom of their feet: meaningful dance in Milton and the Stuart masque', *English Literary Renaissance*, 37 (2007), 74–99.
75. See David Loewenstein, '"Fair offspring nurs't in princely lore": on the question of Milton's early radicalism', *Milton Studies*, 28 (1992), 45–6.
76. Brown, *Milton's Aristocratic Entertainments*, 105–10.
77. Brown, *Milton's Aristocratic Entertainments*, 130.

Index of masques and entertainments

General index